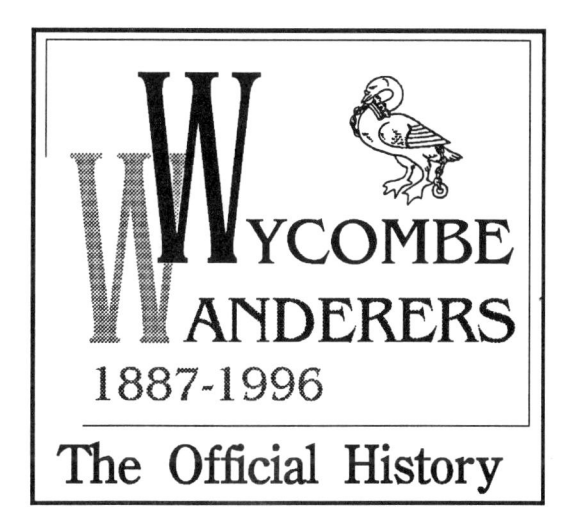

Wycombe Wanderers
1887-1996
The Official History

Dave Finch
&
Steve Peart

WYCOMBE WANDERERS F.C.
1887 - 1996
The Official History

By:
Dave Finch & Steve Peart

Published by:
Yore Publications
12 The Furrows, Harefield,
Middx. UB9 6AT.

© Dave Finch & Steve Peart 1996

....

All rights reserved.
No part of this publication may be reproduced or copied in any manner without the prior permission in writing of the copyright holders.

British Library Cataloguing-in-Publication Data.
A catalogue record for this book
is available from the British Library.

ISBN 1 874427 76 3

Printed and bound by The Bath Press

WYCOMBE WANDERERS F.C.
1887 - 1996
The Official History

By Dave Finch & Steve Peart

DEDICATION

This book is dedicated to the memory
of Roger Vere who sadly died in August 1996.

His company, Verco Office Furniture Ltd.,
as Club sponsors since 1988,
helped pave the way to so much success.

Contents

Chapter:			Page:
		Introduction	6
1	(1887-1895)	The Early Years Of Struggle	8
2	(1895-1914)	Loakes Park And A Rise In Status	16
3	(1919-1945)	Amateur Cup Winners... But Little Else	30
4	(1945-1961)	Wycombe Reach The Top	39
5	(1961-1976)	A Fall... Then The Glory Years Return	48
6	(1976-1987)	The Last Years With The Isthmians	57
7	(1987-1990)	Conference Consolidation	65
8	(1990-1996)	The Irish Messiah And The Football League	73
	Appendix A:	Formation Date	94
	Appendix B:	Smoking Concerts	95
		The Grounds	96
		Great Games	102
		Two Dozen Of The Best	116
		Programme Parade	137
		(Non-League) Players Who's Who (1963-1993)	143
		Football League Players Who's Who	150
		Football League Players - Pre 1992/93 Season	151
		Honours...Records...Statistics	153
		Seasonal Statistics and Team Groups	156
		Advanced Subscribers	254
		Yore Publications	256

INTRODUCTION

All football clubs have interesting histories and Wycombe Wanderers are certainly no exception. What makes them unique amongst the current Premiership/Football League clubs is their dogged adherence to amateur status, right up to its abolition by the Football Association in 1974. For nearly 100 years the club was one of the great bastions of amateur football with little interest in turning professional. In 1896 *The Evening News* asked the club's early guiding light, secretary Charley Harper, whether the team would ever turn professional. *"Of course the time may come when we shall have a professional team here. But I believe in remaining an amateur club as long as you can keep the football up to a good standard."* The club enjoyed a very successful period in the 1950's with huge crowds packing Loakes Park but even in the Amateur Cup Final season of 1956-57, secretary Bill Hayter shunned all notions of turning professional. *"I cannot see Wycombe ever becoming a professional club. We get far too much fun out of amateur soccer. We are convinced our supporters would not like to see any change because interest in first class amateur games is now deep rooted here. Why should we ever consider becoming a professional club? We play in the premier amateur league and there is no fear of a soccer slump while we provide bright football."* The great success in the 1970's was achieved under a manager, Brian Lee, who believed strongly in playing football for the right reasons, namely for the love of the game. In fact the club only seriously set about becoming a Football League member ten years ago, culminating in the most successful period when promotion was achieved under manager Martin O'Neill and chairman Ivor Beeks. Apart from an isolated Amateur Cup win in 1931, these are the only sustained periods of success in the 110 year period.

As you might expect the history dwells on recent years but the period before the First World War is also dealt with extensively because of the fascinating story of a club trying to establish itself in a still infant sport. The town of High Wycombe, surrounded by the beech laden Chiltern Hills, became the centre of the country's furniture making industry in the 19th century. Nestling as it does in a steep valley, the town has always been a very tight-knit community, certainly up to the period of great expansion after the Second World War. Town and football club always enjoyed a very supportive relationship as the two grew hand in hand. Only once has the town let the club down when, in the 1980's, Wycombe Wanderers searched in vain for a site to build a new ground on. The local council's refusal to offer any help was a shameful chapter in High Wycombe's history.

We would like to thank all the people who have helped in the making of this history, particularly Wycombe Wanderers FC who have been so supportive. Those who have contributed are Derek Alldridge M.B.E. (Metropolitan Police F.C.), Phil Ball, Paul Bates, Ivor L Beeks, Mike Bondy (MJB Research), Paul Clayton (Charlton Athletic), Tom Cook (WWFC Programme Shop), John Delaney, Paul Dennis, Billy Gallacher, Ronald Goodearl, Denis Gray, Mr & Mrs S Grimsley, Brian Hanley (Wycombe Chair Museum), Percy Hawes, Julie Hayward, Ray Howson, Tony Horseman, Alan Hutchinson, Brian Lee, Paul Lewis, Steve Maguire, John Maskell, Jock McCallum, Jill Osborne, Alan Parry, Graham Peart, Dave Phillips, Larry Pritchard, Keith Searle, Alan Smith (Slough Town), Mark Smith and Andy Ross (Maidenhead United), Brian Southam, Mrs Spanna, Gordon Summerfield, John D Taylor, Dick Tunmer and Mike Wilson. Please accept our apologies to any contributor who we have not mentioned.

Most of the photographs have been supplied by the club, particularly the team line-ups, and a large number are from the Bucks Free Press which have been provided by players, officials and supporters. Brian Southam and Paul Dennis took most of the photographs in the last seven years and Phil Ball came up with some stunning early photographs, some of which were previously unknown. Where known, the copyright has been acknowledged. The majority, which are thus untitled are believed to be from the Bucks Free Press, and we apologise for any untraceable omissions. In some cases original prints were not found and therefore, in order to provide the greatest variety in time span and importance, these examples have been included, despite the inferior source quality. To those named our grateful thanks for permission to include same.

We would still be interested in hearing from anyone with photos or momentoes not shown in this book. There is very little surviving between the two wars and we are keen to track down an original of the earliest ever photograph taken of the team in 1890, reproduced in this book from a very faded newspaper cutting. Similarly we would be glad to receive comments and corrections on any points in this history. Regarding the records section of the book we decided it was not a good idea to overload things with complete line-ups for every single season. However, it is hoped at a later date to publish one or two supplements which would include these. Friendly games have been included in the records until 1914 as they were considered at the time to be just as important as competitive games.

Dave's Foreword

Little did I realise where it would lead when I allowed the then co-programme editor, Bob Cairney, to persuade me to write the "Back in Time" page after Steve Maguire had decided to give it up after several fine years. That was back in August 1990, and not long afterwards I was then asked to take over the statistical pages as Steve Peart, my co-conspirator, was finding less time to do them due to pressure of work. The first thing I realised was that the club themselves do not keep records, so I decided that it would be a good idea to compile my own (I already had a record of every game I have seen anyway). Steve happened to remark that it would be good to see them in book form combined with a history of the club. Things were left at that until, during the double season of 1992-93, I asked him if he was serious in bringing out a book. Like a fool he remarked in the affirmative! So began a three-year sentence and hours of painstaking research, mainly at High Wycombe Reference Library. The staff there have probably got fed up with the sight of us, and it is a huge relief that all is now finished. I sincerely hope the end product is as interesting to you as it has been to me during my research. My thanks go out to all those people listed above, who have given their assistance, but especially to my dear wife, Lynden, the most patient and understanding person I have ever met.

Steve's Foreword

Shortly after moving to Adams Park in 1990, Dave and myself first discussed the possibility of writing a detailed history of the club. Early in 1993, as the team were poised to win the Conference, we realised that the Football League's newest club would be lacking a detailed statistical history. Certainly there had been excellent histories before, Ted Rolph in 1957, Steve Daglish in 1984 and John Goldsworthy in 1990, but none with a complete list of results. Unfortunately, like the vast majority of non-League clubs, Wycombe Wanderers' have never had a policy of archiving match details or reports. The only source of information for every game was to be found in the local reference library, where the local newspapers were stored on microfilm. For three years we spent Monday and Thursday evenings, and Saturday mornings, reading every single match report, Dave concentrating on the line-ups and results and myself on the history. We would like to thank Valerie Beadle and all her colleagues at High Wycombe Reference Library for putting up with us for so long! Publisher Dave Twydell has shown great patience in guiding two first-time authors throughout.

My wife Katie deserves a special mention for her wonderful support since I first met her two years ago, particularly in the final frantic months when she temporarily "lost" me. Another supporter was my company, The National House-Building Council, who probably did not have my full attention in the run-up to the publication of this book!

Finally we would like to thank Martin O'Neill on behalf of all Wycombe Wanderers supporters for five wonderfully exciting years, something which all football fans dream about.

Dave Finch and Steve Peart, September 1996

THE HISTORY OF WYCOMBE WANDERERS FOOTBALL CLUB
CHAPTER 1 (1887-1895)
THE EARLY YEARS OF STRUGGLE

- The oldest known Wycombe Wanderers team group (unnamed) - 1889/90 Season -

Football, in the modern sense, can be traced back in High Wycombe to a 20-a-side match in 1863 on the Rye Mead, still a long stretch of public land to the East of the town centre. In 1871 High Wycombe F.C. played its inaugural match there, a 0-0 draw with Marlow, and that decade saw a rapid growth of the town, hand in hand with the countless furniture making factories (the origin of the Club's nickname 'Chairboys') and paper mills. By the 1880's competition for pitches on the Rye had become fierce; space was limited due to the cattle which were allowed to graze and the entrance was made deep with mud as they were brought in early in the morning and returned to their sheds around the town in the afternoon. According to an unwritten law in those days, goalposts could be erected immediately after the Parish Church had struck midnight on Friday. Sometimes the posts would be found uprooted in the morning because of the rivalry which existed between clubs.

By the time Wanderers began to play, there were a handful of junior clubs in the town, the biggest being High Wycombe F.C., who sometimes played under the name of Wycombe Ramblers. Their importance was on the wane as they found it increasingly hard to attract players, who were mostly tradesmen and white collar workers. In 1887 an attempt was made to amalgamate all of the town teams into one, but the fierce club loyalties prevented this. Overshadowing all football in the area were the mighty Marlow F.C., F A Cup semi-finalists in 1882 and still one of the top ten clubs in the South of England. Their achievement was the more extraordinary because of the smallness of Marlow village. The intense rivalry between Marlow and Wycombe Wanderers was to become one of the main themes of developing football in South Buckinghamshire.

In 1957 the Club marked its 75th anniversary with the first published history following, written by Ted Rolph, vice-president. The following revised and unpublished notes from 1959 is the only source of information for the formation period:

"It was the writer's privilege to discuss with John Randell, the first Wycombe Wanderers goalkeeper, on the 8th July 1958, when he was 92 years of age, the early days of the Club in an effort to obtain the information to establish for all time just exactly how it all began.

"John Randell stated that he gave up playing football when he joined the Bucks Volunteer Rifle Corps in 1888, when he was a little over 21 years of age. Before that he had played for the North Town Wanderers, a team of young lads, living in the area of High Wycombe known as Wheeler's Field. Very few of the boys could read or write, he himself could a little because he went to the British School in Queens Square - now Woolworths Shop - where he paid 2d per week. 'Datchet' Webb, whose father was a cane seat framer and lived at 29 Duke Street, got a ball from somewhere and he charged the other boys who had left school and were working, a penny to play with it. These youngsters began to learn the rudiments of the game on the Rye Mead. So in 1884 they decided to start a club to play matches against some of the smaller villages.

"John Randell said that Harry Rolph (father of Ted), a coachman, who had played for Marlow and won a Berks & Bucks Senior Cup medal in 1881 and was considered the best player on the Rye, taught the boys many tricks about the game and acted in what we would now term as coach.

"The first meeting was held in the woodhouse at the rear garden to 29 Duke Street, with the privy in the corner, upon which 'Datchet' Webb sat, he being "cock of the gang" and owner of the ball, to control the business transacted, which so far as can be ascertained was to force agreement upon the payment of 3d per week contribution.

> 'Datchet upon the throne sat he,
> Gazed down upon his motley gang;
> The first captain to be,
> Before the Press the Wanders' praises sang.'

"So wrote a sage years afterwards. 'Datchet' was full of enthusiasm and energy and possessed a dominating personality. He extracted the best out of everybody, inspiring the team to almost to desperation in difficult circumstances to overcome strong opposition and kept the boys together, thereby contributing a big part in the consolidation of the Club. He went down with others to Stone's Sawmills, London Road, between Harlow Road and the Nags Head, and got the four goalposts cut, pieces of rope being used for the crossbar. He owned the ball for the time being and a great problem was blowing it up; there were no cycle pumps and a kind of hand bellows was used. Nevertheless the boys slowly overcame all obstacles. No records were kept, but we do know that in 1886 football requisites were purchased from Joe Norton, who had been the secretary and the captain of the [Wycombe] Rangers F.C., and consisted of two top bars, four goalposts, six boundaries, with flags orange and blue, together with one ball, all for 18/6d. Joe Norton became the first president of the Wanderers F.C..

"The lads in 1887 felt that they may do well if they went in for junior football and play against better clubs. They had been playing against scratch elevens got together by young individuals from chair shop and village green. So a meeting was called by Jim Ray, who was a good writer, backed by 'Datchet' Webb, now the star footballer amongst them, to take place at the Steam Engine, Station Road, where Willie Woods was the licensee. They persuaded Billy Dimmock, brewers drayman, to be the chairman. The first item on the agenda was the name of the Club. Billy invited suggestions by asking "What the name shall be?" Noel Curtis proposed "The name shall be North Town Wanderers." John Randell, who resided in Lilys Walk, off St Marys Street, disagreed on the grounds that whilst he recognised that most of the players came from Wheelers Field, then known as North Town, there were now some players who lived in other parts of the town, as he did himself. So he proposed that "the name be Wycombe Wanderers." This was agreed after a heated discussion. 'Datchet' Webb was elected captain, Jim Ray was made the Club's secretary. He played for years and was a glutton for work, indefatigable in his efforts to further the Club's interests. He tramped all over the place for players, his was the task to arrange for the horse and wagonette and many other services for the well being of the Club. These two played a big part in the development of the early Wanderers. George Cook was elected treasurer and his widow continues to live in Duke Street. We have had talks with her and she has the earliest photograph of the Wanderers in 1890 [whereabouts unknown]. She is 91 years of age, lives alone and does all her work. It was also agreed to pay 6d per week contribution and that the colours shall be two blues."

Traditionally 1884 is the formation date of Wycombe Wanderers but the authors of this book feel that 1887 is the historically correct date (see Appendix A for a more detailed discussion). It is probable that North Town Wanderers was used as a name for at least some of those pre-formation years. In fact the local paper uses that name rather than Wycombe Wanderers when reporting on the match against Wycombe Rovers on 22nd October 1887, which suggests that someone supplying the match details had either not got out of the habit of using the old name or had not been aware of the change.

It is also highly likely that the Club was named 'Wanderers' after the famous Wanderers, first winners of the F.A. Cup in 1872, who had visited the town on 15th December 1877 and defeated High Wycombe 9-0 on the way to their fifth and last F.A. Cup Final win. On the same day, Queen Victoria visited the town to see the Prime Minister, Lord Beaconsfield, better known as Benjamin Disraeli, at his home of Hughenden Manor.

The colours of light and dark blue are often referred to as the 'varsity' colours of Oxford and Cambridge Universities. It may seem surprising that an apparently wholly working class club should want an affinity with the rarefied heights of academia but all references to the colours in match reports straight after the formation refer to the 'varsity' colours. In fact on the 15 December 1893 the *Bucks Standard* comments: *"For the first time, the Wycombe Wanderers appeared in their true colours - Oxford and Cambridge blue - last Saturday, each member wearing a new shirt."* 'First time' meant that season and the strip referred to can be seen in the 1893-94 team photograph.

The line-up from the first ever game, against Wycombe Nose Club on 24 September 1887, is unknown but the team for the second game, four weeks later against Wycombe Rovers, does survive:

Noel Curtis, Datchet Webb, Jim Hearne, A. Thorne, George Johnson, R Stallwood, Joe Norton, John Randell, Ted Ball, George Cook, Jim Ray.

Secretary Jim Ray scored the goal in the 3-1 defeat and became the first ever goalscorer for the Club, but no other goalscorers are known for that season. In between the opening two games secretary Ray advertised in the *South Bucks Free Press*:

Club now open to receive challenges from junior clubs, James W Ray, 6 Aveling Villas, Wycombe.

At the same time he acknowledged a donation of 5/- from Lord Curzon, MP, the first of his many donations. The Club's first competitive game took place on 21st January 1888 in the High Wycombe Challenge Cup.

WYCOMBE CUP
WYCOMBE RAMBLERS v WYCOMBE WANDERERS

This, the only match in the first round of the above Cup, the other three clubs entered having byes, was played in the Rye on Saturday last. There was a fair attendance of spectators present when the game began about 3 o'clock. From start to finish the play was very one-sided and uninteresting, the Wanderers proving themselves a team in want of a lot of practice, and beyond stating that the Ramblers won by 14 goals to nil, no further description of the game is necessary.

John Randell, the goalkeeper, remembered the match well: *"A strong wind was blowing down the pitch, there was nobody behind the goal and I had to run a long way to retrieve the ball every time they scored, as there were no nets at that time."* The thrashing evidently had a salutary effect - the team did not venture on to the pitch again for six weeks, no doubt to put in the extra practice.

When they did emerge, with several positional changes, they won their final six matches. Only seven line-ups of the fourteen matches that season survive, and twenty different players are known.

The following season saw a change of headquarters from the Steam Engine when new landlord Sam Hayden took over and wanted to charge for use of the club room. So the Masons Arms in Saffron Platt was adopted, probably at a meeting on 1 December 1888, although the landlord Charlie Durham charged 1/- (5p) a week for providing a tub of cold water in the yard, for washing down after games. It was also decided to run a reserve side and a challenge was placed in the *Free Press* to play other junior teams aged 18 to 19 years.

Meanwhile Wycombe Ramblers changed their name back to High Wycombe and secured the use of the newly opened town cricket ground, on the Rye. It had the distinct advantage of being enclosed so that the Club could charge spectators and keep out the rowdy element which afflicted all football at that time. The results of four advertised games in 1888-89 are not known although one of these, against Wycombe Marsh on 27th October, is referred to in the controversial return match on Christmas Day. At this time football matches were controlled by two umpires, one supplied from each club, and the obvious potential for conflict was realised when Marsh, losing by three goals to one, pulled a goal back only to have it disallowed for offside by the Wanderers official, Joe Norton. The Marsh umpire Plumridge allowed the goal because the crowd and not the players had appealed for the infringement. The dispute could not be settled and the Marsh team left the pitch with a quarter of an hour still to play.

Season 1889-90 opened with another change of headquarters, this time to the Nags Head which was handily situated opposite the Rye. The previous season, landlord Bill Pearce, a keen football fan, had invited Wycombe Rovers to use his pub as their headquarters. But he would have been able to watch Wanderers playing from his premises and he began to follow their progress with increasing interest. He induced them to switch pubs by donating £1 and offering free use of a room for changing, club meetings and dinners - an offer which could not be refused! His encouragement was crucial in the early development of the Club, helping to attract better players and influential supporters. At one of the monthly smoking concerts, held in November that season, newly elected President Joe Norton proudly noted that 30 new members had joined that season.

Just before Christmas, Wanderers played High Wycombe, losing 3-0 in a rather bad tempered game: *Several of the*

Town club did not appear to approve of their late member (Morris) playing against them, and commenced playing very roughly, and the ground being in a wretched condition, the boys could not stand up to it so well as their opponents. Sid Morris had only recently defected from High Wycombe F.C. and he immediately became the best player in the Wanderers team. Making a rare first team appearance for Wanderers in goal that day was Police Constable Tugwell. On the same day the committee met and decided to enter, in great secrecy, two teams in the High Wycombe Challenge Cup, the reserves were entered as Wycombe Wanderers and the first team adopted the name Wild West F.C.. Each club could have two representatives on the High Wycombe Football Association but by entering two clubs, the Wanderers would have four. The reserves lost to High Wycombe 6-1 in one semi-final while in the other, Wild West defeated Mr Birch's Factory 3-0 on the Rye *'in the presence of the largest crowd that had assembled there for some years, there being about 500 spectators, many of whom seemed just a little disappointed at seeing so little rough play and such a pleasant game'.*

Making their first appearance at a Wycombe game was what was described as a 'North Country "Plan" of cards' with 'Play up Wanderers' written on them. The final was played at Wrights's Meadow, Wycombe Marsh, with Wild West equalising and High Wycombe declining to play extra time because of injury to two of their players. In the replay Wild West scored five minutes from the end only for High Wycombe to equalise one minute later. Wild West lodged a protest afterwards about the qualifications of one of their opponents, and of the decisions of the officials, but nothing came of it. The *Free Press* enthused over the Wanderers' first cup win:

The third game in the final round for the above Cup took place on Saturday on the usual ground at the Marsh, with the result that at the third time of asking the better team were able to make the object of their ambition a fait accompli, the Wild West winning by two goals to nil. The Wild West (or Wanderers) are to be congratulated on their plucky fight on all three occasions against the town club; and to have finally secured possession of the coveted trophy is abundant proof of their rapid rise in the local football scene since the Club's formation three years ago, when in their first year of existence the Wycombe club disposed of them in the first round of the competition to the tune of 14 goals to nil. Its success practically dates from the time when the Club shifted to its present headquarters and is in some measure due to the indefatigable efforts of its president (Mr J W Norton), who found willing helpers in the captain (Mr E Webb) and Mr S Morris...about 15 minutes from the kick-off, the forwards worked the ball up to the Wycombe end, Webb passing to Ray, and the latter scored the first goal for the Wild West, amid cheers...some time before the usual interval, they managed to score their second and last, as it transpired, goal, out of a scrimmage, Crook doing the needful.

The Wycombe team in all three final matches was: Jim Ball, George Beckett, Frank Howlett, George Bowles, Jim Putnam, C Nash, 'Sunny' Lane, 'Datchet' Webb, Sid Morris, Edward Crook, Jim Ray. After the game, the Cup was presented by the Mayor of High Wycombe and the medals by Miss Thurlow. In his Captain's speech, Datchet Webb said: *"They were all glad to have won for the Wanderers, despite the name employed".* The Club tried unsuccessfully to have Wycombe Wanderers rather than Wild West inscribed on the Cup and it appears that the underhand tactic of entering two teams caused an enormous amount of bad feeling in the town. In the following years that season would be described as 'those dark days' and it appears that there was a real danger of the Club folding at the time.

The winning team met with an enthusiastic welcome on arriving at their temporary room at the "Red Lion", Wycombe Marsh, and the Cup was quickly filled by the following gentlemen:- Mr T Thurlow (twice), Mr W Pearce (twice), Mr B L Reynolds, and Mr W Clark. The health of the various gentlemen was drunk with musical honours. When all had a drink out of the cup, a start was made for their headquarters, "Nag's Head", London-road, where a crowd of their supporters awaited their arrival. So wild was the enthusiasm that the two men had difficulty to obtain an entrance, and on the Captain placing the trophy on the shelf it will adorn, the scene 'baffled description'.

After the final game of the season, against Finsbury Polytechnic, *'the visitors left by the last train thoroughly satisfied by their visit, and saying they had never played in such a friendly game, as their was no dispute whatsoever'.* Two hundred Wycombe supporters saw them off on the 10 o'clock train, which would have arrived at Paddington via Marlow at 11.25 am.

Season 1890-91 began with Bill Pearce taking over from George Cook as Treasurer, and Jim Ball becoming joint captain with Datchet Webb. The latter two had both been playing since the first season. It was also decided that the committee would meet every Monday evening to pick the team for the following Saturday - this method of selection continued up to 1968! The Wycombe Challenge Cup was again entered, this time with 'A' and 'B' teams, and the Berks & Bucks Junior Cup for the first time. The winter was particularly cold, with heavy frost and snow; even the Thames at Marlow was frozen.

When play resumed Wanderers managed to secure the use of the Cricket Ground for the first time, for the Junior Cup tie with Chesham Reserves. A large crowd paid to see the game, in spite of there being an inch of snow on the pitch *'...the pavilion was rammed full of spectators, who evidently preferred the dry boards and friendly shelter to standing about in the snow, and boundary was tolerably well lined'.* The 3-2 win put them into the semi-final against Maidenhead Norfolkians at Marlow's Crown Ground. The 2-1 win which put them into the final was marred by an incident 15 minutes from time when the Wycombe players discovered that their opponents' goalkeeper was wearing 'tipped and nailed' boots. Appeals to the referee to have him ordered off the pitch came to no avail. The victory was greeted enthusiastically by the hundreds of travelling Wycombe fans who followed the High Wycombe Drum and Fife Band down Marlow High Street, to the amazement of the locals, on the way back to the station.

The Final at Maidenhead drew a crowd of 1,500, the first time the Wanderers had played in front of a four figure crowd, and their opponents, hot favourites Reading Albion were surprisingly held to a 2-2 draw. The replay two weeks later drew another large crowd, although reduced by the wet weather, and the Wycombe supporters, sporting 'rosettes of two-hued blue' were disappointed to find that two key players, Morris and Howlett, were missing with illness, replaced by two 'guest' players, Hutchinson of Wycombe Rovers and Corby of Marlow. Helped by a strong following wind, Reading took a 2-0 lead at half-time but within fifteen minutes of the restart, Wycombe had levelled. Then the wind, which was now helping Wanderers, dropped, heavy rain fell, and Reading took advantage, running out easy 6-2 winners. A fine run in the Wycombe Challenge Cup saw a second successive final appearance at Wright's Meadow, this time against Wycombe Marsh. Favourites to win at odds of 6-4, Wanderers dominated the first half, helped by a strong wind, but failed to score because of wayward shooting. Marsh had no such problems after the break and scored three without reply. Wycombe lodged an unsuccessful formal protest that one of the Marsh players, Clifford, lived in Well End, outside the four mile radius from the town centre which the competition stipulated.

During this season we learn something more of Wycombe's style of play when against Burnham they are described as *'fast and athletic'* and the match against Wycombe Rovers brought the comment *'...both teams went in for plenty of charging.'* In previous seasons the local press had sometimes used the word 'rough' with their style of play; when Wanderers defeated High Wycombe in the Challenge Cup, the *Free Press* complained:

'[High Wycombe] played much better football than the Wanderers from start to finish - the winners going in for any amount of charging, and descending to tricks which I thought they were above...[Wanderers] *spoilt their play by indulging in rough play and sometimes deliberate tripping to such an extent as to make it appear to all impartial observers that such actions were pre-arranged'.*

Commenting on the same match, The *Bucks Standard* was also critical: *'The town club showed superior, scientific passing, whilst the Wanderers, I am sorry to say, indulged in tripping and charging much too freely. I was particularly struck with the gentlemanly conduct of the town club players, who had, on several occasions, to appeal to the referee for free kicks and foul play. The sooner the Wanderers pay more attention to the ball than to the man than they did on Saturday the better it will be for them and their "reputation".* This may have been a natural establishment bias for the older Club who were drawn from the more genteel middle class. Wanderers were the young upstarts - lower class - although the Club's supporters were becoming increasingly well connected. There may also been an element of frustration that Wanderers refused to merge with the town club. In April 1891 the *Free Press* pessimistically said: *"...an amalgamation of forces is sadly wanted at Wycombe, and until this has become a fait accompli, I see little hope of the town ever making its mark in the local football world."*

At the end of season dinner, Robert Wood, in the chair, alluded to the feelings against the Club: *"The Wycombe Wanderers should not be despised, they deserved far more respect than they got. He had watched the reports in the local papers, and he was sorry to see that they had backed the outsiders to win, and had not encouraged the home team to win, but he knows that a little had been done towards their success by the Press, who had sometimes said a kindly word for them. He hoped next season they would be able to get a ground for the Wanderers to play on; he did not see why the* [High] *Wycombe F.C. should go on the cricket ground any more than the other Wycombe clubs, and he hoped next year they would be able to get the cricket ground for our cup ties."*

Mr B L Reynolds, captain of Wycombe Marsh, also spoke at the dinner about the football problem in the town: *"...the clubs were always ready to support one another, but he was sorry to see how the other clubs in the town held aloof from them* [Wanderers]. *He was very sorry for some reasons that the Wycombe Cup was in existence, because it not only engendered a great deal of discontent, but caused so many little clubs to start in Wycombe, and there was in consequence no really good club among them. If that Cup were done away with, however, they might be able to amalgamate and form a really strong Club. (Applause). He was sorry the people of Wycombe did not have any interest in sport of any kind, and he was surprised they regarded football as a dangerous game."*

The 1891-92 season began with major changes at the Club. Joe Norton, President since 1888, stepped down, to be replaced by Robert Wood, a solicitor recently arrived in town. Jim Ray, Player/Secretary since the beginning, retired from both of his roles because of family commitments, with talented forward Frank Jennings taking over. Another retiring from the game was the captain Sid Morris, and goalkeeper Jim 'Chummy' Ball assumed responsibility.

The question of playing on the cricket ground had been resolved and Wanderers were granted its use provided High Wycombe F.C. had no use of it. The season on the pitch was notable only for some controversial matches. After the home defeat to Slough in the Berks & Bucks Junior Cup on 14 November 1891, some *"loud-mouthed rowdies, who know nothing about, still less understand football"*, assaulted the Slough linesman outside the Nags Head. The presence of a plain clothes policeman (possibly PC Tugwell) prevented a more serious incidence. The match which caused the most problems, however, was a Maidenhead Norfolkians Charity Cup match against Maidenhead Reserves on the 9 January 1892. This was a second attempt to complete the tie - the first, on the 21st November at Wycombe, was played over a mutually agreed 40 minutes each way, because the visitors had arrived late. Wanderers won 2-0 but it was ruled invalid because the match had not lasted 90 minutes, and the second match, on the cricket ground, again suffered from a late start.

Maidenhead had arrived on time in the town but, thinking the snow covered pitch would prevent play, failed to appear until the referee appealed to them a second time. By this time the crowd, frozen stiff, had become extremely restless, and gave the visitors an unwelcome reception when they finally appeared. The Maidenhead goalkeeper was continually pelted with snowballs during the match and one of the linesmen refused to change to the rowdier side at half time. Maidenhead were holding a 2-1 lead when the match had to be abandoned ten minutes form time due to poor light - it was played to a conclusion the following week at Maidenhead, with Wycombe losing 1-0. The events which followed the second abandoned game at the cricket ground brought national notoriety to Wycombe Wanderers. The local Maidenhead paper reported that some Wycombe followers tried to shut the gate, to prevent the Maidenhead team from leaving. Gilroy, their captain, was punched in the eye and hit out; another player was nearly 'limbed' climbing over the metal gate at the cricket ground entrance.

When the team got onto the road they were then pelted with snowballs, some with stones in, and one player had to scramble over a cottage wall before arriving safely at the Nags Head. Another Maidenhead player who was limping because of an injury, was knocked over and hit with a stick. This version of events, which appeared in such national publications as *The People* and *The Sportsman*, was hotly disputed by the Wycombe President Robert Wood, who described them as *'untrue and malicious statements'* in a letter to the *Bucks Standard*.

The Club's absence, however, was conspicuous at a special meeting of the Berks & Bucks Junior Association a week later, to discuss the *'disgraceful scenes'*. Several Maidenhead players confirmed the worst of the allegations, although the Wycombe players were exonerated from any blame and in fact tried their best to prevent the attacks. The Association declared that the situation would normally have meant the closure of the ground for the remainder of the season. But as High Wycombe owned the ground, this would unfairly penalise them, and The Wycombe Cup Final and a County Senior Cup semi-final scheduled there would have had to be cancelled. It was resolved that the Football Association be requested to *'remonstrate'* with Wycombe Wanderers for not taking enough precautions to prevent the disgraceful behaviour of their supporters. The national body were not impressed by this 'buck passing' and, on the 17 February 1892, Charles Alcock informed the county body of the resolutions of the FA's Southern Committee:

1. That the committee views with regret that the Berks & Bucks Junior Association did not deal with the matter severely, so as to prevent the future occurrence of such disgraceful conduct, and that, as the Wycombe ground is now closed for preparation of the cricket team, they are unable to inflict punishment by closing the ground for the remainder of the season.
2. That the Wycombe Wanderers Club be censored for not having taken precautions to ensure the proper conduct of the spectators at and after the match.

The only bright spots of the season were the debuts of two important players:- Charley Harper, 29 years old, who had played for High Wycombe when they beat Wanderers 14-0 in 1888 and would go on to become one of the club's most influential personalities. The Reverend Alfred Baines, a graduate of Keble College, Oxford, quickly established a reputation as an outstanding full back.

Centre back Jim Putnam took over as Captain for the 1892-93 season and the Club, preferring not to play on the Rye if at all possible, had two blank Saturdays in September as they waited for the cricket club to finish with their ground. *The Evening News and Sun* bemoaned the uncertain future of the town club: *High Wycombe seems to be in a parlous state. No matches have yet been arranged, and it seems doubtful whether an Association eleven will be raised. The hoped-for amalgamation with the Wanderers is not likely to take place.* High Wycombe did not take the field again and Wanderers effectively became the town's leading club. The Club's growing influence in local football was shown by the fact that the management of the Wycombe Challenge Cup had been entrusted to the Wanderers Committee. Sadly, ugly crowd scenes were again witnessed when a Maidenhead team visited town, this time the Norfolkians, in a Wycombe Cup tie. Maidenhead won by a hotly disputed goal and after the game, when challenged by the home crowd outside the ground, the referee apologised for awarding the goal. This only made matters worse and two policemen had to accompany him to the Nags Head where a crowd of 100 were waiting outside. The visiting players were jostled as they entered, one receiving a black eye, and the referee was threatened with a ducking in the adjacent River Wye, which he managed to escape.

Wanderers had no luck in the Berks & Bucks Junior Cup when, after defeating Chesham Generals 2-1 on Christmas Eve, the organising committee upheld a protest from Chesham over one of the goals and ordered a replay which Wycombe lost 4-2. On 23rd February a benefit match was staged for the former Wycombe captain Frank Howlett who was gravely ill. He had sustained concussion when heading a ball against Finsbury Polytechnic on 30th March 1891 and had not played since. Twelve Wanderers comfortably won 4-0, against a team of eighteen veterans from various clubs in the town. The match raised the large sum of £7-12s (£7-60) but sadly Frank Howlett died on 9th February 1893.

The Club received a severe shock in the summer when Frank Jennings, Secretary, left Wanderers to play for Loudwater Lilliputians. His brother Charles was also unavailable because of an injury picked up the previous season. Jim Ray took over temporarily but Charley Harper soon stepped into the breach, both as Secretary and player, where he occupied the right-back position. His influence was felt immediately, arranging twenty friendlies compared with just eleven the previous season, and, crucially, renting Spring Meadow in Spring Gardens for £5 per annum. At last the Club could escape the uncertainties of playing on the Rye, with the accompanying hooliganism, and a better standard of team could be enticed to the town.

Although larger than the rather cramped cricket ground, Spring Meadow was not ideal, with many comments made about its 'peculiar shape'. It sloped upwards at both ends and, after a Berks & Bucks Junior tie with Burnham in January, the visitors protested, unsuccessfully, that the ground was not fit for a cup-tie. It was, however, the only piece of ground in the town available to the Club and the gamble quickly paid off. Spectators at the opening game, however, were greeted by protestors angry that the pitch lay across a footpath to Tylers Green. Access to the ground was through Coniger Farm and over the railway bridge on the Bourne End line.

Crowds reached record levels - on 28th December a remarkable 2,000 people saw the friendly with Wolverton and three other crowds reached four figures. The Club had much success on the pitch with a total of thirteen cup-ties played. The first match in the Wycombe Challenge Cup ended with Wycombe Marsh 2-1 winners, but the match ended 15 minutes early, the referee relying on the Marsh linesman and secretary to keep time. The affair was shrouded in mystery but Wycombe's protest had little chance of failing as the Challenge Cup committee was headed by the Club's president Robert Wood! Wanderers easily won the replay 7-0 and went on to win the trophy in the final against Marlow Reserves at Wright's Meadow. The Maidenhead Norfolkians Cup was also won, with an easy 5-1 win over Windsor & Eton Victoria at Maidenhead. Three hundred supporters had travelled by rail, and when the team arrived back on the 8 o'clock train, they paraded around the town in a two horse brake, accompanied by a crowd of 1,000 well-wishers. A 'treble' was thwarted by Chesham Reserves in the semi-finals of the Berks & Bucks Junior Cup and although the first team never won this competition, the reserves did so in 1924..

This means that the Club has won, at least once, every cup competition entered as a non-League club, barring the F.A. Cup. The most talked about match was sandwiched in between the two cup wins. Middlesbrough Ironopolis, a professional team in the Second Division of the Football League, had been enticed down by Charley Harper for the considerable sum of £17-10s (£17-50). The match was arranged to reward the Club's ever growing band of supporters and the 1,600 who attended, paying 6d instead of the usual 3d, vindicated the secretary's foresight. Only £3 was required from a guarantee fund to cover the total expenses of £23. A hard and fast match saw the visitors held until just before half time, the Nops eventually winning 3-0 and becoming the first visiting team to win on Spring Meadow.

After the game the result was telegraphed to 32 different sources, indicating the growing interest in Wycombe

Wanderers. The first choice team in this, the most successful season so far was:- Jim Ball, Charley Harper (capt.), Owen Ball, Albert Turner, Bob Collier, George Stevens, Sunny Lane, Datchet Webb, Ted Jones, Bill Buchanan and Fred Abbott. Top scorer was Bill Buchanan with 27 goals in 32 games, his first full season in what turned out to be a prolific career. Another new player destined for widespread fame was left-winger Fred Abbott, very fast and a great crosser of the ball. One of the reasons why the gates had increased so dramatically was due to women who were attending along with their men-folk. On the 30th March 1894, *The Bucks Standard* noted that *"there is one thing very evident this week at the football matches on the Wanderers ground, and that is the growing interest of the fair sex of the town. Two out of the three matches, I should think, the ladies have been in the majority."*

Fred Abbott: dashing left-winger in the 1890's.

After such a successful season, it seemed natural that the players would want to turn 'senior' but Charley Harper found it difficult to convince all of them. Some of the players wanted to win the Junior Cup first but, at a June Meeting of Club members, a compromise was struck, that the Club would join the senior association but not enter for the Berks & Bucks Senior Cup. Discontent simmered until another meeting was called on the 20th July 1894 at the Nags Head. Alderman Deacon, in the chair, became impatient with the players opposed to entering the Senior cup, saying *"Should any player be against it, I would remind them that there were as good fish in the sea as ever came out of it."* George Stevens retorted: *"Yes Mr Chairman, but they want a lot of bloody catching!"*

George Beckett proposed and George Bowles seconded *"That the Wanderers enter for the Berks & Bucks Senior Cup and the F.A. Amateur Cup and the English Cup"*. The motion was carried unanimously and it was also decided to enter the East Berks & South Bucks Junior League, in which the first team played the first five matches and then allowed the reserves to continue for the rest of the season.

Admission prices were set at 6d for men and 3d for children, ladies to be admitted free; two committees, 'General' and 'Match', ran the Club.

The Club's first venture into the Amateur Cup, then in its second season, ended abruptly at West Herts with a 5-1 defeat. The team travelled by brake to Great Missenden and then by train to Watford, changing at Rickmansworth. West Herts scored after five minutes and led 2-1 at the break, after Buchanan had scored Wycombe's first goal in the competition. Heavy rain then fell and the home team quickly scored three more, although penned in their own half by Wycombe for the last twenty minutes.

Afterwards right-half Albert Turner suffered the misfortune of losing his job because he had taken time off to play. After a surprising 4-0 win in the County Cup at Slough, Wolverton were drawn away in the next round but were persuaded to play at Spring Meadow for a guarantee of £12. The match drew record receipts of £21 17s 6d and, in spite of Wycombe's domination, Wolverton won with a 'soft' first half goal. For the second successive season the finals of both the Maidenhead Norfolkians Charity Cup and the Wycombe Challenge Cup were reached. The former saw a humbling 6-1 defeat at the hands of the powerful 1st Scots Guards at Kidwells Park in Maidenhead.

Three days later, however, the town cup was won for the third time, and in the last season that the first team entered. Maidenhead Norfolkians themselves, who had just won the East Berks & South Bucks Junior League, were easily defeated 5-0 at Wright's Meadow. Again Bill Buchanan finished the season averaging more than a goal a game (37 in 33 games), this time playing in the inside-left position; new centre forward was Billy Lloyd.

15

CHAPTER 2 (1895-1914)
LOAKES PARK.... AND A RISE IN STATUS

As soon as the 1894-95 season ended, the Club learnt that Spring Meadow had been sold and was no longer available for football (it would soon be built over by the London Marylebone railway line. A ground committee of six was formed, to try and purchase land next to Spring Meadow, but this idea was quickly abandoned when the asking price of £600 became known. It would also have cost a further £200 to make the pitch playable so an approach was made to Lord Carrington who owned Wycombe Abbey and the surrounding estate, which included Loakes Park. The Club received the following letter from Mr G. Gardner, tenant of Loakes Park:

Market Place
High Wycombe, August 21st 1895
Dear Sirs
A letter has been received from Lord Carrington, offering no objections to the football club using Loakes Park, with a proviso that no annoyance is given to the tenants of Wycombe Abbey or Loakes House. Presuming, Gentlemen, that you will take every precaution that no damage is done to the fences.

I remain, Gentlemen,
Yours etc.
(Signed) G Gardner

Mr Wertheimer, then tenant of Wycombe Abbey, also had no objections. No rent was to be charged for the first year and discussions would then take place to fix the terms of the lease. These arrangements were agreed to at the AGM and the General Committee was enlarged to fifteen members, with six on the Match Committee. A heated discussion took place over the future of the reserve side. Some members, including surprisingly Charley Harper, questioned whether the annual running costs of £20 were worth it; a close vote, however, saw their continued existence. Harper took over from Bill Pearce as Treasurer, and, although the Nags Head remained the headquarters, teams would now change in the Red Lion Hotel, High Street, a site now occupied by Woolworths. Players would cross over the High Street, walk down Crown Lane, into St Marys Street and up Marlow Hill to

R.S.Wood
Club President (1891-1908)

the only entrance, where the General Hospital now stands.

Loakes Park comprised two large fields for the use of Wycombe Abbey tenants, separated by a fence running down from Barracks Road to a plantation of trees, where Queen Alexandra Road now runs. In front of these were gardens and greenhouses where the tenants would grow fruit and vegetables.

The site was not ideal for playing football on - the bottom of Tom Burts Hill, where the pitch was located, had a considerable slope and the surface was rough and stony. The ground was first used for football on Saturday 1st September 1895, when the first and reserve teams held a practice session. The opening match was held the following Saturday, when Park Grove were the visitors. On a hot and sultry day, the crowd was numbered in 'hundreds', and before the game they were issued with notices warning against making "uncalled remarks against the referee both on and off the ground". Bill Buchanan became the first goalscorer on the new ground, with the only goal of the game, and the line-up was: Jim Ball, Albert Hutchinson, Harry Turner, Fred Keen, Bob Collier, George Stevens, G Wooster, Frank Jennings (newly returned), Billy Lloyd, Bill Buchanan and Fred Abbott. The new ground helped to attract a better class of opponents from further afield and, after a few weeks of the season, *The Football Sun* was prompted to say: *"The chair metropolis is one of the rising football centres in Berks and Bucks."*

The first competitive game at Loakes Park was an F.A. Cup First Qualifying Round tie against Wolverton L & NWR from the Southern League Division Two. *"Great enthusiasm and a record gate! A grand game! Hard lines for the Wanderers! Lucky Wolverton!"* were the headlines in the *Free Press*. It was the Wanderers first ever game in the F.A. Cup, and produced record receipts of £30-14s-6d (£30-72). Loakes Park was, *"in the pink of condition for which the ground committee deserved a word of praise; Wolverton expressed themselves highly pleased with it.*

16

"The attendance of spectators that assembled was far and away beyond anything that had been seen at a football match before, and for impartial behaviour they, too, are entitle to a little praise."

The first half was goalless with the Wolves having the upper hand and after half-time they quickly scored three goals. Wycombe reorganised the attack, with Jennings switching from inside-right to centre forward and soon scored the Club's first F.A. Cup goal. Abbott added a second, shots rained in on the visitors goal, hitting post and cross-bar, but the North Bucks side held on for a 3-2 win. The following week a match with Tottenham Hotspur Reserves was arranged, at their then Northumberland Park ground, to give the players a break from home fixtures. Wycombe raced to a 4-0 lead, urged on by a large contingent of former residents, before the home side scored three goals in the last twenty minutes. The *Free Press* noted that the welcome voice of Captain Harper urging his forwards to shoot induced one local to remark: *"Are the Wanderers a professional team because I observe they have a trainer! Comment is needless."*

Charley Harper's enterprise continued when the Amateur Cup holders Middlebrough F.C., then on a Southern tour, were enticed to Loakes Park for a £15 guarantee. The previous week The 'Boro had drawn 3-3 with the mighty Corinthians, creating great interest in Wycombe. The match was played on a Monday afternoon, much to the detriment of the local furniture industry, but the Wanderers put on a good display in losing 3-1. Another Monday afternoon match, on the 11th November 1895, saw the first female football game at Loakes Park, when The North defeated The South 4-0. Remarkably the game produced receipts of £18, £2 more than for the visit of Middlesbrough, with many more viewing from the 'free gallery' at the top of Tom Burts Hill. *The Free Press* noted:

"The play was of a very original order, only one or two of the performers having advanced beyond the alphabet of the game; but they put any amount of spirit into it, and seemed to enjoy themselves as much as the spectators, who were very hilarious."

The highlight of the season was a protracted run in the Amateur Cup. The final qualifying round meant a journey to the 2nd East Lancashire Regiment in Aldershot, after the soldiers turned down the chance to play at Loakes Park. They were a crack army team who had already disposed of Reading Amateurs, Ealing, and Chesham Generals in that season's competition. Taking the 10.06 am train from High Wycombe, the party of 29 arrived at 1.15 pm and were met by a guide who then led them on a three mile journey over rough ground.

"We would not suggest that this was done to 'fag out' the blues, but it looked as though 'Tommy' was not particular how far he took the Wanderers", the *Free Press* noted.

When they got to the ground, they found that the goalposts were a foot too short, the crossbar dipped in the centre, the grass was in a pitiful state and there were no chalk markings - two soldiers were trying to mark the pitch with dry whitening, a third followed breaking up the hard pieces. The referee judged the pitch unfit for a cup-tie and Charley Harper lodged a formal protest. The two teams agreed to play a friendly match, with Wycombe winning 3-2, but afterwards the soldiers claimed the tie because Wycombe had not lodged the protest correctly. The Football Association ruled that, as the match had been played, it must count as a cup-tie (Amateur Cup, Rule 12) and nothing else mattered.

So Wanderers found themselves champions of their qualifying division and facing a trip to Marlow in the First Round Proper. They had already met in two friendlies earlier in the season, the first ever matches between the respective first teams and the start of an intense and, at times, bitter rivalry. Marlow still retained a considerable national reputation, however their fixtures were still largely against the increasingly less influential old boys teams, as professionalism took root in the South.

Wycombe were the young pretenders in the area, progressive and with much bigger support, and the match created great interest in the area. The crowd at the Crown Ground, paying £74 9s 3d, numbered 2,700, the largest ever seen in the area, surpassing the 2,421 crowd when Middlesbrough Ironopolis played there in the F.A. Cup three seasons before. Some 1,500 made their way from Wycombe, many walking the five miles, and the passion of the occasion was underlined by the many flare-ups between rival players, some coming to blows. Jennings put Wycombe into the lead after 28 minutes but Shaw equalised soon after. Five minutes before the break Buchanan restored Wycombe's lead - *"the scene was almost indescribable, hats and sticks being thrown into the air, while the shouts were stentorian."* Marlow quickly levelled maters after half-time and the Riversiders' continued pressure paid when Ellerton *"notched up a clinking goal four minutes to time."*

The following Saturday, eleven Wycombe players and Charley Harper, who rarely took the field now, were awarded Cambridge and Oxford blue silk caps, emblazoned with "W.W.F.C. 1895-96", in honour of their Amateur Cup exploits that season. Another big match that season was a friendly with West Bromwich Albion, twice winners of the F.A. Cup and beaten finalists the previous season.

They would finish this season bottom of the First Division but escape relegation in the Test Matches. A guarantee of £30 was required but the 2,000 crowd paid more than £50 to see many past and future England internationals. Because the ground was soaked, Councillor Flint lent a large quantity of boards for the spectators to stand on, the first (temporary) terracing at Loakes Park. Wycombe strengthened the side with guest players Len Reynolds from Oxford University and Fred Handsombody, Marlow's best player. Buchanan unexpectedly gave the home side the lead but Albion equalised before half-time and ran out easy 4-1 winners, "fatigue" overcoming the amateurs.

In the evening, the members and their visitors held a 'smoker' at the Nags Head (see Appendix B). The final game of the season at Loakes Park was a replayed Berks & Bucks Senior Cup Final when a crowd of 1,237 saw Maidenhead win 1-0 after extra time against Wolverton 1-0, newly crowned champions of the Southern League Division Two. Datchet Webb played his final game that season and Bill Buchanan scored a goal a game for the third consecutive season. The success of the first season at Loakes Park was reflected in the gate receipts of £320-17s-9, more than double the previous season's take of £146-19s-3d. Five years before, the income amounted to just £9-3s-0d. A loss of £14-11s was made, however, in this inaugural season, largely because of £182 paid in guarantees to opposing clubs. The Club had also learnt in May that their application to join the Southern League Division Two had been accepted.

Entering the League was a big gamble, with away games as far as Bristol and Southampton, but the Club was keen to get away from a staple diet of friendly games and provide more attractive home games for their supporters. Throughout the summer of 1896 rumours of Wanderers turning professional circulated the town. Wolverton had decided to 'cross the Rubicon', as it was termed, for the coming season in the First Division, a disastrous decision as it turned out. But Wycombe saw no immediate need to do so and soon had 26 players signed on League forms. A party of 40 travelled by brake to Amersham, and then by train for the opening fixture at West Herts. They witnessed a much closer game then the 5-0 defeat suggests, and after the game the referee apologised for not allowing two apparently good goals for the visitors.

A 2-1 home defeat followed at the hands of Uxbridge, and afterwards the referee reported the Club to the F.A., for the spectators behaviour towards him and the visitors; Wycombe were let off with a caution. From this game, the Club began issuing a free match programme, available in the morning and detailing the match details, line-ups and fixtures for the season. A 9-0 defeat at Dartford

> **SOUTHERN LEAGUE.—DIVISION II.**
> **WYCOMBE WANDERERS v. WEST HERTS.**
> COMMENCEMENT OF THE LEAGUE CAMPAIGN.
> WYCOMBE'S FIRST LEAGUE TEAM; A HEAVY LOSS.
> REFEREE GREGORY EXTREMELY SORRY HE MADE MISTAKES.
>
> The above-named clubs made their initial appearance in the Southern League on Saturday last at Watford, and the outcome of such a meeting was looked forward to with great interest by the partisans of both clubs. Saturday will prove a memorable day from more than one standpoint in local football annals, for the town of chairs had never contributed a League team before, and the importance of such an undertaking was perhaps not realised to its fullest extent. West Herts and the Wanderers had previously met at Watford some two years ago, when the Hertfordshire men, after a good game, won by the margin of 5 goals to 2. It had been hoped that the Wanderers would have whipped up a good team in order to save, if possible, the loss of a couple of points, but the anticipated help was not forthcoming, and so "our boys" undertook the journey with their usual eleven, and against such formidable opponents they went down somewhat heavily, although not after by any means a one-sided game. The journey to Watford was by brake to Amersham, then by train to the desired destination, arriving at which with an hour to spare before play was commenced. In all the Wycombe party numbered 40, and with ideal football weather, and the turf in good trim, everything pointed to a pleasant encounter.
>
> **THE TEAMS.**
> Kick-off was announced for 3.30, but it was a few minutes after that hour when the teams put in an appearance, which was the signal for an outburst of applause from their respective supporters, the old familiar "Good old Wanderers" being heard from all quarters of the ground. Referee Gregory, R A., of Uxbridge, was the knight of the whistle, and when all were in readiness the teams were seen facing each other in the following order:—Wycombe Wanderers:— J. Ball, goal; A. W. Keen and H. Turner, backs; F. C. Keen, R. Collier, and G. Stevens, half-backs; W. Lloyd and F. G. Jennings, right wing; R. White, centre; F. W. Abbott (capt.) and W. Buchanan, left wing. West Herts:—S. King, goal; G. Davenport and J. R. Paull (capt.), backs; G. E. Green, F. C. Robins, and A. O. Ardley, half-backs; H. Wood and W. Saunders, right wing; R. G. Wright, centre; H. G. Anderson and R. Blyth, left wing.
> The duties of linesmen were shared by Mr. O. E. Russell (West Herts), and Mr. C. W. Harper (Wycombe Wanderers). Wycombe won the toss, and amid a general cheer Wright started
>
> **THE GAME.**
> Give and take play marked the opening exchanges; then the home team was forced to retreat by a big kick from A. W. Keen. Collier and Green were a bit conspicuous in mid-field, following which Abbott tried hard to break away, and although the "blues" had to stand back for a moment, they were the first to get in anything like dangerous quarters,

caused further alarm but the team grew stronger and finished the season in a creditable fifth position out of thirteen. Defeat in the F.A. Cup at Norwich Church Of England Young Mens Society was partly attributable to fatigue - the team had begun their journey at 8pm on Friday evening from Wycombe station.

Excused the qualifying rounds in the Amateur Cup because of their progress the previous season, the town was gripped with excitement at the prospect of playing the famous Casuals at Loakes Park in the First Round. Heavy snow had put the match in jeopardy so, the day before, 30 men with horses, carts and wheelbarrows, were paid a sum of £6-14s-8d to clear the pitch. By the evening only half the work had been done but, overnight, a thaw set in and the match had become a quagmire when the match eventually started.

Casuals had not arrived with their strongest team, although R.R. Barker, a full England player was included. Their superior passing and marking helped them to a 2-0 half-time lead but Wycombe fought back gamely and equalised three minutes before full-time. Both teams were happy to settle for a replay but the referee called for extra time; Casuals scored three more before the change around and finished 5-3 winners.

The rivalry with Marlow continued, including an incident packed match at the Crown Ground in November. Some players were wearing a jersey on top of their shirt and the referee asked all players to take them off because he could not distinguish the two sides. All agreed except for Marlow's Handsombody, then the other players claimed that all or none should remove them. Eventually the game was restarted and Wycombe's left-back, the Reverend Baines, fouled Marlow's captain C.A. Shaw. He went to retaliate but Albert Keen intervened, saying: *"If you hit Baines, you hit me. I'm not a parson, if he is."* Three minutes before the end Handsombody left the pitch to catch a train and immediately afterwards Abbott scored the only goal of the game. It was Marlow's first defeat of the season but Wycombe's rough play was roundly condemned afterwards. In February, Councillor Deacon made what was described as *"a bitter and unsportsmanlike attack"* on Marlow FC at a Wanderers dinner, only helping to fan the growing rivalry.

On 27 March, the two sides met once again but this time it was in the Final of the Berks & Bucks Senior Cup at Maidenhead. The interest was enormous - it was the biggest match in Wycombe's history and Marlow had just been knocked out of the Amateur Cup at the semi-final stage. The match drew a crowd of 4,000, paying over £122, a record for the district, with more than half coming from Wycombe. Shortly after the game had started, tragedy stuck Marlow's left-back Morton, when he broke two bones in his leg in a tackle with Jennings. Attended by three doctors, he was carried to the Cottage Hospital on the Press table and afterwards he exonerated Jennings from any blame. Helped by a strong wind, Marlow managed to score two goals just before half-time, through Davis and Hatton. After the five minute break, Jennings quickly pulled a goal back and the Wanderers appeared to have equalised when White, the Marlow goalkeeper, handled a shot behind the goal line. The referee, strangely, gave a corner and after the game, both neutral linesmen agreed that a goal should have been awarded. In spite of heavy Wycombe pressure, Marlow's ten men bravely held on to win.

Further controversy followed the final whistle when the usual presentation ceremony did not follow. The Berks and Bucks FA had decided beforehand that if Wycombe won, the presentation would be after the match. Marlow, if successful, would receive it at one of their future dinners, the inference being that the Wanderers did not have the grace to allow their opponents to receive the trophy.

The close season was a busy time for the Club. In August 1897 Robert Wood had met with Lord Carrington and a leasehold agreement for another 14 years was signed. The Earl also agreed to widen Lily's Walk, which led up to the ground from the town. Complaints had been made that spectators were using the woods at the bottom of the ground as a public toilet so it was decided to build a soakaway urinal; in October turnstiles were used for the first time. The Club had made over £100 last season, and, with £40 in the bank, could afford these necessary ground improvements. It seems that Charley Harper's efforts in bettering the Club did not meet with everyone's approval and he only narrowly defeated F. Owen in the election for Secretary. George Horwood stepped down as trainer and Messrs Plumridge and Neville took over his duties. Bill Trinder was appointed groundsman and, in an effort to clear the pitch of stones, he would collect up boys after school finished and set them to work, rewarding them with free entry on the Saturday. The Club's headquarters were changed to the Swan Hotel, Pauls Row, where the teams would also change. Bill Pearce was heartily thanked for all that he had done for the Club at the Nags Head.

Wycombe Phoenix, the Berk & Bucks Junior Cup holders, merged with the Wanderers and would provide most of the reserve players. On the pitch Chesham Generals accounted for Wycombe in both the opening games in the F.A. Cup and the Berks & Bucks Senior Cup, the latter having a large body of policemen present at Loakes Park because of trouble both on and off the pitch at Chesham in the F.A. Cup.

The Amateur Cup, however, produced a memorable run beginning at Old Deer Park, Richmond, when the favourites to win the competition, Old Westminsters, were sensationally defeated 5-0. After disposing of 2nd Coldstream Guards 3-1 at Loakes Park, Uxbridge were drawn way in the Quarter Finals. More than a thousand Wanderers fans saw Charlie Buchanan score a dramatic equaliser a few minutes before time. Before the replay the following Saturday, the draw for the semi-finals had taken place, pitching the winners of the tie against Old Malvernians. The F.A. appeared to anticipate Wycombe winning because the semi-final would take place at Marlow, however Uxbridge won the replay 4-2, never falling behind, and went on to the final, losing to Middlesbrough 2-1 at Crystal Palace.

19

In the League the team began to struggle as standards improved, meanwhile two more teams, St Albans and West Herts, had turned professional. In December Royal Artillery (Portsmouth), the eventual champions, visited Loakes Park. Wycombe had played magnificently to lead 1-0 at half-time, but trailed 3-1 with a few minutes to go when Fred Abbott barged the Portsmouth keeper, Gunner Reilly, to the ground as he patted the ball upfield. He got up and brandished his fists at Abbott and then ran 15 yards to a spectator who was urging the referee to send him off. Reilly struck a certain J.Payne, apparently not the originator of the comment, who fell back into the arms of a policeman. The crowd then rushed onto the pitch but order was eventually restored and the match finished. Two weeks later at an F.A. disciplinary hearing, Reilly was suspended for two weeks and Loakes Park was closed for one week, from Monday 10 January 1898, with no games to played within three miles.

Bowing out that season was Jim Ball, the last remaining player since the opening season and goalkeeper since 1889, with the former Marlow player Ernie Wheeler taking his place. The Club received a huge blow when captain Fred Abbott joined the Metropolitan Police in June. He did play a few odd games the following season but his enormous influence was essentially lost. Abbott was probably the best Wycombe player at the time, and at the start of the season he had turned down the large offer of £2 a week to go professional with another team. The Christmas Day edition of the Bristol Mercury had said of him after playing at Warmley: *"In Abbott, who is captain, they have a brilliant outside-left, who can shoot and centre grandly, while his pace is extraordinary, and he often shewed the Warmley back a clean pair of heals."* His leadership qualities were quickly noticed in his new career and in 1936 Frederick William Abbott retired as Deputy Assistant Commissioner of the Metropolitan Police. Before his death on 28 December 1940, he had been made an Officer of the British Empire, a Member of the Royal Victorian Order and been presented with the Kings Police Medal.

Fred Keen was elected captain for the 1898-99 season, one of the best half backs in the county. Charlie Johnson was appointed groundsman in place of Bill Trinder who had a grievance about unpaid wages, which he claimed for extra work on the turnstiles. A constant problem since moving to Loakes Park had been spectators playing football on the pitch before kick-off, during half-time, and after the game. So goalposts were erected on another part of the ground to prevent damage to the pitch. Charlie Buchanan was offered professional terms by Reading and, while he considered his future, he refused to sign League forms, only doing so in mid-October. In the meantime new signing E.G. Hatton played at centre forward, reputedly the fastest sprinter in Berks & Bucks and able to cover 120 yards in 10½ seconds. Playing against Chesham, the match report wryly noted that he did not cover that distance in ten minutes and , after four games, he left the Club. Professionalism was the burning issue as Wycombe remained one of the few amateur clubs in the Southern League.

The *Free Press* stated *"discontent appears to reign generally amongst their supporters, and the question is asked 'Will they turn pros'"* - a vice-president even offered to pay 10s (50p) a week towards the players wages. At this time the town of High Wycombe had a population of 18,000 and, given the level of attendances, could well have supported a full-time team. The members of the Club, however, were a conservative body and feared getting into financial difficulty, especially as the annual rent for Loakes Park had just been raised from £14 to £30 for the next 14 years. The Club had entered a second league this season, the Bucks and Contiguous Counties League, so named because the Hertfordshire F.A. refused to allow their name to be used in the title. The second game in the new League saw an 8-0 half-time deficit finish in a 15-0 defeat at Watford, to date the Club's joint record defeat. Four months later Wycombe won 3-1 at Watford in the Southern League, with just five players remaining from the first game.

Wycombe first met Brentford this season, initially in the Southern League, (at the Cross Roads Ground, South Ealing), when the Bees won 9-2, seven of the goals coming from dead-ball situations. In January the sides met on a frost bound pitch at Loakes Park and, in spite of leading 2-1 at half-time, Wycombe lost 3-2 to a goal which the home crowd felt was clearly offside; the referee, Royston Bourke, needed a police escort after the game. It was Brentford's only game in the Amateur Cup - they scratched to Grimsby Albany in the next round, probably due to their impending switch to professionalism. Fulham were also new opponents that season in the Southern League, and when the teams met at Craven Cottage in December, the *Bucks Standard* reporter noted: *"The Craven Cottage ground is situated about a mile from everywhere, and is approached by dirty, narrow lanes"!* Making his debut in that match for the Wanderers was the talented goalkeeper F.C.'Tibby' Johnson, who had left Maidenhead in acrimonious circumstances. The *Football Sun* said: *"He is a splendid man between the sticks but he has his own terms, and these must be accepted by any club - amateur or professional - who deserves his services. Maidenhead could not see their way to complying with "F C J's" conditions."* This slur on both player and club caused uproar in Wycombe and both Charlie Harper and Johnson strenuously denied the allegation in the press.

The Berks & Bucks Senior Cup Final was reached for the second time, and once again the old enemy Marlow were the opponents. They had already beaten Wycombe at Loakes Park in the F.A. Cup this season and so great was the interest that an enormous crowd of 7,752 paid on the day at Maidenhead, with several hundred more having paid in advance. In fact it was the biggest amateur gate nationally that season. Some 4,000 travelled from Wycombe, *"chair vans were gaily trimmed with the Oxford and Cambridge colours"*, while many walked the ten miles. Temporary stands were erected and 1,000 supporters had to stand on the railway embankment at the York Road ground. Marlow support numbered 1,000, which was the population of the village at the time, and the duties of fifteen police officers present consisted principally of saying, *"Pass on please"*! Goalless at half-time, Marlow scored two goals in the first eight minutes after the break, through Hawkes and a Shaw penalty. Charlie Buchanan pulled a goal back with an overhead kick but Marlow once again won 2-1.

At the end of the season the Club decided that the infamous Loakes Park pitch must be levelled and a sum of £225 was set aside for the task, to be carried out by Lee & Son. A shilling ground fund was set up with the hope that a thousand people would pay a shilling each. It was optimistically thought that the ground would be ready for the coming season but just in case, the High Wycombe Cricket Club was approached in July 1899. They learnt that rent on the Wanderers old stomping ground would be £3 per match for a minimum of twelve matches, and the pitch would have to be put in good order before the cricket season started, at the football Club's expense. The cricket club were not well off, having only raised £6 to £7 the previous season, and Wanderers rejected the terms. They then turned to Captain Williams, Commanding Officer of the Third Oxford Light Infantry at Wycombe Barracks. He kindly agreed to the Club using Barrack Meadow, adjoining Loakes Park on the West side. The first match there was a friendly against Wandsworth on 16 September 1899 with the Reverend Oakley, a former Corinthian, playing his only game for the Club. He was killed on a motor bike in many years later, and a huge crowd attended his funeral.

The third match, against Wolverton on 7 October, was the last at this venue, for the Club were informed on the morning of the match by the War Office that it was against military rules to charge admission on Barrack Meadow. The Club hurriedly called a meeting and resolved to approach Earl Carrington who generously agreed to them playing rent free in Wycombe Abbey Park, on a former hockey pitch, and where peacocks freely roamed. His lordship would not allow the main entrance to be used, the Rupert Gates then situated on the High Street and now situated half way up Marlow Hill. Instead the Club had to build a bridge across the Dyke from the Rye, Lee & Son completing the job in seven days at a cost of £37. The rather flimsy looking trestle bridge, in soft wood, lasted until the First World War and stood half way between the open air swimming pool and Wendover Way. The one turnstile was on the Park side and the pitch is now covered with trees, under Keep Hill. The opening match at the Park was against Bowes Park on 14 October, with Earl and Lady Carrington coming down from the Abbey to see some of the match, the first of many they watched that season.

The only F.A. Cup game played there saw the powerful Reading professionals, including famous England international J Holt, win 8-0, still Wycombe's record home defeat in a cup-tie. Two train loads of Reading fans arrived, many with biscuits hanging from their lapels (after the Reading biscuit factory of H & P Palmer). Wycombe fans sported miniature wooden chairs, and afterwards Mayor Robert Wood had to separate a group of rival fans fighting, while the Reading Band paraded around the High Street. The team bounced back the following week at Maidenhead, with a 6-0 win in the Amateur Cup, *"the Wycombe followers shouted the goals after Reading's style: 1-2-3-4-5-6, with a long breath for the last named figure."* Wycombe battled through the Amateur Cup qualifying rounds and lost to Marlow in a First Round replay after a draw at Daws Hill in front of 3,000, the record crowd for that ground. Marlow were again the opponents in the Berks & Bucks Senior Cup Final at Maidenhead on Easter Monday, in front of a smaller crowd on this occasion. A very sporting 1-1 draw gave little indication of the controversy that was to come in the replay the following Saturday on the same ground.

The game kicked off at 5pm and the 2,200 Wycombe fans were soon celebrating as Tom Barlow scored after eight minutes. Marlow's Captain Ted Shaw had a goal disallowed for offside and Wycombe retained their lead at the break. Shortly after the restart, another Marlow goal was ruled offside. Almost immediately they got the ball into the net again and this time the referee, Mr Muir from Southampton, consulted with his linesman before ruling offside once more. This was all too much for the Marlow Captain who walked off the pitch, in protest, followed by the goalkeeper. The game continued and the President of the Berks & Bucks F.A., R.F. Lunnon, who was also a Marlow vice-president, hurried down to the pitch and persuaded the two players to rejoin. This they did after a lengthy conversation with the referee and soon afterwards Marlow equalised through James. Ten minutes from time Wycombe were awarded a penalty for a trip, in spite of Marlow's claim for an offside.

Bill Buchanan converted and Wycombe appeared to be home and dry until the last minute when Ernie Wheeler, the Wanderers goalkeeper, held onto the ball for too long and was unceremoniously bundled into the net by a posse of Marlow forwards; with little protection for keepers in those days, the goal was given.

The referee called for extra time but 15 minutes were lost as the Wycombe players refused to continue, a *"severe attack of the sulks"* as The Maidenhead Advertiser described it. Eventually play started in the gathering gloom and by the turn around, Marlow were leading 3-2 through a Hawkes goal. The second quarter began at 7.25 pm and an injury to a Wycombe player brought further delay before Marlow added a fourth goal, with no none able to see who scored it. All around spectators lit matches and held burning newspapers in the air. Bob White pulled a goal back for Wycombe, although few saw it, and then with six minutes left to play the ball was kicked onto the railway embankment. The crowd refused to give it back and suddenly the pitch was engulfed by supporters. The referee abandoned the match with Marlow leading 4-3 and he was escorted back to the pavilion by the police.

The following Wednesday the Berks and Bucks F.A. held a special meeting to consider the events and decreed that the remaining six minutes of play should be played the following Friday at Maidenhead. Alfred Davis, secretary of both Marlow F.C. and the Berks & Bucks F.A., had submitted a written statement, much to the annoyance of the Wycombe Committee whose version of events was not formally put forward. Marlow claimed that the Wycombe players had not assembled on the pitch until 10 minutes after the official kick-off time, had wasted 15 minutes before starting extra time and took an extra five minutes at the changeover. The referee supported the claim that the match would have been completed but for Wycombe's time wasting.

In their reply Wycombe said that their train, due to arrive at 4.30 pm, did not arrive until 4.46 pm and anyway the match officials took the field after the Wycombe players. The alleged time wasting was also greatly exaggerated they said, and if the referee had really felt that Wycombe wasted time after 90 minutes, then he could have awarded the tie to Marlow. They also pointed out that two previous games between the clubs that season, one in the Amateur Cup and the other a reserve game, were both abandoned due to poor light and replayed over a full 90 minutes. Wycombe refused to play the extra six minutes and the cup was subsequently awarded to Marlow. This affair shook the local football world and although the town of High Wycombe was, as ever, solidly behind their team, other clubs sided with Marlow.

It was a real watershed for football in Buckinghamshire. Although it was Marlow's eleventh win in the twenty two years of the competition, it turned out to be their last for 91 years, marking the gradual lessening of their importance in the increasingly competitive world of football. Wycombe, on the other hand, were poised to dominate local football completely.

The following season Wycombe refused to enter the County Cup as a protest, a measure which would hit the County body hard in the pocket. As a result, the Berks & Bucks F.A. amended their rules and insisted that all member clubs must enter the competition. Instead Wycombe applied to join the London League for the 1900-01 season, but their application was refused by the F.A., under the recommendation of the Berks & Bucks F.A. and influenced by Wycombe's refusal to enter the County Cup. Chesham Town and Chesham Generals were also unwittingly caught up in the affair as their applications were also refused. As the fixture list had been published Wycombe still played the matches against the reserve sides of Woolwich Arsenal, Tottenham Hotspur, Queens Park Rangers and Millwall Athletic as friendlies. The levelling of Loakes Park had been completed but the grass had not grown sufficiently so Daws Hill would be used for a second season. R. Howland took over from Charlie Deacon as Chairman.

C.W.Deacon:
President (1908-13) and Chairman (1900-1902)

The opening Southern League game at home, against Shepherds Bush, saw yet more controversy. Many of the spectators from Wycombe had been drinking heavily before the game because the General Election result had been declared in the morning. They continually abused the visiting players and the referee, who was hustled as he left the pitch, and Charlie Harper had to appeal for calm. Two Wycombe players were sent off for the first time in the Club's history, Charlie Buchanan for a bad foul and Archie Green for dissent. Afterwards the referee claimed that Green had said to him: *"How much have you been paid to square this job?"* The player later said that his comment of *"How much did you get for that?"* was aimed at another player's appointment during the election. The Club committee met the following Wednesday and decided to ban two of the troublemakers from home games for the rest of the season and four more for one month.

Wycombe were reported to the F.A. and Buchanan was banned from football for two weeks and Green for one month. Daws Hill Park was closed for two weeks from 29 October and the Club was banned from playing football within a ten mile radius. This was the third time the Club had got into serious trouble with the Football Association, and the second time its ground was closed. The closure meant that the scheduled F.A. Cup Third Qualifying Round tie at home to Richmond Association on 3 November would have to be played away. The Club, however, decided to scratch from the competition rather than lose money as the expected tiny attendance would not cover travelling costs (the previous match at Richmond in 1898 had only netted £2-5s); this showed the lack of importance the competition then held for the Club. Richmond Association were beaten in the Amateur Cup at Daws Hill Park but Wycombe lost 5-2 at Ealing in the Second Round, playing against a deaf and dumb goalkeeper (Finley).

Results went badly in the Southern League with many heavy defeats. The 11-1 defeat at Brentford was partly explained by only ten men taking the field - captain Fred Keen failed to catch the train at Loudwater and it was rumoured that he had gone ice skating instead! Keen was sent off in the 4-0 friendly against Millwall for rough play and the following week the team travelled to Millwall and lost 8-0, with only one foul given in the whole game. The biggest disaster happened when only one first-teamer, the goalkeeper Eddie Reynolds who had taken over from Ernie Wheeler earlier in the season, was prepared to play at Grays in a League fixture. The team, including people picked up on the way *"who had hardly touched a ball"*, crashed to a 15-0 defeat, equalling the record defeat at Watford the previous season.

There was much criticism at that summer's AGM of the previous season's playing record and because gate receipts were down to £200 from the usual £300 plus. Bill Buchanan took over as captain and half back Bob Collier had played his last game, eight years after first playing for the team. The good news was that Loakes Park was ready again for use, with just an eleven foot slope from corner flag to corner flag, and a letter was sent to Lord Carrington thanking him for the use of Daws Hill Park rent free. Up to now ladies had been admitted free to home games but it was decided to charge them 3d admission or 2/6d for a season ticket. The 1901-02 season began at Loakes Park with a match against Mr.E. Shaw's XI, a combined team of Marlow and Maidenhead players, arranged to dispel the bad feeling still lingering from the 1900 County Cup final.

A new League had been formed, the Berks & Bucks Senior League with just four teams, and results improved in the Southern League. The season, though was remembered for good cup runs, in particular the Berks & Bucks Senior Cup when the final was reached for the fourth time in six years. This time Slough were the opponents, not the bogey side Marlow, and the Wycombe supporters travelled full of expectation. Receipts were £217-11s-7d, and there is an intriguing mention of £5 lost to forged tickets. In an entertaining game, Wycombe were slightly superior in skill and tactics. Bill Buchanan opened the scoring after five minutes, three minutes later a mistake by the Slough full-back Fidler allowed Bob White to score and Fidler again was lax when he let Fred 'Sunny' Rouse run through the defence to complete the scoring. Wycombe supporters were overjoyed, for they had endured much heartache in this competition, but now that the coveted trophy was won, the Club's first win as senior side,, they felt that the Club had truly established itself.

The presentation of the Cup, by the Mayor of Maidenhead, was followed by a high tea in the town hall. The team arrived back at Wycombe station at 7pm where a crowd of thousands was waiting to greet them. The team were pulled on a wagonette to the Swan Hotel, where the cup was filled again and again. Celebrations continued for many days as the players took the cup around the town's many different pubs. One of the dinners the players attended served the following menu: Mayonnaise of Lobster, Game Pie, Pigeon Pie, Ham, Roast Beef, Press Beef, Potatoes, Mutton Cutlets in Aspic, Galantines, Brawn, Tongues, Roast Fowl, Mixed Salads, Compote of Pears, Cold Rice, Jellies, Creams and Apple Tart. A photograph was taken of the winning team before the match with Brighton the next day.

Opening day of the High Wycombe Tennis Club, at Loakes Park.

(May 1903)

The Maidenhead Norfolkians Charity Cup was also won against the Norfolkians and the Cup was presented by Lord Carrington standing next to the Press Table, situated by the half-way line. Receipts that season totalled a record £533-2s-8d, and more than half the cost of levelling the pitch had been cleared. In spite of the healthy financial state of affairs, a motion to reduce admission from 6d to 4d was heavily defeated. George Stokes was elected Collector, responsible for both collecting money at the turnstiles and from the annual members subscriptions. A former Army NCO, all local children feared him in his role as High Wycombe's school attendance officer.

Top scorer from the previous season, Fred Rouse, had signed professional forms for Shepherds Bush and went on to a long Football League career with Grimsby Town (37 apps, 15 goals), Stoke City (69, 28), Everton (9,2), Chelsea (38,11) and W.B.A. (5,2), before returning to the Southern League with Croydon Common and Brentford. Only six teams were entered for Division Two of the Southern League, with Maidenhead fined £20 for their late withdrawal. A notice was posted to the entrance at Loakes Park warning all members to show their membership cards or pay to go in as some people were getting in free by saying *"that they were members"*.

Later that month, when Chesham Generals visited Loakes Park in March for a County League fixture, the referee, Mr Neale from London, wanted to play ten minutes short each way so that he could catch an early train; the teams refused and the official wasted no time at all during the afternoon! In April the Berks & Bucks Senior Cup Final was held at Loakes Park, a crowd of 6,000 seeing Slough beat Aylesbury 3-0. This was the largest crowd ever seen at the ground, with another 1,000 watching free from Tom Burt's Hill, and the gates were only opened one hour before the game.

Fred Rouse
Wycombe's first professional player

In Remembrance of
Wycombe Wanderers,
Who succumbed from a severe attack of indigestion brought on by attempting to eat Aylesbury Ducks,
On Saturday Feb. 21st, 1903.

Oh it was a very dreadful blow,
That for another year has laid us low.
But in season 1904,
We hope to lift that cup once more.

After defeat by Aylesbury in the Berks. & Bucks Cup, hundreds of these cards were circulated in High Wycombe by a Ducks supporter!

Wycombe wanted £10 from the county association for the use of the ground, twice what they were normally charged at Maidenhead, but eventually agreed to £5.

Bunny Hooper was elected captain for the 1903-04 season and Lord Carrington was proposed as President, but Robert Wood easily won the vote. A private entrance for the players and members was built during the summer and, on 23 October 1903, Harry Browning of the Red Lion Hotel, initiated a fund to build a stand at Loakes Park at a meeting of supporters. The cost would be £400 and shares of £1 each would be issued, paying 4% interest until the Club had paid the capital back. Holders of ten shares would have free use of the stand until it became the absolute property of the Club. £250 worth of shares were taken up at the meeting, and a total of £411 was eventually subscribed.

The £400 tender of H. Flint, Easton Street, was accepted and the stand was opened for the visit of Southampton Reserves on 9 January 1904. It measured 150 feet long, with four rows of benches seating 400 people and at either end were dressing rooms 20 feet wide. The one at the eastern end was thatched and more ornamental, to blend in with the local architecture, and this was used by the opposing players. Zinc baths were heated up on stoves, just enough to remove the worst of the mud - proper baths were yet to come. Apart from providing more comfort for spectators and making visits by top teams even more attractive, the main aim was to block the view from the steeply rising ground behind the pitch, a source of constant irritation to the Club since Loakes Park opened.

Half back George Stevens made his last appearance in a quartered shirt in September, ten years after his first game. At Christmas 1903 the Club was shaken when both the president, Robert Wood, and Charlie Harper handed in their resignations. Harper by now had moved to London to teach but both men were persuaded to stay on. The 1903-04 season was notable for an F.A. Cup run which saw Wycombe face Brentford at Loakes Park, one game away from the First Round Proper. Early in the match the Wanderers goalkeeper Eddie Reynolds received a severe kick on the right thigh from the opposing forward Buchanan. He was carried off and returned gingerly 20 minutes later, with the Brentford players careful not to charge him again! The Bees won 4-1 and after the game there was an incident 300 yards from the ground, which was reported to the referee.

One of the visiting players stood up in a brake and invited the home supporters to go to their hotel, the Desborough Arms, if they *"wanted anything - a punch on the nose by way of change."*

At the 1904 AGM it was announced that the pitch levelling account had been paid off and that the Club had secured a bank overdraft, enabling them to pay off all tradesmen bar one. The High Wycombe Tennis Club rented the pitch in the summer for £10, helping to keep the grass in good order; they used netting to stop the balls rolling down the hill. Wycombe now found themselves the only amateur club in the Southern League, following Chesham Town's withdrawal and Southall's decision to turn professional. The problem of the 'free gallery' was still present, although these spectators were now forced further up Tom Burt's Hill.

The *Bucks Free Press* noted in December 1904: *"A collection was made on Monday, the occasion of the Marlow v Wycombe match, among the "sportsmen" patronising the "free gallery" which overlooks Loakes Park. The proceeds, without deducting anything for expenses, amounted to 10d! Every coin ought to be studded with diamonds and kept in a glass case at Headquarters."* The receipts for the match amounted to £20. Charlie Harper again tendered his resignation at the 1905 AGM as he was finding it difficult to get down from London. He agreed to continue provided he was given help, so George Bunce became the Assistant Secretary. It was a gloomy meeting as George Miles also handed in his resignation, which was not accepted.

Attendances had fallen because of the poor results so it was decided to let ladies into the enclosure free. The despondency was lifted by a stirring F.A. Cup run, successfully coming through four qualifying rounds before failing once again at the hands of Brentford, this time 4-0 at Griffin Park. An appalling accident happened in November 1905, in a Berks & Bucks match at home to Chesham Generals. The visitor's right-back, A. Bone, sustained a badly broken leg in a challenge with Wanderers's half back M Ray. A stretcher was fetched from Newlands Police Station and he was taken to Dr Bradshaw's surgery in Easton Street and then to the Cottage Hospital, Priory Road. A collection of £6 was raised at the game but later the leg had to be amputated. Wanderers paid for his twelve week stay in hospital and on 26 March a benefit match against the Generals was staged at Loakes Park, raising £25 5s 6d towards the fund. The Berks & Bucks F.A. and the Football Association donated £20-10s and £25 respectively, eventually enabling the unfortunate player to set himself up in business.

When Fulham Reserves visited in January 1906, the General Election campaign was in full swing and Seddon Cripps, the Tory candidate, kicked off the first half and Arnold Herbert the second. Herbert's was the bigger kick and he was later elected MP.

At the end of the season the Club held a smoking concert at the Swan Hotel and presented a medal and a smoker's cabinet to left-back Widdy Busby, to commemorate 111 consecutive appearances. Charlie Tilbury also received a special presentation for only missing two games in six seasons. At the AGM that summer, a lively debate took place on *"Should professionalism be embraced in order to compete with opponents?"* The Club had finished bottom of the League for the first time but there was no likelihood of turning its back on the amateur game. Nor was there any chance of failing to be re-elected to the Southern League as all of the visiting teams enjoyed their train trips to one of the best amateur grounds and pitches in the South.

At the beginning of the 1906-07 season, Tom Phillips, the new landlord of the Swan Hotel, presented the Club with a solid silver spirit flask, for use when the players were injured! One side was beautifully engraved with the Wycombe Swan, the other was engraved *"The Swan is chained, the trainer is Free so if you are hurt rely on me"*. The trainer, Fred 'Ladder' Free, was delighted with his new aid. In November, former player Sunny Rouse was transferred from Stoke to Everton for £600 and Charley Harper tried unsuccessfully to get Everton to play at Loakes Park. Stoke, however, were willing and the match was held on Fair Monday, 19 November, when farm workers, looking for work, would come to Wycombe to be hired under the Guildhall. The game attracted a big crowd of 3,000 and receipts of £35-10s; generously Stoke only took £22-10s, after originally wanting a minimum of £20 and all receipts over £30. The Royal Grammar School boys successfully petitioned the headmaster, Mr Arnison, to change the school half-day from Tuesday to Monday! In those days the school was situated opposite the Rye, close to Loakes Park, and a source of players for the Club. Stoke's golkeeper Dr Leigh Richmond Walsh was in sparkling form as the professionals won 3-1.

On 25 January 1907 the Club's headquarters was connected with the National Telephone Company, number 128. Another disappointing season in the League, bottom again, was partly made up by a good run through the qualifying rounds of the Amateur Cup, only to lose in the First Round at home to 2nd Grenadier Guards. The Berks & Bucks Senior Cup Final was held at Loakes Park in April and in the Maidenhead Norfolkians side to face Marlow was the famous one legged goalkeeper, C Gyngell, with a wooden stump below his knee. There had been much controversy in the national press whether he should be allowed to play but the F.A., backed by Marlow, decreed he was eligible. Surprisingly mobile, he received a lot of protection from his defence, and picked up a winners medal in a replay after the first game ended in a 1-1 draw.

The 1907-08 season goes down as the worst season the Club has ever had in a League. The opening 13 Southern League games were all lost and the team had to wait until 1 April for the first points of the season, a 4-0 win against second from bottom club Brighton. The AGM on the 27 July 1908 was perhaps the most depressing in the Club's history. Gate receipts were down to just £165, subscriptions were only £34 and liabilities amounted to £244-14s, with only £1-3s-2d at the bank.

The members listened gloomily as the deaths were reported of Sammy Ellis, the promising inside-right who had fallen ill the previous October, and W.K. Melsome, the former landlord of the Swan Hotel, who had done so much for the Club after the move to Loakes Park. Charley Harper handed in his resignation for a third time, and this time it was accepted with much regret, the members realising that it was impossible for him to carry out his duties as Secretary while based in London. He was made a vice-president, along with Bunny Hooper who handed the captaincy over to Charlie Tilbury, and J.N.F. Vale was elected the new Secretary, polling 24 votes to George Vickers' 16.

The Southern League again invited Wanderers to retain their membership but the offer was declined as the professional league was clearly no longer a place for amateurs. The Club needed the income that local derbies could generate and became members of the Great Western Suburban League, in existence since 1904-05, and covering West London and the Thames Valley. Admission charges were reduced to 4d for men, and 2d for women and children. In September, Tom Gilson, a former professional with Aston Villa, Brentford, Bristol City and Clapton Orient, joined the Club as a re-instated amateur. He had found local employment and became the regular left-back for the next three seasons.

Wycombe enjoyed their best League season ever to finish third out of thirteen teams, the opening game seeing a 4-3 home win against old rivals Maidenhead. Maidenhead also appeared at Loakes Park in a controversial F.A. Cup game in October, when their right-back, Warwick, refused to leave the field after being sent off for hitting George Payne. Warwick was subsequently suspended for one month and Payne for two weeks.

A promising Amateur Cup run was surprisingly halted by Caversham Rovers at Loakes Park but it was the Berks & Bucks Senior Cup which provided the most excitement. In the Final at Marlow, Chesham Generals were defeated 3-0 and Wanderers won the Cup without conceding a goal in the competition. The Cup was presented by R.A. Lunnon, the President of the Berks & Bucks F.A., and he paid tribute to captain Charlie Tilbury saying *"that a man so small in physique had reached a high standard in skill and sportsmanship."* On the way back the team left the train at Loudwater and travelled by brake to town, cheered by thousands of people. On the London Road the horses were taken out and the brake was pulled to the Swan Hotel where drink was taken from the Cup. The gold medals had to be inscribed and were presented twelve days after, at the match with Reading Reserves, by Lady Myee Carrington.

In attendance were Lord Wendover and Lady Carrington, local MP Arnold Herbert, Viscount Bury and the Reverend E D Shaw, the Vicar of High Wycombe and the first English cricketer to carry his bat through the innings against the Australians. The match ball used in the final was purchased by Charlie Deacon and can still be seen in the boardroom at Adams Park. New Secretary Vale had been busy making his mark that first season. A bicycle stand was opened at Loakes Park in January 1909, to prevent them being left untidily all over the ground, and an attendant charged a small fee. A series of whist drives was held at the Swan Hotel, the first one raising £5 from the 100 tickets sold, and a concert in March raised the large sum of £30.

The 1909-10 season was even more of a success, third position once more in the League and the Club's all time record score, when Staines were defeated 18-1 at Loakes Park. The visitors apparently fielded their first team and afterwards were at a loss to explain the humiliating scoreline. Fred Pheby's seven goals in that game is still an individual Wycombe record in a League game, and he went on to average more than a goal a game that season. Rouse finally made his return to his old Club when he played for West Bromwich Albion on the September Fair Monday, a crowd of over 3,000 turning out to see the 1-1 draw. There were four exciting cup runs as well, beginning with the F.A. Cup.

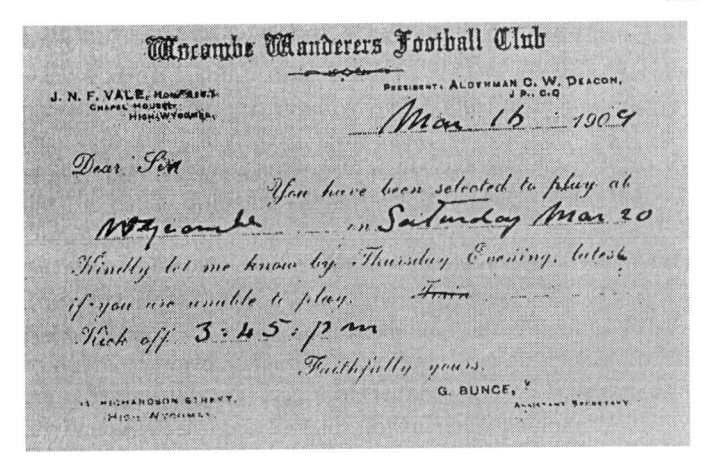

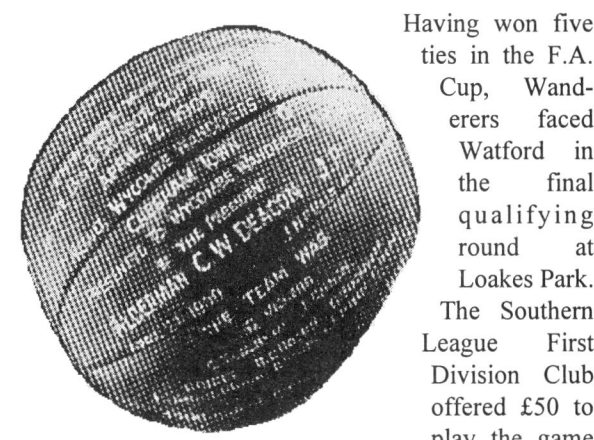

The 1909 B.& B. Final match ball

Having won five ties in the F.A. Cup, Wanderers faced Watford in the final qualifying round at Loakes Park. The Southern League First Division Club offered £50 to play the game at Watford, but it was turned down and the 4,500 crowd paid £85 2s 9d. The professionals won 4-0 and lost to Woolwich Arsenal in the First Round.

The Amateur Cup was no less exciting and, after a splendid 5-3 win against the powerful Leytonstone side, second in the Isthmian League the previous season, they faced the Cup holders themselves, Clapton, in the Fourth Round. The Oxford & Bucks Territorial Band travelled with the team to the Spotted Dog ground and entertained the spectators. Many neutrals had tipped Wanderers to win the Cup after the win in the previous round but Clapton were too good a side and won 4-1. The Wycombe players found the small pitch and cramped ground not at all to their liking and in AGM the following summer, chairman, Charlie Deacon, said *"we may have won the Amateur Cup, if the game had been at Loakes Park, instead of the 'toy ground', the Spotted Dog."* The Berks & Bucks Senior Cup Final was again reached, this time the opponents were Wokingham Athletic at Marlow. A physically hard game ended 0-0, with Frank Langley having to leave the pitch with an injury. He also missed the replay when his team mates won the cup for the second successive season.

Notification to player George Payne of his selection by the Committee, who met every Monday evening.

Nearly 10,000 saw the two games and afterwards Alfred Davis Jnr, secretary of the Berks & Bucks F.A., said that *"his Association always recognised it as a matter of relief when Wycombe was in the Final."* The team shared the Bucks Charity Cup that season, after a 1-1 draw with Aylesbury in the final. In the semi-final against Wolverton, police had to be called in to protect the Wycombe team as they left the pitch at Aylesbury. Charlie Tilbury was threatened with a ducking in the nearby canal! Reading F.C., whose reserve side won the Great Western Suburban League that season, made the unusual request of financial assistance from Wycombe Wanderers.

The general committee agreed to donate £2-2s if the other clubs in the League did likewise. Secretary Vale had to tender his resignation in the summer, because work commitments would take him out of the district and the popular half back Bernard Hooper was elected in his place.

The 1910-11 season started without the services of inside-right, Bly Brion, because the Berks & Bucks F.A. had suspended him from football for four months. Once again the Fourth round of the Amateur Cup was reached; in the First Round, Swindon Victoria drew at Loakes Park but gave up the right to use their ground in the replay, eager for a big pay day. Further home victories followed over Woking and 1st Kings Royal Rifles before 2nd Coldstream Guards came to Loakes Park for a Fourth Round tie. Once again Wanderers felt confident of winning the most cherished of all competitions and a thrilling match ended 1-1 at 90 minutes. Roberts put Wycombe into the lead in extra time but then the soldiers equalised with a soft goal and then dramatically snatched the winner in the last minute. After Christmas 1910, the Club set off on their first overseas tour, playing a match at Weymouth before catching a ferry to Guernsey, where they drew 1-1 with a representative side.

Loakes Park - County Final Venue.

The AGM of 1911 was pleased to hear that there was a balance in hand of £43-4s, the first time for some years. Charlie Tilbury expressed a strong desire to stand down from the captaincy and George Buchanan was elected in his place. The opening match of the 1911-12 season was a benefit match against Fulham St Andrews for Tom Gilson who had left the district in the summer and fallen seriously ill. He died from cancer the following February aged 33. The match raised £30 and making his debut in that game was Frank Adams, four days after his twentieth birthday. Before the season had started Queen Park Rangers had invited both him and Billy O'Gorman for a trial. They returned but were not selected to play and when they were picked again, they failed to put in appearance. Captain George Buchanan created a sensation on the day of the opening League game - for he resigned from the Club and never played football again. Marlow joined the Great Western Suburban League this season and surprisingly took three points off Wanderers.

Their winning goal in the November win at Marlow was scored by former Wycombe player Bly Brion. Prolific scorer Fred Pheby was now playing on the left-wing and Joey Goodchild was top scorer in his debut season with 29 goals in 29 games. This included nine goals in League games against Ravenscourt Amateurs, seven in the 13-0 win, both games later expunged when the Club withdrew from the League with pitch problems.

The AGM of July 1912 decided to change headquarters to the Red Lion Hotel, where the new proprietor, Mr.D. Adams, had been showing an interest in the Club. Billy O'Gorman was elected Captain and Frank Adams left the Club to play for Shepherds Bush, prompting much criticism from supporters of the fifteen man match selection committee. In the Amateur Cup, Abingdon visited Loakes Park on 9th November, not arriving until 4.15 pm.

The match was abandoned at half time with spectators lighting small paper fires around the ground in an effort to see. It was replayed the following week, with Abingdon sensationally winning 6-2. In the F.A. Cup old rivals Uxbridge won 4-3 at Loakes Park, with Joey Goodchild missing a penalty with the last kick of the match, after he had been brought down when clean through.

Charlie Deacon, President, Chairman and an influential supporter of the Club since their junior days, died on 27 February 1912, aged 62. Once gain Wycombe contested the Berks & Bucks Senior Cup Final, against Maidenhead at Marlow. The game ended 1-1 and top scorer Billy O'Gorman missed the replay through illness, the returning Frank Adams stepping in and helping to secure the Club's fourth win in the competition with an extra time goal from Pheby. Adams was elected captain for the following season, beginning 70 years of devotion to the Club. George Miles became Chairman, and the Marquess of Lincolnshire, now the senior title of Lord Carrington, finally became President.

On 27 September 1913 the team first made use of motorised transport for a game when Alec Stacey's "Blue Bird" took the team to Maidenhead in the F.A. Cup. Gates at Loakes Park were seriously affected during a major industrial dispute in the furniture trade in High Wycombe.

All workers were locked out for twelve weeks from 13th October to the following February. Bunny Hooper, Charlie Tilbury and Fred Pheby all played their final games before the season ended. Walter Harvey had a remarkable season, scoring 107 goals for both Wycombe Wanderers Reserves and Wycombe Wednesday, including 27 hat-tricks. He was given a try out in the first team in November, scoring two goals on his debut against Maidenhead, but failed to score in the next two games and returned to the reserves. In those days there was little movement between first team and reserves and it may be that he preferred to play with his old team mates.

During the close season the Club's application to join the Spartan League was accepted but membership of the Great Western Suburban League would continue, the intention being to field sides of equal strength in each competition. The Great War, however, broke out before the season started and Wycombe players began to join the two companies of Territorials and the Bucks Battalion, all based in the town. The Club withdrew from the Spartan League and decided not to arrange any fixtures, scratching from the scheduled F.A. Cup game at Maidenhead Norfolkians on 26 September. The Royal Field Artillery was being concentrated in High Wycombe, barracks and stables were built in Daws Hill Park, and it soon became an important centre for training artillarymen to ride the horses which pulled the guns. The Marquess of Lincolnshire requested Wanderers to allow free use of Loakes Park to the Military so the Club ceased to be active for the duration of the war.

In early 1919, as former players began to return home from service, George Miles, Chairman and Treasurer, called a meeting to discuss contacting other clubs. Much of the Club's pre-war gear had been loaned to the Military, and was either missing or in poor condition but on 15 February 1919 two local sides contested the first match on Loakes Park, Nelson Rolfe's side beating Frank Didcock's 2-1. George Bunce acted as Secretary as Bunny Hooper was still on active service and the first side to visit were 49 Wing RAF. Mayor Haines kicked off and proceeds from the match were donated to the Wycombe War Memorial Hospital Fund, including a 3d raffle for the match ball. On 10 April the RFA Officers fund made a generous contribution of £50, a large enough amount to free the Club from financial worry. A game against Chesham United, newly formed from the merger of Chesham Generals and Chesham, attracted a gate of £71, but the Club was staggered when they learnt that £18 was due for the new Entertainment Tax. Eventually football managed to organise itself and Wycombe entered their usual pre-war competitions and became members of the Spartan League.

On 14 July 1919 the Club held its AGM at the Red Lion Hotel and all stood for those who had lost their lives in the Great War.

The players who died were:-
Charlie Buchanan, George Buchanan, Pat Carter, Bunny Fowler, Frank Langley, Jock Love, Jim McDermott, Edward Reynolds, A. Saunders and Harry Stallwood.

Other fatalities were vice-presidents Viscount Wendover, Dr R.A. Hobbs and Frank Elliott; Members R. North, R. Harrell, B.R.P. Wood, G.A. Priest, H. Dunn and J. Baker. Officials remained the same as before the war and Charlie Tilbury became the groundsman. Twelve members would form the General Committee, with five each on Finance and Emergency, and the unwieldy Match Selection Committee was reduced to seven.

The Great Western Suburban League side easily won their opening game 13-0 against 1st Scots Guards, Frank Adams and F. Rose scoring five each; they eventually finished 7th out of 12. On the same day the Spartan League side won their inaugural game 4-3 at St Albans, with Fred Crook scoring all four after the Wanderers had been three goals down. Frank Adams was then elected captain of the Spartan League side and this became the senior side, although there was much mixing throughout the season. Fifteen goals were scored in the F.A. Cup ties against Slough. The first game at Slough ended 3-3, with Klon Smith equalising for Wycombe with a direct free kick from within his own half. The replay, in midweek, saw Wanderers victorious by the odd one in a nine goal thriller.

Smith scored 28 goals in the 28 competitive games that season, although top scorer was Tommy Jackman with 31 from 27 games. They helped the Club to its best League record, either before or since, and only three points were dropped in the 20 games. The 114 goals scored, another all time record, averaged out at a 5.7 per game. The team also reached the Final of the Berks & Bucks Charity Cup, against Chesham United. Played at Aylesbury, the match was abandoned seven minutes from the end when the referee sent off Archie Gomm, and Wycombe supporters in the big 5,000 crowd invaded the pitch. Chesham were leading 1-0 at the time and were subsequently awarded the Cup.

Gomm, Wycombe's talented centre half, was invited for a trial at Aston Villa on 17 January 1920. In the summer he joined Millwall as one of the country's first stopper centre halves; he had a fine physique and was exceptionally good in the air. In all he made 187 League appearances for Millwall, scoring 13 goals, before joining Carlisle United in 1931 for two seasons (67 apps). After Wanderers became champions, a visiting 'Rest of the League' eleven won 5-4, the only side to win at Loakes Park that season. After the game a moving memorial service was conducted in front of the large crowd; three buglers played the Last Post in memory of the Wanderers who died in the War, and Mayor Stratford unveiled a memorial tablet in the pavilion.

CHAPTER 3 (1919-1945)
AMATEUR CUP-WINNERS.... BUT LITTLE ELSE!

The Reserve side in 1920, who played in the Great Western Combination - the venue?

The AGM in July 1920 was in an upbeat mood as Chairman George Miles reported that the gate receipts from the 1919-20 season totalled a remarkable £1771. This compared with £440 in the last season before the War, but the Club had to pay £301-17s-7d in Entertainment Tax. During the close season a dressing room for the match officials was provided and the players' washing facilities were improved. The Club had hoped to be playing in the Isthmian League this season but their application registered on 30 April 1920 had been unsuccessful.

Another Spartan League season began without Reggie Boreham, who had been invited for a trial at Notts County. He played three Football League games for them that season and was offered attractive terms to go professional, but he chose to continue playing as an amateur for Wycombe. He scored 41 goals in 33 games this season, to add to his 18 from 17 games the previous, and became the first Wanderer to play for an FA XI (against Oxford University); he also played for South v North. The opening ten Spartan League fixtures were all won, making 21 consecutive League wins in all with the 11 from the end of the previous season, still a Club record. This time four points were dropped out of 44 (three to runners up Slough), and another century of goals scored, but, like last season, it was not a runaway championship. At this time the Spartan League had some very good teams but also some extremely weak ones. Another fine run in the FA Cup saw Wycombe drawn away to Kettering in the Fifth Qualifying Round, two rounds away from the competition proper. Fifteen minutes from time Wanderers were leading the professionals 1-0, but Kettering equalised and won a corner three minutes from time. As the kick came over goalkeeper Jim Wicks shouted 'Right!' to 'Salt' Smith, who let the ball go. The 'keeper misjudged the bounce and the ball rolled up his arm and into the net, to give the professionals a 2-1 victory.

The Amateur Cup proved no less exciting that season and a thrilling 4-3 win at home to Barnet was followed by an excellent 2-1 victory at top Isthmian League side Tufnell Park. Loftus Albion were drawn away in the Quarter-Finals and hopes were high of winning the Cup. The long journey to the North Riding the previous day left the team stiff and Wanderers disappointingly lost 2-0.

Three weeks later, on 18 March 1921, High Wycombe was celebrating after their application to join the Isthmian League had been accepted this time, along with Wimbledon. On 30 April the FA picked Loakes Park as the venue for a possible Amateur Cup Final replay, a little surprising perhaps as the ground still only had 400 seats and had no made up terracing. In the event, however, Bishop Auckland beat Swindon Victoria.

The Berks and Bucks Senior Cup was also won and the 9,875 crowd who saw the Final at Reading against Slough was the biggest crowd the Club had played in front of.

The Club were now financially much better off and donated £50 to the Mayor's fund to relieve distress through unemployment and £121 10s 3d to the Wycombe Hospital Fund. George Bunce retired after 21 years of service to the Club as Assistant Secretary and became the Club's first life member. For the first time accident insurance was taken out for all of the players, prompted by the step up to a higher league. The first game in the Isthmian League was a hard fought 4-3 defeat at Leytonstone and presaged a period of little success in this competition for the next thirty years.

One immediate problem was the loss of Reggie Boreham after Arsenal invited him to play for them in December 1921. He scored 10 goals in 22 appearances for the First Division side and was widely credited with saving them from relegation that season. He went on to make 51 appearances for Arsenal, scoring 18 goals, before rejoining Wycombe permanently in January 1924. Before he joined the Gunners, Boreham became the first Wycombe player to earn a full amateur cap when he represented England against Ireland at Leicester on 14 November 1921. At the end of the season Arsenal lost 2-1 in a friendly at Loakes Park. The London club took no expenses and were much taken with the charming ground and the usefulness of the team.

A new cup was presented by the Marchioness of Lincolnshire, called the Wycombe Memorial Hospital Cup, and Wycombe won the first of the annual matches, beating Tufnell Park 4-1 in front of 5,000 people. After the game plans were announced to extend the stand along the length of the pitch and build changing rooms at the rear. The money was to be raised by a loan and work began in December. During the season the Marquess had been asked about selling the ground to the Club but in the event a fourteen year lease was signed, to start from 21 September 1921 (it was extended to 21 years in 1923). The lower part of Loakes Park was to be let to Mr De Lana and Miss Dicks for use as a tent theatre.

Two players turned professional in the summer. Goalkeeper Jim Wicks joined Nottingham Forest and centre-back George Harris, who had played three games for Southend during the 1921-22 season, left for Notts County. The 1922-23 season opened disastrously at Nunhead as Wanderers lost 7-1. New goalkeeper Jim Munday was injured and Nunhead sportingly allowed Walter Ball to deputise at half-time, the first time Wycombe used a substitute in a competitive match. The Amateur Cup game at home to Kings Lynn in the same month was filmed and subsequently shown at the Palace Cinema in Frogmore, in the town centre. The next round against St Albans, on 20 January, was also filmed *(where are these films now?)* when the extension to the stand was officially opened. A crowd of 7,000, the biggest thus far recorded at Loakes Park, paid £222 to see the visitors win 2-1. The county cup was won, however, 4-0 against Maidenhead at Slough and the 11,500 crowd was another record gate for a Wycombe game. An end of season tour was undertaken to France with a 3-0 win over Olympic FC (Paris), a 4-3 defeat against Cette FC and a 3-3 draw with Bordeaux. The party were involved in a motor accident but the Club received a telegram to say that only bruises were suffered.

In August 1923 left-winger Alf Fryer became the first Wycombe player to represent the Middlesex Wanderers, on their tour to Sweden. The first League game of the season, against Nunhead on 25 August, saw the new changing rooms used for the first time, and the total cost of the stand redevelopment had cost £1,500. In the opening five League games, Wycombe scored 29 goals, including nine against eventual champions St Albans, and finished top scorers with 88 goals from 26 games. The first defeat did not come until 15 December and the final position of fourth was only bettered once before the Second World War. Tim Hinton was now the leading scorer at the Club and this season scored 38 in 31 games.

Botwell Mission from Hayes caused a shock in the FA Cup by winning in a replay at Loakes Park, but it was the Amateur Cup which once again provided the main excitement. In the First Round Wycombe defeated St.

31

Albans in a replay at Loakes Park, Weaver scoring with the last kick of the game. The powerful Ilford side, Isthmian champions in 1921 and 1922, were beaten at home in the next round and after a win at Staines Lagonda, London Caledonians were drawn at home in the Quarter-Finals. The visitors put on a brilliant display to win 3-0 in front of 9,288, a new record Loakes Park crowd.

On 22 March 1924 right-winger Joey Grace became the second Wanderer to play for his country when he represented Wales against England at Llandudno. He played one game for Wycombe at the start of the following season but then transferred to Newbury. Inside-right Alec Weaver left at the end of his only season for the Club and turned professional with Sheffield Wednesday. Centre-back Walter Keen left for Millwall but he had to wait three seasons before making his Football League debut.

The first visitors of the 1924-25 season were a touring South African XI who won 5-2. The only real success saw another Berks & Bucks Senior Cup win in a final replay at Slough against Windsor & Eton. The first game at Reading attracted a crowd of over 10,000 and Tim Hinton missed a penalty in the 0-0 draw. The Wycombe Hospital Cup was shared with League champions London Caledonians after playing 150 minutes in an effort to break the 2-2 deadlock. Centre-back Jim Baker was the latest recruit to the professional game, signing for Watford during the season, and during the following campaign he was joined at Vicarage Road by inside-right Cyril Foster.

At the AGM on 19 July 1925 Bernard Hooper resigned as secretary as he had taken a hotel at Dunmow. He ended a 27 year association with the Club and was replaced by W.Howland as General Secretary and Charlie Allen as Match Secretary. It was also announced that talented goalkeeper Jim Kipping had signed for Queens Park Rangers but he never made the first team and returned to Wycombe in October the following season. The 1925-26 season saw an extraordinary number of goals scored, the highest number in the Club's history. The 26 League games produced 180 goals, an average of 6.9 per match, and the 33 competitive games produced 231 goals, averaging exactly seven per game. Tim Hinton scored 50 goals, and in his career at Wycombe scored 168 goals in 155 games, the best goals per game ratio by a Wanderer. At the end of the season he signed for Millwall but only went on to make 5 appearances, scoring 3 goals. In the summer George Miles stepped down as Treasurer, a position he had held since 1898, because he felt unable to combine those duties with that of Chairman; George Bunce became the new Treasurer.

In October 1926 Wycombe lost 9-0 at Slough in the First Qualifying Round of the FA Cup, still the Club's record defeat in any cup competition as a senior side. Three weeks later they lost 9-0 at St Albans, which is the biggest losing margin they ever suffered in the Isthmian League. The Supporters Club received its first mention when a Recreation Room, costing £414 7s 6d and built with their own funds, was opened at the rear of the stand on 17 November 1926. The deeds were presented to the football club in 1929. Once again the Club reached the Amateur Cup Quarter-Finals but were unlucky to lose 3-2 at Barking Town. Reggie Boreham made his last appearance for Wycombe Wanderers in January 1927 but by now the Club's leading scorer was Bill Brown.

The team that played at Tufnell Park on Feb.28 1925 (a 2-1 victory) McDermott, Foster, Brooks, Gates, Kipping, Gammon, Fryer, Adams, Boreham, Beeson and Smith

George Miles announced, in July 1927, that a 50 year lease on Loakes Park had been signed, backdated to October 1926, after he and Mr Winter-Taylor, the Club's solicitor, had negotiated a £50 annual rent with the Marquess of Lincolnshire. Charlie Allen resigned as Match Secretary and A.J.Gardner succeeded him. When right-winger Billy Coward joined Queens Park Rangers in October, he became the eleventh Wanderer to turn professional in the nine seasons since the Great War. It would another 50 years before the Club saw a similar exodus and there is little doubt that this was the major factor in the disappointing finishes in the Isthmian League in the Twenties and Thirties.

In December 1927 the Club welcomed back Joey Grace and he scored in the 1-1 draw in the Amateur Cup at Cambridge Town. The replay at Loakes Park was a disaster, the visitors winning 8-3, which is the highest number of goals the Club has ever conceded in that competition.

The members were shocked to hear at the AGM of 13 July 1928 that the FA had demanded the Club's accounting books, which were kept for six weeks. It was alleged that a member of the Club had secretly reported the Club but the FA found the books to be in perfect order.

All stood in memory of the Marquess of Lincolnshire who had died on 13 June 1928, he had been President of the Club since 1913 and an important benefactor since 1895.

The Marchioness, who had always shown a keen interest in the Club, was fittingly elected President.

(Above) The Marquess of Lincolnshire (Club President 1913-1928)

(Above right) The Marchioness who was elected President on his death.

(Left) Thousands lined the streets of High Wycombe for the Marquess' funeral procession.

A packed Loakes Park crowd look on during the Amateur Cup-tie with Romford - 1930/31 season.

W.Howland resigned as General Secretary for business reasons, replaced by R.J.Gardner, but continued in office in the newly created role of Financial Secretary. One of the few highlights in a disappointing season was an 11-1 FA Cup Preliminary Round win against Henley Town. Eight of the goals were scored by Bill Brown and this remains as the Club's all time individual scoring record in any first team game. In February 1929 Frank Adams, now aged 37 and made a life member in the summer, played his last game for the Club but his greatest contribution to the Club was yet to come.

George Miles became President in July 1929 after the Marchioness of Lincolnshire had moved from Wycombe Abbey and felt it inappropriate to continue in office. In September 1929 a Chelsea XI visited Loakes Park, drawing 1-1 in a game specially arranged for Marlow FC's new ground fund. Results were very disappointing, however, and in the league the forwards struggled to score goals with the first games in the three cup competitions all lost. The Club embarked on an April tour to Germany, beating Marburg 6-2, Fulda 7-0 and losing 5-4 to SV Waldhof (Mannheim).

In complete contrast to the previous season, the 1930-31 season proved to be the most successful up to that time. Wycombe finished third in the Isthmian League, their best position so far, and were one of only two teams to beat the champions Wimbledon.

The season, however, will always be remembered for the Clubs exploits in the Amateur Cup. It all began in the First Round with a wonderful 4-1 win away to London Caledonians, who only scored a late consolation. It was a result which caused much surprise in amateur circles and a splendidly balanced Wycombe side, quick, skilful and very fit, easily disposed of Walthamstow in the next round by 6-1. A crowd of just under 10,000 saw Romford fall to a similar fate - 6-2 - in the following round at Loakes Park, and the Quarter-Final draw produced a tricky away game against the Metropolitan Police, the reigning champions of the Spartan League and considered one of the best amateur teams in the South despite their lower league status.

Three thousand Wycombe supporters travelled to Thames Ditton and saw a tense, hard fought, but very clean game. Brown opened the scoring for Wanderers in the 27th minute, after a scramble in front of goal, but the Police equalised six minutes later when Avey sent an unstoppable shot into the top corner. Extra time was played but nothing could separate two very even teams.

The following Saturday a record crowd of 10,881 packed into Loakes Park for the replay and making an emotional return to his former stomping ground was Fred Abbott, now Deputy Assistant Commissioner in the Metropolitan Police. He saw his Police side take the lead on 30 minutes when Avey broke clear and scored with a powerful shot. This stirred the home side into action and Braisher equalised soon after with a long range shot. In the second-half Avey missed an open goal before, ten minutes from time, Vernon dribbled past defender after defender and scored a dramatic winner from close in. At last, after six previous defeats in the Quarter-Finals, Wycombe Wanderers had qualified for the Semi-Finals.

The draw was favourable as their opponents, Woking, were struggling near the bottom of the Isthmian League. The town hardly had time to catch its breath as the Semi-Final took place the following Saturday at Ilford.

Woking were a robust side and held Wycombe 0-0 at half-time, but in the second-half Wycombe's class began to tell and Britnell opened the scoring. Brown drove in the rebound for the second after Simmons had hit the bar, and Britnell scored a fluke goal ten minutes from time to make the final score 3-0. The thousands of Wycombe fans went wild with delight and were even happier when they learnt that the final would be against Hayes who had surprisingly beaten Bishop Auckland 1-0 in the other Semi-Final. Some 4,000 from High Wycombe travelled up to Highbury for the final on 11 April 1931, part of a crowd of 32,000 paying £2,222.

Captain Pat Badrick proudly displays the Cup.

One Wycombe supporter even carried a chair to the game and back!

Goalkeeper Kipping returned to the side after splitting an eardrum in the Semi-Final but captain John Timberlake had to miss the game after an injury incurred against Metropolitan Police. Right-back Sid Crump had to leave the field early in the game with an injury and Hayes, with a very experienced team, had the better of the goalless first-half.

Crump returned in the second-half, when Wycombe began to take control, and six minutes from time Bill Brown's shot hit the bottom of the post after a scramble in front of goal. The Hayes defender Caesar deliberately handled the rebound and a penalty was awarded. Brown took the kick but Holding, the Hayes keeper, punched the ball clear. Alf Britnell responded the quickest and shot into the top right hand corner. It proved to be the winning goal and Wycombe Wanderers had achieved the ultimate for an amateur club.

Sir Charles Clegg, The President of the FA, presented the famous cup, and it went with the team on the London Underground as they took the same route home via Marylebone.

No official preparations had been made at High Wycombe but thousands lined the approach to the station when the train pulled in at 9pm. The team climbed aboard a brake which someone had fetched from Wooburn and it was pulled to the Guildhall where speeches were made and Pat Badrick proudly showed the cup to a crowd estimated at 10,000. Later the Club held a celebratory dinner for 400 at the town hall when clocks were presented to George Harris, the trainer, and Charlie Tilbury, the groundsman. John Timberlake received a specially struck winners medal for the part he played in the earlier rounds.

A happy group of Wycombe supporters at Highbury. Note the man with his 'lucky' mascot - a commode (potty) chair, the boy in 'replica' shirt (1931 style), and the home-made berets.

Goalmouth action at Highbury

Every player except for Doug Vernon, an RAF man stationed nearby, lived within a five mile radius of the town centre, a town with a population of 20,000. Even though the Club has since gone onto greater successes, High Wycombe has probably never since experienced the special thrill of that extraordinary day in April 1931 when that most coveted trophy was brought home.

The extended cup run had meant something of a fixture backlog and on the last day of the season Wycombe played Kingstonian twice! The first match at Kingstonian kicked off at 3 pm with the home side winning 2-0. Everyone travelled back to Loakes Park for the return match at 6.30 pm. This time Wycombe won 4-0 thanks to a hat-trick for Bill Brown who was the only Wanderer not to have played in the first game. The team took a well earned 'break', if it can be called that, with a May tour to Holland. Five games were played in nine days, and four were won; Zebruggia (2-1), Northern Provinces (6-4), Ado FC (the only defeat - 4-2), Hilversum (5-2), and Dordecht (1-0).

The sizeable profits from the cup run were immediately put to use when a 360' corrugated cover (affectionately known as the 'cowshed') was built, which ran the entire length of the lower side of the ground. It was opened on 13 February 1932 and it was said that Wycombe Wanderers became the first amateur club to have stands on opposite sides of the pitch. Almost inevitably the Amateur Cup success was not repeated in the 1931-32 season; a Third Round match at Bracken Edge, Leeds, against the unknown Yorkshire Amateurs, ended in a disastrous 4-0 defeat. Strangely enough the Yorkshire side played in light and dark blue quartered shirts. There was a good FA Cup run, but in the last qualifying round, the team crashed 6-1 at Enfield. There was more disappointment in the Berks & Bucks Senior Cup Final when Maidenhead defeated Wanderers at Reading in front of over 10,000, when they scored the winner with the last kick of the game. League form was still good and the team ended up in fourth position, only three points behind champions Wimbledon.

In the close season more of the money from the cup run was spent on further ground improvements. The changing rooms were enlarged with tiled baths large enough for a whole team; the referee's room also now had a bath. George Miles stepped down as Chairman after serving the Club for 44 years and former player Bob Spatchett was elected in place. The 1932-33 season witnessed another landmark in the Club's history when the First Round of the FA Cup was reached for the first time. Drawn away to Gillingham from the Third Division South, Wycombe surprised their professional opponents by deservedly scoring an equaliser through Braisher. The replay took place on the following Wednesday afternoon when a crowd of 7,597 saw Wycombe get off to a bad start when Dickie Cox put through his own goal. By half-time Wanderers had taken the lead with goals from Brown and a Braisher penalty, and could have had another one after Brown missed a sitter. Gillingham, however, took control after the break and were relieved to run out eventual 4-2 winners.

The 1933-34 season saw no joy in either of the FA competitions, and for the second successive season Chesham United were the opponents in the Berks & Bucks Senior Cup Final. This time United won in a replayed final after Wycombe had beaten them the previous year. League form was disappointing and in fact the team failed to win away; only their good home form prevented a very low finish. On 28 February 1934 Frank Jordan died of meningitis only 25 days after playing his last game, and his 32 games as centre-forward had produced 30 goals. Reading played a benefit match at Loakes Park on 30 April 1934, winning 6-5, and all proceeds from the 3,000 crowd went to Frank's widowed mother. At the end of the season right-back Gerry Darvill signed for Reading, the last player to turn professional before the Second World War.

The 1934-35 season was an even worse season in the League, finishing second from bottom, and having to apply for re-election. The Berks & Bucks Senior Cup was won however, overcoming Aylesbury 3-0 in the Blues' fourth consecutive final appearance. After such a bad season the Club decided to advertise for a Trainer/Coach in the Athletic News, The Daily Express and the News Chronicle.

Out of the 70 applicants, a short list was drawn up and a special sub-committee comprising of Spatchett, Adams, Howland and Vine offered the job to James Seddon for a period of one year from 1 August 1935, at £5 per week during the playing season and £3 10s during the close. Seddon was a vastly experienced former Bolton Wanderers player, who had made 342 League appearances between 1913/14 and 1931/32. He refused the terms, however, and at the AGM that summer it was decided to re-elect George Harris to his old job.

Earlier in the season floodlighting was installed for training purposes. The relative demise of the side was underlined by the fact that for 1935-36, the team had had to start in the qualifying rounds of the Amateur Cup, only four seasons after winning it, and for the first time since the 1913/14 season. They successfully came through only to lose at home to Casuals, the eventual winners, in the Second Round. The League form, however, was much improved, and the team finished in the top half of the table. The General Secretary, Ralph Gardner, resigned in December because he was leaving the town, and Reggie Boreham was a popular replacement.

There was plenty of cup activity in the 1936-37 season, notably in January and February when nine consecutive cup ties were played. A promising run in the Amateur Cup ended at Stockton, three times winners, in the Third Round by four goals to one in front of over 7,000. In 1937-38 Wycombe reached the Final of the Berks & Bucks Senior Cup, and lost for the second successive season to Windsor & Eton; Wycombe were finalists for the sixth time in the previous seven seasons, and were successful on three occasions.

War loomed across the English Channel and the Club allowed the ground to be used for Gas Chamber demonstrations during the 1938-39 campaign. A rather unfortunate situation developed at this time between the Club and the Trustees of Loakes Park. The representative to the Trustees of the Carrington Estate, Mr Carter Jonus, objected to the bank being made up at the eastern end of the ground. He ordered the Club committee to remove and to restore it to its proper state, as it was a contravention of the terms of the lease, and further, they had to make good any damage. The Club sent a letter regretting the situation but the Borough Council were now querying whether it was a breech of local bylaws. Eventually agreement was reached that the Club could shape up the bank and sow grass seed but that the mound must be cleared away within one year of the lease expiring, a strange stipulation as the lease was due to run until 1977. On 21 June the local Military and the Civil Defence began to use the ground, and the stands and changing rooms were taken over by the Billeting Authority and the Police. They explained, however, that they would not use their authority unless absolutely necessary.

The 1939-40 season began as normal and Wycombe beat Woking 4-0 in the opening Isthmian League fixture on 26 August at Loakes Park. The following Saturday the team won 3-0 at Hounslow Town, in the Extra Preliminary Round of the FA Cup, in front of only 250. It was one of just 28 FA Cup games played that season, because, the following day - 3 September 1939 - Great Britain declared war on Germany.

The Isthmian League was suspended, so the Club Committee decided to enter the Great Western Combination and the services of Trainer George Harris were dispensed with. The team was largely the same as the previous season and finished second in the League, well behind Hayes, but won the Berks & Bucks Emergency Senior cup. Played at Loakes Park on Boxing Day 1939, the gate of 5,000 was the only crowd figure released for a Wanderers game during the war. On 2 July 1940, Pat Badrick, captain of the Amateur Cup winning team, and Jack Turner, were reported missing in action. Meanwhile the team gradually changed during the 1940-41 season as players were called up, but the side was ably captained and run by Jock McCallum, unable to join the war because of a perforated ear drum. He searched high and low for players, calling on former Wanderers long since retired, to put on the quartered shirt once more. One of the major problems during the War was transport because of fuel rationing. After one game at Slough the team had to walk 15 miles back to High Wycombe!

In 1943, the Chairman George Miles died after 46 years serving the Club as President, Chairman and Treasurer, and C P Vine was elected to the position. During this time the High Wycombe Civil Defence Authority approached the General Committee to use the stand in the event of the town being blitzed. George Bunce, the Treasurer, successfully appealed to the Rating Authority and obtained a reduction of 75%; he also reported that the bank overdraft had been reduced to £470. The final war season, 1944-45, and the last in the Combination saw Wycombe finish champions, winning the final nine games. The side included many players from before the war, for Jock McCallum, Bill Ing, Bert Crump, Alf Britnell, Tommy Andrews, Jack Meeks, and Fred Gearing all played their part.

CHAPTER 4 (1945-1961)
WYCOMBE REACH THE TOP

The presentation at the handover of the ground to the Club in 1947

Peace in Europe was declared on 8 May 1945 and football returned to normality remarkably quickly. Club officials remained the same as, to a large extent, did the team and the opening Isthmian League game at Loakes Park against newcomers Walthamstow saw a 4-3 win for the Londoners. Walthamstow caused a sensation that season by winning the title at their first attempt, equalling Wimbledon's points record of 42 and becoming the first team to score 100 goals. Frank Avery top scored for Wycombe with 37 goals, closely followed by Jock McCallum with 36, both from 37 games.

The 1946-47 season witnessed one of the most important chapters in the history of the Club. Frank Adams had been negotiating since 1944 with the Carrington Estate to buy Loakes Park for the Club and end any uncertainty about its future. Lord Carrington then, and now, is Lord Peter Carrington KG GCMG CH MC PC, and was Minister of State under Prime Minister Margaret Thatcher. He was a great nephew of the Marquess and Marchioness of Lincolnshire who had done so much for the Club, and Peter Carrington succeeded his father to the title in 1938 (he is still a life vice-president of Wycombe Wanderers). The ceremonial presentation of the deeds to President Vine was made before the game with Corinthian Casuals on 19 April 1947. In his speech to the 5,000 crowd, Frank Adams said: *"If future generations obtain the same enjoyment out of Loakes Park as it has given me in the past, then this gift will have been worthwhile."* This extremely generous act was one of the most important single events in the Club's history as it paved the way for the Club's later rapid rise in football. Also at the game a presentation of a cheque for £100 was made to Charlie Tilbury, who had decided to retire. His association with the Club stretched back to 1898 as a player and captain, and he had been the groundsman since 1919.

The 1947-48 season was notable for the Blues' first appearance in the Amateur Cup Quarter-Finals since the 1930-31 Cup-winning season. Once again they failed to successfully negotiate a long journey North and crashed 6-2 to Bishop Auckland in front of over 10,000. To reach this stage Wycombe had played two thrilling matches with St Albans. The first game had ended 2-2 after 90 minutes and 3-3 after extra time.

The replay at Loakes Park remained goalless at 90 minutes, but St Albans took the lead in extra time. During an attack by the visitors, centre-forward Jock McCallum switched position to the left-wing just inside his own half in a pre-determined move. This caused some confusion in the St Albans defence and, with his marker now on the wrong side, the ball was cleared over McCallum's head down the wing. He raced onto the ball and homed in on the goal, sending a tremendous banana shot past a surprised keeper for the equaliser. A few minutes from time McCallum took a corner which Ken Butler toe-poked into the net for a dramatic winner. McCallum was famous for his swerving shots but only found out how he did it after retiring from the game. He took up golf and discovered the principle of slicing the ball!

At the AGM of 1949, Reggie Boreham retired as General Secretary and Bill Hayter, the Reserve Secretary, was elected in his place. The 1949-50 season started badly, with just two wins out of ten in the League, and an early exit in the FA Cup. Part-time coach W.Brown reversed the fortunes of the team as they embarked on another Amateur Cup run. In fact the team were lucky to escape past the final qualifying round at Maidenhead. Trailing 5-4, Wycombe were relived when the fog came down and caused the game to be abandoned. After a 0-0 draw in the replayed match, Wycombe eventually won 2-1 at Loakes Park, thanks to some smart goalkeeping by Reg Williams.

```
Lucky No 1986
BUNGAY TOWN FOOTBALL CLUB
Headquarters: The "Fleece" Hotel, Bungay

Amateur Cup—1st Round Competition Proper

BUNGAY TOWN F.C.
Winners, Norfolk & Suffolk League Cup 1946/7, 1947/8, 1948/9
Applegate Cup 1947/8, 1948/9   Beccles Hospital Cup 1947/8, 1948/9

v.

WYCOMBE WANDERERS
KICK-OFF 2.30 P.M.
Saturday, 14th January, 1950

Holders of the Lucky Numbers will receive
a Voucher Prize which can be exchanged for
Goods to the Value of FIVE SHILLINGS

OFFICIAL PROGRAMME    PRICE TWOPENCE
```

In the First Round, 500 Wycombe fans were part of the 2,500 crowd packed into the tiny Suffolk ground of Bungay Town. Without a stand, 20-30 officials perched on an old farm cart that had been pulled into the ground and before the game Wycombe's captain, Peter Birdseye, presented a full sized Windsor chair to the Bungay captain Deacon. It was a match marred by injuries, the worst being when Birdseye and Tufts, the Bungay goalkeeper, clashed heads. Both were taken to hospital but returned to the field in the second-half, the goalkeeper playing on the wing as a 'nuisance' player; Slatcher for Bungay and Blizzard for Wycombe also had to leave the pitch. After taking a first-half lead, Wanderers scored three times in the last 20 minutes to go through and meet Crook Town at Loakes Park.

Crook were developing into one of the great teams after the war and went on to win the Amateur Cup four times between 1954 and 1964. In a classic struggle in front of a 10,000 crowd (1,000 from Crook), McCallum scored the only goal 17 minutes from time, when a perfectly judged lob over the advancing 'keeper just crept over the line. Afterwards the old boys behind the goal joked with Jock that they had sucked the ball into the net! Even more spectators turned up for the Third Round tie against Dulwich Hamlet, the gate of 13,607 was a new record for Loakes Park, and Wycombe won an exciting game 3-1. Johnny Blizzard put Wycombe one-up in the first minute, McCallum scored the second from a narrow angle on 25 minutes and Mikrut added the third three minutes later.

In the Quarter-Finals Wycombe were again blessed with a home tie and the attendance of 15,850 against St Albans remains the Club's record for a home game. Eighty coaches carried 2,000 away supporters to the ground. McCallum scored the opening goal on 25 minutes, rushing between two defenders, controlling the ball, and shooting powerfully into the net. Ken Butler scored the second five minutes later with a hard shot after a solo run down the wing. Sayers for the visitors pulled one back six minutes later but one minute after the break McCallum scored his second. Mikrut made the final score 4-1 with a great header in the 72nd minute and Wycombe were then drawn against the mighty Bishop Auckland at Brentford.

Thirty thousand spectators and a television audience watched a thrilling match. The Bishops converted a dubious penalty after half an hour and scored a second, freak goal, nine minutes after half-time. Wycombe then took over the match, pulled one back twenty minutes from time through Johnny Way, and only some brilliant goalkeeping saw Bishop Auckland hold on for the win (they lost to Willington in the final).

The Wycombe team that day was: Chris Lodge, Jim Flippance, George Jackson, Fred Gearing, Mieczystra Krupa, Johnny Way, Johnny Blizzard, Jock McCallum, Henri Mikrut, Ken Butler, and Peter Birdseye. The Berks & Bucks Senior Cup provided some consolation with a replayed final win over Slough Town, who the Blues also beat in the previous season's final.

A poor season in the League in 1950-51 prompted the Club to engage a full-time coach for the first time. James McCormick was appointed, a very experienced 39 year old former professional who began his career with Rotherham United (19 appearances) in 1930-31, and went on to play for Chesterfield (14), Tottenham Hotspur (137), Fulham (9), Lincoln City (64), and ending with Crystal Palace (13) in 1948/49. Bob Spatchett stepped down as Chairman after first joining the Club in 1899 as a player, and he was presented with a television set. John Timberlake, the captain in the Amateur Cup winning year was elected the new Chairman.

The new Coach immediately arranged three pre-season friendlies against his former clubs, Crystal Palace, Fulham and Tottenham Hotspur, a novel idea for the Club as they only normally played one game before the League season opened. He played in the 0-0 draw against Spurs, a game which attracted a gate of 5,000. One of McCormick's first decisions was to leave out Jock McCallum for all League games, who was now getting on in years but still an effective goalscorer. The player left the Club, joining Aylesbury United, and he came back to haunt his old club when he scored the winning goal for the Ducks in the FA Cup at Loakes Park that season, in front of 9,000 people. In the previous round Wycombe had lost 3-2 at Headington United (the former name of Oxford United and then a big club in the Southern League). But their goalkeeper C.McDonald was already registered for another club, and this fact was brought to the attention of the FA who deemed him ineligible and awarded the tie to Wanderers.

Results improved in the League and the Club reached the Quarter-Finals of the Amateur Cup, but lost 2-0 at Barnet in front of 11,026, still a crowd record for the Hertfordshire club. In May 1952 the Club toured Holland and played four matches in seven days versus Dordrecht (lost 2-1), Sparta Rotterdam (lost 1-0), Wageningen (a 3-2 victory), and Roosendaal (lost 5-4). The match against Sparta Rotterdam was played in front of 3,000 and the hosts only made one change from the side which beat Leeds United (including John Charles) 2-1 just two days earlier!

McCormick ruffled rather too many feathers in his attempt to modernise the Club and left at the end of the season (he died in a car crash in Spain in 1968).

The Club engaged Sid Cann as coach for the 1952-53 season, another former professional, who between 1928 and 1938 had made 101 league appearances for Torquay United, Manchester City and Charlton Athletic. He also had a spell as the Secretary/Manger of Southampton FC and was a qualified FA coach. Headington got their revenge in the FA Cup, beating Wycombe 6-2 at the Manor Ground and in the FA Amateur Cup, Ken Butler scored an amazing winner in the Second Round at home to Barnet, with just ten minutes of the game remaining. Romford, however, created an enormous shock in the next round by winning 5-0 at Loakes Park, after losing there 3-2 in the League four weeks earlier.

The 1953-54 season saw the side finish third, their highest placing since 1930-31, and win the Berks & Bucks Senior Cup against Slough Centre, winners of the Cup in the previous two seasons. The Amateur Cup had seen a tremendous struggle with Leytonstone in the Second Round. Two 0-0 draws home and away were followed by a midweek replay at Dulwich Hamlet. The winner in extra time came directly from a Leytonstone goal kick when Geoff Truett drove the ball back into the net before the goalkeeper had time to recover his ground. The FA forced the Club to play the next round the following Saturday, three days later, and against Wycombe's wishes. The match at Dulwich had been played on a frozen pitch and Hounslow took advantage of the Wycombe players' blistered feet to win 3-0 at Loakes Park. A 19 year old inside-forward called Ron Rafferty made his debut in January 1954 and by the end of the season had scored 10 goals in 14 games. He turned professional with First Division Portsmouth in the summer and later became a prolific scorer with Grimsby Town.

During the close season the tennis courts behind the main stand were replaced with a floodlit training pitch, which was financed by the Supporters Club. John Timberlake took over from retiring President C.P.Vine and George Partridge became the new Chairman.

There was more drama in the Amateur Cup in 1954-55. After defeating three Isthmian League sides, Wycombe were drawn at home to the famous Pegasus team, a team of Oxford and Cambridge Old Boys and then managed by Joe Mercer, who went on to managerial fame with Manchester City and England. The original tie on 13 February was postponed due to snow but the following Saturday a crowd of 14,000 saw Wanderers do everything but score in a 0-0 draw. The replay at Iffley Road, Oxford, attracted a capacity crowd of 6,500, and Wycombe came from behind to win with two goals in the last twenty minutes, the second scored by Jackie Tomlin in the last minute.

F.A. AMATEUR CHALLENGE CUP FOURTH ROUND REPLAY

N.º 1524

PEGASUS versus WYCOMBE WANDERERS
Iffley Road Running Ground, Oxford, Saturday, March 5th, 1955
Kick-off 2.45 p.m.

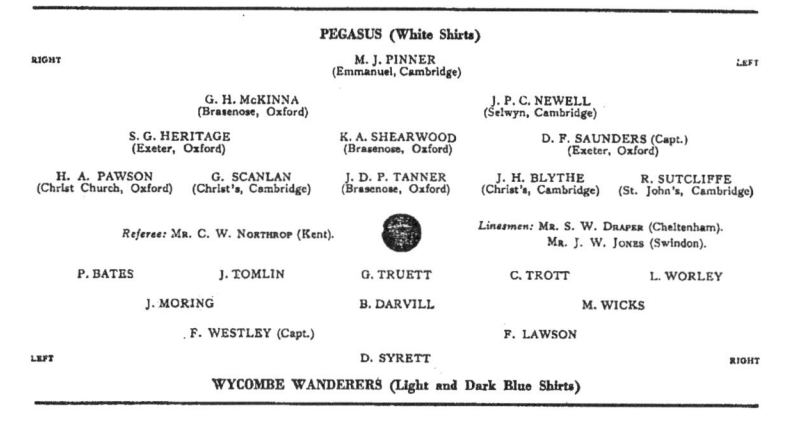

PEGASUS (White Shirts)

RIGHT

M. J. PINNER
(Emmanuel, Cambridge)

LEFT

G. H. McKINNA
(Brasenose, Oxford)

J. P. C. NEWELL
(Selwyn, Cambridge)

S. G. HERITAGE
(Exeter, Oxford)

K. A. SHEARWOOD
(Brasenose, Oxford)

D. F. SAUNDERS (Capt.)
(Exeter, Oxford)

H. A. PAWSON
(Christ Church, Oxford)

G. SCANLAN
(Christ's, Cambridge)

J. D. P. TANNER
(Brasenose, Oxford)

J. H. BLYTHE
(Christ's, Cambridge)

R. SUTCLIFFE
(St. John's, Cambridge)

Referee: Mr. C. W. Northrop (Kent).

Linesmen: Mr. S. W. Draper (Cheltenham).
Mr. J. W. Jones (Swindon).

P. BATES   J. TOMLIN   G. TRUETT   C. TROTT   L. WORLEY

J. MORING   B. DARVILL   M. WICKS

F. WESTLEY (Capt.)   F. LAWSON

LEFT

D. SYRETT

RIGHT

WYCOMBE WANDERERS (Light and Dark Blue Shirts)

(Left) Another packed Loakes Park, when Wanderers fought a goalless draw with Pegasus.

(Above) The match programme (a single sheet card) for the replay.

Wanderers could have drawn Hendon or Hounslow in the Semi-Final, but instead again faced the powerful Bishop Auckland side, Amateur Cup finalists the previous season, and victors of Tranmere Rovers earlier in the season in the FA Cup. This time the match was 'away' at Doncaster Rovers and 5,000 fans in six train loads were part of the 24,800 crowd.

The Club missed the services of Malcolm Hunt, the Club's free scoring centre-forward, who had been injured just before the Pegasus games and would take no further part that season. Barry Darvill declared himself fit for the Semi-Final, even though he was suffering with a 100 degree temperature, and had a wonderful game at centre-half.

Running rings around the Bishop's defence was Wycombe's right-winger, the precociously talented 17 year-old Len Worley, playing in his first season for the Club and destined to become one of the Club's all time great players.

Goalless at half-time courtesy, of a penalty miss by the Durham side in the 13th minute, Bates had a chance to put Wycombe ahead in the 70th minute. Clean through he bore down on goal at an angle but delayed his shot too long and a defender smothered his attempt. Seconds later Oliver scored the only goal of the game for the Bishops, to put them into the final when they beat Hendon. The team at Doncaster was: Dennis Syrett, Freddie Lawson, Frank Westley, Michael Wicks, Barry Darvill, Jim Moring, Len Worley, Cliff Trott, Geoff Truett, Jackie Tomlin, and Paul Bates.

Towards the end of the season 19 year old defender Terry Long played five games for Wycombe and signed for Crystal Palace in the summer. He went on to make more than 400 league appearances for Palace in a career that stretched until 1969.

The 1955-56 season started with a match at Loakes Park against FC Schaffhausen, on tour from Switzerland. Several members of the Swiss Embassy came down from London to watch Wycombe win 1-0, and afterwards the Mayor of High Wycombe entertained the party in the Town Hall. A bizarre FA Cup Preliminary Round tie at Witney Town followed soon after. The match ended goalless with Witney missing a penalty after ten minutes and spurning several other chances to beat their lacklustre opponents. The replay on the following Wednesday afternoon saw the visitors miss two early chances, then, in the twentieth minute, Wycombe scored the first of four goals in eight minutes, partly due to an injured goalkeeper who soon left the field, and were leading 8-0 at half-time! Seven more goals followed for Wycombe, with five goals each for Bates and Truett, and a consolation goal for Witney. The 15-1 win remains Wycombe's record score in a Cup-tie. Wanderers went on to the First Round for only the second time in their history, but lost 3-1 at home to Birmingham & District League side Burton Albion; the Midland's team reached the Third Round, eventually losing 7-0 at Charlton.

Hitchin Town attracted a record crowd of 7,860 for the visit of Wycombe in the Amateur Cup Third Round, a record which still stands and, on a snow bound pitch, the Hertfordshire side scored a freak winner.

On the last day of 1955, Wycombe went top of the Isthmian League for the first time and remained there until the end of the season. They actually won the title on 21 April with a 3-0 win against Dulwich in front of 6,000 wildly enthusiastic supporters at Loakes Park. It had been a long wait, 29 seasons since entering the Isthmian League, but now at last the Club could claim to be the top amateur side in the South of England. Top scorers that season in all matches were Paul Bates with 39 in 40 games and Geoff Truett with 33 in 39.

All season scouts had been coming to Loakes Park, mostly to check up on Len Worley and Geoff Truett. Worley was offered terms by Charlton which he turned down although the following season he did play one game as an amateur for the London club in the Football League. He also made one League appearance for Tottenham Hotspur in the 1959-60 season and again he turned down a contract. Truett turned down an offer from Arsenal and Paul Bates signed amateur forms for Reading although he never played in the Football League. Centre-half Barry Darvill was another talented player who attracted the scouts' attention but he also resolved to remain an amateur.

Soon after the 1956-57 season began George Partridge resigned as Chairman due to business commitments and Eric Webb took over. The team began with a three match tour of Switzerland, drawing 1-1 with FC Schaffhausen, and beating Cantonal (3-0) and Winterthur (4-1). On their return, the Club were honoured when the FA asked them to entertain the touring Ugandan side in their first match, the first time a side from Uganda had come to Britain. The match attracted intense interest in the country and film crews from the BBC, ITV and Pathe News all attended the midweek match on 29 August, which attracted a crowd of 7,500. Part of the great interest was due to many of the visitors who played barefoot. Wycombe were in fine form that day and won 10-1, and afterwards the Club entertained the Ugandans to dinner at the Red Lion Hotel. Amongst the many personalities from Africa and the football world was Sir Stanley Rous, who told the visitors not to be too despondent about losing by such a big score as they had played the possible winners of the Amateur Cup. They were so nearly prophetic words as the Club reached the Amateur Cup Final after a truly exciting run.

After wins against St Albans and Clapton, some 5,000 Wycombe fans travelled to Ilford in 160 coaches and three special trains. Four hours of torrential rain before the game had made the pitch a quagmire. Ilford took the lead within minutes when Butler headed home, but by half-time Wycombe were leading with two goals in four minutes, a Truett penalty and a Trott shot. Ilford equalised with a speculative 25 yard lob from Whittall but Wanderers quickly took the lead again, when Truett's 30 yard throw-in was headed home by Trott. Ten minutes from the end Ilford equalised with a free kick and had chances to win, but the Wycombe defence held out.

15,500 crammed into Loakes Park for the Amateur Cup Quarter-Final replay against Ilford

43

It had been a thrilling game and both teams knew that Corinthian Casuals would be the opponents in the Semi-Final as they stepped out for the replay the following Saturday. In the event the game never matched the excitement of the previous week. The score remained goalless until seven minutes into the second-half, when Worley's cross was chipped by Tomlin to Frank Smith who headed home. Wycombe's second goal was nodded in by Trott in the 70th minute after a corner was deflected by Bates.

The Semi-Final against Corinthian Casuals on 16 March 1957 turned out to be one of the most thrilling of games in the Club's history. Casuals belied their bottom placing in the Isthmian League and took the lead in the first minute direct from a Kerruish corner, but Bates headed the equaliser within four minutes and scored a second fifteen minutes later with a fierce drive. Ten minutes later Casuals equalised, and at half-time the score was 2-2. Fifteen minutes after the break Wycombe's captain Frank Westley hobbled off and a minute later Wanderers were down to nine men after Smith dislocated a shoulder. Goalkeeper Syrett was also badly injured after colliding with a post, but when Westley returned to the pitch, no more than a nuisance player on the wing, Wycombe rallied and remarkably scored twice more through Len Worley, to take them through to their first Wembley appearance.

The Club received an allocation of 15,000 standing and 6,000 seat tickets; 10,000 of the holders travelled to the game by train. The official attendance was 90,000, the largest crowd a Wycombe team has ever played in front of. Interest in South Bucks was enormous, and even Amersham Town chose to go to Wembley rather than play a Spartan League game. They were fined £3-15s, but the Wanderers Committee later decided to pay it.

Both teams chose to play in red, but Wycombe won the toss and so turned out in their away colours of that colour. Their opponents, Bishop Auckland, were hot favourites having won the two previous Finals. Inspired by the famous England international Bob Hardisty, by then 36 years old, they were soon in control and took the lead in the 13th minute when Russell tricked Wicks and beat Syrett with a low shot. The Bishops laid siege to the Wycombe goal, but gradually Wanderers got back into the game, and Jim Truett's header was well saved by the goalkeeper. The Blues equalised in the 38th minute when Geoff Truett sent a crisp pass down the middle to Smith. He was tackled and the ball rolled away, but he regained possession, tricked the defence into thinking he was going to pass the ball, and scored with a fierce shot. Within two minutes, however, the Bishops had regained the lead, Lewin scoring from close range, and the Northerners continued on top after the break.

Gradually, however, Wycombe took control with Worley now showing his best form. The Bishops's keeper Sharratt brilliantly stopped Worley's point-blank shot and a Bates header was also well saved. Then Wycombe were on the defensive, and Auckland wasted two golden chances before finally scoring the final goal in the 71st minute.

Cliff Trott (right) challenges the Bishop Auckland 'keeper Sharratt, in the Wembley Final.

'A GALLANT FIGHT AGAINST ODDS' SAY THE CRITICS

As Others Saw The Wanderers' Bid

"A COURAGEOUS FIGHT against the overwhelming odds presented by Bishop Auckland's machine-like efficiency"—that was how the national newspaper critics summed up Wycombe Wanderers' Wembley performance. "Wycombe's task was hopeless but how gallantly they fought as if it wasn't" commented one writer.

'FINEST MACHINE' PROVED TOO SLICK

Michael Wicks, hero of Wycombe's gallant defence, heads clear during an Auckland attack, with Westley and Jimmy Truett covering.

Wycombe could not clear after a corner and the ball fell to Bradley who shot through a crowd of players into the net. Bishop Auckland fully deserved the 3-1 win in their third successive final and they demonstrated that they were the country's top amateur side. It was their 10th win in all, an all-time record, but it was their last appearance at Wembley and this match marked the end of an era. The Bishops' skipper said afterwards: *"I don't think anyone will deny we deserved to win, but Wycombe certainly let us know we were in a game."*

Wycombe team: Dennis Syrett, Freddie Lawson, Frank Westley, Geoff Truett, Michael Wicks, Jeff Truett, Len Worley, Cliff Trott, Paul Bates, Jackie Tomlin and Frank Smith. Jim Moring, Wycombe's regular left-half, had broken his arm in January but played in the two League games prior to the Final. Unfortunately he was not deemed fit enough and missed out on the big game.

This is how the national papers saw it:
SUNDAY PICTORIAL: "Bishops' superiority in skill and experience told in both attack and defence. Wycombe's rearguard was often too easy prey for a long pass up the middle. Yet Wycombe fought every inch of the way."
TIMES: "The brothers Truett played heroically at wing-half for Wycombe, especially Geoff Truett, with his fine physique and inexhaustible energy, but there were no weak links for them to destroy."
DAILY TELEGRAPH: "Wycombe were able only on occasions to reproduce that fire and determination that had shocked Casuals."
GUARDIAN: "For a brief period in the second-half Wycombe were kept at bay by Sharratt and Cresswell."
SUNDAY EXPRESS: "Frank Smith was the losers' best forward. Fighting Wycombe were beaten by the finest machine in amateur football. The Southerners were never disgraced."

REYNOLDS NEWS: "Bishops' brilliant football outclassed and outmanoeuvred the slap-happy stuff of the Southerners. Wycombe's lone star was left-winger Frank Smith."
PEOPLE: "Wanderers fought valiantly but the edge always remained with Bishop Auckland."
OBSERVER: "The Wanderers' passes were short and obvious but, Wycombe's brief moment of glory came shortly after the interval as they fought to draw level."
EMPIRE NEWS: "The Wanderers were honest triers. It was left to Smith and Bates to do the damage."
DAILY MAIL: "Wycombe deserve full praise for the way they came off defence into attack.....but they did not have the poise of the holders."
SUNDAY TIMES: ".....a match of such entertainment as to make a very sharp contrast with the dreary England v Scotland international. Wycombe had a right-half of exceptional quality in Geoff Truett."

In spite of the defeat thousands lined the High Street to greet the returning team who had boarded an open top bus at the cricket ground, and each player took a bow on the portico of the Red Lion Hotel.

There was still much to play for on the pitch and the Isthmian League was won for the second successive season, but this time the team had to wait until the final day. A 3-2 win at home to Corinthian Casuals ensured the title by one point from Woking. Len Worley missed this game after fracturing his leg the previous week playing for the Army while doing his National Service.

Both Len Worley and Paul Bates won their England amateur caps that season, the first players to do so since Reggie Boreham in the 1920's. Geoff Truett left at the end of the season and signed for Crystal Palace.

Amateur Cup - 3rd round at Ilford (8 February 1958).
Before a crowd of nearly 10,000, Syrett punches clear from Ilford's Winch.

For the 1957-58 season the Club began broadcasting match commentaries to the neighbouring hospital, a practice which continued until the last game at Loakes Park. The public address system was also upgraded at the same time. As Amateur Cup finalists, Wycombe were exempted from the qualifying rounds of the FA Cup for the first time but lost 3-2 at Dorchester. Progress in the Amateur Cup strangely brought them up against Ilford in the Third Round again, but this time the match was a dour affair, Ilford winning 2-1 with all three goals coming from penalties.

The team failed to win the League for a third time, and finished second, four points behind Tooting & Mitcham, in spite of taking three points from them. In the summer of 1958 Dennis Syrett was picked by the FA to tour Ghana and Nigeria, and Sid Cann was put in charge of the England Youth side. The Supporters Club were also busy at that time, installing wrought iron gates at the main entrance and fencing down the west side of the ground.

The gates, which can still be seen in the car park at Adams Park, were officially opened in October 1958 when Loakes Park staged an Amateur International for the first time, England v South Africa.

The early League form was exceptional, the first six games being won with 34 goals scored, and the team won ten and drew two of the first twelve games. However a formidable Wimbledon side eventually won the League with a record 47 points. Wycombe were a little unlucky to lose a First Round FA Cup match at Fourth Division Northampton, conceding the two goals in the last 20 minutes.

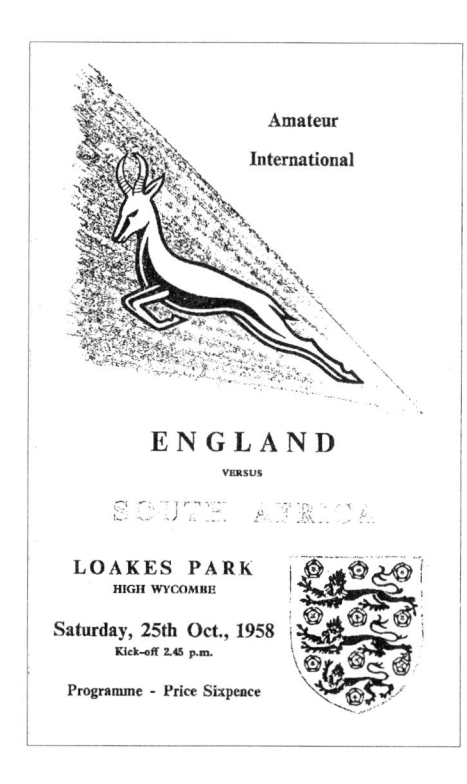

Amateur International

ENGLAND
VERSUS
SOUTH AFRICA
LOAKES PARK
HIGH WYCOMBE
Saturday, 25th Oct., 1958
Kick-off 2.45 p.m.
Programme - Price Sixpence

In the Amateur Cup Third Round Wycombe were leading 2-0 at half-time at Barnet, but the Bees drew level and won 1-0 in the replay at Loakes Park.

46

An extraordinary Berks & Bucks Senior Cup Semi-Final, saw Wycombe 5-1 down at half-time, draw 6-6 with Aylesbury after extra time, but then lose the replay, with Mick Rockell breaking a leg. Paul Bates was picked for England, along with inside-right Dennis Edwards who turned professional with Charlton in February 1959. Bates ended the season with 40 goals, the first player to do so since Tim Hinton in the 1925-26 season.

In November 1959, Wycombe won a First Round FA Cup match for the first time. They won 4-2 at home to Southern League Premier Division side Wisbech Town in front of 7,900. The reward was an attractive local derby at Watford, then in the Fourth Division, and 5,000 from Wycombe swelled the crowd to 23,907, the largest attendance since Manchester United had visited Vicarage Road in 1952.

The home side scored after eight minutes through Uphill, with a powerful well placed shot, but Atkins equalised 11 minutes later with a free kick from outside the penalty area. Wycombe were playing well, however, in the 40th minute Uphill scored again, with a header, and Holton scored the third a few seconds before half-time.

Trott went close just after the break but McNeice scored Wayford's fourth in the 51st minute with a 40 yard dipper which deceived Dennis Syrett in goal. Paul Bates for Wyc-ombe had a penalty saved by the goalkeeper two minutes from time and a minute later Watford were awar-ded a penalty, Holton mak-ing the final score 5-1, which is still Wanderers' record defeat in a first class cup game. Watford beat First Div-ision Birmingham City in the Third Round and eventually lost to Sheffield United in the Fifth Round.

Wycombe beat Ilford 10-0 at Loakes Park in February, their record score in the Isthmian League, but four weeks later lost 2-1 at home to Tooting & Mitcham, who went on to win the League on the last day of the season by just one point from Wanderers. Long serving players Dennis Syrett, Jim Moring, Ron Fryer and Jim Truett all played their last games that season and it seemed to mark the end of the Club's most successful period thus far. By Christmas in the 1960-61 season, only five League games out of 19 had been won and the Club finished eighth, losing more games than they won for the first time in ten years.

The Loakes Park crowd before the record 10-0 Isthmian League defeat of Ilford in February 1960.

47

CHAPTER 5 (1961-1976)
A FALL.... THEN THE GLORY YEARS RETURN

1962 - a former players reunion (standing): Jim Moring, Jim Kipping, Ben Newell, Bill Hayter, Joey Grace, Frank Didcock, Reg Maskell, Pat Badrick, (sitting): Nelson Rolfe, Fred Gates, Archie Gomm, Klon Smith, Frank Adams, Reggie Boreham, Billy O'Gorman and Tommy Jackman.

Sid Cann left the Club at the end of the 1960-61 season to return to the Football League with Norwich. After a long and painstaking search for a new coach, 30 year old Colin McDonald was appointed on 29 August 1961, Burnley's goalkeeper between 1953 and 1959, when he made 186 First Division appearances. In 1958 he became England's first choice 'keeper and had won eight caps before breaking a leg playing for the Football League in Ireland in March 1959, an injury which ended his career at the age of 28. It was quite a coup for Wycombe Wanderers and since he was living in Bury, the Supporters Club bought a house for him locally to live in. He was found employment in the Sports Department in Murrays department store in High Wycombe. Two weeks later he returned home for a family illness and never returned - on 20 September he resigned as manager for "domestic reasons", just three weeks after being appointed. Wycombe's shortest serving coach was succeeded by Graham Adams, a former Oxford United full back.

In October 1961 a young Tony Horseman scored on his debut for the team in a 3-2 defeat at Oxford City. He played most of his games that season on the left-wing, scoring 9 goals in 31 games, but he would soon start his career as an inside-forward and become the Club's most prolific scorer ever. Paul Bates, captain the previous season, started the season at Tooting & Mitcham but rejoined Wycombe in October. Another Amateur international was staged at Loakes Park on 16 September 1961 when England played Iceland. In the annual end of season Wycombe Hospital match, Mike Keen (Queens Park Rangers) and former players Geoff Truett and Dennis Edwards all guested in the 5-1 win over Loughborough Colleges. Graham Adams left at the end of the season and Don Welsh became the new coach, a former inside-forward with Torquay (80 appearances between 1932 and 1935) and Charlton Athletic (199 appearances, with 44 goals between 1934 and 1948).

The Supporters Club held a Sports Forum in 1963. Amongst the invited guests were: (sitting): Jimmy Greaves, Alf Ramsey and Billy Wright.

The severe winter of the 1962-63 season meant that effectively there was no football from Boxing Day until March. The Amateur Cup First Round tie with Uxbridge was due to be played on 5 January but eventually took place on 2 March, Wycombe winning 2-0 on an icy pitch. The next round, the following Saturday, was played in the pouring rain, when Barking were a little unlucky to lose 3-2. But Wycombe's promising run ended at Hitchin 3-2, in spite of a second-half recovery. The 1963-64 season saw the Isthmian League extended by another four clubs, Enfield, Hendon, Hitchin Town and Sutton United all joining from the Athenian League. The newcomers immediately showed their quality and Enfield, Sutton and Hendon all finished in the top five, the latter scoring 124 goals, an all-time record in the Isthmian League. Wimbledon, however, won the League for the third successive season, turned professional and joined the Southern League. A future Wimbledon stalwart, 19 year old Dave Bassett, played 14 games for Wycombe in the first part of the season as an inside-forward, centre-forward and left-winger; one of his three goals was in the 6-3 FA Cup defeat at Barnet.

A larger League meant midweek matches, so Wycombe installed floodlights which were used for the first time on 25 September 1963, when Enfield were the visitors. The team strip changed from quarters to light and dark blue stripes, a traditional colour for the Reserves but not used by the First Team since before the First World War. It was an unpopular choice and the quarters were reinstated for the following season.

The *Bucks Free Press* came to the rescue when Wanderers only turned up with ten men for a midweek game at Ilford on 21 April 1964. Reporter John Taylor happened to be a Wycombe youth player and, luckily, was registered for the Isthmian League. He played on the left-wing and after the match submitted his match report as normal! He later went on to a television career with ITV, producing *Football Italia* in the 1990's, and also produced *The Loakes Park Years 1895-1990*, the only video history of the Club.

John Maskell joined the Club at the start of the 1964-65 season, the first of sixteen seasons as the first choice goalkeeper. He broke an ankle, however, in a disastrous 7-0 FA Cup defeat at Hayes in October. Coach Don Welsh resigned in December 1964 after a 9-2 defeat at Hendon, and former player Barry Darvill took over and even played one game in the Isthmian League in his old centre-half position. The Club were in a precarious position in the League but he eventually turned results around, winning seven and drawing two of the last 12 games. Chairman Eric Webb died in February and Jack Smethurst was appointed in his place.

The revival continued in 1965-66 when the Club finished fourth, their best placing for six seasons, and scored 100 goals for the first time in the Isthmian League. Paul Bates scored 45 goals in all first team games, supported by Tony Horseman with 34 and Keith Samuels with 23 goals.

In the FA Cup, Len Worley scored a brilliant last minute goal to force a 2-2 draw at Guildford City in the FA Cup First Round. An attractive draw at Queen Park Rangers awaited the winners of the replay but Guildford won 1-0 and then lost 3-0 at Loftus Road. The Quarter-Finals of the Amateur Cup were reached for the first time since the Wembley season of 1956-57, but Wanderers lost 2-1 at Hendon, the Cup holders who went on to lose to Wealdstone in the final. Wycombe entered a new midweek competition, the Wycombe Floodlight League Cup, for teams in the Thames Valley.

1966-67 saw another good season in the League, with a finish in third place, and Tony Horseman created a new scoring record which still stands. He netted 60 goals in 51 first team games, including a run of nine consecutive matches when he scored, and he also produced 14 goals in other games that season. The season is best remembered for an extraordinary FA Cup First Round tie with Southern League Bedford Town which ran to four games and 6½ hours, and was watched by a total of 32,000 spectators. In the first match at Loakes Park, Bedford took the lead after half-time but Keith Samuels equalised with five minutes to go.

In the replay at the Eyrie it was Bedford's turn to equalise a few minutes from time. Wycombe took the lead in extra time but again Bedford equalised, with two minutes left from a controversial penalty. Wycombe won the toss for choice of venues for the second replay but at 1-1, the game was abandoned at the start of extra time because of a waterlogged pitch. The result stood and in the third replay at Bedford, Wycombe finally lost 3-2. This was the season when the substitute was introduced in English football, and on 24 September 1966 Martin Priestley became Wycombe's first to come on during a game when John Maskell went off injured, at home to Barking.

Paul Bates played his last game in October 1967 and the team struggled to finish fourteenth in the League. There were immediate exits in the two FA competitions, including an embarrassing exit at unknown City of Norwich School Old Boys in the Amateur Cup. Only the Berks & Bucks Senior Cup brought any joy with a Final win over Slough Town. Mike Keen, a native of High Wycombe, left Queens Park Rangers after over 400 games for the Club. Rangers visited Loakes Park on 14 May and a crowd of just under 4,000 saw Wycombe win 1-0 in a special benefit match for Keen.

Results improved, but in December coach Barry Darvill resigned. George Thompson, on the Club's Committee, approached Brian Lee who had been recommended by the Football Association. At the time he was coach to the Oxford University football team and managing Bisham Abbey National Sports Centre. He agreed to come after the Varsity match in December had been played, and for the same pay that he received as a staff coach for the FA, namely 6 guineas (£6 6s.) per week during the season.

Wary of his previous experience as manager of Wellington Town (now Telford United) and the factions which occurred in its 29 man General Committee, he invited all of Wanderers' Committee down to Bisham Abbey one Sunday morning. He asked each man in turn *"Do you want me to come?"* and all said *"Yes"*. He was appointed before the Amateur Cup tie at Oxford City on 14 December, but his first game in charge was a 0-0 draw at Clapton on 28 December.

As amateurs, no player had a contract, and their relationship with the Club hinged on trust and loyalty. Lee was keen that integrity and honesty remained the most important values at the Club and the first thing he said to the players was *"You will let me down, I will not let you down"*.

Tony Horseman: A career with Wycombe which spanned from 1961 to 1978. The Club's all-time record number of appearances holder and top goalscorer.

Within a month Lee was picking the side, after disbanding the Selection Committee which had met every Monday at 8pm and notified by post the players selected for the following Saturday's match. John Reardon, who had managed Chesham United to the Amateur Cup Final in 1968, soon joined as Assistant Manager. At the end of the season the Reserve side had been disbanded because, due to the Club's limited resources, it had no Coach and it was felt too many of the players were content not to challenge for First Team places. Some of the established players took time to settle to the new regime, including leading scorer Tony Horseman, who was suspended for two weeks in January after a disagreement. But results improved and the team finished fourth in the League, losing just two such games out of fifteen after Lee took over. At the end of the season reserve 'keeper John Pratt signed for Reading, the first of ten players who would go on to play in the Football League after playing under Brian Lee.

The new manager had stuck with the players that he inherited, but the following season he began rebuilding the team. Schoolteachers Geoff Anthony and Peter Suddaby were recruited from the University circuit, centre-half John Delaney arrived as the new captain, Keith Blunt joined from Dulwich and John Reardon was instrumental in bringing Johnny Hutchinson and Keith Searle, one of the finest amateur strikers in the country, from Wealdstone. One of the most difficult decisions Brian Lee had to make was dropping Len Worley, the first choice right-winger since 1954 but still only 32 years old. He made his final appearance for the Club as a substitute in the Amateur Cup at Croydon Amateurs on 13 December 1969, and left soon after.

The new team went unbeaten in the League from 6 September to the end of the season, a run of 30 matches, and finished second, just one point behind champions Enfield. The side played a large number of fixtures - 79 in all including friendlies and the Premier Midweek Floodlit League. The manager was keen that all members of the squad should get a regular game and it set the pattern in the following seasons. In January 1970, Viv Busby, who had played everywhere in the Wanderers forward line, signed for Luton Town and went on to play for Newcastle United, Fulham (FA Cup Finalist in 1975), Norwich, Stoke, Sheffield United, Blackburn Rovers and York City, in a distinguished career. In and out of the Wycombe side for four seasons, it was felt that Busby's undoubted talent would benefit from the discipline of the professional game. At the end of the season Peter Suddaby joined Blackpool and enjoyed a long career as captain of the Seasiders.

Important new signings for the 1970-71 season included Ted Powell, one of the great centre-backs of the amateur game, and who won 51 England caps, 15 of them whilst with Wycombe. The extremely gifted Sutton midfielder Larry Pritchard signed, as did right-back Paul Fuschillo (he left at the end of the season for a professional career with Blackpool and Brighton), and this talented team won the Isthmian League for the third time in the Club's history by just one point from Sutton. For the second successive season the Amateur Cup Quarter-Final was reached, but a crowd of over 10,000 at Loakes Park were stunned when Skelmersdale United won 3-0; the Lancashire Club won the Cup that season, beating Dagenham in the final.

(Left: Ted Powell, and (Right): Peter Suddaby.

Two players who each returned to the Club later as Manager for short spells (in 1976 and 1987 respectively)

The Club took part in the Channel Islands FA celebrations at Easter, beating a Jersey FA XI 3-0, a Jersey League XI 5-1 but losing 2-0 to a Guernsey FA XI, and they also toured Gibraltar at the end of the season.

Wealdstone joined the Southern League and were replaced by Bishops Stortford plus Walton & Hersham for the 1971-72 season. The new intake included right-back Paul Birdseye, son of Peter - the Wanderers captain after the Second World War - Micky Holifield, Trevor Waughman, Rob Williams and, later in the season, Derek Gamblin and Micky Mellows. The latter had already played 70 games for Reading as an Amateur and turned professional with Portsmouth in 1973. Keith Searle had started the season at Hayes but returned to Wycombe just two weeks later. Brian Lee warned the supporters that it would be harder to retain the Championship than it had been to win it, but Wycombe got off to a flying start, winning 19 and drawing two of the first 22 games, which included 11 wins on the trot. The 40 League games produced 102 goals for and just 20 against, and three of the six defeats were incurred in the final five matches, after Wycombe had already won the title
.

The team also had an excellent chance of doing the 'double', but their Amateur Cup campaign nearly finished in the First Round at Aveley when, two goals down, Wycombe forced a draw and easily won the replay. In the Third Round at Walton & Hersham Larry Pritchard suffered two cracked ribs and missed the rest of the season. Keith Searle scored the only goal in the Quarter-Final match with Hayes who included in their line-up Jim Kelman, a future Wycombe Wanderers manager. The Semi-Final draw paired the Blues with Hendon at Brentford, but, because of postponements due to international call-ups, Wycombe had to play the third round, Quarter-Final and Semi-Final, on consecutive Saturdays. The majority of the near 10,000 crowd at Griffin Park were from Wycombe, but they saw Hendon take the lead after 14 minutes, against the run of play. Keith Searle laid on Wycombe's equalising goal for Johnny Hutchinson on 60 minutes, but Peter Deadman scored the winner for Hendon with a long-range shot, in spite of vociferous protests from the Wycombe defence that a player was in an offside position.

It was a huge disappointment for the Club, especially as it was a match Wycombe should have won and perhaps would have if Larry Pritchard had not been injured. Hendon, a much more experienced side, coped better with the pressure of the occasion and beat Enfield 2-0 in the Final. At the end of the season the Club went on tour to Greece and beat a Greek National Youth XI 1-0 and then, in front of 39,000, played a Panathanikos Under-23 side.

This preceded a match at this level between Greece and Czechoslovakia. Yet, in very hot conditions, Wanderers took a 3-0 lead before the home side scored a late goal. John Maskell played the match of his life between the posts and was warmly applauded by the Greeks at the end of the match.

The 1972-73 season was relatively disappointing and, in spite of winning the opening six League games, the team only finished fourth in the Isthmian competition. At the end of the season captain John Delaney, at the age of 31, turned professional with Bournemouth where he made 25 appearances in the following two seasons. It was a huge loss for the Club, for as a player he was a commanding centre-half who hardly ever fouled and scored an amazing number of headed goals from set pieces. He was also an exemplary leader, who hated cheating and knew how to get the best out of his colleagues. It is perhaps true to say that the Club have never replaced him.

Another player to turn professional was Kenny Swain, a 21 year old right-winger who Lee had spotted playing in a college match at Loakes Park that season. He played in the final seven games of the season, never appearing on the losing side, and signed for Chelsea in the summer after Dario Gradi saw one of his outstanding performances. Because he was a non-contract player his signing on fee was just £500. He is perhaps the most distinguished of the Wycombe players who turned professional, making 379 First Division appearances for Chelsea, Aston Villa and Nottingham Forest, and over 600 in total in the Football League in a long career. Two other players were also spotted in a college game - goalkeeper Paul Barron played two games the following season and then, from Slough Town, went on to play for Plymouth, Arsenal, Crystal Palace, West Bromwich Albion, Queens Park Rangers and Reading. The other was left-winger Steve Perrin who became a very successful centre-forward for Wycombe, before a professional career with Crystal Palace, Plymouth, Portsmouth and Northampton Town. He returned to the Club in the 1980's and helped secure another Isthmian League championship.

The forward line of Searle, Horseman and Perrin notched up over 70 goals in the 1973-74 season. New players Keith Mead, Terry Reardon and Roger Grant added an element of steel to an already skilful side and Wycombe brought the Isthmian League championship home again, remaining unbeaten at Loakes Park. Rothmans began their sponsorship of the League and introduced three points for a win, a world first. There was prize money for sporting behaviour and Wycombe only picked up one booking all season!

With three games in the final five days of the season, Wycombe crucially overturned a 1-0 deficit at Leytonstone to win with two goals in the final 11 minutes. Wanderers then beat the same team at home on the final day of the season to claim the Championship by two points.

The main excitement, however, surrounded the FA Cup and a run which began with a 1-0 win at Tilbury in the First Qualifying Round. In the Third Qualifying Round, Wycombe sensationally won 7-0 at Chatham Town, a semi-professional side in the Kent League who, the previous evening on local radio, expressed their confidence at beating an 'amateur' team! A 3-0 win at Worthing ensured a home tie with Newport County in the First Round, a struggling Fourth Division side who were clearly unprepared mentally for a game against an amateur eleven. In spite of continued pressure from Wycombe, the game remained goalless at half-time. After the break Newport came into the game but Wycombe ran riot midway through the half, scoring three goals in nine minutes from Perrin (2) and Evans, with Newport scoring a consolation goal seven minutes from time.

It was Wycombe's first victory over a Football League Club, but their opponents in the Second Round, Fourth Division leaders Peterborough United, took no chances, for they stayed nearby before the game, and even trained on a sloping pitch. In an even first-half, Larry Pritchard equalised just before half-time but Peterborough took control and ran out 3-1 winners.

The Amateur Cup was in its last season but sadly Wycombe failed in their bid to win it one more time. Progress was halted in the Third Round by the top amateur team in the North, Blyth Spartans, after Keith Mead scored an unfortunate own goal. The three day working week, brought on by the Coal Miners strike, meant that Wycombe played their first ever game on a Sunday. The 2,200 crowd at Loakes Park on 13 January 1974 saw Wycombe overcome bottom side Corinthian Casuals by 7-0.

Wycombe Wanderers' claim to be the best non-League side in the country was underlined in the 1974-75 season, the most memorable in the Club's history to that time. It was the first season after the divide between amateur and professionals had been abolished by the Football Association - now everyone was a 'player'. Larry Pritchard had returned to Sutton but the new blood included teacher Howard Kennedy, Dave Alexander and an experienced pair from Hendon, Alan Phillips and Gary Hand.

In spite of the previous season's FA Cup heroics, the team had to battle through the qualifying rounds this season because they forgot to send in the qualifying round exemption form! Marlow proved tough opponents and could have taken the lead before Steve Perrin scored the only goal late in the game.

Later wins over Milton Keynes, Chesham and Margate saw Wycombe face Cheltenham Town at home in the First Round. The referee in this match controversially awarded a penalty to Wycombe in the first-half after Dylan Evans was fouled in an off-the-ball incident in the penalty area, long after the ball had been cleared. Horseman converted and Wycombe's 3-1 win was rounded off by a truly stunning solo effort by right-back Paul Birdseye, who beat player after player before thumping the ball into the net. The reward was a home tie to Bournemouth in the Second Round, an emotional home coming for John Delaney who captained the visitors. Kevin Charlton was outstanding in the Bournemouth goal and was the only reason why the game ended 0-0.

The replay at Dean Court, however, was one of the most exciting of nights in the Club's history. Bournemouth, crucially missing Delaney through injury, started the match with a vengeance, scored after nine minutes and could have had several more. But Wycombe managed to keep the scoreline to 1-0 at half-time, when Brian Lee, out of character, read the riot act in the changing room. Kevin Charlton, the Bournemouth goalkeeper, had picked up an injury early in the first-half and right-winger John Wingate took over after the break. Wycombe quickly took control, equalising through Tony Horseman before that player's shot was deflected off the back of Steve Perrin, for a dramatic winner. That evening at Dean Court remains one of the most exciting nights in the Club's history, and the reward was a home tie in the Third Round against Middlesbrough. At the time, the League team was managed by Jack Charlton and were second only on goal difference to First Division leaders Ipswich.

A 12,000 capacity crowd packed into Loakes Park on Saturday 4 January 1975 for the game which was covered by London Weekend's *Big Match* cameras, with highlights being shown the following afternoon. The game ended goalless but Wycombe were the better team on the day and were unlucky not to win. The best chances of the game fell to Wycombe - on 47 minutes a Horseman cross was toe-poked just wide by Perrin, and in the 72nd minute central defender Phillips sent a fierce, diving header into the side netting. The outstanding players of the game were Reardon, who got the better of Graeme Souness in their midfield battle, and central defender Keith Mead who repelled all that Boro' could throw at him. The First Division side really were hanging on at the end and Reardon said afterwards: *"Quite a few of them let their heads drop when things were not going their way. Twenty minutes from time Souness was yelling at his team to shut up shop. What an indictment of First Division football that is."*

Jack Charlton, relieved to have got the draw, was first to congratulate the Wycombe team in the changing room: *"You were great"*, he told them. *"We have not been put on the rack like that for months. This must count as one of my worst days as a manager. The slope was frightening for my lads but that's no excuse. No team in the world could have scored against them today."* He added ominously: *"Our pitch at Ayresome is very big and very flat - and we are going to give them a chasing."* Before the replay on the following Tuesday, Charlton controversially condemned the Loakes Park pitch, saying it was wrong for top professional clubs to play on *'degrading pitches'*. *"I know a lot of people will say that professional footballers should play on any surface. But I say it is ridiculous to ask top players to turn out in such situations."* Brain Lee was in a realistic, if not pessimistic mood, when he forecast: *"I think Middlesbrough will murder us. Football is not a game of fantasy. My view has not changed because we caught them on an off day last week."* As it turned out Wanderers played the game of their lives and once again severely frightened their more illustrious opponents.

Both sides had chances to score, the Boro' goalkeeper Jim Platt twice superbly saved from Howard Kennedy, but the score was scoreless when, a minute from time, Souness spotted Armstrong in space in the box. The blond striker cut inside, beat one defender and slipped the ball past Maskell into the net. When the final whistle went the 30,000 crowd chanted *'Wycombe! Wycombe!'* and the home players applauded the Wycombe players off the pitch. The Middlesbrough Chairman provided a case of champagne for the gallant losers. It was the greatest performance a Wycombe team had ever given and all of those present from the Club still remember it as one of the most emotional moments they have ever experienced. Brain Lee said afterwards: *"We'd started to flag in the last ten minutes. I'm glad Boro' scored when they did. If we'd lasted another minute and gone into extra time we could have lost 6-0."*

(Top): Alan Phillips leads out the Wycombe team for the F.A.Cup match at Loakes Park versus Bournemouth in December 1974. (Below) How close they came to winning in the next round

Brave Wanderers give Charlton's men the shock of their lives

Wycombe Wanderers 0, Middlesbrough 0
STUART EARP AT LOAKES PARK

Wycombe returned to the seemingly impossible task of winning the Isthmian League. Sixteen points behind leaders Enfield with only one game in hand, they travelled to Oxford City the following Saturday. It would have been easy for Wycombe to have remained on 'cloud nine' but, showing great determination, the Wanderers ground out a 1-0 victory and started one of the most amazing League runs in their history. Nine straight victories were recorded and of the final 21 games played after Middlesbrough, 16 were won and 5 drawn. With four games to go Wycombe missed the chance to beat Enfield in a tense 0-0 draw at Loakes Park, and it all came down to the final day of the season and a tough home match against third placed Dagenham. Wanderers were top, but level on points with Enfield, and knew that probably only a win would keep them in first place.

It was a cold, wet day and Wycombe showed their nerves in a desperately tense match. Dave Alexander missed a good chance to put Wycombe ahead but the match appeared destined to finish 0-0. Then, five minutes from time, Keith Searle received a throw-in on the topside at the Gasworks end; he turned, and, from the corner of the penalty area, unleashed a shot into the far corner of the net. The terrace behind the goal erupted and the sheer ecstasy has rarely been repeated - before the goal went in the damp, cold supporters, were in a mental state of severe depression at the thought of bitter rivals Enfield winning the League! The score remained 1-0 and Wycombe won the championship for the second successive season by just 0.1 on goal difference.

The scene inside the Wycombe dressing-room, after the Dagenham victory, which sealed the Isthmian League Championship.

Steve Perrin is foiled by the Thatcham 'keeper Palmer in the 1975 Berks.& Bucks. Senior Cup Final at Chesham.

It was without doubt the most memorable season the Club had ever experienced, but there was one other match that season that deserves mention, one of the strangest in the Club's history. Back in March, Wycombe had qualified for the Final of the Berks & Bucks Senior Cup against Thatcham Town. Played at Chesham United, Wycombe were on the receiving end of some bizarre decisions by referee Ken Walker. After eleven minutes the referee booked Wycombe's Terry Reardon for swearing - before the game he had gone into the Thatcham changing room and warned that any swearing would be severely punished but had not entered Wycombe's to give the same warning.

Keith Mead then made a comment to his team mate Reardon, using a swear word, and was booked. Mead began walking back to his position but the referee called him back and dismissed him from the pitch (the player later successfully appealed against the dismissal). Soon after Keith Searle broke through the defence and, despite being fouled by a defender, drove the ball home for what looked like Wycombe's first goal. The referee then blew his whistle for the foul on Searle and awarded a free kick which came to nothing. A similar thing happened when Steve Perrin collided with the 'keeper and a defender on the edge of the penalty area.

Perrin was first to react and slotted the loose ball home but again the referee awarded a free kick to Wycombe instead. The Hellenic League side gamely held Wycombe to 0-0 after ninety minutes, but their inferior fitness told in extra time and a hat trick from Tony and a Searle goal ensured a 4-0 win for Wycombe. The Wanderers players applauded Thatcham off the pitch and then went straight to the changing room. After some minutes the Thatcham players collected their losers medals but the Berks & Bucks officials waited in vain to present the Cup. By now the supporters were chanting: *"We want to play in the London Senior Cup"*, and if they did not know before, the County officials realised that Wanderers were protesting against the Berks & Bucks FA's refusal to allow them to compete in the one of the top non-League competitions of the day, the semi-finalists of which could enter the London Challenge Cup and play against top Football League sides.

For three successive seasons the Berks & Bucks FA had turned down Wycombe's application to play in the London Senior Cup, the last refusal had been two weeks before. What had really incensed Brian Lee was not so much the refusal, but the fact that no reason was given, even when repeatedly asked for. The manager had decided before the game that if Wycombe were successful, the Club would not collect the Cup as a protest. Consequently Thatcham were classified as the holders, Wycombe were expelled from that season's competition, and officially there are no winners of the Berks & Bucks Senior Cup for 1974-75, as neither finalist has ever claimed to be so. The Berks & Bucks FA subsequently reported Wycombe to the FA who severely censured Brain Lee and the Club. The county body then 'punished' Wycombe Wanderers by forcing them to compete next season from the First Round instead of the Third Round, and depriving them of the small amount of their share of pooled receipts.

Charles Twelftree, the Berks & Bucks FA Secretary, consequently said that the county was not an overlapping county, which means that it does not overlap into the 15 mile radius of the London FA, but if counties do overlap, they are entitled to enter the competition. At the time every other Home Counties' FA allowed all of their top non-League sides to enter for the competition. Afterwards Lee said: *"This is our protest against the Berks & Bucks FA. For too long it has been one way traffic - we do everything for them and they do nothing for us. We didn't want to spoil Thatcham's day so this was a mild protest, but we feel we have been badly treated."*

Since the abolition of the amateur code other top non-League clubs had been able to pay their players more than Wycombe and the great side from the previous season began to break up. Keith Searle, Alan Phillips and Gary Hand left, Steve Perrin turned professional with Crystal Palace, but former players John Delaney and Geoff Anthony returned. Searle's departure to Enfield was probably the difference between the two clubs, and this time Enfield finished champions of the Isthmian League, five points ahead of Wycombe. The second match in the League saw Wycombe lose 1-0 at home to Slough, the first side to win a League game there for 52 matches, a run which stretched back to December 1972.

The Club enjoyed exemption to the last qualifying round of the FA Cup but found themselves two goals down at Croydon before drawing 2-2. After winning the replay 5-2, Wycombe were paired with Bedford Town, and a repeat of the marathon in the Sixties looked possible at one stage. The first game at Loakes Park was a 0-0 draw, the replay ended 2-2 after extra time but Wanderers eventually won 2-1 in the pouring rain at Loakes Park. The reward was a trip to Cardiff City where Wycombe were unlucky to lose to a Tony Evans goal two minutes before half-time. Wycombe's Dylan Evans had smacked the ball against the upright in the 10th minute, and had several chances before Cardiff scored the only goal of the game two minutes before the interval and deserved at least a draw.

Early in the season Wycombe were invited to play in the Anglo-Italian Trophy, beating A C Monza 2-1 over two legs. At the end of the season they took part in the Anglo-Italian Semi-Professional Tournament, together with Enfield, but went out in spite of winning two of the four group games. There was more drama in the Berks & Bucks Senior Cup after winning 4-2 at Chesham United in the Semi-Final. Wycombe's opening goal was an own goal, believed to be the fastest ever in this country, but afterwards the Club withdrew from the competition when they realised that they had played an ineligible player; Chesham went on to win the competition.

Frank Adams donated the F.A. Vase (the Amateur Cup equivalent) in 1975.

CHAPTER 6 (1976-1987)
THE LAST YEARS WITH THE ISTHMIANS

Former player Reg Williams became Chairman after Jack Smethurst died during the 1975/76 season after a long illness. The previous season he had watched the Middlesbrough game from the adjoining Wycombe General Hospital which sadly he never left. He had enjoyed a remarkably good relationship with Brian Lee who, in November 1975, announced that he would resign as manager at the end of the season as his commitments at Bisham Abbey prevented from his spending enough time at the Club (The National Sports Centre had become enlarged in June 1974). It was the end of a quite remarkable period in the Club's history - four League wins, two runners-up spots and glory in the FA Cup. The teams included a dazzling array of talent and many of those players went on to successful Football League careers. The Club invited him to stay on as Vice-Chairman and he continued to advise the Club on playing matters.

For the 1976-7 season former favourite Ted Powell was appointed as manager on Brian Lee's recommendation. However in March he announced that he had accepted the offer of a coaching job in Malawi and the Club thought it best if he left the Club immediately; John Reardon acted as manager until the end of the season. The Club finished second again to Enfield, a championship which went to the final day of the season. Much of the good form was down to new striker Ian Pearson, a very skilful and beautifully balanced player who caught the attention of Millwall. They signed him at the end of the season although he did not enjoy the career his talent suggested.

Another appearance in the FA Cup Second Round saw Wycombe face Reading at Loakes Park. On a frost bound pitch the Royals lead 2-0 at the break, but Pearson pulled one back in the 68th minute and then hit the post as Wycombe were unlucky not to earn a replay. Long serving players John Maskell and Tony Horseman were awarded a joint testimonial in November 1976 and a 3,000 crowd saw a team of former players beaten 5-4.

John Reardon continued as manager for the 1977-78 season and the team finished third, a staggering 35 points behind an all conquering Enfield team who won 35 of the 42 League games, to amass a record 110 points. Wycombe continued to win sportsmanship awards and at the season's end had incurred only six bookings in the previous five seasons!

The Club were exempted to the First Round of the FA Cup for only the second time in their history, but lost 2-0 at Minehead, going a goal down just before half-time and conceding the second a minute from time. Tony Horseman hung up his boots at the end of the season, 17 years after making his debut. In a total of 746 competitive games for the Club, he scored an incredible 416 goals, a total which is unlikely to be surpassed.

The former Enfield and England Amateur international goalkeeper Andy Williams took charge of the team for the 1978-79 season after John Reardon had departed from the Club. The League finish of sixth was the lowest for ten years but in the FA Trophy the team progressed past the Second Round for the first time. To do so they gained the notable scalp of Blyth Spartans - who were seconds away from reaching the FA Cup Quarter-Finals the previous season - winning 3-0 in a replay at Loakes Park. However Wycombe lost at struggling Hayes in a replay in the Third Round, in a competition which Wanderers had never really got to grips with. The Club again received exemption to the First Round of the FA Cup and dominated the game at Maidstone but fell to the only goal of the game when 'keeper Peter Spittle unfortunately tipped an indirect free-kick into the net.

The only joy was in the Berks & Bucks Senior Cup which was won for the second time in successive seasons and rather fortuitously. Wycombe only equalised in the final minute with a penalty at Marlow. In the replay at Slough, opponents Hungerford again took the lead before Wanderers eventually won 3-1. Goalkeeper John Maskell retired at the end of the season after over 600 games for the Club in a career which had started in 1964.

The 1979-80 season saw a another major upheaval in the non-League world when the Alliance Premier League was formed from 13 Southern League and 7 Northern Premier League teams. The League would be the pinnacle of a pyramid of non-League football, with relegation to and from the Southern and Northern Premier Leagues. The main objective was that the Alliance champions alone would apply for membership of the Football League, so concentrating all of the efforts of the non-League world behind one candidate and avoiding a split vote. It is true that four clubs in the seventies had gained election (Cambridge United 1970, Hereford United 1972, Wimbledon 1977 and Wigan Athletic in 1978) but the Football League was still notorious for being a 'closed

Blues apply to join Football League

Wycombe drop a bombshell

Story by MICHAEL KNOX

shop', with the struggling clubs at the bottom of the Fourth Division desperate to cling onto their coveted membership.

The only problem for the Alliance was the non co-operation of the Isthmian League, which contained many of the top non-League sides in the country, who refused to join the pyramid structure.

WYCOMBE Wanderers dropped a football bombshell over the Easter holiday by applying to join the Football League next season.

This shock announcement, which will send reverberations around the non-league world, means that for the first time in their history Wycombe are aiming to join the elite.

Indeed improvements might have to be made to the press area.

There must be severe doubts as to whether Wycombe would pass this inspection, although Mr Goldsworthy defends the pitch by saying: "If you can't play on that surface, you anywhere."

Even if hard their exceptional non-league record, failed to beat strugglers Rochdale in a vote la-year. There are no su- vious candidate thrown out of th time.

has received support from the Isthmian League, can only benef else it sho not hav

easily won 3-0 in the rain. Reserve team football returned for the first time since 1969, with a team entered in the Suburban League (North).

Early in 1981 Brian Lee was elected Chairman after Reg Williams stepped down, and one of his earliest decisions was that Wycombe Wanderers should apply to join the Football League, which they did in April 1981. This caused considerable surprise in the non-League world, but Brain Lee took this action partly as a protest against the Alliance Premier League's assertion that only their champions could apply - this was a notion that the Football Association had never endorsed. Jim Thompson, the Chairman of the Alliance Premier League, was extremely unhappy with this development, as were champions Altrincham who feared a split non-League vote. As champions the previous season Atrincham missed out on election by just one vote in farcical circumstances when two supporters for the Club's election (they later found out) failed to vote - Luton's representative got stuck in traffic and Grimsby Town's misunderstood when to vote; Rochdale survived by the skin of their teeth!

Wycombe Wanderers were invited to become Alliance founder-members, along with Enfield and Dagenham, but all declined the offer as they found the idea of a national semi-professional league very unattractive, with the increased travelling costs and probable loss of existing players.

Andy Williams departed from Wycombe, and Brian Lee took temporary charge at the start of the 1979-80 season before Mike Keen, a sports shop owner in High Wycombe, took over in January 1980. The former Queens Park Rangers, Watford and Luton midfielder inherited a team which unusually found itself in the bottom half of the table. He quickly improved results and won the final seven League games to finish in tenth position. That season Mike Phillips became the Club's first full-time Commercial Manager and went on to develop one of the most successful football club lotteries in this country with Canvasser John Simmonds. Without this source of income the Club would never have been able to achieve so much in the next 15 years.

Good results continued in 1980-81 as the team finished third, seven points behind champions Slough Town who were managed by former player Terry Reardon. The FA Cup First Round tie with Bournemouth failed to bring back happy memories when the Dorset club, managed by Mike Keens' former boss at QPR and Luton, Alec Stock,

Brian Lee also wanted to see whether Loakes Park would pass the Ground Inspection test and a team of three Football League representatives, Sir Matt Busby, Jack Wiseman from Birmingham City, and George Readle, came down and duly passed Loakes Park fit for the Football League, with one or two minor modifications required. The point made, Wycombe withdrew their application before the Football League's AGM, much to the relief of Altrincham who subsequently failed to gain election.

That same summer Enfield and Dagenham accepted the invitation to join the Alliance Premier League and the Isthmian lost two of its consistently strongest sides. Since joining in 1963, Enfield had only ever finished once in the bottom half, winning the championship seven times.

**Brian Lee and Sir Matt Busby.
Sir Matt was part of the Football League
Ground Inspection Committee in 1981.**

Dagenham, since winning promotion to the Isthmian League Premier Division in 1974, had never finished below half-way and had been runners-up four times and third on two occasions. Fearing further defections, the Isthmian decided to join the Pyramid, and from the 1981-82 season the champions would qualify for election to the Alliance Premier league. As it turned out Leytonstone/Ilford finished top but declined the elevation, as did Sutton in second place and Wycombe in third place who still found the idea of national part-time football unattractive.

Wycombe enjoyed its best season since the days when Brain Lee was manager and the highlight was an extended run in the FA Trophy. It begun at Walthamstow Avenue on a wet January evening in front of just 280 people. The match ended 1-1 (with Steve Toll scoring his only goal for the club), as did the replay, but Wycombe finally went through 5-1, after winning the toss for the third match venue. The second round saw a visit to Northern Premier League Hyde United and, in spite of some scintillating runs by Hyde's left-winger George Oghani, Wycombe held on to a 0-0 draw and beat them 3-2 in the replay. Howard Kennedy scored a memorable winner five minutes from time with a free-kick from outside the penalty area. The Third Round was a wallow in nostalgia as Bishop Auckland, the Club's arch rivals in the Fifties, visited Loakes Park. The two teams from the 1957 Amateur Cup Final were special guests at the match, and Wycombe played some excellent football to win 4-1.

A tricky Quarter-Final tie at Kidderminster Harriers saw the team give a great performance, as Terry Glynn scored the only goal in the second-half. The Semi-Final opponents were the mighty Altrincham, and nearly a thousand Wycombe supporters, who had travelled up for the away leg on a specially chartered train, saw Ken Wilson give their side a 1-0 lead before the home side agonisingly equalised in the dying minutes through a defensive error. It was still an excellent result and Wycombe felt confident of finally reaching Wembley again. The Second Leg turned out to be the Club's biggest disappointment since losing in the Amateur Cup Semi-Final in 1972. Reserve 'keeper Chris Way came into the side in place of Gary Lester, who was injured, and the whole team gave a very nervy performance on a hard pitch. By half-time Alty were two up, added a third after the break, and gave a very professional performance to go through 4-1 on aggregate.

In between the two legs the Club were humbled by Hungerford Town in the Berks & Bucks Senior Cup Final at Wokingham, losing 1-0 with the players minds' clearly on the Second Leg Trophy game against Altrincham. Further disappointment followed when Kingstonian knocked Wycombe out of the Hitachi League Cup at the Semi-Final stage, and to cap it all, two League matches were lost at Sutton and Dulwich, which effectively put paid to any hopes of the championship. In just twelve traumatic days, Wanderers had lost hopes of winning four trophies. It was still a very enjoyable season and the talented team included a strike duo of Terry Glynn, a goal-poacher supreme with 38 in 64 games that season, and Steve Long, who was very fast and skilful, who scored 21. The midfield was anchored by the hard working Bobby Dell and Howard Kennedy, an excellent distributor of the ball, who chipped in with 20 goals, mostly from long range shooting. Ken Wilson laid on many crosses from the left-wing and Anton Vircavs was one of the best non-League central defenders at the time.

The team was strengthened for the 1982-83 season when left-back Mark Hill joined, along with former players Peter Suddaby and Steve Perrin. In September, the manager's son Kevin Keen, became the youngest Wycombe player to play in a first team game, when aged 15 years and 209 days, on his debut at Hendon. He showed remarkable maturity in his three games that season and went on to a Football League career with West Ham, Wolves and Stoke. The team went to the top of the table on 16 October and stayed there until the end of the season. At the end of February the chasing pack had plenty of games in hand to go top, but Wycombe ended the season with a remarkable run of nine wins and one draw in the last ten games to win their seventh Isthmian championship. In the FA Cup First Round at Eastville, Bristol Rovers were a little fortunate to beat Wanderers 1-0, after Mark Hill found himself clean through against the goalkeeper but the ball bobbled and he blasted over for what would have been the equaliser.

In April the Club were invited to Italy to compete in the Gigi Peronace Cup, with Padua, Cosenza and Chelmsford City. They lost 4-0 to Cosenza but beat Chelmsford on penalties after a 2-2 draw to claim Third Place.

Again Wycombe declined promotion to the Alliance Premier League, as did Leytonstone/Ilford and Harrow Borough below them. It was still felt that the move up would require a complete change of officials and playing staff because of the increased travelling. It may have been as well as the 1983-84 season proved something of an anti-climax, with an indifferent League campaign which was partially rescued by just three defeats in the second-half of the season. The team lost to Sutton United in the Hitachi League Cup Final for the second successive season and, at the end of the season, the Club decided not to offer manager Mike Keen a new contract.

In 1984-85 Wycombe Wanderers appointed Paul Bence as manager, a former defender with over 200 Football League appearances for Brentford in the early Seventies. He was given the brief of getting the Club into the Alliance Premier League, now known as the Gola League, as the Club now realised it could no longer afford to stand still. He rebuilt the side, and in particular brought in two strikers, Declan Link and Simon Read, from Staines Town. Both players in this deadly partnership scored 30 goals that season as the team shot from 15th place at the turn of the year, with just 24 points from 19 games, to third place at the finish. The final 21 League games produced 16 wins and two draws, proving once again that Wycombe Wanderers have a happy knack of finishing strongly in their League.

The run began with the debut of a young Mark West, a native of High Wycombe whose Football League career at West Ham and Reading had never got off the ground. He went on to become one of the all-time great strikers in the Club's history. There was a shock in the FA Cup when the team lost at Burton Albion in the Fourth Qualifying Round. It was the first time since the 1972-73 season that the side had failed to compete in the First Round, an unbroken 11 year run which was a non-League record.

The FA Trophy First Round tie against Dartford was played on a snowbound Loakes Park marked with blue lines, and Wycombe trounced the Gola League side 6-1 with the visitors clearly not relishing the conditions. The Club did win the Hitachi Cup for the first time, beating Farnborough, and the trophy was presented by Sir Stanley Rous who had just celebrated his 90th birthday. The (premature) centenary celebrations included a match against Leicester City who were also celebrating 100 years. Gary Lineker played for Leicester in the 0-0 draw on 3 October, a match marred by Wycombe's John Richardson breaking a leg, and the Club also held a special dinner at Phyllis Court, Henley, with Sir Stanley Rous being one of 100 guests.

There was joy at the end of the season when it was announced that champions Sutton and second placed Worthing could not enter the Gola League because of ground difficulties, but that Wycombe Wanderers had been accepted.

The opening Gola League game in 1985-86 saw a 1-0 home defeat to Runcorn and showed just how difficult this season would be; the visitors scored early on and then closed up shop. The only new signings were Neal Stanley, Sean Price and Des McMahon, all from Paul Bence's old side Wokingham Town, but until the middle of March the team held their own. The second game produced a victory, 1-0 at Barnet, when the home side tore into Wycombe but could not beat Gary Lester performing heroics on the day. Just before half-time Neal Stanley was brought down in the box and the penalty converted by Link. After the break Lester again held Barnet at bay, even saving a penalty five minutes from time, and Wycombe held on. The next game was a brilliantly entertaining match at Altrincham when the home side took a 2-0 lead and could have had more. Wycombe fought back superbly in the second-half to 3-3 but lost to a late goal.

Wycombe were the only team to do the double over Enfield, the eventual League champions, and the 3-2 win in North London in January had an incredible finish.

Enfield were leading 2-1 in a match they had completely dominated, but with the watch showing 90 minutes, Wycombe converted a penalty and then Mark West popped up with the winner. However the 2-1 home defeat to Telford on 22 March began a terrible run of just one win and two draws in the final 14 League games. Fixture congestion meant that a total of 23 first team games were played in the final nine weeks of the season, an impossible schedule. The tiredness really showed in a humbling 8-2 defeat at Kidderminster but, as it turned out, the turning point came in the penultimate game, a Wednesday evening match at home to Altrincham. With the score at 0-0, Wycombe's left-back Graham Pearce lobbed the ball 30 yards back to his 'keeper Gary Lester, who unfortunately was rushing out of his goal and could only watch it sail into the net for the only goal of the game.

The final match was at home to Kettering on the Saturday, but the situation was not desperate. Two sides were already relegated and as long as one of the other three candidates for the final relegation place, Nuneaton, Maidstone or Dagenham, lost, then Wycombe could afford to draw or even lose. The match with Kettering ended 0-0, with Wycombe never really threatening. Unfortunately Nuneaton and Maidstone picked up points so it all came down to Dagenham's Sunday game at home to Runcorn - in sixth place - and due to play in the Trophy final two weeks later. Just forty seconds after the start, the Dagenham 'keeper punted the ball upfield and, caught by the wind, it bounced once and was helped into the net for a goal by the Runcorn goalkeeper Peter Eales, who had not held a first team place for some time. That clearance was Dagenham's only real attempt all afternoon and, although Runcorn equalised in the second-half, they had their precious point. Wycombe were relegated for the only time in their history, on goal difference and equal on points with three other clubs.

The fixture backlog was partly caused by an extended run in the FA Trophy which fell foul of the weather. In the First Round at Barnet, Wycombe again defended in siege like conditions and again scored the only goal of the game with a penalty. Barnet's manager, Roger Thompson, was sacked after the game by Stan Flashman, paving the way for the return of Barry Fry. A 2-0 win in the mud at Crawley was followed by a Third Round Tie against Leek Town which took a month to complete. The first game, postponed once because of snow, finished 2-2 at Loakes Park on a skating rink of a pitch. The replay was one of the most exciting games the Club had ever played in. Four times Wycombe led before the match finished 4-4 at 90 minutes and ended 5-5 after extra time. Eventually Wanderers went through 1-0 but lost in the Quarter-Finals at Kettering.

There was also a good run in the FA cup when Fourth Division Colchester were beaten 2-0 at Loakes Park in the First Round, Mark West heading the first after just three minutes. The match was marred by crowd trouble, but it was the first time a League club had been beaten for 12 years. The Second Round saw Chelmsford also succumb 2-0 at Loakes Park, the highlight being Des McMahon's 30 yard goal.

```
WYCOMBE WANDERERS
FOOTBALL              CLUB
SEASON                1985/86

THE GOLA LEAGUE

versus
Chelmsford City
F.A. CUP - 2nd Round Proper
SATURDAY, 7th DECEMBER 1985  K.O. 3.00 p.m.
Programme No. 21              Price 40p

CLUB SPONSORS
TREND
COMMUNICATIONS
```

The draw for the Third Round was straight after the game and the fans were bitterly disappointed to be drawn away to Third Division York City. A special train took the supporters to the game but they saw York dominate and win 2-0; they beat Altrincham in the next round and then narrowly lost to Liverpool after extra time in a replay.

There were two other factors in the Club's downfall that season. Top scorer Declan Link left at the end of November to work in the United States after scoring 17 goals in the first four months of the season. Then following the York defeat in January, manager Paul Bence left the Club because of increased business responsibilities. Assistant Alan Gane, a former player in the early seventies, took over, aided by former goalkeeper John Maskell and, later in the season, John Reardon. They did their best in circumstances which were clearly beyond their control.

While the team were experiencing a fascinating season on the pitch, much was happening off the pitch which would prove to be of enormous importance in the future. At that time the Club was not a limited company but a members' club like any other sporting club in the country. The members, who comprised the various Committees as well as season ticket holders, controlled affairs and what assets there were at the time. In 1980 Wycombe Wanderers Football Club Limited had been registered but had never traded since its formation. Loakes Park was not owned by the Club but had been held in Trust ever since Frank Adams had presented it to the Club in 1947. At that time the three Trustees were Jack Adams (Frank's son), Reg Williams (a former player and Chairman) and John Roberts (a local solicitor). Chairman Brian Lee realised that if the Club was to progress further and ultimately win promotion to the Football League then two things had to happen. Loakes Park would not pass a ground inspection visit this time and there was not enough space to redevelop the ground sufficiently. Even if there was, the Club simply did not have the funds to do so. The only answer was to sell Loakes Park and move to a purpose built ground somewhere else in High Wycombe.

On Christmas Eve 1985, the Club entered into an agreement with property company Westbruton Ltd who would fund the building of a new ground and, when the Club had made the move, acquire Loakes Park for redevelopment (Westbruton subsequently sold their agreement to another company). Brian Lee felt that this would be too great an undertaking for the Committee who had managed the Club extremely well in past years, keeping it solvent, but probably lacked the commercial acumen for what would be a multi-million pound scheme. One of the original stipulations that Frank Adams had made was that the ground should only be used for amateur football and not be sold. The amateur stipulation had long since been lifted, and with the future of the Club dependant on a move, the Trustees had agreed that Loakes Park could be sold.

In January 1986 it was announced that Loakes Park would soon be vacated for another site somewhere in the town. Meanwhile, late in 1985, Brain Lee approached local Builder & Developer Ivor Beeks with a view to becoming involved in the new project. He then approached Gordon Richards and Graham Peart, both of whom owned local businesses, who agreed join him, and the three of them took a background role during that season, observing and learning how a top non-League club was run. On 21 May 1986 these three, together with Brian Lee, John Goldsworthy, the Football Secretary, Gerald Cox, the Treasurer, and John Roberts met for an informal 'board' meeting to begin the 'reconstruction' of the Club. The Committee still continued but had no executive powers.

This upset some of its members who felt, correctly, that they had done nothing wrong, but were now left out of the main picture. Some of the Committee subsequently resigned but the Board felt that it had to take hold of the situation and act very swiftly otherwise an opportunity would be lost.

In October 1986, Wycombe Wanderers Football Club Limited was activated and all assets of the football club transferred to it. At the same time the Trustees handed Loakes Park over to the company and the new Board of Directors comprised Brian Lee (Chairman), John Goldsworthy (Company secretary), Gerald Cox, Ivor Beeks, John Roberts, Gordon Richards and Graham Peart. The Board met formally for the first time on 27 October 1986, and each member became responsible for a particular area of the Club's activities. One of the early discoveries by the Board was that it was not possible to ascertain what the monthly trading figures of the Club were, but only at the year end. Director Graham Peart began looking into the financial records and, to his surprise, found very little. At the time it was the convention for the Chairman to give each week, a lump sum to the Manager who would then pay the players. Records of who got what were minimal, partly because the Club had so few players on contract. Declarations were made to the Inland Revenue and money paid out as PAYE, but it was not clear how it was calculated. The Board felt that this was unsatisfactory and instructed Peart to sort out the situation. He appointed Arthur Howell as accountant for two days a week and after six weeks of delving through records, the two paid a visit to the Inspector of Taxes then based in High Wycombe.

"I will never forget the meeting", Peart says. *"We were shown in and he had his secretary there taking minutes and asked what the problem was and I said that I did not know what the problem is - that is why we are here. There obviously is one because we are paying you money but cannot quantify it precisely. This is not a situation we want to find ourselves in and we need time to sort it out. He asked a number of relevant questions which we could answer because of Arthur Howell's investigations, and we agreed that a line would be drawn under the records as of that day, and that the Inland Revenue would reserve judgement on that period until the Club had decided how it would go forward.*

"The Inspector was being very positive because he was getting to where he wanted to be without being obstructive or indeed threatening. Eventually the two parties agreed on how contract and non-contract players would be paid, and on what expenses were permissible tex-free, and how they would be audited. As it turned out we were one of the very first football clubs to approach the Inland Revenue

and ask for time to sort out our affairs because, within a year, writs were being issued on clubs for vast amounts of money and directors were even being prosecuted. We put our house in order very early and the Inland Revenue eventually asked for a sum of £20,000 to be paid as back payment for PAYE. After long negotiations a figure of £10,000 was finally agreed on, but the Club did not receive an invoice for another eight years.

"The Club unsuccessfully appealed that the claim was out of time, and the Inland Revenue finally agreed to a payment of £5,000. Why there was such a delay I do know but I felt that the Inspector knew that there was a problem and that he wanted someone from the Club to come and tell him so and that he was relieved when someone actually did. Had the Club ended up with a much larger sum to pay straight way, it would not have been possible subsequently to buy and pay the players, and managers, who went on to so much success. The Inspector has since retired but I still see him in the town and he greets me with a knowing look."

Relegation from the Gola League had been an obvious setback but the Board were determined for a swift return and agreed to the manager's request that the player's weekly wage bill be increased by £100 to £650 per week, although this quickly became £750. To raise extra income 'LeagueLine' was instituted, a weekly members draw, and in September Steve Coppell and Alan Parry officially launched it at the Town Hall. There was much movement of players in the close season - long term favourites Anton Vircavs and Bobby Dell left, as did forwards Simon Read and Joe Blochel.

New players included the unknown quantities of Kevin Durham, Paul Hackett and Byron Walton. Most excitingly two very gifted England semi-professional players from Enfield, midfielder/forward Noel Ashford and central defender Keith Barrett, signed for a total fee of only £9,000. Ashford is fondly remembered by those who saw him play as perhaps the most talented non-League player of his day. He was exceptionally skilful and, once he had possession, no-one could get the ball off him. An immaculate passer and scorer of spectacular goals from a midfield position, he would have had no problem in playing at a very high level of professional football. Barrett became a fine team captain after skipper Kevin Collins left for Australia in October.

The main rivals for the championship were Yeovil Town who had failed the previous season to regain their Gola League status, finishing four points behind champions Sutton United. Wanderers, however, immediately stamped their authority by winning the first eight League games.

This run included a 2-1 win over Bognor when goalkeeper Gary Lester went off injured in the second-half and first Noel Ashford and then Graham Bressington took over between the posts. The run came to end with a 2-1 home defeat to Farnborough, followed by a 2-1 defeat at rivals Yeovil who scored a late, undeserved winner in front of over 3,000. The slump continued with a draw at Bishop Stortford and a defeat at Harrow Borough.

The latter was notable for the debut of midfielder Barry Silkman, then aged 34, and with a Football League career stretching back to 1974, notably with Manchester City and Orient. He replaced the injured Kevin Durham and immediately struck up an understanding with Ashford. He only played eight games but his performances were dazzling, and he helped the Club onto winning ways. In fact twelve successive victories were then recorded in the League and other key players joined the Club - Jason Seacole, a former Oxford United midfielder and, in fact their youngest ever player in the Football League, quickly became a favourite with his whole hearted displays; Neil Price, Watford's left-back in the 1984 FA Cup Final against Everton; Kirk Corbin became a very reliable defender, and tall midfielder Andy Graham went on to average a goal every other game.

During this run the team however suffered two embarrassing cup defeats. In the FA Cup, underdogs VS Rugby inflicted a humiliating 5-1 defeat at Loakes Park when the pace of Steve Norris tore the defence to shreds, and Leatherhead surprisingly won an FA Trophy replay two days before Christmas. The League run came to an end with a 1-0 defeat at Croydon, when Mark West was sent off for retaliation, but spirits were lifted by the surprise resignation of Yeovil manager Gerry Gow. Prolific scorer Declan Link made a welcome return to the Club for the next game and he went on to score 14 goals in 19 games. Four more victories were gained and the team by this time was 17 points clear of second placed Yeovil. An extraordinary Berks & Bucks Senior Cup tie at Loakes Park saw Wycombe four goals up in 15 minutes against Windsor & Eton. At half-time the score was 7-0 and the match ended 11-1 with Andy Graham scoring four goals.

Then Wycombe supporters were aghast to see their team take the field at Farnborough for a League game with no Gary Lester in goal. He had aggravated an injury in the morning and no reserve was available, but midfielder Graham Bressington donned the green jersey and played magnificently to earn the team a 0-0 draw. The next game saw Yeovil visit Loakes Park and win 1-0 in a rather violent atmosphere on the terraces, but it was all too late for the Somerset club.

Wycombe won the final seven League games to end the season as champions of the Vauxhall-Opel League, nine points clear of Yeovil in second place. The deciding game came on a misty Monday night at Bognor when Wycombe, a goal down, scored twice in the last 15 minutes to win 2-1 and send players, officials and supporters dancing around the ground in jubilation at the final whistle. The trophy was presented after the final game at Hitchin, when Carl Hoddle, Glen's younger brother, helped the side win 2-1.

The final statistics were remarkable - 32 victories from 42 games, 101 points and 103 goals scored - the Club's best ever record in the Isthmian League. The icing on the cake came in the Berks & Bucks Senior Cup Final when Aylesbury were beaten 3-2 at Wolverton Park. The quaint ground, with possibly the oldest surviving football stand in the country (built before 1900 and still there!), was home of the now defunct Wolverton Town, and a 4,000 crowd fittingly gave it one last moment of glory.

Midfielder Graham Bressington kept a clean sheet in goal at Farnborough

One other trophy captured was the President's Cup, the Capital League's League cup, when Barnet were beaten 3-2 over two legs. A crowd of 1,157 saw a 2-2 draw in the second leg at Loakes Park on 8 May.

It had been a very enjoyable campaign, but it turned rather sour two weeks before the 1987-88 season was due to start, when manager Alan Gane resigned after a friendly against Chelsea on 7 August. He had wanted to sign top non-League players, but the Chairman was unhappy that the wage bill would subsequently soar and rejected the proposed signings. As the season approached, the last season's players had not been re-signed and no new players were in sight. This, combined with the managers' changing situation at work, saw an unamicable parting of the ways.

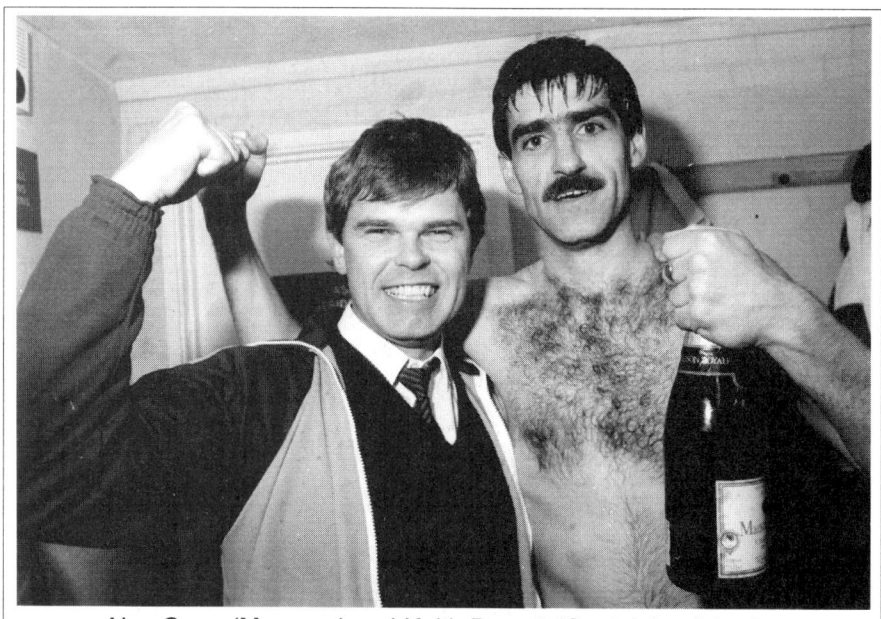

Alan Gane (Manager) and Keith Barrett (Captain) celebrate after clinching the Vauxhall-Opel League at Bognor.

64

CHAPTER 7 (1987-1990)
CONFERENCE CONSOLIDATION

Former player Peter Suddaby, a local schoolteacher, was the Board's first choice as new manager. He accepted the offer and took up his job after the opening fixture of the 1987-88 season, a 4-0 defeat at home to Stafford Rangers which underlined the enormous gap between the Vauxhall-Opel League and the Vauxhall Conference.

The next two games saw very welcome away wins, both largely due to Noel Ashford who won a dubious penalty at Maidstone and laid on two goals for Kevin Durham at Kidderminster. Ashford, however, then signed for Barnet for a fee of £17,000, a record between non-League teams, and his departure was a huge loss for the Club, particularly when the club had no other player to replace him and did not need the money. He was the only significant transfer and there were only two new signings, Nigel Gray, a central defender with nearly 300 Football League games under his belt, mostly with Orient, and Alan Mayes a prolific scorer with Watford, Swindon and Chelsea, having netted 127 Football League goals. The team found themselves in the FA Cup First Qualifying Round for the first time since that great run in 1974-75, but a 2-0 defeat at Aylesbury United was followed by one of the most humiliating defeats in the Club's history.

Supporters watched in stunned silence as a Barnet side, containing Ashford, completely outclassed a demoralised Wycombe team, and won 7-0 - the club's record home league defeat. Nicky Evans scored four goals, including three in nine minutes, and Barnet's performance was described by many as the finest ever seen by a non-League side. Telford caught Wycombe on the rebound the following Saturday at Loakes Park and a long range free kick by Neil Price and a goal by left-winger Graham Westley on his debut gave the Wanderers a much needed 2-1 win. Westley had been signed from Barnet for £7,500 but failed to live up to his early promise and eventually joined Kingstonian.

Another player from Barnet to make his debut in that game was Barry Little, on loan, but he soon returned. Three 2-2 draws were followed by another humiliation at Loakes Park when Enfield won 5-1, with all of their goals scored by Nick Francis, and this match started a run of seven consecutive defeats. A fighting performance at Enfield saw Wycombe equalise twice before losing 3-2. Three more players made their debuts in that game - Phil Lovell, a right-back from Brighton, left-back Sean Norman, who signed from Colchester for £2,500, and Matt Carmichael, a tall centre-forward who had been playing for the Army. A crowd of over 2,000 at Loakes Park saw the visit of second placed Lincoln City gain a rather lucky 2-1 win. One Wanderer who impressed in that game was Graham Bressington and three weeks later Lincoln signed him for £10,000, a generous sum as he was a non-contract player. The Imps had stayed full-time since their relegation from the Fourth Division and were beginning to press Barnet at the top of the table. Bressington was sent off at Boston in the following game as Wycombe conceded all four goals in the first-half.

By now the team were in 19th position, just above the relegation zone, but results improved slightly as Ian Fergusson and Steve Cox joined briefly on loan from Barnet. Dagenham were beaten, and fifth placed Weymouth were held in their impressive new Wessex Stadium. Striker Mark Boyland was another new signing, costing £10,000 from Cheltenham, and he scored a wonderful 30 yard winning goal at Runcorn. He also scored the following week against his former club, but Cheltenham won 3-2 in the FA Trophy First Round. After a comprehensive 3-0 defeat at Kettering on Boxing Day, mid-table Maidstone visited Loakes Park on 2 January 1988. They won 5-1 with Steve Butler scoring a hat-trick, and Wycombe supporters openly expressed their anger and frustration with the manager and officials. With the Club in such a precarious position and no sign of any real improvement in performances the Club asked for the manager's resignation. It was a sad end for a popular former player, and a manager who was liked by his own players.

The Club advertised for the vacancy but faced the important visit to Wealdstone the following Saturday, another team in the relegation zone. Watching manager-less Wycombe battle to a 0-0 draw was Jim Kelman, a former manager of Maidenhead United and Newbury Town, who was working locally as an FA qualified coach. He was one of two on the short list for the job, the other being Martin O'Neill who, after a brilliant career with Nottingham Forest and Northern Ireland, was working for a financial company.

Only two of the seven directors voted for O'Neill, an interesting decision as history would tell! Jim Kelman was the surprise choice, certainly as far as the supporters were concerned, and he took up his post the following Saturday for the home game with Cheltenham Town, who four weeks before had won the FA Trophy clash. A wonderfully entertaining game ended with a 5-3 win for Wycombe and it was if a cloud had lifted from the Club.

There were some sparkling performances, notably against Macclesfield at Loakes Park when a Mark Boyland hat-trick, the first by a Wycombe player in the Conference, contributed to a 5-0 win. A 2,000 crowd at Loakes Park on Easter Monday saw the side all but clinch safety with a 2-1 win over Weymouth, but the team were to play a crucial part in deciding the championship. They visited leaders Barnet the following Saturday and remarkably Kevin Durham gave Wycombe a first-half lead. After the 7-0 thrashing earlier in the season it looked as though Wanderers would pull off an amazing victory but the home side equalised in injury time. Barnet failed to win in their next five games, and on the final Saturday of the season Wycombe travelled to Lincoln City to face the League leaders who were just two points ahead of Barnet but with an inferior goal difference.

Jim Kelman - Wanderers Manager 1988-90

Barnet had lost 2-1 at home to Runcorn two days earlier, but would still go up if they beat Welling and Lincoln failed to beat Wycombe.

The atmosphere at Sincil Bank was as tense as it could be, intimidating even for the 800 Wycombe supporters. The ground was packed and the attendance of 9,432 is still a record in the Conference. Fans even stood on the railway embankment alongside the ground and were shocked when a Lincoln official came along with a collection tin! The match was something of an anti-climax as the Wycombe players froze and found the occasion to much to cope with. Mark Sertori gave Lincoln the lead on 26 minutes and Phil Brown scored the second on 62 minutes. The 2-0 win saw one big party take place on the pitch at the final whistle. Barnet won 2-0 at Welling, but in vain, and four years later Wycombe too would experience exactly what those Barnet players and supporters felt that day. Jim Kelman had done the job he was brought in to do - avoid relegation. When he took over the team had gained just 22 points from 26 games, but in the final 16 games 24 points were won and the team finished nine points clear of the relegation zone.

Kevin Durham beats Andy Lomas for the opening goal at Barnet   (Photo: Gordon Leach)

In spite of the struggles, the Club was the sixth best supported in the Conference with an average of 1,461. Kelman raised the morale of the existing players and brought in many new faces, such as winger Brian Greenaway, a former Fulham player in the late seventies and a wonderful crosser of a ball. The 1-0 win over Wealdstone saw the debut of a 20 year-old central defender, Matt Crossley, signed from Hampshire League side Overton United, who would prove to be a most reliable defender and is currently the longest serving player at the Club. Former Millwall goalkeeper John Granville took over from Gary Lester, and the Trinidad & Tobago international thrilled the crowd with some acrobatic saves and a huge throw which could reach the half-way line. The dogged midfielder Nigel Taylor signed from Basingstoke and two more players came from Colchester, defender John Ray and winger Scott Young.

Most exciting of all perhaps were a duo from Newport County - Adrian Mann had the perfect debut in the 3-1 win against Welling, scoring twice and entertaining the supporters with some skilful forward play. The supporters welcomed him like the new Messiah but he could not keep up the wonderful start and he left at the end of the season. Lawrence Osborne came with him from Newport but he was injured when he arrived, which was to be the story of his all too brief period at Wycombe. He was a very gifted midfield player who was unfortunately plagued with injuries.

The Club entered the summer of 1988 with a great air of optimism. The Club had successfully won the appeal to build a new ground at Sands (to be named 'Adams Park after Frank Adams), some 2½ miles from the town centre, and work began immediately. Ivor Beeks became the new Chairman as Brian Lee took up a full time role with the Club as Development Director, responsible for overseeing the construction of the new stadium. Jim Kelman began working full-time for the Club as a coach in local schools, and was helped by goalkeeper John Granville.

Lincoln on the attack in front of a record Conference crowd of 9,432 at Sincil Bank in May 1988

New faces included midfielders Andy Robinson from Carlisle, and Martin Blackler from Trowbridge.

Steve Abbley from Cheltenham Town began the season as a forceful right-winger but converted to an overlapping right-back half-way through. Both were tough tacklers and the latter proved also to be a gifted player. Another Carlisle player was goalkeeper Steve Crompton who played in the first six games until John Granville returned from the summer break.

Making his debut in the first game at Yeovil was a tall, wiry right-winger named Dave Carroll. He had made some reserve team appearances at the end of the previous season and immediately caught the eye with his ball control and passing ability. In the second game of the season he scored with a wonderful 25 yard shot to put Wycombe 2-0 up against Maidstone, but unfortunately the Kent side won the game 3-2 and went on to win the League. The same thing happened at Chorley the following week when another 2-0 lead ended up in a 3-2 defeat. Northwich easily won 4-1 at Loakes Park and it looked like being another season of struggle, but at last a win was recorded in the fifth match, against Cheltenham, when a gangly right-back from Telford, Andy Kerr, made his debut and would eventually become a great central defender with the Club.

A 3-2 defeat at home to Barnet is remembered for an incident that proved to be so very important to the Club. Mark West was left writhing on the ground, holding his face, after a challenge with Barnet's big central defender Glyn Creaser. The referee sent Creaser off for use of an elbow and after the game Barnet Chairman Stan Flashman angrily asked his manager Barry Fry to get rid of the player. Jim Kelman quickly put in a bid and a £15,000 fee was agreed, a record for the Club, and Glyn Creaser went on to become such an influential figure for the Club, as a commanding centre-half in the 'stopper' tradition and an inspiring club captain. Afterwards Mark West admitted overreacting to the challenge, and Barry Fry would later say that Creaser was the one player that he sold and later regretted. Creaser made his debut the following Saturday at Kettering when Wycombe were unlucky to lose 2-1 after being a goal up at the break. That defeat, however, was the last for nine weeks in the League as the team embarked on a ten match unbeaten run, moving from 20th place to 9th.

Highlights included a 5-0 home win over Newport County at Loakes Park, with three goals coming in the last five minutes, and a 3-0 victory at Weymouth in the pouring rain in a match which came close to being abandoned. One of the goalscorers that night was American John Kerr, playing his second game and about to become something of a legend on the terraces for his great speed and terrific goals. Carroll was unfortunate to break a collar bone in a reserve game in October and miss nearly two months of the season. A 19 year old Dion Dublin, still to make his first team debut for Cambridge United, joined on loan in October but was sent back after just two games, deemed not up to scratch!

Good progress was being made in the FA Cup and a Third Qualifying Round draw saw Wycombe travel to Staines Town, managed by former boss Alan Gane. Mark West scored the only goal of the game and in the next round Kettering proved once again to be a bogey team and won with a late goal at Loakes Park. Defeat in the League finally came at leaders Kidderminster, when captain Keith Barrett conceded a penalty just before half-time, which was converted, and was also sent off. Wycombe defended spiritedly and only a goalkeeping error let the Harriers score a second. That sending off was followed by another the following Saturday, Andy Kerr at Altrincham, after Wycombe threw away a two goal lead to draw 2-2. The Boxing Day clash at newly promoted Aylesbury saw yet another dismissal, the somewhat fiery Martin Blackler this time, late in the game for stamping, as Wycombe cruised to a 2-0 win in a derby match, which was not for the feinthearted.

This was the Club's fifth sending-off of the season and Blackler's second, and he was immediately put on the transfer list. Bath City matched the asking price of £10,000, but eventually the manager relented and took him off the transfer list, realising that he was too good a player to let go. That win at Aylesbury began a run of five successive wins which included an amazing 3-1 victory at leaders Maidstone. Wycombe kept a 2-0 lead, after early goals from John Kerr and Mark West, until 19 minutes from time. The Stones pulled one back and piled on the pressure but, in the 80th minute, Kevin Durham ran from the half-way line and was brought down by the 'keeper.

West converted the penalty for a 3-1 win. Maidstone did not lose another match until after they had secured the championship in May.

The return match with Aylesbury on 2 January featured a stunning first-half snap shot, on the angle, by Mark West from outside of the area. It was the only goal of the game which the Ducks were unlucky to lose, and they were relegated at the end of the season. The attendance was a healthy 3,000, with many more around that figure to come. On 28 January the team paid a League visit to the decaying Somerton Park, home of bottom placed Newport County. A wonderfully entertaining match saw Wycombe lose a 3-1 lead before finally winning 5-3. Playing for County that day was 22 year-old central defender Darren Peacock who went to better things with Queens Park Rangers and Newcastle United. Newport only played two more League games before folding under the weight of their huge debts, a tragedy not only for the Club but for the Conference and non-League football in general. There was something wrong with a system that saw the Football League impose strict financial conditions on the promoted Conference champions yet allow one of its own clubs to incur large debts and coolly pass them onto the Conference, washing their hands of the disruption to follow!

The good League form continued and struggling Stafford Rangers were mercifully dispatched 6-1 at Loakes Park as a Mark West hat-trick was followed by one from John Kerr. An astonishing attendance of 4,239 saw the clash with League leaders Kidderminster at Loakes Park, the first over 4,000 for a League match since the halcyon days of Brian Lee in the Seventies. Wycombe played out of their skins, completely dominating the game and letting the Harriers of with just a 1-0 defeat. The roar when Andy Kerr scored in the 55th minute was deafening, and after the game Brian Lee generously told Jim Kelman that it was the finest performance he had ever seen from a Wycombe team.

Could Wycombe win the League and win promotion to the Football League? It was a tall order, especially as the team were enjoying a fine Trophy run. The Club had already decided that Loakes Park would be brought up to standard if required, even if it was only for one season before the new ground was ready. The Trophy run began in the First Round with a tight 0-0 draw on a January Sunday afternoon at Bath City. The replay three days later was a different affair and Wycombe were in sparkling form as they won 4-0. John Kerr scored a hat-trick and he remains the only Wanderer to do so in the competition. A 1-0 win at Wealdstone in the next round was followed by a 2-0 home win over Merthyr Tydfil on a very muddy pitch, both sides missing penalties.

Wycombe, by now the favourites for the competition, were drawn away to Hyde United who went on to finish second in the HFS Loans (Northern Premier) League.

Around 1,000 Wycombe supporters travelled up North on 11 March, full of optimism with just a slight worry about Hyde's cramped ground and artificial pitch. What a concern it turned out to be as the team completely failed to get to grips with the surface and the high bounce of the ball meant that they could not play their normal passing game. Hyde took full advantage and scored the only goal of the game just after half-time when Harris headed home a free kick. It was a devastating blow for the Club, but Jim Kelman quickly dispersed the gloom when he announced, four days later, that he had signed the Barnet striker Evans for £32,000, a non-League record.

Evans was one of the classiest players outside of the Football League but had been troubled by a persistent knee problem. He made a dream debut on the following Saturday at home to Boston, scoring both goals in the 2-1 win, and ending an 11 match unbeaten run by the Lincolnshire club. The following Saturday he scored again in a 2-1 win at Telford and Wycombe were now in 3rd position, their highest ever in the Conference.

Hopes of the championship were dashed by the visit of leaders Kettering Town on 6 April. Cohen Griffith's harmless looking header was agonisingly deflected past John Granville by Glyn Creaser in the 65th minute and Andy Beesley, in the visitors goal, performed heroics and ensured a 1-0 win for the Poppies. The most remarkable aspect of the game was the gate of 4,890, the biggest in the Conference that season and the largest recorded League attendance at Loakes Park since Enfield drew 5,000 way back on 4 April 1969! It was the end of a 15 match unbeaten League run, but third place was still feasible and the team bounced back three days later with an exciting fixture at Enfield.

Wycombe had scored in the first minute but, with the score 2-2 and ten minutes remaining, Mark West netted

Record non-League signing Nicky Evans.

twice to complete his hat-trick before Enfield secured a late consolation goal. The 4-3 win was followed by two more away victories, and the team ended with a record on their travels of 11 wins (two more than at home), 4 draws and 5 defeats.

The final position of fourth was easily the Club's best finish in the Conference. Under Jim Kelman's astute management, the team had finally come of age and were now no longer a 'soft touch' in the Conference. In the summer, Club Secretary John Goldsworthy resigned as a director, and local TV commentator Alan Parry joined the board. He had had an interest in the Club ever since he visited Loakes Park as a young BBC radio reporter, for the FA Cup match with Middlesbrough in 1975.

The 1989-90 season would be the last at Loakes Park and was looked forward to with even greater optimism. Keith Barrett, who had lost his place towards the end of the previous season, left to join Noel Ashford at Redbridge Forest. The 33 year old former Queens Park Rangers and Chelsea defender Steve Wicks was a surprise signing, although he left after eight games, much to the Club's disappointment, and was a financial loss due to the large signing-on fee paid to him. Another brief stayer was left-winger Paul Sanderson who had impressed for Newport County the previous season, but he was released after six games.

Central defender Paul Franklin also joined, although still struggling with a persistent knee injury which had curtailed his Football League career at Watford and Reading. Simon Stapleton, released by Bristol Rovers after a handful of games, quickly established himself in the left-back spot and proved to be another valuable asset in the following seasons. Two key players were unable to start the season, Nicky Evans with his knee problem and Martin Blackler with an old groin strain which kept him out until the final weeks.

Like the previous season, the team got off to a bad start, losing three and drawing two of the opening five games. Aspirations of winning the League were severely knocked by the visit of relegated Darlington in the third game. Like Lincoln and Newport before them, they had taken the gamble of staying full-time, to have a better chance of returning to the Football League at the first attempt. Managed by Brian Little in his first job as manager, they produced a thoroughly professional performance and gave nothing away at the back. David Cork scored the only goal ten minutes after half-time and they quickly closed the game down. The following Wednesday a 0-0 draw at Welling saw the debut of 20 year-old left-winger Steve Guppy, a Southampton reject but luckily spotted by Wycombe's southern area scout Ian Crossley, father of player Matt.

It was immediately obvious that the new signing had excellent close control and a wonderful left foot with which he curled in some dangerous crosses. The other foot, as the saying goes, was just for standing on. He lacked confidence and needing beefing up as he was too easily knocked off the ball, but he established himself by the end of the season and would prove to be one of the Club's most valuable signings. A trip to Enfield on 19 September provided the first win in yet another exciting game at Southbury Road. The home side scored in the 13th minute, Wycombe quickly replied with two through Carroll and Stapleton, but Enfield led 3-2 at half-time.

West equalised on 67 minutes with a penalty, Stapleton scored his second 7 minutes later and David Gipp, on loan from Barnet (where else?) wrapped up a 5-3 win for Wanderers, six minutes from time. The following game was equally exciting as the home encounter with Kidderminster saw John Kerr make a dramatic return to the Club. Trailing 3-1, Wycombe pulled a goal back on 84 minutes through Mark West and then, as if working to a script, John Kerr raced in to head home the equaliser in the final minute. Resounding home victories followed, 6-1 against Fisher and 5-0 against Runcorn, but the team was also losing matches they would have won the previous campaign, and were languishing near the relegation zone.

Starting from the First Qualifying Round again in the FA Cup, the team had comfortably disposed of Baldock and Boreham Wood. It then took three matches to overcome Southern League Gravesend, after two 1-1 draws, the second of which saw Wycombe fall behind in extra time before Guppy equalised. Gravesend won the toss for the Second Replay venue which was dominated by a returning Nicky Evans simply oozing class at every touch. He inspired Wanderers to an easy 3-0 win on a Monday evening at the impressive Stonebridge Road ground. Five days later it was a completely different story as Wycombe crashed out of the competition, 4-1 at Stafford Rangers, on a very windy day. It was a simply wretched performance and the inconsistent form continued, two defeats against Chorley and Yeovil, which were followed by wins against Boston and Barrow. The 4-0 win over Barrow included a stunning second minute solo effort by the fast improving Steve Guppy.

On 1 November Loakes Park staged an international fixture for the first time for many years, and the first women's game there since 1895! England drew 1-1 with the professionals from Italy and afterwards the Italians refused to use the big sunken baths in the changing rooms, saying that they were unhygienic. Instead, they were taken in their team strip up to the Crest Hotel for a shower!

A December home win against high flying Barnet, courtesy of a mis-hit Martin Lambert shot, was followed by an excellent 2-1 win at Sutton on Boxing Day. In this game Jim Kelman scrapped his favoured sweeper system and successfully reverted to a 4-4-2 formation. Four days later, however, a Cheltenham side, including the Scottish international Andy Gray, cruised to an embarrassingly easy 4-0 win, thanks to a Mark Buckland hat-trick.

After a return win against Sutton and a heavy 4-1 defeat at Telford United, who had just appointed Gerry Daly as player/manager, Wycombe faced Metropolitan Police at home in the First Round of the FA Trophy. The game has gone down in the Club's history as one of the most embarrassing defeats. The hard working Vauxhall-Opel League side out-thought a tactically unprepared Wycombe team, and recorded a shock 3-1 win.

A few days later Jim Kelman resigned as manager, although it is a misconception to assume it was wholly because of the Trophy defeat. Disagreements between the manager and the Club had been developing, and Kelman felt unable to continue. The great period of success that followed his departure has perhaps underplayed his contribution to the Club. When he arrived team morale was at an all-time low, but he quickly got to grips with the danger of relegation and steered the team to safety.

The following season he made the team a real force to be reckoned with in the Conference and it should be noted that he left with the team in a relatively safe 13th position after languishing in the relegation zone at the start of the season. Perhaps unbeknown at that time, Jim Kelman had laid a very solid foundation from which the Club was able to achieve unparalleled success. Before he came, the Club had had little involvement with local schools but, in his capacity as an FA Coach, he toured around the Buckinghamshire schools giving coaching lessons and getting the youngsters, the future supporters, interested in Wycombe Wanderers. He was the manager who had the foresight to sign Steve Guppy, Dave Carroll, Glyn

Creaser, Matt Crossley, Andy Kerr and Simon Stapleton, the core of the team which would win promotion to the Football League three years later.

John Reardon took temporary charge of the team and gained a morale boosting 3-0 win at Barrow the following Saturday. The Club advertised for the vacancy and attracted a very high calibre of applications - the new stadium to be opened the following season had made the Club an attractive proposition for ambitious managers. The two shortlisted candidates were Alan Harris, Terry Venables' assistant at Barcelona and Tottenham Hotspur, and 37 year old Kenny Swain, a former Wanderer who had gone on to a distinguished Football League career. He was then coach to Dario Gradi at Crewe Alexandra and it was Swain who impressed in the interviews the Club held on the weekend of 27/28 January, whereupon he was offered the position. He went away to think over the offer but on the Sunday that same weekend, Alan Parry was commentating on the Norwich City v Liverpool FA Cup-tie and after the match bumped into Martin O'Neill, then a radio summariser, in the Directors Toilets at Carrow Road.

Parry asked Martin whether he had applied for the job as he could not recall seeing his application and he replied that he did not know that it had been advertised. O'Neill did not want to apply and be turned down again, but Parry convinced him that he was the man for the job although he pointed out that it might already be too late. He duly applied and the following Wednesday Kenny Swain turned down the offer and accepted the upgraded position of assistant manager at Crewe. On the same day Martin O'Neill came down to Wycombe, visited Adams Park and made a very favourable impression on the Directors. They unanimously agreed to offer him the job and five years of unbroken success were about to unfold.

The Club were getting a former player who had won the Football League, European Cup and League Cup under Brian Clough at Nottingham Forest. He had won 64 caps for Northern Ireland between 1972 and 1985 and, moreover, had captained the team when they reached the Quarter-Finals of the World Cup in 1982 in Spain. A knee injury had forced him to give up the game in 1984 and his only managerial experience since then had been with two non-League clubs. He spent the 1987-88 and 1988-89 seasons with Beazer Homes Midland side Grantham Town, finishing third and fifth respectively, and discovered Gary Crosby who he sold to Forest for £20,000.

In the summer of 1989 he became manager of HFS Loans Premier Division side Shepshed Charterhouse, but left after just seven weeks of an uneasy relationship with the Chairman. He was still based in Nottingham but agreed to manage Wycombe part-time and continue with his full time job with 'Save & Prosper'.

Martin O'Neill signs for Wycombe. The beginning of a great partnership with Chairman Ivor Beeks.

Martin O'Neill took over on 7 February and his first game in charge was the Conference fixture at Merthyr Tydfil on 10 February 1990. He met the team coach at Aust Services, at the Severn Bridge, and as he climbed aboard he wondered that there was any room for the players as so many officials were on the coach. It is a tradition in non-League football that Club workers are allowed to travel with the team but by the start of the next season the coach had become the preserve of the players. O'Neill quickly abolished other 'traditions' as he tried to get the Club thinking about a Football League future and not the glories of their amateur days. The match at Merthyr ended 1-1 in the pouring rain; Mark West gave Wycombe a 36th minute lead but Dave Webley equalised five minutes after half-time.

One of the new manager's earliest problems was the strong influence of of right-back Steve Abbley in the changing room. Martin O'Neill almost felt that the team had two managers and he was none too keen either on the player's preference for playing more as a right-winger. Abbley was dropped after four games and was then substituted in a reserve game one night and was asked him to sit on the bench for the rest of the game. He refused and after the game O'Neill told him not to bother turning up again. The manager told the chairman what he had done and was pleasantly surprised to hear Ivor Beeks say: *"You're the manager, that's fine"*.

WYCOMBE WANDERERS

These words gave Martin O'Neill enormous encouragement. Results improved and the team finished in 10th position in the Conference, winning eight and drawing four of the final 16 matches.

The Bob Lord Trophy (the Conference Cup) Semi-Final was reached and Wycombe were unlucky to lose on away goals to Yeovil. Wycombe were leading the tie in the second leg at Loakes Park when a last minute Yeovil goal took the game into extra-time. The new manager did have some silverware to show at the end of the season when Slough Town were beaten 2-1 at Hungerford in the Berks & Bucks Senior Cup Final it was Wycombe's 25th win in the competition and their last.

The final League game played at Loakes Park took place on a Thursday evening when Stafford Rangers were beaten 2-1 in front of 1,818 spectators, Dave Carroll scoring the last competitive goals on the ground. The very last action on a ground, which had home in 1895, took place on Monday 7 May. Nearly 4,000 fans paid their last respects as Wycombe Wanderers lost 8-4 to an International XI including George Best. Even Martin O'Neill risked his dodgy knee and played a part in the match and actor Warren Clarke made a surprise substitute appearance - the start of his support for the Club. The match was refereed by John Martin and the two teams were:

Wycombe Wanderers: John Granville, Matt Crossley, Simon Stapleton, Paul Franklin, Andy Kerr, Kevin Durham, Dave Carroll, Martin Lambert, Mark West, Martin Blackler, Steve Guppy.
Subs: Nicky Evans, Ricky Pearson.
International XI: Jim McDonough, Joe Kinnear, Mark Lawrenson, Alan McDonald, Glyn Creaser, John McClelland, Danny Wilson, Gerry Armstrong, John Robertson, Robert Thorpe, George Best.
Subs: Andy Robinson, Spencer Tuckerman, Alan Parry, Martin O'Neill, Nazim Bashir, Warren Clarke.

After the game supporters dug up turves from the famous 11'-6" sloping pitch and took whatever souvenirs they could find. Seven days later the Club had moved out its belongings and closed the door on 95 years of history.

George Best scores in the final game at Loakes Park.

CHAPTER 8 (1990-1996)
THE IRISH MESSIAH
&
THE FOOTBALL LEAGUE

The history of the move to the new stadium is long, and sadly, for both the town and Club, somewhat bitter. It began in 1968 when the Health Authority sought discussions with the Club with a view to acquiring part of Loakes Park for the neighbouring Wycombe General Hospital. Two years later a 'blueprint' was released showing Hospital expansion over the whole of Loakes Park. The Football Club were shocked that such a document had been produced without their consent. The Trustees of Loakes Park, however, felt it wise to explore the possibility of moving, especially as the Health Authority could apply for a Compulsory Purchase Order and purchase the ground for under the market value.

Throughout the Seventies a succession of sites around High Wycombe were investigated and eventually one at Four Ashes, nearly two miles north of the town, was chosen by the Club but rejected by Wycombe District Council. The big problem was that any spare land of sufficient size around the town was in the Green belt and could therefore not be built on. Many developers approached the Club at this time inquiring whether Loakes Park was for sale. They were pleasantly surprised to be given a positive answer but the condition that another site be found in the town was always the stumbling block. In the early Eighties Wycombe District Council released a Structure Plan for the town. It showed Loakes Park redeveloped for housing but nowhere on the plan could Wycombe Wanderers Football Club be found. This embarrassing mistake perhaps revealed what the local authority really thought of its leading football club.

Eventually a site at the end of the Hillbottom Road Industrial Estate at Sands was chosen, the 13th possible site the Club had looked at. Pat Day, the Planning Officer, indicated that it was the only one in High Wycombe that the Council could possibly entertain. At last the Club had been given some encouragement but the site was not ideal, for as it was situated in the bottom of a valley it would need substantial levelling, and it only had one access road.

It was Green Belt land and, moreover, designated as an Area of Outstanding Natural Beauty, but it was all that the Club could find. On Christmas Eve 1985 a deal was signed between Wycombe Wanderers Football Club, property developers Westbruton Ltd., and Sir Francis Dashwood, the owner of the site at Sands. Westbruton would pay for the building of the new ground and, when completed, would acquire Loakes Park for development for a price of £3.4 million - the Hospital would buy 2/5ths and the rest would be for sheltered housing.

Brian Lee was completely opposed to groundsharing and made absolutely sure that the Club would only move when the new ground was ready. The outline block planning application for the new ground at Sands was rejected by the elected councillors, although the professionals in the Planning Department at Wycombe District Council were in favour. With nowhere else to go the Football Club had no choice but to appeal to the Department of the Environment, a process which took 18 months and cost the Club over £100,000. On 11 March 1988 the Appeal Inspector ruled in favour of the Club probably because if Loakes Park was not vacated then the Hospital would be unable to complete the expansion it so desperately needed. A 30,000 signature petition urging the local Council to agree to the move had also played an important part.

The Appeal showed very clearly what Wycombe District Council thought of Wycombe Wanderers. When the Inspector had asked the Council's representative: *"If you do not want the Club to go to Sands, can you suggest an alternative site?"* The reply was: *"It is not the responsibility of the local authority to find the Football Club an alternative site."* Such blatant unhelpfulness contrasted sharply with the co-operation and encouragement other Councils around the country were affording their local football clubs. A good example was Yeovil Town who, as it happens, opened their new Huish stadium on the same day that Adams Park was opened.

Their local authority not only helped find a new site but actually paid for the land! Wycombe District Council failed to realise that Wycombe Wanderers was, and would continue to be, an enormous benefit to the town. Since the decline of the furniture industry, the Football Club was now the most famous attribute of High Wycombe, providing a great deal of positive and free publicity. It would have been in everyone's interest for all parties to find a more suitable site in the town, with less nuisance for residents and better access, but that sadly never happened.

In September 1988 full consent was given by the local authority and the Football Club invited tenders for the building of Adams Park, but received a set-back when all of the quotations were a long way over budget. The directors were determined that the Club only spent on the new ground what they received for Loakes Park, and not incur large debts which would inhibit the push for promotion to the Football League. As it turned out the new stadium only cost £70,000 more than was received for Loakes Park.

Abandoning the original design in steelwork, the Club opted for reinforced concrete which allowed for a much cheaper and quicker construction. Bill O'Neill, then Chairman of Boreham Wood FC, acted as a consultant and became the site manager. Bob Pearson was employed as the architect and three contractors were chosen to build the stadium; McKenna & Lehane carried out all of the groundworks, Atcost Buildings erected the concrete frames, and Neary & Picot were responsible for the distinctive brickwork.

Work commenced in April 1989 and the adjacent land was leased to deposit 65,000 cubic metres of chalk that was removed in levelling the site. A water main and sewer unexpectedly had to be diverted at a cost of £86,000, but by July the pitch was completed with its five miles of drainage pipes and a 40 head 'pop-up' watering system serviced from a 1,000 gallon tank. The pitch is sand based, drains quickly and therefore needs constant watering. Structural work on the stands and terracing began in August and was completed in January 1990.

Internal work had begun in October and by July 1990 the stadium was essentially finished although the contractors did not finally leave site until October, 18 months after work began. The main stand, 102 metres long, seated 1,267 in seven rows and included a press box, hospital broadcast facilities and a police control box. The other three sides of the ground were all covered but had no seats and the initial capacity was set at 6,000 by the licensing authority, much lower than the 10,000 it could actually have held because of concerns over parking and access.

Behind the main stand were extensive facilities including a suite of offices, gymnasium, physiotherapy room and well appointed changing rooms. Rather than build sports facilities to generate extra income, the Board of Directors chose catering, a considerable gamble as none of the directors had any experience in that area. The extensive social facilities included the Vere banqueting room which can seat 240 for dinner or 300 for conferences and is used on matchdays as a members club. There is also a smaller room for 100 people, two sponsors lounges and a pub, The Centre Spot, which has two stained glass windows and an unusual sign of two supporters shaking hands, one suited and the other casually dressed in jeans and a red shirt (based on a Manchester United logo!). Outside is a large house-like building comprising two flats for the groundsman and bars manager, whilst at ground level there is a Club Shop (a second shop was later opened in the town) and Ticket Office. Each corner of the ground contained turnstiles, tea bars and toilets. The team benches were clear perspex shelters as used on the continent, and one of the earliest usages in this country.

The car park accommodates over 300 vehicles and just inside the entrance can be seen the Loakes Park gates, re-erected and now used as the entrance to an overflow car park. The Club had also applied to build an artificial training pitch next to the car park on a hill but this was turned down by the Council who would only agree to its construction if built at a much lower level. Because of the prohibitive cost of moving so much chalk, the Club have abandoned this idea and simply use the site as a car park.

The opening match at Adams Park took place on 9 August 1990, a warm Thursday evening which attracted a crowd of 4,810. Brian Clough brought down a full strength Nottingham Forest side and an entertaining match ended 1-1, with Wycombe's Mark West scoring the first goal on the ground. Gary Smith was the first player to score in the opening League match at the new venue, in the 4-1 win against Welling.

(Above) Mark West scores the first goal at Adams Park in the game versus Nottingham Forest.
(Photo Dave Twydell)

(Below) Adams Park in the early days - Summer 1990

The only new face in the team was right-back Steve Whitby, a free transfer from Berkhamsted, and he was soon joined by his cousin Keith Ryan who became such an influential player. Martin O'Neill made his first money signing at the end of August, paying £7,000 to Eastwood Town for right-winger Simon Hutchinson. Midfielder Kevin Durham left after four years at Wycombe and signed for Barnet for £15,000. A true two-footed player with a tremendous shot, he had never really shown his best form under Martin O'Neill.

Matches at Barnet are always incident packed and the game on a Tuesday September evening was no exception. The kick-off had been delayed for 15 minutes because of the large crowd, with 4,500 still trying to get in. Second-placed Barnet opened the scoring with a controversial fourth minute penalty and added two more before half-time through the explosive winger Andy Clarke, who was soon to become a Premier League player with Wimbledon. Wanderers staged a stirring fightback after the break with two opportunist strikes from Mark West, which came either side of the dismissal of Matt Crossley for a professional foul, and the Blues were unlucky not to take a point from the game.

Trowbridge Town, two levels below in the Beazer Southern Division, provided stiff opposition in the FA Cup Second Qualifying Round. Only goalkeeper John Granville kept Wycombe in the tie at Trowbridge with some splendid one-on-one saves. The replay at Adams Park was equally difficult and Steve Lester gave the Wiltshire side a 52nd minute lead which they held until the third minute of injury time. Andy Robinson, a 78th minute substitute, prevented a major shock when his header glanced off Nicky Evans and took the game into extra time. It looked like a second replay until, three minutes from time, Nicky Evans picked the ball up just inside the Trowbridge half, beat two defenders, and from twenty yards out struck a tremendous left foot winner for Wycombe into the top corner.

The opening November game saw the visit of unbeaten Conference leaders Kettering Town, with 12 wins and three draws in their opening 15 games. Wanderers gave one of the great performances at Adams Park to simply overwhelm their opponents 5-1, with Mark West getting a memorable four goal haul, two headers, a chip over the 'keeper and a close in shot. Wycombe reached the First Round of the FA Cup for the first time in five years and drew 1-1 at Boston after taking the lead. The replay was watched by a large midweek crowd of just under 5,000 at Adams Park, and Boston impressed the most in the first half but fell behind just before the break to a Mark West goal. The Wycombe man added a second on 49 minutes with a brilliant header and Wycombe added two late goals, for the homesters to end up 4-0 winners.

The following Saturday Wycombe visited Colchester who had won all eight Conference matches at Layer Road. Relegated from the Fourth Division, they had stayed full-time and were favourites to go straight back up, but Wycombe gained a memorable 2-2 draw, twice taking the lead through Keith Ryan playing as a make-shift striker. In December Kidderminster Harriers became the first visiting team to win at Adams Park in spite of falling behind in the second minute.

A masterful display by left-winger Delwyn Humphreys, who scored two goals, helped Harriers to a 3-2 win.

The BBC had decided to feature the Wycombe v Peterborough FA Cup Second Round game on "Match of the Day". As the Posh team approached the outskirts of High Wycombe, they were astonished to see snow on the ground and even more astonished that the referee had postponed the game because of the conditions. It did, however, allow for a classic piece of footage to be shot, as a rather fed-up looking John Motson in sheepskin coat and hat, stood alone on a snowbound pitch, apparently in the middle of a blizzard - years after the BBC continues to show the clip.

The match was played the following Wednesday in freezing conditions and on a frostbound pitch. It was the first time a Wycombe game had been featured on television since Middlesbrough in 1975 and the attendance of 5,695 was a new record for Adams Park.

Wycombe had much the better of the first-half but time after time Peterborough's 'keeper Carl Bradshaw pulled off some amazing saves, mostly from Nicky Evans efforts. Martin Blackler deservedly gave Wanderers the lead in the 58th minute with a 15 yard shot, but nine minutes later substitute Paul Culpin took advantage of a defensive error to equalise and earn his side a 1-1 draw.

After a 4-1 League win against Sutton, with Mark West once again scoring four goals, Wycombe travelled up for the Cup replay in good spirits. It all went terribly wrong in the first minute when Peterborough's right-back Noel Luke left Simon Stapleton motionless on the floor after a tackle ruled legal by the referee. After a six minute delay the midfielder was stretchered off to hospital where he received 16 stitches, but the stuffing had been knocked out of Wycombe. Within eight minutes of restarting Peterborough were leading 2-0, through Halsall and Culpin, then the 800 Wycombe supporters saw their side play like they had never played before.

Mark West was inspirational up front and one minute after going two down, he won possession in the Peterborough penalty area, passed to Dave Carroll who slammed the ball against the post from ten yards. Martin Blackler ran in for the rebound and he too shot against the same post, before Mark West 'scored' with this rebound, only for the referee to disallow the goal for handball. Granville in the Wycombe goal was another hero, preventing more goals as Posh were now playing more on the break. West laid on a chance for Nicky Evans on 37 minutes but the jinx from the first game continued, and Bradshaw save brilliantly.

Evans had another good chance after half-time, just clearing the bar with a lob, and by now Wycombe were in control with Martin Blackler in outstanding form in midfield and giving one of those 'all time great' performances by a Wycombe player. He should have scored when clean through but slipped the ball past the post as the away fans roared their team on. Keith Ryan, another outstanding performer that night, headed against the bar with 16 minutes remaining but inevitably the part-timers tired and Peterborough were relieved to finish 2-0 winners.

Afterwards Martin O'Neill praised his players but was very disappointed that they had not won the match. *"It's getting non-League players to believe they're good enough to compete. There was a lack of real, real belief that they could do it. It's just my opinion, but I'm right."* A revealing comment, it showed that the manager knew he had a good set of players and it just needed his motivation skills to turn them into winners.

At the turn of the year the team were in fifth place in the Conference but just two wins in ten away games only gave them an outside chance of the championship. Nicky Evans made his last appearance in January after requesting a transfer following a fine for not turning up for training one evening. His suspect knee meant that he could only play half a season and he had wanted to return to his spiritual home of Barnet for some time; Barry Fry eagerly took back his former goalscoring ace for £28,750.

Mickey Nuttell was signed as a replacement from Cheltenham for £6,000, a big target man with excellent ball control. He produced a good goalscoring ratio in his short stay at the Club but never really became a big favourite with the supporters. In March, Nuttell lost his place to Keith Scott, another big target man who had been languishing in the reserves at Lincoln City, where manager Steve Thompson had told him he would never make it in the Football League.

Scott's eventual transfer fee was £30,000, but he started on loan, scored on his debut against Slough, and quickly became an enormously effective and popular player. Another player who made his debut against Slough was left-back Stuart Cash, a loan signing from Nottingham Forest, whose wholehearted displays proved so important for the remainder of the season.

If the Conference was becoming out of reach them, an FA Trophy run was looking more and more promising. Keith Scott's brace of goals in four minutes at Northwich ensured a Semi-Final place against Altrincham, Wycombe's conquerors in the 1982 Semi-Final.

The Cheshire side led the Conference by one point from Barnet, had two games in hand, and with nine games remaining looked a good bet for the championship. The first leg at Adams Park saw Altrincham score after only five minutes, Paul Rowlands heading home a Paul Showler cross. Seven minutes later Wycombe equalised when a Harry Wiggins back pass fell short and Dave Carroll nipped in to place the ball past Jeff Wealands.

An even match looked like ending in a draw when, on 72 minutes, Matt Crossley attempted to find Keith Scott in the area. It should have been the 'keeper's ball but some close attention from the Wycombe centre-forward saw him hesitate, miss the ball, and Scotty darted in to run the ball into an empty net. It was a superb piece of opportunism and gave Wycombe a vital one goal advantage at Moss Lane for the return leg where a sell out crowd was limited to just 3,500 because of safety problems.

The 1,500 travelling supporters created a wonderful atmosphere and released a deluge of light and dark blue balloons when the teams came out.

This was the club's most important match for a decade and would should show whether the lessons of Peterborough had been learnt and that the team could win big matches. Wanderers turned in a scintillating performance, for Altrincham simply could make no impression on the defence superbly marshalled by captain Glyn Creaser who won a classic battle with Alty's dangerous forward Ken McKenna.

Goalless at half-time, Wycombe scored the all important goal when Mark West slotted in a far post cross from a few yards out. For two seconds there was an eerie silence before the Wycombe fans at the far end had realised what had happened. Silence, that is, except for an ecstatic Westy who ran screaming in delight towards the corner flag before being engulfed by his team mates.

It was one of those memorable moments which are treasured by football supporters for the rest of their lives - at last Wycombe Wanderers would be appearing at Wembley for the first time in 34 years. A last minute penalty by Keith Scott wrapped up a 2-0 win and the best side in the Conference had been beaten 4-1 over the two legs (Altrincham fell apart afterwards and finished third at the end of the season).

The mounting excitement in the High Wycombe area was slightly dimmed by pop star Michael Jackson, of all people, when he refused to allow the team to release a specially recorded version of 'The Wanderer', to which he owned exclusive rights.

Keith Scott scores the opening goal in the 1991 Trophy Final.
(Photo: Brian Southam)

The Final itself was one of the greatest days in the Club's history as some 23,000 Wycombe supporters swelled the crowd to a over 34,000, a record for a Trophy Final. In a very tense atmosphere, Keith Scott settled down the nerves when he bundled home the ball (along with 'keeper Paul Jones and defender Dave Barnett!) at the second attempt in the 18th minute. The match came to life on the hour when Dave Hadley's long range effort seemed to be covered by John Granville, but it slipped under his body into the net for the equaliser. Five minutes later Wembley saw one the greatest goals scored in the hallowed stadium, when Keith Scott ran down the right-wing and crossed for Mark West to send a brave, diving header into the net.

The twenty-five minutes until the final whistle seemed like an eternity, but the 2-1 victory was greeted with a huge roar at the final whistle. The rest of that Saturday was one big party in High Wycombe, and the following day the team toured the town in an open top bus as thousands lined the streets to cheer their heroes. Mark West rounded off a perfect season by being voted Conference Player of the Year and gaining his first England semi-professional cap, against Wales.

The opening season at Adams Park had been an enormous success and there is no doubt that the impressive surroundings had helped to get the best out of the players.

The new ground swelled the average attendance to 2,800, nearly 1,000 more than that of the previous season. The Club ended the season in a very healthy financial position, mostly due to the Trophy run, and in the three weeks before the Final, Club Shop sales totalled more than £100,000. Over £500,000 was taken in ticket sales and although a large percentage of that went to the FA and Kidderminster, the Board realised what sort of income the Club was capable of earning. In fact the profit made from that first season at Adams Park kept the club going in the first two seasons of the Football League, when the wage bill increased dramatically. Alain Thibault brought catering experience to the Board in the Summer, replacing John Roberts who sadly died of Cancer in 1994.

(Left) Glyn Creaser leads the celebrations.

There were two major signings for the start of the 1991-92 season. Steve Walford, the former Arsenal, Norwich and West Ham defender who had won an FA Cup winners medal for the Gunners in 1979, and Paul Hyde, a £15,000 signing from Hayes who replaced departed goalkeeper John Granville.

Colchester, as the only full-timers, were favourites for the title this season, but it was Wycombe who set the early pace and recorded seven consecutive wins at the start, still a Conference record. Ironically Keith Scott missed this run with an injury but stand-in Mickey Nuttell scored six goals, including a hat-trick against Altrincham.

The first away match of the season, at Witton, saw three players sent off - Simon Stapleton and Witton's Jim Connor for an altercation, closely followed by the home side's Andy Grimshaw for a second bookable offence. They were the first of many dismissals in Wycombe games this season. The Championship Shield, the Conference version of the Charity Shield, was also won when Barnet were beaten 1-0 at Adams Park. Wycombe's share of the gate receipts were donated to a fund for Kevin Durham's son after the former Wanderer had died that summer of a brain haemorrhage, after joining Barnet.

The first defeat of the season came in somewhat controversial circumstances when Macclesfield won 1-0 at Adams Park, after John Timmons handled the ball before scoring (his manager later admitting this infringement).

An incident which nearly set the game alight! A factory burns during the F.A. Trophy match with Salisbury (Photo: Paul Dennis)

The referee, Royston Osborne, sent off two Wycombe players - Nuttell and Cousins - during the game and was escorted by the Police from the time he left the pitch until he left the environs of High Wycombe.

The next time Mr Osborne refereed a Wycombe game, at Chel-tenham in February, he sent off Simon Hutch-inson and reported Martin O'Neill to the FA for comments made afterwards. He was fined £200 for 'insulting and improper behaviour', and the manager fell foul of referee Eddie Green the following month, at Adams Park against Northwich Victoria. He was ordered from the dugout and later fined £100 for 'ungentlemanly and improper behaviour'.

Martin O'Neill, a passionate man, found it hard to contain himself after a bad refereeing decision, or indeed sub-standard play by his team. The home defeat by Macclesfield was followed by an even bigger disaster when second placed Colchester visited. A record League crowd at Adams Park of over 5,000 saw Colchester's Nicky Smith score first after the break and then Steve Guppy equalise seven minutes later. In injury time, just as both sides seemed to have settled for a draw, the visitor's 'keeper, Scott Barrett, launched an enormous punt which bounced once in the penalty area and, caught by a gust of wind, sailed over Paul Hyde's head into the net for an amazing winner.

The return match at Layer Road in December saw Wycombe have the upper hand for 33 minutes before Paul Hyde allowed a deflected Gary Bennett shot to squirm under his body into the net. The U's took over and Steve McGavin scored two more goals for the home side, one a superb curling shot from the edge of the penalty area. Nine days later Wycombe won 6-2 in the fog at Layer Road, in the Bob Lord Trophy.

As Trophy winners, Wycombe received exemption to the First Round of the FA Cup and should have won at Kettering but could only draw 1-1. With the game goalless in the replay, Dave Carroll, the scorer in the first game, dribbled past five defenders in the 58th minute to within six yards of the goal and flicked the ball past the 'keeper but on to the post. Eleven minutes later Glyn Creaser missed his kick and allowed Phil Brown to score the opening goal for Kettering, and John Graham scored a breakaway second six minutes from time.

The FA Trophy began with an unusual match at home to Salisbury in January 1992. As the game approached half-time a huge cloud of smoke began to rise from behind the ground, with flames leaping into the air. A plastics factory had caught fire on the industrial estate but fortunately there were no casualties, and the game continued amidst a strange red glow, with cinders dropping into the stadium. By the time the fire service had gained controlled, Wycombe had completed a rather unexciting 2-0 win, but another promising Trophy run was underway.

It was disappointingly cut short by Witton Albion who deservedly won 2-1 at Adams Park in the Quarter-Final. Goalless at the break, Mike Lutkevitch scored five minutes after the break, Karl Thomas added a second in the 89th minute, and Mark West netted with a consolation penalty immediately after. It was Wycombe's first defeat in the FA Trophy for 26 months, but winning the Conference was still a real possibility. By the new year Colchester and Wycombe were pulling away from the chasing pack, with Wycombe seven points behind although with three games in hand.

The third placed club was Farnborough, and on a freezing Monday evening at the end of January the two clubs met at Adams Park. The visitors scored after eight minutes with a goal from Andy Bye but a very unfortunate accident happened eleven minutes later when Wycombe's Kim Casey, a £9,000 buy from Cheltenham two weeks before and a legendary goalscorer in non-League football, ran on to a Keith Scott flick. The Farnborough 'keeper, John Power, ran out to meet him but the ball just ran ahead of Casey on the frozen pitch.

He tried to flick it past the goalkeeper but missed his kick and Power kicked the bottom of Casey's foot and fell to the ground with a broken leg. After a six minute delay he was stretchered off and replaced by Wayne Stemp. Two minutes after the break Steve Guppy equalised with a rare header but as conditions became colder, the pitch became more dangerous, and after 62 minutes the referee abandoned the game - Wycombe won the replayed match in March, 2-1.

Other new signings included midfielder Steve Thompson from Slough in February, one of the most sought after players in non-League football, and one who Martin O'Neill had been chasing for some time. Paying £25,000 for him was a big gamble as he was in the RAF and therefore could not be put on a contract, but he proved an invaluable acquisition. Prolific 'scorer Dennis Greene joined for £15,000 from Chelmsford and he netted on his debut in the Bob Lord Trophy Semi-Final against Yeovil.

On 7 April, Wycombe completed a two-leg Bob Lord Trophy Final win over Runcorn, the first time the Club had won the Conference version of the League Cup. The following Saturday Greene scored all of the goals in the 4-0 thrashing at Altrincham, the last Wycombe player to score four goals in a game. That game saw Wycombe go three points clear at the top, with the same number of games played as Colchester, but it only lasted until the following Tuesday when a 3-1 defeat at Macclesfield allowed the Essex club to go top on goal difference. After dropping two points at Kettering, Wycombe travelled to Gateshead, now two points behind Colchester and in need of a favour from Macclesfield who entertained United that day.

The huge stand at the Gateshead International stadium reverberated to the sound of the 500 Wycombe fans in the 900 crowd, but it was the home team who scored first on 29 minutes, following news on the radio that Colchester had taken an early 2-0 lead. Macclesfield pulled a goal back in that other game, and then Keith Scott equalised for Wycombe with a penalty in the 39th minute, after a foul on Kim Casey. A Glyn Creaser header 14 minutes after the break gave Wycombe the lead and then, right on cue, news filtered through that Macclesfield may just have twice taken the lead.

The fans shouted the news at the bench, confusion reigned as no one seemed to know what the truth was, but Alan Lamb cut short any premature celebrations when he scored his, and Gateshead's second, in the 63rd minute. By now Martin O'Neill had thrown Simon Hutchinson and Dennis Greene on as subs in an all out attempt to score the vital winner and possibly overtake Colchester.

With four minutes remaining, Kim Casey made room for himself on the right hand edge of the penalty area, sent a low shot towards goal which Gateshead 'keeper Smith could only parry, and it looped up for Keith Scott to volley home the winner from close range. The supporters went wild and at the final whistle joyfully invaded the pitch unaware that Colchester had equalised at Macclesfield in the 75th minute, to make the final score 4-4. At least Wycombe were level on points with two games to play, but there was no let up from Colchester as they beat Kettering 3-1 at home the following Tuesday.

Both teams were at home on the final Saturday of the season, Colchester facing bottom club Barrow who were already relegated. Wycombe travelled to Dagenham on the Thursday evening before to face Redbridge Forest, knowing that they not only had to win but score an avalanche of goals to dent Colchester's goal difference advantage of 13.

Redbridge were a good side with many England semi-pro internationals and one former full international in Peter Taylor. Their record in the latter half of the season was as good as Wycombe's, but all that counted for nothing as Wanderers put on a display that many present ranked as the finest performance ever by a non-League team.

Looking like avenging angels in their all white strip under the floodlights, Wanderers ripped the Redbridge defence to shreds with some incisive forward play. A Keith Scott penalty started the scoring in the 15th minute and by half-time Scott and Casey had made it 3-0. Two minutes after the restart Casey and Caroll unbelievingly increased the score to 5-0, and you could almost hear the mental arithmetic as the away supporters worked out that another five goals and a thrashing of Witton on Saturday could win the championship on goal difference. Sadly no more goals followed, as the Wycombe players felt the incredible pace, and Redbridge finally clawed themselves into the game. Hundreds of Colchester supporters had turned up for the game but were disappointed that a Wycombe defeat had failed to materialise.

Saturday arrived and Wanderers did all that they could, and comfortably beat Witton Albion 4-0. Colchester's Roy McDonough had boasted that Barrow would be a pushover and he was right - Colchester won 5-0 and took the Conference title on goal difference. Both teams had gained a Conference record of 94 points and were 21 points clear of third placed Kettering Town. Wycombe's total of 30 wins was also a Conference record, but it all meant nothing to the gutted players, officials and supporters at Adams Park. Martin O'Neill said afterwards that the only reason why they had finished second was because Colchester were full-time and Wycombe part-time.

All was not lost, because Aldershot's demise during the season meant that the Fourth Division would be one club light, and a campaign was instigated to have Wycombe promoted to the Football League as well as Colchester.

Predictably the campaign to get Wanderers promoted along with Colchester failed and it was ironic that Maidstone liquidated soon after the season started. It was to the great credit of Martin O'Neill and his players that they picked themselves off the floor and set about winning the Conference 'again'.

Central-defender Matt Crossley

The manager had proved that his squad was good enough and consequently made no additions. With no team relegated from the Football League, Wycombe were odds-on favourites to become champions and began the campaign with a 1-1 draw at Macclesfield, but won the next nine League games - another Conference record - equalling Altrincham's feat in 1984-85. After ten games the team had scored 28 goals and conceded just three, and had taken 61 points out of a possible 66, since losing to Yeovil on 7 March. Moreover they were ten points clear of second-placed Slough after just four weeks of the season.

But defeat finally came on a wet Tuesday evening at Twerton Park, when Bath scored twice in the opening 18 minutes for a 2-0 Bath City win. A week later Colchester were enjoyably beaten at Adams Park for the Vauxhall Conference Shield, and the only cloud on the horizon was Andy Kerr's transfer request which had been lodged at the start of the season.

The talented central defender had been on trial with Wimbledon but Martin O'Neill had turned down a request from the First Division side for an extension, arguing that they would be depriving Wycombe of a key player and that they should a make a firm offer if interested.

A bad tempered match at Bromsgrove Rovers then followed in front of 3,675, the Midlanders best League attendance since the Second World War, and Glyn Creaser was sent off in a stormy finale as Wycombe lost 1-0. After defeating Merthyr Tydfil in the FA Cup First Round, Wycombe were drawn at home to Second Division West Bromwich Albion, who were managed by Ossie Ardiles and a match considered attractive enough by Sky Television. They covered the match live on a Sunday afternoon in December, and the game started in dramatic fashion, when Keith Scott, surging down the left-wing, sent in a perfect cross for Kim Casey, whose brave diving header from point blank just went wide. He dislocated his shoulder as he collided with The Baggies' goalkeeper Stuart Naylor.

It was a cruel blow and the visitors quickly took control, scoring through Bradley on 11 minutes and Taylor three minutes before half-time.

The lead could have been bigger at the break, and Martin O'Neill told his team that they were not doing themselves justice. He decided to give it fifteen minutes after the interval before 'going for broke'. But in that time West Brom should have increased their lead with Garner (soon to be a Wanderer), Strodder and Taylor all going close.

Only Paul Hyde kept Wycombe in the game, brilliantly tipping a Taylor header onto the underside of the bar. Then O'Neill pushed up Simon Stapleton from full-back, helping Wanderers gain control of midfield, and it was a Stapleton run which won a corner, and Steve Guppy curled the ball in for Glyn Creaser to thump home a header in the 70th minute. Wycombe had chances to equalise but the game looked like ending in defeat until, five minutes from time, Steve Thompson picked up a pass from Carroll, ran forward and sent a shot into the net from 25 yards, Naylor misreading the bounce. An enjoyable game ended in a fair 2-2 draw, and the replay nine days later was just as dramatic.

An amazing 4,500 Wycombe fans travelled up to the Hawthorns for the midweek fixture which drew a crowd of over 17,000 and was again covered live by Sky. Wycombe matched the home side all the way, with Steve Thompson in inspirational form, and Keith Scott saw a first-half shot smack against the outside of the post. Wycombe suffered a devastating blow nine minutes from time when Bob Taylor scored for West Brom, with a left-foot shot from outside of the area.

Deep into injury time Steve Guppy just failed to connect with a Simon Hutchinson far post cross and Wanderers ended the game 1-0 losers, but having gained the admiration of the country. The Club was also over £100,000 better off after the tie.

Wycombe continued to head the Conference but the team began to stutter at the end of February. A run of two draws and two defeats, including an awful 3-0 reverse at Yeovil, was followed by a crucial home game with Slough, four points behind but having played two games more. It was an unforgettable night for the record 7,230 crowd at Adams Park, and hundreds more were locked out and watched from the bank above the Woodland Terrace. Anton Vircavs, a former player in the early Eighties, made his return to the Club in that match after his transfer from Cheltenham. He had been signed as cover for the central defence after captain Glyn Creaser suffered an appalling accident at work in January when a fork lift truck had run over his foot.

Playing his second game for Wycombe that night was Tim Langford, a nippy little striker signed from Telford for £15,000. Keith Scott gave Wycombe the lead on 27 minutes when he slotted home the rebound after the Slough 'keeper Emberson had parried his header. Scott left the field soon after with a twisted ankle, prompting Slough to waste three good chances. Early in the second-half Wycombe captain Andy Kerr was sent off for violent conduct, but with the home crowd roaring their support, Wanderers hung on for an important 1-0 win.

Other thrilling evenings followed at Adams Park, including a 3-3 draw against Boston which saw Wycombe score two goals in the final twelve minutes to gain a point. Steve Guppy scored his most memorable goal in a 5-1 thrashing of Runcorn, running from his own half down the left-wing, before cutting in to chip the 'keeper. In March four Wycombe players, Kerr, Guppy, Thompson and Stapleton, all represented England in a sem-professional international against Wales. The championship was won in mid-April on a Sunday afternoon at Gateshead, the fifth game in eight days, when the team had flown up and gained a 1-0 win.

The Trophy was presented on the final day of the season when Macclesfield gained a surprise 1-0 win which saved them from relegation. After the match, Martin O'Neill having achieved the job he was hired to do, walked around the ground positively beaming with delight as he proudly showed off the pyramid shaped trophy to his adoring fans. Wycombe had finished 15 points clear of second-placed Bromsgrove, a record winning margin in the Conference, and the average attendance of 4,602 was also a record.

The championship would probably have been won much earlier but for the injury to Glyn Creaser and a gruelling end of season finish which saw 20 games played in the final eight weeks. The team were poised for a unique non-League 'treble', but lost in the Drinkwise (League) Cup final to Northwich Victoria.

Club Captain Glyn Creaser missed the Trophy Final through injury - but still 'collected' the Cup
(Photo: Paul Dennis)

The FA trophy was still very much on when Sutton United were entertained in the Semi-Final First Leg, but the Diadora League side, managed by former Wycombe manager Alan Gane, gained a surprise 3-2 win, after taking the lead three times. The return leg at Gander Green Lane is the game Martin O'Neill remembers most fondly in his time at Wycombe. He desperately wanted to get to Wembley for a second time and his team played magnificently on the day to crush Sutton 4-0 and go through 6-3 on aggregate.

Central defender Matt Crossley scored a rare brace, and the two games were watched by over 10,000 spectators. Runcorn were the opponents in the Final at Wembley on Sunday 9 May but they must have felt they were intruding on someone's party. The crowd of 32,968 included some 28,000 from Wycombe and the stadium was a sea of blue - even the programme cover was coloured light and dark blue! Jason Cousins got the Wanderers off to the best possible start, with a third minute goal, curling a low free kick into the right hand corner after a foul on Keith Scott on the edge of the penalty area. This immediately stirred Runcorn into action with Robertson shooting just over with a 25 yard free kick, and both Cousins and Crossley blocked when McKenna was clean through.

Wycombe's response was to score a second on 21 minutes when an outswinging Dave Carroll cross near the edge of the penalty area was neatly headed in by Andy Kerr on the six yard line. The two combined again in the 36th minute when a Kerr header from a Carroll corner was just tipped over. A minute later Runcorn had a golden opportunity to pull one back when Bates broke into the area and forced a fine save from the oncoming Paul Hyde.

Runcorn scored the goal they deserved three minutes before half-time when Shaughnessy raced through the centre and netted with an excellent 22 yard shot into the corner. Keith Scott almost immediately restored the two goal lead when lobbing onto the bar from ten yards and then Brabin, shooting wide, and McKenna, with a shot saved by Hyde, threatened for Runcorn straight after the break.

An inswinging Steve Guppy corner in the 54th minute was met in a crowd of players by Steve Thompson who headed home from six yards to give Wycombe a 3-1 lead. Keith Scott nearly added a fourth twelve minutes later when his point blank shot was brilliantly saved by Williams in the Runcorn goal.

Chances were now falling to both sides and it was Runcorn who came closest when, eight minutes from time, McKenna headed against the inside of the post and Hyde amazingly scooped the ball off the line. Had that gone in Wycombe would have suffered a nervous last few minutes, but it was the Blues who dominated the closing stages and Dave Carroll made the score 4-1 in the final minute when his speculative shot was mishandled by the 'keeper and only helped into the net.

The scenes at the final whistle were one of unrestrained joy as captain Andy Kerr lifted the Trophy. It was probably the happiest day in the Club's history - promotion to the Football League was assured and the team had just won a Wembley Final by 4-1.

Another 'Double' was won in the 1992/93 season, when Martin O'Neill won the 'Conference Manager of the Year' award, and Steve Guppy picked up the 'Conference Player of the Year' trophy.
(Photo: Paul Dennis)

The only cloud on the horizon was the possible departure of Martin O'Neill, who had become the hottest property in the managerial market. Brian Clough had announced that he would retire at the end of this season and Nottingham Forest chairman Fred Reacher was keen to secure the Wycombe man, the supporters choice, as the new manager. Ivor Beeks had told both O'Neill and Reacher that nothing could be discussed until after the Trophy Final as he did not want the matter to unsettle the players.

The Forest chairman was so keen that as soon as the presentations were over, he came to the Wembley banqueting suite and asked Ivor Beeks for permission to talk to Martin O'Neill. The Wycombe chairman agreed but it was not the first time that a Football League club had come in for Martin. In 1991 O'Neill had turned down offers to manage both Bristol Rovers and Leicester City, and later Ipswich Town were refused permission to talk to him.

O'Neill opens 'another' Adams Park- at nearby Bekonscot Model Village.
(Photo: Alan Hutchinson)

Nottingham Forest, however, was his old team where he had won so many honours under Brian Clough.

As the town celebrated the team's exploits the following day with another parade on an open top bus and a civic reception at the Town Hall, Martin O'Neill was visibly moved by the enthusiastic turnout and the chants of 'Don't go, Martin, don't go'.

He travelled up to Nottingham the following day on the understanding that he report back to Ivor Beeks to discuss asked when a League club had approached him in the past. He met Fred Reacher at 9.30am to discuss terms and, at two minutes past two that afternoon, the Forest chairman telephoned Martin O'Neill and offered him the job, saying *"I am your new chairman"*.

Martin drove back to Wycombe and met Ivor Beeks at 5.15pm when the Forest offer was discussed. The Wycombe chairman did his best to persuade him to stay, offering him a new two year contract with a big salary increase. The two went home and had several telephone conversations that evening until, at 11.45pm on the Tuesday evening, Martin O'Neill phoned Ivor Beeks and told him that he was staying. The improved contract was a factor but it was the reception he had received on the balcony of the Town Hall which finally swayed it, and the following morning a press Conference was called at Adams Park to announce that he would be staying. He still had this nonsensical dream, as he put it, of taking the Club up to the Premier League. Nottingham Forest appointed their second choice, Frank Clark, as manager and inaccurately claimed that O'Neill had never been offered the job.

There was a surprise win for the club in the *Evening Standard* Five-A-Sise competition at Wembley Arena, when four Premiership sides were beaten, to take the £10,000 first prize. Remarkably the feat was repeated the following year, and both wins were largely due to goalkeeper Chuck Moussaddik.

There was much work to be done off the pitch as the squad was still part-time but, one by one, players were offered full-time contracts. Steve Thompson, Glyn Creaser and Mark West remained part-time however, and the only significant signing was former Barnet skipper Duncan Horton.

There would be no problem with either finances or the ground. Back in January a Football League representative had visited Adams Park to ensure that the Club would pass the then current criteria for entry to the competition. The ground, he concluded, would need some minor additional building work such as crush barriers on the Woodland terrace and the building of a matchday security control box. CCTV would also need to be installed and The Football Trust would contribute 70% of all these costs.

The League man then moved onto financial affairs and began by asking how the Club serviced its overdraft. He was surprised to hear that there was no overdraft and became even more surprised to learn that the Club had no loans and no rent to pay on the ground. He found it hard to grasp that Wycombe Wanderers Football Club had no debts and, indeed, were one of the very few clubs in the country in such a sound financial state. He also put two very tough constraints on the Club, one that a profit had to be shown for the first six months of that financial year - which is extremely difficult for any football club to achieve. Wycombe's financial year ran from June which meant that the low income summer months were included in that period, since the majority of home games are played in the second half.

More by luck than judgement, the Club were actually showing a profit by the end of November, and the other stipulation, that a bond of £250,000 be lodged in the eventuality that the players wages were not paid, was also no problem. After the experiences of financially unstable Maidstone and Barnet, the Football League were very wary about admitting any more non-League clubs, and Wycombe Wanderers always felt that they were looking for any loophole to prevent their entry. Wycombe Wanderers were in fact the only non-League side to be voted into the Football League under such stringent conditions.

The judge's comments, that the League's refusal to allow Stevenage Borough to be promoted from the Conference in 1996 was a 'restraint of trade', will almost certainly see a relaxation of the entry conditions.

The historic first match in the Football League

The team which won promotion to the Football League
John Reardon (Asst.Manager), Martin O'Neill, Jim Melvin (Reserve
& Youth Manager), Paul Franklin (Coach) and Dave Jones (Physio)

Wycombe's first Football League goal, put into his own net by Carlisle's Chris Curran (kneeling). Kerr (no.4), Crossley and Scott celebrate. *(Photo: Brian Southam)*

The feeling that Wycombe were not exactly being welcomed into the League were heightened by the fact that they were given an opening fixture, the most significant in the Club's history, at Carlisle.

The 500 mile trip was the longest possible that season and an unnecessary hardship for the travelling supporters who would naturally turn out in greater than normal numbers. As it was nearly 2,000 made the trip on 14 August 1996 as a crowd of 7,752 saw history made, and Wycombe

Wanderers became the first League club from Buckinghamshire. Those who made the trip remember it firstly for the nervous feeling in their stomachs and the fear that it would all be too much for the players. In the event it was an extremely exciting day and the team gained an admirable 2-2 draw. Carlisle scored first when Rod Thomas drove home an Oghani cross after 19 minutes, but after half-an-hour Wycombe began to relax. Then, in the 40th minute, Wanderers scored that historic first Football League goal when a Dave Carroll corner was headed into his own net by Carlisle's Chris Curran as he attempted to clear. Early in the second-half Tim Langford came on for the injured Horton and joined Keith Scott up front.

The team line-ups in the programme for the first home League match

Wycombe piled on the pressure and deservedly took the lead in the 76th minute when a low, far post cross from Carroll on the right was just missed by Langford, but Guppy joyfully connected and became the first Wycombe player to score in the League. It seemed unbelievable that a win was minutes away, but all of the pressure and the emotion of the occasion took its toll and it was as much tiredness as anything else which allowed Thomas to back-heel to Chris Curran, who amde amends for his earlier lapse, and equalised with a 15 yard shot seven minutes from time. A draw was a fair result and everybody connected with the Club - players, officials and supporters - were emotionally as well as physically drained at the end of the match.

The excitement that day gave a taste of what was to come. Three days later Wycombe travelled to Leyton Orient, then in the Second Division, for the Coca-Cola Cup First Round First Leg tie. It was a thrilling game and Wycombe deservedly won 2-0 with an opportunist strike from Steve Thompson and a spectacular goal from Tim Langford, who sprinted down the wing from the halfway line and scoring from an exceptionally tight angle. The defence, and goalkeeper Paul Hyde in particular, repelled everything Orient could throw at them.

The following Saturday Adams Park saw its first Football League game as Chester City were beaten by an 8th minute goal from Keith Scott, laid on by Man-of-the-match Steve Guppy who was attracting widespread interest amongst Premier League scouts. Impressive away victories were recorded at Hereford (4-3, another thriller and the debut of giant defender Terry Evans who quickly became a legend), and Bury (2-1) before Colchester ended an unbeaten eight match run. Wycombe's arch-rivals stunned the Adams Park crowd with a 5-2 win after twice going behind, but eventually took advantage of the dismissal of Jason Cousins for handball.

Coventry City were the opponents in the Coca-Cola Cup Second Round but Wanderers froze in the first leg at Highfield Road and lost 3-0. The second leg two weeks later saw perhaps the most exciting match yet at Adams Park. Wycombe eagerly set about the seemingly impossible task of overturning the Premier Leaguers three goal lead. Keith Ryan led the way with a stunning 25 yard opening goal on 32 minutes, Keith Scott headed home a corner in the 64th minute and then, three minutes from time, captain Terry Evans beat Steve Ogrizovic to the ball, heading the equalising goal. The fairytale continued as Jason Cousins gave Wycombe the lead in extra-time with a 30 yard free kick, but Coventry took advantage of their tiring opponents and scored two late goals through Morgan and Babb, to go through 5-4 on aggregate.

A 2-1 win at Bristol Rovers in the FA Cup saw top 'scorer Keith Scott make his last appearance for Wanderers, before he signed for Premier League Swindon Town. The fee was an eventual £375,000, which is currently the Club's record transfer fee, although Lincoln City received 20% of this as their sell-on share.

Scott by then had scored 14 goals in the opening 22 games and was still top 'scorer at the end of the season. Explosive winger Tony Hemmings teamed up with Langford for a diminutive but extremely quick strike force.

It was Hemmings with two goals who starred in an impressive 3-1 win in the next match at home to Crewe, then second in the Division.

"Even Martin O'Neill would approve of this ref".

O.Neill knew how to draw the worst out of referees!

Cartoon by lifelong supporter David Langdon.

Wycombe went one better in the next game, winning 3-2 at leaders Preston, who were performing in the last season on their artificial pitch. Langford had twice given Wanderers the lead but Hakan Hayrettin scored the winner deep into injury-time with an astonishing 35 yard shot which left the 'keeper rooted to the spot. The game was notable for the Football League debut of Club captain Glyn Creaser, at the age of 34, who had bravely battled back from nearly losing his foot in the work accident 18 months before.

That win pushed Wycombe up to fourth place, their ninth unbeaten away game in the League, although Chester City ended that particular run in the next away game on 11 December. The FA Cup saw a Third Round place for the first time since 1985-86, when Norwich City came to Adams Park without manager Mike Walker who had been sacked days before. The Premier League side gave a very professional performance and won 2-0 with some clinical finishing from Chris Sutton.

There was Cup drama at Craven Cottage in February when Fulham entertained Wanderers in the Autoglass Trophy Quarter-Final. It was another one of those magical evenings as 2,500 fans from Wycombe swelled the crowd to nearly 9,000. The game saw the debut of the inspirational Simon Garner, Blackburn's all-time record 'scorer with 192 goals, and a bargain free transfer from West Bromwich. He teamed up with Tim Langford who played the game of his life and scored two goals. A thrilling end to end encounter went to extra-time and then penalties, when Jason Cousins scored the winner amongst jubilant scenes at the away end. The victory came at a heavy price as both Terry Evans and Duncan Horton received injuries which sidelined them for the rest of the season.

Wycombe narrowly lost in the Southern Area Final over two legs to Swansea City, but promotion was still a distinct possibility and further new faces included the £60,000 signing of Steve Brown, the talented midfielder captain of Northampton Town, Nicky Reid, another free transfer from West Brom., and Tony Cunningham, a much travelled 36 year-old striker. The March League encounter with Colchester saw the resumption of bitter rivalry between both sets of supporters which boiled over after Wycombe took a 2-0 lead in the 89th minute. Police had to prevent home fans from advancing on the away end, but two managed to invade the pitch, angrily gesticulating towards the Wycombe supporters. The referee stopped the match with time still to play rather than risk any more pitch invasions.

April saw Wycombe begin to stutter, although they still held third place (and automatic promotion) when they travelled to fourth placed Crewe on the penultimate Saturday of the season. A near capacity crowd of just over 6,000 saw Crewe score in the first minute after a defensive mistake let Ashley Ward in. Wanderers equalised after 15 minutes with an own goal from Rowbotham and were happily holding onto a point when Paul Hyde failed to gather a cross 14 minutes from time and Ward nipped in for the winner. It was a devastating blow as Crewe exchanged places with Wycombe, who could only draw with Preston at home on the final Saturday. It did not matter as Crewe won at Chester and took the last automatic promotion place, consigning Wycombe to the Play-offs.

Their opponents were Carlisle United, the form team of the Division who had risen from 13th at the end of March to finish in the final play-off position, with six wins in eight games. Wycombe played some of their best football of the season to win the first leg 2-0 at Carlisle, with goals in either half from Thompson and Garner, and complete a 4-1 aggregate win to qualify for the Final against Preston.

Dave Carroll and Simon Garner celebrate the latter's play-off goal at Carlisle.

It was the third Wembley appearance in just four years but this was a difficult one for the Wycombe fans to enjoy with so much was at stake. Another season in the largely northern Third Division was not an attractive proposition and it would probably be less difficult to gain promotion this season with the aided momentum of recent promotion from the Conference.

Only 16,000 supporters travelled from High Wycombe, much less than in the previous finals, but the attendance of over 40,000 was a record for a Third Division Play-off Final. Preston had finished three points below Wycombe in fifth place, beating Torquay 4-3 in the play-offs, and they found themselves with a surprising 2-1 lead at half-time, in spite of Wycombe's domination.

Steve Guppy should have given Wycombe an early lead but hit his point blank shot straight at the goalkeeper. Preston scored with their first real chance, on 31 minutes, when a long throw was flicked on to Bryson whose overhead kick left Paul Hyde stranded. Steve Thompson replied within sixty seconds, breaking away and seeing his cross-come-shot helped into the net, but Raynor restored Preston's lead four minutes later with a glancing header.

The second half, however, belonged completely to Wycombe, and a smartly taken equaliser from Simon Garner just two minutes after the restart filled the team with confidence. Ten minutes later a flowing four man move saw Garner send a clever pass to Carroll who calmly shot home at an angle. Carroll scored the best goal of the game when he started a mazy run from his own half, checking on the 18 yard line, and then sending a shot off the post into the net.

The final score of 4-2 reflected a very entertaining game and ranks as the greatest ever performance by a Wycombe team. The side was superbly captained by Glyn Creaser who had come into the side again when Terry Evans was injured in February. The forward play of Garner and Thompson was excellent, Carroll produced one of his best ever performances, and Nicky Reid held the midfield together and passed with assured accuracy.

Gaining promotion via the play-offs may be bad for the nerves but it is very good for the bank balance and the Club's share of the Wembley gate receipts amounted to over £100,000, a large sum of money for a small club such as Wycombe. With two promotions in successive seasons, confidence was sky high at the Club, but there was one major problem during the summer.

Influential left-winger Steve Guppy refused to accept the terms of a new contract, and the manager consequently refused to play him in the opening weeks of the season. He was probably the one player who had contributed the most to the glory years, possessing a magical left foot which had laid on so many goals. He was also a very hard working player who dropped back when required to defend and was often referred to as the best left-back in the Club. Newcastle came in for him and issued a take it or leave it offer of £150,000 - if Wycombe went to arbitration then the deal would be called off. Everyone knew that he was worth more than that, but Martin O'Neill did not want his unsettling affect on the rest of the team to continue and he reluctantly accepted the offer. Guppy made a few substitute appearances for Newcastle and was then sold to Port Vale for £225,000. It was a big blow to Wycombe, the end of the famous twin wing partnership with Dave Carroll which had become the main trademark of the Martin O'Neill team.

The Preston 'keeper, Woods, relieves Simon Garner's cramp during the Wembley Play-off Final
(Photo: Paul Dennis)

Cyrille Regis was the only notable addition to the squad and became the first former England player to wear a Wycombe shirt. He had a good start to the season and had scored 8 goals when he sustained an injury in early November. He returned on Boxing Day but was never the same potent player after that.

The season started promisingly and included some excellent away wins, at Huddersfield when Garner spoilt the party with the only goal on the day their new stadium was opened, and Birmingham, where Wycombe defended in siege-like conditions after Regis had scored a breakaway goal. Both of those sides eventually gained promotion and Wycombe kept in close touch with the leaders, reaching the dizzy heights of second place in December and, on Boxing Day, recorded an emphatic 2-0 win at leaders Oxford United, courtesy of goals from Ryan and Garner.

It was Garner who became the first Wycombe player to score a first class hat-trick, in the 5-0 win at Hitchin in the FA Cup Second Round. Struggling West Ham visited Adams Park in the Third Round in a game touted as a potential giantkilling by the media. However like Norwich the previous season, the Hammers gave a very clinical performance and won with two second-half goals from Cottee and Brown in front of 9,007, the current record for the ground.

New players began to arrive - Mickey Bell, a forceful left-winger signed from Northampton for £45,000, midfielder Gary Patterson from Shrewsbury for £70,000, experienced defender Terry Howard, a bargain free transfer after being released by Leyton Orient, and striker Steve McGavin, the Club's record buy at £140,000 from Birmingham, who had always been a thorn in the side when playing for Colchester. Most exciting of all perhaps was 23 year-old striker Miquel Desouza, an £80,000 buy from Birmingham, and an exceptionally fast striker. He scored two goals on his debut at Chester City on a soaking wet January evening and had scored six times in his first six games before a training injury put him out until the final match that season. His absence was sorely missed as an eight match run without a win saw the side sink to tenth place at the end of March.

A good spell at the end of the season saw 20 points reaped from 10 games, but it was not enough and the side finished in sixth place, an agonizing three points behind Huddersfield in the last play-off spot. Sixth place would normally have been enough but the Football League was reorganising itself and only promoted two instead of the normal three clubs that season. The final game of the season at Orient was unusual in that Anthony Clark became the youngest Wycombe player in the Football League at 18 years and 29 days, and Cyrille Regis the oldest at 37 years and 86 days, the latter even scoring on his last appearance for the Club.

It had been a very good season on the pitch with many good results and the average attendance of 5,856 was 386 up on the previous season. However everyone at the Club, including the manager, had realised that the dream of going all the way to the Premiership was still just a dream.

At this time, the team lay seventh in the table. It was to be one of O'Neill's last games in charge

Reaching the First Division was possible but there was not the money to launch a serious assault beyond that. The most significant moment that season came after an awful midweek encounter at York City on 14 March, a game which ended 0-0. The Chairman Ivor Beeks went into the changing room afterwards, as he normally did to give Martin O'Neill the other results. Before leaving he said to the manager: *"The team played without passion and desire"*.

O'Neill took those few words very personally as he, and only he, was responsible for instilling such emotions in the players. He drove back that night with assistant manager Paul Franklin, scout John Robertson, and directors Graham Peart and Alan Parry, and could not get over what his chairman had said. He was also very concerned that the Club's plans for a new stand costing nearly £2 million would eat into the playing budget, and it is probably true to say that Martin O'Neill, subconsciously at least, decided to leave Wycombe Wanderers that night.

There were other incidents which led him to feel that perhaps, just perhaps, he had outstayed his welcome. About a month before the end of the season the directors were holding a board meeting and wanted some information which they knew was in the manager's office. Graham Peart had a master key and he, Ivor Beeks and Alan Parry went in and were confronted by what they felt was an unreasonably untidy office.

The next day the Chairman told the manager to clean up the room, an instruction which Martin O'Neill reacted very unfavourably to. He not only cleaned it but cleared everything out and left the door open to make sure that the Chairman noticed. He never went back inside that room.

At the end of the season Ivor Beeks went on holiday to Portugal, but on the day he left, Robert Chase the Norwich City chairman, rang the Club asking for permission to talk to the manager. Martin O'Neill still had a year to run on his contract but, in Ivor Beeks' absence, Graham Peart decided that it would be unreasonable to refuse.

He told Chase that he had permission but that he would ask Martin whether he wanted to talk to him. Peart met O'Neill and explained that the Norwich chairman wished to speak to him and asked him if he wanted to go.

O'Neill questioned: *"Are you trying to get rid of me?"* Peart replied: *"No, this is the situation. I want to know whether you want to talk him - if you are going to this is his private number to ring him."*

Twenty-four hours later the Norwich chairman phoned Peart and asked: *"Does your manager want to talk to me?"*. *"I really don't know, I'm surprised that he hasn't talked to you already"*, he replied. Peart then phoned O'Neill and asked him whether he was going to speak to Robert Chase and received the reply: *"I think I will."*. The Norwich chairman met Martin O'Neill at Heathrow Airport, an offer was made and accepted, and before going up to Norwich for the press conference to announce his arrival, Martin O'Neill met Graham Peart to tie up some financial loose ends.

"It was very difficult", Peart said, *"because all those wonderful times with Martin ran through my mind, the three Wembley games, two promotions, all those big cup games. We needed this manager to stay but the subconscious message I was getting was that the time had come for Martin to go and do something different. I found it very hard to come to terms with this, but I knew that it was all over. I did try to pusuade him to stay, but I knew that he wanted to get away."*

The chairman was still in Portugal as he could not fly home and leave his car there, but he did speak to Martin one last time at Adams Park, where he was being interviewed by the Club's Press Officer Alan Hutchinson. Martin said that he would ring him back after he had finished, but the call was never made and Martin O'Neill and Ivor Beeks have never spoken since.

It was a rather sad end to five unbelievably wonderful years at the Club, all the more so because, although it was Martin O'Neill's brilliant managership which took the team so far, it was Ivor Beeks who had created the environment for it all to happen. Time and time again his canny business sense secured the best for the Club in many situations and the importance of the excellent relationship he enjoyed with the manager is often underplayed. He never interfered with team affairs, which is highly unusual for a Football League chairman.

Martin O'Neill is the supreme motivator of players in the game, a deep thinker, a proven winner and a thoroughly charming individual. He believes that his team always has a chance of winning any game and proved his ability to carry off the big games time and time again.

The fact that he fell out with the Norwich chairman so quickly underlined Ivor Beeks's ability to work successfully with quite a volatile individual. It was no surprise to Wycombe fans when O'Neill guided his new club Leicester City to the final play-off spot on the last day of the season and no-one had any doubts whatsoever that he would triumph in the final at Wembley.

On the Saturday following O'Neill's departure, the Club advertised in the Daily Mail for a new manager - over 60 applications were received, but the only person to be interviewed was Brian Lee's old acquaintance Alan Smith, who then met Ivor Beeks and his recommendation that he become the next manager was unanimously accepted by the other directors. He was a high profile manager who had just left Crystal Palace after his contract had not been renewed, following the Club's relegation to the First Division. He had, however, enjoyed some success with them, including Semi-Final appearances in both the FA Cup and the Coca-Cola Cup in that final season, and he had also led them to the First Division Championship in 1994.

Smith began the season with only one new player, left-back Paul Hardyman from Bristol Rovers, but had soon signed full-back Jason Rowbotham, promising left-winger David Farrell from Aston Villa for £100,000 and John Williams, an extremely quick striker from Coventry City for a new record fee of £150,000. The latter struggled initially but came back strongly after an injury.

The team gained the reputation for being hard to beat, with just four defeats in the League at the end of the year. In November fourth place was reached, the highest of the season, but there was little success in the Cups. A First Round Coca-Cola Cup win over Leyton Orient included the sending off of goalkeeper Paul Hyde for a professional foul. His suspension ended a run of 120 consecutive first team appearances, allowing eternal understudy Chuck Moussaddik to make his one and only first class start.

In November Hyde fell out with the manager and two loan 'keepers spent long spells in the team, Ben Roberts from Middlesbrough and Sieb Dykstra from Queens Park Rangers.

A very disappointing performance at Maine Road in the next round saw the team crash out 4-0 to crisis-torn Manchester City. Sky television chose to cover the FA Cup First Round tie against Gillingham at Adams Park but, in spite of a spectacular 25 yard volley from Gary Patterson, Wycombe drew 1-1 and deservedly lost the replay 1-0.

Desouza was in prolific form early in the season, with eight goals after the opening seven games, and at Bradford in September he became the first Wycombe player to score a hat-trick in the Football League, remarkably repeating the feat in the return match at Adams Park in March. His goals however dried up between the end of October and mid-February, but he finished strongly and ended with twenty goals for the season, goals which prevented a relegation battle.

The second-half of the season was spent in mid-table with a final position of twelfth summing up a frustrating year. Brilliant performances were often followed by some awful ones, but Martin O'Neill was always going to be a very difficult act to follow, perhaps an impossible one.

In the final weeks of the season the first major development at Adams Park began with the construction of a new 5,000 seater stand on the Woodland Terrace. With two tiers, a large family stand and 20 private boxes, the final cost of £1.8 million was substantially covered by grants of £1.1 million (which would not have to be paid back), interest free loans, and advance subscriptions from the boxes. Not a penny was used from the playing budget and the stand signified the Club's determination to continue its self betterment. For the first time for some years, the Club made an operating loss on the season. Gates were down on average by 1,300 to 4,573, and it was becoming even clearer that income from outside of the Club was essential, even to survive in the Second Division.

Action from the Second Division 1995/96 season.

Terry Howard rises high and heads home Dave Farrell's corner to make it 2-0 at Oxford, in the surpise 4-1 October victory.

(Photo: Paul Dennis)

The constitution of Wycombe Wanderers Football Club is almost unique - only Nottingham Forest are similar but they have a much larger support. Instead of the usual situation of clubs owned by a handful of shareholders who continually contribute money (or not as the case may be), Wycombe are a company limited by guarantee with just over 200 shareholders whose only financial contribution is the original £1 for each share. They elect a board of directors who also do not put extra money in, but do contribute a lot of time, and this set-up has kept the Club very stable over the last ten years, preventing the uncertainty of takeovers and those inherent problems. Wycombe Wanderers have always managed to generate enough income internally to fund the team for their level of football, but any thoughts of a further rise in the League may well mean a change of constitution. The current shareholders will probably have to face relinquishing control of the Club to attract outside money. Relations between the Club and Wycombe District Council have improved slightly - the councillors now understand the significance of having a Football League club in town - but any plans for future development at Adams Park will probably still involve a battle.

None the less the Club is in very good shape financially. To quote Deloitte & Touche's Annual Review of Football Finance (August 1996): *At the end of their 1994/5 financial years, the five clubs with positive reserves over £3 million were Arsenal (£11.1 million), Aston Villa (£7.2 million), Manchester United (£24.1 million), Tottenham Hotspur (£19.2 million) and Wycombe Wanderers (£3.6 million). This only formed the main source of funding for Aston Villa and Wycombe Wanderers who have no bank borrowings nor significant shareholder investment, although Wycombe Wanderers are limited by guarantee and do not have a share capital as such."* The Chairboys are indeed in good company!

The Club has a stadium which it owns and has all but paid off any borrowings. The Youth Team has been revitalised under Neil Smillie's guidance, and for the first time for years it looks as though the Club will produce home grown talent for the Senior Team. There is certainly no reason why Wycombe Wanderers should not progress to the First Division within the next few seasons.

APPENDIX A - Formation Date

The formation date of the club has long been held to be 1884 but research for this history suggests that 1887 is the correct date. Documentary evidence from those early years is confined to a few revealing newspaper references in the South Bucks Free Press. The first mention of the club in print occurred on the 16th September 1887:

HIGH WYCOMBE FOOTBALL ASSOCIATION

The annual meeting of the above was held at the Coach and Horses Inn on Wednesday evening last. There was a large attendance of football players, the following clubs being represented - Ramblers, Rangers, Rovers and **Wanderers**, *Marsh, Loudwater and the "Nose Club".*

No other club in the town was called Wanderers and their attendance at the meeting signified a request for junior status. On the 4th April 1890 the report on Wanderer's win in the High Wycombe Challenge Cup stated:

...to have finally secured possession of the coveted trophy is abundant proof of their rapid rise in the local football scale since the club's formation **three years ago...**

One week later, the same paper carried a review of Wanderer's 1889-90 season, ending with the season by season playing records headed:

CLUB'S RECORD SINCE FORMATION, SEASON 1887-88

Finally on the 1st May 1891, a report of Wycombe Wanderers end of season dinner at the Nags Head included the following comments by the Chairman for the evening, Robert Wood, who was the club's President:

The Chairman proposed the toast of the evening, "Success to the Wycombe Wanderers Football Club." He mentioned the fact that the club had been in existence for **four seasons** *and referred to the fact that the club was composed entirely of working lads.*

In 1933 the club was preparing to celebrate its jubilee the following autumn but, on the 15th September, the 'Goalpost' column in the Bucks Free Press asserted that it was too soon. Quoting match reports in the local paper in the 1890s, the columnist mistakenly tries to prove that the correct year is 1889, thinking that a reference to 'the first match of Wycombe Wanderers' that season meant the first ever. However the anonymous 'Goalpost' intriguingly refers to the Club's first ever meeting:

'Tich' Webb was the individual who called a meeting in the wood-house in Duke Street, High Wycombe, and I had the pleasure of being present. We paid our "coppers" per week towards the funds.

It is difficult to make a case for continuing to adopt 1884 as the formation date. The direct newspaper references are our best source as they date from a time when memories were fresh. It should also be noted that there are no references in the local press before 16th September 1887 to either a team called 'Wanderers' or to any of the players we know played in the first season. Indeed Ted Rolph's notes make it clear that the Club we now know came into being at the Steam Engine meeting, which probably took place just before their first game in September 1887. There is no good reason to doubt that a team of some sort did exist before 1887, but it was only a scratch side, had no official status and was almost certainly not called Wycombe Wanderers. Some time before the jubilee in 1934, and probably after the First World War, 1884 was adopted instead of 1887, possibly at the prompting of some of the original players, and these rather vague early years were included as part of the history.

APPENDIX B - Smoking Concerts

In the early years of the club, smoking concerts, all male affairs and which the club continues with the modern day Sportsmens Dinners, were held every month at the club's headquarters, often after a big game. One such was held after West Bromwich Albion had visited Loakes Park on 21st November 1895 and the following account in the Bucks Free Press gives a charming portrait of the simple pleasures of an evening of song around a piano:

SMOKING CONCERT

In the evening, at the Wanderer's head-quarters (the "Nag's-head" London-road), a capital smoking concert took place. Mr. B.M. Lockyer (the referee in the match) occupied the chair, and was supported by Mr.C.W. Harper (captain and hon. Sec. of the W.F.C.), and Messrs. Higgins, Richards, and Swinnerton (West Bromwich F.C.), and Mr. Holden (formerly of West Bromwich Reserves). The attendance was large, and great enthusiasm prevailed during the whole of the evening, and with toast and song, a very pleasant time was spent. The programme was a lengthy and well arranged one, and encores were frequent. During the evening Mr. Harper proposed "The West Bromwich Albion F.C.," and referred to the gentlemanly part played by them in the match during the afternoon, and said that the same spirit had characterised the whole of the matches played while on tour. (Applause). It was a great speculation for a club like the Wanderers to guarantee such a sum of money, and it was gratifying to observe the support given to the club in the undertaking, which had for its object the raising of the tone of football in the town. He hoped that West Bromwich would not be the last First League team they would have at Wycombe this season - The Wycombe Challenge Cup was then filled up, and the Chairman gave "The Wanderers," which was received with "three time three."- Mr. H. Millbourn gave "Our Chairman," a toast that was done justice to by the company, the singing of "For he's a jolly good fellow" following. At eleven o'clock the proceedings terminated with "to our next merry meeting," which was fixed for April 4th. Appended is the programme:-Pianoforte solo, Mr. E.Crook; song, "Going to 'Ampstead in a van," Mr.J. East; song, "Baby," Mr Bristowe; song, "Little sister's gone to sleep," Mr. Woods; song, "I shall be there," Mr.J. McDermott; song, "Stammering sweethearts" (encore, "For me"), Mr.B.M. Lockyer; song; "That's a thing he'd never done before," Mr. Rolfe; song, "Widow McCarthy," Mr.C. Heath; song, "Queen of my heart," Mr. Youens; banjo solo, Mr. Wall; song, "Oh, that Gorgonzola cheese" ("It's a great big shame"), Mr.E. Sandilands; song, "India's reply" (encore, "Getting ready for my mother-in-law"), Mr. Higgins; concertina solo, Mr.E. Crook; song "Tableaux vivante," Private Strange; song, "The old musketeer," Mr.T. Price; song, "Ting-a-ling" (encore, "Pink-ponky-poo"), Mr.B.M. Lockyer; song, "The day I backed the winner" (encore, "One of the J's"), Mr.E. Sandilands; pianolo solo, "Canary valse," Mr. J. Howard; "Auld lang syne."

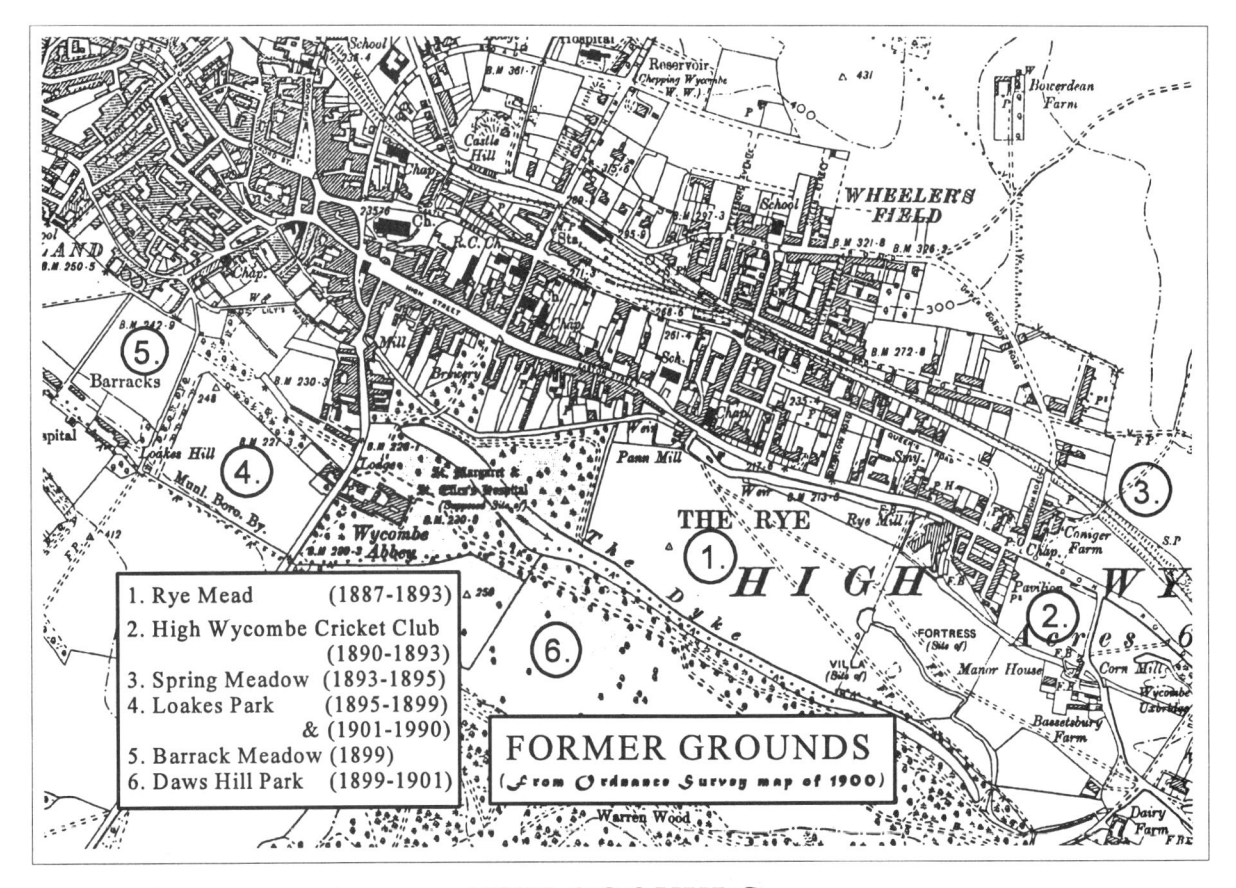

1. Rye Mead   (1887-1893)
2. High Wycombe Cricket Club
                      (1890-1893)
3. Spring Meadow (1893-1895)
4. Loakes Park   (1895-1899)
             & (1901-1990)
5. Barrack Meadow (1899)
6. Daws Hill Park   (1899-1901)

FORMER GROUNDS
(from Ordnance Survey map of 1900)

- THE GROUNDS -

(Above) Rye Mead
(Below) Cricket Ground
Both c.1900

Early years at Loakes Park: (Above) c.1890 before a ball was kicked.........
....and (below) work commences on laying out the Ground in 1894

11 November 1895 (Monday morning) A well attended match at Loakes Park, When the Northern Ladies played Southern Ladies.

A more conventional match in the late 1890's..... Note the large crowd, but no spectator facilities!

However, a few years later (in 1904), the main Stand was built.

1915....

And Loakes Park is used for the War effort.

Note the small embankment at the Hospital end.

(Above) By the late 1920's/early 30's, there had been little change.......

(Below)........ but by 1945, the full length enclosure on the Town side had appeared.

(Left) An inside view of the main seated Stand that lasted for so many years.

February 1990. A fine view of Loakes Park from the adjacent hospital.
But the venue had only a few weeks remaining as a football stadium. Meanwhile.....

..... a virgin site had been selected at nearby Sands, for the construction of a new Ground.

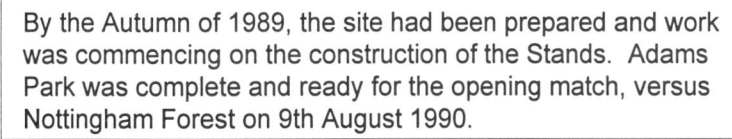

By the Autumn of 1989, the site had been prepared and work was commencing on the construction of the Stands. Adams Park was complete and ready for the opening match, versus Nottingham Forest on 9th August 1990.

September 1990.
The sad site of Loakes Park. During a period of over 90 years it had staged so many memorable matches By now the pitch had become a car park, and later all remnants of the Ground soon disappeared

GREAT GAMES

March 31st 1902: Wycombe 3 - Slough 0

First Senior Cup Success

This was Wycombe's fourth appearance in the Berks & Bucks Senior Cup Final and they were looking for their first win, having lost the other three to their old rivals, Marlow. This time their opponents at Maidenhead on Easter Monday were Slough. The Wanderers had beaten Maidenhead themselves, Aylesbury and Chesham Generals (holders of the trophy) on the way to the final, while Slough had accounted for Marlow (after two drawn games) and Reading Amateurs. Slough had undergone strict training in readiness for the game but Wycombe, who were quietly confident, never bothered with any special preparations. Slough were dealt a blow in the week preceding the match when their influential captain, G.Werrell, failed a fitness test, which consisted of a practice match in those days. Wycombe, too, had injury problems and decided not to risk either Archie Green or Dick Pugh and they fielded the line-up that had played in their most recent games.

The game attracted much attention from the Wycombe public and three special trains were run from Wycombe station with over 2,000 people on board, while hundreds more travelled by road on all sorts of transportation. The gates opened some time before kick off and a crowd of 6,500, paying receipts of £214.7s, assembled in brilliant sunshine. The attendance would have been bigger but for the fact that several counterfeit tickets were sold. The huge crowd were entertained by the Slough and Chalvey Brass Band until the two teams arrived. Wycombe appeared first, led by Bill Buchanan, to a rousing reception, with Slough following three minutes later.

Buchanan won the toss for Wycombe and asked Slough to kick into a strong wind and with the sun in their eyes. The Wanderers wasted no time in taking advantage of this and, after five minutes, Tom Barlow headed on a cross for Buchanan to head past Crocker. Wycombe's supporters went wild with loud cheering, while hats, sticks and umbrellas were flung in the air. Three minutes later, they were two up as Fidler failed to cut out a pass from Fred Rouse and Bob White fired home. The rest of the first half continued in the same vein as Wycombe surged forward with one superb move after another. Crocker, in the Slough goal, made save after save, and both Buchanan and Rouse had "goals" disallowed for offside, the first to the displeasure of the crowd, who booed the referee loudly.

With the conditions in their favour, Slough started the second half with high hopes, but they reckoned without Wycombe's resolve and, within minutes of the restart, Rouse had struck the post with a great shot. In a rare counter attack, Denton outpaced Charlie Tilbury and crossed into the middle, where both Poole and Wright missed the ball with the goal at their mercy. This was just a brief respite and, after Rouse, Albert Hearn and Buchanan had all gone close, Rouse added a third with a fine solo effort. The game was all over now and Slough offered only token resistance as Wycombe could easily have added to their score. When they did attack, Albert Keen thwarted them on several occasions by booting the ball into touch, bringing forward cries of "Marlow" from the Wycombe contingent, in reference to their main rivals' supposed style of play!

After the game both teams were treated to a "high tea" in the Maidenhead Town Hall, where Wycombe were then presented with the Cup. The team then travelled back to Wycombe by train and were met at the station just after 7 o'clock by a crowd of several thousand. The players and officials boarded a brake and were taken via Crendon Street to their headquarters at the Swan Hotel, Pauls Row, cheered on by the mass of people lining the streets. Needless to say an enjoyable evening followed as the Cup was filled time and time again with appropriate refreshment!

Wycombe line-up: Reynolds, Tilbury, A.Keen, F.Keen, Hooper, Stevens, White, Rouse, W.Buchanan, Hearn, Barlow.

April 11st 1931: Wycombe 1 - Hayes 0

Amateur Cup Triumph

The Blues' first appearance in a national final, which was played at Highbury. In getting there they had been in superb form and had scored 22 goals in defeating London Caledonians, Walthamstow Avenue, Romford, Metropolitan Police and Woking. Hayes, of the Athenian League, had reached the final in amazing fashion, coming all the way through from the qualifying rounds and playing all nine games away from home. They caused a surprise though when they named their team, by including new signing, Bill Caesar, at left-half instead of the regular, A.Butcher. Caesar was to play an important part in proceedings later on. Wycombe had also changed their left-half in recent weeks due to the injury to John Timberlake, the captain, in an earlier round. Pat Badrick took over as skipper.

Like the Berks & Bucks Cup almost thirty years previous, the game had gripped the imagination of the town and thousands travelled by train to swell the crowd to a figure of 32,489. They looked resplendent in their blue and blue, with miniature chairs fixed to lapels.

Hayes, the favourites, had slightly the better of what was a disappointing first half, with both sides seemingly affected by the occasion. Wycombe were dealt a blow after fifteen minutes when Sid Crump was forced to leave the field with a head injury. When he returned, he played on the right wing for the remainder of the half, with Bill Brown dropping back. He resumed his normal position in the second half. During his absence Jim Kipping was called upon to save well from Rowe and Eric Caesar, while at the other end, Doug Vernon twice headed over from Alf Britnell's crosses. Vernon was the only non-local in Wycombe's team. He was stationed in the R.A.F. at Halton and was playing his only season for the club, during which he scored 25 goals in just 21 games.

The two Captains, Rowe of Hayes and Pat Badrick, shake hands before the kick-off.

Ten minutes before half-time Dick Braisher let fly a superb shot only for Holding to make a great save. After the interval the game livened up considerably and Wycombe began to gain the upper hand. Arthur Greenwell saw Holding make another fine save from his shot, while Bill Brown hit another fierce effort just wide. Britnell also skimmed the bar following a free kick. At the other end Lloyd wasted a good chance for Hayes, while there was a real scare when Crump appeared to handle in the area. The referee, Mr Graham, thought otherwise and awarded a free kick outside the area. Then, ten minutes from the end, and only a few minutes after this incident, Wycombe were awarded a penalty. Bill Caesar handled the ball whilst laid on the ground in a goalmouth melée. Brown took the kick and, although he struck it well, hit it straight at Holding. However, the ball rebounded off the keeper and in a flash Britnell had fired it home.

Wycombe had no problems in holding out after this and Badrick went up to collect the cup amid joyful scenes of celebration.

Back in the town the team were met by thousands of people as they made their way to the Guildhall. Later that week a celebration dinner was held in the Town Hall. Four hundred people attended, including several players from the past.

Wycombe line-up: Kipping, Crump, Cox, Rance, Badrick, Greenwell, Simmons, Brown, Vernon, Braisher, Britnell.

Doug Vernon on the attack

November 26th 1932: Gillingham 1 - Wycombe 1

This was the first time that Wycombe had reached the First Round Proper of the F.A. Cup and the first time they met Football League opposition, the Gills being in Division Three (South).

Gillingham won the toss and kicked off in front of a crowd of 6,400 with a strong wind at their backs, hoping to unsettle the Blues early on. However, they tended to bunch their attack through the middle and were kept at bay by stout defending from Sid Crump, Dickie Cox and Pat Badrick. Wycombe made more use of their wings and Holland, in the home goal, was soon in action. The game ebbed and flowed and Jim Kipping made fine saves from Liddle, Raleigh and Nicol, while, at the other end, Bill Brown and A.Varney went close. Then Holland made a great double save from Brown and Dick Braisher. Gillingham took the lead in the 39th minute when Liddle's long range shot caught in the wind and swerved past Kipping's outstretched hand. A minute later Liddle tried again, but this time Kipping saved.

Gritty Display in Kent

In the second half Wycombe had the advantage of the wind, but found Gillingham pushing hard for the second goal and Purcell went close with one effort. However, the Blues weathered the storm and, with fifteen minutes left, equalised. Alf Britnell got clear of his marker and slipped the ball across to Braisher, who ran through the defence and hit a shot into the corner of the net. According to the Bucks Free Press, this was met with great excitement from the Wycombe supporters who hugged each other, somebody beat on a loud drum, and one fan threw his bowler hat at a policeman's helmet!

After the equaliser, both sides went close in an exciting finale. Gillingham had several shots blocked in an almighty goalmouth scramble and, at the other end, Brown broke clear, but Holland charged out of his goal to deflect the shot for a corner.

Dick Braisher, scorer of Wycombe's goal

In the replay, on the following Wednesday afternoon, Wycombe conceded a first minute own goal through Cox, then went 2-1 in front through Brown and Braisher (penalty), before eventually losing 4-2. Despite people having to have time off work to attend the game, there was a crowd of 7,597 at Loakes Park.

Wycombe line-up (both games): Kipping, Crump, Cox, Rance, Badrick, Greenwell, Varney, Simmons, Brown, Braisher, Britnell.

February 25th 1950: Wycombe 4 - St. Albans City 1

Amateur Cup Quarter-final day and the biggest ever gate at Loakes Park 15,850, including 2,000 from St. Albans turned up to see the Blues reach the semi-final for the first time in nineteen years. There were still long queues outside when the two teams took the field.

Wycombe, who made one change to their regular line-up when they brought in Frank Westley, a newcomer from Barnet in place of Peter Birdseye, started off at a terrific pace and Jock McCallum (twice) and Westley went close in the opening minutes. The visitors held out though and Sperrin headed over at the other end. The Blues took the lead in startling fashion in the 25th minute. George Jackson's free-kick looked to be drifting out when McCallum somehow reached it. Controlling the ball in mid-air, he flashed in a shot which gave City keeper Sullivan no chance. Five minutes later, the homesters were two up. Henrik Mikrut chased Jimmy Flippance's long clearance only to stumble over the ball. However, Ken Butler followed up and, with the St. Albans' defence caught off guard by Mikrut's antics, he hammered home a fierce shot. Six minutes further on though Wycombe's defence were caught napping as the unmarked Sayers picked up a pass from Lucas to score. Moments later there was a scare when Chris Lodge dropped a shot from Lucas, but the ball was scrambled clear.

A Record Crowd

Dead on half-time Mikrut headed Fred Gearing's free-kick onto the crossbar and then, a minute after the interval, McCallum made it 3-1, when he ran on to Mikrut's pass, then outpaced both full backs and the 'keeper to score. This effectively put paid to the visitors' hopes and Mikrut added a splendid fourth 18 minutes from the end with a diving header from Westley's cross. The Blues could have added one or two more after this, with Mikrut ballooning one effort over.

Wycombe line-up: Lodge, Flippance, Jackson, Gearing, Krupa, Way, Blizzard, McCallum, Mikrut, Butler, Westley.

Fred Gearing leads out the Wycombe team, followed by Johnny Blizzard, Jimmy Flippance, Johnny Way, Henrik Mikrut and Mieczystow Krupa

March 16th 1957: Wycombe 4 - Corinthian Casuals 2

Wycombe reached Wembley for the first time with an astounding win in the Amateur Cup semi-final at Highbury in front of a crowd of 28,197.

The thrills started in the very first minute when Casuals' outside-left, Kerruish netted direct from a corner. 'Keeper Dennis Syrett fell awkwardly in trying to keep the ball out and played the rest of the game in great pain. Undeterred by this early blow, the Wanderers hit back and equalised in the fourth minute when Len Worley retrieved a wayward free-kick and sent over a perfect cross for Paul Bates to head home. The game continued at a furious pace for another twenty minutes, before they took the lead. Bates latched onto Worley's long ball and dribbled past Buchanan and Cowan before beating Ahm, in Casuals' goal, with a superb left-foot drive, hiding the fact he was playing with blistered feet.

Walking Wounded Clinch Famous Victory

Wycombe were well on top now and Ahm saved Cliff Trott's shot at point-blank range. Suddenly though Casuals equalised when Tracey and Laybourne combined for the latter to beat Syrett with a neat lob. Bates nearly netted with an overhead kick shortly after, while, close on half-time Ahm brought off an excellent save from Frank Smith.

The second-half started off as the first had finished and Ahm made a remarkable save from Bates in the 50th minute. However, the Blues were dealt a double blow ten minutes later when Frank Westley collided with Shuttleworth and was carried off with a knee injury. As soon as the game restarted, Smith became the next casualty with a dislocated shoulder. On hearing of this latest incident, Westley bravely returned to the fray, spending the rest of the game limping on the wing. After Shuttleworth had crashed a shot against the underside of the Wycombe bar, the Blues amazingly grabbed the lead. Bates swerved his way past two defenders before crossing for Worley to head in. Casuals again hit the Woodwork when Tracey's shot hit the bar, before Worley delivered the coup-de-grace with five minutes left. The heroic Westley side-footed to Trott and his measured pass put Worley through and he finished with a splendid drive.

Thankfully, the injuries had cleared up in time for the Final a month later.

Wycombe line-up: Syrett, Lawson, Westley, G.Truett, Wicks, J.Truett, Worley, Trott, Bates, Tomlin, Smith.

November 30th 1966: Bedford Town 3 - Wycombe 3

A disputed penalty two minutes from the end robbed Wycombe of F.A. Cup glory against their Southern League opponents. It was the second game of a four match saga in the First Round of the competition, after a 1-1 draw at Loakes Park four days previously. A crowd of 7,641 packed Bedford's Eyrie ground. They saw Bedford give the Blues a run-around in the first half and Sturrock give them the lead with a speculative shot that deceived John Maskell in the 40th minute. However, the Blues staged a great comeback after the interval and had equalised within thirteen minutes when Paul Bates fired home from a free-kick after having his initial effort blocked. With a large contingent from Wycombe urging them on, they took the lead with ten minutes left. John Beck floated over a perfect cross and Tony Horseman out-jumped his markers to head home. A minute later though, at the other end, Skinn ran into the area to head in a corner kick.

Late Penalty Drama

The game went from end to end in the closing minutes and Les Merrick fired a shot over for the Blues, while Sturrock shot wide when well-placed. The game went into extra time and after six minutes Wycombe went back in front. Len Worley broke away on the right and passed inside to Merrick who coolly rounded Collier before scoring. Benning then hit the bar for Bedford and Maskell made a good save from Sturrock, before Ian Rundle was adjudged to have handled a bouncing ball in the area and the referee, Mr Sinclair, pointed to the penalty spot, despite Wycombe's vehement protests. Sturrock shot past Maskell to send the tie into a third game, which was again drawn 1-1. Bedford finally triumphed 3-2 in the third replay, at The Eyrie, to earn a second round trip to Oxford United.

The total attendance at the four games was over 32,000.

Wycombe line-up (in all four games): Maskell, Beck, Roystone, Baker, Rundle, Gale, Worley, Samuels, Bates, Horseman, Merrick.

24th November 1973: Wycombe 3 - Newport County 1

Three goals in a nine-minute spell saw the Blues record their first ever win over a Football League side when Fourth Division Newport visited for a F.A. Cup First Round game.

Three-Goal Burst Wins The Day

The first half was a close affair with neither side giving much away. There was an anxious moment in the Wycombe penalty area after 14 minutes when John Maskell fumbled a cross under pressure and Dave Bullock had to hack clear. Two minutes later, Steve Perrin broke clear at the other end but screwed his shot wide. As the half progressed, Wycombe began to get a grip of midfield, with Terry Reardon playing his first full game for the club, in commanding form. The Blues carved out a great chance in the 23rd minute, only for Dylan Evans, playing in place of the injured Keith Searle, to blaze it high over the bar. Six minutes later they were dealt a blow though when right-back Rob Williams went off injured. However, his replacement, Tony Brothers, had a great game.

There was no hint of the excitement to come as Newport dominated the early second half play. The visitors came desperately close to opening the scoring when, after just three minutes of the half, Jones struck the crossbar with a lob over Maskell. With Wycombe visibly rattled, both Jones (again) and Coldrick went close. After surviving this spell of pressure with their goal intact Wycombe suddenly struck in deadly fashion. In the 62nd minute Tony Horseman put Perrin through with an astute chip. The young striker outran the County defence and hammered in a great shot from an acute angle. Five minutes later, Roger Grant hit a free-kick hard across the area, County keeper Macey failed to hold it cleanly, and Perrin tucked in the rebound. The crowd had hardly finished celebrating when Evans took a pass from Horseman and beat a defender before firing in a superb third.

Newport were truly stunned by these events, and only some fine saves by Macey prevented them conceding more goals, although they did pull one back, six minutes from the end, through their substitute Hooper.

The attendance on this historical afternoon was 6,888.

Wycombe line-up: Maskell, Williams (Brothers), Grant, Mead, Bullock, Reardon, Horseman, Pritchard, Evans, Holifield, Perrin.

7th January 1975: Middlesbrough 1 - Wycombe 0

Possibly Wycombe's finest performance in their history. Division One leaders Middlesbrough had gained a rather fortunate goalless draw at Loakes Park three days earlier and had to pull out all the stops to snatch victory in this F.A. Cup Third Round replay at Ayresome Park after a superb rearguard action by the Blues.

John Maskell played the game of his life and had already made a couple of fine saves before pulling off a superb stop from Souness' 20 yard volley midway through the first half. Shortly after, Wycombe produced their best move of the game with Paul Birdseye, Keith Searle and Steve Perrin all involved. Platt was perfectly positioned to deal with Perrin's effort though.

During the first half, 'Boro had wasted a lot of chances and the crowd had got on their backs, but after the interval they really turned the screw, with Armstrong a constant danger. The introduction of substitute Willey for the ineffectual Foggon also caused problems. He **Last-Minute Goal Denies Brave Blues** almost gave 'Boro the lead when his header struck the post with twenty minutes left. Maskell then pulled off two more saves inside a minute as first Mills, then Willey looked certain to score. With time running out and Wycombe's defence still doggedly holding on, a goal finally arrived. Armstrong ran on to a pass from Souness, and cutting inside, he beat a defender before slipping the ball past Maskell.

Although it was a killer blow, with just seconds remaining, it was felt that Wycombe could have capsized in extra time. They had made a big impression on the home fans though and the whole crowd of 30,128 stood to chant *"Wycombe, Wycombe"* as the teams left the field.

Wycombe line-up: Maskell, Birdseye, Hand, Mead, Phillips, Reardon, Perrin, Kennedy, Searle, Holifield, Horseman (Evans).

The Middlesbrough players line-up to applaud Wycombe off the pitch, led by Stuart Boam (shaking hands with Gary Hand). Behind Hand is Mickey Holifield, while to the right, Graeme Souness applauds.

11th May 1991: Wycombe 2 - Kidderminster Harriers 1

An estimated 25,000 Wycombe supporters helped create a record attendance of 34,842 for the F.A. Trophy Final.

The Blues got off to a lively start when Dave Carroll's near post cross caused first minute problems for the Harriers' defence. They then took the lead in the 18th minute when Mark West sprung the offside trap. Running onto Steve Guppy's long ball, he crossed low to the near post. Jones fumbled the ball on the line and Keith Scott ran in to force it home. Jones redeemed himself later with a great save from Scott's well-struck shot. At the other end, John Granville, playing with a broken thumb, made a good save from Lilwall, while Joseph wasted a good chance.

The second half started with a superb run by West, before Kidderminster took a grip of the game, and equalised in the 61st minute. Hadley took on and beat Glyn Creaser and although his shot wasn't hit hard, it squirmed under Granville's grasp. This stung Wycombe back into action and, four minutes later, they regained the lead with a glorious goal. **West seals First Win at Wembley** Creaser put Scott clear down the wing and his cross was met by a brilliant diving header from West. Jones then saved well from both Guppy and Carroll as the Blues surged forward.

Harriers hit back late in the game, but Granville foiled Lilwall with a good low save, while McGrath volleyed over.

The next day, the team travelled on an open top bus through the town, when a huge crowd greeted them outside the Town Hall, where a civic reception was held for them.

Wycombe line-up: Granville, Crossley, Cash, Kerr, Creaser, Carroll, Ryan, Stapleton, West, Scott, Guppy (Hutchinson).

A quartet of players celebrate after the game. (L.to R.):

John Granville, Mark West, Keith Scott and Stuart Cash.
(Photo: Paul Dennis)

30th April 1992: Redbridge Forest 0 - Wycombe 5

Four Goal Burst In Vain

Wycombe travelled to East London knowing that they needed a big score to stand any chance of catching leaders Colchester. That they ultimately lost out on the GM Vauxhall Conference title shouldn't detract from this superb performance. They tore into their hosts from the kick-off and were awarded an early penalty, which Keith Scott duly converted after 15 minutes. The same player then made it two, six minutes before half-time, flicking home a cross from Keith Ryan. This was the start of an incredible burst of scoring either side of the interval. Kim Casey slotted home the third four minutes later, followed by Dave Carroll's deflected shot a minute after the break and Casey's second a minute after this. Four goals in eight minutes! Although that was the end of the scoring, the action continued thick and fast as both Carroll and Ryan saw efforts kicked off the line. Dennis Greene and Simon Hutchinson were also sent on to keep the momentum going.

A crowd of 2,891, Redbridge's highest of the season and including a large Colchester contingent, watched the match.

Wycombe line-up: Hyde, Cousins, Crossley, Kerr, Creaser, Ryan (Hutchinson), Carroll, Stapleton, Casey, Scott, Guppy (Greene).

Keith Scott
two goals at Redbridge
(Photo: Paul Dennis)

5th October 1993: Wycombe 4 - Coventry City 2

When Coventry comprehensively won 3-0 at Highfield Road in the first leg, it looked as though this Coca Cola Cup, Second round, second leg game would just be a formality. However, the crowd of 5,933 were treated to an incredible display by the Blues on a pitch made very wet by heavy rain earlier in the day.

The first half was rather low key, with few chances created at either end, although Keith Ryan opened the scoring in the 32nd minute with a low 25 yard shot. The second half started with Dave Carroll shooting just wide and Paul Hyde saving well from Williams and Gayle at the other end. Then Keith Scott set the ground alight with a superb header from a 64th minute corner. Wycombe began to believe a shock result was possible and Ogrizovic had to be at his best to keep out a full-bloodied drive from Tony Hemmings. Five minutes from the end, substitute, Simon Hutchinson, got to the byeline and sent over a cross which Ogrizovic lost in a crowd of players. Terry Evans bundled the ball over the line for the equaliser on aggregate. Two minutes into extra time, the Blues were in the lead when Jason Cousins sent a free kick low into the corner of the net and then celebrated by sliding across the wet surface.

Brave Blues Just Miss Out

Unfortunately, it was this wet surface that played an important part in Coventry rescuing the game. With just eight minutes of the extra period left, Hutchinson slipped as he went to tackle Morgan, and the City player ran on to blast the ball home. The visitors scored again five minutes later when Babb's shot looped up off of Cousins over Hyde's head.

Although beaten over the two legs, to defeat a Premier side in their first season in the Football League was a marvellous achievement.

Wycombe line-up: Hyde, Cousins, Crossley, Kerr, Evans, Ryan, Carroll, Hayrettin (Hutchinson), Hemmings (Horton), Scott, Guppy.

8th February 1994: Fulham 2 - Wycombe Wanderers 2 (Decided on penalty shoot-out)

This Autoglass Trophy, Southern semi-final had just about everything, keeping the crowd of 8,733 on their toes throughout over two hours.

It started in startling fashion with Brazil giving Fulham a first-minute lead, with a superb volley from 20 yards. The Cottagers then proceeded to dominate the rest of the first half, their slick passing causing the Blues to chase shadows. To make matters worse two defenders, Terry Evans just before half-time and Duncan Horton during the interval, went off injured. However, the tactical changes caused by their departures paid dividends as the Blues completely reversed the first half. It was their turn to dominate and play some great football. One of the substitutes, Tim Langford, equalised in the 62nd minute when he controlled Paul Hyde's long kick, and slotted the ball past Stannard. After this, Simon Garner, making his debut for the club, and Dave Carroll, both had good chances, while Steve Guppy hit the bar with a cross-shot.

Langford grabbed a glorious second goal three minutes into extra time when he hooked a bouncing ball home from 20 yards. After both sides had seen efforts scrambled off the line, Fulham equalised in the 113th minute when Baah crossed low for Brazil to lash home his second of the match.

Penalty Shoot-Out Thriller

With no further score, it was into the penalty shoot-out. Langford scored from the first, while Hyde saved from Pike. Andy Kerr, Brazil, Carroll and Tierling were then successful, before Simon Stapleton's kick was saved by Stannard. Hyde then matched this when he saved Jupp's effort. This left Jason Cousins with the chance of winning the game. He tucked away his shot comfortably, before being submerged under his joyous teammates.

Wycombe line-up: Hyde, Cousins, Horton (Langford), Crossley, Evans (Kerr), Ryan, Carroll, Thompson, Stapleton, Garner, Guppy.

Injured Terry Evans is surrounded by his joyful team-mates after the game, with two-goal hero Tim Langford at the front
(Photo Paul Dennis).

28th May 1994: Wycombe 4 - Preston North End 2

Play-Off Triumph

Both Wycombe and Preston had let slip an automatic promotion place in the last few weeks of the season, but they served up a feast of football in this Division Three Play-off Final at Wembley before a crowd of 40,109.

The Blues started off at a hectic pace and could have been two up in no time. Steve Thompson twice went close, Steve Guppy missed a great chance, and both Nicky Reid and Simon Garner saw shots blocked during this opening spell. As is often the case, it was Preston who took the lead though when, on the half hour mark, Bryson scored with an overhead kick after a long throw had fooled the Wycombe defence. From the restart Wycombe equalised when Thompson ran onto Garner's pass and slipped the ball past Woods. Within four minutes though Preston were back in front with Ellis crossing for the unmarked Raynor to head home.

Undeterred by this the Blues came out in the second-half and tore Preston apart. Garner equalised after two minutes when he controlled a long ball from David Titterton in expert fashion before firing home. Nine minutes later, a superb flowing move put the Blues in front for the first time. Guppy started the move with a pass to Thompson, he in turn fed Garner, who then laid the ball perfectly into Dave Carroll's path. With the goal at his mercy, the ball was side-footed home. Glyn Greaser then struck the bar with a glancing header before Carroll sealed victory in the 70th minute with a goal to savour for all time. Picking the ball up twenty-five yards out, he jinked his way backwards and forwards across the edge of the area, going past several defenders, before unleashing a left-foot shot that went in off the inside of the post.

Preston staged a late fightback, but Paul Hyde saved well from Ellis and Cartwright shot over.

Emotional scenes greeted the final whistle as Wycombe had clinched promotion in their first season.

Wycombe line-up: Hyde, Cousins, Titterton, Crossley, Creaser, Ryan, Carroll, Thompson, Reid, Garner, Guppy.

Simon Garner fires home Wycombe's second goal. (Photo: Paul Dennis)

'TWO DOZEN OF THE BEST'

CHARLEY HARPER

Go ahead player and secretary, who led the club from junior to senior ranks and from open pitches on the Rye to their own ground, first at Spring Gardens, then at Loakes Park.

He was born in Hereford on 5th December 1862 and played for his home town club and county before moving to High Wycombe in 1880, where he took up a teaching post at Priory Road School. He played for three leading local clubs, Wycombe Alexandra, Wycombe Ramblers and High Wycombe before joining the Wanderers in 1891. At the start of the 1893-94 season he was elected as secretary and captain. Described as a dapper man, slightly balding on top with a waxed moustache stretched to a fine point at both sides, but full of energy and self-confidence, he began to make changes from the start. First of all, he instigated the move away from the Rye, where there was no control over crowds and there was fierce competition for pitches. He urged the club to rent Spring Meadow, where they could take a gate and he could organise prestige friendlies against professional opposition. After a successful first season there, the club decided to adopt senior status and they entered the F.A. Amateur Cup and the Berks & Bucks Senior Cup. This was followed by the move to Loakes Park, entry to the Southern League (which he was surprisingly against) and a first appearance in the F.A. Cup. The latter season coincided with his retirement as a player, although he turned out in an emergency on a few occasions. Although he was essentially a full-back, he could play anywhere and even played several games in goal. He was also a good cricketer and played for High Wycombe C.C. for many years.

In July 1908 he finally resigned as secretary, after twice being persuaded to stay on after two previous attempts to leave, although there was no rift with the club. He had by this time become a school master in London and found it impossible to carry on (travel wasn't easy in those days). He remained in the capital until his death in December 1923, three days after his 61st birthday.

THE BUCHANANS

Four brothers who played for the club at the turn of the century.

The first to appear and the most famous was **Bill** (christened William), a skilful forward who formed a high-scoring left-wing partnership with Fred Abbott at Spring Gardens and the early Loakes Park years. Born in 1875, he made his debut for the Wanderers toward the end of the 1892-93 season, shortly after helping Wycombe Marsh win the Maidenhead Norfolkians' Cup. He continued to play for the club for thirteen years and was a member of the team in the first ever game at Loakes Park on 7th September 1895. Later that same season he scored six times in a 9-1 win over Peckham at Loakes Park. He finished leading scorer, as he had in the two previous seasons. He also led the scoring list in 1899-1900. His highest tally in a season was in 1894-95 when he scored 37 goals.

Bill also captained the side for several seasons, leading them to their first major success in 1901-02, when they won the Berks & Bucks Senior Cup and scoring the first goal in the 3-0 win over Slough at Maidenhead. He was also a regular in the County team. In all he made 386 known appearances and scored 228 goals.

His fame was enhanced in one particular incidence, when Lord George Sanger's Circus came to the town, and he played a game against an elephant, using a gigantic ball! He was presented with a cup for his exhibition. After playing his last game for the club in 1906 he took over the Squirrel public house, at Booker, and turned out frequently for the local cricket club. After three and a half years there he moved to the Half Moon, where he was still residing when he died from bronchitis and pleurisy on 5th April 1918.

There is still a connection with the club today, for great-grandson, Phil Ball helped edit the programme at Loakes Park for five seasons during the 1980's and is still a regular supporter.

Charlie, born in 1878, played one game in 1895-96, a handful the following season (in various positions), before gaining a regular place in 1897-98 at centre-forward, from where he scored 20 goals. After turning down professional terms with Reading at the start of the next campaign, he lost the knack of scoring during the season and was tried at full-back with great success and stayed there for the remainder of his career. He soon gained a reputation as a fearless tackler, although he blotted his copy-book when he became the first Wycombe player to be sent off during a Southern League match at home to Shepherd's Bush in October 1900. It was only by a matter of minutes though, for Archie Green was also dismissed later in the game! Charlie was suspended for two weeks for his indiscretion.

He played his last game in March 1908 after 248 appearances and 30 goals, although he missed the Berks & Bucks Senior Cup success in 1902 through injury. He also represented the County on several occasions. Employed in the furniture trade, where he was held in high esteem, he enlisted during the early months of the First World War and was killed in action in France in July 1918.

Albert, born in 1879, is the least known of the brothers. He played just two matches in the first team, one at Wolverton in February, 1899 and the other at home to Grays a year later, although he was a regular in the reserves for several seasons. Also played for Wycombe Generals and Wycombe Alexandra. Troubled by an eye complaint for some time, he was almost blind when he died after a long illness on 6th October 1911, aged just 32.

George was born in 1884 and played for West End Rovers before joining Wycombe. He played regularly for the reserves before making his first team debut in a 1-0 defeat at Fulham in March 1905 in the Southern League. Gained a regular place two seasons later at left-half, forming a formidable half-back line with Harry Gates and Bernard Hooper. Featured in the Berks & Bucks Senior Cup successes of 1909 and 1910, scoring twice in the latter game from the inside-left position. He surprisingly retired at the end of the following season (1910/11) after 160 appearances and 23 goals, despite the fact that he had been elected as captain for the following campaign. Like Bill and Charlie, he represented the County (the only case of three brothers from the Wanderers to do so). Was also an accomplished cricketer with Marsh Green.

A member of the Bucks and Oxford Light Infantry, he joined the First World War at the start. He was killed in action at the Front on 22nd July 1917, one year before Charlie's death.

BERNARD HOOPER

Long-serving player and secretary and main instigator of the club's move into the Isthmian League.

Born c.1884 as Bernard Charles, but known throughout his career as Bunny, he came to live in High Wycombe when nine years old and quickly took to watching the Wanderers play. He first came to prominence as a player with the Royal Grammar School and actually played his first game for Wycombe Reserves whilst still there, aged just 14. On leaving school he played for Wycombe St. Johns before joining Wycombe on a permanent basis, making his first team debut in September 1900 at the age of 16, one of the club's youngest ever players. Although he played in several positions, it was at centre-half that he gained a regular place the following season, during which he gained a Berks & Bucks Senior Cup winners' medal and made his first appearance for the county.

A natural leader, he was elected captain in 1903 at just 18 (the club's youngest ever), a position he held for several seasons, during which time the club won the Berks & Bucks Senior Cup on three more occasions. When J.N.F. Vale retired as secretary in 1910, Bunny duly took on that post as well. He was also secretary of Wycombe Lawn Tennis Club. He carried on playing until 1919, when he made his last appearance in a pre-season friendly. In all he played 390 games for the club, scoring 33 goals. He also represented Wycombe on the council of the Great Western Suburban League and then saw the side enter the Spartan League. After two successive championships he pleaded with the committee to put in an application to join the Isthmian League. They did so and the club was duly elected. He continued as secretary until leaving the town to live in Bedford in 1925. He was made a life member of the club for his services over the years.

FRANK ADAMS

Player, administrator and patron, whose affiliation with the club lasted seventy years.

He was born in Downley on 5th September 1891 and left school at the age of 12 to become an apprentice photographer. Because he had to work on Saturdays, he started his football career in the local Wednesday League. However, a change of employment saw him have weekends free and he was invited for a trial at Loakes Park during the 1910-11 season and, after making an impression in the reserves, made his first team debut at Maidenhead in the last Great Western Suburban League fixture of the season. Playing at inside-left he helped Wycombe to a 3-2 win. The following season saw him gain a regular place, mainly at inside-right. He then left to join Shepherd's Bush of the Isthmian League at the start of the 1912-13 season, but had returned to the club before the end of that campaign. The following season he was elected captain, a position he kept until his retirement in 1929. He also made a successful switch to centre-half when football restarted after the First World War, although he was at home in almost any position. He featured in two Spartan League championships, three Berks & Bucks Senior Cup wins, as well as in Maidenhead and Oxford Hospital Cup wins. In all he scored 104 goals in 331 appearances. His representative

He was a sportsman in the true sense of the word and this is summed up by an incident in a Berks & Bucks Senior Cup game against Aylesbury at Loakes Park in 1921. A Wycombe shot appeared to have gone over the line, and an Aylesbury defender caught the ball and kicked it back to the centre circle thinking a goal had been scored. However, the referee hadn't blown (he was unsighted) and had no choice but to award a penalty. Frank took the kick and deliberately shot wide!

He was also a good administrator and served on Wycombe's committee after his retirement, as well as organising football overseas for the forces in both wars. In 1947 he was elected to the Football Association and served on several committees, including the International committee.

Frank - in his playing days....

He had also been a sound businessmen with a photography and sports outfitters' shop in Oxford Road. At the close of the Second World War he began negotiations with Lord Carrington to purchase the freehold at Loakes Park. Two years later, having acquired this, he gifted the ground to the Wanderers and the deeds were formally presented on 19th April 1947 before the Isthmian League match with Corinthian Casuals. In his speech he declared, *"If future generations obtain the same enjoyment out of Loakes Park as it has given me, then this gift will have been worthwhile"*. The club immediately responded by making Frank their patron, a position he held until his death in 1981, shortly after his 90th birthday. He was succeeded by his son, Jack, who is still patron to this day. He will always be remembered by virtue of the present ground being named in his honour.

.... and as Club Patron.

REG BOREHAM

Prolific goalscorer of the early twenties and the club's first international.

Born in High Wycombe on 27th May, 1896 and christened Reginald Walter, he first played football for Wycombe All Saints in the Wycombe Junior League and was with them at the outbreak of war. During the War he served in India and played for his regiment and garrison. On his return to these shores in 1919 he signed for the Wanderers and made his debut in December in the 7-1 Spartan League win over 2nd Coldstream Guards at Loakes Park. Although he didn't score, he made up for it in the remainder of the season by netting 22 goals in 16 games from the centre-forward position, and helping the club to the League championship. This drew the attention of Football League clubs and, at the start of the following season, he signed amateur forms for Notts County. He found the travelling a bugbear though and after just three appearances returned to Loakes Park, where he again helped Wycombe to the Spartan League championship, finishing the season as leading scorer with 42 goals. He also became the club's first international when he played for the England Amateur side against Ireland on 14th November, 1921. A month later he signed for Arsenal (still an amateur) and played a big part in the Gunners' successful battle to avoid relegation. He played regularly for the Gunners, scoring 18 goals in 51 appearances, before returning to Wycombe during the 1923-24 season. Whilst at Highbury he gained a second international cap against Wales in January 1922 and also played for the F.A. XI several times, captaining them on one occasion against Oxford University. He was also in the Arsenal team that won the London Challenge Cup.

At Wycombe, apart from the Spartan League successes, he was also in two Berks & Bucks Senior Cup winning sides. He played for the County team, and was part of their 1924 Southern Counties championship success as well as representing the Spartan and Isthmian Leagues. In all he made 157 appearances for the Blues and scored 141 goals. During the 1926-27 season, he left to join Maidenhead, along with his brother Edgar who had also played for Wycombe the previous season. Surprisingly, he retired at the end of that season. He was also a keen cricketer and played in the Wycombe & District League for Church Room C.C. for over twenty years.

In 1936 he returned to Wycombe as secretary, a post he held for thirteen years. He continued to follow Wycombe's fortunes until ill heath prevented him from going to games in the early seventies. He died after a long illness in January 1976, aged 79.

ALF BRITNELL

Long-serving winger and scorer of the F.A. Amateur Cup winning goal in 1931.

He was born at Wheeler End on 19th May, 1907 and played for West Wycombe Minors and Lane End before joining Wycombe in 1928. After just two games in the reserves he made his debut at outside-left in the 6-2 Isthmian League defeat at Ilford on 3rd November. Despite the result, he kept his place (and position) for the rest of the season, and for the rest of his career, despite the fact he had actually joined the club as a centre-forward. When he finally retired, after playing in a handful of games in Wycombe's Great Western Combination winning side of 1944-45, he had made 427 appearances and scored 74 goals.

His greatest moment, of course, was that winning goal in the 1931 Amateur Cup Final. He had also scored twice in the semi-final win over Woking. This was the first medal that he won, but not his last for he appeared in eight Berks & Bucks Senior Cup Finals alone.

At the end of the 1930-31 season he toured Holland with Middlesex Wanderers and also represented the F.A., the Isthmian League and the Berks & Bucks F.A. (both at senior and junior level). After his last game for the club he joined Ernest Turners as coach, and under his guidance they won several honours in local football, until his retirement in 1956; he also played cricket for them. Alf kept in touch with Wycombe as a spectator until his death in 1984.

JOCK McCALLUM

One of Wycombe's most prolific goalscorers, he was born William McCallum on 9th September, 1913 in Coatbridge, Scotland. He played junior football in the Ayrshire League, before moving to High Wycombe in search of work in 1934 due to the depression. Once settled, he joined Bledlow Ridge in the Wycombe Combination, scoring four goals during the first half of his debut game. Word soon spread of his prowess and Wycombe sent a scout to watch him before signing him during the 1934-35 season. He made his debut in the latter part of the following season in the 6-3 Isthmian League win over Nunhead at Loakes Park. Playing at inside-right he scored a hat-trick. Despite such a start, he never gained a regular place and was released at the end of the 1936-37 season and joined Holmer Green. However, he returned to the club during the 1938-39 season.

Due to perforating an eardrum during his National Service in the Royal Navy, Jock wasn't accepted for active duty when the Second World War began, so he continued to play for the Blues, captaining the side and helping to run things with secretary Reg Boreham. Under his leadership, the Great Western Combination was won (in 1944-45), as well as the Berks & Bucks Senior and

Benevolent Cups. He continued to play into his late thirties and featured in the Amateur Cup run of 1949-50, when the team reached the semi-final. In all he played 348 games and scored 224 goals, finishing leading scorer on four occasions, with his best season being 1945-46 when he scored 37 times.

With the introduction of a lot of young players at the start of the 1951-52 season, Jock became surplus to requirements and left to join Aylesbury. Ironically the Ducks were drawn at Wycombe in the F.A. Cup that season and Jock had the satisfaction of scoring the winning goal in his new club's 2-1 win. He finally retired in 1954 at the age of 41 after playing in the same line-up with his son John. Amazingly throughout his career at Loakes Park his surname was spelt incorrectly as 'McCullum'!

He still lives locally, not far from Adams Park, and is often seen at matches there.

Jock McCallum scores one of the goals in the Amateur Cup win over St.Albans, before Loakes Park's record crowd.

JOCK SHEPPARD

Player, trainer, groundsman, spectator, Jock was involved in everything.

Christened Ronald George and born in Glasgow on 12th July, 1918, he moved south at the age of 10 and lived at Wooburn Green, where he stayed for the rest of his life. He played for Loudwater in the thirties before serving in the Army as a P.T. instructor for four years, during which time he captained his battalion football team.

He joined Wycombe after the Second World War as a wing-half and made his debut in the 9-1 home win over Wolverton Town in the Berks & Bucks Benevolent Cup in February 1946. Although he stayed at the club for four seasons, his first team appearances were limited to just 8. He was however, a member of the reserves' championship winning side of 1946-47 (the first Isthmian League title won by the club). After leaving Wycombe he played for Maidenhead, Chesham and Flackwell Heath before coming back to Loakes Park in 1958 as trainer. In this capacity he served under nine different managers.

When Brian Lee became manager in December 1968, Wycombe did not have a full-time groundsman. Jock gave up his job as a french polisher to take this on, whilst doubling up as team attendant. He was great for team spirit, having a wonderful sense of humour and an infectious laugh. He also acted as trainer for the Amateur F.A. XI, the Isthmian League representative team and Bucks County rugby team, before retiring in 1982. The club held a testimonial match for him in April 1984 when two teams of ex-players turned out. He remained a regular supporter, both home and away, and his voice could often be heard in the stands at both grounds. He died after a long illness in December 1993.

SID CANN

Innovative coach of Wycombe's successful sides of the 1950's.

Born Sidney Thomas Cann on 30th October, 1911 in Torquay and educated at Babbacombe School, he won two England Schoolboys caps before signing professional with Torquay United in November 1928. He made 44 appearances (3 goals) at full-back before joining Manchester City in March 1930. He stayed there for five years, although only making 42 appearances. However, one of these was in the 1933 F.A. Cup Final, when City lost to Everton at Wembley. In the summer of 1935 he joined Charlton Athletic for £400, but again his appearances were limited, a total of 85 in eleven years, one in the Football League South Cup Final of 1943 (against Arsenal).

Just before the War he qualified as a physiotherapist and when he left Charlton to join Southampton in May 1946, it was as reserve team trainer and masseur. In 1949 he was promoted to secretary-manager and was the first to introduce floodlights for training as well as being in charge of the first floodlit game at The Dell in 1950. He also became F.A. coach for Hampshire, a F.A. examiner of coaches and a qualified referee! He stood down as manager in 1951, but stayed on as secretary until joining Wycombe as coach on 7th July 1952.

There then began one of the most successful periods in the club's history and before he left to join Norwich as coach in 1961, Wycombe had won two Isthmian League championships and had finished runners-up twice. They reached the Amateur Cup Final in 1957, the semi-final in 1955, won the Berks & Bucks Senior Cup three times and had been runners-up twice. He also toured with the England Youth squad and was even called on to give special tuition to Prince Charles at Cheam School!

His successes didn't stop there though. After just a year at Norwich, he went to Sutton and, in his first season, took them to Wembley in the Amateur Cup final where they lost 4-2 to Wimbledon. Another Wembley visit followed six years later, when the team lost to North Shields, while in 1966-67 they won the Isthmian League Championship. There was also the F.A. Cup run of 1969-70, when Sutton reached the 4th Round, losing to mighty Leeds United.

He retired in 1972 and has lived in Surrey ever since. Sadly, at the time of writing, he is seriously ill in hospital.

PAUL BATES

Centre-forward in Wycombe's successful sides of the 1950's and scorer of over 300 goals.

Paul was born in High Wycombe on 10th March 1935 and attended Green Street and Mill End schools, where he first showed his football skills. His first appearance at Loakes Park was for the latter in the Thurlow Cup final of 1949/50. He first came to Wycombe's notice while playing for Castlefield Minors, with whom he won an England Youth Cap v. Wales in 1952.

He signed for the Blues at the start of the 1953/54 season and scored twice on his debut for the reserves. He not only finished that season as leading scorer for the second string with 45 goals, but also made his first team debut in the Amateur Cup match at Leytonstone on January 30th, which finished goalless. The following season he gained a regular place in the first team, originally at outside-left. However, due to a serious injury to centre-forward Malcolm Hunt, he was switched to lead the attack. From them on he never looked back and finished leading scorer for the next six seasons, winning two Isthmian League Championship medals, an Amateur Cup Runners-up medal and two Berks & Bucks Senior Cup winning medals, as well as various other honours.

He scored twice in the famous Amateur Cup semi-final win over Corinthian Casuals at Highbury, despite playing with blistered feet! He was also capped twice by the England Amateur side, against Iceland in Reykjavik (1956) and Finland at Dulwich (1958), while appearing regularly for the county and Isthmian League sides.

At the end of the 1960/61 season he left to join Tooting & Mitcham United, but by November, he was back at Loakes Park. However, when the season finished he was on the move again and joined Hendon for a short spell before going onto Sutton United, for whom he appeared in the 1963 Amateur Cup final defeat against Wimbledon. He returned to Wycombe once more in October 1964, scoring in a 3-1 home defeat against St. Albans in his first game back. He soon found his old goalscoring ability and finished leading scorer in 1965/66 with 45 goals, his best ever tally for the first team. He played his last game in October 1967 after 416 appearances and 309 goals, including five in a game twice. He continued to play for, and also manage, the reserves until their disbandment in 1969, when he joined Chesham United. After that, he managed Aylesbury United for a short while and then Ernest Turners until they folded in 1974.

Since his retirement his main interest in football has been Aston Villa and he goes to watch them as often as possible. He was also a fine cricketer and played for many years for Ernest Turners and Bledlow Ridge.

Both his father, Harry and an uncle, Jack, played for the Blues in the 1920's. Harry was later a committee man for several years and a life member of the club.

LEN WORLEY

The "Stanley Matthews" of Amateur football. Just like his idol, Len was a right-winger who dribbled round defenders and delivered deadly crosses.

He was born at Chalfont St. Peter on 29th June 1937 and played for Chalfont Youth Club before joining Chalfont St. Peter when aged sixteen. At the end of the 1953/54 season he played in a friendly against Wycombe and made such an impression on coach Sid Cann, that he promptly signed Len for the following season. After just four reserve outings he came into the first team for the F.A. Cup game at Slough Centre on 25th September 1954. He held his place for the rest of the season and helped the team reach the Amateur Cup semi-final, which they lost 1-0 to Bishop Auckland at Doncaster. Two Isthmian League Championships followed and then the Amateur Cup run of 1956/57, which culminated in another defeat at the hands of the Bishops in the Wembley final. He scored twice in the action packed semi-final at Highbury against Corinthian Casuals.

To cap a memorable season he played twice for his country in Amateur Internationals against Wales (at Peterborough) and against Scotland (at Hampden Park). Unfortunately the campaign ended on a sour note when he broke his leg on 30th April playing for the Army at Woolwich. On his recovery from this injury during the following season he signed Amateur forms for Charlton Athletic and played once for them in Division One before returning to Loakes Park.

At the start of the 1959/60 season he once more featured in Division One (still as an amateur), this time for Tottenham, who tried to persuade him to sign on professional terms. He declined and again returned to Wycombe, where he continued to be a permanent fixture for the next ten years. He took his international appearances to seven, played for the Great Britain Olympic Team, Middlesex Wanderers, F.A. XI's, the Isthmian League, and the County side. He also broke his leg again, in January 1967, during an Isthmian League match at St. Albans, but had recovered by the time the return match was played at Loakes Park in May.

With the changing tactics of the late 60's, an out and out winger became surplus to requirements, and Len played his last game for the club when he came on as substitute in the Amateur Cup game at Croydon on 13th December 1969. In all he played 512 games and scored 67 goals. He joined Chesham shortly after, and continued playing for Wealdstone, Slough, and Hayes plus Sunday League football for Chalfont, before calling it a day in the mid-seventies.

Always supremely fit, he also played a lot of tennis. A successful businessman in property development and sports retail, he still lives in the area of his birth, at Chalfont St. Giles, and is a frequent visitor to Adams Park.

TONY HORSEMAN

Loakes Park legend who has made the most appearances (749) for the club and also scored the most goals (416).

Born at 13, Underwood Road, on 12th May 1941, he played football as a youngster on the sloping field behind the Morning Star pub, which obviously stood him in good stead for his career at Loakes Park! He played minor football for East End, then had two seasons with Wallaby Sports before signing for Wycombe in 1961.

He made his debut at Oxford City on 23rd October of that year and scored in the 3-2 Isthmian League defeat. He kept his place for the rest of the season, mainly on the left wing, before moving to inside forward the following season. He finished leading scorer with 20 goals, including all five in the Isthmian League win over Clapton at Loakes Park. He kept a regular place in the team for the next fourteen seasons, finishing leading scorer in half of them, and broke the club's scoring record with 60 goals in 1966-67 (in all games played he actually scored about 90 times). Despite being on the small side for a striker at 5ft 8ins, he was good in the air and was deadly in the six yard box.

At the start of the 1976-77 season, Wycombe signed Ian Pearson and Tony found his appearances limited that season, but, on Pearson's departure to Millwall, he once more gained a regular place the following season, which was to be his last at Loakes Park, when he scored 13 goals.

In his time at Wycombe, the Blues won four Isthmian League Championships and were runners-up twice. There was an Amateur Cup semi-final appearance in 1972, several memorable F.A. Cup runs, as well as Berks & Bucks Senior Cup and other honours. He also actually retired three times, in 1964, 1969 and 1972, but never stayed out of the game for long and quickly returned to the side each time. He gained personal honours with various F.A. XI's, Isthmian League and the County, but, unbelievably was never selected for his Country! The nearest he came to an international honour was 45 minutes for the Great Britain Olympic team against Germany in November 1967.

On finishing with Wycombe, he had short spells at Tring and Flackwell Heath to help out old team mates John Delaney and Ian Rundle, who were the respective managers.

Nicknamed "Bodger", because of his employment in the furniture trade, he works as a sander for the club's sponsor Verco and still lives locally at Downley. Although he doesn't attend matches at Adams Park, he does visit the club for lunch and some of the sportsmens' dinners.

In typical action, Tony rounding the keeper....... to score one of his many goals.

JOHN MASKELL

Longest serving and arguably the finest goalkeeper in the club's history.

Born at Oxford on 1st May 1943 he played for Eynsham's senior team when just 15. He then signed for Headington United, playing for their youth and reserve teams, before joining Oxford City, ironically making his first team debut against Wycombe. After a year and a half at the White House Ground, he signed for Wycombe at the start of the 1964/65 season and made his debut in the opening League fixture on 22nd August (a 1-1 draw with Kingstonian at Loakes Park). Inside two months though he had broken his leg in a F.A. Cup game at Hayes. On his return from injury he soon regained his place and held it until 1976/77, when he shared duties with Peter Spittle for two seasons. A few games followed in 1979/80, before the signing of another stalwart Gary Lester. In all he made 616 appearances, a record for a goalkeeper and second only to Tony Horseman for the club.

John shows off the Isthmian League Trophy - end of the 1973/74 season.

A superb all-round 'keeper with terrific reflexes he featured in all of the club's successes of the late 60's - mid 70's period. One of his most momentous games was the F.A. Cup match at Middlesbrough, where he kept the Boro's forward line at bay for ninety minutes. He gained various representative honours for Oxfordshire, Berks & Bucks, F.A. XI's and the Isthmian League, but never received an International call-up, although he did turn down an opportunity to tour Scandinavia one year with the England squad.

In 1980 he was appointed manager for the reserve team and was responsible for introducing some good players to the club, Anton Vircavs being a fine example. He then left to take over as manager of his old club, Oxford City, before returning to Loakes Park in January 1986 as assistant to Alan Gane. His spell this time was just a short one and he left at the end of the season. Since then he has helped out at Abingdon Town and Witney as goalkeeping coach before a hip replacement operation forced him to retire. However, he has since been persuaded to help out at his son's local Sunday team as manager. Lives at Toot Boldon, a small village near Oxford.

BRIAN LEE

Wycombe's first manager, in the true sense of the word, who was in charge of the successful 1970's team.

Born in Sale, Cheshire, in 1936, Brian was a good all round sportsman at school. He played for his district at football and, when he later attended Sale Grammar School, he captained the school's rugby team and represented the county. On leaving school he joined Altrincham before going on to Port Vale. However, before he had a chance of playing in the Football League, he broke a toe which turned arthritic and was advised by doctors to give up the game. He then decided to take up coaching and, after passing the Preliminary Coaching Award, was appointed the youngest F.A. Staff Coach in the country at the age of 18.

He then took up teaching as a career and had reached the position of deputy headmaster of Holt School, Norfolk, when he left the profession to become Assistant Warden at Lilleshall in 1960. He was later coach with the England Youth Team and was involved in the administration of the 1966 World Cup, as well as playing for and managing Wellington Town (now Telford United).

In 1967 he was appointed Director of Bisham Abbey and also coach to Oxford University. In December 1968 he was appointed manager of Wycombe after Barry Darvill's resignation. When he retired in 1976 to concentrate on the development of Bisham Abbey as a Centre of Excellence, Wycombe had won the Isthmian League Championship four times, been runners-up twice and had finished fourth twice. They were Amateur Cup semi-finalists in 1972, competed in five Berks & Bucks Senior Cup finals in successive years (including the infamous 1975 one), had beaten two Football League sides in the F.A. Cup, and had won the Anglo-Italian Trophy.

All of this was achieved with good, attacking football and a real sense of sportsmanship. In a four-year spell there were only two bookings! Several of his players went on to Football League careers or became Amateur Internationals (some achieved both). He also took charge of various representative sides and managed the first England semi-Professional team against Italy.

After his retirement as manager he was appointed Vice-chairman of the club and then Founder-Chairman of the Company in 1980. He was instrumental in forming the club into a Limited Company by Guarantee with Jack Adams and the late John Roberts, and recommending for appointment three new directors - Ivor Beeks, Graham Peart and Gordon Richards - who have become the backbone of the club's meteoric rise. The job of overseer for the move to Adams Park was taken, and, after getting the club settled, he reverted to a Board Director and moved into the golf world by taking charge of a complex in Dorset.

He is married with two sons, one of whom, Tim, played for the Blues before moving to America. Brian has also been on the committees of the Norfolk F.A., Shropshire F.A., a founder member of the Isthmian League Management committee, Vice-chairman of the GM Vauxhall Conference and a magistrate in High Wycombe for over twenty years!

JOHN DELANEY

Powerful, goal-scoring centre-half and captain in the early 1970's.

Born in Slough on 3rd February 1942, he started as a goalkeeper and played for the Slough & District schools team before joining Queen's Park Rangers. After failing to make the grade, he then played for two works' teams, Horlicks and Coopers, at centre-half and, after a successful time with the later, joined Slough Town in 1963. In his first season the team won promotion to the Premier Division of the Athenian League. He gained representative honours with the League and with Berks & Bucks before joining Wycombe in the summer of 1969. He was immediately appointed captain and made his debut on 9th August in the opening League fixture, a 5-0 win over Bromley at Loakes Park. Later that season he won the first of his 17 England Amateur International caps, coming on as sub. in Ireland, and then starting the next game in Wales. He also played for Great Britain in the Olympic qualifier in Bulgaria. He went on to lead Wycombe to two successive Isthmian Championships, an Amateur Cup semi-final appearance, plus three Berks & Bucks Senior Cup finals (one won, two lost).

At the end of the 1972/73 season, Wycombe played AFC Bournemouth in a friendly and John obviously made a big impression for he joined the Cherries shortly after. He spent two seasons at Dean Court and came up against the Blues in their F.A. Cup run of 1974/75. He captained Bournemouth in the goalless draw at Loakes Park, but missed the replay through injury.

He returned to Wycombe for the 1975/76 season, then joined Hayes for the next. Spells at Tring Town (as player-manager) and Oxford City (as player and manager) followed, before work commitments at Heathrow Airport made it difficult for him to get to matches and he gave up the game.

As well as being a forceful leader and an excellent stopper, he was a prolific goalscorer for a defender, and scored several important goals from corners as well as being the club's regular penalty-taker. He always seemed to do well against old adversaries Enfield and scored two memorable goals in the Amateur Cup win over them at Loakes Park in 1970/71. The following season he scored a hat-trick at Enfield in the 4-0 Isthmian League win - two penalties and a rebound after the 'keeper had saved a third penalty. He actually scored 19 goals in the 1970/71 season and 65 altogether in 228 appearances, a record that some modern strikers would be happy with.

Now a grandfather after 35 years of marriage to Carole, he lives at Holmer Green and often frequents the Queens Head at Hazlemere, where an old adversary from his Cooper's playing day, John Harvey, is landlord.

KEITH SEARLE

Talented striker of the 1970's who formed a dynamic partnership with Tony Horseman.

Keith was born in Hammersmith, West London, on 20th September 1947, and then moved to Harrow, where he went to Blackwell Secondary Modern School. Represented his school at all sports before being selected for Middlesex County Youth F.A. in 1964. Joined Wealdstone in 1965 after a successful trial and played for them for two seasons before joining Barnet. He stayed there for a season before returning to Wealdstone, and came to Loakes Park in 1969. He made his debut on 11th October in a 3-0 win over Walthamstow Avenue at Loakes Park, marking his first appearance with a goal after 24 minutes; he finished the season with 17. He then became leading scorer for the next three seasons, despite leaving the club twice for short spells. He scored the goal that clinched the 1970/71 Isthmian League championship at Oxford City, but shocked everyone by joining Hayes during the close season. However, within two weeks of the new season starting he was back in Wycombe's colours and delighted the crowd by scoring in his first game back, a 4-1 home win over St. Albans. Later that season he scored the only goal of the game against Hayes in the 4th Round Amateur Cup tie at Loakes Park, which put the Blues into the semi-final.

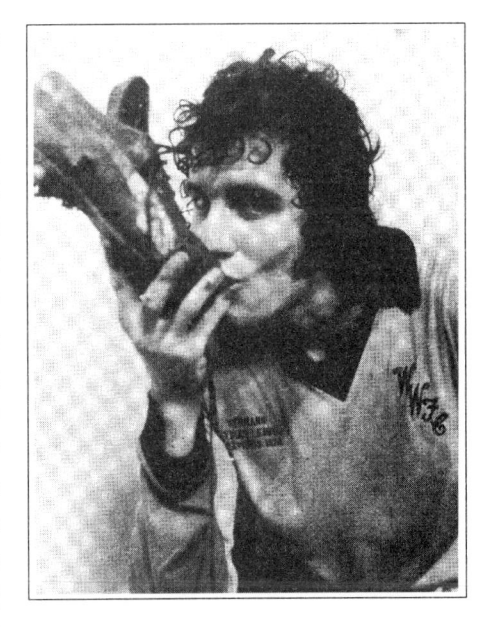

His next move was in November 1972 when he joined Hendon. Again it wasn't long before he was back at Loakes Park, in March, and he still finished top goalscorer! The following season saw him sustain a bad injury at Walthamstow, in a game made famous by Dylan Evans scoring all four goals in the 4-0 win. He unfortunately missed out on the F.A. Cup triumph over Newport and was out for five months, but came back in April to play an important part in Wycombe's third Championship success in four years. This was extended to four in five the next season and Keith again grabbed the decisive goal, five minutes from the end, as Wycombe beat Dagenham 1-0. In the run-in to the championship he scored three hat-tricks inside 17 days against Bromley (home and away) and Barking. He of course also featured in the memorable F.A. Cup run of that season.

At the end of the season he was off on his travels again and joined Enfield. Amazingly, in his first two seasons there they won the League title. So he then had six championship successes in seven seasons.

During his career at Wycombe he made 249 appearances and scored 124 goals, which included 101 League goals in 196 appearances. He won various representative honours with Middlesex, London, and Berks & Bucks, as well as F.A. XI's. He also made one appearance for the England Amateur side when he came on as substitute in the UEFA competition match against West Germany at Wembley in October 1973. He scored the only goal of the game 15 minutes from the end. His injury and the abolition of the Amateur game at the end of the season curtailed his International career, although he did feature in the England semi-Professional squad without winning a cap.

He played for Enfield until 1979, when work commitments caused him to retire, although he was persuaded to play for Oxford City for a spell in 1984, when he played in a Hitachi Cup game at Loakes Park. He again came out of retirement in 1987 to play centre-half for Shenley & Loughton and then Emberton, before finally calling it a day in 1992 at the age of 45. He joined Buckingham Town, for whom his son Steve played, as assistant manager for the 1993/94 season before work commitments again caused him to quit.

Lives and works in Milton Keynes.

LARRY PRITCHARD

Wycombe's most capped player and gifted midfielder from the 1970's.

Born in Epsom on 25th November 1944, he began his career at his local club, Epsom and Ewell, as a 15 year old. From Epsom he went on to Walton & Hersham and Leatherhead, before joining Sutton United in 1965. For two seasons he was leading scorer before moving into midfield. During this first spell at Gander Green Lane he won his first England Amateur International cap, in Austria, won his first Isthmian League Championship, and played in the 1969 Amateur Cup Final, as well as the famous F.A. Cup game against Leeds.

He joined Wycombe in the summer of 1970, making his debut when he came on as substitute in the 3-2 home win over Walthamstow Avenue on 15th August. He then played his first full game in the next match at Wealdstone and scored twice in a superb 6-1 win. Was a key figure in the Blues' midfield for the next four seasons making 199 appearances and scoring 57 goals, including all four in a 4-0 win at Woking in the 1971/72 season. Featured in three Isthmian League championships and the F.A. Cup run of 1973/74, but missed out on the Amateur Cup semi-final in 1972 after sustaining an injury at Walton & Hersham in a bruising third round battle. Won several representative honours during his stay, the highlight being his 26 England caps to add to 22 whilst at Sutton.

Rejoined Sutton in 1974/75 and carried on playing until 1985, bringing his total of appearances for them to 781 (a club record).

He was appointed assistant to manager Barrie Williams in 1980 (his testimonial year) and played in the 1981 F.A. Trophy Final when Williams moved 'upstairs' and then left in 1986 to manage Walton. He left them in 1989 and then came out of retirement a year later to play for Redhill in the Sussex County League, aged 45! Returned to Sutton, yet again, as manager in 1994/95 but has since left (again!).

Still lives in the Epsom area.

MARK WEST

Local legend, who played an integral part in the club's rise to the top of non-League football.

Born in High Wycombe on 12th February 1966, he first made his name as a prolific scorer in the successful High Wycombe Schools' team of 1981. He scored the only goal of the two-legged final against Sunderland. He also won four Schoolboy International caps for England and scored a wonderful goal against West Germany at Wembley. He then joined West Ham, where he played in their youth and reserve teams, before being released after three years. Trained with Reading for a while, then played locally for Stokenchurch, before joining Wycombe in December 1984. After making an impression in the reserves, he made his first team debut when he came on as substitute in the 1-0 home win over Hayes in the Isthmian League on 5th February 1985. Continued in the squad for the remainder of the season, helping the club gain promotion to the Gola League and scoring one of the goals as they defeated Farnborough 5-1 on aggregate to win the Hitachi Cup Final. From then on he was a regular, but, until Simon Read's departure, it was as a wide player. Scored one of the goals in the defeat of Colchester during the F.A. Cup run of 1985/86, but tasted disappointment at the season's end when the club were relegated for the first time in their history.

With Read's departure, he played as a central striker with immediate effect, and finished the next season as leading scorer as the club broke all records by running away with the Vauxhall Opel League Championship. He was also top goalscorer for the next four seasons, and was voted player of the year in 1987/88. He reached his peak in the inaugural season at Adams Park with 38 goals, including four in a game twice, once in a great 5-1 win over previously unbeaten Kettering at Adams Park, and all four in the 4-1 home win over Sutton. His crowning glory though came later that season when he scored the winning goal in the F.A. Trophy Final triumph over Kidderminster at Wembley. He was voted The Mail on Sunday Conference Player of the Season and chosen as the Non-League Directory's Semi-Professional Footballer of the Year, as well as being included in the Conference Team of the Year, and being voted Wycombe's Player of the Year for the second time. It didn't stop there! He won an England semi-Professional cap against Wales at Stafford on 17th May and scored on his debut for Middlesex Wanderers a few days later at Adams Park.

Sadly, he never produced this form again and then a back and a foot injury (plus illness) limited his appearances in the latter part of 1991/92, and throughout the following double season, of 1992/93. He was granted a Testimonial, and Wycombe played Portsmouth at the beginning of their first Football League season. Unfortunately he never featured in League action and was loaned out to Kidderminster, only to break his leg in his first game. He recovered from this and went out on loan to Yeovil before finishing the season on a high note when he was a member of the Wycombe squad that won the London 5-a-side championship. He was released at the end of the season and joined Slough, where he has finished leading scorer for the last two seasons.

Altogether for the Blues he made 381 appearances and scored 171 goals, including 99 in the GM Vauxhall Conference. Newport's demise in 1988/89 and the subsequent deleting of the two results robbed him of his 100th, which he eventually achieved at Yeovil.

DAVE CARROLL

Good all-round midfielder who has been a permanent fixture in the Wycombe line-up for eight years.

Born in Paisley, Scotland on 20th September 1966, he moved to London at an early age and started his career at Fulham, where he won three England Youth caps, before joining Wembley and then Ruislip Manor. Impressed in Wycombe's friendly against a Swedish side, FBK Karlstad, in April 1988, he played in the Capital League President's Cup Final against Brentford a month later, and then signed in the summer for £6,000. Made his debut in the opening GM Vauxhall Conference fixture of the 1988/89 season, a 1-1 draw at Yeovil, and has been first choice ever since under three different managers.

His play on the right flank was a perfect foil to that of Steve Guppy's on the left, giving Wycombe a deadly two-wing attack in their successes of the last five years.

(Photo: Paul Dennis)

Has the ability to go past several defenders at a time and has scored some spectacular goals in this way, as Welling, Merthyr, Preston (in that never-to-be-forgotten match at Wembley) and Stockport will testify. His skills are not confined to attack though and he is often seen as the last line of defence with timely and important clearances.

During his non-League career, he represented the F.A. XI and Middlesex Wanderers but was prevented from playing for the England Semi-Professional side (despite being selected) by virtue of his Scottish birth place.

Stands in eleventh place in the club's all-time appearances chart with 391 (76 goals) which includes 128 out of a possible 134 in the Football League. Was ever-present in 1995/96, a record which deservedly won him Player of the Year awards from three different sources.

STEVE GUPPY

Exciting winger who played a big part in the club's rise to the Football League.

Born in Winchester on 29th March 1969, he served an apprenticeship at Southampton before being released towards the end of the 1988/89 season. Played a few games in Wycombe's Capital League side before signing the following season after turning down an offer from Exeter City. Made his debut away to Welling United on 6th September 1989 in a 0-0 GM Vauxhall Conference fixture when he came on as substitute. By the end of the season he had gained a regular place and from there went on to play an integral part in Wycombe's rapid rise to Division Two status.

Although a winger in the old fashioned sense, he could defend as well and Martin O'Neill often described him as the best left-back at the club. Scored one of the best goals ever seen at Adams Park when he finished a 70 yard run with a chip over the 'keeper in Wycombe's 5-1 win over Runcorn, which virtually sealed the Conference Championship in 1993. This was a great season for Steve as he was voted the Conference Player of the Year and selected in the Conference Team of the Year. He also made his debut for the England Semi-Professional team in their 2-1 win over Wales at Cheltenham. Additionally he was voted man of the match on eight occasions at Adams Park during the season.

(Photo: Brian Southam)

When Wycombe won promotion to the Football League, Steve created history by scoring the first ever League goal by a Wycombe player, in the 2-2 draw at Carlisle (the first was an own goal). He went on to score a creditable eight League goals and help secure promotion first time round for the Blues. Before the start of the next season though he signed for Newcastle for £150,000, but, after making just one substitute appearance for the Magpies, he left to join Port Vale three months later in a deal worth £225,000. Has settled in well at Vale Park and earned some good reviews during the 1995/96 season. During his career at Wycombe he made 253 appearances and scored 37 goals.

MARTIN O'NEILL

Charismatic manager of Wycombe's most successful spell in their history, taking them from mid-table in the GM Vauxhall Conference to sixth place in the Football League Division Two in the space of five years, plus three successful visits to Wembley.

Born in Kilrea, County Derry in Northern Ireland on 1st March 1952, he started his playing career with Derry City before signing for Nottingham Forest in 1971. he enjoyed a successful ten year spell at the City Ground, winning League championship, European Cup and League Cup medals. He then went on to play for Norwich (two spells), Manchester City and Notts County before a knee injury ended his career in 1985. In all he played 428 Football League games and scored 66 goals. He also won 64 caps (8 goals) for Northern Ireland and was captain when they reached the Quarter-Finals of the 1982 World Cup in Spain. He received the MBE shortly after for his services to football.

He then turned to management with Grantham and Shepshed Charterhouse before retiring to concentrate on business commitments.

Martin proudly displays the F.A.Trophy after the 1993 win.
(Photo: Paul Dennis)

A chance meeting with Alan Perry then brought about his surprise appointment at Wycombe in February 1990, following the resignation of Jim Kelman. His first game in charge was at Merthyr Tydfil, where, on a soaking wet afternoon, the Blues grabbed a 1-1 draw in the GM Vauxhall Conference. Two months later he had won his first trophy as the Blues defeated Slough 2-1 at Hungerford in the final of the Berks & Bucks Senior Cup. The rest, of course, is history.

A highly emotional man, who always got the best out of his players, he often let his heart rule his head, especially when he elected to stay at Wycombe when the managers' seat was on offer at Bristol Rovers, Nottingham Forest and Leicester.

Eventually though he succumbed and accepted the post at Norwich in June 1995. His stay was shortlived though, and he was soon on his way to Leicester where he successfully guided them through the play-offs into the Premiership.

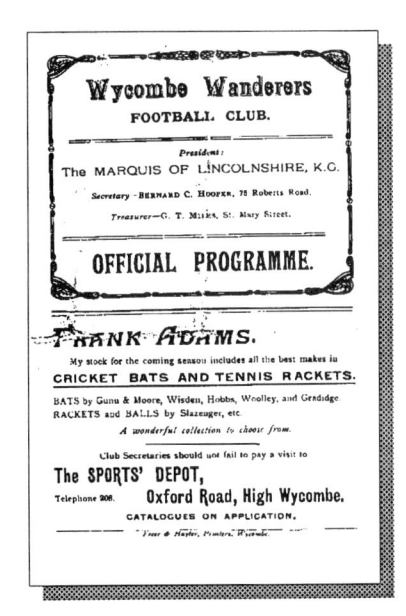

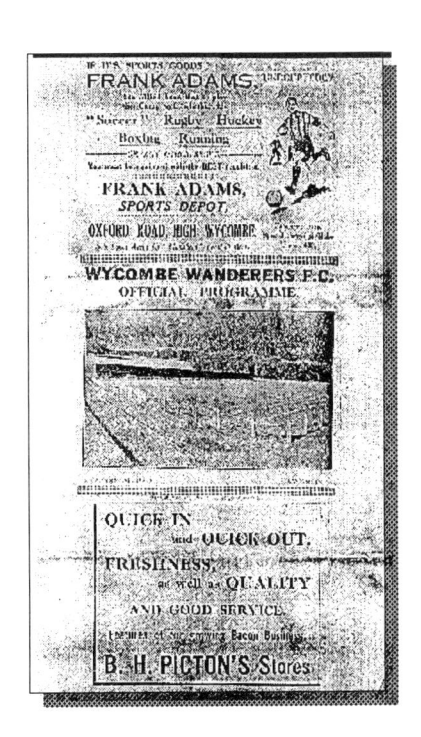

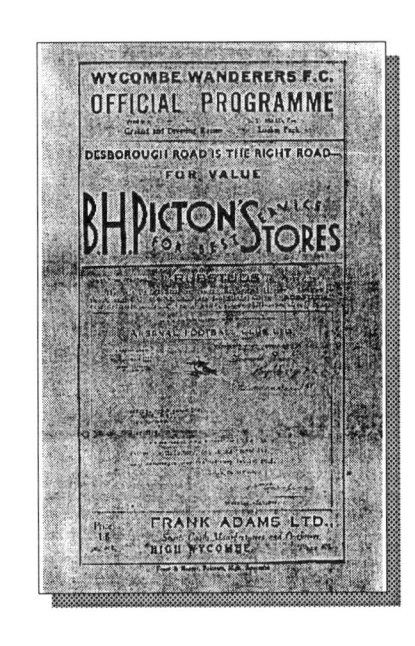

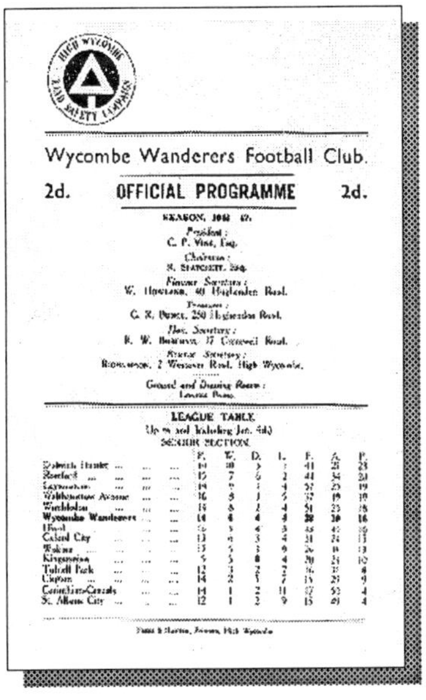

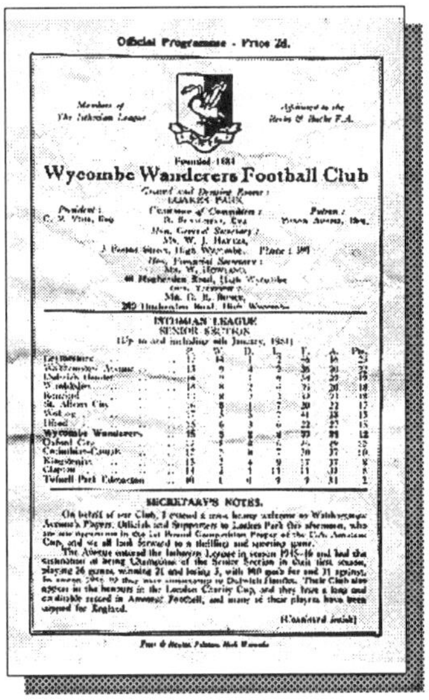

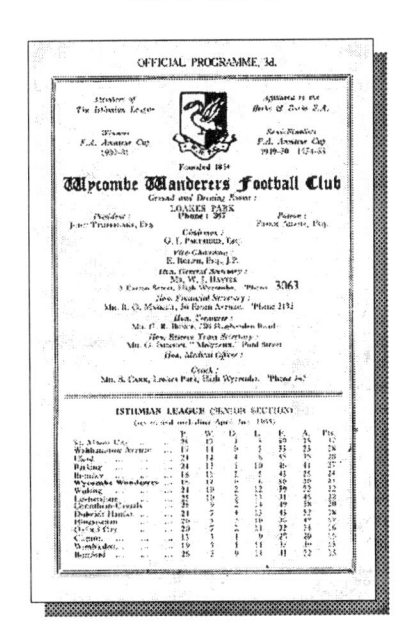

1928/29

1954/55

1920/21

1936/37

1946/47

1950/51

PROGRAMME PARADE

(Covers reproduced, with thanks, from Alan Hutchinson collection)

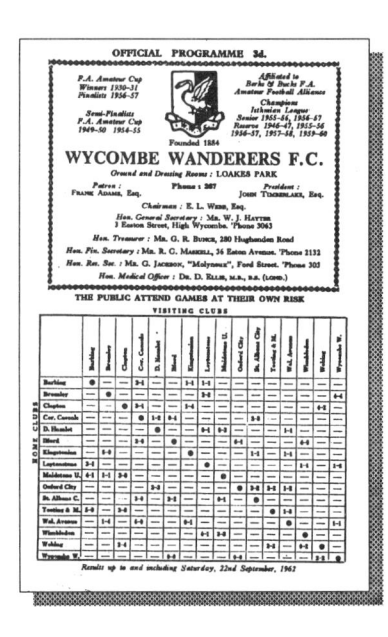

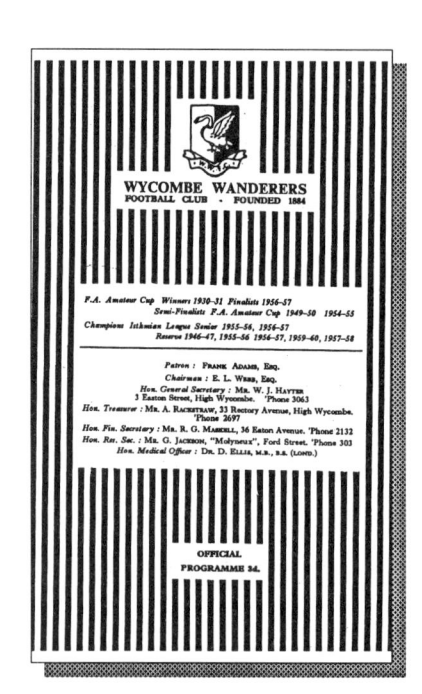

1963/64

1969/70 (1)

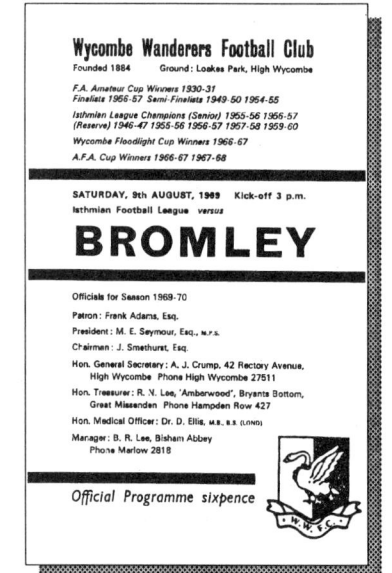

1962/63

1968/69

1967/68

1969/70 (2)

1970/71(1)    1970/71(2)    1971/72

1973/74    1974/75    1975/76

1976/77

1977/78

1978/79

1979/80

1983/84

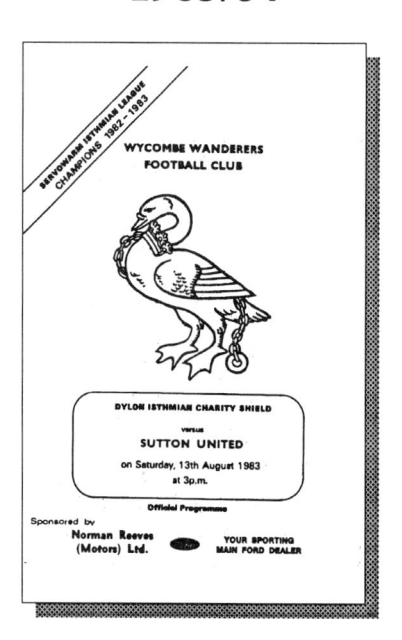

1981/82

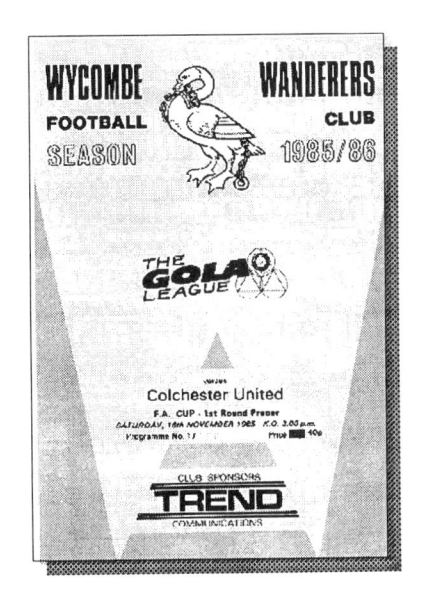

1984/85

1985/86

1986/87

1987/88

1989/90

1988/89

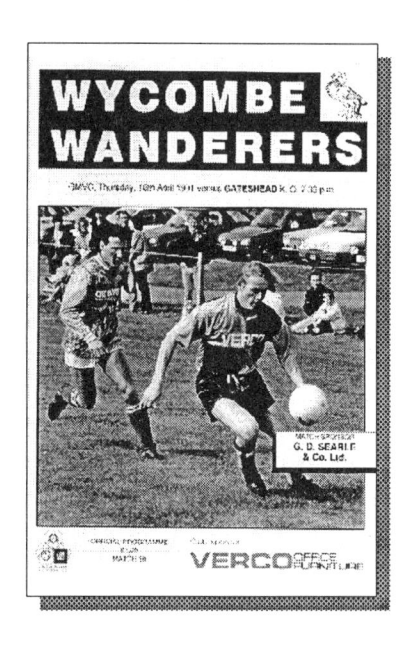

1990/91   1991/92   1992/93

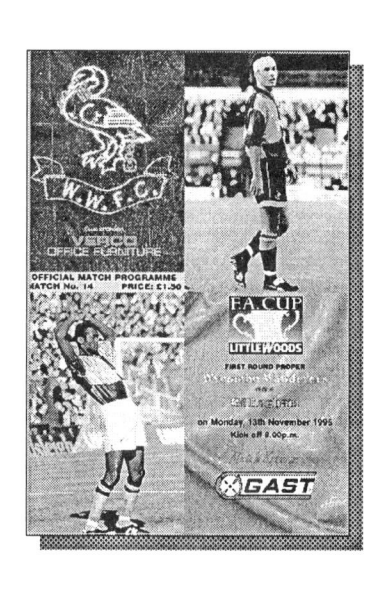

1993/94   1994/95   1995/96

142

(NON-LEAGUE) PLAYERS WHO'S - WHO: 1963 - 1993

Page 1 — Abbley - Carroll

NAME	Seasons Played	Appearances League	Appearances FA Comp	Appearances Others	Goals League	Goals FA Comp	Goals Others	TOTAL Apps.	TOTAL Goals
ABBLEY Steve	1988-90	61 + 2	17	6	1	.	.	84 + 2	1
ALEXANDER Dave	1974-76	40 + 12	2 + 5	14 + 2	6	.	5	56 + 19	11
ALLANSON Dave	1978-80	27	.	.	2	.	.	27	2
AMOS Tony	1972-73	24 + 5	3	2 + 1	7	.	2	29 + 6	9
ANDERSON Peter	1973-74	2	.	.	.	.	.	2	.
ANTHONY Geoff	1969-72, 1975-76	81 + 17	19	11 + 2	28	3	1	111 + 9	32
ASHFORD Noel	1986-88	41	3	6	12	.	1	50	13
ATKINS Stewart	1978-79	25 + 1	4 + 1	7	13	1	2	36 + 2	16
AUSTIN Chris	1971-72	12	.	2	.	.	.	14	.
AYLOTT Trevor	1992-93	3	1	1	.	.	.	5	.
BAKER Barry	1963-71	250	38	60	4	1	7	348	12
BALSON John	1963-64	10	4	2	5	2	4	16	11
BANTOCK Tony	1965-66	17	1	2	3	.	.	20	3
BARNES Michael	1987-88	1	.	.	.	.	.	1	.
BARR Ian	1979-80	1 + 1	.	.	.	.	.	1 + 1	.
BARRETT Keith	1986-89	102 + 1	12	13	5	.	.	127 + 1	5
BARRON Paul	1973-74	2	.	.	.	.	.	2	.
BARROWCLIFF Paul	1992-93	1 + 1	.	5	.	.	.	6 + 1	.
BARRY Tim	1987-88	3	.	1	.	.	.	4	.
BASSETT Dave	1963-64	13	1	.	2	1	.	14	3
BATES Jamie	1986-87	1	.	.	.	.	.	1	.
BATES Paul	1964-68	100 + 1	16	27	68	4	15	143 + 1	87
BECK John	1963-68	130 + 1	22	26	5	1	.	178 + 1	6
BEDFORD Dick	1963-64	1	.	.	1	.	.	1	1
BIRCH John	1964-65	17	1	.	.	.	.	18	.
BIRDSEYE Paul	1971-82	345 + 5	54 + 2	52 + 1	10	1	3	451 + 8	14
BLACKLER Martin	1988-92	39 + 9	15 + 1	5 + 2	3	2	1	59 + 12	6
BLOCHEL Jozef	1985-86	21 + 1	9	4	4	1	.	34 + 1	5
BLUE Richard	1986-87	6	.	1	.	.	.	7	.
BLUNT Keith	1969-71	41 + 2	10 + 3	3 + 1	2	2	1	54 + 6	5
BORG George	1979-84	115 + 3	24	22 + 1	14	.	5	161 + 4	19
BOWEN Keith	1987-88	.	.	1	.	.	.	1	.
BOYLE Gary	1985-86	1 + 3	.	.	.	.	.	1 + 3	.
BOYLAND Mark	1987-89	20	1	2	8	1	1	23	10
BRADLEY Dave	1985-86	1	.	.	.	.	.	1	.
BRADSHAW Dave	1964-66	50	10	10	.	.	.	70	.
BRADY Mike	1988-89	.	.	2	.	.	.	2	.
BREMER Bernie	1970-72	38 + 6	10 + 1	2 + 2	15	1	.	50 + 9	16
BRESSINGTON Graham	1985-88	48 + 7	1 + 1	4 + 1	4	.	1	53 + 9	5
BRITNELL Darren	1987-88	.	.	1	.	.	.	1	.
BROOME Brian	1984-85	3	.	.	.	.	.	3	.
BROTHERS Tony	1973-74	11	1 + 1	.	1	.	.	12 + 1	1
BUCKLE Paul	1992-93	1 + 1	1	.	.	.	.	2 + 1	.
BULLIS Dave	1977-78	1	.	0 + 1	.	.	.	1 + 1	.
BULLOCK Dave	1971-77	104 + 6	22 + 1	16	3	1	1	142 + 7	5
BUNTING Colin	1963-64, 1965-68	19	2	8	.	.	.	29	.
BUNTING Trevor	1985-86	.	.	0 + 1	.	.	.	0 + 1	.
BURGESS Dave	1984-88	90 + 2	16	21 + 1	5	.	4	127 + 3	9
BUSBY Viv	1966-70	48 + 2	7	30 + 3	19	3	28	85 + 5	50
BUTLER Mark	1988-90	1 + 5	0 + 1	.	.	.	.	1 + 6	.
BUTTERFIELD John	1975-76	.	.	2	.	.	.	2	.
CALVERT Micky	1976-68	1	0 + 1	1 + 2	.	.	.	2 + 3	.
CARMICHAEL Matt	1987-88	8 + 2	1	.	2	.	.	9 + 2	2
CARROLL Dave *	1988-93	166 + 4	43 + 2	20	35	12	4	229 + 6	51

143

NAME	Seasons Played	Appearances League	Appearances FA Comp	Appearances Others	Goals League	Goals FA Comp	Goals Others	TOTAL Apps.	TOTAL Goals
CASEY Kim	1991-93	29 + 10	8	3	15	2	3	40 + 10	20
CASH Stuart	1990-91	11 + 1	4	1	.	.	.	16 + 1	.
CHALWIN Mark	1991-92	.	.	1	.	.	.	1	.
CLEARY George	1976-77	5	.	.	.	.	.	5	.
COLLIER Rick	1986-87	1	.	.	.	.	.	1	.
COLLINS Kevin	1984-87	77 + 2	12	15	4	.	1	104 + 2	5
COLLINS Paul	1987-88	3	.	.	.	.	.	3	.
CONNOLLY Kevin	1985-87	8 + 2	1	1	2	.	.	10 + 2	2
COOK Mike	1990-91	1 + 1	.	.	.	.	.	1 + 1	.
COOPER Geoff	1991-93	9 + 3	4	4 + 1	.	.	.	17 + 4	.
COOPER John	1963-65	23	.	1	1	.	.	24	1
COOPER Micky	1972-73	5	.	.	.	.	.	5	.
CORBIN Kirk	1986-88	46 + 4	3	7	.	.	1	56 + 4	1
COTTRELL Derek	1975-76	3 + 1	1	2	.	.	.	6 + 1	.
COUSINS Jason *	1991-93	79	18	8	1	1	.	105	2
COVINGTON Gavin	1991-93	4	1	2	.	.	.	7	.
COX Steve	1987-88	3	.	.	.	.	.	3	.
CREASER Glyn *	1988-93	162	41	26	11	5	2	229	8
CROMPTON Steve	1988-89	6	.	2	.	.	.	8	.
CROOK Dave	1983-84	4 + 1	.	1	.	.	.	5 + 1	.
CROSSLEY Matt *	1987-88	145 + 5	33	27	2	2	2	312 + 6	6
CRUSE Peter	1976-77	9 + 1	2	4	.	.	.	51 + 1	.
DALE Steve	1988-89	.	.	1	.	.	.	1	.
DARVILL Barry	1964-65	1	.	.	.	.	.	1	.
DAVIES Alan	1976-77, 1982-83	9 + 2	0 + 1	0 + 1	1	.	.	9 + 4	1
DAVIES Barrie	1972-73	8	.	.	.	.	.	8	.
DAVIES Bobby	1975-79, 1980-82	170 + 3	22 + 1	27 + 1	4	1	1	219 + 5	6
DAVIES Peter	1967-68	3	.	1	.	.	.	4	.
DAWBER Mark	1986-88	9 + 9	.	2 + 1	2	.	.	11 + 10	2
DAY Kevin	1986-89	66 + 3	5 + 2	7 + 1	3	.	.	78 + 6	3
DAY Roger	1977-78	16 + 1	1	2	1	.	.	19 + 1	1
DEAKIN John	1991-92	8 + 5	4 + 1	4 + 1	.	.	.	16 + 7	.
DEAN Nick	1988-89	.	.	2	.	.	.	2	.
DELANEY John	1969-73, 1975-76	168	37	23	48	10	7	228	65
DELL Anthony	1983-84	0 + 1	.	.	.	.	.	0 + 1	.
DELL Bobby	1979-86	227 + 1	41	50	21	2	9	318 + 1	32
DEWHURST Rob	1992-93	2	2	.	1	.	.	4	1
DEXTER Simon	1980-81	3	.	.	.	.	.	3	.
DODDS Rowan	1987-88	8 + 3	0 + 1	1 + 1	3	.	.	9 + 5	3
DOHERTY Mike	1984-85	6 + 3	1	2	.	.	.	9 + 3	.
DUBLIN Dion	1988-89	1	.	1	.	.	.	2	.
DURHAM Kevin	1986-91	137 + 10	18	18 + 1	28	4	1	173 + 11	33
EATON Gary	1992-93	.	.	0 + 1	.	.	.	0 + 1	.
EATON Ray	1975-76, 1979-80	67	5	13 + 2	.	.	.	85 + 2	.
EDE Brian	1971-72	1	.	1	.	.	.	2	.
EDWARDS Kevin	1983-84	11 + 7	.	3 + 2	2	.	.	14 + 9	2
ELWORTHY Matt	1988-89	.	.	1	.	.	.	1	.
EVANS Dylan	1973-79	157 + 31	23 + 8	24 + 5	56	5	10	204 + 44	71
EVANS Nicky	1988-91	29	10	1 + 1	14	7	.	40 + 1	21
EVANS Terry *	1993-94	.	.	1	.	.	.	1	.
EYRES Pete	1964-68	30 + 1	3	11	.	.	.	44 + 1	.
FAIRCHILD Roy	1984-86	24 + 9	1 + 1	3 + 3	2	.	1	28 + 13	3
FAULKNER Vince	1963-71	106 + 9	6 + 2	42 + 1	9	1	3	154 + 12	13

NAME	Seasons Played	Appearances League	Appearances FA Comp	Appearances Others	Goals League	Goals FA Comp	Goals Others	TOTAL Apps.	TOTAL Goals
FERGUSSON Ian	1987-88	3	.	.	.	.	.	3	.
FISHER Simon	1986-87	1 + 1	.	.	.	.	.	1 + 1	.
FORDE Clevere	1987-88	.	.	1	.	.	.	1	.
FOWLES Gary	1978-81	36	3	2	3	.	.	41	3
FRANKLIN Paul	1989-90	17 + 3	1	1 + 1	1	.	.	19 + 4	1
FRASER Gavin	1976-77	13 + 1	2 + 1	1 + 1	1	.	.	16 + 3	1
FRENCH Brian	1963-67	35	4	10 + 1	7	1	2	49 + 1	10
FUSCHILLO Paul	1970-71	18 + 1	10	3	.	.	.	31 + 1	.
GALE Charlie	1963-71	239	25	58	15	.	3	322	18
GALLACHER Billy	1963-64	2	.	.	.	.	.	2	.
GAMBLIN Derek	1971-74	51 + 2	7	11 + 1	1	.	1	69 + 3	2
GANE Alan	1972-73	20 + 6	2 + 1	3	2	.	.	25 + 7	2
GIAMATTEI Aaron	1992-93	.	.	1	.	.	.	1	.
GILLIGAN Martin	1975-76	.	.	0 + 2	.	.	.	0 + 2	.
GIPP David	1989-90	2 + 3	.	.	4	.	.	2 + 3	4
GLASS David	1965-66	3	.	.	2	.	.	3	2
GLYNN Terry	1980-84	133 + 3	24	26	62	10	18	183 + 3	90
GOODEN Ty	1991-93	4 + 7	.	8 + 1	.	.	1	12 + 8	1
GRAHAM Andy	1986-88	51 + 6	5	8 + 2	17	.	7	64 + 8	24
GRANT Roger	1973-74	41	9	3	.	.	.	53	.
GRANVILLE John	1987-91	120	28	15	.	.	.	163	.
GRAVES Roger	1965-66	1	.	.	.	.	.	1	.
GRAY Nigel	1987-88	17 + 4	2	3	1	.	.	22 + 4	1
GREENAWAY Brian	1987-89	9 + 9	1 + 2	2 + 1	2	.	.	12 + 12	2
GREENE Dennis	1991-93	20 + 20	3 + 2	5 + 3	11	.	2	28 + 25	13
GRIFFITHS Paul	1974-75	5	.	1	.	.	.	6	.
GUMBS David	1989-90	1	.	.	.	.	.	1	.
GUPPY Steve	1989-93	124 + 13	27 + 4	23 + 4	17	4	6	174 + 21	27
HACKETT Paul	1986-87	6 + 2	.	.	.	.	.	6 + 2	.
HALL Dave	1968-69	0 + 1	.	1	.	.	.	1 + 1	.
HAND Gary	1974-75	35	9	2	.	.	.	46	.
HANLAN Matthew	1990-91	2	.	1 + 1	.	.	.	3 + 1	.
HARDWICK Steve	1978-81	83 + 1	14	12 + 1	2	1	.	109 + 2	3
HARMAN Andy	1981-86	49 + 10	8 + 2	13 + 6	.	.	1	70 + 18	1
HARRIS Derek	1975-76, 1977-79	41 + 7	2	8 + 2	10	.	4	51 + 9	14
HARTRIDGE Les	1970-71	4 + 1	3	.	.	.	.	7 + 1	.
HATT Bobby	1969-70	8	.	.	2	.	.	8	2
HAY Jimmy	1963-64	3	.	.	3	.	.	3	3
HAYRETTIN Hakan *	1992-93	5	2 + 1	3	.	.	.	10 + 1	.
HAYTER John	1963-64	1	.	.	.	.	.	1	.
HEMMINGS Tony *	1993-94	.	.	1	.	.	.	1	.
HILL Mark	1982-84	68	11	18	3	1	1	97	5
HILL Steve	1976-77	4 + 3	.	.	2	.	.	4 + 3	2
HINTON Tim	1988-89	.	.	1	.	.	.	1	.
HODDLE Carl	1986-87	2	.	.	.	.	.	2	.
HODGES Paul	1963-64	29	5	3	7	.	2	37	9
HOLIFIELD Micky	1971-81	321 + 9	48	43 + 1	69	10	5	412 + 10	84
HOLLIDAY Mike	1964-65	7	.	2	.	.	.	9	.
HOLMES Steve	1967-68	19	1	12	4	.	2	32	6
HONEYMAN Dick	1967-69	1 + 1	.	2	1	.	.	3 + 1	1
HORSEMAN Tony	1963-78	483 + 29	79 + 5	74 + 5	283	37	67	636 + 39	387
HORTON Duncan *	1993-94	.	.	1	.	.	.	1	.
HOW Trevor	1983-85	67 + 1	8	15	4	.	1	90 + 1	5
HUBBICK Billy	1982-83, 1985-86	1 + 1	1	2 + 2	.	.	1	4 + 3	1

NAME	Seasons Played	Appearances League	Appearances FA Comp	Appearances Others	Goals League	Goals FA Comp	Goals Others	TOTAL Apps.	TOTAL Goals
HUNT Andy	1981-82	2 + 5	0 + 1	1 + 2	1	.	1	3 + 8	2
HUNT Barry	1966-67	1	.	.	.	.	.	1	.
HUTCHINSON Johnny	1969-73	104 + 4	23 + 2	11 + 1	24	6	3	138 + 7	33
HUTCHINSON Simon *	1990-93	55 + 26	17 + 13	10 + 7	11	1	3	82 + 46	15
HYDE Paul *	1991-93	82	18	12	.	.	.	112	.
JACOBS Jimmy	1979-85	157 + 8	31	35 + 2	13	.	4	223 + 10	17
JAMES Tommy	1975-76	3 + 1	.	0 + 1	.	.	.	3 + 2	.
JAMESON Keith	1972-73	8	1	1	1	.	.	10	1
JOHNSON Peter	1991-92	8	1	1	.	.	.	10	.
JONES Cliff	1982-83	1	.	.	.	.	.	1	.
JUDD Mark	1978-79	2 + 2	1 + 2	1	.	1	1	4 + 4	2
KEEN Kevin	1982-83	1 + 2	.	.	.	.	.	1 + 2	.
KEEN Matthew	1992-93	.	1	.	.	.	.	1	.
KELLOWAY Paul	1991-92	.	.	0 + 1	.	.	.	0 + 1	.
KENNEDY Howard	1974-83	284 + 16	54	51 + 2	67	9	24	389 + 18	100
KERR Andy	1988-93	165	39	31	17	10	3	235	30
KERR John	1988-90	33	12	3	13	6	3	48	22
KETTLEBOROUGH Howard	1976-77	29	2	5	11	1	4	36	16
KIELY Micky	1982-83	3	.	.	.	.	.	3	.
KIPPING Darren	1988-89	.	.	1	.	.	.	1	.
KNOX Tony	1964-65	21	2	4	4	.	3	27	7
KOTVICS Joe	1982-84	8 + 2	2	2 + 1	.	1	1	12 + 3	2
LAILEY Julian	1968-70	77	12	14	.	.	2	103	2
LAMBERT Martin	1989-91	19 + 4	1	7 + 1	5	.	5	27 + 5	10
LANE Keith	1968-69	0 + 1	.	.	.	.	.	0 + 1	.
LANGFIELD Brian	1972-73	7 + 1	.	.	3	.	.	7 + 1	3
LANGFORD Tim	1992-93	11 + 1	.	.	5	.	.	11 + 1	5
LAVENDER Roy	1964-65	4	.	.	.	.	.	4	.
LEE Tim	1981-82	3 + 1	.	.	.	.	.	3 + 1	.
LESTER Gary	1979-90	309	51	60	.	.	.	420	.
LINK Declan	1984-87	71 + 3	6	16	44	1	16	93 + 3	61
LINK George	1986-88	9 + 4	1 + 1	2	1	.	1	12 + 5	2
LITTLE Barry	1987-88	5	.	.	.	.	.	5	.
LONG Steve	1978-85	188 + 19	35 + 2	30 + 1	73	11	14	253 + 22	98
LONGSTAFF Andy	1981-83, 1985-86	12 + 7	0 + 1	3 + 1	3	.	1	15 + 9	4
LOVELL Phil	1987-88	6	.	.	1	.	.	6	1
LOWEN Peter	1963-64	14	4	3	13	5	7	21	25
MACKENZIE Graham	1973-78	60 + 11	4	10 + 4	11	.	4	74 + 15	15
MACLEAN Iain	1970-71	11 + 1	1	1	1	.	.	13 + 1	1
MAHARG George	1963-64	7	4	1	.	.	.	12	.
MANN Adrian	1987-88	8	.	.	3	.	.	8	3
MARCHAM Bobby	1971-72	0 + 1	.	.	.	.	.	0 + 1	.
MARKWELL Adam	1988-89	.	.	1	.	.	.	1	.
MARTIN Peter	1967-68	2	.	5 + 1	.	.	.	7 + 1	.
MASKELL John	1964-80	468	86	62	.	.	.	616	.
MAYES Alan	1987-88	4 + 6	1	2	.	.	1	7 + 6	1
McCARTHY Jim	1979-80	10 + 7	1	1 + 1	2	.	.	12 + 8	2
McCRAE Bruce	1975-76	4 + 4	.	3 + 1	1	.	2	7 + 5	3
McGILLICUDDY Peter	1973-74	0 + 1	.	.	.	.	.	0 + 1	.
McMAHON Des	1985-86	18 + 2	5 + 2	5	.	1	1	28 + 4	2
MEAD Keith	1973-82	272 + 1	38	41	9	1	4	351 + 1	14
MELI David	1988-89	.	.	0 + 2	.	.	.	0 + 2	.

NAME	Seasons Played	Appearances League	Appearances FA Comp	Appearances Others	Goals League	Goals FA Comp	Goals Others	TOTAL Apps.	TOTAL Goals
MELLOWS Micky	1971-72	7 + 1	6	3	1	3	.	16 + 1	4
MERRICK Les	1963-69	128	13	43	31	2	14	184	47
MESSITT Leroy	1987-88	.	.	1	.	.	.	1	.
MIKURENDA Richard	1983-85	20	3	5	1	.	.	28	1
MILES Paul	1979-81	27 + 8	3	0 + 1	9	1	.	30 + 9	10
MOORE Roger	1983-84	4 + 2	.	2	1	.	.	6 + 2	1
MOORE Steve	1986-87	0 + 3	0 + 2	0 + 4	.	.	2	0 + 9	2
MOUSSADDIK Chuck	1990-93	11	2	6	.	.	.	19	.
MURPHY Mick	1981-82	0 + 1	.	0 + 1	.	.	.	0 + 2	.
MURRAY John	1979-80	6	.	.	1	.	.	6	1
MUTTOCK Jon	1991-92	.	.	1	.	.	.	1	.
MYATT John	1991-92	.	.	1	.	.	.	1	.
MYERS Alan	1987-88	9 + 2	1	1 + 1	.	.	.	11 + 3	.
NORMAN Alec	1991-93	0 + 1	.	1 + 1	.	.	.	2 + 1	.
NORMAN Sean	1987-89	61 + 3	8 + 1	4 + 1	5	.	1	73 + 5	6
NORMAN Steve	1982-83, 1987-88	15 + 3	1	4	1	.	1	20 + 3	2
NUTTELL Mickey	1990-92	17 + 6	2	3 + 1	9	.	4	22 + 7	13
O'BRIEN Kevin	1969-73	25	5	6	.	.	.	36	.
O'DRISCOLL Paul	1989-90	.	.	0 + 1	.	.	.	0 + 1	.
OLSON Gerry	1972-73	24 + 1	3	.	.	.	.	27 + 1	.
OSBORNE Lawrence	1987-89	14 + 4	2 + 1	2 + 1	1	.	.	18 + 6	1
OWEN Danny	1992-93	.	.	1	.	.	.	1	.
PACQUETTE Henry	1983-84	20	2	.	6	1	.	22	7
PAGE Mick	1963-64	4	.	.	.	.	.	4	.
PATRICK Phil	1963-64	7	.	1	.	.	.	8	.
PEARCE Graham	1978-79, 1983-87	80 + 2	4	16 + 3	2	1	.	100 + 5	3
PEARSON Ian	1976-77	41	5	5	24	2	3	51	29
PEARSON Ricky	1989-90	10 + 1	1	3	.	.	.	14 + 1	.
PENTLAND Simon	1984-85	6 + 2	1 + 1	4	.	.	2	11 + 3	2
PERRIN Steve	1973-76, 1982-84	126 + 7	30	25	49	13	6	181 + 7	68
PETIT Denis	1966-67	2	.	1	.	.	.	3	.
PHILLIPS Alan	1974-75, 1976-79	154 + 1	23	21	12	1	2	198 + 1	15
PICKING Stan	1964-65	7	.	1	.	.	.	8	.
PIPER Chris	1989-90	0 + 1	.	.	.	.	.	0 + 1	.
POFFLEY Nathan	1992-93	.	.	1	.	.	.	1	.
POOLE Michael	1991-93	.	.	1 + 1	.	.	.	1 + 1	.
POWELL Ted	1970-72	76	17	4	.	.	.	97	.
POWLES Ian	1979-80	1	.	.	.	.	.	1	.
PRATT John	1968-69	2	.	6	.	.	.	8	.
PRATT Steve	1977-78	0 + 3	.	.	1	.	.	0 + 3	1
PRICE Jonathan	1990-91	3	.	.	.	.	.	3	.
PRICE Neil	1985-88	51	4	8	2	.	.	63	2
PRICE Sean	1985-86	6	1	2	.	.	.	9	.
PRICE Tony	1973-77, 1979-81	53 + 14	6 + 2	7	19	.	2	66 + 16	21
PRIESTLEY John	1975-80	78 + 6	9 + 1	14 + 1	7	1	1	101 + 8	9
PRIESTLEY Martin	1963-67	2 + 3	.	2	.	.	.	4 + 3	.
PRITCHARD Larry	1970-74	155 + 2	28	14	37	12	8	198 + 2	57
PULLIN George	1963-64	29	5	3	3	.	.	37	3
QURAISHI Faroukh	1977-78	13	1	1	.	.	.	15	.
RAINE Kevin	1973-74	5	.	1	.	.	.	6	.
RAY John	1987-88	1	.	.	.	.	.	1	.

NAME	Seasons Played	Appearances League	Appearances FA Comp	Appearances Others	Goals League	Goals FA Comp	Goals Others	TOTAL Apps.	TOTAL Goals
READ Simon	1984-86	76 + 1	15	16	34	10	13	107 + 1	57
REARDON Terry	1973-76	95 + 2	19 + 3	13	4	1	1	127 + 5	6
REED Les	1978-79	16 + 2	.	4	.	.	.	20 + 2	.
REGAN John	1988-89	2 + 1	2	1	.	1	1	5 + 1	2
RICHARDSON Jimmy	1980-81	3 + 1	.	.	.	.	.	3 + 1	.
RICHARDSON John	1984-86	10 + 1	.	1	2	.	.	11 + 1	2
RILEY Anthony	1983-87	58 + 8	11	11 + 4	1	.	1	80 + 12	2
ROBINSON Andy	1988-91	89 + 12	19 + 4	15	6	1	2	123 + 16	9
RODERICK Martin	1987-89	1 + 2	.	.	.	.	.	1 + 2	.
ROFFEY Trevor	1991-92	.	.	2	.	.	.	2	.
ROYSTONE Pete	1963-64, 1965-68	92	17	19	5	2	3	128	10
RUNDLE Ian	1965-74	250 + 7	41 + 1	56 + 2	2	1	2	347 + 10	5
RUSSELL Andy	1988-89	1 + 2	.	.	1	.	.	1 + 2	1
RUSSELL Dave	1984-85	11	2	.	1	1	.	13	2
RUTLEDGE Brian	1981-82	2 + 2	.	1 + 1	.	.	.	3 + 3	.
RYAN Keith	1990-93	48 + 18	13 + 9	15 + 3	9	1	3	76 + 30	13
SAMUELS Keith	1963-70	172 + 3	23	49	83	7	25	244 + 3	115
SANDERSON Paul	1989-90	5	1	.	.	.	.	6	.
SCIARAFFA Mark	1990-93	.	.	2 + 1	.	.	.	2 + 1	.
SCOPE David	1990-91	1 + 2	.	.	1	.	.	1 + 2	1
SCOTT Keith *	1990-93	79 + 2	21	12	44	12	5	112 + 2	61
SCOTT Terry	1978-81	66 + 8	13	8	28	3	5	87 + 8	36
SEACOLE Jason	1986-88	36 + 7	4	8 + 2	10	1	3	48 + 9	14
SEARLE Keith	1969-75	194 + 2	40	13	101	19	4	247 + 2	124
SEWELL Peter	1963-65	21	.	2	.	.	.	23	.
SHERBOURNE Vic	1966-67	3 + 2	.	.	.	.	.	3 + 2	.
SHILLINGFORD Stuart	1964-65	4	.	.	.	.	.	4	.
SIDLEY Scott	1988-89	1 + 1	.	.	.	.	.	1 + 1	.
SILKMAN Barry	1986-87	6	1	1	.	.	.	8	.
SIMPSON Rob	1986-87	0 + 1	.	.	.	.	.	0 + 1	.
SLATER Peter	1968-69	5	.	2	.	.	1	7	1
SMITH Gary	1989-92	52 + 14	11 + 4	5 + 1	4	.	.	68 + 19	4
SMITH Martin	1981-82	0 + 1	.	.	.	.	.	0 + 1	.
SMITH Steve	1979-80	10 + 1	0 + 1	1	2	.	.	11 + 2	2
SNOW Martin	1985-86	2	.	1	.	.	.	3	.
SORENSON Micky	1976-77	7	.	.	.	.	.	7	.
SORRELL Tony	1992-93	0 + 1	.	.	.	.	.	0 + 1	.
SPALDING Lee	1991-92	.	.	1	.	.	.	1	.
SPITTLE Peter	1972-73, 1975-79	67	6	22	.	.	.	95	.
SPURR Andy	1988-89	.	.	1	.	.	.	1	.
STANLEY Neal	1985-86	37 + 2	10 + 1	6 + 1	4	2	3	53 + 4	9
STAPLETON Simon	1989-93	147 + 3	37	21 + 1	19	3	.	205 + 4	22
STEPHENSON Keith	1968-70	17	4	5	.	.	.	26	.
STEVENTON Brian	1974-75	.	1	.	.	.	.	1	.
STRONG Richard	1977-78	9 + 1	.	2	.	.	.	11 + 1	.
STYLES Peter	1963-65	6	.	.	3	.	.	6	3
SUDDABY Peter	1969-70, 1982-83	27	5	5	4	.	2	37	6
SULLIVAN Keiran	1988-89	.	.	1	.	.	.	1	.
SUSSAMS Paul	1975-76	.	.	1	.	.	.	1	.
SWABY Glenn	1976-77	0 + 1	.	.	.	.	.	0 + 1	.
SWAIN Kenny	1972-73	6	.	1	1	.	.	7	1
SYRETT Dennis	1963-65	18	3	.	.	.	.	21	.
TATE Colin	1983-85	15 + 2	.	0 + 2	3	.	2	15 + 4	5
TAYLOR John	1963-64	1	.	.	.	.	.	1	.

NAME	Seasons Played	Appearances League	Appearances FA Comp	Appearances Others	Goals League	Goals FA Comp	Goals Others	TOTAL Apps.	TOTAL Goals
TAYLOR Mike	1964-65	1	.	.	.	.	.	1	.
TAYLOR Nigel	1987-89	20	.	.	.	.	.	20	.
TEMEL Lou	1968-70	34 + 1	4	7	1	.	.	45 + 1	1
THOMAS Dave	1963-64, 1968-70	65 + 2	6 + 1	12	5	.	.	83 + 3	5
THOMAS John	1963-64	3	.	.	1	.	.	3	1
THOMPSON Les	1992-93	7	2	1	.	.	.	10	.
THOMPSON Steve	1991-93	41 + 2	10	2 + 1	7	2	.	53 + 3	9
THOMPSON Stuart	1965-69	26 + 2	2	7	1	.	2	35 + 2	3
THORNE Steve	1982-84	14 + 7	0 + 1	8 + 5	3	.	1	22 + 13	4
THORPE Robert	1989-91	0 + 10	0 + 1	1 + 3	2	.	.	1 + 14	2
TILLEY Kevin	1984-85	39	3	8	.	.	.	50	.
TILLY Graham	1991-92	.	.	1	.	.	.	1	.
TINSLEY Ron	1967-68	2 + 1	.	.	.	.	.	2 + 1	.
TOLL Gary	1979-82	33 + 3	3 + 2	4	10	.	1	40 + 5	11
TOLL Steve	1980-83, 1985-86	90	20 + 1	19	.	1	.	129 + 1	1
TRINI Gerhard	1967-68	2	.	.	.	.	.	2	.
VASS Steve	1977-78	9 + 1	.	.	1	.	.	9 + 1	1
VIRCAVS Anton	1981-86, 1992-93	167 + 3	38	43	8	6	8	248 + 3	22
VOUSDEN Brian	1967-68	3	.	.	.	.	.	3	.
WAITMAN Gerald	1992-93	.	.	1	.	.	.	1	.
WALFORD Steve	1990-92	26	8	4	.	.	.	38	.
WALTON Byron	1986-87	17 + 2	1 + 2	3	8	.	.	21 + 4	8
WANKLYN Wayne	1984-85	1	.	.	.	.	.	1	.
WARD Kenny	1969-70	9 + 1	.	1	.	.	.	10 + 1	.
WATSON Peter	1975-76	.	.	1 + 1	.	.	.	1 + 1	.
WAUGHMAN Trevor	1971-73	28 + 7	1	2	10	.	1	31 + 7	11
WAY Chris	1978-84	53	2	9	.	.	.	64	.
WELLS Howard	1965-67	3	.	5	.	.	.	8	.
WEST Mark	1984-93	244 + 37	49 + 5	45 + 1	122	23	26	338 + 43	171
WEST Paul	1980-84	63 + 11	7 + 7	15 + 7	3	.	3	85 + 25	6
WESTLEY Graham	1987-88	15 + 5	1	2	4	1	.	18 + 5	5
WHEWAY Chris	1987-88	.	.	1	.	.	.	1	.
WHITBY Steve	1990-91	24 + 2	7	6 + 1	.	.	.	37 + 3	.
WICKS Steve	1989-90	7	1	.	.	.	.	8	.
WILLIAMS Rob	1971-74	89 + 3	17	8	5	1	1	114 + 3	7
WILLIAMS Tony	1963-64	1	.	.	.	.	.	1	.
WILSON Ken	1980-85	114 + 18	22 + 3	30 + 2	22	5	10	166 + 23	37
WILSON Mat	1988-89	.	.	0 + 2	.	.	.	0 + 2	.
WOOD Gareth	1992-93	.	.	0 + 1	.	.	.	0 + 1	.
WOOD Phil	1973-74	35 + 1	9	3	.	.	.	47 + 1	.
WOODALL Martin	1987-88	9	.	2	.	.	.	11	.
WOODBRIDGE Dave	1973-74	1 + 1	.	.	.	.	.	1 + 1	.
WORLEY Dave	1963-65	20	1	2	1	.	.	23	1
WORLEY Len	1963-70	199	28 + 1	42	27	5	3	269 + 1	35
WRIGHT Dave	1971-72, 1973-74	5	.	.	.	.	.	5	.
WRIGHT Peter	1964-65	5	.	.	1	.	.	5	1
YOUNG Scott	1987-89	11 + 9	0 + 3	1 + 1	.	1	2	12 + 13	3

* Includes Conference Championship Shield 1993 (played in 1993/94 season).

League   Isthmian (1963-85), Gola (1985-86), Vauxhall-Opel (1986-87), GM Vauxhall Conference (1987-93).
F.A. Comps   F.A. Cup (1963-93), F.A. Amateur Cup (1963-74), F.A. Trophy (1974-93).
Other Comps   Berks & Bucks Senior Cup (1963-93), A.F.A. Invitation Cup (1964-69), Wycombe Floodlight League/Cup (1965-69), Mithras Cup (1968-69), Anglo-Italian Trophy (1975-76), Anglo-Italian Semi-Professional Tournament (1975-76), Isthmian League Cup/Hitachi Cup (1975-85), Dylon Charity Shield (1981, 1983, 1985, 1987), Bob Lord Trophy/Drinkwise Cup (1985-86, 1989-93), A.C. Delco Cup (1986-87), GMAC/Clubcall Cup (1986-89), Conference Championship Shield (1991, 1992, 1993).

FOOTBALL LEAGUE PLAYERS - WHO'S WHO

NAME	Born	Birthplace	Joined	Left	Pos	Appearances League	Appearances Cup	Goals Lge.	Goals Cup
BELL Mickey	15 Nov 1971	Newcastle	October 1994	-	M/D	71 + 1	8 + 1	3	2
BLATHERWICK Steve *	20 Sep 1973	Nottingham	February 1994	March 1994	D	2	1	.	.
BLISSETT Gary *	29 Jun 1964	Manchester	December 1995	January 1996	S	4	.	2	.
BROWN Steve	6 Jul 1966	Northampton	February 1994	-	M/D	84 + 3	13 + 2	2	.
CARROLL Dave	20 Sep 1966	Paisley	May 1988	-	M/S	128	28	21	4
CASTLEDINE Stewart *	22 Jan 1973	Wandsworth	August 1995	September 1995	M	7	.	3	.
CLARK Anthony	7 Apr 1977	London	August 1993	-	S	2 + 2	.	.	.
COOPER Mark	18 Dec 1968	Wakefield	January 1994	February 1994	M	0 + 2	.	1	.
COUSINS Jason	4 Oct 1970	Hayes	August 1991	-	D	106 + 2	29	3	1
CREASER Glyn	1 Sep 1959	London	September 1988	August 1995	D	17 + 2	10 + 2	2	2
CROSSLEY Matt	18 Mar 1968	Basingstoke	February 1988	-	D	86 + 1	21	3	1
CUNNINGHAM Tony	12 Nov 1957	Jamaica	March 1994	June 1994	S	4 + 1	.	.	.
CUSACK Nick *	24 Dec 1965	Maltby	March 1994	May 1994	S	2 + 2	.	1	.
DESOUZA Miquel	11 Feb 1970	Mewham	January 1995	-	S	44 + 6	8	24	2
DYKSTRA Sieb *	20 Oct 1966	Kerkrade, Holland	May 1996	April 1996	G	13	.	.	.
EVANS Terry	12 Apr 1965	Hammersmith	August 1993	-	D	90 + 4	14	14	2
FARRELL David	11 Nov 1971	Birmingham	September 1995	-	M	27 + 6	6	5	.
FORAN Mark *	30 Oct 1973	Aldershot	August 1995	September 1995	D	5	2	.	.
GARLAND Peter *	20 Jan 1971	Croydon	March 1995	April 1995	M	5	.	.	.
GARNER Simon	23 Nov 1959	Boston	March 1994	May 1996	S	53 + 13	12 + 3	16	7
GUPPY Steve	29 Mar 1969	Winchester	August 1989	August 1994	M	41	17	8	2
HARDYMAN Paul	11 Mar 1964	Portsmouth	July 1995	May 1996	M	12 + 3	5	.	.
HAYRETTIN Hakan	4 Feb 1970	Enfield	March 1993	June 1994	M	15 + 4	6 + 2	1	.
HEMMINGS Tony	21 Sep 1967	Burton	September 1993	September 1995	S	28 + 21	6 + 10	12	2
HODGES Lee *	4 Sep 1973	Epping	December 1993	January 1994	S	2 + 2	2	.	.
HORTON Duncan	18 Feb 1967	Maidstone	August 1993	September 1994	D	15	6 + 2	.	.
HOWARD Terry	26 Feb 1966	Stepney	February 1995	May 1996	D	56 + 3	7	2	1
HUTCHINSON Simon	24 Sep 1969	Sheffield	July 1993	August 1995	M	2 + 10	2 + 3	.	.
HYDE Paul	7 Apr 1963	Hayes	August 1991	February 1996	G	105	31	.	.
KERR Andy	7 Apr 1966	West Bromwich	September 1988	June 1994	D	12 + 2	5 + 1	3	.
KERR Paul	9 Jun 1964	Portsmouth	October 1994	March 1995	S	0 + 1	1	1	.
LANGFORD Tim	12 Sep 1965	Kingswinford	March 1993	May 1995	S	19 + 16	6 + 7	8	5
LAWRENCE Matthew	19 Jun 1974	Northampton	January 1996	-	M	1 + 2	.	.	.
MARKMAN Damien	7 Jan 1978	Slough	July 1995	-	S	0 + 2	.	.	.
McGAVIN Steve	24 Jan 1969	North Walsham	March 1995	-	S	34 + 9	3 + 3	4	.
McGORRY Brian	16 Apr 1970	Liverpool	August 1995	-	M	0 + 4	1	.	.
MOUSSADDIK Chuck	23 Feb 1970	Morocco	December 1989	December 1995	G	1	0 + 1	.	.
NORMAN Alec	14 Feb 1975	Reading	August 1990	June 1994	S	.	0 + 1	.	.
PATTERSON Gary	27 Nov 1972	Newcastle	December 1994	-	M	40 + 10	4 + 1	2	1
POTTER Graham *	20 May 1975	Solihull	September 1993	October 1993	D	2 + 1	2	.	.
REGIS Cyrille	9 Feb 1958	French Guyana	August 1994	July 1995	S	30 + 5	3	9	1
REID Nicky	30 Oct 1960	Urmston	March 1994	May 1995	M	6 + 2	5 + 1	.	.
ROBERTS Ben *	22 Jun 1975	Bishop Auckland	December 1995	March 1996	G	15	.	.	.
ROGERS Darren *	9 Apr 1970	Birmingham	November 1993	December 1993	D	0 + 1	1	.	.
ROWBOTHAM Jason	3 Jan 1969	Cardiff	September 1995	-	D	27	6	.	.
RYAN Keith	25 Jun 1970	Northampton	July 1990	-	M/S	84 + 5	22 + 1	9	3
SCOTT Keith	10 Jun 1967	London	March 1991	November 1993	S	15	7	10	4
SHEPSTONE Paul	8 Nov 1970	Coventry	December 1993	March 1994	M	.	1 + 1	.	.
SKINNER Justin *	17 Sep 1972	Dorking	August 1994	September 1994	D	4 + 1	.	.	.
SKIVERTON Terry	26 Jun 1975	Mile End	February 1995 * March 1996	May 1995 -	D	11 + 3	.	1	.
SOLOMAN Jason	6 Oct 1970	Welwyn Garden City	March 1995	May 1996	D/M	11 + 2	1	1	.
STAPLETON Simon	10 Dec 1968	Oxford	August 1988	May 1996	D/M	46 + 3	10 + 1	3	2
THOMPSON Steve	12 Jan 1963	Plymouth	February 1992	September 1995	M/S	41 + 21	15 + 3	3	3
TITTERTON David	25 Sep 1971	Warwick	August 1993	May 1995	D	15 + 4	7 + 1	1	.
TURNBULL Lee	27 Sep 1967	Stockton	January 1994	May 1995	S	8 + 3	2 + 1	1	1
TURNER Andy *	28 Mar 1975	Woolwich	August 1994	September 1994	M	3 + 1	.	.	.
WALLACE Danny	21 Jan 1964	Greenwich	March 1995	May 1995	M	0 + 1	.	.	.
WILLIAMS John	11 May 1968	Birmingham	September 1995	-	S	23 + 6	5	7	.

* Player on loan.   A blank in the 'Left' column indicates player still at Club (at start of 1996/97 season).
(Cup totals include F.A. Cup, Coco-Cola Cup, Autoglass/Auto Windscreens Shield and Division Three Play-offs). All details are correct as at 1 September 1996.

FOOTBALL LEAGUE PLAYERS - Pre 1992/93 season.

Below is a list of players who have made made at least one first team appearances for Wycombe Wanderers when a non-League team, and subsequently played in the Premier/Football League for another club. Players who continued into the Football League with Wycombe and then joined another club have been excluded. The names are ordered by the season when the player made a Premier/Football League appearance after playing for Wycombe. Season only includes first year i.e. 1960 signifies 1960-61, 1960-62 signifies 1960-61 to 1962-63 incl. Loan players, denoted by italics, have been included, as full-time players joining a part-time club remains an uncommon occurrence. In the case of Dion Dublin, he made two Conference appearances for Wycombe before making his Football League debut with Cambridge United. Loan appearances in the Premier/Football League are also shown in italics.

Player	Wycombe seasons	Football Lge. club	Seasons	FL Apps	FL Goals
Fred ROUSE (CF)	1900-01	Grimsby Town	1902-03	37	5
		Stoke	1903-06	69	28
		Everton	1906-07	9	2
		Chelsea	1907-08	38	11
		West Brom.Alb.	1909	5	2
Archie GOMM (CB)	1919	Millwall(via Cheshunt)	1920-30	87	13
		Carlisle United	1931-32	67	
Reggie BOREHAM(CF/IF)	1919-26	Notts County	1920	3	
		Arsenal	1921-23	51	18
George HARRIS (HB)	1920-21	Southend United	1921	3	
		Notts County	1922-23	49	
		Queens Park Rang.	1924-25	38	
		Fulham	1926-27	8	1
John 'Jim' WICKS (G)	1920-21	Notts County			
		Reading	1923	6	
		Queens Park Rang.	1924	5	
Alex WEAVER (IR)	1923	Sheffield Wed.	1924	6	1
Jim BAKER (CB)	1924	Watford	1924-25	9	2
Cyril FOSTER (IR)	1924-25	Watford	1925-27	70	24
		Queens Park Rang.	1928-29	5	
Robert'Tim'HINTON (CF)	1920-25	Millwall	1926	5	3
Walter KEEN (CB)	1922-23	Millwall	1926-28	6	
		Clapton O(via Fulham)	1932-34	53	2
Billy COWARD (RW/IF)	1926-27	Queens Park Rang.	1927-31	126	22
		Walsall	1932	35	8
Gerry DARVILL (RB)	1932-33	Reading			
		Mansfield Town	1935	13	
		Wolverhampton W			
Alec BLAKEMAN (RB/IF)	1945	Brentford(Via Oxford C)	1946-48	42	7
		Sheffield United	1948	5	
		Bournemouth	1948-49	25	8
Ron RAFFERTY (IF)	1953	Portsmouth	1954-56	23	5
		Grimsby Town	1956-62	264	145
		Hull City	1963-64	16	6
		Aldershot	1966-68	81	10
Terry LONG (D)	1954	Crystal Palace	1955-68	442	15
Len WORLEY (RW)	1954-69	Charlton Athletic	1956	1	
		Tottenham Hotspur	1959	1	
Geoff TRUETT (WH)	1952-56	Crystal Palace	1957-61	38	5
Dennis EDWARDS (CF)	1957	Charlton Athletic	1958-64	171	61
		Portsmouth	1964-67	71	14
		Brentford	*1967*	*11*	*2*
		Aldershot	1967	14	1
Steve HYDE (LW)	1960-61	Oxford United	1964-65	9	
John PRATT (G)	1968	Reading	1969-71	29	
Viv BUSBY (F)	1966-70	Luton Town	1969-72	77	16
		Newcastle United	*1971*	*4*	*2*
		Fulham	1973-76	118	29
		Norwich City	1976-77	22	11
		Stoke City	1977-79	50	9
		Sheffield United	*1979*	*3*	*1*
		Blackburn Rovers	1980	8	1
		York City	1982-83	19	4
Peter SUDDABY (CD)	1969, 82	Blackpool(via Skelm.)	1970-79	332	9
		Brighton & Hove A.	1979	23	
		Wimbledon	1981	6	
Paul FUSCHILLO (RB)	1970	Blackpool	1971-73	11	
Kenny SWAIN (RW/RB)	1972	Chelsea	1973-78	119	26
		Aston Villa	1978-82	148	4
		Nottingham Forest	1982-84	112	2
		Portsmouth	1985-87	113	
		West Bromwich A	*1987*	*7*	*1*
		Crewe Alexandra	1988-91	126	1
John DELANEY (CD)	1969-72,75	Bournemouth	1973-74	25	
Mickey MELLOWS (M)	1971	Reading(Am.via Sutton)	1970	16	2
		Portsmouth	1973-77	181	16
Alan GANE (M)	1972	Hereford United	1973	9	1
Paul BARRON (G)	1973	Plymouth A(via Slough)	1976-77	44	
		Arsenal	1978-79	8	
		Crystal Palace	1980-82	90	
		West Bromwich Alb.	1982-84	63	
		Stoke City	*1984*	*1*	
		Queens Park Rang.	1985-86	32	
		Reading	1986	4	

Player	Wycombe seasons	Football Lge. club	Seasons	FL Apps	FL Goals
Steve PERRIN (F)	1973-75,82-83	Crystal Palace	1976-77	48	13
		Plymouth Argyle	1977-79	35	6
		Portsmouth	1979-80	28	3
		Northampton Town	1981-82	22	5
Ian PEARSON (F)	1976	Plymouth A(via Goole)	1974-75	12	
		Millwall	1977-78	44	9
		Exeter City	1978-80	69	10
		Plymouth A(v Bideford)	1983	8	1
Dave BASSETT (D)	1963	Wimbledon	1977	35	
Kevin KEEN (M)	1982	West Ham United	1986-92	219	21
		Wolverhampton W	1993-94	42	7
		Stoke City	1994-95	54	5
Jamie BATES (CD)	1986	Brentford	1986-95	315	14
Dion DUBLIN (F)	1988-89	Cambridge United	1988-91	156	52
		Manchester United	1992-93	12	2
		Coventry City	1994	65	27
Graham BRESSINGTON(M/CD)	1985-87	Lincoln City	1988-92	141	7
		Southend United	1993-94	47	5
Carl HODDLE	1986	Leyton O			
	(via Bishops Stortford)		1989-90	28	2
		Barnet	1991-94	94	3
Matt CARMICHAEL(F/CD)	1987-88	Lincoln C(via B'stoke)	1989-92	133	18
		Scunthorpe United	1993	62	20
		Barnet	1994	3	
		Preston North End	1994	10	3
		Mansfield Town	1995	1	1
		Doncaster Rovers	1995	27	4
		Darlington	1995	13	2
Lawrence OSBORNE (M)	1987-88	Newport County	1987	15	
		Maidstone U (via Redbridge For.)	1990-91	53	8
		Gillingham	1991	5	

Player	Wycombe seasons	Football Lge. club	Seasons	FL Apps	FL Goals
Nicky EVANS (F)	1988-90	Barnet	1991-93	39	8
Mike COOK (M)	1990	York City(via Coventry)	1987	6	1
		Cambridge United	1989-90	17	1
David SCOPE (M)	1990	Northampton Town	1989-91	19	1
John KERR (F)	1988-89	Portsmouth(via Harrow)	1987	4	
		Peterborough United	1987	10	1
		Millwall(via Chertsey)	1992-4	43	8
		Walsall	1995	1	
Gary SMITH (M)	1990-91	Fulham	1985	1	
		Colchester United	1987	11	
		Barnet	1993-4	16	
Paul BUCKLE (M)	1992	Brentford	1987-92	57	1
		Torquay United	1993-95	59	9
		Exeter City	1995	22	2
Geoff COOPER (LB/LM)	1992	Brighton & Hove A	1987-88	5	
		Barnet	1991-92	31	1
		"	1993-94	37	3
Rob DEWHURST (CD)	1992	Blackburn Rovers	1990	13	
		Darlington	1991	11	1
		Huddersfield T	1992	7	
		Hull City	1993-95	84	10
Les THOMPSON (LB)	1992	Hull City	1987-90	35	2
		Scarborough	1988	3	1
		Maidstone United	1991	38	
		Burnley	1992-3	39	
Ty GOODEN (RW)	1991-2	Swindon Town	1993-95	46	5
Hakan HAYRETTIN (M)	1992-3	Barnet	1991-92	6	
		Torquay United	1992	4	
		Cambridge United	1994	17	

HONOURS...RECORDS...STATISTICS
(Applies up to and including 1995/96 season)

Endsleigh Insurance League Division Three
Play off winners: 1993/94
GM Vauxhall Conference
Champions: 1992/93
Runners Up: 1991/92
Bob Lord/Drinkwise Trophy
Winners: 1991/92
Runners Up: 1992/93
Championship Shield
Winners: 1991/92, 1992/93, 1993/94
Isthmian/Vauxhall-Opel League
Champions: 1955/56, 1956/57, 1970/71, 1971/72, 1973/74, 1974/75, 1982/83, 1986/87
Runners Up: 1957/58, 1959/60, 1969/70, 1975/76, 1976/77
Hitachi League Cup
Winners: 1984/85
Runners Up: 1982/83, 1983/84
Dylon/Vauxhall Charity Shield
Winners: 1981/82, 1983/84, 1985/86, 1987/88
Spartan League
Champions: 1919/20, 1920/21
Great Western Combination
Champions: 1944/45
Runners Up: 1939/40
F.A. Trophy
Winners: 1990/91, 1992/93
Semi-Finalists: 1981/82
F.A. Amateur Cup
Winners: 1930/31
Runners Up: 1956/57
Semi-Finalists: 1949/50, 1954/55, 1971/72

Anglo-Italian Trophy
Winners: 1975/76
Berks & Bucks Senior Cup
Winners: 1901/02, 1908/09, 1909/10, 1912/13, 1920/21, 1922/23, 1924/25, 1932/33, 1934/35, 1939/40, 1946/47, 1948/49, 1949/50, 1953/54, 1957/58, 1959/60, 1963/64, 1967/68, 1972/73, 1973/74, 1977/78, 1978/79, 1986/87, 1989/90
Berks & Bucks Benevolent Cup
Winners: 1931/32, 1942/43, 1945/46*
Bucks Charity Cup
Winners: 1909/10*, 1932/33
Wycombe Floodlight League Cup
Winners: 1966/67
High Wycombe Challenge Cup
Winners: 1889/90, 1893/94, 1894/95
Maidenhead Norfolkians Charity Cup
Winners: 1893/94, 1901/02, 1902/03*
Maidenhead Hospital Cup
Winners: 1923/24, 1924/25
Oxford Hospital Cup
Winners: 1921/22, 1927/28, 1930/31*
Windsor Hospital Cup
Winners: 1935/36
A.F.A. Invitation Cup
Winners: 1959/60, 1960/61, 1964/65, 1966/67, 1967/68
Smith Memorial Cup
Winners: 1960/61
Note
* Trophy shared

BIGGEST WINS

Home:	18-1	v Staines (Great Western Suburban League)	1909-10
	15-1	v Witney Town (F.A. Cup)	1955-56
	13-0	v Wycombe Trinity (Friendly)	1889-90
		v Ravenscroft Amateurs (Friendly)**	1911-12
		v Amersham Town (F.A. Cup)	1950-51
Away:	14-0	v 2nd Coldstream Guards (Spartan League)	1919-20
	8-0	v Datchet (Berks & Bucks Junior Cup)	1893-94
		v St. Albans City (Isthmian League)	1958-59
		v Maidenhead United (Wycombe Floodlight League Cup)	1967-68
		v Oxford City (Isthmian Leauge)	1972-73

HEAVIEST DEFEATS

Home:	2-10	v Bristol City (Friendly)	1912-13
	0-8	v Reading (F.A. Cup)	1899-1900
	0-7	v Barnet (GM Vauxhall Conference)	1987-88
Away:	0-15	v Watford (Bucks & Contigious Counties League)	1898-99
		v Grays United (Southern League)	1900-01
	0-14	v Wycombe Ramblers (High Wycombe Challenge Cup)	1887-88

(N.B. Friendlies count as first team games until the First World War)

** Match played as Great Western Suburban League game, then deleted from the records after Ravenscourt Amateurs folded.

LONGEST UNBEATEN RUN
All games: 27 (16 Mar - 6 Oct 1970)
League: 43 (30 Aug 1969 - 6 Oct 1970)

LONGEST RUN WITHOUT A WIN
All games: 14 (31 Mar - 29 Sep 1900)
League: 17 (6 Apr 1907 - 1 Apr 1908)

MOST CONSECUTIVE WINS
All games: 16 (14 Oct 1893 - 10 Feb 1894)
League: 21 (10 Jan 1920 - 5 Feb 1921)

MOST CONSECUTIVE DEFEATS
All games: 8 (3 times in 1898/99, 1907/08 and 1987/88)
League: 14 (22 Apr 1907 - 21 Mar 1908)

General Notes:
Appearances and Goals refer to competitive matches (i.e. league games and cup matches), plus Friendly games upto First World War Figures in brackets indicate actual appearances and substitute appearances. Years referred to are beginning of first season to end of last season, e.g.: 1961-1978 is 1961/62 - 1977/78.

MOST GOALS IN A GAME
8 - Bill Brown v Henley Town (home) F.A. Cup 1928-29
7 - Fred Pheby v Staines (home) Great Western Suburban League 1909-10
7 - Joey Goodchild v Ravenscourt Amateurs (home) Friendly 1911-12

MOST GOALS IN A SEASON
All games: 60 - Tony Horseman 1966-67
League: 39 - Tim Hinton 1925-26

ATTENDANCE RECORDS
Loakes Park: 15,850 v St. Albans (F.A. Amatuer Cup) 25 Feb 1950
Adams Park: 9,007 v West Ham United (F.A. Cup) 7 Jan 1995
Away Ground: 30,128 at Middlesbrough (F.A. Cup) 7 Jan 1975
Neutral Ground: 90,000 at Wembley v Bishop Auckland (F.A. Amateur Cup Final) 13 Apr 1957

PLAYERS WITH 300 APPEARANCES OR MORE:

749 (710 + 39)	Tony Horseman	1961-1978
616	John Maskell	1964-1980
512 (511 + 1)	Len Worley	1954-1970
459 (451 + 8)	Paul Birdseye	1971-1982
427	Alf Britnell	1928-1945
422 (412 + 10)	Micky Holifield	1971-1981
420	Gary Lester	1979-1990
417 (416 + 1)	Paul Bates	1953-1962, 1964-1968
413	Charlie Gale	1961-1971
407 (389 + 18)	Howard Kennedy	1974-1983
391 (385 + 6)	Dave Carroll	1988-1996
390	Bernard Hooper	1900-1914
388	Charlie Tilbury	1900-1914
386	Bill Buchanan	1892-1906
381 (338 + 43)	Mark West	1984-1993
375	George Stevens	1893-1905
365	Dickie Cox	1929-1938, 1940-1945
359 (358 + 1)	John Beck	1957-1968
357 (347 + 10)	Ian Rundle	1965-1974
352 (351 + 1)	Keith Mead	1973-1982
348	Barry Baker	1963-1971
348	Jock McCallum	1935-1937, 1938-1951
331	Frank Adams	1910-1914, 1919-1929
319 (318 + 1)	Bobby Dell	1979-1986
318 (312 + 6)	Matt Crossley	1987-1996

SCORERS OF 100 GOALS OR MORE:

416	Tony Horseman	1961-1978
309	Paul Bates	1953-1962, 1964-1968
228	Bill Buchanan	1892-1906
224	Jock McCallum	1935-1937, 1938-1951
190	Bill Brown	1925-1936, 1938-1939
171	Mark West	1984-1993
168	Tim Hinton	1920-1926
158	Cliff Trott	1954-1961
157	Fred Pheby	1903-1906, 1907-1914
149	Tommy Andrews	1934-1950
144	Albert Smith	1912-1914, 1919-1925
141	Reggie Boreham	1919-1927
124	Keith Searle	1969-1975
115	Keith Samuels	1963-1970
114	Ralph Roberts	1904-1913
113	Norman Turner	1933-1946
107	Fred Abbott	1893-1899
107	Walter Brion	1902-1911, 1912-1913
107	Billy O'Gorman	1909-1914, 1919-1924
106	Frank Jennings	1889-1893, 1895-1900
104	Frank Adams	1910-1914, 1919-1929
100	Howard Kennedy	1974-1983

CLUB OFFICIALS

President		Chairman		Secretary	
J Norton	1888-1891	W Dimmock		J Ray	1887-1891
R S Wood	1891-1908	C W Deacon	1898-1900	F Jennings	1891-1893
C W Ceacon	1908-1913	R Howland	1900-1902	C W Harper	1893-1908
Marquess of Lincolnshire	1913-1928	C W Deacon	1902-1913	J N F Vale	1908-1910
Marchioness of Lincolnshire	1928-1929	G T Miles	1913-1932	B C Hooper	1910-1925
G T Miles	1929-1943	R Spatchett	1932-1951	W Howland	1928-1935
C P Vine	1943-1954	J Timberlake	1951-1954	R J Gardner	1928-1935
J Timberlake	1954-1964	G Partridge	1954-1956	W Howland	1935-1936
G Hodsdon	1964-1966	E L Webb	1956-1965	R G Boreham	1936-1949
M E Seymour	1966-	J Smethurst	1965-1975	W J Hayter	1949-1969
		R H Williams	1975-1981	A J Crump	1969-1975
		B R Lee	1981-1988	A J Mahoney	1975-
		I L Beeks	1988-	J Goldsworthy	1975-1990
				A Hutchinson	1990-
				J Goldsworthy	1990-1994
				J Reardon	1994-

Treasurer		Coaches		
G Cook	1887-1890	J McCormick	1951-1952	
W Pearce	1890-1895	S Cann	1952-1961	
C W Harper	1895-1896	C McDonald	1961-	
R Howland Jnr	1896-1898	G Adams	1961-1962	
G T Miles	1898-1926	D Welsh	1962-1964	
G R Bunce	1926-1963	B Darvill	1964-1968	
A Rackstraw	1963-1968			
R G Maskell	1968-1969	**Managers**		
R N Lee	1969-1975	B R Lee	1968-1976	
A F Ward	1975-1977	E W Powell	1976-1977	
G B Cox	1977-1986	J Reardon	1977-1978	
		A Williams	1978-1980	
Directors		M Keen	1980-1984	
B R Lee	1986-	P Bence	1984-1986	
J Goldsworthy	1986-1989	A Gane	1986-1987	
I L Beeks	1986-	P J Suddaby	1987-1988	
G F Peart	1986-	J Kelman	1988-1990	
G Richards	1986-	M O'Neill	1990-1995	
G B Cox	1986-	A Smith	1995-	
J H P Roberts	1986-1991			
A Parry	1989-			
A Thibault	1991			

INTERNATIONAL PLAYERS

England Amateur
R W Boreham
P A Bates
D Edwards
L F Worley
A Horseman
J J Delaney
L Pritchard
P J Suddaby
E W Powell
P M Fuschillo

Wales Amateur
A V Grace
J Fisher
G Anthony

STATISTICS RECORDS: 1887 - 1996

The seasonal statistics pages that follow have been designed for easy reference, and are generally self-explanatory, however the following notes are added to avoid confusion:

Left hand column signifies the match no. or the round number in a Cup competition, i.e. PR = Preliminary round, 1R = 1st round, etc., 1QR = 1st qualifying round, F = Final. A 'r' suffix indicates a replay. The second column provides the date (months abbreviated). Third column shows the opposing team (Upper case - capital letters - a Wycombe 'home' match, lower case - 'away'. Neutral venues are indicated separately). Fourth column - the match result. Fifth column, attendance (where known). Sixth column - goalscorers (where known); brackets indicate number of goals scored by that player, (pen) = goal scored from penalty; O.G. an own goal. (Where space is limited, players' names may be abbreviated).

Right-hand 'players' table - 1963/64 to 1995/96 inclusive:
The numbers refer to the shirt number worn by that player in the starting line-up. Used substitutes; no.12 replaced player with asterisk suffix (e.g. 10*), no. 14 replaced player with hash suffix (e.g. 7#), and no.13 replaced player with quote marks (e.g. 4").

(N.B. Space has precluded the inclusion of pre-1963 line-ups, the majority of which the Authors have records)

SEASON 1887-88
FRIENDLIES

No.	Date	Opposition	Res.	Att.	Goalscorers
1	24 Sep	Wycombe Nose Club	0-0		
2	22 Oct	WYCOMBE ROVERS	1-3		Ray
3	19 Nov	Flackwell Heath Ramblers	1-1		
4	26	Booker	2-0		
5	3 Dec	West Wycombe Rovers	0-0		
6	26	MARLOW ALBION	0-3		
7	*	WYCOMBE WILD WEST	0-3		
8	3 Mar	WYCOMBE NOSE CLUB	2-1		
9	10	BOOKER	5-0		
10	17	Wycombe Wild West	3-0		
11	24	FLACKWELL HEATH RAMBLERS	4-1		
12	2 Apr	WYCOMBE ROVERS	1-0		
13	3	WEST WYCOMBE ROVERS	8-0		

* Date unknown

HIGH WYCOMBE CHALLENGE CUP

1R	21 Jan	Wycombe Ramblers	0-14		

SEASON 1888-89
FRIENDLIES

No.	Date	Opposition	Res.	Att.	Goalscorers
1	10 Nov	West Wycombe Rovers	3-0		Webb(2), A.Lane
2	24	WELL END RED STAR	4-4		
3	15 Dec	Marlow Rangers	1-3		
4	22	WYCOMBE WEST END	11-0		
5	25	WYCOMBE MARSH	3-1		T.Luker(2), Webb
6	26	MARLOW RANGERS	1-1		
7	12 Jan	WYCOMBE MARSH	0-6		
8	9 Feb	Well End Red Star	1-1		
9	30 Mar	FLACKWELL HEATH RAMBLERS	1-1		

HIGH WYCOMBE CHALLENGE CUP

1R	26 Jan	WEST WYCOMBE ROVERS	5-0		Howlett, Webb(2), A.Lane, Harris
SF	23 Feb	Wycombe Marsh	1-3		

SEASON 1889-90
FRIENDLIES

No.	Date	Opposition	Res.	Att.	Goalscorers
1	28 Sep	Well End Red Star	3-0		
2	5 Oct	Wycombe Marsh	0-4		
3	2 Nov	WYCOMBE TRINITY	13-0		Morris(5), Webb(3), A.Lane(3), J.Ball, Ray
4	16	CHESHAM GENERAL BAPTIST	3-0		A.Lane, Morris(2)
5	30	Stokenchurch Reindeer	1-0		A.Lane
6	14 Dec	Marlow Juniors	2-7		
7	21	High Wycombe	0-3		
8	25	WYCOMBE ROVERS	3-0		
9	26	MARLOW RANGERS	3-2		Morris(2), Ray
10	28	Chesham General Baptist	0-1		
11	11 Jan	STOCKENCHURCH REINDEER	4-0		
12	1 Feb	MARLOW JUNIORS	2-2		Webb, Ray
13	8	Boyne Hill Y.M.F.S.	3-1		Webb, F.Jennings(2)
14	15	BOYNE HILL Y.M.F.S.	1-0		Lee
15	20	MR B.L. REYNOLDS' XI	1-0		Janes
16	5 Apr	J.KEEN'S XI	2-0		A.Lane(2)
17	7	FINSBURY POLYTECHNIC	5-1		A.Lane, Webb(2), F.Jennings(2)

HIGH WYCOMBE CHALLENGE CUP

SF	22 Feb	Birch's Factory	3-0	500	Ray(2), Morris
F*	15 Mar	High Wycombe	1-1		
Fr*	22	High Wycombe	1-1		
F2r*	29	High Wycombe	2-0		Ray, Crook

* Played at Wycombe Marsh

SEASON 1890-91
FRIENDLIES

No.	Date	Opposition	Res.	Att.	Goalscorers
1	20 Sep	CHESHAM GENERALS	4-1		Ray, Webb, A.Lane, unknown(1)
2	27	Boyne Hill Y.M.F.S.	1-1		Bowles
3	4 Oct	Wycombe Marsh	2-0		Webb(2)
4	1 Nov	BOYNE HILL Y.M.F.S.	1-0		
5	8	CHESHAM RESERVES	3-1	250	A.Lane(3)
6	22	Burnham	3-0		
7	6 Dec	Boyne Hill Y.M.F.S.	1-0		F.Jennings
8	13	High Wycombe	0-2		
9	7 Feb	Chesham Generals	0-4		
10	14	Sir W.Borlase's School	7-0		
11	7 Mar	Marlow Reserves	1-0		
12	14	MARLOW RESERVES	1-0		Webb
13	30	FINSBURY POLYTECHNIC	3-1		A.Lane, Beckett, unknown(1)

BERKS & BUCKS JUNIOR CUP

1R	18 Oct	WYCOMBE MARSH	4-0		Webb, A.Lane(2), F.Jennings
2R	15 Nov	STANTONBURY UNITY	5-1	500	Ray, F.Jennings(2), Webb(2)
3R	17 Jan	CHESHAM RESERVES	3-2		F.Jennings, Webb, A.Lane
SF*	21 Feb	Maidenhead Norfolkians	2-1	750	Webb, O.G.
F#	21 Mar	Reading Albion	2-2	1500	Ray, F.Jennings
Fr#	4 Apr	Reading Albion	2-6	1000	Ray, Webb

* Played at Marlow
# Played at Maidenhead Town Ground

HIGH WYCOMBE CHALLENGE CUP

1R	31 Jan	High Wycombe	2-1		F.Jennings, unknown(1)
SF	25 Feb	Wycombe Rovers	5-0		F.Jennings, White, Ray(2), Webb
F*	28 Mar	Wycombe Marsh	0-3	250	

* Played at Wycombe Marsh

SEASON 1891-92
FRIENDLIES

No.	Date	Opposition	Res.	Att.	Goalscorers
1	26 Sep	Wycombe Marsh	3-2		C.Jennings, Webb, F.Jennings
2	3 Oct	MAIDENHEAD RESERVES	1-1		Webb
3	10	AYLESBURY PRINTING WORKS	2-4		Webb, unknown(1)
4	24	Wooburn	2-3		C.Jennings, Clark
5	7 Nov	Maidenhead Norfolkians	1-0		F.Jennings
6	5 Dec	Wycombe Marsh	1-0		C.Jennings
7	26	High Wycombe	0-0		
8	27 Feb	Marlow Reserves	0-3		
9	5 Mar	Thame	1-4		
10	19	Aylesbury Printing Works	3-3		
11	2 Apr	MARLOW RESERVES	4-1		C.Jennings(2), Harper, Webb
12	16	HIGH WYCOMBE	3-3		A.Lane, F.Jennings, Webb
13	18	FINSBURY POLYTECHNIC	5-1		Webb(3), F.Jennings(2)

BERKS & BUCKS JUNIOR CUP

1R	17 Oct	BURNHAM	5-1	400	F.Jennings(3), Beckett, Webb
2R	14 Nov	SLOUGH	1-3	700	A.Lane

HIGH WYCOMBE CHALLENGE CUP

1R	12 Dec	Maidenhead Forfolkians	1-2		A.Lane

MAIDENHEAD NORFOLKIANS' CHARITY CUP

1R	31 Oct	MAIDENHEAD FORFOLKIANS	2-1	500	Webb(2)
2R	16 Jan	Maidenhead Reserves	0-1		

SEASON 1892/93
FRIENDLIES

No.	Date	Opposition	Res.	Att.	Goalscorers
1	10 Sep	CHESHAM RESERVES	2-0		Eustace, Bowles
2	17	Windsor & Eton Victoria	1-2		F.Jennings
3	8 Oct	Maidenhead	0-6		
4	15	BURNHAM	2-0		F.Jennings(2)
5	29	Aylesbury Printing Works	5-0		C.Jennings,F.Jennings,Harper,Webb,A.Lane
6	4 Feb	Chesham Generals	0-5		
7	11	Wycombe Marsh	0-1		
8	18	Marlow Reserves	0-1		
9	25	Wycombe Marsh	5-1		
10	4 Mar	Chesham	0-5		
11	18	MARLOW RESERVES	6-1		F.Jennings(3),A.Turner,Webb,unknown(1)
12	3 Apr	FINSBURY POLYTECHNIC	1-1		F.Jennings

BERKS & BUCKS JUNIOR CUP

1R	22 Oct	CHESHAM RESERVES	5-0		F.Jennings(2), Webb(2), unknown(1)
2R	26 Nov	WOLVERTON L. & N.W.R. RES.	2-2		A.Lane, F.Jennings
2Rr	3 Dec	Wolverton L. & N.W.R. Reserves	1-1		Harper
2R2r	17	WOLVERTON L. & N.W.R. RES.	2-0		F.Jennings(2)
3R	28 Jan	Chesham Gererals	2-4		Harper, F.Jennings

HIGH WYCOMBE CHALLENGE CUP

PR	5 Nov	Wycombe West End United	4-0		Webb(2), C.Jennings, A.Turner
1R	10 Dec	Wycombe Marsh Gordons	7-0		A.Lne(2),J.Putnm,C.Jnnings,Wbb,F.Jnnings(2)
2R	14 Jan	MAIDENHEAD NORFOLKIANS	0-1		

MAIDENHEAD NORFOLKIANS' CHARITY CUP

1R	19 Nov	WINDSOR & ETON RESERVES	2-1		A.Lane, J.Putnam
2R	26 Dec	TAPLOW Y.M.F.S.	2-0		
SF*	1 Apr	Wycombe Marsh	1-3		

* Played at Kidwell's Park, Maidenhead

SEASON 1893/94
FRIENDLIES

No.	Date	Opposition	Res.	Att.	Goalscorers
1	9 Sep	Chesham Reserves	3-3		W.Hearn, Webb, W.Buchanan
2	16	AYLESBURY PRINTING WORKS	4-1		Webb, W.Buchanan, Bowles, O.G.
3	23	Henley	2-2		Unknown
4	30	Marlow Reserves	3-0		Butterfield, A.Lane, Jones
5	7 Oct	Burnham	2-3		Webb(2)
6	14	WOLVERTON L. & N.W.R. RES.	3-2		Jones, Unknown(2)
7	11 Nov	ROYAL HORSEGUARDS (BLUE)	3-0	400	Webb(2), A.Lane
8	23 Dec	HENLEY	5-1		W.Buchanan, Harper(2), Abbott(2)
9	26	MAIDENHEAD NORFOLKIANS	4-0	550	Jones(2), W.Buchanan, Webb
10	28	WOLVERTON L. & N.W.R.	2-0	2000	W.Buchanan, O.G.
11	13 Jan	CHESHAM RESERVES	7-0		W.Buchanan(3), Abbott(2), Jones(2)
12	17 Feb	Maidenhead Norfolkians	2-1		Webb, W.Buchanan
13	24	Wycombe Marsh	7-1		W.Buchanan(3),Jones,A.Lane,Harpr,Webb
14	10 Mar	1ST COLDSTREAM GUARDS	2-2	300	Jones(2)
15	10	MIDDLESBROUGH IRONOPOLIS	0-3	1600	
16	24	ROYAL ORDNANCE FACTORIES	1-2		Stevens
17	26	FINSBURY POLYTECHNIC	1-0		W.Buchanan
18	28	1ST COLDSTREAM GUARDS	1-4		Abbott
19	31	Royal Horseguards (Blue)	0-4		
20	21 Apr	MR H. MAISEY'S XI	1-1		W.Buchanan

BERKS & BUCKS JUNIOR CUP

1R	21 Oct	Datchet	8-0		A.Lne,Harpr(3),Jnes(2),W.Bchann,Webb
2R	25 Nov	Wycombe Marsh	4-0	500	A.Turner(pen), Webb, Abbott, Jones
3R	16 Dec	MARLOW RESERVES	2-1	600	Stevens, W.Buchanan
4R	20 Jan	BURNHAM	5-1	1268	A.Lane, Webb(2), W.Buchanan, Jones
SF*	10 Feb	Chesham Reserves	1-2	500	Jones

* Played at Marlow

HIGH WYCOMBE CHALLENGE CUP

PR	4 Nov	Wycombe Marsh	7-0	600	A.Lne(2),Cllier,Abbtt,W.Bchann(2),Webb
1R	9 Dec	BURNHAM	4-1	600	Jones, Webb, W.Buchanan(2)
2R	30	Bourne End Excelsior	1-0		Jones
SF*	3 Feb	Stokenchurch	5-0	400	Webb, A.Lane, W.Buchanan(2), Abbott
F*	3 Mar	Marlow Reserves	3-1	1000	W.Buchanan, Jones(2)

* Played at Wycombe Marsh

MAIDENHEAD NORFOLKIANS' CHARITY CUP

1R	2 Dec	Maidenhead Norfolkians	2-1		Abbott, Jones
SF*	27 Jan	Slough	3-1		W.Buchanan, Abbott(2)
F#	17 Mar	Windsor & Eton Victoria	5-1		W.Buchanan(2), Webb, Jones(2)

* Played at St. Ives' Meadow, Maidenhead
# Played at Maidenhead Town Ground

SEASON 1894/95
FRIENDLIES

No.	Date	Opposition	Res.	Att.	Goalscorers
1	8 Sep	Wycombe Marsh	8-0		Abbtt(2),W.Bchann,Lloyd(3),Valentine,A.Turnr
2	15	Maidenhead Resreves	4-1		W.Buchanan(2), Abbott, A.Turner
3	22	1ST SCOTS GUARDS	0-3		
4*	29	BOURNE END EXCELSIOR	11-0		Abbtt(2),W.Bchann(4),Llyd(3),Hddock,Stvns
5*	6 Oct	Burnham	7-1	200	Abbott(3(, Jones, O.G., Harper, Lloyd
6*	13	LOUDWATER	6-2		Abbott(3), W.Buchanan(3)
7	20	Royal Horseguards (Blue)	1-3		Abbott
8*	27	MAIDENHEAD NORFOLKIANS	1-3		W.Buchanan
9*	3 Nov	MAIDENHEAD RESERVES	6-0		Abbott(3), Jones, Lloyd, A.Putnam
10	24	SOUTHALL	2-1		Abbott(2)
11	15 Dec	HANWELL	4-1		Lloyd(2), O.G., Abbott
12	22	SOUTHALL	2-2		Abbott, Biggs
13	24	WOLVERTON L. & N.W.R. RES.	6-0		W.Buchanan(3), Webb(2), Abbott
14	27	1ST SCOTS GUARDS	3-0	1000	Abbott(2), Hutchinson
15	29	HENLEY	4-0		A.Turner, Abbott, O.G., W.Buchanan
16	19 Jan	OLYMPIANS	8-1		Htchinsn,W.Buchanan(4),Llyd,Abbtt,A.Lane
17	23 Feb	Uxbridge	6-6		Hutchinson(2), Lloyd(3), Abbott
18	2 Mar	EAST SURREY REGIMENT	5-0		Hutchinson, Lloyd(2), W.Buchanan, Ward
19	16	OLYMPIANS	3-0		W.Buchanan, Abbott(2)
20	23	PARK GROVE	1-0		W.Buchanan(pen)
21	6 Apr	1ST COLDSTREAM GUARDS	3-2		W.Buchanan, Webb(2)
22	12	KILDARE	3-1		Lloyd(2), Hutchinson
23	13	PARK GROVE	3-1		Hutchinson, W.Buchanan, Abbott
24	16	SOUTH LONDON	1-1		Lloyd
25	20	UPTON PARK	2-1		W.Buchanan(2)

* These matches were played in the East Berks & South Bucks Junior League before the first team withdrew. The remaining fixtures were later taken over by the reserve team.

F.A. AMATEUR CUP

2R	10 Nov	West Herts	1-5		W.Buchanan

BERKS & BUCKS SENIOR CUP

1R	8 Dec	Slough	4-0		O.G. Lloyd, W.Buchanan(2)
2R	5 Jan	WOLVERTON L & N.W.R.	0-1		

HIGH WYCOMBE CHALLENGE CUP

1R	1 Dec	Stokenchurch	2-0		W.Buchanan(2)
2R	28	Chesham Generals	3-2		W.Buchanan(2), Jones
SF*	26 Jan	Marlow Reserves	5-1		W.Buchanan, Abbott(2), Hutchinson(2)
F*	27 Apr	Maidenhead Norfolkians	5-0		Lloyd, Abbott(2), A.Lane, W.Buchanan

* Played at Wycombe Marsh

MAIDENHEAD NORFOLKIANS' CHARITY CUP

SF*	30 Mar	Slough	3-1	250	O.G., Lloyd, W.Buchanan
F*	24 Apr	1st Scots Guards	1-6		W.Buchanan

* Played at Kidwell's Park, Maidenhead

SEASON 1895/96
FRIENDLIES

No.	Date	Opposition	Res.	Att.	Goalscorers
1	7 Sep	PARK GROVE	1-0		W. Buchanan
2	14	ROMFORD	6-4		F.Keen,Abbtt,W.Bchann,F.Jnnings,Woostr,Llyd
3	21	OLD ST. STEPHENS	3-1		F.Jennings, W.Buchanan, Wooster
4	28	CIVIL SERVICE	2-1		Hutchinson, Wooster
5	5 Oct	WEST HAM GARFIELD	1-1		W.Buchanan
6	19	Tottenham Hotspur	4-3		W.Buchanan(2), F.Jennings, Lloyd
7	26	UPTON PARK	5-1		W.Buchanan(3), A.Lane, Abbott
8	28	MIDDLESBROUGH	1-3		F.Jennings
9	16 Nov	UNIVERSITY COLLEGE HOSPITAL	5-0		A.Putnam(3), Jennings, O.G.
10	30	Marlow	2-2	1500	Abbott, Randell
11	7 Dec	49TH REGIMENTAL DISTRICT	5-0		W.Buchanan(3), White, J.Lane
12	21	MARLOW	4-2	2000	Abbott(4)
13	26	1ST SCOTS GUARDS	3-3	1200	W.Buchanan, F.Jennings, Randell
14	27	ROYAL ORDNANCE FACTORIES	1-3		A.Hearn
15	28	THE IDLERS	3-0		Abbott(2), A.Hearn
16	4 Jan	OLYMPIANS	11-1		Abbott(3),Llyd,W.Bchanan(3),F.Jnnings(4)
17	11	PECKHAM	9-1		O.G., W.Buchanan(6), F.Jennings, Webb
18	18	Eastville Rovers	2-2	1000	W.Buchanan, Abbott
19	8 Feb	BARKING WOODSIDE	1-1		Randell
20	22	ERITH UNITED	4-0		W.Buchanan, Abbott(2), Lloyd
21	7 Mar	OLD. ST. MARKS	7-1		F.Jennings(2), Lloyd(3), Abbott, O.G.
22	14	HANWELL	1-0		F.Jennings
23	21	WEST BROMWICH ALBION	1-4	2000	W.Buchanan
24	28	LEYTON	5-2		R.Turner, Lloyd(3), Abbott
25	3 Apr	KILDARE	6-0		Lloyd, Abbott, Randell(3), R.Turner
26	4	MAIDENHEAD	9-0	800	R.Turnr(3),W.Bchann(3),Llyd,F.Jnnings,Cllier
27	7	MR LOCKYER'S XI	3-2		Lloyd(2), Abbott
28	11	VAMPIRES	2-3		W.Buchanan, King
29	18	LONDON CALEDONIANS RES.	4-1		Lloyd, F.Jennings(3)

F.A. CUP

1QR	12 Oct	WOLVERTON L. & N.W.R.	2-3	1500	F.Jennings, Abbott

F.A. AMATEUR CUP

2QR	2 Nov	NEWBURY	1-0		F.Jennings
3QR	23	ROYAL SCOTS FUSILIERS	9-0		W.Bchann(2),Abbtt(3),Cllier,Bains(2),F.Jnnings
4QR	14 Dec	East Lancs. Regiment	3-2		F.Jennings, W.Buchanan, Abbott
1R	1 Feb	Marlow	2-3	2700	W.Buchanan, F.Jennings

BERKS & BUCKS SENIOR CUP

1R	9 Nov	Chesham	1-2		W.Buchanan

MAIDENHEAD NORFOLKIANS' CHARITY CUP

1R	25 Jan	Reading Redlands	3-2		Randell(2), Janes
SF	29 Feb	READING TEMPERANCE	6-1		W.Buchanan(2),F.Keen,F.Jnnings,Llyd,Abbtt
F*	22 Apr	Maidenhead Norfolkians	1-2		O.G.

* Played at Kidwell's Park, Maidenhead

Season 1893/94
A.Turner, T. Ball, Harper, Collier, O.Ball, Stevens, Lane, Webb, W.Buchanan, Abbott, Jones

Season 1896/97: (Back) Harper (Secretary), A.Keen, F.Keen, J.Ball, Stevens, H.Turner, Howland (Treas.). (Middle) C.Buchanan, R.Collier. (Front) Green, Abbott, Jennings, W.Buchanan

SEASON 1896/97
SOUTHERN LEAGUE DIVISION TWO

No.	Date	Opposition	Res.	Att.	Goalscorers
1	19 Sep	West Herts	0-5		
2	26	UXBRIDGE	1-2		Abbott
3	3 Oct	Dartford	0-9	1200	
4	17	SOUTHALL	3-3		W.Carter, King, Abbott
5	24	Chesham	1-0	450	W.Buchanan
6	14 Nov	Old St. Stephens	2-0		Abbott(2)
7	5 Dec	R.E.T.B. (Chatham)	1-3		W.Buchanan
8	19	WARMLEY	2-1		W.Buchanan, Green
9	25	MAIDENHEAD	2-2		F.Jennings(2)
10	26	FREEMANTLE	3-2		Davies, Green(2)
11	9 Jan	WEST HERTS	2-1		Stevens, Green
12	6 Feb	1ST SCOTS GUARDS	0-5		
13	13	OLD ST. STEPHENS	3-1		F.Jennings, Abbott(2)
14	15	1ST COLDSTREAM GUARDS	3-2		F.Jennings, E.Shaw, W.Buchanan
15	20	CHESHAM	2-2	1000	Abbott, F.Jennings
16	6 Mar	1ST SCOTS GUARDS	2-2		Davies, W.Buchanan
17	8	Warmley	1-0	1000	Abbott
18	13	Maidenhead	2-4	1200	Davies, Green
19	20	1ST COLDSTREAM GUARDS	2-0		F.Jennings, Abbott
20	3 Apr	R.E.T.B. (CHATHAM)	1-1		F.Jennings
21	10	Uxbridge	1-1		F.Keen
22	12	DARTFORD	1-0		W.Buchanan
23	17	Southall	1-4		F.Keen
24	19	Freemantle	1-4		F.Keen

N.B. Both games against 1st Scots Guards and 1st Coldstream Guards played at Loakes Park.

F.A. CUP

1QR	31 Oct	Norwich C.E.Y.M.S.	1-2	1400	W.Buchanan(pen)

F.A. AMATEUR CUP

1R	30 Jan	CASUALS	3-5		Green(2), F.Jennings

BERKS & BUCKS SENIOR CUP

2R	16 Jan	NEWBURY	1-0		O.G.
SF*	27 Feb	Chesham Generals	1-0	1700	Abbott
F#	27 Mar	Marlow	1-2	4000	F.Jennings

* Played at Aylesbury
# Played at Maidenhead

Final League Table

		P.	W.	D.	L.	F.	A.	Pts.
1	Dartford	24	16	4	4	83	19	36
2	Royal Engineers Training Btn.	24	11	9	4	49	37	31
3	Freemantle	24	12	4	8	58	40	28
4	Uxbridge	24	11	5	8	62	37	27
5	Wycombe Wanderers	24	10	6	8	37	54	26
6	Chesham	24	11	3	10	41	55	25
7	Southall	24	9	6	9	55	52	24
8	1st Scots Guards	24	9	6	9	49	50	24
9	Warmley (Bristol)	24	10	3	11	44	43	23
10	West Herts	24	11	1	12	41	49	23
11	Old St Stephen's	24	5	7	12	36	52	17
12	Maidenhead	24	4	8	12	33	64	16
13	1st Coldstream Guards	24	3	6	15	30	86	12

SEASON 1897/98
SOUTHERN LEAGUE DIVISION TWO

No.	Date	Opposition	Res.	Att.	Goalscorers
1	2 Oct	ST. ALBANS	2-1		C.Buchanan, W.Buchanan
2	9	Warmley	0-4	600	
3	6 Nov	WEST HERTS	1-2		C.Buchanan
4	13	OLD ST. STEPHENS	0-2		
5	20	R.E.T.B. (CHATHAM)	4-1		Abbott(3), F.Jennings
6	18 Dec	Southall	2-6		F.Jennings(2)
7	20	ROYAL ART. (PORTSMOUTH)	1-3		H.Butler
8	1 Jan	MAIDENHEAD	0-0	1000	
9	8	St. Albans	1-2	400	W.Buchanan
10	22	R.E.T.B. (Chatham)	1-3		F.Keen
11	5 Feb	Dartford	3-5		C.Buchanan, Abbott(2)
12	19	Maidenhead	5-1		Green(2), W.Buchanan(3)
13	9 Mar	Royal Artillery (Portsmouth)	0-6	1500	
14	12	Old St. Stephens	3-2		C.Buchanan, Abbott(2,1pen)
15	19	WARMLEY	2-6		Abbott(pen), C.Buchanan
16	2 Apr	West Herts	2-4		W.Buchanan, J.Lane
17	6	UXBRIDGE	3-1		W.Buchanan, Abbott, F.Keen
18	9	Chesham	0-3		
19	12	DARTFORD	4-1		Collier, Green, C.Buchanan(2)
20	13	CHESHAM	0-1		
21	16	Uxbridge	1-1		Green
22	20	SOUTHALL	2-0		Abbott, W.Buchanan

F.A. CUP

1QR	25 Sep	Chesham Generals	0-3		

F.A. AMATUER CUP

1R	29 Jan	Old Westminsters	5-0		C.Buchanan(2),W.Buchann,Green,Abbtt
2R	12 Feb	2ND COLDSTREAM GUARDS	3-1	1100	F.Jennings, C.Buchanan, O.G.
3R	26	Uxbridge	1-1	2500	C.Buchanan
3Rr	5 Mar	UXBRIDGE	2-4	2500	C.Buchanan, Abbott(pen)

BERKS & BUCKS SENIOR CUP

2R	4 Dec	CHESHAM GENERALS	0-2		

Final League Table

		P.	W.	D.	L.	F.	A.	Pts.
1	Royal Artillery (Portsmouth)	22	19	1	2	75	22	39
2	Warmley (Bristol)	22	19	0	3	108	15	38
3	West Herts	22	11	6	5	50	48	28
4	Uxbridge	22	11	2	9	39	57	24
5	St Albans	22	9	5	8	47	41	23
6	Dartford	22	11	0	11	68	55	22
7	Southall	22	8	2	12	49	61	18
8	Chesham	22	8	2	12	38	48	18
9	Old St Stephen's	22	7	2	13	47	66	16
10	Wycombe Wanderers	22	7	2	13	37	55	16
11	Maidenhead	22	4	4	14	27	81	12
12	Royal Engineers Training Btn.	22	4	2	16	26	62	10

c.1897 Reserve team: (Back) Harper (Sec.), Butler, ? , ? , ? , Maine, Miles (Treas.).
(Middle) ? , A Buchanan, ? , ? , T Barlow. (Front) ?

1898/99 Season: (Back) Horwood, Harper (Sec.), Wheeler, H.Turner, Plumridge, Miles (Treasurer)
(Middle) F.Keen (Capt.), White, R.Collier, W.Buchanan, Stevens (Vice-Capt.) (Front) Green, A.Keen, Jennings, Aldridge

SEASON 1898/99
SOUTHERN LEAGUE DIVISION TWO

No.	Date	Opposition	Res.	Att.	Goalscorers
1	17 Sep	CHESHAM TOWN	1-2	800	Green
2	1 Oct	Maidenhead	0-7	250	
3	8	SOUTHALL	4-5	450	R.Butler, W.Buchanan, Aldridge(2)
4	15	Brentford	2-9		White(2)
5	22	Wolverton L. & N.W.R.	2-4		White(2)
6	29	THAMES IRONWORKS	4-1		Aldridge(3), White
7	5 Nov	ST. ALBANS	5-0	500	F.Jnnings,Stevns(2),C.Bchanan,W.Bchanan
8	19	Uxbridge	3-0		F.F.Jennings, Aldridge, C.Buchanan
9	26	WOLVERTON L. & N.W.R.	4-3		H.Turner(p),Aldridge,Abbott,W.Buchanan
10	17 Dec	Fulham	1-3	650	Aldridge
11	24	SHEPHERD'S BUSH	6-1		F.Jnnings(2),White(2),Aldridge,C.Bchanan
12	14 Jan	Thames Ironworks	1-4		F.Keen(pen)
13	21	Watford	3-1	800	C.Buchanan(3)
14	4 Feb	Southall	1-0	700	White
15	4 Mar	WATFORD	2-2	1000	F.F.Jennings, W.Buchanan
16	25	Chesham Town	2-4		Aldridge, White
17	1 Apr	Shepherd's Bush	0-4	1500	
18	10	FULHAM	4-1		Aldridge(pen), Rolfe, Collier, W.Buchanan
19	17	UXBRIDGE	5-1		A.Keen, Rolfe(2), White(2)
20	20	St. Albans	0-4		
21	22	BRENTFORD	1-1		F.F.Jennings
22	24	MAIDENHEAD	4-0	200	Aldridge(pen), W.Buchanan, F.Keen

BUCKS & CONTIGUOUS COUNTIES' LEAGUE

No.	Date	Opposition	Res.	Att.	Goalscorers
1	10 Sep	CHESHAM GENERALS	0-2	1500	
2	14	Watford	0-15		
3	12 Nov	Chesham Town	1-3		W.Buchanan
4	5 Dec	WATFORD	1-2		F.Jennings
5	31	Aylesbury United	5-2	100	J.Aldridge(2), F.Jennings(3)
6	25 Feb	Wolverton L. & N.W.R.	1-7	200	R.Janes
7	18 Mar	Chesham Generals	0-2		
8	8 Apr	AYLESBURY UNITED	9-0	500	W.Bchanan(4),Green,Rlfe,White,F.Jnnings,Stvnsa
9	15	WOLVERTON L. & N.W.R.	2-2		W.Buchanan, J.Aldridge
10	29	CHESHAM TOWN	1-0	700	H.Aldridge

F.A. CUP

PR	24 Sep	MARLOW	1-2	1900	W.Buchanan

F.A. AMATEUR CUP

1R	28 Jan	BRENTFORD	2-3	1200	White, W.Buchanan

BERKS & BUCKS SENIOR CUP

2R	3 Dec	SLOUGH	2-1	1800	F.Jennings, Green
SF*	18 Feb	Aylesbury United	1-1	2638	W.Buchanan
SFr*	11 Mar	Aylesbury United	3-0	2777	W.Buchanan, Aldridge, F.Jennings
F#	3 Apr	Marlow	1-2	7752	W.Buchanan

* Played at Marlow
# Played at Maidenhead

Final League Table

		P.	W.	D	L	F	A	Pts.
1	Thames Ironworks	22	19	1	2	64	16	39
2	Wolverton L. & N.W. Rly	22	13	4	5	88	43	30
3	Watford	22	14	2	6	62	35	30
4	Brentford	22	11	3	8	59	39	25
5	Wycombe Wanderers	22	10	2	10	55	57	22
6	Southall	22	11	0	11	44	55	22
7	Chesham	22	9	2	11	45	62	20
8	St Albans	22	8	3	11	45	59	19
9	Shepherd's Bush	22	7	3	12	37	53	17
10	Fulham	22	6	4	12	36	44	16
11	Uxbridge	22	7	2	13	29	48	16
12	Maidenhead	22	3	2	17	33	86	8

SEASON 1899-1900
SOUTHERN LEAGUE DIVISION TWO

No.	Date	Opposition	Res.	Att.	Goalscorers
1	2 Sep	Chesham Town	0-4		
2	9	Brentford	0-1		
3	23	Southall	2-0		F.Jennings, Barlow
4	7 Oct	WOLVERTON L. & N.W.R.	3-1		A.Keen, W.Buchanan, White
5	11 Nov	SHEPHERD'S BUSH	2-1	500	W.Buchanan, J.Aldridge
6	25	WATFORD	2-1		J.Aldridge(pen), Unknown(1)
7	6 Jan	MAIDENHEAD	6-0		Barlow(2),White(2),W.Bchanan,F.Jnnings
8	13	GRAYS UNITED	2-2		W.Buchanan(2,1pen)
9	24 Feb	SOUTHALL	1-0	800	O.G.
10	10 Mar	Watford	0-1		
11	17	Maidenhead	1-0		W.Buchanan
12	21	DARTFORD	6-1		White(2), W.Buchanan(2), Stevens, O.G.
13	31	Shepherd's Bush	2-3		W.Buchanan, Barlow
14	7 Apr	CHESHAM TOWN	5-5	500	Redington,Barlow(2),W.Buchanan(2,1pen)
15	14	Fulham	0-2		
16	18	Dartford	0-6		
17	21	Wolverton L. & N.W.R.	0-5		
18	25	FULHAM	0-6		
19	28	Grays United	0-9		
20	30	BRENTFORD	2-2	100	O.G. Carter

F.A. CUP

3QR	28 Oct	READING	0-8	2800	

F.A. AMATEUR CUP

1QR	21 Oct	SLOUGH	3-1	900	Green, Stevens, W.Buchanan
2QR	4 Nov	Maidenhead	6-0		F.Jennings,W.Buchanan(2),J.Aldridge(p) *
3QR	18	OXFORD CITY	2-0	1000	Green, F.Jennings
4QR	9 Dec	Reading Amateurs	3-0		F.Jennings
1R	20 Jan	MARLOW	1-1	3000	White
1Rr	27	Marlow	0-1	2500	

* Extra scorers = A.Keen, Green

BERKS & BUCKS SENIOR CUP

2R	2 Dec	Aylesbury United	2-1		J.Aldridge, F.Jennings
SF*	3 Mar	Maidenhead Norfolkians	3-1	1500	W.Buchanan, White(2)
F#	16 Apr	Marlow	1-1	5363	W.Buchanan
Fr#	23	Marlow	3-4	4000	Barlow, W.Buchanan(pen), White

* Played at Marlow
# Played at Maidenhed

Final League Table

		P.	W.	D	L	F	A	Pts.
1	Watford	20	14	2	4	56	25	30
2	Fulham	20	10	5	5	44	19	25
3	Chesham Town	20	9	6	5	46	34	24
4	Wolverton L. & N.W. Rly	20	11	2	7	43	38	24
5	Grays United	20	8	6	6	61	29	22
6	Shepherd's Bush	20	8	5	7	41	36	21
7	Wycombe Wanderers	20	8	3	9	35	50	19
8	Dartford	20	7	3	10	35	42	17
9	Brentford	20	5	7	8	31	48	17
10	Southall	20	6	3	11	20	42	15
11	Maidenhead	20	2	2	16	18	64	6

SEASON 1900-01
SOUTHERN LEAGUE DIVISION TWO

No.	Date	Opposition	Res.	Att.	Goalscorers
1	6 Oct	Southall	0-2		
2	13	SHEPHERD'S BUSH	0-3	500	
3	17 Nov	Sheppey United	1-10	500	Snell
4	24	BRENTFORD	1-4	1000	Rouse
5	15 Dec	MAIDENHEAD	1-2	500	Rouse
6	26	Chesham Town	1-5		Rouse
7	27	GRAYS UNITED	2-2		Rouse(2)
8	16 Feb	Brentford	1-11	1000	W.Buchanan
9	9 Mar	Maidenhead	3-2		Barlow, O.G., Rouse
10	16	Fulham	0-5	1000	
11	6 Apr	Shepherd's Bush	0-3		
12	8	CHESHAM TOWN	1-0		Barlow
13	10	Grays uNITED	0-15		
14	13	SOUTHALL	9-1		Barlow(3), Rouse(4), Green(2)
15	27	SHEPPEY UNITED	1-0		Rouse
16	29	FULHAM	2-3		Rouse, W.Buchanan

F.A. AMATEUR CUP

| 1R | 19 Jan | RICHMOND ASSOCIATION | 2-1 | 1500 | Saville, Rouse |
| 2R | 9 Feb | Ealing | 2-5 | 1000 | Barlow(2) |

Final League Table

	P.	W.	D.	L.	F.	A.	Pts.
1 Brentford	16	14	2	0	63	11	30
2 Grays United	16	12	2	2	62	12	26
3 Sheppey United	16	8	1	7	44	26	17
4 Shepherd's Bush	16	8	1	7	30	30	17
5 Fulham	16	8	0	8	38	26	16
6 Chesham Town	16	5	1	10	26	39	11
7 Maidenhead	16	4	1	11	21	49	9
8 Wycombe Wanderers	16	4	1	11	23	68	9
9 Southall	16	4	1	11	22	68	9

SEASON 1901-02
SOUTHERN LEAGUE DIVISION TWO

No.	Date	Opposition	Res.	Att.	Goalscorers
1	28 Sep	Maidenhead	3-0		Barlow, W.Buchanan, Rouse
2	12 Oct	Chesham Town	3-2		W.Buchanan, White, Rouse
3	19	FULHAM	1-2	1000	Barlow
4	28 Dec	Shepherd's Bush	0-5	600	
5	11 Jan	SOUTHALL	11-0		F.Keen(3), Rouse(2), W.Buchanan(2), *
6	25	MAIDENHEAD	3-0		W.Buchanan, White, Unknown(1)
7	1 Feb	GRAYS UNITED	1-2		Barlow
8	1 Mar	Grays United	0-6		
9	8	Brighton & Hove Albion	0-1	1500	
10	15	WEST HAMPSTEAD	1-1	1000	Hearn
11	1 Apr	BRIGHTON & HOVE ALBION	2-0		W.Buchanan, Rouse
12	5	CHESHAM TOWN	6-0		Rouse(3), W.Buchanan(3)
13	12	Fulham	0-8		
14	14	West Hampstead	2-2		Hearn, Barlow
15	21	SHEPHERD'S BUSH	2-0	500	F.Keen, Barlow
16	26	Southall	1-1		Hearn

* Extra scorers = White(2), Tilbury, Barlow

BERKS & BUCKS SENIOR LEAGUE

1	14 Sep	SLOUGH	2-0		Barlow, Rouse
2	21 Dec	Slough	0-3		
3	4 Jan	Maidenhead Norfolkians	0-4	150	
4	24 Feb	MARLOW	0-0	300	
5	5 Mar	MAIDENHEAD NORFOLKIANS	1-3		Hearn
6	12	Marlow	0-3		

F.A. CUP

3QR	2 Nov	MAIDENHEAD	1-1	1000	Rouse(pen)
3QRr	7	Maidenhead	2-0	400	Pugh, White
4QR	16	OXFORD CITY	2-5	2000	W.Buchanan, Rouse(pen)

F.A. AMATEUR CUP

1QR	26 Oct	CHESHAM GENERALS	3-1	2000	O.G., A.Keen, Barlow
2QR	9 Nov	Slough	2-0	950	F.Keen, W.Buchanan
3QR	23	CHESHAM TOWN	5-0	1450	White, Rouse(2), Pugh(2)
4QR	7 Dec	Oxford City	1-2	1000	Hearn

BERKS & BUCKS SENIOR CUP

1R	30 Nov	Maidenhead	4-1		Green, White, Rouse, Stevens
2R	14 Dec	Aylesbury United	2-1		Hearn, Green
SF*	22 Feb	Chesham Generals	2-1	3000	Rouse, Pugh
F#	31 Mar	Slough	3-0	6500	W.Buchanan, White, Rouse

* Played at Marlow
# Played at Maidenhead

(Southern League) Final League Table

	P.	W.	D.	L.	F.	A.	Pts.
1 Fulham	16	13	0	3	51	19	26
2 Grays United	16	12	1	3	49	14	25
3 Brighton & Hove Albion	16	11	0	5	34	17	22
4 Wycombe Wanderers	16	7	3	6	36	30	17
5 West Hampstead	16	6	4	6	39	29	16
6 Shepherd's Bush	16	6	1	9	31	31	13
7 Southall	16	5	2	9	28	52	12
8 Maidenhead	16	3	1	12	23	59	7
9 Chesham Town	16	2	2	12	24	64	6

(Berks & Bucks Senior League - South Bucks & East Berks. Div.) Final league Table

	P.	W.	D.	L.	F.	A.	Pts.
1 Marlow	6	3	2	1	7	5	8
2 Maidenhead Norf'olkians	6	4	1	1	15	4	7*
3 Slough	6	1	2	3	5	8	4
4 Wycombe Wanderers	6	1	1	4	3	13	3

* 2 points deducted for fielding an ineligible player 1901/02

Season 1901/02. Berks & Bucks Senior Cup Winners: (Back) Free (Trainer), Weston (Committee), Tilbury, Reynolds, Horwood, A Keen (Middle) Harper (Secretary), F Keen, Tilbury, Stevens, Howland (VP) (Front) White, Rouse, W Buchanan, Hearn, T Barlow

Season 1903/04 (Reserve Team)
(Back) Harper (Hon. Sec.) Griffin, W.Barlow (Vice-Capt.), Vickers, Busby, Butler (Linesman), Melsome. (Middle) Standage (Capt.), J.Luker, Plumridge, Curtis (Front) Saunders, Spatchett, Carter, H.Luker

SEASON 1902-03
SOUTHERN LEAGUE DIVISION TWO

No.	Date	Opposition	Res.	Att.	Goalscorers
1	27 Sep	Grays United	0-2		
2	25 Oct	Fulham	0-5		
3	15 Nov	CHESHAM TOWN	4-1		W.Buchanan(3,1pen), Russell
4	27 Dec	Brighton & Hove Albion	0-5	3000	
5	7 Feb	BRIGHTON & HOVE ALBION	1-1	550	F.Keen
6	7 Mar	Southall	2-4		Brion, Unknown(1)
7	14	Chesham Town	1-1		White
8	21	GRAYS UNITED	2-0	700	Brion(2)
9	14 Apr	FULHAM	0-0		
10	18	SOUTHALL	3-0		Brion(2), Barlow

BERKS & BUCKS SENIOR LEAGUE

1	13 Sep	MAIDENHEAD NORFOLKIANS	1-1		F.Keen
2	20 Dec	Maidenhead	2-2		W.Buchanan, Barlow
3	3 Jan	Maidenhead Norfolkians	0-4		
4	10	CHESHAM GENERALS	3-3		Stevens(2), Barlow
5	17	AYLESBURY UNITED	3-2	350	Brion(2), Barlow
6	24	MAIDENHEAD	3-1	400	W.Buchanan, Russell, O.G.
7	28 Feb	Chesham Generals	2-4		Barlow, W.Buchanan
8	28 Mar	Aylesbury United	1-6		Unknown
9*	4 Apr	SLOUGH	3-1		Pugh(2), W.Buchanan
10	15	Slough	1-4		Pugh

* Abandoned after 73 minutes (waterlogged pitch), result stood.

F.A. CUP

2QR	18 Oct	Aylesbury United	0-2	500	

F.A. AMATEUR CUP

2QR	8 Nov	MAIDENHEAD NORFOLKIANS	0-2		

BERKS & BUCKS SENIOR CUP

2R	6 Dec	CHESHAM TOWN	4-0		W.Buchanan(2,1pen), Russell, Barlow
SF*	21 Feb	Aylesbury United	0-2	2360	

* Played at Marlow

(Southern League) Final Table

		P.	W.	D	L	F	A	Pts.
1	Fulham	10	7	1	2	27	7	15
2	Brighton & Hove Albion	10	7	1	2	34	11	15
3	Grays United	10	7	0	3	28	12	14
4	Wycombe Wanderers	10	3	3	4	13	19	9
5	Chesham Town	10	2	1	7	9	37	5
6	Southall	10	1	0	9	10	35	2

(Berks & Bucks Senior League) Final League Table

		P.	W.	D	L	F	A	Pts.
1	Chesham Generals	10	6	2	2	27	15	14
2	Aylesbury United	10	5	2	3	30	21	12
3	Maidenhead Norfolkians	10	4	3	3	16	15	11
4	Slough	10	4	2	4	19	18	10
5	Wycombe Wanderers	10	3	3	4	19	28	9
6	Maidenhead	10	0	4	6	12	26	4

SEASON 1903-04
SOUTHERN LEAGUE DIVISION TWO

No.	Date	Opposition	Res.	Att.	Goalscorers
1	12 Sep	SWINDON TOWN RESERVES	2-2		Pheby(2)
2	26	Watford	0-9	3500	
3	3 Oct	READING RESERVES	4-4		Pheby, Barlow(2), W.Buchanan
4	17	PORTSMOUTH RESERVES	1-4	1500	Barlow
5	19 Dec	Southall	2-1	200	Pheby, Bass
6	30	Swindon Town Reserves	1-2		Tilbury
7	9 Jan	SOUTHAMPTON RESERVES	2-2	1000	Pheby, Spriggs
8	16	Fulham Reserves	0-2	3000	
9	30	Reading Reserves	0-6	200	
10	20 Feb	Southampton Reserves	1-1		O.G.
11	5 Mar	WATFORD	0-5		
12	12	Portsmouth Reserves	0-8	1000	
13	19	CHESHAM TOWN	0-0		
14	26	GRAYS UNITED	3-0		Pheby(3,1pen)
15	2 Apr	SOUTHALL	2-1		Spriggs, Pheby(pen)
16	6	Chesham Town	2-1		Spriggs(2)
17	9	FULHAM RESERVES	1-1		Pheby(pen)
18	16	Grays United	1-3		Bass
19	23	MILLWALL ATHLETIC RESERVES	7-1		Bass,Hawes(3),Pheby,W.Bchanan,Stevens
20	30	Millwall Athletic Reserves	0-3	1200	

F.A. CUP

3QR	31 Oct	RICHMOND ASSOCIATION	2-1	1000	Bass, Pheby
4QR	14 Nov	SLOUGH	5-2	2000	Bass(2), Spriggs(pen), OG, W.Buchanan
5QR	28	BRENTFORD	1-4	2250	Spriggs

F.A. AMATEUR CUP

2QR	7 Nov	Reading Amateurs	2-1	200	W.Buchanan, Russell
3QR	21	Maidenhead Norfolkians	1-2	1000	Bass

BERKS & BUCKS SENIOR CUP

1R	5 Dec	Chesham Town	1-4	450	Bass

Final League Table

		P.	W.	D	L	F	A	Pts.
1	Watford	20	18	2	0	70	15	38
2	Portsmouth (Res.)	20	15	2	3	85	25	32
3	Millwall Athletic (Res.)	20	9	4	7	35	39	22
4	Southampton (Res.)	20	9	3	8	59	35	21
5	Grays United	20	9	3	8	25	55	21
6	Fulham (Res.)	20	8	4	8	40	34	20
7	Swindon Town (Res.)	20	8	3	9	50	44	19
8	Reading (Res.)	20	8	2	10	43	42	18
9	Wycombe Wanderers	20	5	5	10	29	64	15
10	Southall	20	4	2	14	25	62	10
11	Chesham Town	20	1	2	17	19	65	4

SEASON 1904-05
SOUTHERN LEAGUE DIVISION TWO

No.	Date	Opposition	Res.	Att.	Goalscorers
1	3 Sep	Brighton & Hove Albion Reserves	0-6	2000	
2	17	Southampton Reserves	3-4		Langley(2), Bass
3	24	FULHAM RESERVES	1-3	800	Pheby
4	1 Oct	SOUTHALL	1-2	400	Hawes
5	15	Portsmouth Reserves	1-11	2000	Hawes
6	22	READING RESERVES	3-5	450	W.Buchanan(2,1pen), Blatchford
7	17 Dec	PORTSMOUTH RESERVES	0-3	700	
8	31	SOUTHAMPTON RESERVES	3-1	1000	Pheby, Brion, Langley
9	7 Jan	Grays United	1-10		Langley
10	21	CLAPTON ORIENT	6-4	600	W.Buchanan(2), Brion(3), Langley
11	28	Swindon Town Reserves	1-3	1500	Pheby
12	8 Feb	Southall	3-0		Bass(2), Langley
13	11	GRAYS UNITED	0-2	600	
14	18	Reading Reserves	0-3	350	
15	4 Mar	Clapton Orient	1-1	1500	Brion
16	11	BRIGHTON & HOVE ALB. RES.	2-4		W.Buchanan(pen), Langley
17	25	Watford Reserves	1-1		Pheby
18	27	Fulham Reserves	0-1		
19	1 Apr	WATFORD RESERVES	2-0		Langley(2)
20	8	West Ham United Reserves	3-5		Finch(2), Pheby
21	15	WEST HAM UNITED RESERVES	4-1		Langley(2), Hawes(2)
22	26	SWINDON TOWN RESERVES	1-0		Finch

F.A. CUP

3QR	29 Oct	Oxford City	0-3	2000	

F.A. AMATEUR CUP

1QR	8 Oct	HENLEY	11-0	400	Pheby(2), Langley(3), W.Buchanan(3) *
2QR	5 Nov	2ND GRENADIER GUARDS	3-0	1000	Blatchford, Langley, Pheby
3QR	19	Maidenhead Norfolkians	2-4	1100	Pheby, Langley

* Extra scorers - Brion(2), Blatchford

BERKS & BUCKS SENIOR CUP

1R	12 Nov	Marlow	3-1	1900	Pheby(3)
2R	3 Dec	Aylesbury United	3-1		Bass(2), W.Buchanan
SF*	25 Feb	Chesham Generals	2-2	2000	Bass, W.Buchanan(pen)
SFr*	18 Mar	Chesham Generals	0-1	1800	

* Played at Marlow

Final League Table

		P.	W.	D.	L	F	A	Pts.
1	Fulham (Res.)	22	16	4	2	78	25	36
2	Portsmouth (Res.)	22	14	2	6	75	28	30
3	Swindon Town (Res.)	22	12	3	7	54	47	27
4	Grays United	22	11	3	8	61	40	25
5	Southampton (Res.)	22	10	5	7	52	35	25
6	Brighton & H. A. (Res.)	22	9	3	10	48	49	21
7	West Ham Utd. (Res.)	22	8	5	9	45	47	21
8	Clapton Orient	22	7	7	8	47	56	21
9	Watford (Res.)	22	5	6	11	30	62	16
10	Southall	22	7	2	13	31	66	16
11	Wycombe Wanderers	22	6	2	14	37	70	14
12	Reading (Res.)	22	4	4	14	24	57	12

SEASON 1905-06
SOUTHERN LEAGUE DIVISION TWO

No.	Date	Opposition	Res.	Att.	Goalscorers
1	9 Sep	ST. LEONARD'S UNITED	0-4		
2	16	WEST HAM UNITED RESERVES	2-0		Hawes, Finch
3	30	WATFORD RESERVES	2-1	600	Roberts(2)
4	21 Oct	READING RESERVES	3-6	400	Blatchford, Finch, Busby(pen)
5	23 Dec	Southern United	3-3	700	Tilbury, Brion(2)
6	26	SOUTHAMPTON RESERVES	1-1	2500	Brion
7	30	St. Leonard's United	2-6		Langley(2)
8	6 Jan	CRYSTAL PALACE	1-4	500	Langley
9	13	FULHAM RESERVES	3-4		Finch(2), Roberts
10	20	Leyton	0-9		
11	27	Portsmouth Reserves	0-4	2000	
12	3 Feb	SWINDON TOWN RESERVES	2-1		Brion, Blatchford
13	10	LEYTON	1-7		Finch
14	24	Reading Reserves	0-6		
15	3 Mar	Swindon Town Reserves	1-4	1200	Roberts
16	10	GRAYS UNITED	5-0		Tilbury, Seymour, Busby(2,pens), Finch
17	17	West Ham United Reserves	1-1		Unknown
18	24	PORTSMOUTH RESERVES	1-5		Finch
19	7 Apr	Watford Reserves	1-2	500	Roberts
20	13	Southampton Reserves	1-4		Blatchford
21	14	Crystal Palace	0-4		
22	17	Grays United	1-2		Hutchinson
23	21	Fulham Reserves	3-5		Unknown
24	28	SOUTHERN UNITED	2-0		Blatchford, Busby(pen)

F.A. CUP

PR	23 Sep	Marlow	1-0	500	Langley
1QR	7 Oct	Aylesbury United	2-2	200	Roberts(pen), Finch
1QRr	11	AYLESBURY UNITED	2-0	400	Roberts, Pheby
2QR	28	Maidenhead	3-1	400	Langley, Roberts(2)
3QR	18 Nov	SLOUGH	4-1	1350	Roberts, Brion(2), Blatchford
4QR	9 Dec	Brentford	0-4	4000	

F.A. AMATEUR CUP

1QR	14 Oct	Chesham Town	0-2	300	

BERKS & BUCKS SENIOR CUP

1R	11 Nov	CHESHAM GENERALS	2-0	500	Brion, Finch
2R	2 Dec	MAIDENHEAD	4-3	400	Roberts(pen), Brion, Hooper, Langley
SF*	17 Feb	Maidenhead Norfolkians	2-2		Brion, Langley
SFr*	31 Mar	Maidenhead Norfolkians	1-4	3000	Brion

* Played at Marlow

Final League Table

		P.	W.	D.	L.	F.	A.	Pts.
1	Crystal Palace	24	19	4	1	66	14	42
2	Leyton	24	16	6	2	61	18	38
3	Portsmouth (Res)	24	12	8	4	52	24	32
4	Fulham (Res)	24	11	6	7	52	39	28
5	Southampton (Res)	24	7	9	8	39	41	23
6	Southern United	24	8	7	9	45	49	23
7	St. Leonards United	24	9	4	11	54	50	22
8	Watford (Res)	24	8	5	11	43	47	21
9	West Ham Utd. (Res)	24	7	5	12	46	48	19
10	Grays United	24	8	3	13	24	77	19
11	Reading (Res)	24	6	5	13	36	49	17
12	Swindon Town (Res)	24	5	5	14	38	51	15
13	Wycombe Wanderers	24	5	3	16	36	83	13

Season 1905/06 (Reserve Team) (Back) Cooper, Coventry, W.Barlow, F.Collier, G.Buchanan, Standage (Middle) Bunce (Asst.Sec.), Williams, Butler, Spatchett, Melsome, Esq. (Front) Saunders (Capt.), Burnham, Ellis, Cheese, Hutchinson

Season 1906/07 (First Team- players only) (Back) Spicer, Vickers, Tilbury (Middle) Rose, Lyford, Brion, Roberts, Cambridge (Front) Langley, Hooper, G Buchanan

SEASON 1906-07
SOUTHERN LEAGUE DIVISION TWO

No.	Date	Opposition	Res.	Att.	Goalscorers
1	1 Sep	Reading Reserves	2-2		Hooper, Langley
2	29	Hastings & St. Leonard's	0-3		
3	17 Nov	Salisbury City	0-10		
4	24	Swindon Town Reserves	1-5		Brion
5	15 Dec	Portsmouth Reserves	0-7	2000	
6	22	SOUTHEND UNITED	2-2		Roberts, Busby(pen)
7	29	Tunbridge Wells Rangers	1-6		Busby(pen)
8	12 Jan	SALISBURY CITY	3-2	900	Roberts(2), Brion
9	19	Royal Engineers (Aldershot)	0-1		
10	26	Southampton Reserves	3-0		Hutchinson, Langley, Tilbury
11	2 Feb	FULHAM RESERVES	2-2	1000	Spriggs(2)
12	16	WEST HAM UNITED RESERVES	0-5	1000	
13	23	Fulham Reserves	0-3		
14	2 Mar	HASTINGS & ST. LEONARD'S	2-4	1000	Brion, Roberts
15	9	Southend United	0-3		
16	11	TUNBRIDGE WELLS RANGERS	0-2	300	
17	16	SOUTHAMPTON RESERVES	3-0		Lyford, Brion(2)
18	3 Apr	ROYAL ENG. (ALDERSHOT)	3-2		O.G., Lyford(2)
19	6	PORTSMOUTH RESERVES	2-2	800	Roberts, Rose
20	13	SWINDON TOWN RESERVES	2-2		G.Buchanan, Lyford
21	20	READING RESERVES	2-2		Rose, Lyford
22	22	West Ham United Reserves	0-3		

F.A. CUP

2QR	20 Oct	AYLESBURY UNITED	3-1	1200	Roberts, Busby(pen), Langley
3QR	3 Nov	CHESHAM TOWN	1-1	2000	Finch
3QRr	7	Chesham Town	1-2	500	Langley

F.A. AMATEUR CUP

1QR	13 Oct	Aylesbury United	3-2		Roberts(2), Rose
2QR	10 Nov	CHESHAM TOWN	4-2	1500	Tilbury, Langley, Roberts(2)
3QR	17	LUTON CLARENCE	5-0	1100	Roberts(3), Brion, Langley
4QR	8 Dec	READING AMATEURS	1-0		Finch
1R	5 Jan	2ND GRENADIER GUARDS	3-5		Brion, Busby(pen), Roberts

BERKS & BUCKS SENIOR CUP

1R	1 Dec	Chesham Town	3-4	800	Spriggs, Brion(2)

Final League Table

		P.	W.	D.	L.	F.	A.	Pts.
1	Southend United	22	14	5	3	58	23	33
2	West Ham Utd. (Res.)	22	14	3	5	64	30	31
3	Portsmouth (Res.)	22	11	6	5	53	24	28
4	Fulham (Res.)	22	11	4	7	47	32	26
5	Hastings & St Leonards	21	10	4	7	46	31	24*
6	Tunbridge Wells Rang.	22	10	1	11	46	36	21
7	Salisbury City	22	9	2	11	40	42	20
8	Southampton (Res.)	22	8	2	12	37	56	18
9	Swindon Town (Res.)	22	7	3	12	15	46	17
10	Reading (Res.)	22	6	4	12	32	47	16
11	Royal Engineers (A'shot)	21	5	4	12	27	58	14*
12	Wycombe Wanderers	22	4	6	12	28	68	14

* One match not played

SEASON 1907-08
SOUTHERN LEAGUE DIVISION TWO

No.	Date	Opposition	Res.	Att.	Goalscorers
1	7 Sep	Southend United	0-5		
2	14	TUNBRIDGE WELLS RANGERS	2-4		Cambridge, Ellis
3	28	Salisbury City	0-4	750	
4	12 Oct	Southampton Reserves	2-6		Langley, Brion
5	9 Nov	Swindon Town Reserves	0-8		
6	21 Dec	Portsmouth Reserves	0-3	2000	
7	28	SWINDON TOWN RESERVES	0-4	800	
8	8 Feb	SOUTHAMPTON RESERVES	1-3		Brion
9	22	CROYDON COMMON	0-2		
10	29	Hastings & St. Leonard's	1-6		Brion
11	9 Mar	HASTINGS & ST. LEONARD'S	0-5		
12	14	Brighton & Hove Albion Reserves	1-3		Hutchinson
13	21	Tunbridge Wells Rangers	0-6		
14	1 Apr	BRIGHTON & HOVE ALB. RES.	4-0		Brion(3), O.G.
15	4	PORTSMOUTH RESERVES	0-2		
16	11	Croydon Common	2-5		Brion, Roberts
17	18	SALISBURY CITY	2-2		Winter(2)
18	28	SOUTHEND UNITED	1-4	40	Pheby

F.A. CUP

PR	21 Sep	READING AMATEURS	5-3		Cambridge, Roberts(pen), Lngley, Ells(2)
1QR	5 Oct	SHEPHERDS BUSH	1-1		Roberts(pen)
1QRr	10	Shepherds Bush	0-1	800	

F.A. AMATEUR CUP

1R	4 Jan	Reading Amatuers	0-0		
1Rr	11	READING AMATEURS	5-3		Winter(2), Brion(3)
2R	25	Maidenhead Norfolkians	0-6		

BERKS & BUCKS SENIOR CUP

1R	7 Dec	Aylesbury United	0-0		
1Rr	14	AYLESBURY UNITED	3-2		Brion, Newell, Hutchinson
2R	18 Jan	Chesham Town	1-2	1000	Cambridge

Final League Table

		P.	W.	D.	L.	F.	A.	Pts.
1	Southend United	18	13	3	2	47	16	29
2	Portsmouth (Res.)	18	10	5	3	39	22	25
3	Croydon Common	18	10	3	5	35	25	23
4	Hastings & St Leonards	18	10	2	6	43	29	22
5	Southampton (Res.)	18	7	4	7	54	46	18
6	Tunbridge Wells Rang.	18	7	3	8	42	38	17
7	Salisbury City	18	6	4	8	35	46	16
8	Swindon Town (Res.)	18	5	5	8	36	40	15
9	Brighton & H. A. (Res.)	18	4	4	10	34	47	12
10	Wycombe Wanderers	18	1	1	16	16	72	3

SEASON 1908/09
GREAT WESTERN SUBURBAN LEAGUE

No.	Date	Opposition	Res.	Att.	Goalscorers
1	5 Sep	MAIDENHEAD	4-3	700	Brion, Langley, Pheby(2)
2	12	WINDSOR & ETON	4-2		Brion(2), Hooper, Winter
3	21	Brentford Reserves	0-0		
4	26	SOUTHALL	3-1		Pheby, Brion, Hooper
5	31 Oct	Southall	0-4	700	
6	14 Nov	STAINES	4-0		Langley, Roberts, Brion, G.Buchanan
7	21	1ST IRISH GUARDS	2-0	1000	Pheby, Hooper
8	12 Dec	SLOUGH	4-1	700	Langley, Brion, Hooper, Winter
9	19	MAIDENHEAD NORFOLKIANS	0-1	550	
10	26	UXBRIDGE	1-1	1900	Langley
11	28	Reading Reserves	0-6		
12	2 Jan	BRENTFORD RESERVES	3-1	1350	Pheby(3)
13	9	Slough	2-1		Pheby(2)
14	23	Hounslow	0-0	180	
15	6 Feb	Maidenhead Norfolkians	1-0	500	Pheby
16	13	Hanwell	1-0	300	Hooper
17	20	HANWELL	7-0	900	Pheby(5,1pen), Brion, Roberts
18	27	Windsor & Eton	0-0	170	
19	3 Apr	Staines	1-1	300	Winter
20	13	Uxbridge	1-5		Pheby
21	19	HOUNSLOW	3-1		Roberts, Brion(2)
22	21	Maidenhead	0-0		
23	24	READING RESERVES	2-0	1500	Roberts(2)
24	28	1st Irish Guards	3-2		Pheby(2), Brion

F.A. CUP

PR	19 Sep	Slough	3-1		Winter(2), Brion
1QR	3 Oct	MAIDENHEAD	3-2		Langley, Brion(2)
2QR	17	Uxbridge	1-1	800	G.Buchanan
2QRr	21	UXBRIDGE	3-4	1000	Langley, H.Gates, Pheby(pen)

F.A. AMATEUR CUP

2QR	24 Oct	THAME	9-1	800	Winter,Pheby(2),Brion(4),Hooper,H.Gtes
3QR	7 Nov	MAIDENHEAD NORFOLKIANS	4-3	1000	Brion, Hooper, Roberts(2)
4QR	28	CAVERSHAM ROVERS	3-4	800	Payne, Winter, Pheby(pen)

BERKS & BUCKS SENIOR CUP

1R	5 Dec	AYLESBURY UNITED	2-0	1000	Lyford, Winter
2R	30 Jan	READING GROVELANDS	2-0	1000	Roberts(2,1pen)
SF*	13 Mar	Marlow	2-0	2000	Roberts, H.Gates
F#	12 Apr	Chesham Town	3-0	5874	Brion, Payne, Roberts

* Played at Maidenhead
# Played at Marlow

Final League Table

		P.	W.	D	L	F	A	Pts.
1	Brentford Reserves	24	17	5	2	70	28	39
2	Reading Reserves	24	17	3	4	108	22	37
3	Wycombe Wanderers	24	14	6	4	46	30	34
4	Hounslow	24	11	7	6	36	31	29
5	Windsor & Eton	24	9	8	7	35	38	26
6	Maidenhead	24	11	3	10	47	47	25
7	Maidenhead Norfolkians	24	9	5	10	43	52	23
8	Southall	24	9	3	12	48	52	21
9	Hanwell	24	8	5	11	40	55	21
10	1st Irish Guards	24	8	3	13	49	62	19
11	Uxbridge	24	6	5	13	40	59	17
12	Staines	24	4	4	16	24	64	12
13	Slough	24	3	3	18	19	65	9

SEASON 1909-10
GREAT WESTERN SUBURBAN LEAGUE

No.	Date	Opposition	Res.	Att.	Goalscorers
1	4 Sep	MAIDENHEAD	3-0		Brion, Pheby, Roberts
2	11	UXBRIDGE	2-1	1000	Pheby, Roberts(pen)
3	25	Southall	1-0	500	Pheby
4	9 Oct	Reading Reserves	1-4		Pheby
5	23	BRENTFORD RESERVES	3-2		Pheby(2), Roberts(pen)
6	30	Slough	3-2	300	Roberts(pen), Langley, Brion
7	27 Dec	STAINES	18-1	1200	Phby(7),Rbrts(5),Brion(3),Vckrs(p),H.Gtes,Hoopr
8	28	2ND SCOTS GUARDS	8-1		Pheby(3), Hooper, Langley, Brion(3)
9	1 Jan	SLOUGH	5-1		Payne, Pheby(2), Roberts(2, 1 pen)
10	5 Feb	Maidenhead Norfolkians	5-1	250	Roberts, Hooper, Payne(2), Pheby
11	19	READING RESERVES	2-2	2000	Pheby(2,1pen)
12	12 Mar	WINDSOR & ETON	3-1		Pheby, Hooper, Brion
13	26	HANWELL	7-1		Winter, H.Gates, Pheby(4), Brion
14	29	Maidenhead	0-4		
15	2 Apr	Brentford Reserves	0-3		
16	4	Windsor & Eton	0-4	200	
17	11	2nd Scots Guards	1-0		O'Gorman
18	18	Hanwell	0-1		
19	23	SOUTHALL	0-2		
20	24	Staines	1-0		O.G.
21	27	MAIDENHEAD NORFOLKIANS	0-2		
22	30	Uxbridge	2-0		Roberts, G.Buchanan

F.A. CUP

PR	18 Sep	Aylesbury United	4-3	850	Langley(2), Roberts, Brion
1QR	2 Oct	SOUTHALL	1-0	800	Roberts
2QR	16	Maidenhead Norfolkians	3-1	800	Roberts(2,1pen), G.Buchanan
3QR	6 Nov	UXBRIDGE	1-0	2500	Roberts
4QR	20	Summerstown	3-1	1800	Pheby, Roberts, Langley
5QR	4 Dec	WATFORD	0-4	4500	

F.A. AMATEUR CUP

1R	8 Jan	CAVERSHAM ROVERS	5-0	1000	Pheby(3), Roberts, Brion
2R	22	LUTON CLARENCE	2-0		Pheby(2)
3R	12 Feb	LEYTONSTONE	5-3	3000	Brion,Roberts(2),H.Gates,G.Buchanan
4R	5 Mar	Clapton	1-4	3000	Pheby

BERKS & BUCKS SENIOR CUP

1R	11 Dec	Aylesbury Unted	2-0	800	Roberts(2)
2R	29 Jan	MAIDENHEAD NORFOLKIANS	2-0		Roberts, Payne
SF*	26 Feb	Maidenhead	1-0	3000	Brion
F*	28 Mar	Wokingham Athletic	0-0	6490	
Fr*	9 Apr	Wokingham Athletic	3-0	3260	G.Buchanan(2), Brion

* Played at Marlow

Final League Table

		P.	W.	D	L	F	A	Pts.
1	Reading Reserves	22	19	2	1	110	21	38 *
2	Brentford Reserves	22	18	1	3	95	21	37
3	Wycombe Wanderers	22	14	1	7	85	33	29
4	Windsor & Eton	22	14	1	7	46	33	29
5	Southall	22	10	3	9	37	38	23
6	Maidenhead	22	10	3	9	45	48	23
7	Uxbridge	22	8	4	10	53	44	20
8	2nd Scots Guards	22	8	1	13	44	57	17
9	Hanwell	22	6	3	13	30	79	15
10	Maidenhead Norfolkians	22	4	2	16	28	80	10
11	Staines	22	4	4	14	26	86	10 *
12	Slough	22	3	3	16	24	83	9

* 2pts deducted for fielding an ineligible player

Season 1908/09 Berks & Bucks Senior Cup Winners: (Back) Free (Trainer), Tilbury, Vickers, Gilson (Middle) Langley, Brion, Roberts, Pheby, Payne (Front) Gates, Hooper, G Buchanan

Season 1909/10 Berks & Bucks Senior Cup Winners (left), Wycombe Charity Cup Winners
(Back - behind players) unknown. (Second Row) Spatchett, Standage, Tilbury, Vickers, Gilson, Holland, Free (Train.), Phillips (Swan Landlord) (Third Row) Deacon (Pres./Chair.), Langley, Brion, Roberts, Pheby, Payne, Winter, Bunce (Asst. Sec.) (Front) Cooper, Mrtin, Gates, Hooper, Buchanan, Vale (Sec.), unknown

SEASON 1910-11
GREAT WESTERN SUBURBAN LEAGUE

No.	Date	Opposition	Res.	Att.	Goalscorers
1	10 Sep	SLOUGH	7-0		Roberts(3), Pheby(2), G.Buchanan(2)
2	24	1ST COLDSTREAM GUARDS	0-3		
3	8 Oct	Royal Horseguards (Blue)	3-0		O.G., O'Gorman, Bird
4	22	1st Coldstream Guards	1-2	200	O'Gorman
5	29	SOUTHALL	1-2		Roberts
6	5 Nov	Brentford Reserves	3-10	1000	Pheby, G.Buchanan(pen), O'Gorman
7	19	Southall	1-4		Pheby
8	17 Dec	WINDSOR & ETON	4-0		O'Gorman(2), G.Buchanan, Roberts
9	24	Staines	3-1		Roberts(2), O'Gorman
10	26	READING RESERVES	0-1	2500	
11	27	UXBRIDGE	1-1	2000	O'Gorman
12	25 Feb	ROYAL HORSEGUARDS (BLUE)	8-1		Brion(4), O'Gorman(2), Pheby, Roberts
13	11 Mar	Uxbridge	1-1		Pheby(pen)
14	18	Hanwell	0-3		
15	25	BRENTFORD RESERVES	1-5		Pheby(pen)
16	1 Apr	STAINES	1-3		O'Gorman
17	8	MAIDENHEAD	4-0	300	Hooper, Roberts, O'Gorman, Pheby
18	13	Windsor & Eton	1-2		H.Chown
19	15	MAIDENHEAD NORFOLKIANS	5-0		O'Gorman(3), Blake(2)
20	17	Reading Reserves	1-1		Pheby(pen)
21	18	HANWELL	10-0	250	O'Gormn(5),Phby(2),Rberts,Blke,G.Bchann(p)
22	19	Slough	1-0		P.Chown
23	22	Maidenhead Norfolkians	2-1		Stone, Pheby
24	27	Maidenhead	3-2		P.Chown(2), O.G.

F.A. CUP

PR	17 Sep	Kilburn	2-2	3000	Pheby, Spriggs
PRr	21	KILBURN	2-1		Morris, Payne
1QR	1 Oct	CITY OF WESTMINSTER	1-1		O'Gorman
1QRr	5	CITY OF WESTMINSTER	4-2		G.Buchanan(3), O'Gorman
2QR	15	1ST GRENADIER GUARDS	0-1		

Both games againt City of Westminster played at Loakes Park.

F.A. AMATEUR CUP

1R	7 Jan	SWINDON VICTORIA	1-1		O'Gorman
1Rr	14	SWINDON VICTORIA	2-1		G.Buchanan(pen), Pheby
2R	21	WOKING	4-3		O.G., Payne, Hooper, O'Gorman
3R	11 Feb	KING'S ROYAL RIFLES	4-2		O'Gorman(2), Langley, O.G.
4R	4 Mar	2ND COLDSTREAM GUARDS	2-3		Roberts(2)

Both games against Swindon Victoria played at Loakes Park.

BERKS & BUCKS SENIOR CUP

1R	3 Dec	1ST COLDSTREAM GUARDS	5-0		O'Gorman(2),G.Buchanan(2pens),Roberts
2R	28 Jan	WINDSOR & ETON	1-1		Roberts
2Rr	4 Feb	Windsor & Eton	0-0		
2R2r	18	Windsor & Eton *	1-2		Brion

* Played at Marlow

Final League Table

		P.	W.	D.	L.	F.	A.	Pts.
1	Brentford Reserves	24	22	2	0	103	15	46
2	Uxbridge	24	15	7	2	52	21	37
3	Southall	24	15	4	5	80	32	34
4	1st Coldstream Guards	23	14	3	6	56	27	31 †
5	Wycombe Wanderers	24	11	3	10	62	43	25
6	Windsor & Eton	24	9	3	12	40	47	21
7	Maidenhead Norfolkians	24	8	4	12	38	51	20
8	Maidenhead	24	9	4	11	40	57	20 *
9	Hanwell	24	8	3	13	43	65	19
10	Staines	24	7	4	13	44	53	18
11	Reading Reserves	24	12	1	11	48	42	13 **
12	Slough	24	1	5	18	17	77	5 *
13	Royal Horse Guards (Blue)	23	2	1	20	21	114	5 †

* 2 pts deducted   **12pts deducted   † 1 match not played

SEASON 1911-12
GREAT WESTERN SUBURBAN LEAGUE

No.	Date	Opposition	Res.	Att.	Goalscorers
1	23 Sep	HANWELL	5-3		Goodchild(2), Payne(2), O.G.
2	7 Oct	SOUTHALL	3-2		Goodchild, Pheby(pen), O.G.
3	21	Hanwell	3-2		O'Gorman(2), Goodchild
4	4 Nov	STAINES	1-0	800	Payne
5	18	2nd Grenadier Guards	1-2	25	Roberts
6	25	Marlow	0-1		
7	9 Dec	2ND GRENADIER GUARDS	2-2	1000	Collings, O'Gorman
8	16	MAIDENHEAD NORFOLKIANS	3-1		Pheby(pen), Adams, Rolfe
9	23	UXBRIDGE	6-1		Goodchild,Hooper,Adms,Phby,O'Gormn(2)
10	30	Maidenhead	2-5		Spriggs, Payne
11	20 Jan	Windsor & Eton	5-2	350	Adams(3), Goodchild(2)
12	3 Feb	MARLOW	0-0	1400	
13	10	Staines	1-5		Harvey
14	17	Maidenhead Norfolkians	1-4		Adams
15	16 Mar	Southall	3-5		Goodchild, Pheby(pen), O'Gorman
16	23	SLOUGH	10-2		Rbrts,Hoopr(3),Goodchld,Phby,O'Grmn(3),Adms
17	30	Slough	1-1	500	Roberts
18	6 Apr	Uxbridge	1-0		O.G.
19	13	MAIDENHEAD	6-0		Adams(2), Goodchild(3), Pheby
20	27	WINDSOR & ETON	2-1		Hooper, Pheby

F.A. CUP

1QR	30 Sep	Uxbridge	4-1		Goodchild, Adams, Pheby(2 pens)
2QR	14 Oct	SOUTHALL	1-1		Goodchild
2QRr	18	Southall	1-2		Goodchild

F.A. AMATEUR CUP

| 1R | 13 Jan | Shepherds Bush | 0-2 | 500 | |

BERKS & BUCKS SENIOR CUP

1R	2 Dec	Chesham Generals	3-1		O'Gorman, Adams, Goodchild
2R	27 Jan	SLOUGH	3-1	1500	Goodchild, O'Gorman, Payne
SF*	9 Mar	Maidenhead	1-2	1793	O'Gorman

* Played at Marlow

Final League Table

		P.	W.	D.	L.	F.	A.	Pts.
1	2nd Grenadier Guards	20	17	2	1	79	21	36
2	Staines	20	12	3	5	43	30	27
3	Wycombe Wanderers	20	11	3	6	56	39	25
4	Maidenhead	20	10	2	8	52	45	22
5	Windsor & Eton	20	10	2	8	39	34	22
6	Maidenhead Norfolkians	20	9	1	10	49	38	19
7	Southall	20	7	3	10	43	50	17
8	Uxbridge	20	7	3	10	32	42	17
9	Slough	20	5	5	10	25	41	15
10	Marlow	20	6	3	11	22	46	13 *
11	Hanwell	20	2	1	17	27	83	5

* 2pts deducted for fielding an ineligible player

Season 1911/12 (Reserve Team) (Back) Clark, Janes, Reynolds (Capt.), Keating, Burnham (Vice-Capt.), Bunce (Asst.Sec.), Martin (Middle) McDermott, Jolliffe, Spriggs, Harvey, Holt, Collings (Front) Brocklehurst, Stratford, Withers, Crook

Season 1913/14 (Reserves) All Unknown, except: (Back) (4th) Stratford, (7th) Clark, (Front) (1st) McDermott.

SEASON 1912-13
GREAT WESTERN SUBURBAN LEAGUE

No.	Date	Opposition	Res.	Att.	Goalscorers
1	21 Sep	SOUTHALL	1-2	800	O'Gorman
2	5 Oct	MARLOW	4-1		Roberts, O.G., Pheby, Goodchild
3	23 Nov	Slough	1-1		Roberts
4	30	19TH HUSSARS	0-2		
5	14 Dec	Staines	0-1	200	
6	21	MAIDENHEAD	3-2		O.G., Collings, Goodchild
7	4 Jan	3RD COLDSTREAM GUARDS	7-2		Pheby(4), Roberts, Goodchild, O'Gorman
8	11	Maidenhead Norfolkians	2-2		Roberts, Didcock
9	18	3rd Coldstream Guards	2-3		Goodchild, Roberts
10	25	Marlow	1-2	1000	O'Gorman
11	8 Feb	Maidenhead	1-2		Pheby(pen)
12	15	WINDSOR & ETON	1-3		Goodchild
13	22	Windsor & Eton	1-5		Pheby
14	22 Mar	19th Hussars	0-2		
15	29	Uxbridge	0-4		
16	12 Apr	STAINES	5-0		A.Smith(3), Harvey(2)
17	19	UXBRIDGE	3-2		Harvey, Pheby, A.Smith
18	23	SLOUGH	5-3		A.Smith(2), Pheby(2), O'Gorman
19	26	Southall	1-2		Roberts
20	30	MAIDENHEAD NORFOLKIANS	6-2		Gdchild(2),A.Smth,Phby,Tilbury,Pyne(pen)

F.A. CUP

PR	28 Sep	Maidenhead Norfolkians	4-3	500	Pheby(2), Goodchild(2)
1QR	12 Oct	WINDSOR & ETON	3-1		Pheby, Goodchild, O'Gorman
2QR	2 Nov	UXBRIDGE	3-4		Pheby, Goodchild, O.G.

F.A. AMATEUR CUP

2QR	19 Oct	READING GROVELANDS	5-0		Goodchild 2(1pen), Pheby(3)
3QR	16 Nov	ABINGDON	2-6		Pheby(pen), Goodchild

BERKS & BUCKS SENIOR CUP

1R	7 Dec	CHESHAM GENERALS	3-2		Goodchild(2), Pheby(pen)
2R	1 Feb	CHESHAM TOWN	4-0		Goodchild(2), Roberts, Pheby
SF*	8 Mar	Slough	2-0	2250	Pheby, Roberts
F*	24	Maidenhead Norfolkians	1-1	6752	Pheby
Fr*	5 Apr	Maidenhead Norfolkians	2-1	2032	Goodchild, Pheby

* Played at Marlow

Final League Table

		P.	W.	D	L	F	A	Pts.
1	Southall	20	14	3	3	53	21	31
2	19th Hussars	20	11	4	5	51	37	26
3	Windsor & Eton	20	11	3	6	55	35	25
4	Uxbridge	20	10	4	6	40	29	24
5	3rd Coldstream Guards	20	11	1	8	60	49	23
6	Slough	20	6	8	6	34	40	20
7	Wycombe Wanderers	20	7	2	11	44	43	16
8	Maidenhead Norfolkians	20	6	3	11	30	60	15
9	Staines	20	6	2	12	25	38	14
10	Maidenhead	20	5	2	13	32	47	12
11	Marlow	20	5	4	11	23	48	12*

* 2 pts deducted for fielding an ineligible player

SEASON 1913-14
GREAT WESTERN SUBURBAN LEAGUE

No.	Date	Opposition	Res.	Att.	Goalscorers
1	20 Sep	MARLOW	3-1		Goodchild, A.Smith, Adams
2	8 Nov	Southall	0-4		
3	15	MAIDENHEAD	4-1		Pheby, Harvey(2), Payne
4	22	19th Hussars	1-5		Payne
5	3 Jan	WINDSOR & ETON	3-2		A.Smith, F.E.Crook, Stallwood
6	10	Marlow	2-3	600	O'Gorman, A.Smith(pen)
7	17	MAIDENHEAD FORFOLKIANS	1-5		A.Smith
8	24	Windsor & Eton	1-1		Baker
9	31	SLOUGH	3-1		Payne, A.Smith, Baker
10	14 Feb	Maidenhead	0-4		
11	21	Slough	5-1		F.E.Crook(2), Stoner, A.Smith, Baker
12	7 Mar	Maidenhead Norfolkians	1-2		Payne
13	21	Uxbridge	5-1		A.Smith, Adams(2), F.E.Crook, O'Gorman
14	28	3rd Coldstream Guards	0-0	200	
15	11 Apr	SOUTHALL	1-1		A.Smith
16	18	3RD COLDSTREAM GUARDS	5-2		F.E.Crook, A.Smith(2), Adams(2)
17	23	19TH HUSSARS	4-1		Adams(2,1pen), A.Smith, Baker
18	25	UXBRIDGE	10-0		A.Smth(3),Stonr(3),Ddcock(p),FE.Crook(2),Pyne

F.A. CUP

PR	27 Sep	Maidenhead	1-0		Adams
1QR	11 Oct	Oxford City	0-5		

F.A. AMATEUR CUP

1QR	4 Oct	NEWBURY TOWN	5-2		O'Gorman,Goodchild(2),Adams,A.Smith
2QR	18	ABINGDON	6-0		Stoner, A.Smith, Pheby(3), Love
3QR	1 Nov	Windsor & Eton	2-5		A.Smith, O'Gorman

BERKS & BUCKS SENIOR CUP

1R	6 Dec	WOLVERTON TOWN	1-1		Pheby
1Rr	13	Wolverton Town	1-3		Goodchild

Final League Table

		P.	W.	D	L	F	A	Pts.
1	19th Hussars	18	13	1	4	48	20	27
2	Maidenhead Norfolkians	18	12	2	4	34	19	26
3	Southall	18	10	5	3	47	17	25
4	Wycombe Wanderers	18	9	3	6	49	35	21
5	Maidenhead	18	8	4	6	42	32	20
6	3rd Coldstream Guards	18	5	6	7	31	44	16
7	Windsor & Eton	18	6	3	9	29	37	15
8	Marlow	18	3	5	10	25	48	11
9	Slough	18	4	2	12	21	36	10
10	Uxbridge	18	3	3	12	18	54	7*

* 2 pts deducted for fielding an ineligible player

Season 1919/20 (Back) Hooper (Sec.), Didcock, Ball, Rolfe, Martin, Tilbury (Groundsman)
(Middle) Grace, Jackman, Boreham, A.Smith, O'Gorman (Front) Fane, Adams, Gomm, F.Gates.

Season 1920/21 Spartan League Champions (left) Berks & Bucks Senior Cup Winners
(Back) Martin, Didcock, Wicks, Rolfe, Cooper, Gardner (Middle) Hooper (Sec.), Grace, Jackman,
Boreham, A Smith, O'Gorman, Vickers (Front) Harris, W Smith, Adams, F Gates

SEASON 1919-20
SPARTAN LEAGUE

No.	Date	Opposition	Res.	Att.	Goalscorers
1	6 Sep	St. Albans City	4-3	1000	E.Crook(4)
2	13	Great Eastern Railway	1-1		A.Smith
3	18 Oct	Aylesbury United	5-2		A.Smith(2), O'Gorman, Jackman, Adams
4	15 Nov	Great Western Railway	8-3		Adams(3),Jackmn(2),Fane,A.Smith,Grace
5	22	AYLESBURY UNITED	4-0		Jackman, Adams(2), Clarke
6	6 Dec	GREAT EASTERN RAILWAY	3-1		Adams, A.Smith(pen), Grace
7	20	2ND COLDSTREAM GUARDS	7-1		A.Smith(6), O'Gorman
8	26	CHESHAM UNITED	6-0		O'Gormn,A.Smth(pen),Brehm(2),Jckmn(2)
9	27	Chesham United	2-3		A.Smith(pen), Boreham
10	10 Jan	2nd Goldstream Guards	14-0		Gomm,Brehm(4),A.Smth(2),Jckmn(3),Grce(2)
11	17	Sutton Court	4-0		A.Smith(2), Jackman(2)
12	24	ST. ALBANS CITY	4-1		O'Gorman, Boreham, Grace, Jackman
13	21 Feb	NEWPORTONIANS	5-1		A.Smith(2,1pen), Jackman(2), Grace
14	28	TUFNELL SPARTANS	9-2		Brehm(3),Grce,A.Smth,Jackmn(3),O'Grmn
15	6 Mar	LONDON POLYTECHNIC	8-2		Grce(2),Brehm(2),O'Grmn,A.Smth(2),Gomm
16	13	NEWPORTONIANS	6-0		Boreham(3), Jackman(2), Grace
17	27	GREAT EASTERN RAILWAY	4-0		Jackman, A.Smith, O'Gorman, Boreham
18	2 Apr	LONDON POLYTECHNIC	5-0		Adams, Jackman(3), Boreham
19	3	SUTTON COURT	7-1		Jackman(4), Boreham(2), O'Gorman
20	24	TUFNELL SPARTANS	8-3		O'Gorman(2),Boreham(2),Grace,A.Smth(3)

Match 10 - extra goalscorer - O'Gorman(2)
N.b. Both games against London Polytechnic, Newportonians and Tufnell Spartans played at Loakes Park.

F.A. CUP

PR	27 Sep	READING UNITED	6-2		Adams(3),A.Smith,O'Gorman,Jackman
1QR	11 Oct	MAIDENHEAD UNITED	2-1	3000	Adams, Jackman
2QR	25	SLOUGH	3-3	3300	Jackman, Smith, Gomm(pen)
2QRr	29	Slough	5-4		Adams(2), O'Gorman(2), A.Smith
3QR	8 Nov	Hampstead Town	1-4	3000	Jackman

F.A. AMATEUR CUP

| 1R | 3 Jan | Tufnell Park | 2-6 | 1000 | Jackman, Adams |

BERKS & BUCKS SENIOR CUP

| 1R | 29 Nov | Maidenhead United | 2-3 | | Adams, Gomm(pen) |

Final League Table

	P.	W.	D.	L.	F.	A.	Pts.
1 Wycombe Wanderers	20	18	1	1	114	24	37
2 Great Eastern Railway Romford	20	17	1	2	88	19	35
3 St. Albans City	20	13	1	6	64	35	27
4 Aylesbury United	20	12	2	6	49	31	26
5 Chesham United	20	11	2	7	58	46	24
6 Sutton Court	20	11	2	7	54	45	24
7 Polytechnic	19	6	0	13	42	65	12
8 Tufnell Spartans	20	5	1	14	41	70	11
9 Newportonians	20	4	3	13	25	67	11
10 Great Western Railway	20	3	0	17	20	79	6
11 2nd Coldstream Guards	19	2	1	16	19	93	5

SEASON 1920-21
SPARTAN LEAGUE

No.	Date	Opposition	Res.	Att.	Goalscorers
1	11 Sep	Great Eastern Railway	4-1		Jackman, Adams, O'Gorman, Harris
2	18	NEWPORTONIANS	6-1		Jackman,Boreham(2),A.Smith(2),O'Gorm'n
3	25	Great Western Railway	6-1		Boreham, A.Smith(3), Adams, Jackman
4	2 Oct	Wood Green	5-1		Grace, O'Gorman(2), A.Smith, McDermott
5	16	SUTTON COURT	11-2		Brehm(3),Grce,A.Smth,O'Gorman,Jckmn(3),Adms(2)
6	30	GREAT WESTERN RAILWAY	9-3		Brehm(4,2p),Jackmn,O'Gormn(2),Adms,A.Smth
7	18 Dec	AYLESBURY UNITED	7-0		Boreham, A.Smith(5), Adams
8	27	Chesham United	4-2	4000	Boreham(3), A.Smith
9	28	CHESHAM UNITED	3-2	5000	Grace, A.Smith, Boreham
10	5 Feb	NEWPORTONIANS	6-0		Adams,Jackman(2),Grace,O.G.,O'Gorman
11	5 Mar	SLOUGH	1-1	4000	Adams
12	19	Slough	0-3		
13	25	LONDON POLYTECHNIC	4-2		O'Gorman,W.Smith(p),A.Smith,Boreham
14	26	SUTTON COURT	2-2		O.G., Adams
15	28	WOOD GREEN	5-2	5000	Boreham(2), W.Smith(2pens),A.Smith
16	6 Apr	LEAVESDEN MENTAL HOSPITAL	4-1	2000	Boreham(2), A.Smith, McDermott
17	9	GREAT EASTERN RAILWAY	4-1		Boreham(2), A.Smith, W.Smith(pen)
18	16	Leavesden Mental Hospital	2-1		Boreham, Adams
19	19	LONDON POLYTECHNIC	5-2	3000	Boreham(2), O'Gorman(2), A.Smith
20	23	Aylesbury United	3-1		Boreham(2), O'Gorman
21	27	1ST WELSH GUARDS	5-0	3000	Jackman(2), Boreham(2), W.Smith
22	4 May	1ST WELSH GUARDS	12-0	1000	Hinton(5), Grace(3), Mitchell(2), Bass(2)

N.b. Both games against London Polytechnic, Newportonians, Sutton Court and 1st Welsh Guards played at Loakes Park.

F.A. CUP

1QR	9 Oct	SOUTHALL	4-1		Adams, Boreham(2), A.Smith
2QR	23	WINDSOR & ETON	2-0	5508	Boreham, A.Smith
3QR	6 Nov	SLOUGH	2-2	6250	Adams, Jackman
3QRr	10	Slough	7-2		Grace,Boreham(3),Jackmn,A.Smith,Adms
4QR	20	GREAT EASTERN RAILWAY	3-2	5000	Jackman(2), A.Smith
5QR	4 Dec	Kettering	1-2	6000	A.Smith

F.A. AMATEUR CUP

1R	1 Jan	SIGNAL SERVICE	3-2		Jackman, Boreham, Adams
2R	15	BARNET	4-3		Jackman(2), O'Gorman(2)
3R	12 Feb	Tufnell Park	2-1	5000	F.Gates, O'Gorman
4R	26	Loftus Albion	0-2	5000	

BERKS & BUCKS SENIOR CUP

1R	27 Nov	SLOUGH TRADING COMPANY	2-0		O'Gorman, A.Smith
2R	29 Jan	CUBITT'S (AYLESBURY)	4-0	2905	Boreham(2), Jackman(2)
SF*	19 Feb	Windsor & Eton	4-0	5000	Adams, Boreham, O'Gorman, Jackman
F#	2 Apr	Slough	5-2	9875	Boreham(2), A.Smith, Grace, Jackman

* Played at Slough
# Played at Reading

Final League Table

	P.	W.	D.	L.	F.	A.	Pts.
1 Wycombe Wanderers	22	19	2	1	108	29	40
2 Slough	22	16	4	2	74	20	36
3 Chesham United	22	16	3	3	88	34	35
4 Great Eastern Railway	22	15	1	6	87	36	31
5 Leavesden Mental Hospital	22	13	4	5	42	29	30
6 Wood Green	22	9	5	8	55	54	23
7 Aylesbury United	22	10	1	11	44	52	21
8 Sutton Court	22	6	4	12	47	71	16
9 Polytechnic	22	5	5	12	37	63	15
10 Great Western Railway	22	2	2	18	34	100	6
11 1st Welsh Guards	22	1	4	17	24	79	6
12 Newportonians	22	0	5	17	18	79	5

(Reserve Team)

Season 1921/22 (Back) White (Trainer), Beeson, Keating, Hodson (Capt.), Hooper (Sec.) (Middle) Stallwood (Trainer), Thompson, Saunders, Webster, Newell (Vice-Captain), Abbott (Linesman) (Front) McDermott, Pierce, Dancer, Bass, Nash.

Season 1922/23   Tour to France (May 1923)
(L.toR.) O'Gorman, ? , ? , ? ,Hooper, Harris, Foates, ? , ? , Martin, Rolfe, A.Smith, Grace, Didcock, Jackman, Vickers

SEASON 1921-22
ISTHMIAN LEAGUE

No.	Date	Opposition	Res.	Att.	Goalscorers
1	3 Sep	Leytonstone	3-4		O'Gorman, Jackman(2)
2	10	CASUALS	7-2		Borehm,OG,Adms(2),Jackmn,O'Gormn(2)
3	17	Tufnell Park	1-0	2500	Jackman
4	24	NUNHEAD	2-1	5000	Grace, O'Gorman
5	1 Oct	Wimbledon	4-3	6000	W.Smith(pen), Boreham(2), Jackman
6	15	London Caledonians	0-3	4000	
7	22	Nunhead	3-2	3000	Boreham(2), Grace
8	29	West Norwood	1-2		Styles
9	5 Nov	DULWICH HAMLET	2-4	5500	W.Smith(pen), Grace
10	12	CASUALS	6-2	3500	Harris, Hinton(2), Jackman(3)
11	19	WOKING	1-3	3500	Hinton
12	3 Dec	Woking	1-3	2500	Boreham
13	24	LEYTONSTONE	1-1	5000	Jackman
14	27	CLAPTON	2-3	7000	Grace, Jackman
15	31	OXFORD CITY	3-1	5000	Jackman(2), Bass
16	7 Jan	Oxford City	1-2		Jackman
17	4 Feb	Civil Service	1-2		A.Smith
18	11	TUFNELL PARK	1-0	4000	Hinton
19	25	Wimbledon	7-1		Jackmn,O'Gormn,A.Smth,Grce,Hintn(2),W.Smt
20	4 Mar	Clapton	2-3		Jackman, Hinton
21	18	WEST NORWOOD	4-2	4000	Hinton, Adams, Harris(2pens)
22	1 Apr	LONDON CALEDONIANS	2-1	4000	Hinton(2)
23	8	Dulwich Hamlet	0-7	3000	
24	15	CIVIL SERVICE	2-2	3000	Grace, Hinton
25	22	ILFORD	3-1	4000	Hinton(2), A.Smith
26	27	Ilford	1-9		Pierce

N.b. Both games against Casuals played at Loakes Park

F.A. CUP

| 1QR | 8 Oct | SLOUGH | 2-2 | 7787 | Boreham, Adams |
| 1QRr | 12 | Slough | 1-3 | 5000 | Jackman |

F.A. AMATEUR CUP

| 1R | 10 Dec | ENFIELD | 7-2 | 4218 | Boreham(2),Hinton(3,1p),Grace,Jackmn |
| 2R | 14 Jan | Bromley | 0-6 | | |

BERKS & BUCKS SENIOR CUP

1R	26 Nov	AYLESBURY UNITED	5-1	5000	Jackman, Boreham(2), Hinton, Adams
2R	28 Jan	READING B.W.I.	4-1	3300	O'Gorman, Bass, Hinton, Jackman
SF*	11 Mar	Maidenhead United	2-2	6000	O'Gorman(2)
SFr*	25	Maidenhead United	5-1	5000	O'Gorman, Jackman(4)
F*	17 Apr	Chesham United	1-1	10100	Hinton
Fr*	29	Chesham United	0-2	5400	

* Played at Slough

Final League Table

		P.	W.	D.	L.	F.	A.	Pts.
1	Ilford	26	17	4	5	66	34	38
2	Dulwich Hamlet	26	15	7	4	65	24	37
3	London Caledonians	26	16	3	7	41	21	35
4	Nunhead	26	12	5	9	65	41	29
5	Clapton	26	13	3	10	51	46	29
6	Tufnell Park	26	10	7	9	44	39	27
7	Oxford City	26	12	2	12	48	47	26
8	Wycombe Wanderers	26	12	2	12	61	64	26
9	Civil Service	26	9	8	9	40	48	26
10	Woking	26	10	6	10	39	49	26
11	Leytonstone	26	9	6	11	41	48	24
12	West Norwood	26	8	5	13	43	57	21
13	Wimbledon	26	7	4	15	52	56	18
14	Casuals	26	0	2	24	25	107	2

SEASON 1922-23
ISTHMIAN LEAGUE

No.	Date	Opposition	Res.	Att.	Goalscorers
1	26 Aug	NUNHEAD	1-7	5000	Hinton
2	2 Sep	Ilford	1-5	2500	Jackman
3	9	LEYTONSTONE	4-2	4000	Grace, A.Smith, Adams(2)
4	16	Clapton	1-3		A.Smith
5	30	TUFNELL PARK	3-0	4000	Adams, A.Smith, Jackman
6	14 Oct	Tufnell Park	1-0		Jackman
7	28	LONDON CALEDONIANS	1-2		Jackman
8	4 Nov	Woking	1-1	2000	Adams
9	11	CLAPTON	5-1		F.Gates,Adams,Grace,A.Smith(2)
10	18	WEST NORWOOD	0-1	3000	
11	2 Dec	CASUALS	3-4		Jackman, Adams, Grace
12	23	Oxford City	5-4		Jackman, Adams(2), A.Smith(2)
13	30	OXFORD CITY	3-2	4000	Jackman, Rose, Adams
14	27 Jan	CIVIL SERVICE	1-1	3000	Grace
15	10 Feb	WEST NORWOOD	1-2	3500	Boreham
16	17	WIMBLEDON	5-4		A.Smith,Jackman,Adams,McDermott(2)
17	24	London Caledonians	2-0		Hinton, A.Smith
18	3 Mar	Wimbledon	2-4		Rose, A.Smith
19	24	Nunhead	5-1		A.Smith(4), Jackman
20	31	Civil Service	1-4		A.Smith
21	7 Apr	Leytonstone	0-1	3000	
22	14	WOKING	9-4	3000	Hinton(5), A.Smith(3,1pen), Fryer
23	18	Casuals	2-2		Grace, Hinton
24	21	ILFORD	2-2	3000	Crook, Hinton
25	23	Dulwich Hamlet	0-3		
26	28	DULWICH HAMLET	2-1	3000	A.Smith, W.Smith(pen)

N.b. Both games against West Norwood were played at Loakes Park.

F.A. CUP

PR	23 Sep	MARLOW	7-1		Rose(2),Hinton(3),A.Smith(p),Saunders
1QR	7 Oct	Uxbridge	6-1	1500	Grace(2),Rose,A.Smith,Jackman,Hinton
2QR	21	SLOUGH	0-2	6000	

F.A. AMATEUR CUP

| 1R | 9 Dec | KING'S LYNN | 6-4 | 4000 | Adams(2), Jackman, A.Smith(3) |
| 2R | 20 Jan | ST. ALBANS CITY | 1-2 | 7000 | Grace |

BERKS & BUCKS SENIOR CUP

1R	25 Nov	SLOUGH	2-1	5000	A.Smith, W.Smith
SF*	10 Mar	Reading B.W.I.	4-0	4000	Hinton(2), A.Smith(2)
F#	2 Apr	Maidenhead United	4-0	11500	Hinton(2), A.Smith, Jackman

N.b. Second round - drawn at home to Wantage who withdrew.
* Played at Maidenhead
# Played at Slough

Final League Table

		P.	W.	D.	L.	F.	A.	Pts.
1	Clapton	26	15	7	4	51	33	37
2	Nunhead	26	15	5	6	52	32	35
3	London Caledonians	26	13	7	6	43	26	33
4	Ilford	26	11	7	8	57	38	29
5	Casuals	26	12	5	9	68	51	29
6	Civil Service	26	9	10	7	39	36	28
7	Wycombe Wanderers	26	11	4	11	61	61	26
8	Dulwich Hamlet	26	9	7	10	60	44	25
9	Leytonstone	26	9	7	10	45	56	25
10	Tufnell Park	26	9	5	12	41	45	23
11	Wimbledon	26	10	2	14	49	50	22
12	Woking	26	7	6	13	42	67	20
13	Oxford City	26	6	5	15	45	68	17
14	West Norwood	26	5	5	16	25	71	15

SEASON 1923-24
ISTHMIAN LEAGUE

No.	Date	Opposition	Res.	Att.	Goalscorers
1	25 Aug	NUNHEAD	5-2	5000	Boreham(2), Hinton(3)
2	1 Sep	Woking	6-1		Hinton(3), A.Smith(3)
3	8	TUFNELL PARK	1-1	4000	Grace
4	15	Ilford	8-1	2000	Hintn(3), Walter Keen, Fryr, A.Smth, Grce(2)
5	29	ST. ALBANS CITY	9-1		Grace(2,1p), Hinton(3), A.Smith(2), Weaver, Fryer
6	13 Oct	CIVIL SERVICE	4-1	5000	O.G., Hinton, Weaver(2,1pen)
7	27	Leytonstone	3-2		Weaver, Adams, A.Smith
8	10 Nov	Wimbledon	1-1		Weaver
9	1 Dec	LEYTONSTONE	3-3	3000	Weaver, Hinton(2)
10	8	WOKING	2-2	3500	Hinton(2,1pen)
11	15	Dulwich Hamlet	2-4	6500	W.Smith, Hinton
12	22	St. Albans City	0-5		
13	29	Oxford City	1-6	2500	Adams
14	2 Feb	Clapton	3-2		Weaver(2), Boreham
15	9	OXFORD CITY	5-2	4000	A.Smith(2), Grace(2), Boreham
16	15 Mar	Nunhead	2-2		Boreham, Walter Keen
17	29	LONDON CALEDONIANS	7-1		Boreham(2), Hinton(3), Fryer, Weaver
18	3 Apr	Tufnell Park	1-0	500	Adams
19	5	CASUALS	5-4	5000	Hinton(3), Boreham(2)
20	9	WIMBLEDON	8-0		Hinton(4), Boreham(2), Weaver, Fryer
21	12	Civil Service	0-6		
22	14	CLAPTON	4-3	3000	Grace, Weaver(2), Boreham
23	16	DULWICH HAMLET	4-2	5000	Boreham(2), Weaver, Hinton
24	26	Ilford	2-3	3000	Fryer, Weaver
25	28	London Caledonians	0-4		
26	3 May	Casuals	2-6		Hinton(2)

F.A. CUP

PR	22 Sep	Chesham United	4-2	3000	Weaver(2), A.Smith, Hinton
1QR	6 Oct	HOUNSLOW	8-2	4500	Hinton(4), Fryer, Weaver(2), A.Smith
2QR	20	Botwell Mission	4-4	4500	A.Smith, Walter Keen, Hinton, Weaver(p)
2QRr	24	BOTWELL MISSION	1-2	5000	Hinton

F.A. AMATEUR CUP

1R	5 Jan	St. Albans City	1-1	4500	Hinton
1Rr	12	ST. ALBANS CITY	2-1	4944	Weaver(2),
2R	19	ILFORD	1-0	6000	A.Smith
3R	16 Feb	Staines Lagonda	2-1	3125	Boreham, Weaver
4R	1 Mar	LONDON CALEDONIANS	0-3	9288	

BERKS & BUCKS SENIOR CUP

1R	24 Nov	STOKENCHURCH	12-1	2000	Hintn(2), A.Smth(3), OG, Walter Keen(2)*
2R	26 Jan	Slough	2-5	5000	Boreham, F.Gates

* Extra goalscores:- Fryer(2), Adams(2)

Final League Table

		P.	W.	D.	L.	F.	A.	Pts.
1	St. Albans City	26	17	5	4	72	38	39
2	Dulwich Hamlet	26	15	6	5	49	28	36
3	Clapton	26	14	5	7	73	50	33
4	Wycombe Wanderers	26	14	5	7	88	65	33
5	London Caledonians	26	14	3	9	53	49	31
6	Civil Service	26	12	5	9	52	47	29
7	Casuals	26	13	1	12	65	55	27
8	Ilford	26	9	6	11	56	59	24
9	Nunhead	26	8	8	10	42	46	24
10	Wimbledon	26	8	4	14	43	62	20
11	Tufnell Park	26	8	2	16	38	53	18
12	Woking	26	5	8	13	31	62	18
13	Oxford City	26	7	2	17	53	74	16
14	Leytonstone	26	6	4	16	41	68	16

SEASON 1924-25
ISTHMIAN LEAGUE

No.	Date	Opposition	Res.	Att.	Goalscorers
1	30 Aug	ST. ALBANS CITY	3-6	5000	Hinton(3)
2	6 Sep	St. Albans City	0-4		
3	11	Ilford	1-5		Hinton
4	17	ILFORD	4-2		Hinton(3), Johnson
5	27	CIVIL SERVICE	1-1	4000	Hinton
6	11 Oct	Casuals	3-5	3000	Hinton(2), Woolford
7	25	TUFNELL PARK	3-2	3000	Johnson, Hinton(2,1pen)
8	1 Nov	Woking	2-4		Hinton(2)
9	8	Dulwich Hamlet	4-0	5000	Boreham(2), Hinton, Fryer
10	15	NUNHEAD	2-1	4000	Foster, Hinton
11	22	Wimbledon	5-4		Hinton, Foster, Fryer(2), Boreham
12	29	OXFORD CITY	7-1		Johnson(3), Hinton(3), Boreham
13	13 Dec	Oxford City	2-3		A.Smith, Boreham
14	27	WOKING	1-1		Hinton
15	17 Jan	CASUALS	0-3		
16	24	LONDON CALEDONIANS	4-1	5000	R.Simmons, Foster(3)
17	7 Feb	WIMBLEDON	1-4		Boreham
18	14	Leytonstone	1-2		Foster
19	28	Tufnell Park	2-1		Adams, Foster
20	14 Mar	Civil Service	3-0		Foster(2), R.Simmons
21	30	DULWICH HAMLET	5-0		Foster(2), Hinton, Boreham
22	4 Apr	LEYTONSTONE	1-2	4000	Boreham
23	25	London Caledonians	0-3		
24	27	CLAPTON	2-1		Boreham(2)
25	29	Nunhead	0-3		
26	29	Clapton	1-2		F.Gates

F.A. CUP

PR	20 Sep	YIEWSLEY	9-1		Hinton(3), Boreham(3), A.Smith(2), Rose
1QR	4 Oct	BOTWELL MISSION	4-0	5000	Boreham, Hinton(2), Fryer
2QR	18	SOUTHALL	0-0	6002	
2QRr	22	Southall	1-4		Hinton

F.A. AMATEUR CUP

1R	3 Jan	Aldershot Traction Company	1-3		Foster

BERKS & BUCKS SENIOR CUP

2R	31 Jan	READING B.W.I.	5-2	3000	Boreham, R.Simmons, Brooks, Foster(2)
SF*	7 Mar	Newbury Town	0-0		
SFr#	28	Newbury Town	1-0	3000	Foster
F+	13 Apr	Windsor & Eton	0-0	10504	
Fr#	18	Windsor & Eton	2-0	5600	Hinton, Boreham

* Played at Maidenhead
# Played at Slough
+ Played at Reading

Final League Table

		P.	W.	D.	L.	F.	A.	Pts.
1	London Caledonians	26	18	5	3	76	36	41
2	Clapton	26	19	1	6	64	34	39
3	St. Albans City	26	16	2	8	69	39	34
4	Tufnell Park	26	11	4	11	47	41	26
5	Ilford	26	11	4	11	46	42	26
6	Leytonstone	26	12	2	12	55	63	26
7	Casuals	26	12	1	13	55	58	25
8	Wycombe Wanderers	26	11	2	13	58	61	24
9	Civil Service	26	10	4	12	52	64	24
10	Nunhead	26	9	5	12	45	43	23
11	Wimbledon	26	10	2	14	50	54	22
12	Dulwich Hamlet	26	8	5	13	42	57	21
13	Oxford City	26	9	2	15	38	71	20
14	Woking	26	5	3	18	33	67	13

SEASON 1925-26
ISTHMIAN LEAGUE

No.	Date	Opposition	Res.	Att.	Goalscorers
1	2 Sep	OXFORD CITY	6-2		Foster, Beeson(pen), Hinton(4)
2	10	Oxford City	2-7	1500	Fryer, Hinton
3	12	Dulwich Hamlet	1-3	6000	Hinton
4	26	London Caledonians	1-9	3000	Timberlake
5	3 Oct	St. Albans City	1-4		Boreham
6	10	CASUALS	1-2	4000	Beeson(pen)
7	24	Wimbledon	4-2	3000	Hinton(2), Fryer, Clarke
8	7 Nov	LEYTONSTONE	3-3	3000	Boreham, Fryer(2)
9	14	Leytonstone	1-4		Fryer
10	21	ILFORD	7-6		Fryr,Hintn(2),Clrke,Adms,Borehm,Beesn(p)
11	5 Dec	CIVIL SERVICE	5-4		Hinton(2), Boreham(2), Adams
12	12	NUNHEAD	2-1	3000	Fryer, Boreham
13	19	Woking	5-3		Adams, Clarke, Hinton(2), Fryer
14	9 Jan	Ilford	6-4		Hinton(4), Fryer(2)
15	6 Feb	WIMBLEDON	9-2		Hinton(5), Boreham(2), Slade, Gates
16	13	Civil Service	5-6		Boreham, Hinton(2), Brooks, Slade
17	20	WOKING	6-4		Slade(2), Hinton(2), Boreham, Druce
18	27	Casuals	1-1	2000	Slade
19	6 Mar	LONDON CALEDONIANS	4-5	4000	Adams(2), Slade, Hinton
20	13	DULWICH HAMLET	4-1	4500	Adams, Hinton(3)
21	20	Clapton	1-2	2500	Brooks
22	17 Apr	Tufnell Park	4-2	1900	Hinton(2), Boreham, Fryer
23	19	TUFNELL PARK	4-1		Hinton(2), Clarke(2)
24	24	Nunhead	1-0	1000	Fryer
25	26	CLAPTON	9-1		Clrke(2),Brown(2),OG,Fryr,Borehm,Hintn(2)
26	1 May	ST. ALBANS CITY	4-4		Hinton(2), Boreham, Beeson(pen)

F.A. CUP

PR	19 Sep	NEWBURY TOWN	1-6	2000	Boreham

F.A. AMATEUR CUP

1R	2 Jan	HOVE	10-2	5000	Hinton(5), Druce(2), Boreham(3)
2R	23	Hampstead Town	0-1	3500	

BERKS & BUCKS SENIOR CUP

2R	30 Jan	WINDSOR & ETON	2-7	4000	Boreham, Hinton

Final League Table

		P.	W.	D.	L.	F.	A.	Pts.
1	Dulwich Hamlet	26	20	1	5	80	49	41
2	London Caledonians	26	15	1	7	81	44	37
3	Clapton	26	14	4	8	64	50	32
4	Wycombe Wanderers	26	14	3	9	97	83	31
5	St. Albans City	26	12	6	8	76	54	30
6	Nunhead	26	13	4	9	49	43	30
7	Ilford	26	13	2	11	81	70	28
8	Leytonstone	26	12	1	13	75	63	25
9	Woking	26	8	6	12	56	73	22
10	Tufnell Park	26	8	5	13	36	53	21
11	Casuals	26	8	4	14	48	61	20
12	Wimbledon	26	9	1	16	61	77	19
13	Oxford City	26	8	1	17	48	76	17
14	Civil Service	26	5	1	20	43	99	11

SEASON 1926-27
ISTHMIAN LEAGUE

No.	Date	Opposition	Res.	Att.	Goalscorers
1	28 Aug	Oxford City	1-2		Brown
2	1 Sep	OXFORD CITY	6-2		Clarke,Adams,Fryer,Boreham(2),Brown
3	4	Ilford	1-5	3000	Clarke
4	11	ST. ALBANS CITY	2-6	3000	Brown, Fryer
5	16	Clapton	3-4		Lacey(3)
6	25	Nunhead	2-3		Brown, Vickers
7	9 Oct	TUFNELL PARK	6-3		Adams(pen),R.Simmons,Lacey(3),Meakes
8	16	CASUALS	3-1		Lacey, Boreham(2)
9	23	St. Albans City	0-9		
10	30	LEYTONSTONE	3-2	3500	Lacey(2), Brown
11	20 Nov	CIVIL SERVICE	4-3		Fryer(2), Timberlake(2)
12	27	Casuals	3-1		Lacey, Fryer, Finch
13	4 Dec	CLAPTON	1-4		Timberlake
14	11	Tufnell Park	2-2		Fryer, Lacey
15	18	Woking	3-3	2500	Brown, Lacey, Fryer
16	8 Jan	CIVIL SERVICE	0-6		
17	29	Dulwich Hamlet	1-8	4000	Murphy
18	19 Feb	Woking	1-5		O.G.
19	12 Mar	WIMBLEDON	3-1	2000	Coward, Brown(2)
20	19	London Caledonians	0-3	1845	
21	26	Leytonstone	1-4		Finch
22	2 Apr	ILFORD	4-1	2000	Brown(2pens), Meakes, Coward
23	9	LONDON CALEDONIANS	3-4		Adams, Brown(2)
24	20	Wimbledon	0-3		
25	27	DULWICH HAMLET	5-1		Adams(3), Coward(2,1pen)
26	30	NUNHEAD	1-0	3000	Brown

F.A. CUP

PR	18 Sep	BOTWELL MISSION	4-1		Vickers, Lacey(2), O.G.
1QR	2 Oct	Slough	0-9		

F.A. AMATEUR CUP

1R	1 Jan	WALTHAMSTOW AVENUE	3-2	4000	Brown(2), Adams
2R	15	LONDON CALEDONIANS	3-2	5000	R.Boreham, Brown(2)
3R	12 Feb	CHILTON COLLIERY	3-1	6000	Adams, Brown, Timberlake
4R	26	Barking Town	2-3	6084	Finch, Burnard

BERKS & BUCKS SENIOR CUP

2R	5 Feb	Maidenhead United	3-6	3000	Brown(3)

Final League Table

		P.	W.	D.	L.	F.	A.	Pts.
1	St. Albans City	26	20	1	5	96	34	41
2	Ilford	26	17	0	9	76	57	34
3	Wimbledon	26	15	3	8	72	45	33
4	Nunhead	26	11	8	7	51	33	30
5	Woking	26	12	6	8	68	60	30
6	London Caledonians	26	11	7	8	58	47	29
7	Clapton	26	11	4	11	58	60	26
8	Leytonstone	26	11	1	14	54	78	23
9	Dulwich Hamlet	26	9	4	13	60	58	22
10	Wycombe Wanderers	26	10	2	14	59	86	22
11	Tufnell Park	26	8	4	14	45	55	20
12	Oxford City	26	7	5	14	46	72	19
13	Casuals	26	8	3	15	37	78	19
14	Civil Service	26	6	4	16	48	65	16

(Reserve Team)

Season 1923/24: (Back) Stallwood (Trainer), Gammon, Watts, Phipps, White (Trainer) (Middle) Miles (Chairman & Treas.), McDermott, Reynolds, Thomas, Johnson, Vickers, Garland (Front) Hodson (Vice-Capt.), Mitchell, Newell (Capt.), Wethered

Season 1929/30 (Back) Harris (Trainer), Crump, Kipping (Capt.), Cox, Gardner (Sec.) (Middle) Simmons, Brown, Vernon, Braisher, Britnell   (Front) Tapping, Badrick, Timberlake

SEASON 1927-28
ISTHMIAN LEAGUE

No.	Date	Opposition	Res.	Att.	Goalscorers
1	1 Sep	Oxford City	1-1		Slade
2	3	Ilford	0-5		
3	7	OXFORD CITY	3-3		Brown(pen), Slade(2)
4	10	TUFNELL PARK	8-1		Meakes,Brown(3),H.Bates,Cward(2),Slde
5	24	Tufnell Park	2-1	1809	Slade, Brown
6	8 Oct	WOKING	3-1	4000	Slade, Brown(2)
7	15	Woking	1-1		Adams
8	22	Dulwich Hamlet	1-2		Burnard
9	29	Leytonstone	1-2		Braisher
10	5 Nov	Wimbledon	1-6		Vickers
11	19	LONDON CALEDONIANS	2-7		Brown, S.Stratford
12	3 Dec	CLAPTON	4-4		Slade(3), Grace
13	10	Clapton	0-2		
14	17	CASUALS	4-2		Braisher, Slade(2), Grace
15	24	St. Albans City	1-6		Slade
16	18 Feb	ST. ALBANS CITY	3-5		Grace, Braisher, Brown(pen)
17	25	CIVIL SERVICE	3-2		Lacey, Brown(2)
18	3 Mar	NUNHEAD	3-4		H.Bates, Grace, Brown
19	17	Civil Service	1-3		Brown
20	31	ILFORD	3-1		Vickers(2), Brown
21	12 Apr	London Caledonians	2-2		Timberlake(2)
22	21	DULWICH HAMLET	4-2		Finch(2), S.Crump(pen), Braisher
23	26	Nunhead	1-3		Brown
24	25	LEYTONSTONE	1-2		S.Crump(pen)
25	2 May	WIMBLEDON	4-0		Brown(3), H.Bates
26	5	CASUALS	3-1		S.Crump(pen), Timberlake, Finch

N.b. Both games against Casuals played at Loakes Park.

F.A. CUP

PR	17 Sep	UXBRIDGE TOWN	4-4	5000	Slade, Brown, Adams(2)
PRr	21	Uxbridge Town	4-0		Slade, S.Stratford, Vickers(2)
1QR	1 Oct	Hounslow	1-4	1500	Brown

F.A. AMATEUR CUP

1R	7 Jan	SOUTHWICK	4-2	3485	Grace, Brown(2), O.G.
2R	21	Cambridge Town	1-1	3469	Grace
2Rr	28	CAMBRIDGE TOWN	3-8	2900	Brown, O.G., Slade

BERKS & BUCKS SENIOR CUP

2R	4 Feb	FARNHAM UNITED	3-1		Lacey(2), Grace
SF*	10 Mar	Slough	2-1		Grace, Brown
F#	9 Apr	Maidenhead United	0-1	8500	

* Played at Maidenhead
# Played at Slough

Final League Table

		P.	W.	D.	L.	F.	A.	Pts.
1	St. Albans City	26	15	5	6	86	50	35
2	London Caledonians	26	12	9	5	63	38	33
3	Ilford	26	14	4	8	72	54	32
4	Woking	26	13	5	8	72	56	31
5	Nunhead	26	13	2	11	57	54	28
6	Wimbledon	26	12	3	11	57	48	27
7	Leytonstone	26	13	1	12	53	56	27
8	Clapton	26	8	10	8	52	47	26
9	Dulwich Hamlet	26	8	9	9	56	49	25
10	Casuals	26	8	8	10	54	58	24
11	Wycombe Wanderers	26	9	5	12	60	69	23
12	Oxford City	26	7	7	12	36	57	21
13	Civil Service	26	8	4	14	38	76	20
14	Tufnell Park	26	4	4	18	38	82	12

SEASON 1928-29
ISTHMIAN LEAGUE

No.	Date	Opposition	Res.	Att.	Goalscorers
1	1 Sep	WIMBLEDON	4-3	2000	Wells, Brown(3)
2	8	OXFORD CITY	4-2		Wells, Grace, Timberlake, Brown
3	22	London Caledonians	1-1		Grace
4	6 Oct	CLAPTON	3-0		Grace, Wells, Brown
5	13	Civil Service	4-2		Timberlake(2), Wells, Brown
6	20	ILFORD	4-2		Wells(2), Braisher(2)
7	27	St. Albans City	0-2		
8	3 Nov	Ilford	2-6		Brown, Timberlake
9	10	NUNHEAD	2-0		Brown(2)
10	17	TUFNELL PARK	4-2		S.Crump(pen),Brown,Wells,Timberlake
11	24	Wimbledon	0-2		
12	1 Dec	Nunhead	2-3		Brown(2)
13	8	Casuals	1-1		Britnell
14	22	DULWICH HAMLET	3-4		S.Crump(pen), Grace, Brown
15	29	Dulwich Hamlet	0-6		
16	5 Jan	Woking	0-1		
17	12	ST. ALBANS CITY	3-0		Braisher, H.Stratford, Timberlake
18	23 Feb	Oxford City	1-4		Tapping
19	9 Mar	LEYTONSTONE	2-3		Collins, Tapping
20	16	LONDON CALEDONIANS	1-2		Grace
21	23	CASUALS	0-0		
22	6 Apr	CIVIL SERVICE	2-4		Brown(2)
23	20	WOKING	7-1		Brown(3),Braisher(2),Britnell,Timberlke
24	24	Tufnell Park	2-3		Britnell, Braisher
25	27	Clapton	5-3		Britnell,Brown,Grace,Wilf Keen,Braishr
26	4 May	Leytonstone	1-3		Brown

F.A. CUP

PR	15 Sep	HENLEY TOWN	11-1	2000	Brown(8), Braisher(2), Wells
1QR	29	Southall	3-3	3688	Grace(2), Brown
1QRr	3 Oct	SOUTHALL	1-5		Brown

F.A. AMATEUR CUP

1R	15 Dec	AYLESBURY UNITED	3-1	4000	Brown(2), Wilf Keen
2R	19 Jan	B/MOUTH GASWORKS ATH.	5-2	5109	Tapping(2),Braisher,Britnell,Timberlake
3R	9 Feb	Dulwich Hamlet	1-7		O.G.

BERKS & BUCKS SENIOR CUP

2R	26 Jan	MARLOW	7-2	2420	Braisher(2),S.Crmp(p),Tpping(3),W.Brwn
SF*	2 Mar	Chesham United	1-2		Wilf Keen

* Played at Aylesbury

Final League Table

		P.	W.	D.	L.	F.	A.	Pts.
1	Nunhead	26	15	6	5	47	35	36
2	London Caledonians	26	15	4	7	65	33	34
3	Dulwich Hamlet	26	14	6	6	85	34	34
4	Wimbledon	26	9	10	7	66	54	28
5	Ilford	26	12	3	11	67	52	27
6	Clapton	26	11	5	10	60	55	27
7	Tufnell Park	26	11	5	10	58	55	27
8	St. Albans City	26	12	3	11	63	89	27
9	Leytonstone	26	11	3	12	56	79	25
10	Wycombe Wanderers	26	10	3	13	58	60	23
11	Oxford City	26	10	3	13	61	71	23
12	Casuals	26	8	5	13	49	60	21
13	Woking	26	8	3	15	39	65	19
14	Civil Service	26	4	5	17	39	71	13

SEASON 1929-30
ISTHMIAN LEAGUE

No.	Date	Opposition	Res.	Att.	Goalscorers
1	31 Aug	CLAPTON	2-1		O.G., F.Bates
2	5 Sep	Oxford City	0-0		
3	7	Leytonstone	0-2		
4	11	OXFORD CITY	4-1		G.Smith, R.Simmons(2), Timberlake
5	14	CASUALS	3-2		Brown, R.Simmons, S.Crump(pen)
6	28	ILFORD	1-0		F.Bates
7	5 Oct	Woking	2-2		Britnell, O.G.
8	19	LONDON CALEDONIANS	2-2		Brown(2)
9	26	London Caledonians	1-2		Brown
10	2 Nov	Nunhead	1-3		G.Smith
11	9	ST. ALBANS CITY	4-0		C.Simmons, Brown(2), G.Smith
12	23	Kingstonian	0-2		
13	30	TUFNELL PARK	2-3		C.Simmons(2)
14	7 Dec	Casuals	2-2		G.Smith, Finch
15	21	LEYTONSTONE	4-2		Finch, C.Simmons(3)
16	28	KINGSTONIAN	0-2		
17	4 Jan	DULWICH HAMLET	2-0		Cubbage(2)
18	18	St. Albans City	2-3		S.Crump(pen), Tapping
19	8 Feb	WOKING	6-0		Brown(2),Tapping(2),C.Simmons,Serjent
20	15	Dulwich Hamlet	0-7		
21	8 Mar	Tufnell Park	0-2		
22	15	Clapton	1-7		Cubbage
23	22	NUNHEAD	4-1		C.Simmons, Brown(2), Tapping
24	12 Apr	Wimbledon	1-3		Brown
25	26	Ilford	1-2		Braisher
26	28	WIMBLEDON	4-1		Cubbage(3), Brown

F.A. CUP

PR	21 Sep	Maidenhead United	0-1		

F.A. AMATEUR CUP

1R	14 Dec	Bournemouth Gasworks Athletic	1-2	1500	C.Simmons

BERKS & BUCKS SENIOR CUP

2R	1 Feb	Slough	0-1		

Final League Table

		P.	W.	D.	L.	F.	A.	Pts.
1	Nunhead	26	19	3	4	69	36	41
2	Dulwich Hamlet	26	15	6	5	74	39	36
3	Kingstonian	26	15	4	7	57	37	34
4	Ilford	26	16	1	9	84	60	33
5	Woking	26	11	5	10	66	85	27
6	Wimbledon	26	11	2	13	64	66	24
7	Wycombe Wanderers	26	10	4	12	49	52	24
8	Casuals	26	8	7	11	50	51	23
9	Oxford City	26	10	3	13	45	80	23
10	St. Albans City	26	9	4	13	54	77	22
11	Clapton	26	8	4	14	47	56	20
12	Tufnell Park	26	6	7	13	34	54	19
13	London Caledonians	26	8	3	15	49	69	19
14	Leytonstone	26	8	3	15	48	68	19

SEASON 1930-31
ISTHMIAN LEAGUE

No.	Date	Opposition	Res.	Att.	Goalscorers
1	30 Aug	CLAPTON	6-1	2000	Brown(3), Braisher(2), C.Simmons
2	3 Sep	OXFORD CITY	2-2		Brown, Tapping
3	6	Nunhead	1-2		C.Simmons
4	11	Oxford City	5-0		Brown(2), Vernon(2), Timberlake
5	13	CASUALS	3-3		Vernon(3)
6	27	ILFORD	2-2		Feesey, C.Simmons
7	4 Oct	St. Albans City	1-3		Vernon
8	11	WOKING	1-0		Braisher
9	25	Leytonstone	3-1		Channer, Brown, Britnell
10	1 Nov	Wimbledon	1-3		Channer
11	15	ST. ALBANS CITY	2-4		Vernon, Brown
12	22	LONDON CALEDONIANS	3-3		Vernon(3)
13	29	Clapton	1-5		C.Simmons
14	6 Dec	Ilford	2-0		Braisher, Brown
15	20	WOKING	4-1		Brown(2), Vernon(2)
16	27	NUNHEAD	5-2		Tapping(2), Brown, Britnell, Cox
17	3 Jan	DULWICH HAMLET	3-1		Tapping, O.G., Brown
18	14 Feb	Dulwich Hamlet	2-2		Braisher(2)
19	21 Mar	London Caledonians	0-1		
20	28	WIMBLEDON	1-0		Braisher
21	18 Apr	LEYTONSTONE	4-1		Braisher, Richards, C.Simmons, Vernon
22	20	Tufnell Park	3-3		Rance, Tapping(2)
23	22	Casuals	0-3		
24	30	TUFNELL PARK	8-0		Rnce,Vrnon(3),Badrck,Brwn,Braishr,C.Simmn
25	2 May	Kingstonian	0-2		
26	2	KINGSTONIAN	4-0		Brown(3), O.G.

Matches No. 25 & 26 played on the same day with 3.00pm and 6.30pm kick-offs respectively.

F.A. CUP

PR	20 Sep	Uxbridge Town	0-1	2500	

F.A. AMATEUR CUP

1R	13 Dec	London Caledonians	4-1	1879	Brown(2), Vernon(2)
2R	17 Jan	WALTHAMSTOW AVENUE	6-1	6232	Tapping(4), Brown(2)
3R	7 Feb	ROMFORD	6-2	9014	Timberlake,Britnell,Vernon(2),Rance(2)
4R	21	Metropolitan Police	1-1	5000	Brown
4Rr	28	METROPOLITAN POLICE	2-1	10881	Braisher, Vernon
SF*	7 Mar	Woking	3-0	7500	Britnell(2), Brown
F#	11 Apr	Hayes	1-0	32489	Britnell

* Played at Ilford
\# Played at Highbury

BERKS & BUCKS SENIOR CUP

2R	31 Jan	SLOUGH	6-3		Vernon(4), Braisher(2)
SF*	14 Mar	Chesham United	2-4	6000	Tapping(2)

* Played at Maidenhead

Final League Table

		P.	W.	D.	L.	F.	A.	Pts.
1	Wimbledon	26	18	6	2	69	37	42
2	Dulwich Hamlet	26	12	9	5	51	39	33
3	Wycombe Wanderers	26	12	6	8	67	45	30
4	Casuals	26	12	6	8	71	58	30
5	St. Albans City	26	11	7	8	67	66	29
6	Ilford	26	10	6	10	70	62	26
7	Oxford City	26	10	5	11	43	48	25
8	London Caledonians	26	8	8	10	43	53	24
9	Kingstonian	26	10	4	12	49	64	24
10	Tufnell Park	26	9	5	12	46	61	23
11	Nunhead	26	9	4	13	49	54	22
12	Woking	26	9	4	13	56	64	22
13	Clapton	26	7	4	15	62	75	15
14	Leytonstone	26	6	4	16	46	65	16

SEASON 1931-32
ISTHMIAN LEAGUE

No.	Date	Opposition	Res.	Att.	Goalscorers
1	29 Aug	ILFORD	2-2	5000	Braisher, C.Simmons
2	3 Sep	Oxford City	5-4		Tapping(2), Richards, Braisher(2)
3	9	OXFORD CITY	4-1	2000	C.Simmons, Brown, Braisher(2)
4	12	London Caledonians	1-1		Tapping
5	10 Oct	Casuals	2-1		C.Simmons, Tapping
6	24	LONDON CALEDONIANS	6-1		Stne(2),Braishr,W.Brwn,S.Crmp(p),C.Simmns
7	7 Nov	WIMBLEDON	3-2	5500	Stone(2), Braisher
8	21	CLAPTON	2-2		Braisher(2)
9	28	Kingstonian	2-2		Braisher, Burnham
10	5 Dec	LEYTONSTONE	9-2		C.Simms,Braishr(5),S.Crmp(2,1p),Vickrs
11	19	Ilford	1-5		O.G.
12	2 Jan	TUFNELL PARK	3-2		Rance, Tapping, Vickers
13	20 Feb	Tufnell Park	1-3		S.Crump(pen)
14	5 Mar	Leytonstone	1-3	4000	Britnell
15	12	WOKING	2-1		Britnell, Vickers
16	19	Woking	1-1		Vickers
17	2 Apr	Clapton	2-1		Brown, C.Simmons
18	9	NUNHEAD	3-4		Braisher(2), Greenwell
19	16	St. Albans City	5-1		Braisher, Vickers, Brown(2), Loveday
20	20	Wimbledon	0-3		
21	25	DULWICH HAMLET	5-2		C.Simmons(3), Braisher, Britnell
22	28	Nunhead	2-0		C.Simmons, Brown
23	30	ST. ALBANS CITY	1-2		Brown
24	2 May	KINGSTONIAN	6-2		Pritchard(3), Vickers(2), C.Simmons
25	5	Dulwich Hamlet	1-2		Pritchard
26	7	CASUALS	2-0		Braisher, C.Simmons

F.A. CUP

EXPR	5 Sep	MORRIS MOTORS	9-1		Tapping(6), Braisher(2), Brown
PR	19	UXBRIDGE TOWN	7-0		W.Brwn(2),C.Smmns(2),Brtnll,S.Crmp(p),Braishr
1QR	3 Oct	PARK ROYAL	5-3	4500	Braisher(2), Brown(3)
2QR	17	MAIDENHEAD UNITED	4-0	7500	Brown(2), Timberlake(2)
3QR	31	SOUTHALL	2-1	7300	S.Crump(p), Braisher
4QR	14 Nov	Enfield Town	1-6		Braisher

F.A. AMATEUR CUP

1R	12 Dec	Barking Town	3-2	7000	C.Simmons, Braisher(2)
2R	16 Jan	EPSOM TOWN	7-2	7000	Vickers, Waite(4), C.Simmons
3R	6 Feb	Yorkshire Amateurs	0-4	2000	

BERKS & BUCKS SENIOR CUP

2R	30 Jan	Wolverton Town	1-1	2000	G.Smith
2Rr	13 Feb	WOLVERTON TOWN	4-2	3500	Braisher(2), Vickers(2)
SF*	27	Slough	4-0		Vickers,Badrick,C.Simmons,Timberlake
F#	28 Mar	Maidenhead United	1-2	10760	Vickers

* Played at Maidenhead
# Played at Reading

Final League Table

		P	W	D	L	F	A	Pts
1	Wimbledon	26	17	2	7	60	35	36
2	Ilford	26	13	9	4	71	45	35
3	Dulwich Hamlet	26	15	3	8	59	43	33
4	Wycombe Wanderers	26	14	5	7	72	50	33
5	Oxford City	26	15	2	9	63	49	32
6	Kingstonians	26	13	3	10	71	50	29
7	Tufnell Park	26	9	7	10	50	48	25
8	Nunhead	26	9	7	10	54	61	25
9	The Casuals	26	10	4	12	59	65	24
10	Clapton	26	9	5	12	50	57	23
11	Leytonstone	26	9	3	14	36	61	21
12	St. Albans City	26	8	4	14	57	78	20
13	Woking	26	6	5	15	44	64	17
14	London Caledonians	26	2	7	17	24	74	11

SEASON 1932-33
ISTHMIAN LEAGUE

No.	Date	Opposition	Res.	Att.	Goalscorers
1	27 Aug	TUFNELL PARK	3-0	4000	Braisher, Downer(2)
2	31	OXFORD CITY	2-1	2500	C.Simmons, Downer
3	3 Sep	London Caledonians	0-2		
4	8	Oxford City	3-0		Brown(2), C.Simmons
5	10	Casuals	1-2		Brown
6	8 Oct	KINGSTONIAN	1-5		Braisher
7	22	DULWICH HAMLET	0-6	6000	
8	5 Nov	LONDON CALEDONIANS	2-1		Brown, Varney
9	19	LEYTONSTONE	2-1		Braisher, Brown
10	3 Dec	NUNHEAD	2-1		Brown(2)
11	17	Woking	1-5		Braisher
12	24	ST. ALBANS CITY	0-3		
13	26	St. Albans City	0-4		
14	31	Clapton	0-3		
15	7 Jan	Leytonstone	1-2		Britnell
16	4 Feb	Wimbledon	3-2		Brown, Britnell, Youens
17	11	CASUALS	2-2	2800	Jordan(2)
18	18	WIMBLEDON	2-2		Brown, Jordan
19	25	Tufnell Park	2-2		Greenwell, C.Simmons
20	4 Mar	Ilford	3-5		O.G.(2), Brown
21	18	ILFORD	5-1	3000	Jordan(2), Youens(2), Brown
22	1 Apr	Nunhead	0-0		
23	15	CLAPTON	6-0	3000	Jordan(2), Brown, Braisher(2), Britnell
24	20	Dulwich Hamlet	2-3		Brown, Jordan
25	3 May	Kingstonian	1-3		Jordan
26	6	WOKING	3-0		Brown(2), C.Simmons

F.A. CUP

PR	17 Sep	GRADWELL'S SPORTS CLUB	2-0	2000	Brown, C.Simmons
1QR	1 Oct	MAIDENHEAD UNITED	3-2		Braisher(2), C.Simmons
2QR	15	PARK ROYAL	6-1		C.Simmons(3), Braisher(2), S.Crump(pen)
3QR	29	Slough	3-2		Britnell, Badrick, Braisher
4QR	12 Nov	Camberley & Yorktown	4-0	2050	Brown(3), Britnell
1R	26	Gillingham	1-1	6428	Braisher
1Rr	30	GILLINGHAM	2-4	7597	Brown, Braisher(pen)

F.A. AMATEUR CUP

1R	10 Dec	WIMBLEDON	1-2	4002	Braisher

BERKS & BUCKS SENIOR CUP

2R	28 Jan	SLOUGH	2-0		Brown, O.G.
SF*	11 Mar	Wolverton Town	4-1	5000	Brown(3), Youens
F#	17 Apr	Chesham United	1-0	7339	Youens

* Played at Aylesbury
# Played at Maidenhead

Final League Table

		P	W	D	L	F	A	Pts
1	Dulwich Hamlet	26	15	6	5	71	45	36
2	Leytonstone	26	16	4	6	66	43	36
3	Kingstonian	26	15	2	9	77	49	32
4	Ilford	26	14	0	12	60	55	28
5	Casuals	26	12	2	12	48	38	26
6	Tufnell Park	26	11	3	12	51	51	25
7	St. Albans City	26	12	1	13	57	63	25
8	Clapton	26	10	5	11	51	65	25
9	Oxford City	26	9	6	11	49	54	24
10	Woking	26	10	4	12	53	61	24
11	Wycombe Wanderers	26	10	4	12	47	56	24
12	Nunhead	26	8	6	12	42	50	22
13	Wimbledon	26	8	5	13	55	67	21
14	London Caledonians	26	5	6	15	35	64	16

SEASON 1933-34
ISTHMIAN LEAGUE

No.	Date	Opposition	Res.	Att.	Goalscorers
1	26 Aug	Wimbledon	1-4		Jordan
2	31	Oxford City	1-2		O.G.
3	2 Sep	Clapton	1-1		Jordan
4	6	OXFORD CITY	6-1	2500	Jordan(3), Britnell, Hardy, Braisher
5	9	CASUALS	3-1		Turner, Loveday, Jordan
6	16	WIMBLEDON	1-2	5000	Britnell
7	23	Ilford	1-2		Greenwell
8	7 Oct	LONDON CALEDONIANS	1-2		Darvill(pen)
9	14	WOKING	4-0		Jordan, Turner(2), Badrick
10	21	ILFORD	6-3		Greenwell, Turner(2), Badrick(p), Walker(2)
11	4 Nov	LEYTONSTONE	2-1		Walker, Jordan
12	18	KINGSTONIAN	2-4		J.E.Gearing, Jordan
13	25	Woking	1-3		Walker
14	2 Dec	Leytonstone	2-2		J.E.Gearing, Walker
15	16	DULWICH HAMLET	1-5		J.E.Gearing
16	25	St. Albans City	2-4	1000	Brown(2)
17	26	ST. ALBANS CITY	5-1	2000	Jordan(4), Britnell
18	3 Feb	Kingstonian	2-7		Anthony, Wilf Keen
19	10	Casuals	0-2		
20	10 Mar	Tufnell Park	0-3		
21	17	TUFNELL PARK	8-0		Britnell, JE.Gearing(3), Turner(2), Lovedy(2)
22	24	CLAPTON	2-0	2500	J.E.Gearing, Turner
23	7 Apr	London Caledonians	0-2		
24	14	Dulwich Hamlet	0-2	8500	
25	21	Nunhead	0-5		
26	28	NUNHEAD	5-1		Brown(3), Ayres(2)

F.A. CUP

4QR	11 Nov	Dulwich Hamlet	0-1	7568	

F.A. AMATEUR CUP

1R	9 Dec	KINGSTONIAN	0-1	5050	

BERKS & BUCKS SENIOR CUP

2R	27 Jan	Marlow	3-2	3000	Britnell, Turner, Jordan
SF*	3 Mar	Maidenhead United	2-1	3000	Wilf Keen(pen), Loveday
F#	2 Apr	Chesham United	0-0	9000	
Fr+	5 May	Chesham United	0-3		

* Played at Marlow
# Played at Maidenhead
+ Played at Reading

Final League Table

		P	W	D	L	F	A	Pts
1	Kingstonian	26	15	7	4	80	42	37
2	Dulwich Hamlet	26	15	5	6	68	36	35
3	Wimbledon	26	13	7	6	63	35	33
4	Tufnell Park	26	13	5	8	55	50	33
5	Ilford	26	15	2	9	60	56	32
6	The Casuals	26	13	5	8	47	32	31
7	Leytonstone	26	13	3	10	55	48	29
8	Nunhead	26	10	5	11	48	44	25
9	London Caledonians	26	7	8	11	29	51	22
10	Wycombe Wanderers	26	9	2	15	57	60	20
11	St. Albans City	26	8	4	14	44	75	20
12	Oxford City	26	7	4	15	45	57	18
13	Clapton	26	5	6	15	35	62	16
14	Woking	26	6	1	19	43	78	13

SEASON 1934/35
ISTHMIAN LEAGUE

No.	Date	Opposition	Res.	Att.	Goalscorers
1	25 Aug	CASUALS	3-1		Ayres(2), Rowe
2	29	OXFORD CITY	2-3		Brown(2)
3	1 Sep	DULWICH HAMLET	3-2		Pitts, Turner(2)
4	6	Oxford City	2-5		Ayres, Wilf Keen
5	8	WOKING	2-3		Rowe, Britnell
6	22	Kingstonian	2-1		Ward(2)
7	29	CLAPTON	2-2	4000	Ayres, Ward
8	6 Oct	London Caledonians	2-6		Harvey, Ayres
9	20	Clapton	2-2		Harvey, Ayres
10	27	Wimbledon	1-4	3700	Ayres
11	3 Nov	NUNHEAD	3-1		Andrews, Britnell, Harvey
12	10	Tufnell Park	2-2		Wilf Keen, O.G.
13	17	TUFNELL PARK	1-0	3000	Andrews
14	24	Woking	3-4		Rhodes(2), Britnell
15	8 Dec	Ilford	1-2		Williams
16	15	Leytonstone	1-3		Andrews
17	22	WIMBLEDON	1-1	3000	Young
18	25	ST. ALBANS CITY	2-2		Warfield, J.A.Gearing
19	26	St. Albans City	2-6		Brown, Willmoth
20	29	Casuals	4-4		Britnell, Brown(2), Andrews
21	5 Jan	LONDON CALEDONIANS	1-2	3000	Brown
22	16 Mar	ILFORD	2-3		Newns(pen), Britnell
23	23	Nunhead	0-3		
24	13 Apr	LEYTONSTONE	2-1		Brown, Newns(pen)
25	20	KINGSTONIAN	3-1		Brown, Britnell, Andrews
26	4 May	Dulwich Hamlet	2-5		Newns, Brown

F.A. CUP

PR	15 Sep	Aylesbury United	0-3		

F.A. AMATUER CUP

1R	12 Jan	Hastings & St. Leonards	1-1	4300	Warfield
1Rr	19	HASTINGS & ST. LEONARDS	4-2	6507	Willmoth(3), Andrews
2R	2 Feb	Bromley	1-2	4300	Young

BERKS & BUCKS SENIOR CUP

2R	9 Feb	Slough	1-0		Ayres
SF*	9 Mar	Wolverton Town	3-1		Brown, Young, Newns
F#	22 Apr	Aylesbury United	3-0	7000	Brown, Newns, Young

* Played at Chesham
# Played at Reading

Final League Table

		P	W	D	L	F	A	Pts
1	Wimbledon	26	14	7	5	63	30	35
2	Oxford City	26	14	4	8	69	50	32
3	Leytonstone	26	15	2	9	49	36	32
4	Dulwich Hamlet	26	11	7	8	66	45	29
5	Tufnell Park	26	11	7	8	53	44	29
6	Kingstonian	26	11	6	9	44	40	28
7	Nunhead	26	10	7	9	35	34	27
8	London Caledonians	26	9	7	10	40	41	25
9	St. Albans City	26	9	6	11	61	50	24
10	Ilford	26	9	6	11	40	56	24
11	Clapton	26	7	7	12	46	48	21
12	Woking	26	9	3	14	44	68	21
13	Wycombe Wanderers	26	7	6	13	51	69	20
14	The Casuals	26	6	5	15	37	57	17

Season 1930/31:
(Back) Harris (Trainer Coach), Rance, Crump, Kipping, Cox, Timberlake, Gardner (Sec.)
(Front) Badrick (back), Simmons, Brown, Vernon, Braisher, Britnell, Greenwell (front)

Season 1936/37: (Back) Spatchett (Chair.), J.E.Gearing, Smith, Cox (Vice-Capt.), Boreham (Hon.Sec.)
(Middle) Young, Andrews, Turner, Atkinson, Britnell (Capt.) (Front) Green, Crump, J.A.Gearing

SEASON 1935-36
ISTHMIAN LEAGUE

No.	Date	Opposition	Res.	Att.	Goalscorers
1	5 Sep	Oxford City	1-1	1600	Andrews
2	7	Leytonstone	2-3		Andrews(2)
3	11	OXFORD CITY	2-1		Atkinson, Andrews
4	14	Woking	1-5		Newns
5	28	WOKING	5-1		Andrews, Atkinson, Britnell, Newns, Young
6	2 Nov	LEYTONSTONE	3-0		Atkinson, Britnell, Young
7	16	Tufnell Park	2-0	500	Britnell, Atkinson
8	30	Ilford	1-7		Atkinson
9	7 Dec	LONDON CALEDONIANS	4-1		Andrews(3), Cox(pen)
10	14	KINGSTONIAN	3-2		Brown, Andrews, Claydon
11	21	WIMBLEDON	2-6		Andrews, Brown
12	25	St. Albans City	2-9		Claydon, Britnell
13	26	ST. ALBANS CITY	5-0		Andrews, Atkinson(2), Young(2)
14	28	Clapton	3-1		Andrews, Atkinson, Young
15	11 Jan	CLAPTON	2-1		O.G., Turner
16	18	CASUALS	2-5		Britnell, Andrews
17	8 Feb	Nunhead	0-5		
18	22	NUNHEAD	6-3		Andrews(2), Turner, McCallum(3)
19	29	Dulwich Hamlet	1-5		Andrews
20	14 Mar	Casuals	3-2		Turner(2), Britnell
21	21	Kingstonian	1-5		Turner
22	28	DULWICH HAMLET	2-3		Britnell, Brown(pen)
23	4 Apr	Wimbledon	0-1		
24	18	London Caledonians	0-0		
25	21	ILFORD	4-0	750	Atkinson, Andrews(2,1pen), Turner
26	2 May	TUFNELL PARK	3-1		Andrews(pen), Britnell, Turner

F.A. CUP

PR	21 Sep	SLOUGH	4-3	3200	Britnell, Newns(2), Turner
1QR	5 Oct	R.A.F. Halton	4-1		Newns(4)
2QR	19	SOUTHALL	2-7	4441	Newns, Read(pen)

F.A. AMATEUR CUP

1QR	12 Oct	BICESTER TOWN	5-2		Young, Brown(2), Read(pen), Carr
2QR	26	Henley Town	8-4		Turnr,W.Brwn(3),Andrws,OG,Britnll,Read(p)
3QR	9 Nov	MARLOW	3-1	5048	Newns, Andrews, Atkinson
4QR	23	COWLEY	3-0	4000	Young, Cox(pen), Brown
1R	4 Jan	NUNHEAD	2-1	4844	Atkinson, Green
2R	1 Feb	CASUALS	0-2	6300	

BERKS & BUCKS SENIOR CUP

2R	25 Feb	SLOUGH	3-4	2400	Atkinson(2), Carr

Final League Table

		P	W	D	L	F	A	Pts
1	Wimbledon	26	19	2	5	82	29	40
2	The Casuals	26	19	5	7	60	45	33
3	Ilford	26	13	3	10	67	47	29
4	Dulwich Hamlet	26	10	8	8	64	47	28
5	Nunhead	26	11	6	9	51	40	28
6	Wycombe Wanderers	26	13	2	11	60	68	28
7	Clapton	26	11	5	10	42	46	27
8	Oxford City	26	11	4	11	60	55	26
9	St. Albans City	26	11	2	13	59	64	24
10	Woking	26	9	4	13	43	62	22
11	Tufnell Park	26	9	3	14	42	61	21
12	London Caledonians	26	9	3	14	35	52	21
13	Kingstonian	26	9	2	15	43	56	20
14	Leytonstone	26	7	5	16	34	67	17

SEASON 1936-37
ISTHMIAN LEAGUE

No.	Date	Opposition	Res.	Att.	Goalscorers
1	29 Aug	WOKING	4-2	2000	Young, Atkinson(2), Andrews
2	3 Sep	Oxford City	1-2	1100	Turner
3	5	Clapton	0-0		
4	9	OXFORD CITY	5-0		Turner(4), Atkinson
5	12	Casuals	0-4		
6	26	LONDON CALEDONIANS	5-1		Andrews(4), Turner
7	10 Oct	CASUALS	2-1		Andrews(pen), Atkinson
8	24	Leytonstone	2-5		Andrews(2)
9	7 Nov	Kingstonian	2-2		Britnell, Andrews
10	14	Nunhead	3-5		A.Crump, Atkinson, Turner
11	21	NUNHEAD	0-2		
12	28	London Caledonians	0-2	200	
13	12 Dec	LEYTONSTONE	2-0	1500	Turner(2)
14	19	Woking	2-3		Brooks, Carr
15	25	ST. ALBANS CITY	1-1		Brooks(pen)
16	26	St. Albans City	1-4		McCallum
17	2 Jan	ILFORD	2-3	2000	Brooks, Britnell
18	13 Mar	CLAPTON	1-2		O.G.
19	20	TUFNELL PARK	3-1	2000	Turner(2), Britnell
20	27	KINGSTONIAN	2-0	3000	Andrews, Thompson
21	3 Apr	Ilford	0-6	2000	
22	10	WIMBLEDON	2-1		Young, Andrews(pen)
23	17	Wimbledon	2-2		Turner(2)
24	19	Tufnell Park	2-2		Britnell, Turner
25	22	Dulwich Hamlet	5-1		Turner(3), Young, Thompson
26	28	DULWICH HAMLET	6-0		Andrews(3,1p),Thompson,Britnell,Turner

F.A. CUP

PR	19 Sep	Aylesbury United	2-1		Atkinson, Turner
1QR	3 Oct	Banbury Spencer	3-1		Turner, Andrews(pen), Young
2QR	17	WINDSOR & ETON	3-1		Britnell, Turner(2)
3QR	31	Hayes	1-5		Turner

F.A. AMATEUR CUP

1R	9 Jan	Gorleston	0-0	1000	
1Rr	16	GORLESTON	3-2	4208	Andrews(3)
2R	6 Feb	NUNHEAD	4-2	5000	Young(2), Atkinson(2)
3R	20	Stockton	1-4	7559	Andrews

BERKS & BUCKS SENIOR CUP

2R	23 Jan	SLOUGH	4-4	2000	Turner, Andrews(2), Atkinson
2Rr	30	Slough	2-2		Andrews(2)
2R2r*	13 Feb	Slough	2-2		Carr, Turner
2R3r#	27	Slough	2-1	2500	Turner, Britnell
SF#	6 Mar	Wellingford Town	4-2		Andrews(3,1pen), Young
F#	29	Windsor & Eton	1-3	7245	Young

* Played at Marlow
# Played at Maidenhead

Final League Table

		P	W	D	L	F	A	Pts
1	Kingstonian	26	18	3	5	63	43	39
2	Nunhead	26	17	3	6	77	32	37
3	Leytonstone	26	16	4	6	71	42	36
4	Ilford	26	14	5	7	86	39	33
5	Dulwich Hamlet	26	12	6	8	64	48	30
6	Wycombe Wanderers	26	10	5	11	55	52	25
7	Wimbledon	26	9	7	10	52	53	25
8	Clapton	26	10	5	11	42	51	25
9	The Casuals	26	10	3	13	46	58	23
10	Woking	26	9	4	13	53	69	22
11	Oxford City	26	8	5	13	56	89	21
12	St. Albans City	26	7	5	14	44	62	19
13	Tufnell Park	26	4	7	15	43	74	15
14	London Caledonians	26	5	4	17	26	66	14

SEASON 1937-38
ISTHMIAN LEAGUE

No.	Date	Opposition	Res.	Att.	Goalscorers
1	28 Aug	DULWICH HAMLET	3-1	3000	Turner(2), Thompson
2	1 Sep	OXFORD CITY	7-0	1500	Britnll,Turnr(2),Thompsn,Young,OG,Green
3	4	Leytonstone	2-6		Turner, Andrews
4	9	Oxford City	2-3		Turner, Thompson
5	11	CLAPTON	4-2	3000	Andrews, Turner(2), Thompson
6	25	LONDON CALEDONIANS	2-1	3000	Turner, Thompson
7	2 Oct	Casuals	2-3		Milton, Andrews
8	9	LEYTONSTONE	1-2	4000	Alkinson
9	16	Nunhead	1-1		Thompson
10	23	Ilford	1-1		Andrews
11	30	Clapton	2-1		Thompson, Turner
12	6 Nov	TUFNELL PARK	5-1	3500	Joys, Turner(3), Thompson
13	13	WOKING	7-1	3500	Andrws(2),Turnr(2),Meeks(p),Thompsn(2)
14	20	Dulwich Hamlet	3-3	6000	Turner(2), Young
15	27	London Caledonians	2-4		Andrews, Thompson
16	25 Dec	St. Albans City	2-2		Meeks(pen), Turner
17	26	ST. ALBANS CITY	3-2	4000	Andrews, Thompson(2)
18	1 Jan	KINGSTONIAN	4-0	3000	Meeks(pen),Andrews,Thompson,Turner
19	8	Woking	3-2		Turner(2), Thompson
20	19 Feb	ILFORD	4-1	3000	Turner, Thompson, Joys, Britnell
21	26	CASUALS	0-4		
22	12 Mar	Tufnell Park	0-3		
23	2 Apr	WIMBLEDON	2-2		Turner(2)
24	9	Wimbledon	1-3		Turner
25	30	Kingstonian	1-3		Joys
26	7 May	NUNHEAD	5-3		Turner(2), Joys(2), Young

F.A. CUP

PR	18 Sep	Slough	0-4		

F.A. AMATUER CUP

1R	15 Jan	Portland United	4-1		Thompson(2), Andrews(2)
2R	5 Feb	Aylesford Paper Mills	2-4	3400	Turner, Carr

BERKS & BUCKS SENIOR CUP

2R	29 Jan	AYLESBURY UNITED	3-1	4000	Britnell, Joys, Turner
SF*	5 Mar	Marlow	2-2	3500	Turner(2)
SFr*	19	Marlow	1-1	4000	Thompson
SF2r#	26	Marlow	6-0	4500	Turnr(2),Meeks(p),Young,Joys,Thompsn
F+	18 Apr	Windsor & Eton	0-1	6500	

* Played at Maidenhead
# Played at Slough
+ Played at Reading

Final League Table

	P	W	D	L	F	A	Pts
1 Leytonstone	26	17	6	3	72	34	40
2 Ilford	26	17	3	6	70	39	37
3 Tufnell Park	26	15	2	9	63	47	32
4 Nunhead	26	14	5	9	52	44	31
5 Wycombe Wanderers	26	12	5	9	60	55	29
6 Dulwich Hamlet	26	13	3	10	57	46	29
7 Kingstonian	26	12	4	10	51	46	28
8 Clapton	26	9	6	11	40	53	24
9 Wimbledon	26	10	3	13	62	49	23
10 London Caledonians	26	9	4	13	44	55	22
11 Oxford City	26	7	7	12	35	71	21
12 The Casuals	26	8	3	15	51	74	19
13 Woking	26	7	2	17	41	72	16
14 St. Albans City	26	4	5	17	31	60	13

SEASON 1938-39
ISTHMIAN LEAGUE

No.	Date	Opposition	Res.	Att.	Goalscorers
1	27 Aug	CASUALS	2-2	3000	Turner(2)
2	10 Sep	Kingstonian	0-2		
3	17	Woking	1-5		Young
4	22	Oxford City	2-2		Britnell, Thompson
5	24	WOKING	2-0		Brooks, Thompson
6	1 Oct	CLAPTON	2-0	3000	Andrews, Thompson
7	8	Ilford	0-0	3500	
8	15	TUFNELL PARK	4-4	3000	Britnell, Turner, Andrews, F.Gearing
9	22	ILFORD	4-1		Andrews(3), Thompson
10	29	Nunhead	4-3		Abdrews, Turner, Britnell, Thompson
11	5 Nov	TUFNELL PARK	4-2		Turner, Andrews(2), F.Gearing
12	12	London Caledonians	2-2		Turner(pen), Brown
13	19	Clapton	0-3		
14	26	OXFORD CITY	5-0		Thompson(2),Andrews,Meeks(pen),Turner
15	3 Dec	Leytonstone	3-3		Thompson, Brooks(2)
16	10	LEYTONSTONE	1-2	4000	Turner
17	7 Jan	Casuals	2-4		Andrews(2)
18	4 Feb	NUNHEAD	1-4		Townsend
19	25	LONDON CALEDONIANS	5-2	1900	Andrews(3), Britnell, Walker
20	4 Mar	Wimbledon	3-9		Turner(2), Andrews
21	11	DULWICH HAMLET	0-2	3000	
22	18	Dulwich Hamlet	1-4		Turner
23	1 Apr	WIMBLEDON	4-3		Turner, Andrews(2), Britnell
24	15	ST. ALBANS CITY	5-2		McCallum(2), Turner(2), Walker
25	22	St. Albans City	0-1		
26	3 May	KINGSTONIAN	5-0		McCallum,Meeks(p),Townsend(2),Andrws

N.b. Both games against Tufnell Park were played at Loakes Park.

F.A. CUP

EXPR	3 Sep	HAYES	2-5	3500	Joys(2)

F.A. AMATEUR CUP

1R	14 Jan	SLOUGH	1-5	4000	Walker

BERKS & BUCKS SENIOR CUP

2R	28 Jan	Maidenhead United	2-3		Townsend, Andrews

Final League Table

	P	W	D	L	F	A	Pts
1 Leytonstone	26	18	4	4	68	32	40
2 Ilford	26	17	4	5	68	32	38
3 Kingstonian	26	16	3	8	62	39	37
4 Dulwich Hamlet	26	15	5	6	60	32	35
5 Wimbledon	26	14	3	9	88	56	31
6 Nunhead	26	11	6	9	54	44	28
7 The Casuals	26	11	6	9	54	51	28
8 Clapton	26	12	2	12	69	61	26
9 Wycombe Wanderers	26	10	6	10	62	62	26
10 St. Albans City	26	8	5	13	44	50	21
11 Woking	26	9	2	15	35	56	20
12 Oxford City	26	4	4	15	44	84	12
13 Tufnell Park	26	4	4	18	33	87	12
14 London Caledonians	26	3	4	19	26	81	10

SEASON 1939-40
GREAT WESTERN COMBINATION

No.	Date	Opposition	Res.	Att.	Goalscorers
1	21 Oct	Henley Town	2-3		Andrews, Turner
2	11 Nov	WINDSOR & ETON	7-1		D.Busby(3), Andrews(3), F.Gearing
3	18	Hayes	1-7		McCullum
4	2 Dec	Uxbridge Town	7-1		D.Busby(3), McCullm, Britnll, Meeks(p), Andrws
5	16	WYCOMBE REDFORDS	2-1		D.Busby, Meeks(pen)
6	23	Maidenhead United	1-0		Turner
7	30	CHESHAM UNITED	4-3		McCullum(2), D.Busby, Andrews
8	7 Jan	Slough	1-2		Britnell
9	14	Windsor & Eton	3-1	2000	Turner, McCullum, Andrews
10	24 Feb	SLOUGH	4-2		McCullum, D.Busby(2), Andrews
11	2 Mar	UXBRIDGE TOWN	0-4		
12	16	HENLEY TOWN	6-3		Britnll, F.Gearing, Green(2), McCullum, Andrws
13	22	MARLOW	5-1		Andrws, McCullm(2,1p), Green(p), Walkr(p)
14	23	Chesham United	3-7		McCullum(2), Turner
15	25	MAIDENHEAD UNITED	4-3		McCullum(2), Britnell, Andrews
16	30	Marlow	1-5		Andrews
17	6 Apr	Wycombe Redfords	2-2		Turner(2)
18	13	HAYES	5-3		Green, Andrews(2), Turner(2)

BERKS & BUCKS (EMERGENCY) SENIOR CUP

1R	4 Nov	SLOUGH	3-1		D.Busby, McCullum(2)
2R	25	Windsor & Eton	4-2		Meeks(pen), McCullum(2), Turner
SF	9 Dec	NEWBURY TOWN	6-2		D.Busby, Britnell, Andrews(4)
F	26	WYCOMBE REDFORDS	4-0	5000	D.Busby(2), Andrews, Britnell

Final League Table

	P	W	D	L	F	A	Pts
1 Hayes	18	15	1	2	60	20	31
2 Wycombe Wanderers	18	11	1	6	58	49	23
3 Slough	18	8	5	5	43	37	21
4 Wycombe Redfords	18	7	5	6	41	33	19
5 Chesham United	18	9	1	8	53	43	19
6 Maidenhead United	18	7	4	7	40	36	18
7 Uxbridge Town	18	6	2	10	35	47	14
8 Henley Town	18	6	2	10	47	62	14
9 Marlow	*17	3	5	9	25	42	11
10 Windsor & Eton	*17	3	2	12	32	65	8

* One game not played.

SEASON 1940-41
GREAT WESTERN COMBINATION

No.	Date	Opposition	Res.	Att.	Goalscorers
1	5 Oct	Windsor & Eton	1-6		Ford
2	12	OXFORD CITY	1-3		McCullum
3	19	Wycombe Redfords	1-0		Doe
4	26	Reading Reserves	1-0		Andrews
5	2 Nov	MARLOW	6-0		Cormack(2), Doe, Ing(2), Wharton
6	16	Maidenhead United	2-1		Wharton, D.Busby
7	23	Oxford City	3-4		Wharton(3)
8	30	READING RESERVES	1-2		Britnell
9	7 Dec	HIGH DUTY ALLOYS	3-6		Andrews(3)
10	14	WYCOMBE REDFORDS	2-2		Wharton, McCullum
11	21	Uxbridge Town	2-1		Cormack, Andrews
12	28	CHESHAM UNITED	2-3		Cormack, Andrews
13	4 Jan	MAIDENHEAD UNITED	6-3		Noble(2), Britnell, Ing, James, Hill
14	11	WINDSOR & ETON	4-2		James(2), Noble(2)
15	1 Feb	High Duty Alloys	4-1		Noble(2), Russell(2)
16	8	Marlow	1-3		McCullum
17	15	UXBRIDGE TOWN	3-1		Walker(3)
18	15 Mar	Chesham United	4-3		Andrews(2), McCullum, James

BERKS & BUCKS (EMERGENCY) SENIOR CUP

2R	9 Nov	READING RESERVES	1-4		Andrews

BERKS & BUCKS RED CROSS CUP

1R	22 Feb	Marlow	1-4		Ing

GREAT WESTERN COMBINATION SUBSIDIARY CUP

1R	29 Mar	UXBRIDGE TOWN	1-1		Andrews
1Rr	14 Apr	Uxbridge Town	0-4		

Final League Table

	P	W	D	L	F	A	Pts
1 Oxford City	18	13	3	2	70	30	29
2 Reading Reserves	18	12	3	3	57	40	27
3 Windsor & Eton	18	12	2	4	64	30	26
4 Chesham United	18	10	1	7	51	44	21
5 Wycombe Wanderers	18	10	1	7	47	41	21
6 Marlow	18	8	3	7	46	40	19
7 Uxbridge Town	18	5	2	11	41	43	12
8 Maidenhead United	18	4	1	13	37	74	9
9 High Duty Alloys	18	2	4	12	41	86	8
10 Wycombe Redfords	18	1	6	11	21	47	8

SEASON 1941-42
GREAT WESTERN COMBINATION

No.	Date	Opposition	Res.	Att.	Goalscorers
1	27 Sep	Windsor & Eton	3-6		McCallum(2), Andrews
2	4 Oct	OXFORD CITY	4-8		Noble, Andrews(2), McCallum
3	11	Maidenhead United	5-3		Telling(3), McCallum(2)
4	25	HIGH DUTY ALLOYS	6-0		Turner(3,1pen), Noble(2), McCallum
5	1 Nov	Marlow	3-0		Telling(3)
6	22	CHESHAM UNITED	5-0		Noble(2,1pen), Cubbage(2), Britnell
7	29	Grenadier Guards	5-4		Ing(2), Cubbage(pen), McCallum(2)
8	13 Dec	UXBRIDGE TOWN	4-2		Blamey(2), McCallum(2)
9	20	Chesham United	0-2		
10	27	Reading Reserves	2-1		McCallum, Cubbage
11	21 Feb	WINDSOR & ETON	3-4		Cormack, Cubbage(pen), Noble
12	28	UXBRIDGE TOWN	2-0		McCallum, Hodgson
13	7 Mar	GRENADIER GUARDS	1-3		W.Smith
14	14	High Duty Alloys	4-1		McCallum(2), Clark, O.G.
15	21	READING RESERVES	4-1		Blamey(2), Cubbage(pen), McCallum
16	28	Oxford City	2-6		Cormack(2pens)
17	4 Apr	MARLOW	5-0		McCallum, Blamey(2), Noble, Ing
18	11	MAIDENHEAD UNITED	4-3		W.Smith, Blamey(2), Cormack(pen)

N.b. Both games against Uxbridge Town played at Loakes Park.

BERKS & BUCKS (EMERGENCY) SENIOR CUP

1R	18 Oct	Chesham United	2-0		Telling(2)
2R	8 Nov	MARLOW	5-5		McCallum, Noble, Telling(3,1pen)
2Rr	15	Marlow	3-1		Britnell, McCallum, Noble
SF	6 Dec	SLOUGH	3-2		Britnell, McCallum(2)
F	3 Jan	WINDSOR & ETON	1-1		McCallum
Fr	10	Windsor & Eton	1-4		Cormack

BERKS & BUCKS RED CROSS CUP

1R	31 Jan	HIGH DUTY ALLOYS	5-5		McCallum(3,1pen), Noble, Cormack
1Rr	14 Feb	High Duty Alloys	2-3		Cubbage(pen), McCallum

GREAT WESTERN COMBINATION SUBSIDIARY CUP

1R1	18 Apr	Marlow	3-2		McCallum(2), Spencer
1R2	2 May	MARLOW	2-1		Spencer, McCallum
SF1	9	Oxford City	3-1		Priestley(2), W.Smith
SF2	16	OXFORD CITY	1-3*		Cormack(pen)

* Lost on toss of coin.

Final League Table

	P	W	D	L	F	A	Pts
1 Oxford City	18	15	3	0	78	30	33
2 Grenadier Guards	18	11	2	5	56	37	24
3 Wycombe Wanderers	18	12	0	6	62	44	24
4 Windsor & Eton	18	12	0	6	72	57	24
5 Chesham United	18	7	4	7	35	44	18
6 Marlow	18	7	1	10	45	52	15
7 Reading Reserves	18	7	1	10	53	65	15
8 Uxbridge Town	18	4	3	11	41	46	11
9 Maidenhead United	18	3	4	11	42	63	10
10 High Duty Alloys	18	2	2	14	26	72	6

SEASON 1942-43
GREAT WESTERN COMBINATION

No.	Date	Opposition	Res.	Att.	Goalscorers
1	26 Sep	UXBRIDGE TOWN	2-4		Bass, H.Smith
2	3 Oct	Windsor Works (Slough)	1-0		Priestley
3	10	WINDSOR & ETON	5-0		Bass, R.Hunt, Blamey, Priestley(2)
4	17	Marlow	3-1		Priestley(2), H.Smith
5	31	HIGH DUTY ALLOYS	5-1		Andrews, Blamey(4)
6	7 Nov	WINDSOR WORKS (SLOUGH)	8-6		Priestley(3),Andrews(2),Blamey(2),McCullm
7	21	SLOUGH CENTRE	4-3		Priestley, Andrews(3)
8	28	Windsor & Eton	2-8		Joys(2)
9	5 Dec	Maidenhead United	1-0		Wharton
10	12	OXFORD CITY	4-2		Priestley, Blamey(2), McCallum
11	19	Uxbridge Town	1-2		Bass
12	2 Jan	Slough Centre	3-4		Britnell, Ing(2pens)
13	9	MARLOW	4-0		R.Hunt, Priestley, Larkins, Blamey
14	16	High Duty Alloys	5-2		McCallum, Daniels, Blamey, Ing(2)
15	23	MAIDENHEAD UNITED	4-1		Priestley(2), McCallum(2)
16	6 Feb	Oxford City	2-3		Ing(2)
17	13	GRENADIER GUARDS	2-3		Blamey, F.Gearing
18	27	Grenadier Guards	3-3		O.G., Priestley(2)

BERKS & BUCKS (EMERGENCY) SENIOR CUP

2R	14 Nov	Marlow	0-2		

BERKS & BUCKS RED CROSS CUP

1R	30 Jan	SLOUGH CENTRE	5-2		Blamey, Priestley, R.Hunt(3)
2R	20 Feb	READING CASUALS	6-2		Priestley(4), McCallum(2)
SF	13 Mar	GRENADIER GUARDS	3-0		McCallum(2), Ing
F1	24 Apr	Marlow	2-2		R.Hunt, Joys
F2	8 May	MARLOW	5-1		Joys, Ing(2), Priestley(2,1pen)

GREAT WESTERN COMBINATION SUBSIDIARY CUP

2R	20 Mar	GRENADIER GUARDS	2-1		R.Hunt, McCallum
SF	10 Apr	OXFORD CITY	4-2		Priestley(3), Britnell
F1	17	MARLOW	4-4		Unknown(1), F.Keen, Priestley(pen), Ing
F2	1 May	Marlow	1-4		R.Hunt

Final League Table

	P	W	D	L	F	A	Pts
1 Grenadier Guards	18	13	3	2	75	28	29
2 Uxbridge Town	18	11	2	5	50	38	24
3 Wycombe Wanderers	18	11	1	6	59	43	23
4 Windsor & Eton	18	8	3	7	57	49	19
5 Oxford City	18	7	4	7	43	48	18
6 Windsor Works(Slough)	18	6	4	8	44	49	16
7 Slough Centre	18	5	4	9	35	43	14
8 Marlow	18	5	4	9	37	48	14
9 Maidenhead United	18	5	3	10	35	59	13
10 High Duty Alloys	18	4	2	12	31	61	10

SEASON 1943-44
GREAT WESTERN COMBINATION

No.	Date	Opposition	Res.	Att.	Goalscorers
1	25 Sep	Windsor & Eton	4-2		Chubb(2), McCallum, Christie
2	2 Oct	WINDSOR WORKS (SLOUGH)	1-5		Christie
3	9	Oxford City	2-2		McCallum, Blamey
4	16	Maidenhead United	3-3		Chubb, McCallum, Stanley
5	23	Slough United	0-2		
6	30	R.A.F. (HIGH WYCOMBE)	3-5		Law, Ing, Walker
7	6 Nov	HIGH DUTY ALLOYS	7-1		Keen,McCallum(2),Gaunt,Ing,Walkr,R.Hnt
8	20	MAIDENHEAD UNITED	4-0		R.Hunt, McCallum(3)
9	4 Dec	Marlow	6-4		McCallum(5,1pen), O.G.
10	18	OXFORD CITY	1-1		Jackson(pen)
11	22 Jan	Windsor Works (Slough)	4-1		Ing, Gaunt, Atherton, McCallum
12	5 Feb	MARLOW	1-1		Ing
13	12	High Duty Alloys	2-2		Blamey, Gaunt
14	26	WINDSOR & ETON	3-1		Cox, Ing, Gaunt
15	4 Mar	UXBRIDGE TOWN	2-3		McCallum, Blamey
16	18	SLOUGH UNITED	3-1		Walker(2), Blamey
17	8 Apr	R.A.F. (HIGH WYCOMBE)	4-2		Blamey, R.Hunt, McCallum, Andrews
18	29	UXBRIDGE TOWN	2-2		R.Hunt, Ing

N.b. Both games against R.A.F. (High Wycombe) and Uxbridge Town played at Loakes Park.

BERKS & BUCKS (EMERGENCY) SENIOR CUP

2R	13 Nov	ROYAL AIR FORCE XI	3-1		R.Hunt, McCallum(2)
SF	11 Dec	MAIDENHEAD UNITED	6-0		Palmer, McCallum(3), Jackson, Walker
F1	1 Jan	WINDSOR & ETON	1-2		Blamey
F2	8	Windsor & Eton	4-3		R.Hunt, Ing(2), Blamey
Fr*	29	Windsor & Eton	4-6		Walker(2), McCallum(2)

* Played at Maidenhead

BERKS & BUCKS RED CROSS CUP

2R	19 Feb	R.A.F. (HIGH WYCOMBE)	1-5		McCallum

GREAT WESTERN COMBINATION SUBSIDIARY CUP

1R	25 Mar	OXFORD CITY	0-3		

Final League Table

	P	W	D	L	F	A	Pts
1 Windsor Works (Slough)	18	13	1	4	63	29	27
2 Oxford City	18	12	3	3	44	24	27
3 Marlow	18	9	5	4	53	40	23
4 Wycombe Wanderers	18	8	6	4	52	38	22
5 Slough United	18	7	5	6	36	34	19
6 R.A.F. (High Wycombe)	18	8	1	9	51	51	17
7 Windsor & Eton	18	5	4	9	45	57	14
8 Uxbridge Town	18	4	5	9	36	46	13
9 Maidenhead United	18	3	4	11	30	52	10
10 High Duty Alloys	18	2	4	12	26	65	8

SEASON 1944-45
GREAT WESTERN COMBINATION

No.	Date	Opposition	Res.	Att.	Goalscorers
1	16 Sep	Windsor Works (Slough)	5-6		Glaister, McCallum(3), Ing
2	23	R.A.F. (HIGH WYCOMBE)	4-1		Ing, Wood(2), Glaister
3	30	Maidenhead United	3-2		McCallum, R.Hunt, Avery
4	14 Oct	YIEWSLEY	2-0		R.Hunt, Ing
5	21	OXFORD CITY	2-1		Andrews, McCallum
6	28	MAIDENHEAD UNITED	2-3		Jackson, McCallum
7	18 Nov	Windsor & Eton	3-1		Larkins(3)
8	25	SLOUGH UNITED	6-1		Larkins(2), Jones, R.Hunt(2), McCallum
9	9 Dec	WINDSOR WORKS (SLOUGH)	2-1		Avery(2)
10	16	Reading Reserves	4-5		Andrews(2), Avery, Larkins
11	23	MARLOW	5-0		McCallum,Andrews,Wood,Avery,R.Hunt
12	6 Jan	High Duty Alloys	5-1		McCallum(2), Avery(2), F.Gearing
13	20	Oxford City	1-1		McCallum
14	3 Feb	WINDSOR & ETON	2-1		Ing, McCallum
15	10	Marlow	3-1		Avery, Andrews, McCallum
16	17	Yiewsley	6-5		Avery(3), Andrews, McCallum, R.Hunt
17	3 Mar	Slough United	4-2		Avery, Andrews(2), Blamey
18	10	R.A.F. (HIGH WYCOMBE)	7-0		R.Hnt,Andrws(2),Avry(2),F.Gearng,McCullm
19	24	READING RESERVES	4-2		Parsons, Lewis, R.Hunt(2)
20	31	UXBRIDGE TOWN	7-2		Ing,Avry(2,1p),Andrws(2),McCullm,R.Hnt
21	14 Apr	HIGH DUTY ALLOYS	7-4		McCallum, Avery(4), Andrews, Read
22	28	UXBRIDGE TOWN	3-0		Strong, O.G., Avery

N.b. Both games against Uxbridge Town and R.A.F. (High Wycombe) played at Loakes Park.

BERKS & BUCKS (EMERGENCY) SENIOR CUP

2R	11 Nov	Maidenhead United	6-1		R.Hunt(3), Wood(2), Larkins
SF	2 Dec	R.A.F. (HIGH WYCOMBE)	3-4		Larkins, Ing, McCallum(pen)

BERKS & BUCKS RED CROSS CUP

2R	24 Feb	MARLOW	4-2		Andrews, Avery, Dritnell, McCallum
SF	17 Mar	SLOUGH UNITED	1-2		Avery

GREAT WESTERN COMBINATION SUBSIDIARY CUP

1R1	7 Oct	Reading Reserves	1-6		Glaister
1R2	4 Nov	READING RESERVES	2-2		F.Gearing, Jones

Final League Table

	P	W	D	L	F	A	Pts
1 Wycombe Wanderers	22	18	1	3	87	40	37
2 Maidenhead United	22	15	0	7	68	50	30
3 Windsor & Eton	22	12	3	7	70	49	27
4 Oxford City	22	10	5	7	63	38	25
5 Windsor Works(Slough)	22	12	1	9	63	45	25
6 Marlow	22	9	5	8	64	59	23
7 Uxbridge Town	22	9	3	10	59	56	21
8 Reading Reserves	22	8	2	12	47	70	18
9 Yiewsley	22	8	1	13	46	62	17
10 R.A.F.(High Wycombe)	22	7	2	13	42	74	16
11 Slough United	22	5	4	13	49	84	14
12 High Duty Alloys	22	3	5	14	51	82	11

Season 1944/45 (Back) Spatchett (Chair.), Boreham (Sec.), Keen, Crump, Strong, Hathaway, unknown (Middle) F Gates, R Hunt, McCallum, Avery, Andrews, Ing, O'Gorman (Front) Lewis, Hallwood, Jackson

Season 1946/47: (Back) Willmott, Bunce, Holliman, Birdseye, Spring, Jackson (Front) Gearing, Dean, Crump, McCown, Wharten

SEASON 1945-46
ISTHMIAN LEAGUE

No.	Date	Opposition	Res.	Att.	Goalscorers
1	1 Sep	WALTHAMSTOW AVENUE	3-4		Avery, K.Butler(2pens)
2	15	ILFORD	4-0		K.Butler(2,1pen), McCallum(2)
3	22	Walthamstow Avenue	0-3		
4	29	WOKING	1-2		McCallum
5	6 Oct	Kinstonian	7-3		McCallum(4), Avery(2), F.Gearing
6	13	DULWICH HAMLET	2-6		McCallum, F.Gearing
7	20	Ilford	5-2		Avery(3), McCallum(2)
8	27	TUFNELL PARK	2-6		McCallum, Rouse(pen)
9	3 Nov	Wimbledon	3-4		McCallum, Avery, Blakeman
10	10	KINGSTONIAN	3-3		Avery(3)
11	17	Woking	4-5		Dawkins(2), Hillson, McCallum
12	24	OXFORD CITY	2-6		Avery(2)
13	1 Dec	Oxford City	1-3		Avery(pen)
14	8	WIMBLEDON	4-1		McCallum, Avery, F.Gearing, Jeacock
15	15	LEYTONSTONE	1-1		McCallum
16	22	Romford	3-3		Dawkins(2), Joys
17	29	Tufnell Park	0-3		
18	5 Jan	ROMFORD	2-6		Dawkins, Avery
19	12	St. Albans City	5-3		Avery(3), A.Crump, Vickers
20	2 Mar	Clapton	0-6		
21	23	ST. ALBANS CITY	4-2		McCallum(2), Avery, Dawkins(pen)
22	6 Apr	Dulwich Hamlet	1-3		McCallum
23	20	Leytonstone	5-10		R.Hunt, McCallum(3), Crawford
24	24	Corinthian-Casuals	4-1		R.Hunt(2), Vickers, McCallum
25	27	CLAPTON	9-1		Avery(4),White,R.Hnt(2),McCllum,K.Btler
26	1 May	CORINTHIAN-CASUALS	5-1		McCallum(2), R.Hunt, O.G., Avery

F.A. CUP

PR	8 Sep	SOUTHALL	0-2		

F.A. AMATEUR CUP

1R	19 Jan	Kingstonian	1-1		Avery
1Rr	26	KINGSTONIAN	10-1		Avery(6),F.Gearing,McCallum(2),Batten
2R	2 Feb	WALTHAMSTOW AVENUE	1-1	7000	McCallum
2Rr	9	Walthamstow Avenue	5-7		McCallum(3), K.Butler(pen), Jackson

BERKS & BUCKS SENIOR CUP

2R	23 Feb	SLOUGH UNITED	6-1		McCallum(2,1pen),Dawkins(2),Avery,OG
SF*	9 Mar	Windsor & Eton	2-2	3725	Turner, McCallum
SFr*	30	Windsor & Eton	0-2		

* Played at Maidenhead

Final League Table

		P	W	D	L	F	A	Pts
1	Walthamstow Avenue	26	21	0	5	100	31	42
2	Oxford City	26	17	6	3	91	40	40
3	Romford	26	15	3	8	83	59	38
4	Dulwich Hamlet	26	14	2	10	63	59	30
5	Tufnell Park	26	12	4	10	70	55	28
6	Woking	26	10	7	0	58	51	27
7	Ilford	26	12	2	12	50	71	26
8	Leytonstone	26	11	3	12	61	75	25
9	Wycombe Wanderers	26	9	3	14	50	88	21
10	Wimbledon	26	7	6	13	52	72	20
11	Corinthian Casuals	26	8	4	14	58	93	20
12	Clapton	26	8	3	15	51	62	19
13	St. Albans City	26	6	6	14	48	85	18
14	Kingstonian	26	6	3	17	48	86	15

SEASON 1946-47
ISTHMIAN LEAGUE

No.	Date	Opposition	Res.	Att.	Goalscorers
1	31 Aug	Dulwich Hamlet	1-1		McCallum
2	14 Sep	KINGSTONIAN	1-2		R.Hunt
3	28	WOKING	5-2		McCallum,Dawkins,F.Gearing,H.Hunt(2)
4	12 Oct	Wimbledon	2-2		Birdseye, F.Gearing
5	19	Ilford	2-7		Dawkins, McCallum
6	26	LEYTONSTONE	5-1		Brewster(2),McCallum,F.Gearing,Dawkins
7	2 Nov	Romford	2-2		McCallum(2)
8	9	ILFORD	2-2		O.G., McCallum
9	16	Oxford City	1-2		H.Hunt
10	23	TUFNELL PARK	5-1		McCallum,F.Gearing,Dean,H.Hunt,Dwkins
11	14 Dec	St. Albans City	4-2		McCallum(2), H.Hunt(2)
12	21	WIMBLEDON	4-3		Vickers, Dean, H.Hunt(2)
13	28	Kingstonian	1-2		Andrews
14	4 Jan	OXFORD CITY	3-1		H.Hunt, Dawkins, McCallum
15	11	ROMFORD	3-3		H.Hunt(3)
16	8 Feb	Woking	2-1		K.Butler(pen), McCallum
17	1 Mar	Clapton	2-8		Andrews(2)
18	29	Walthamstow Avenue	2-2		McCallum(2)
19	5 Apr	Tufnell Park	3-4		H.Hunt, Dean, McCallum
20	12	CLAPTON	1-2		H.Hunt
21	19	CORINTHIAN-CASUALS	1-1	5000	Dean
22	26	WALTHAMSTOW AVENUE	2-1		Dean, Blamey
23	1 May	DULWICH HAMLET	5-1	2000	Birdseye(2), Dean(2), F.Gearing(pen)
24	3	CORINTHIAN-CASUALS	2-3		Birdseye, Dean
25	7	Leytonstone	0-4		
26	17	ST. ALBANS CITY	2-2		McCallum, Dawkins

N.b. Both games against Corinthian-Casuals played at Loakes Park

F.A. CUP

ExPR	7 Sep	MARLOW	2-0	4000	McCallum, K.Butler
PR	21	Southall	5-2		Dawkins(2),McCallum,Andrews,H.Hunt
1QR	5 Oct	HAYES	3-4	5300	Dawkins, Andrews, F.Gearing(pen)

F.A. AMATEUR CUP

1R	18 Jan	ENFIELD	3-3	7000	H.Hunt(2), Dean
1Rr	25	Enfield	2-5		F.Gearing, Dawkins

BERKS & BUCKS SENIOR CUP

2R	30 Nov	Huntley & Palmers	2-2		H.Hunt, McCallum
2Rr	7 Dec	HUNTLEY & PALMERS	3-0		H.Hunt(2), McCallum
3R	15 Feb	AYLESBURY UNITED	4-2	2000	Dean, K.Butler(1pen), H.Hunt
SF*	22 Mar	Abingdon Town	6-1		Dean,Birdseye(2),Dawkins,O.G.,Bunce
F#	7 Apr	Slough United	2-1	8237	H.Hunt(2)

* Played at Slough
# Played at Maidenhead

Final League Table

		P	W	D	L	F	A	Pts
1	Leytonstone	26	19	2	5	92	36	40
2	Dulwich Hamlet	26	17	3	6	78	46	37
3	Romford	26	13	8	5	76	52	34
4	Walthamstow Avenue	26	13	4	9	64	37	30
5	Oxford City	26	12	6	8	70	51	30
6	Kingstonian	26	12	4	10	52	57	28
7	Wycombe Wanderers	26	9	8	9	63	62	26
8	Wimbledon	26	10	5	11	68	64	25
9	Ilford	26	7	7	12	66	78	21
10	Tufnell Park	26	8	5	13	45	69	21
11	Woking	26	7	7	12	34	62	21
12	Clapton	26	6	8	12	41	50	20
13	St. Albans City	26	7	5	14	47	79	19
14	Corinthian Casuals	26	4	4	15	36	80	12

SEASON 1947-48
ISTHMIAN LEAGUE

No.	Date	Opposition	Res.	Att.	Goalscorers
1	30 Aug	Romford	2-4		H.Hunt(2)
2	11 Sep	Oxford City	2-5		H.Hunt(2)
3	13	Walthamstow Avenue	0-1		
4	27	Wimbledon	5-5		Birdseye(3), McCallum, Dean
5	11 Oct	CORINTHIAN-CASUALS	3-0	3882	Jackson, H.Hunt, Dean
6	1 Nov	Dulwich Hamlet	1-1		Strong
7	8	ROMFORD	4-0	4709	McCallum, Blamey(2), Avery
8	15	CLAPTON	3-1		Wharton, F.Gearing(2)
9	29	Tufnell Park	1-2		F.Gearing
10	6 Dec	Kingstonian	2-4		Avery, Wharton
11	13	WALTHAMSTOW AVENUE	1-2	4100	Perkins
12	20	Clapton	1-3		Birdseye
13	26	ST. ALBANS CITY	1-3		Avery
14	27	St. Albans City	1-3		Avery
15	10 Jan	WOKING	4-3		Avery, Junger, McCallum, F.Gearing
16	21 Feb	OXFORD CITY	1-1		Avery
17	13 Mar	WIMBLEDON	2-1	3650	Birdseye(2)
18	20	Corinthian-Casuals	0-2		
19	27	Woking	2-4		Barkus, Wegryzk
20	3 Apr	ILFORD	2-2		McCallum, Wegryzk
21	8	Leytonstone	2-7		Wegryzk, Blamey
22	10	KINGSTONIAN	0-3		
23	14	LEYTONSTONE	4-1		Youngman, McCallum(3,1pen)
24	17	Ilford	2-2		Dean(2)
25	24	TUFNELL PARK	2-3		Youngman(2)
26	1 May	DULWICH HAMLET	3-2		Youngman(3)

F.A. CUP

ExPR	6 Sep	HOUNSLOW TOWN	4-2		Dean(2), H.Hunt, McCallum
PR	20	UXBRIDGE	3-1		Dean, H.Hunt, McCallum
1QR	4 Oct	HAYES	1-0	6770	H.Hunt
2QR	18	Southall	3-3		H.Hunt(2), Birdseye
2QRr	25	SOUTHALL	1-2	8825	Birdseye

F.A. AMATEUR CUP

1R	17 Jan	WALTHAMSTOW AVENUE	2-1	5801	McCallum, Barkus
2R	31	St. Albans City	3-3	6844	Vickers, Birdseye(2)
2Rr	7 Feb	ST. ALBANS CITY	2-1	10366	McCallum, K.Butler
3R	14	Ilford	3-2		Birdseye(3)
4R	28	Bishop Auckland	2-6	10129	McCallum, Barkus

BERKS & BUCKS SENIOR CUP

2R	24 Jan	Huntley & Palmers	4-2		K.Butler(2), Birdseye, McCallum
SF*	6 Mar	Slough Centre	3-1	3000	McCallum, Jackson, Birdseye
F#	29	Chesham United	1-2	8578	K.Butler

* Played at Marlow. # Played at Reading.

Final League Table

		P	W	D	L	F	A	Pts
1	Leytonstone	26	19	1	6	87	38	39
2	Kingstonian	26	16	6	4	74	39	38
3	Walthamstow Avenue	26	17	3	6	81	37	37
4	Dulwich Hamlet	26	17	2	7	71	39	36
5	Wimbledon	26	13	6	7	66	40	32
6	Romford	26	14	1	11	53	47	29
7	Oxford City	26	10	5	11	50	68	25
8	Wok;ng	26	10	3	13	63	55	23
9	Ilford	26	7	8	11	51	59	22
10	St. Albans City	26	9	2	15	43	56	20
11	Wycombe Wanderers	26	7	5	14	51	65	19
12	Tufnell Park	26	7	4	15	38	83	15
13	Clapton	26	5	4	17	35	69	14
14	Corinthian Casuals	26	5	2	19	33	81	12

SEASON 1948-49
ISTHMIAN LEAGUE

No.	Date	Opposition	Res.	Att.	Goalscorers
1	28 Aug	ROMFORD	1-2	4000	Walker
2	4 Sep	DULWICH HAMLET	3-4		Youngman, McCallum(2)
3	11	Kingstonian	1-2		Youngman
4	25	WALTHAMSTOW AVENUE	0-3	3000	
5	2 Oct	Leytonstone	1-0		Youngman
6	9	Romford	1-4	6000	Youngman
7	16	ILFORD	4-3	4000	F.Gearing, K.Butler, Youngman, A.Smith
8	23	Oxford City	1-2		Youngman
9	30	CORINTHIAN-CASUALS	2-1		K.Butler(2)
10	6 Nov	Clapton	2-3		McCallum(2)
11	13	TUFNELL PARK	4-1		Youngman, Birdseye(3)
12	20	Dulwich Hamlet	0-7		
13	11 Dec	Wimbledon	1-9		McCallum
14	18	WIMBLEDON	5-1		Chubb,Birdseye(2),Guest,McCallum(pen)
15	25	ST. ALBANS CITY	4-1		McCallum(2), Birdseye(2)
16	26	St. Albans City	3-2		Chubb(2), Stroud
17	8 Jan	Tufnell Park	2-2		O.G., McCallum
18	19 Feb	WOKING	1-3		Rose
19	26	Corinthian-Casuals	2-1		Birdseye, Stroud
20	5 Mar	Woking	2-4		Rose, Stroud
21	19	CLAPTON	1-1		Perkins
22	26	KINGSTONIAN	2-0		McCallum(pen), Perkins
23	2 Apr	Ilford	1-2		Andrews
24	9	Walthamstow Avenue	1-3		McCallum
25	30	LEYTONSTONE	3-0		Thorne, Stroud, Andrews
26	7 May	OXFORD CITY	1-0		McCallum(pen)

F.A. CUP

PR	18 Sep	Uxbridge	3-4		McCallum(3)

F.A. AMATEUR CUP

1R	15 Jan	BARKING	5-5	6000	McCallum, Guest, O.G., Birdseye(2)
1Rr	22	Barking	0-2		

BERKS & BUCKS SENIOR CUP

1R	4 Dec	AMERSHAM TOWN	4-0		Birdseye, Stroud, McCallum, Fenner
2R	5 Feb	Slough Centre	2-2		Perkins, McCallum
2Rr	12	SLOUGH CENTRE	4-3		Stroud(2), Birdseye, McCallum
SF*	12 Mar	Marlow	3-2		Andrews, Guest, Birdseye
F*	18 Apr	Slough Town	0-0		
Fr#	23	Slough Town	2-1		K.Butler, F.Gearing

* Played at Maidenhead
# Played at Chesham

Final League Table

		P	W	D	L	F	A	Pts.
1	Dulwich Hamlet	26	15	6	5	60	31	36
2	Walthamstow Avenue	26	16	4	6	65	36	36
3	Wimbledon	26	15	4	7	64	41	34
4	Ilford	26	14	3	9	56	36	31
5	Oxford City	26	13	5	8	48	34	31
6	Leytonstone	26	12	6	8	49	41	30
7	Woking	26	14	1	11	64	59	29
8	Romford	26	11	3	12	47	54	25
9	Kingstonian	26	10	4	12	43	47	24
10	Corinthian Casuals	26	11	2	13	47	59	24
11	Wycombe Wanderers	26	11	2	13	49	61	24
12	St. Albans City	26	6	6	14	40	60	*16
13	Clapton	26	5	5	16	32	61	15
14	Tufnell Park	26	1	5	20	28	70	7

* Two points deducted

Season 1947/48: (Back) Willmott, Bunce, Holliman, Birdseye, Strong, Jackson
(Front) Gearing, Dean, Crump, McCallum, Wharton

Season 1948/49 (FA Amateur Cup 1st Rnd Replay at Barking, 22/1/49) (Back) Blamey, Bunce, Jackson, Williams, Gearing, Crump, Strong, Hathaway (Front) McCallum, Perkins, Andrews, Guest, Birdseye

SEASON 1949-50
ISTHMIAN LEAGUE

No.	Date	Opposition	Res.	Att.	Goalscorers
1	27 Aug	DULWICH HAMLET	1-4	5000	Mikrut
2	3 Sep	Walthamstow Avenue	4-3		Birdseye(2), Mikrut(2)
3	10	CLAPTON	2-2	6000	Wegryzk, Hobbs
4	1 Oct	TUFNELL PARK	8-1		V.Busby, Birdseye(2), Mikrut(5)
5	8	Romford	2-3		McCullum, Mikrut
6	15	Clapton	0-4		
7	22	ST. ALBANS CITY	0-2		
8	29	Corinthian-Casuals	3-3		Birdseye, Kornas, Blizzard
9	5 Nov	WALTHAMSTOW AVENUE	2-3		K.Butler, Birdseye
10	12	Wimbledon	0-5	4000	
11	10 Dec	OXFORD CITY	1-0		Blizzard
12	17	Tufnell Park	5-2		McCullum, Blizzard, Decker, Mikrut(pen)
13	24	Oxford City	1-1		Blizzard
14	31	ROMFORD	1-1		Mikrut
15	7 Jan	WOKING	2-0	4000	McCullum(2)
16	4 Feb	St. Albans City	2-2		Walker(2)
17	18	Kingstonian	0-2		
18	4 Mar	Ilford	3-4		Mikrut(3)
19	25	WIMBLEDON	4-1		Mikrut(2), K.Butler, Birdseye
20	1 Apr	ILFORD	3-2	4000	McCullum, Mikrut, Birdseye
21	7	Leytonstone	1-2		Birdseye
22	22	Dulwich Hamlet	1-2		McCullum
23	26	Woking	1-1		O.G.
24	29	LEYTONSTONE	1-1		Westley
25	3 May	CORINTHIAN-CASUALS	1-0		McCullum
26	6	KINGSTONIAN	2-1		K.Butler, Blizzard

F.A. CUP

PR	17 Sep	Southall	2-6		Perkins(2)

F.A. AMATEUR CUP

4QR	26 Nov	Maidenhead United	0-0		
4QRr	3 Dec	MAIDENHEAD UNITED	2-1	6000	Mikrut, Birdseye
1R	14 Jan	Bungay Town	4-0	2500	Blizzard, Mikrut(2), McCullum
2R	28	CROOK TOWN	1-0	10087	McCullum
3R	11 Feb	DULWICH HAMLET	3-1	13607	Blizzard, McCullum, Birdseye
4R	25	ST. ALBANS CITY	4-1	15850	McCullum(2), K.Butler, Mikrut
SF*	18 Mar	Bishop Auckland	1-2	30453	J.Way

* Played at Brentford

BERKS & BUCKS SENIOR CUP

2R	21 Jan	ABINGDON TOWN	5-0	4000	Mikrut(5, 1pen)
SF*	11 Mar	Maidenhead United	3-0	4200	McCullum(3)
F#	10 Apr	Slough Town	1-1	4700	Birdseye
Fr	15	Slough Town	1-0		Birdseye

* Played at Chesham
# Played at Maidenhead

Final League Table

	P.	W.	D.	L.	F.	A.	Pts.
Leytonstone	26	17	5	4	77	31	39
Wimbledon	26	18	2	6	72	51	38
Kingstonian	26	16	3	7	59	39	35
Walthamstow Avenue	26	14	6	6	73	42	34
Dulwich Hamlet	26	14	3	9	60	47	31
St. Albans City	26	12	3	11	59	45	27
Woking	26	10	6	10	60	71	26
Wycombe Wanderers	26	9	7	10	51	52	25
Romford	26	10	4	12	46	49	24
Ilford	26	10	4	12	48	53	24
Clapton	26	8	6	12	51	59	22
Oxford City	26	8	6	14	35	54	15
Corinthian Casuals	26	4	5	17	41	69	13
Tufnell Park	26	3	2	21	24	91	8

SEASON 1950-51
ISTHMIAN LEAGUE

No.	Date	Opposition	Res.	Att.	Goalscorers
1	26 Aug	CORINTHIAN CASUALS	9-2	4500	Comben(3), Perkins(3), Westley, O.G., Blizzard
2	9 Sep	WOKING	3-4	6000	Comben(2), Perkins
3	23	LEYTONSTONE	0-2	7000	
4	7 Oct	Romford	3-7		Birdseye, Perkins, McCullum(pen)
5	21	Dulwich Hamlet	3-6	7200	Perkins, McCullum(pen), Partridge
6	4 Nov	TUFNELL PARK EDMONTON	5-0		Westley, Perkins(2), McCullum(2)
7	18	ROMFORD	0-2		
8	25	Woking	2-2		Douglas, F.Gearing
9	2 Dec	ILFORD	2-1		Mikrut(2)
10	9	Leytonstone	0-3		
11	16	DULWICH HAMLET	3-2		Mikrut(3)
12	25	OXFORD CITY	1-3		White
13	26	Oxford City	2-2	3000	K.Butler, Mikrut
14	30	St. Albans	2-0		McCullum(2)
15	6 Jan	ST.ALBANS CITY	2-3		Perkins, Mikrut
16	27	Tufnell Park Edmonton	1-0		Williamson
17	3 Feb	Clapton	1-2		Mikrut(pen)
18	3 Mar	Corinthian Casuals	0-4		
19	17	CLAPTON	3-2		Westley, Mikrut, Perkins
20	31	Ilford	0-2		
21	7 Apr	KINGSTONIAN	0-5		
22	14	Kingstonian	2-1		Baldwin, Comben
23	21	WALTHAMSTOW AVENUE	0-2		
24	25	Wimbledon	1-4		Westley
25	28	WIMBLEDON	0-0		
26	5 May	Walthamstow Avenue	1-3		McCullum

F.A. CUP

ExPR	2 Sep	AMERSHAM TOWN	13-0	5000	P'kins(5), Comben(4), McCul'm, K.But'r(2), Appl'th
PR	16	Maidenhead United	2-0		Comben, McCullum
1QR	30	Chesham United	1-1		Comben
1QRr	4 Oct	CHESHAM UNITED	4-2	4000	Perkins(2), Applegarth, Birdseye
2QR	14	Aylesbury United	2-2	5000	McCullum, Perkins
2QRr	18	AYLESBURY UNITED	2-0	4000	Birdseye, Douglass
3QR	28	Slough Town	1-1		Applegarth
3QRr	1 Nov	SLOUGH TOWN	2-0	3400	Perkins(2)
4QR	11	CHELMSFORD CITY	0-4	10377	

F.A. AMATEUR CUP

1R	13 Jan	WALTHAMSTOW AVENUE	2-2		K.Butler, J.Way
1Rr	20	Walthamstow Avenue	0-3	8000	

BERKS & BUCKS SENIOR CUP

2R	17 Feb	Marlow	1-1		Mikrut
2Rr	24	MARLOW	4-0		Perkins, Mikrut(2), Williamson
SF*	10 Mar	Slough Town	0-1	3300	

* Played at Maidenhead

Final League Table

	P	W	D	L	F	A	Pts
Leytonstone	26	20	3	3	72	26	43
Walthamstow Avenue	26	15	4	7	57	37	34
Romford	26	15	3	8	55	47	33
Wimbledon	26	13	5	8	55	39	31
Dulwich Hamlet	26	14	2	10	54	43	30
Woking	26	11	6	9	65	55	28
Ilford	26	12	4	10	44	45	28
Corinthian Casuals	26	13	0	13	62	60	26
St. Albans City	26	11	4	11	32	36	26
Kingstonian	26	9	4	13	48	54	22
Wycombe Wanderers	26	8	3	15	46	64	19
Oxford City	26	7	4	15	47	65	15
Clapton	26	8	5	15	29	50	17
Tufnell Park Edmonton	26	4	1	21	24	73	9

SEASON 1951-52
ISTHMIAN LEAGUE

No	Date	Opposition	Res.	Att.	Goalscorers
1	25 Aug	Leytonstone	3-3		Applegarth(2), Butler
2	8 Sep	Tufnell Park Edmonton	1-1		Applegarth
3	15	ROMFORD	2-0	5000	Redford(2)
4	22	Ilford	3-0		Redford, Squires, K.Butler
5	6 Oct	ST. ALBANS CITY	2-1	7000	Redford
6	20	DULWICH HAMLET	1-2	7000	Blizzard
7	3 Nov	Walthamstow Avenue	2-5		Blizzard, Lawson
8	10	KINGSTONIAN	7-2	6000	Albert(2), Dorrington, Redford(2), Blizzard(2)
9	17	Romford	0-2		
10	24	WALTHAMSTOW AVENUE	4-2		Albert(2), Hamlin, Redford
11	1 Dec	Woking	1-8		Redford
12	8	CLAPTON	4-0	3000	Albert(3), K.Butler
13	22	Oxford City	3-2		K.Butler, Blizzard, Albert
14	26	OXFORD CITY	3-1	5000	Albert(3)
15	29	LEYTONSTONE	2-2	7000	Blizzard, Atkins
16	5 Jan	WIMBLEDON	2-2		Atkins, O.G.
17	19	WOKING	5-2		Albert, Blizzard, Hamlin, Redford(2)
18	26	Dulwich Hamlet	4-2		Albert(2), O.G., Hamlin
19	2 Feb	Wimbledon	2-4		Albert(2)
20	1 Mar	St. Albans City	1-3		Redford
21	8	Clapton	3-5		Atkins, John, K.Butler
22	15	Kingstonian	1-6		Atkins
23	22	TUFNELL PARK EDMONTON	0-0		
24	5 Apr	ILFORD	2-1		Gaunt, John
25	29	Corinthian-Casuals	2-3		Albert, Redford
26	3 May	CORINTHIAN-CASUALS	4-0		Atkins(pen), Blizzard, Redford, Albert

F.A. CUP

1QR	29 Sep	WINDSOR & ETON	6-1	7000	Redford, K.Butler(3), Applegarth(2)
2QR	13 Oct	Headington United	2-3	9000	K.Butler, Applegarth
3QR	27	AYLESBURY UNITED	1-2	9000	Redford

* Match awarded to Wycombe, Headington fielded an ineligible player.

F.A. AMATEUR CUP

1R	15 Dec	Cheshunt	6-1	2000	Redford, Atkins, Albert(3), Blizzard
2R	12 Jan	ERITH & BELVEDERE	1-0	8000	Albert
3R	9 Feb	MARINE (CROSBY)	1-0	12085	Atkins(pen)
4R	23	Barnet	0-2	11026	

BERKS & BUCKS SENIOR CUP

2R	16 Feb	HUNTLEY & PALMERS	1-3		Chubb

Final League Table

		P	W	D	L	F	A	Pts.
1	Leytonstone	26	13	9	4	63	36	35
2	Wimbledon	26	16	3	7	65	44	35
3	Walthamstow Avenue	26	15	4	7	71	43	34
4	Romford	26	14	4	8	61	42	32
5	Kingstonian	26	11	7	8	62	46	29
6	Wycombe Wanderers	26	12	5	9	64	59	29
7	Woking	26	11	5	10	60	71	27
8	Dulwich Hamlet	26	11	4	11	80	53	26
9	Corinthian Casuals	26	11	4	11	55	66	26
10	St. Albans City	26	9	7	10	48	53	25
11	Ilford	26	8	5	13	32	47	21
12	Clapton	26	9	2	15	50	59	20
13	Oxford City	26	6	3	17	50	72	15
14	Tufnell Park Edmonton	26	2	6	18	25	73	10

SEASON 1952-53
ISTHMIAN LEAGUE

No	Date	Opposition	Res.	Att.	Goalscorers
1	23 Aug	DULWICH HAMLET	5-2	6000	Atkins(3,1pen), Blizzard, John
2	28	Oxford City	3-0	3200	Tunmer, Albert, John
3	30	Romford	0-8		
4	6 Sep	LEYTONSTONE	3-1	7000	Atkins(2), John
5	20	Woking	3-2		Blizzard(2), Atkins
6	4 Oct	WIMBLEDON	1-1	8000	John
7	18	ILFORD	4-0		K.Butler(2), Atkins(2pens)
8	1 Nov	Wimbledon	1-6		K.Butler
9	8	Dulwich Hamlet	1-3		K.Butler
10	15	KINGSTONIAN	3-5		O.G., Atkins(pen), K.Butler
11	22	Corinthian-Casuals	0-4		
12	29	ST. ALBANS CITY	2-1		Redford, Atkins(pen)
13	6 Dec	Leytonstone	1-0		Tomlin
14	26	St. Albans City	3-1	2000	Atkins, Tomlin, Howe
15	3 Jan	Bromley	1-3		Atkins
16	10	ROMFORD	3-2	7000	Atkins, Howe, K.Butler
17	14 Feb	Clapton	3-1		Atkins(3)
18	28	Barking	0-3		
19	7 Mar	CLAPTON	3-1		Tomlin, Atkins(2,1pen)
20	21	WALTHAMSTON AVENUE	0-0		
21	28	BARKING	0-1		
22	3 Apr	BROMLEY	1-3		K.Butler
23	11	Ilford	0-4		
24	16	Walthamstow Avenue	0-4		
25	18	WOKING	1-2		G.Truett
26	22	OXFORD CITY	6-0		Howe, G.Truett(2), Atkins, Redford(2)
27	25	CORINTHIAN CASUALS	4-3		Albert, Atkins(pen), G.Truett, Redford
28	2 May	Kingstonian	2-1		K.Butler, G.Truett

F.A. CUP

PR	13 Sep	Oxford City	4-1		K.Butler(2), Atkins, Blizzard
1QR	27	HUNTLEY & PALMERS	4-2		Atkins(2), Tomlin(2)
2QR	11 Oct	Hemel Hempstead	2-1		Blizzard, Atkins
3QR	25	Headington United	2-6	9900	Tomlin, K.Butler

F.A. AMATEUR CUP

1R	13 Dec	Hitchin Town	0-0	3900	
1Rr	20	HITCHIN TOWN	2-0	4000	John, Moring
2R	24 Jan	BARNET	2-1	9000	Atkins, K.Butler
3R	7 Feb	ROMFORD	0-5	11000	

BERKS & BUCKS SENIOR CUP

1R	17 Jan	Windsor & Eton	3-0		Atkins(2), Tomlin
2R	21 Feb	MAIDENHEAD UNITED	6-3		Atkins, John, K.Butler(2), Tomlin, G.Truett
SF*	14 Mar	Slough Town	0-2		

* Played at Maidenhead

Final League Table

		P	W	D	L	F	A	Pts.
1	Walthamstow Avenue	28	19	6	3	53	25	44
2	Bromley	28	17	4	7	71	35	38
3	Leytonstone	28	14	6	8	60	38	34
4	Wimbledon	28	14	5	9	68	37	33
5	Kingstonian	28	13	6	9	62	50	32
6	Dulwich Hamlet	28	15	2	11	62	52	32
7	Romford	28	12	8	8	62	52	32
8	Wycombe Wanderers	28	14	2	12	54	62	30
9	St. Albans City	28	11	6	11	43	57	28
10	Barking	28	9	7	12	42	51	25
11	Ilford	28	10	4	14	59	57	24
12	Woking	28	10	4	14	57	72	24
13	Corinthian Casuals	28	7	9	12	45	56	23
14	Oxford City	28	5	2	21	37	87	12
15	Clapton	28	2	5	21	27	71	9

Season 1951/52 Tour to Holland May 1952
(Back) Tunmer, Partridge, Westley, Jeffways, Lodge, Mellor (Vice.Chair.), Keen, Blizzard, J.Truett, Atkins, Hayter, Zimmer (Kingstonian), Brewin, Green (Dulwich H.), Braman (Walthamstow), Howland, Butler.
(Front) Partridge, Albert, Rickard, Rackstraw, Hathaway, Young (Walthamstow), John.

Season 1953/54: Tour of South Devon, Easter 1954
(Back Rows) Rafferty, Bates, Westley, Howman, Darvill, Atkins, Burgess, Hathaway, Cartwright, O'Connor, Styles, Campion, Brewin, Moring, Nobbs, Wicks, Rhodes, Hunt, Syrett, Seymour, Hodsdon, Little.
(Front) Cann (Coach), Albert, Lawson, Tomlin, Butler (Capt.), Timberlake (Chairman), Mellor (Vice-Chairman), Hayter (Hon.General Sec.), Mullally (Hon.Medical Officer), Richardson (Hon.Reserve Sec.), Rackstraw, Maskell.

SEASON 1953-54
ISTHMIAN LEAGUE

No.	Date	Opposition	Res.	Att.	Goalscorers
1	22 Aug	Walthamstow Avenue	1-0		Albert
2	27	St. Albans City	0-1		
3	29	WOKING	5-3	4000	Atkins(3,1pen), Redford, K.Butler
4	2 Sep	OXFORD CITY	4-3	3400	G.Truett, Atkins(2,1pen), Redford
5	5	Leytonstone	1-2		Atkins
6	19	ROMFORD	1-2		E.M.Hunt
7	26	Corinthian-Casuals	3-2		E.M.Hunt(3)
8	10 Oct	WALTHAMSTOW AVENUE	1-0	5500	Atkins(pen)
9	17	Bromley	1-2		Atkins
10	24	DULWICH HAMLET	7-2	5000	E.M.Hunt(3), Atkins(3,1pen), C.Burgess
11	31	Barking	1-2		C.Burgess
12	7 Nov	KINGSTONIAN	5-3		E.M.Hunt(3), Wicks, K.Butler
13	14	Clapton	0-2		
14	21	BROMLEY	1-4		Atkins
15	28	Romford	1-1		E.M.Hunt
16	5 Dec	Wimbledon	1-0		Atkins
17	12	BARKING	4-1		Lawson, Cartwright, E.M.Hunt, Atkins
18	26	Dulwich Hamlet	1-2	5000	O.G.
19	9 Jan	ST. ALBANS CITY	3-1		E.M.Hunt, Atkins, Moring
20	16	Kingstonian	2-4		E.M.Hunt, Atkins
21	13 Feb	LEYTONSTONE	4-0	4000	Rafferty(2), Atkins, Lawson
22	20	ILFORD	1-1		Rafferty
23	6 Mar	CORINTHIAN-CASUALS	3-1		E.M.Hunt, Atkins, G.Truett
24	27	Ilford	2-2		Rafferty, Atkins
25	3 Apr	WIMBLEDON	5-2		E.M.Hunt, Atkins(2), Wicks, Tomlin
26	10	Woking	3-0		Moring, Rafferty(2)
27	16	CLAPTON	0-1		
28	29	Oxford City	4-0		E.M.Hunt(2), Cartwright, Tomlin

F.A. CUP

| PR | 12 Sep | Banbury Spencer | 1-2 | | K.Butler |

F.A. AMATEUR CUP

1R	19 Dec	TOOTING & MITCHAM UNITED	5-0		Lawson(2), G.Truett, Atkins(2)
2R	23 Jan	LEYTONSTONE	0-0	9170	
2Rr	30	Leytonstone	0-0	3900	
2R2r*	3 Feb	Leytonstone	2-1		O.G., G.Truett
3R	6	Hounslow Town	0-3	9000	

* Played at Dulwich

BERKS & BUCKS SENIOR CUP

2R	27 Feb	Windsor & Eton	7-1		Rafferty, E.M.Hunt(4), Atkins(2,1pen)
SF*	13 Mar	Wolverton Town	2-1	5000	Rafferty, Atkins
F#	19 Apr	Slough Centre	1-1		Atkins
Fr+	24	Slough Centre	3-1	3700	K.Butler, Rafferty(2)

* Played at Aylesbury
# Played at Maidenhead
+ Played at Chesham

Final League Table

		P	W	D	L	F	A	Pts.
1	Bromley	28	18	3	7	76	45	39
2	Walthamstow Avenue	28	13	7	8	55	30	33
3	Wycombe Wanderers	28	15	3	10	65	44	33
4	Ilford	28	11	10	7	48	44	32
5	Corinthian Casuals	28	12	7	9	59	44	31
6	Woking	28	13	4	11	54	58	30
7	Leytonstone	28	12	5	11	58	48	29
8	St. Albans City	28	11	6	11	54	55	28
9	Dulwich Hamlet	28	11	6	11	55	57	28
10	Romford	28	11	5	12	57	54	27
11	Clapton	28	11	5	12	42	56	27
12	Barking	28	11	2	15	59	84	24
13	Kingstonian	28	8	7	13	59	71	23
14	Wimbledon	28	7	8	13	43	59	22
15	Oxford City	28	4	6	15	49	84	14

SEASON 1954-55
ISTHMIAN LEAGUE

No.	Date	Opposition	Res.	Att.	Goalscorers
1	21 Aug	ILFORD	2-1		Trott, E.M.Hunt
2	28	Leytonstone	1-2		E.M.Hunt
3	4 Sep	Barking	0-2		
4	18	KINGSTONIAN	3-2		J.Truett, G.Truett(2)
5	2 Oct	ROMFORD	8-1		E.M.Hunt(3), Trott(2), Bates(3,1pen)
6	16	Dulwich Hamlet	3-5		Trott, Darvill, Lawson
7	23	WALTHAMSTOW AVENUE	1-0	6000	E.M.Hunt
8	30	Bromley	2-0		Bates, Trott
9	6 Nov	WIMBLEDON	3-0	5000	Trott(2), E.M.Hunt
10	13	Corinthian-Casuals	3-1		E.M.Hunt, Wicks, Trott
11	20	ST. ALBANS CITY	4-1	7000	E.M.Hunt(3), R.Butler
12	27	Romford	3-7		Trott(2), E.M.Hunt
13	4 Dec	St. Albans City	2-3		Trott(2)
14	25	OXFORD CITY	4-0	2000	E.M.Hunt(3), Trott
15	8 Jan	Woking	4-2		Trott(2), R.Butler, L.Worley
16	29	DULWICH HAMLET	4-1		Bates(pen), O.G.(2), E.M.Hunt
17	12 Feb	BARKING	1-2		Trott
18	2 Apr	Ilford	2-0		Bates(2)
19	8	Walthamstow Avenue	2-4		Morris, Trott
20	9	LEYTONSTONE	1-1		R.Butler
21	16	BROMLEY	0-2		
22	18	Wimbledon	3-1		Bates(3)
23	23	CLAPTON	2-1		Trott, R.Butler
24	28	Oxford City	0-1		
25	30	WOKING	3-0		G.Truett(2,1pen), Trott
26	2 May	CORINTHIAN-CASUALS	5-1		R.Butler(2), Trott(2), G.Truett
27	4	Kingstonian	1-1		Trott
28	7	Clapton	1-1		Trott

F.A. CUP

PR	11 Sep	Aylesbury United	1-0		Tomlin
1QR	25	Slough Centre	3-1	1000	E.M.Hunt(2), Trott
2QR	9 Oct	Oxford City	1-4		Bates

F.A. AMATEUR CUP

1R	18 Dec	WEALDSTONE	1-1	7000	E.M.Hunt
1Rr	1 Jan	Wealdstone	2-1		E.M.Hunt, Trott
2R	22	WOKING	4-0	7000	G.Truett, E.M.Hunt(2), Trott
3R	5 Feb	ILFORD	3-1	10000	G.Truett, E.M.Hunt, Bates
4R	26	PEGASUS	0-0	14000	
4Rr	5 Mar	Pegasus	2-1	6500	Trott, Tomlin
SF*	12	Bishop Auckland	0-1	24800	

* Played at Doncaster

BERKS & BUCKS SENIOR CUP

2R	19 Mar	SLOUGH CENTRE	5-1	5000	Bates(2), Tomlin(2), Trott
SF*	26	Newbury Town	3-1		Bates(3,1pen)
F#	11 Apr	Slough Town	1-2	5000	Trott

* Played at Maidenhead
# Played at Chesham

Final League Table

		P	W	D	L	F	A	Pts.
1	Walthamstow Avenue	28	21	1	6	80	38	43
2	St. Albans City	28	18	3	7	61	41	39
3	Bromley	28	15	2	8	66	34	38
4	Wycombe Wanderers	28	16	3	9	68	43	35
5	Ilford	28	13	5	10	64	46	31
6	Barking	28	15	1	12	55	51	31
7	Woking	28	12	3	13	75	79	27
8	Kingstonian	28	10	7	11	47	57	27
9	Leytonstone	28	10	4	14	35	51	24
10	Oxford City	28	10	3	15	43	74	23
11	Clapton	28	9	4	15	41	50	22
12	Wimbledon	28	10	2	16	48	62	22
13	Corinthian Casuals	28	9	3	16	50	65	21
14	Dulwich Hamlet	28	7	5	16	48	60	19
15	Romford	28	4	10	14	43	73	18

Season 1954/55 (Back) Lawson, Hunt, Moring, Syrett, Wicks, G.Truett, L.Worley
(Front) Trott, J.Truett, Westley, Tomlin, Darvill

Season 1955/56 (Back) West, Syrett, Westley (Capt.) (Middle) Hayter (Hon.General Secretary),
Lawson, Wicks, Darvill, Moring (Vice-Capt.), Cann (Coach) (Front) L.Worley, Trott, Bates, Tomlin, G.Truett

SEASON 1955-56
ISTHMIAN LEAGUE

No.	Date	Opposition	Res.	Att.	Goalscorers
1	27 Aug	WALTHAMSTOW AVENUE	0-3		
2	31	Oxford City	3-1		E.M.Hunt, G.Truett(2,1pen)
3	3 Sep	Corinthian-Casuals	0-0		
4	17	CORINTHIAN-CASUALS	6-1		Bates(3), Trott(3)
5	1 Oct	Wimbledon	0-1		
6	15	LEYTONSTONE	5-1		Bates(3), Trott, L.Worley
7	29	Dulwich Hamlet	4-2		G.Truett, Trott, Bates(2)
8	12 Nov	Walthamstow Avenue	4-2		Bates, Trott(2), G.Truett
9	26	BARKING	4-0		Trott(2), Bates(2)
10	3 Dec	Leytonstone	1-2		Bates
11	10	ST. ALBANS CITY	2-2		G.Truett, Rockell
12	17	ILFORD	5-0		Trott(2), G.Truett, Bates(2)
13	26	St. Albans City	1-1		G.Truett
14	27	OXFORD CITY	3-0	3000	Tomlin, G.Truett, Bates
15	31	ROMFORD	6-2		Trott(3), Bates, G.Truett, Tomlin
16	7 Jan	Ilford	3-0		G.Truett(2), Bates
17	14	Romford	3-1		G.Truett, Bates(2)
18	28	Barking	4-3		A.Burgess, G.Truett(3)
19	3 Mar	WIMBLEDON	4-1	4000	Bates(2), Tomlin, Trott
20	17	WOKING	1-3	4000	Trott
21	24	BROMLEY	3-2		Trott, Darvill(2)
22	30	CLAPTON	3-0	4500	Tomlin(2), Bates
23	7 Apr	Woking	2-2		Bates, G.Truett
24	21	DULWICH HAMLET	3-0	6000	Bates, Trott, G.Truett(pen)
25	25	Kingstonian	2-2		Bates(2)
26	28	Clapton	2-0		Trott, L.Worley
27	2 May	KINGSTONIAN	5-2		G.Truett(3,1pen), Bates, F.Smith
28	5	Bromley	3-2		Tomlin(3)

F.A. CUP

PR	10 Sep	Witney Town	0-0		
PRr	14	WITNEY TOWN	15-1		Btes(5),G.Truett(5),Trtt(3),D.Way,L.Wrley
1QR	24	MAIDENHEAD UNITED	4-2		Trott(2), Bates, G.Truett
2QR	8 Oct	Slough Town	3-3		Bates, Westley, G.Truett(pen)
2QRr	12	SLOUGH TOWN	1-0		G.Truett
3QR	22	Banbury Spencer	2-1		Bates, G.Truett(pen)
4QR	5 Nov	FAREHAM TOWN	3-1	7000	L.Worley, D.Way, Trott
1R	19	BURTON ALBION	1-3	9696	Bates

F.A. AMATEUR CUP

1R	21 Jan	DAGENHAM TOWN	4-1	8250	Moring, Trott, G.Truett, Tomlin
2R	11 Feb	Pegasus	2-1	6500	G.Truett(pen), Bates
3R	18	Hitchin Town	0-1	7860	

BERKS & BUCKS SENIOR CUP

2R	25 Feb	Chesham United	2-1		Tomlin(2)
SF*	10 Mar	Newbury Town	3-0	3000	Trott, G.Truett, Tomlin
F#	2 Apr	Maidenhead United	2-2	3000	G.Truett, Tomlin
Fr+	14	Maidenhead United	2-3		Bates(2)

* Played at Maidenhead
# Played at Slough
+ Played at Chesham

Final League Table

	P	W	D	L	F	A	Pts.
1 Wycombe Wanderers	28	19	5	4	82	36	43
2 Bromley	28	12	7	9	54	43	31
3 Leytonstone	28	12	7	9	50	44	31
4 Woking	28	14	3	11	62	60	31
5 Barking	28	12	7	9	41	45	31
6 Kingstonian	28	12	6	10	67	64	30
7 Walthamstow Avenue	28	13	3	12	61	45	29
8 Ilford	28	10	8	10	44	52	28
9 Oxford City	28	10	7	11	48	55	27
10 Clapton	28	9	8	11	45	48	26
11 Wimbledon	28	12	2	4	51	62	26
12 Corinthian Casuals	28	9	7	12	56	56	25
13 Dulwich Hamlet	28	9	6	13	55	67	24
14 Romford	28	9	6	13	42	55	24
15 St. Albans City	28	2	10	16	36	62	14

SEASON 1956-57
ISTHMIAN LEAGUE

No.	Date	Opposition	Res.	Att.	Goalscorers
1	18 Aug	LEYTONSTONE	2-1	5000	Bates, N.West(pen)
2	23	St. Albans City	2-1		Bates, Trott
3	25	TOOTING & MITCHAM UNITED	5-4		Bates(2), F.Smith, Tomlin, G.Truett(pen)
4	1 Sep	Woking	2-3		Bates, G.Truett(pen)
5	5	OXFORD CITY	1-2		Bates
6	8	Corinthian-Casuals	3-1		G.Truett, Bates, D.Way
7	15	DULWICH HAMLET	2-1		Bates, L.Worley
8	22	Ilford	4-1		Tomlin, G.Truett(2), Bates
9	29	KINGSTONIAN	4-1	5000	Trott(2), Bates(2)
10	6 Oct	Barking	2-2		Bates, Trott
11	13	Leytonstone	0-1		
12	20	WALTHAMSTOW AVENUE	4-1		Bates, Trott, F.Smith(2)
13	27	BROMLEY	1-2		Bates
14	10 Nov	Wimbledon	4-1		G.Truett, Moring, Bates, F.Smith
15	17	ROMFORD	4-4		F.Smith(2), Bates, G.Truett
16	24	Kingstonian	6-0		Bates(3), Tomlin, F.Smith, Trott
17	1 Dec	WOKING	5-3		Tomlin,F.Smith,L.Worley,Bates,Moring
18	8	Dulwich Hamlet	3-1		Tomlin, Bates, Trott
19	15	ILFORD	4-3		R.Butler, Tomlin, Rockell, Bates
20	22	BARKING	6-2		Tomlin(2), Bates(3), R.Butler
21	26	Oxford City	0-0		
22	29	Walthamstow Avenue	3-2		Bates(2), Tomlin
23	5 Jan	Romford	2-1		Trott, G.Truett(pen)
24	19	ST. ALBANS CITY	7-0		Bates(2),Trtt,Rckell,G.Truett(2,1p),Atkins
25	2 Feb	Bromley	2-6		Atkins(2)
26	9 Mar	Clapton	1-1		Atkins
27	23	WIMBLEDON	0-0		
28	6 Apr	CLAPTON	3-5		J.Truett, Bates, Tomlin
29	22	Tooting & Mitcham United	1-1		Trott
30	4 May	CORINTHIAN-CASUALS	3-2		Trott, Tomlin(2)

F.A. CUP

4QR	3 Nov	MARGATE	2-4	7000	L.Worley, Trott

F.A. AMATEUR CUP

1R	12 Jan	St. Albans City	4-1	4160	Trott, Bates(2), G.Truett
2R	26	CLAPTON	4-2	10000	Bates(3), Tomlin
3R	9 Feb	HOUNSLOW TOWN	3-1	12000	Bates, G.Truett, Trott
4R	23	Ilford	3-3	12000	G.Truett(pen), Trott(2)
4Rr	2 Mar	ILFORD	2-0	15500	F.Smith, Trott
SF*	16	Corinthian-Casuals	4-2	28197	Bates(2), L.Worley(2)
F#	13 Apr	Bishop Auckland	1-3	90000	F.Smith

* Played at Highbury
# Played at Wembley

BERKS & BUCKS SENIOR CUP

2R	16 Feb	Didcot Town	2-3	3000	Tomlin, Atkins

Final League Table

	P	W	D	L	F	A	Pts.
1 Wycombe Wanderers	30	15	6	6	86	53	42
2 Woking	30	20	1	9	104	47	41
3 Bromley	30	16	5	9	78	60	37
4 Oxford City	30	16	3	11	65	57	35
5 Ilford	30	12	8	10	59	65	32
6 Tooting & Mitcham	30	10	11	9	53	48	31
7 Kingstonian	30	11	9	10	72	77	31
8 Walthamstow Avenue	30	11	8	11	49	46	30
9 Dulwich Hamlet	30	13	3	14	65	54	29
10 St. Albans City	30	13	3	14	62	71	29
11 Leytonstone	30	11	6	13	50	50	28
12 Clapton	30	9	9	12	48	59	27
13 Wimbledon	30	10	5	15	47	66	25
14 Romford	30	10	5	15	53	81	25
15 Barking	30	7	6	17	48	72	20
16 Corinthian Casuals	30	7	4	19	46	78	15

Season 1956/57 (Back) G.Truett, Lawson, Wicks, Syrett, J.Truett, Moring (Vice-Captain), Westley (Capt.), (Front) L.Worley, Trott, Bates, Tomlin, Smith, Atkins.

Season 1958/59:
(Back) M.Brown, Hurley, Moring, Syrett, Wicks, Lawson (Front) Rockell, Trott, Bates, Howson, Tomlin

SEASON 1957-58
ISTHMIAN LEAGUE

No.	Date	Opposition	Res.	Att.	Goalscorers
1	24 Aug	Kingstonian	2-5		Bates, Tomlin
2	37	WALTHAMSTOW AVENUE	4-1		Reardon, Trott(2), Bates
3	4 Sep	Oxford City	1-1	4000	Reardon
4	7	Barking	2-0		Tomlin(2)
5	14	DULWICH HAMLET	5-2		Trott, Rockell, O.G., Lawson, Bates
6	21	Walthamstow Avenue	0-1		
7	28	CLAPTON	4-2		Tomlin(2), Trott(2)
8	5 Oct	Tooting & Mitcham United	1-1		Rockell
9	12	Wimbledon	2-1		Rockell, Reardon
10	19	BROMLEY	2-2		Reardon, Day
11	26	Dulwich Hamlet	1-2		Trott
12	2 Nov	KINGSTONIAN	6-0		Bates(3), Reardon, Trott, Tomlin
13	9	Romford	2-0		Reardon, Trott
14	23	TOOTING & MITCHAM UNITED	2-1		Bates, Rockell
15	30	ST. ALBANS CITY	7-1		Bates(3), Rockell, Reardon(3)
16	7 Dec	Corinthian-Casuals	4-4		Trott(2), Rockell, Bates
17	14	St. Albans City	4-1		Bates(2), Tomlin, Trott
18	21	WIMBLEDON	3-1		Rockell, Tomlin, O.G.
19	26	OXFORD CITY	4-2		Trott(2), Tomlin(2)
20	4 Jan	Woking	1-2		Reardon
21	18	ILFORD	1-0		Tomlin
22	15 Feb	WOKING	0-4		
23	22	Leytonstone	0-1		
24	8 Mar	Clapton	4-3		Edwards(3), Trott
25	29	ROMFORD	6-0		Bates(2), Trott, Tomlin, Rockell(2)
26	19 Apr	Bromley	2-3		Edwards, Howson
27	23	CORINTHIAN-CASUALS	1-0		Edwards
28	26	BARKING	2-0		Bates(2)
29	30	LEYTONSTONE	2-0		Bates, Tomlin
30	1 May	Ilford	3-1		Bates, Rockell(2)

F.A. CUP

1R	16 Nov	Dorchester Town	2-3	3600	Rockell, Reardon

F.A. AMATEUR CUP

1R	11 Jan	LEYTONSTONE	2-0	7209	Trott(2)
2R	25	WINCHESTER CITY	6-0	8031	Bates(2),Rockell,Tomlin,Trott,Reardon
3R	8 Feb	Ilford	1-2	9768	Bates(pen)

BERKS & BUCKS SENIOR CUP

1R	28 Dec	Wolverton Town	8-1		Trott,Bates(2),Reardn(2),Rockll,Tmlin(2)
2R	1 Feb	HUNTLEY & PALMERS	8-3		Trott(5), Reardon, Bates, Tomlin
SF*	1 Mar	Windsor & Eton	2-2		Edwards, Moring
SFr*	15	Windsor & Eton	3-1		Edwards(3)
F#	7 Apr	Maidenhead United	1-0	5000	Edwards

* Played at Maidenhead
# Played at Marlow

Final League Table

	P	W	D	L	F	A	Pts.
1 Tooting & Mitcham United	30	20	6	4	79	33	46
2 Wycombe Wanderers	30	19	4	7	78	42	42
3 Walthamstow Avenue	30	17	5	8	63	35	39
4 Bromley	30	13	9	8	66	51	35
5 Oxford City	30	13	6	11	59	48	32
6 Leytonstone	30	13	6	11	49	48	32
7 Wimbledon	30	15	2	13	64	66	32
8 Corinthian Casuals	30	12	8	10	62	68	32
9 Woking	30	12	7	11	70	58	31
10 Barking	30	10	6	14	49	61	26
11 St. Albans City	30	11	3	16	56	76	25
12 Clapton	30	8	9	13	42	65	25
13 Kingstonian	30	7	8	15	45	66	22
14 Dulwich Hamlet	30	7	7	16	49	64	21
15 Ilford	30	8	4	18	46	70	20
16 Romford	30	6	8	16	45	71	20

SEASON 1958-59
ISTHMIAN LEAGUE

No.	Date	Opposition	Res.	Att.	Goalscorers
1	23 Aug	KINGSTONIAN	6-2		Trott(2), Rockell, Edwards, Bates(2)
2	28	St. Albans City	8-0		Bates(4), Edwards(2), Tomlin, Trott
3	30	Corinthian-Casuals	8-1		O.G., Edwards(4), Trott(2), Bates
4	6 Sep	Walthamstow Avenue	6-3		Trott(2), Edwards(3), Bates
5	10	OXFORD CITY	3-2		Trott, Bates, Edwards
6	13	TOOTING & MITCHAM UNITED	3-0		Rockell, Bates(2,1pen)
7	20	Woking	1-1		Edwards
8	27	BROMLEY	0-0		
9	4 Oct	Kingstonian	2-0		Edwards, Tomlin
10	11	DULWICH HAMLET	4-1		Trott(2), Rockell, L.Worley
11	18	LEYTONSTONE	5-0		Trott(2), Bates(3,1pen)
12	25	Romford	4-3		Trott(3), Bates(pen)
13	8 Nov	CLAPTON	3-3		Tomlin, Bates(2pens)
14	22	Bromley	2-3		Bates, O.G.
15	29	Ilford	2-3		Bates, Edwards
16	6 Dec	ROMFORD	5-1		Tomlin, Fryer, Rockell, Trott(2)
17	13	ST. ALBANS CITY	7-2		Rockell(2),Bates(3,1pen),Trott,L.Worley
18	20	Clapton	3-1		Bates(2,1pen), Tomlin
19	27	Oxford City	2-5		Trott, Bates
20	3 Jan	WOKING	4-0		Edwards(2), Bates, Trott
21	7 Mar	ILFORD	5-2		Bates(4,1pen), Howson
22	14	Dulwich Hamlet	1-3		J.Truett
23	21	BARKING	0-1		
24	30	Leytonstone	0-1	500	
25	4 Apr	WIMBLEDON	1-0		Beck(pen)
26	11	Barking	4-1		Tomlin, Fryer(2), Trott
27	18	CORINTHIAN-CASUALS	3-2		L.Worley, Beck, Fisher
28	23	Tooting & Mitcham United	1-1		Fisher
29	25	Wimbledon	0-4		
30	30	WALTHAMSTOW AVENUE	0-4		

F.A. CUP

4QR	1 Nov	Hendon	3-1	5000	Tomlin, Bates, Trott
1R	15	Northampton Town	0-2	12934	

F.A. AMATUER CUP

1R	17 Jan	Hounslow Town	4-2		Trott(2), Bates(2)
2R	24	DULWICH HAMLET	2-1	8000	Edwards, Trott
3R	7 Feb	Barnet	2-2	8500	Edwards, Trott
3Rr	14	BARNET	0-1	11000	

BERKS & BUCKS SENIOR CUP

2R	31 Jan	WINDSOR & ETON	9-0		Trott(2), Edwards(3),Bates(3), L.Worley
SF*	21 Feb	Aylesbury United	6-6		Bates(3,2pens), Rockell(2), O.G.
SFr*	28	Aylesbury United	1-2	3500	Bates

* Played at Chesham

Final League Table

	P	W	D	L	F	A	Pts.
1 Wimbledon	30	22	3	5	91	38	47
2 Dulwich Hamlet	30	18	5	7	68	44	41
3 Wycombe Wanderers	30	18	4	8	93	50	40
4 Oxford City	30	17	4	9	87	58	38
5 Walthamstow Avenue	30	16	5	9	59	40	37
6 Tooting & Mitcham Utd.	30	15	4	11	84	55	34
7 Barking	30	14	2	14	59	53	30
8 Woking	30	12	6	12	66	66	30
9 Bromley	30	11	7	12	56	55	29
10 Clapton	30	10	6	14	55	67	26
11 Ilford	30	10	6	14	46	57	26
12 Kingstonian	30	9	4	17	54	72	22
13 St. Albans City	30	8	6	16	53	89	22
14 Leytonstone	30	7	6	17	40	87	20
15 Romford	30	7	5	18	54	76	19
16 Corinthian Casuals	30	7	5	18	44	92	19

SEASON 1959-60
ISTHMIAN LEAGUE

No.	Date	Opposition	Res.	Att.	Goalscorers
1	22 Aug	Maidstone United	3-2	2500	Beck(pen), Bates, Atkins
2	29	KINGSTONIAN	2-0		James, Atkins
3	1 Sep	Oxford City	1-3		Free
4	5	Ilford	2-0		James(2)
5	9	ST. ALBANS CITY	5-0		James(2), Atkins(2), Rockell
6	12	WALTHAMSTOW AVENUE	3-1		Trott, Bates(pen), Free
7	26	Wimbledon	1-2		Atkins
8	3 Oct	Tooting & Mitcham United	1-5		Bates(pen)
9	10	CLAPTON	5-2		Bates(2), Atkins, Fryer, Trott
10	17	Bromley	4-2		Howson(2), Trott, Rockell
11	24	BARKING	6-4		Bates(4,1pen), Weaver, Trott
12	7 Nov	CORINTHIAN-CASUALS	3-1		Howson(2), Rockell
13	21	Dulwich Hamlet	2-1		Trott, O.G.
14	28	WOKING	1-1		Rockell
15	12 Dec	MAIDSTONE UNITED	2-1		Bates, Atkins
16	19	Woking	5-3		Trott(2), Bates, Atkins(2)
17	26	OXFORD CITY	3-1		Bates, Weaver, Trott
18	2 Jan	St. Albans City	1-2		Trott
19	23	Clapton	8-1		Free, Fryer(2), Bates(3), Trott, Beck
20	6 Feb	Corinthian-Casuals	0-4		
21	13	DULWICH HAMLET	4-0		Free(2), James, Bates
22	20	ILFORD	10-0		Beck,Bates(3),Trott,Jmes(3),L.Wrley,Free
23	5 Mar	LEYTONSTONE	1-1		James
24	12	Walthamstow Avenue	0-4		
25	19	TOOTING & MITCHAM UNITED	1-2		Bates
26	26	Leytonstone	0-0		
27	2 Apr	Barking	1-2		Atkins
28	9	WIMBLEDON	4-1		Fryer(2), Beck(pen), Trott
29	26	Kingstonian	3-0		Trott, Fryer, Tomlin
30	5 May	BROMLEY	2-0		Bates, L.Worley

F.A. CUP

4QR	31 Oct	OXFORD CITY	1-0	5994	Trott
1R	14 Nov	WISBECH TOWN	4-2	7900	Trott(2), Bates, Rockell
2R	5 Dec	Watford	1-5	23907	Atkins

F.A. AMATEUR CUP

1R	9 Jan	Hounslow Town	0-3	

BERKS & BUCKS SENIOR CUP

2R	30 Jan	SLOUGH TOWN	3-1		Bates(pen), Fryer(2)
SF*	27 Feb	Chesham United	2-1		James, Bates
F#	18 Apr	Maidenhead United	3-0	5358	Fryer, Beck(pen), Tomlin

* Played at Aylesbury
\# Played at Reading

Final League Table

	P	W	D	L	F	A	Pts.
1 Tooting & Mitcham Utd.	30	17	8	5	75	43	42
2 Wycombe Wanderers	30	19	3	8	84	46	41
3 Wimbledon	30	18	3	9	66	36	39
4 Kingstonian	30	18	3	9	76	51	39
5 Corinthian Casuals	30	18	1	11	69	61	37
6 Bromley	30	15	6	9	74	46	36
7 Dulwich Hamlet	30	14	6	10	65	47	34
8 Walthamstow Avenue	30	11	11	8	48	38	33
9 Oxford City	30	10	10	10	57	57	30
10 Leytonstone	30	10	8	12	43	46	28
11 Woking	30	10	6	14	54	61	26
12 St. Albans City	30	10	6	14	50	65	26
13 Maidstone United	30	10	5	15	53	60	25
14 Barking	30	7	4	19	30	75	18
15 Ilford	30	5	6	19	34	86	16
16 Clapton	30	3	4	23	32	92	10

SEASON 1960-61
ISTHMIAN LEAGUE

No.	Date	Opposition	Res.	Att.	Goalscorers
1	20 Aug	LEYTONSTONE	0-3		
2	27	Ilford	0-0		
3	1 Sep	St. Albans City	6-1		Bates(3), Trott(2), Tomlin
4	3	Walthamstow Avenue	1-4		Trott
5	7	OXFORD CITY	1-2		Rockell
6	10	Tooting & Mitcham United	2-3		Bates(2)
7	17	KINGSTONIAN	1-1		Beck(pen)
8	24	Bromley	0-4		
9	1 Oct	WOKING	2-2		Bates, James
10	8	CLAPTON	2-1		Trott, Bates
11	15	Wimbledon	1-2		Tomlin
12	29	MAIDSTONE UNITED	4-2		Atkins, Bressington, Holmes, Bates
13	12 Nov	Kingstonian	3-5		Bressington(2), L.Worley
14	19	DULWICH HAMLET	4-3		Bates(4)
15	26	Leytonstone	1-3		O.G.
16	3 Dec	Maidstone United	0-2		
17	10	BARKING	2-1		James, Ashby
18	17	Corinthian-Casuals	1-5		James
19	27	Oxford City	0-5		
20	31	ILFORD	2-0		Rockell, James
21	7 Jan	Dulwich Hamlet	1-1	2000	Bates
22	14	ST. ALBANS CITY	6-0		Holmes(3), Rockell, Tomlin, Bates
23	18 Feb	TOOTING & MITCHAM UNITED	2-1		Bates(2)
24	11 Mar	CORINTHIAN-CASUALS	7-1		Bates, Trott, Ashby(3), Rockell, Murphy
25	18	Woking	2-4		Trott(2)
26	25	Barking	6-0		Murphy, Ashby(2), Trott(3)
27	8 Apr	Clapton	2-1		Ashby(2)
28	15	BROMLEY	1-2		Bates(pen)
29	29	WALTHAMSTOW AVENUE	1-1		Rockell
30	6 May	WIMBLEDON	2-1		Bates(2)

F.A. CUP

4QR	22 Oct	TOOTING & MITCHAM UNITED	2-1		Bates, Bressington
1R	5 Nov	KETTERING TOWN	1-2	7500	Thomas

F.A. AMATEUR CUP

1R	21 Jan	WIMBLEDON	1-2	5000	Holmes

BEKRS & BUCKS SENIOR CUP

3R	4 Feb	Wokington Town	4-0	Bates(2,1pen), L.Worley, Holmes
SF*	4 Mar	Maidenhead United	1-2	Rockell

* Played at Marlow

Final League Table

	P	W	D	L	F	A	Pts.
1 Bromley	30	20	6	4	89	42	46
2 Walthamstow Avenue	30	20	5	5	87	38	45
3 Wimbledon	30	18	6	6	72	43	42
4 Dulwich Hamlet	30	17	4	9	71	59	38
5 Maidstone United	30	14	8	8	63	39	36
6 Leytonstone	30	15	6	9	46	34	36
7 Tooting & Mitcham Utd.	30	14	3	13	69	51	31
8 Wycombe Wanderers	30	12	5	13	63	61	29
9 St. Albans City	30	12	4	14	45	72	28
10 Oxford City	30	10	7	13	59	59	27
11 Corinthian Casuals	30	9	9	12	49	59	27
12 Kingstonian	30	10	6	14	55	61	26
13 Woking	30	10	6	14	58	71	26
14 Ilford	30	5	8	17	30	69	18
15 Barking	30	3	8	19	30	76	14
16 Clapton	30	3	5	22	25	77	11

Season 1959/60:
(Back) Brown, Grace, Styles, Hodson, Jackson. (Row 2) Aldridge, Little, Fryer, Nobbs, Rackstraw, Conduit, Ing, O'Connor, Shepherd, Cann.
(Row 3) Summerfield, ?, James, Jack Timberlake, Fisher, Morris, Hyde, Worley, Howson, Darvill, Free. (Row 4) Walters, Crook, Bunce (Treas.), Webb, John Timberlake, Dr.Ellis, Haytor, Maskell, M.Brown, H.Brown.
(Row 5) Trott, Worley, Thomas, Fryer, Bates, Moring, Tomlin, Bartholomew, Truett, Beck.

Youth Team
Season 1961/62 (Back) Sewell, Merrick, T.Gomm, Randall, Priestley, Cross
(Front) Fieldhouse, Cooper, Gallacher, Lacey, B.Gomm

SEASON 1961-62
ISTHMIAN LEAGUE

No.	Date	Opposition	Res.	Att.	Goalscorers
1	19 Aug	Leytonstone	1-3		Ashby
2	26	TOOTING & MITCHAM UNITED	1-1		Holmes
3	30	ST. ALBANS CITY	2-1		Holmes(2)
4	2 Sep	Ilford	5-2		James(3), Blair, Holmes
5	16	Kingstonian	1-1		Blair
6	23	CORINTHIAN-CASUALS	0-2		
7	30	Dulwich Hamlet	3-2		James(3)
8	7 Oct	WALTHAMSTOW AVENUE	2-0		L.Worley, Hyde
9	14	Wimbledon	0-2	2692	
10	23	Oxford City	2-3		Blair, Horseman
11	28	MAIDSTONE UNITED	1-0		Beck(pen)
12	11 Nov	Woking	0-3		
13	18	Clapton	2-3		Gale, O.G.
14	25	BROMLEY	3-1		Bates, Beck(pen), Blair
15	2 Dec	Corinthian-Casuals	2-4		Fisher, O.G.
16	16	WOKING	3-1		Horseman(2), Hay
17	26	OXFORD CITY	4-1		James(3), Horseman
18	30	Barking	2-2		James, O.G.
19	27 Jan	KINGSTONIAN	1-3		Bates(pen)
20	24 Feb	BARKING	1-2		O.G.
21	3 Mar	Walthamstow Avenue	1-3		Beck
22	10	CLAPTON	3-3		Hay, James(2)
23	24	WIMBLEDON	0-1		
24	31	St. Albans City	0-0		
25	7 Apr	Maidstone United	2-1		James, Horseman
26	14	ILFORD	2-2		L.Worley, James
27	21	LEYTONSTONE	2-0		Ashby, Pullin
28	28	DULWICH HAMLET	6-0		Horseman(2),Holmes(2),Bates(pen),Gale
29	2 May	Tooting & Mitcham United	2-2		L.Worley(2)
30	5	Bromley	3-2		Gale, Holmes, Thompson

F.A. CUP

4QR	21 Oct	TILBURY	3-1		Blair, L.Worley, Beck(pen)
1R	4 Nov	ASHFORD TOWN	0-0	5500	
1Rr	8	Ashford Town	0-3	3223	

F.A. AMATEUR CUP

1R	20 Jan	ERITH & BELVEDERE	2-1	4003	Holmes, Bates
2R	3 Feb	Sutton United	4-1		James, L.Worley, Bates(2,1pen)
3R	17	Wimbledon	0-1	9254	

BERKS & BUCKS SENIOR CUP

3R	10 Feb	Hazell's (Aylesbury)	7-0	2048	James(2), Bates(3), Blair, Horseman
SF*	17 Mar	Wokingham Town	3-1		James(3)
F#	23 Apr	Windsor & Eton	0-2		

* Played at Marlow
\# Played at Reading

Final League Table

	P	W	D	L	F	A	Pts.
1 Wimbledon	30	19	6	5	68	24	44
2 Leytonstone	30	17	7	6	61	44	41
3 Walthamstow Avenue	30	14	8	8	51	31	36
4 Kingstonian	30	15	5	10	70	48	35
5 Tooting & Mitcham Utd.	30	12	10	8	62	47	34
6 Oxford City	30	12	9	9	56	49	33
7 Wycombe Wanderers	30	12	7	11	57	51	31
8 Corinthian Casuals	30	12	7	11	45	51	31
9 St. Albans City	30	10	9	11	55	60	29
10 Woking	30	9	9	12	51	60	27
11 Dulwich Hamlet	30	11	4	15	55	66	26
12 Barking	30	9	8	13	40	64	26
13 Ilford	30	7	10	13	50	59	24
14 Bromley	30	10	4	16	49	69	24
15 Clapton	30	6	8	16	45	67	20
16 Maidstone United	30	6	7	17	34	59	19

SEASON 1962-63
ISTHMIAN LEAGUE

No.	Date	Opposition	Res.	Att.	Goalscorers
1	18 Aug	ILFORD	0-0		
2	22	OXFORD CITY	0-0		
3	25	Leytonstone	2-1		Hay(2)
4	1 Sep	Bromley	4-4		L.Worley(2), Bressington, Hay
5	15	WOKING	2-2		Bressington, Horseman
6	22	Walthamstow Avenue	1-1		Horseman
7	29	DULWICH HAMLET	1-1		Horseman
8	6 Oct	Clapton	3-0		Thomas(2), Hay
9	13	TOOTING & MITCHAM UNITED	1-2		Hay
10	27	St. Albans City	0-3		
11	10 Nov	WIMBLEDON	3-2		Jackson, Horseman, Thomas(pen)
12	17	BROMLEY	2-2		Cross, Thomas
13	1 Dec	KINGSTONIAN	1-4		Fennel
14	15	Dulwich Hamlet	3-4		Beck, Hay, Jackson
15	26	Oxford City	1-1		O.G.
16	17 Feb	Tooting & Mitcham United	1-2		Hay
17	5 Mar	Kingstonian	3-4		Thomas(pen), Horseman, Gale
18	12	Wimbledon	1-5	2598	L.Worley
19	19	Ilford	1-7		Horseman
20	30	CLAPTON	5-1		Horseman(5,1pen)
21	13 Apr	WALTHAMSTOW AVENUE	2-0		Pullin, D.Worley
22	20	Barking	1-1		Horseman
23	24	ST. ALBANS CITY	1-0		Cross
24	27	CORINTHIAN-CASUALS	4-1		Cross(2), Bedford(2)
25	1 May	Corinthian-Casuals	3-1		Cross, Horseman, Gale
26	4	Woking	2-3		Thomas(pen), Jackson
27	11	Maidstone United	1-6		Horseman
28	14	LEYTONSTONE	2-0		Jackson, Cross
29	18	BARKING	1-1		Bedford
30	24	MAIDSTONE UNITED	4-2		Cross, Gale, Thomas(pen), Horseman

F.A. CUP

4QR	20 Oct	Walthamstow Avenue	1-1	1883	Hay
4QRr	24	WALTHAMSTOW AVENUE	3-1		Cross, L.Worley, Beck
1R	3 Nov	Maidenhead United	3-0	5337	Horseman(2), Hay
2R	24	Gravesend & Northfleet	1-3	6809	Thomas(pen)

F.A. AMATEUR CUP

1R	2 Mar	UXBRIDGE	2-0	4000	Charman, Thomas
2R	9	BARKING	3-2	2008	Fisher, L.Worley(2)
3R	16	Hitchin Town	2-3	4282	Horseman, Jackson

BERKS & BUCKS SENIOR CUP

3R	23 Mar	Slough Town	4-2		Jackson, O.G., Beck(pen), Charman
SF	6 Apr	MAIDENHEAD UNITED	3-3		L.Worley, Thomas(pen), Charman
SFr	15	Maidenhead United	0-1		

Final League Table

	P	W	D	L	F	A	Pts.
1 Wimbledon	30	19	8	3	84	33	46
2 Kingstonian	30	18	8	4	79	37	44
3 Tooting & Mitcham Utd.	30	17	8	5	65	37	42
4 Ilford	30	19	3	8	70	44	41
5 Walthamstow Avenue	30	14	7	9	51	44	35
6 Maidstone United	30	13	8	9	56	45	34
7 Bromley	30	12	10	8	57	51	34
8 Leytonstone	30	12	7	11	48	50	31
9 Wycombe Wanderers	30	10	10	10	56	61	30
10 St. Albans City	30	11	5	14	54	49	27
11 Barking	30	8	10	12	39	50	26
12 Oxford City	30	8	9	13	55	64	25
13 Woking	30	8	8	14	42	66	24
14 Clapton	30	7	4	19	30	71	18
15 Dulwich Hamlet	30	4	5	21	30	71	13
16 Corinthian Casuals	30	4	4	22	28	71	12

Season 1962/63 : (Left to Right) Balson, J.Thomas, Gale, Merrick, Sewell, Wilkes, Cross, Goddard, D.Thomas, Patrick, Cooper, Fieldhouse.

Season 1963/64: (Left to Right) Welsh, Faulkner, Wilkes, Merrick, Gallacher, L.Worley, Pullen, D.Worley, Bunting, Cooper, Hay, Fieldhouse, Birch

SEASON 1963-64
ISTHMIAN LEAGUE

Players (column headers): Patrick P., Lewis A., Pullin G., Worley D., Roystone P., Gale C., Worley L., Bassett D., Thomas D., Hay J., Merrick L., Bunting C., Horseman A., Beck J., Hodges P., Page M., Gallacher W., Syrett D., Cooper J., Balson J., Sewell P., Thomas J., Bedford R., Samuels K., Maharg G., Lowen P., French B., Baker B., Faulkner V., Styles P.

No.	Date	Opposition	Res.	Att.	Goalscorers
1	24 Aug	Maidstone United	2-3		Hay(2)
2	29	St. Albans City	1-4		L.Worley
3	31	KINGSTONIAN	1-3		Hay
4	4 Sep	ST. ALBANS CITY	3-1		Bassett, Pullin(2)
5	7	Enfield	2-2		Horseman, Hodges
6	14	LEYTONSTONE	2-5		Gale, Horseman
7	18	HITCHIN TOWN	0-1		
8	21	Wimbledon	0-1		
9	25	ENFIELD	3-1	3000	Gale, D.Thomas, Beck
10	28	DULWICH HAMLET	4-0		O.G., D.Thomas, Gale, Beck(pen)
11	1 Oct	Hitchin Town	1-4		Gale
12	5	Clapton	6-2	200	Hdges(2), Hrseman(2), L.Wrley, D.Thmas(p
13	9	WIMBLEDON	2-0		Horseman, O.G.
14	26	BROMLEY	3-1		Pullin, Beck, Horseman
15	30	WOKING	2-1		Horseman, Balson
16	2 Nov	Sutton United	1-2		Horseman
17	9	ILFORD	2-3		Balson, Horseman
18	16	Dulwich Hamlet	3-3		Hodges, Bassett, Horseman
19	23	Woking	0-2		
20	30	TOOTING & MITCHAM UTD	3-1		Gale, Hodges, J.Thomas
21	7 Dec	Bromley	1-3		Bedford
22	14	CORINTHIAN-CASUALS	4-1		Horseman, Hodges(2), Samuels
23	21	Corinthian-Casuals	1-3		Horseman
24	28	Oxford City	3-0		Balson, Horseman, Lowen
25	4 Jan	Barking	3-2		L.Worley, Balson(2)
26	18	Walthamstow Avenue	0-0		
27	25	OXFORD CITY	2-4		Samuels, Lowen
28	15 Feb	Hendon	1-2		Lowen
29	7 Mar	HENDON	0-4		
30	21	CLAPTON	4-1		Lowen(3), Roystone
31	8 Apr	SUTTON UNITED	3-5		Horseman, Lowen(2)
32	11	MAIDSTONE UNITED	1-1	1500	Lowen
33	14	Leytonstone	4-2		Horseman, French, Styles, Samuels
34	18	Kingstonian	2-4		Lowen, Horseman
35	21	Ilford	1-4		Lowen
36	25	BARKING	2-2		Lowen, Samuels
37	27	WALTHAMSTOW AVENUE	1-2		Lowen
38	29	Tooting & Mitcham United	0-0		

Extra Players: Match 28 - No.11, Williams A. 35-11, Taylor J. 37-4, Hayter J. 38-2, Priestley, M.

F.A. CUP

Round	Date	Opposition	Res.	Att.	Goalscorers
4QR	19 Oct	Barnet	3-6	3500	L.Worley, Bassett, O.G.

F.A. AMATEUR CUP

Round	Date	Opposition	Res.	Att.	Goalscorers
1R	11 Jan	DULWICH HAMLET	3-0	3300	Balson(2), Lowen
2R	1 Feb	WHITLEY BAY	4-2	6636	Lowen(2), Horseman, L.Worley
3R	22	SPENNYMOOR UNITED	2-2	7394	Roystone(pen), Lowen
3Rr	29	Spennymoor United	1-2	4900	Lowen

BERKS & BUCKS SENIOR CUP

Round	Date	Opposition	Res.	Att.	Goalscorers
3R	8 Feb	ABINGDON TOWN	9-0		Balson(4), Lowen(4), French
SF*	14 Mar	Wokingham Town	5-2		Lowen(3), Hodges, Horseman
F*	30	Windsor & Eton	2-1		Hodges, French

* Played at Maidenhead

Final League Table

	P	W	D	L	F	A	Pts.
1 Wimbledon	38	27	6	5	87	44	60
2 Hendon	38	25	4	9	124	38	54
3 Kingstonian	38	24	4	10	100	62	52
4 Sutton United	38	23	5	10	99	64	51
5 Enfield	38	20	10	8	96	56	50
6 Oxford City	38	20	8	10	90	55	48
7 Tooting & Mitcham Utd.	38	19	8	11	78	51	46
8 St. Albans City	38	14	12	12	62	63	40
9 Ilford	38	16	8	14	75	79	40
10 Maidstone United	38	15	8	15	65	71	38
11 Walthamstow Avenue	38	15	6	17	70	66	36
12 Leytonstone	38	14	8	16	66	71	36
13 Wycombe Wanderers	38	13	6	19	74	80	32
14 Hitchin Town	38	14	4	20	67	100	32
15 Bromley	38	11	8	19	64	75	30
16 Barking	38	10	9	19	46	69	29
17 Woking	38	10	9	19	46	88	29
18 Corinthian Casuals	38	10	4	24	52	92	24
19 Dulwich Hamlet	38	6	12	20	47	97	24
20 Clapton	38	2	5	31	31	100	9

SEASON 1964-65
ISTHMIAN LEAGUE

No.	Date	Opposition	Res.	Att.	Goalscorers
1	22 Aug	KINGSTONIAN	1-1		Samuels
2	25	Leytonstone	1-8		Samuels
3	29	Dulwich Hamlet	1-0		Wright
4	1 Sep	LEYTONSTONE	2-3		Samuels, Cooper(pen)
5	5	Wealdstone	2-4		Samuels, Styles
6	12	WOKING	6-1		Horseman(4), Samuels(2)
7	17	Sutton United	1-2		Styles
8	19	BROMLEY	3-1		D.Worley, Samuels, Horseman
9	26	Walthamstow Avenue	1-2		Samuels
10	30	WEALDSTONE	0-3		
11	3 Oct	Corinthian-Casuals	2-2		Horseman(2)
12	6	ST. ALBANS CITY	1-3	1700	Bates
13	10	BARKING	3-1		Bates, Horseman(2)
14	13	HITCHIN TOWN	6-0		Bates(3), O.G., Baker, Horseman
15	24	CLAPTON	2-3		Horseman, French
16	29	HENDON	3-2		Samuels, French, Bates
17	31	Maidstone United	1-2		Knox(pen)
18	7 Nov	TOOTING & MITCHAM UTD	1-6		Baker
19	14	Barking	2-2		Knox, Horseman
20	21	St. Albans City	1-2		L.Worley
21	1 Dec	Hendon	2-9		French, Bates
22	5	ILFORD	2-2		Baker, L.Worley
23	12	Kingstonian	1-3		French
24	19	WALTHAMSTOW AVENUE	3-3		Bates, Horseman, Samuels
25	26	Oxford City	0-4		
26	16 Jan	ENFIELD	2-3		Gale, Bates
27	23	Tooting & Mitcham United	1-1		French
28	30	CORINTHIAN-CASUALS	3-1		Knox, French, Bates
29	13 Feb	DULWICH HAMLET	2-0		Horseman, O.G.
30	20	Clapton	3-0		Bates(2), Knox
31	24	OXFORD CITY	2-1		Bates, L.Worley
32	27	Enfield	0-4		
33	13 Mar	SUTTON UNITED	1-1		Horseman
34	30	Hitchin Town	1-3		Horseman
35	3 Apr	Bromley	2-0		L.Worley, Horseman
36	10	MAIDSTONE UNITED	2-0		Bates(2,1pen)
37	17	Ilford	0-1		
38	19	Woking	3-1		Horseman(2), Samuels

F.A. CUP

4QR	17 Oct	Hayes	0-7	2469	

F.A. AMATEUR CUP

1R	2 Jan	Leytonstone	2-2	1241	L.Worley, Samuels
1Rr	9	LEYTONSTONE	0-2	3436	

BERKS & BUCKS SENIOR CUP

2R	6 Feb	AYLESBURY UNITED	3-0		Horseman, Bates, Knox
SF*	20 Mar	Chesham United	2-3	1200	O.G., L.Worley

* Played at Aylesbury

Final League Table

	P	W	D	L	F	A	Pts.
1 Hendon	38	28	7	3	123	49	63
2 Enfield	38	29	5	4	98	35	63
3 Kingstonian	38	24	8	6	86	44	56
4 Leytonstone	38	24	5	9	115	62	53
5 Oxford City	38	20	7	11	76	50	47
6 St. Albans City	38	18	9	11	63	43	45
7 Sutton United	38	17	11	10	74	57	45
8 Wealdstone	38	19	6	13	93	68	44
9 Bromley	38	14	11	13	71	80	39
10 Tooting & Mitcham Utd.	38	15	7	16	71	66	37
11 Hitchin Town	38	13	9	16	61	66	35
12 Walthamstow Avenue	38	15	5	18	63	82	35
13 Wycombe Wanderers	38	13	7	18	70	85	33
14 Corinthian Casuals	38	13	7	18	56	77	33
15 Barking	38	10	8	20	59	60	28
16 Ilford	38	8	8	22	43	89	24
17 Maidstone United	38	8	6	24	49	86	22
18 Dulwich Hamlet	38	8	5	25	45	79	21
19 Clapton	38	8	3	27	43	91	19
20 Woking	38	7	4	27	44	113	18

Championship determined by play-off: Hendon 4, Enfield 1.

Season 1964/65: Tour of Holland, June 6th-9th 1965
(Back) Cramp (Driver), Jackson, Knox, Merrick, French, Faulkner, J.Maskell, Gale, Bates, Holliday, Samuels
(Middle) Wicks, Pearce, Thompson, R.Maskell, Wheeler, Hayter, Darvill (Front) Cooper, Birch, Horseman, Baker, Sheppard

Season 1965/66
(Back) Baker, Rundle, Maskell, Beck, Gale, Bates.
(Front) L.Worley, Samuels, Bradshaw, Horseman, Merrick.

SEASON 1965-66
ISTHMIAN LEAGUE

No.	Date	Opposition	Res.	Att.	Goalscorers
1	21 Aug	Walthamstow Avenue	3-5		Bates(2), Thompson
2	25	WOKING	3-0		Bates(2,1pen), Samuels
3	28	CLAPTON	6-1		Bates(4,1pen), Samuels, Horseman
4	30	Barking	1-0		Samuels
5	8 Sep	HITCHIN TOWN	5-0		Samuels, Horseman, Bates(2), Gale
6	11	ILFORD	6-3		Bantock(2), Bates(2,pens), O.G., Worley
7	14	Enfield	2-6		Samuels, Worley
8	18	HENDON	1-1		Bates
9	23	Corinthian-Casuals	4-2		Gale, Bates, O.G., Samuels
10	25	Sutton United	1-1		Bates(pen)
11	29	WEALDSTONE	2-1		Bates, Gale
12	2 Oct	Tooting & Mitcham United	2-1		Horseman, O.G.
13	5	Hitchin Town	4-3		Samuels, Horseman, Bantock, Bates
14	9	KINGSTONIAN	3-1		Horseman, Bates(2)
15	20	ENFIELD	1-0	4000	Bates(pen)
16	23	Maidstone United	0-2		
17	30	TOOTING & MITCHAM UTD	2-1		Bates, Gale
18	6 Nov	Kingstonian	1-1		Horseman
19	19	Oxford City	3-2		Samuels(2), Horseman
20	27	DULWICH HAMLET	4-1		Bates(2), Samuels, Horseman
21	4 Dec	Leytonstone	3-9		Horseman, Bates, Merrick
22	11	Bromley	6-2		Bates(3), Horseman(2), Merrick
23	18	SUTTON UNITED	3-2		Worley, Horseman, Merrick
24	27	OXFORD CITY	1-1		Samuels
25	8 Jan	St. Albans City	1-2	1139	Merrick
26	15	WALTHAMSTOW AVENUE	4-1		Horseman(3), Samuels
27	29	MAIDSTONE UNITED	3-0	2500	Merrick, Bates(2,1pen)
28	5 Mar	BARKING	2-1		Horseman, Bates
29	21	Wealdstone	1-1		Samuels
30	25	Woking	3-1		Merrick, Horseman, Bates(pen)
31	30	Dulwich Hamlet	5-1		O.G., Merrick, Gale, Samuels, Glass
32	2 Apr	CORINTHIAN-CASUALS	2-1		Bates(2)
33	5	Hendon	3-1		Horseman, Samuels, Merrick
34	8	LEYTONSTONE	1-1	5800	Horseman
35	11	Clapton	4-2		Bates, Glass, Horseman, Gale
36	23	BROMLEY	0-3		
37	30	Ilford	0-4		
38	3 May	ST. ALBANS CITY	4-0		Horseman(2), Bates(2,1pen)

F.A. CUP

Rd	Date	Opposition	Res.	Att.	Goalscorers
4QR	16 Oct	Metropolitan Police	3-2	1334	Horseman(2), Samuels
1R	13 Nov	Guildford City	2-2	5300	Samuels, Worley
1Rr	17	GUILDFORD CITY	0-1	6811	

F.A. AMATEUR CUP

Rd	Date	Opposition	Res.	Att.	Goalscorers
1R	1 Jan	AVELEY	2-1	3600	Horseman, Bates
2R	22	PENRITH	1-0	5100	Roystone
3R	12 Feb	ST. ALBANS CITY	1-1	5964	Horseman
3Rr	19	St. Albans City	3-0	5088	Merrick, Horseman, Samuels
4R	26	Hendon	1-2	5489	Horseman

BERKS & BUCKS SENIOR CUP

Rd	Date	Opposition	Res.	Att.	Goalscorers
2R	26 Jan	THATCHAM	12-0	888	Bates(5), Horseman(2), Roystone, #
3R	5 Feb	CHESHAM UNITED	4-3	2611	Bates(2,1pen), Merrick(2)
SF*	12 Mar	Maidenhead United	2-2	2230	Samuels, Horseman
SFr*	19	Maidenhead United	0-1	2300	

* Played at Chesham # Extra scorers = Baker, Merrick, Samuels(2)

Final League Table

	P	W	D	L	F	A	Pts.
Leytonstone	38	27	7	4	98	33	61
Hendon	38	27	5	6	111	55	59
Enfield	38	24	8	6	104	54	56
Wycombe Wanderers	38	25	6	7	100	65	56
Kingstonian	38	24	5	9	94	55	53
Wealdstone	36	20	6	12	90	64	46
Maidstone United	38	19	6	13	74	61	44
St. Albans City	38	19	5	14	57	56	43
Sutton United	38	17	7	14	83	72	41
Tooting & Mitcham Utd.	38	16	7	15	65	58	39
Corinthian Casuals	38	17	5	16	74	67	39
Woking	38	12	10	16	60	83	34
Walthamstow Avenue	38	12	9	17	81	75	33
Oxford City	38	10	9	19	49	72	29
Barking	38	10	7	21	51	72	27
Bromley	38	10	5	23	69	101	25
Ilford	38	7	10	21	50	84	24
Hitchin Town	38	6	8	24	57	118	20
Clapton	38	5	6	27	46	103	16
Dulwich Hamlet	38	5	5	28	30	95	15

SEASON 1966-67
ISTHMIAN LEAGUE

Players: Wells H., Roystone P., Beck J., Baker B., Rundle I., Gale C., Worley L., Samuels K., Bates P., Horseman A., Merrick L., Maskell J., Thompson S., Hunt B., French B., Sherbourne V., Priestley M., Busby V., Eyres P., Faulkner V., Petit D.

No.	Date	Opposition	Res.	Att.	Goalscorers
1	20 Aug	CLAPTON	4-1		Horseman(3), Samuels
2	23	Hitchin	3-1		Horseman, Samuels(2)
3	27	Kingstonian	0-1		
4	29	OXFORD CITY	3-2		Bates, Samuels, Beck
5	3 Sep	Hendon	0-0		
6	7	DULWICH HAMLET	3-0		Samuels, Horseman(2)
7	10	Bromley	2-3		Horseman(2)
8	14	ENFIELD	1-0	3000	Horseman
9	17	ILFORD	0-0		
10	20	St. Albans City	1-4	1102	Samuels
11	24	Maidstone United	4-0		Samuels(2), Horseman(2)
12	1 Oct	BARKING	4-1		Bates(3,2pens), Gale
13	6	Walthamstow Avenue	1-1		Horseman
14	8	Tooting & Mitcham United	5-2		Smuels,Gale,Mrrick,Horsemn,Btes(p)
15	24	ST. ALBANS CITY	7-1		Samuels(3),Horseman,Merrick,Btes
16	29	MAIDSTONE UNITED	5-0		Bates(3), Horseman, Samuels
17	5 Nov	Corinthian-Casuals	4-0		Bates(2), Samuels, Worley
18	8	WEALDSTONE	2-5	3000	Bates(2)
19	12	LEYTONSTONE	0-4		
20	19	Woking	6-2		Horseman(3), Samuels(2), Busby
21	3 Dec	BROMLEY	3-0	2100	Roystone, Busby, Worley
22	17	Sutton United	1-1	900	Bates
23	21	WALTHAMSTOW AVENUE	2-6		Merrick, O.G.
24	27	Oxford City	3-3		Merrick, Horseman(2)
25	31	CORINTHIAN-CASUALS	1-0		Bates(pen)
26	7 Jan	Barking	1-1		Samuels
27	21	TOOTING & MITCHAM UTD	4-0		Horseman(3,1pen), Merrick
28	28	SUTTON UNITED	1-1		Horseman
29	18 Feb	HITCHIN TOWN	2-1		Horseman(2)
30	4 Mar	Ilford	5-1		Horseman(3), Merrick, Busby
31	18	WOKING	2-1		Horseman, Samuels
32	1 Apr	Dulwich Hamlet	3-0		Busby, Worley, Samuels
33	12	HENDON	4-2		Roystone, Samuels(2), Bates
34	15	Wealdstone	0-7		
35	19	KINGSTONIAN	1-0		Samuels
36	24	Enfield	2-1		Busby, Samuels
37	6 Mar	Clapton	1-1		Samuels
38	11	Leytonstone	1-0		Samuels

F.A. CUP

Round	Date	Opposition	Res.	Att.	Goalscorers
4QR	15 Oct	CHESHUNT	8-0	3187	Smuels,Hrsemn(4),Btes(2,1p),Frnch
1R	26 Nov	BEDFORD TOWN	1-1	7488	Samuels
1Rr	30	Bedford Town	3-3	7641	Bates, Horseman, Merrick
1R2r	5 Dec	BEDFORD TOWN	1-1	8821	Samuels
1R3r	8	Bedford Town	2-3	8105	Horseman(2)

F.A. AMATEUR CUP

Round	Date	Opposition	Res.	Att.	Goalscorers
1R	14 Jan	Leytonstone	2-4	2455	Beck, Horseman(pen)

BERKS & BUCKS SENIOR CUP

Round	Date	Opposition	Res.	Att.	Goalscorers
3R	4 Feb	PRINCES RISBOROUGH T.	6-0	2200	Busby(3), Samuels(2), Horseman
SF*	25	Aylesbury United	5-0		Horsemn(2),Worley,Mrrick,Smuels
F#	27 Mar	Chesham United	1-2		Merrick

* Played at Marlow # Played at Maidenhead * Replaced by substitute

Final League Table

	P	W	D	L	F	A	Pts
Sutton United	38	26	7	5	89	33	59
Walthamstow Avenue	38	22	12	4	89	47	56
Wycombe Wanderers	38	23	8	7	92	54	54
Enfield	38	25	2	11	87	33	52
Hendon	38	20	9	9	64	37	49
Tooting & Mitcham Utd.	38	19	10	9	76	60	48
Leytonstone	38	19	9	10	67	38	47
St. Albans City	38	16	12	10	59	45	44
Kingstonian	38	18	8	12	60	49	44
Oxford City	38	15	9	14	74	61	39
Woking	38	13	10	15	65	71	36
Wealdstone	38	13	8	17	72	73	34
Barking	38	11	12	15	56	61	34
Bromley	36	12	7	19	50	67	31
Clapton	38	10	8	20	49	92	28
Ilford	38	8	10	20	43	77	26
Corinthian Casuals	38	9	7	22	45	68	25
Maidstone United	38	6	10	22	43	90	22
Hitchin Town	38	8	6	24	39	89	22
Dulwich Hamlet	36	3	4	31	33	107	10

SEASON 1967-68
ISTHMIAN LEAGUE

No.	Date	Opposition	Res.	Att.	Goalscorers
1	19 Aug	Walthamstow Avenue	2-4		Samuels, Horseman
2	22	HITCHIN TOWN	6-1		Hrseman(3), Wrley, Smuels, Roystne
3	26	DULWICH HAMLET	3-0		Horseman, Merrick, Worley
4	28	St. Albans City	1-2	1109	Worley
5	2 Sep	Kingstonian	2-0		Horseman(pen), Roystone
6	5	HENDON	2-3		Merrick, Horseman
7	9	CLAPTON	4-0		Horseman(3), Busby
8	12	Woking	3-3		Busby, Horseman(2,1pen)
9	16	Enfield	0-1		
10	19	WOKING	2-4		Samuels, Worley
11	23	CORINTHIAN-CASUALS	1-1		Horseman
12	26	Ilford	2-1		Samuels, Bates
13	30	Wealdstone	0-2		
14	7 Oct	LEYTONSTONE	2-4		Horseman(pen), Samuels
15	10	ST. ALBANS CITY	0-0		
16	14	Barking	1-3		Samuels
17	21	TOOTING & MITCHAM UTD	2-3		Merrick, Horseman
18	24	BARKING	5-2		Samuels(2), Horseman, Hlmes, Wrley
19	18 Nov	WALTHAMSTOW AVENUE	1-2		Baker
20	25	Bromley	1-3		Horseman
21	2 Dec	Maidstone United	2-1	223	Holmes, Horseman(pen)
22	16	Sutton United	1-4		Horseman
23	26	OXFORD CITY	2-3		Samuels(2)
24	30	ILFORD	0-0		
25	6 Jan	Hitchin Town	3-3		Merrick, Horseman(2)
26	27	MAIDSTONE UNITED	4-1		Horseman(2,1pen), Samuels(2)
27	10 Feb	Tooting & Mitcham United	3-2		Merrick, Busby, Horseman
28	17	Oxford City	1-3		Holmes
29	24	BROMLEY	4-2		Holmes, Samuels, Busby, Gale
30	16 Mar	ENFIELD	0-2		
31	23	Clapton	5-2		Merrick, Wrley, Busby(2), Horsemn(p)
32	30	KINGSTONIAN	3-2		Busby(2), Merrick
33	6 Apr	Corinthian-Casuals	3-0		Merrick, Worley, Samuels
34	13	Hendon	0-6		
35	17	Dulwich Hamlet	0-5		
36	22	SUTTON UNITED	1-2		Horseman
37	27	Leytonstone	0-5		
38	4 May	WEALDSTONE	1-3		Worley

F.A. CUP

| 4QR | 28 Oct | DAGENHAM | 0-2 | 2000 | |

F.A. AMATEUR CUP

| 1R | 20 Jan | City of Norwich S.O.B.U. | 0-1 | 2003 | |

BERKS & BUCKS SENIOR CUP

3R	3 Feb	Didcot Town	4-1		Samuels(2), Worley, Busby
SF	2 Mar	WOLVERTON TOWN	3-3		Samuels(2), Holmes
SFr	9	Wolverton Town	3-0		Merrick, Busby, Samuels
F*	15 Apr	Slough Town	3-2	3422	Horseman(2), Samuels

* Played at Chesham

Final League Table

	P	W	D	L	F	A	Pts.
Enfield	38	28	8	2	85	22	64
Sutton United	38	22	11	5	89	27	55
Hendon	38	23	6	9	90	36	52
Leytonstone	38	21	10	7	78	41	52
St. Albans City	38	20	8	10	78	41	48
Walthamstow Avenue	38	19	9	10	81	64	47
Wealdstone	38	19	8	11	50	45	46
Tooting & Mitcham Utd.	38	19	5	14	57	45	43
Barking	38	17	8	13	75	57	42
Oxford City	38	17	4	17	59	58	38
Kingstonian	38	14	10	14	56	61	38
Hitchin Town	38	14	9	15	61	73	37
Bromley	38	12	10	16	58	80	34
Wycombe Wanderers	38	13	5	20	73	85	31
Dulwich Hamlet	38	10	7	21	39	66	27
Clapton	38	10	7	21	51	88	27
Woking	38	8	8	22	50	90	24
Corinthian Casuals	38	7	10	21	40	80	24
Ilford	38	7	7	24	41	77	21

C.Gale   P.Roystone
          L.Merrick
A.Horseman
V.Faulkner   V.Busby
   ?   W.Gallacher
M.Priestley T.Anning J.Maskell
K.Samuels   B.French
B.Darvill   V.Beck

Season 1966/67:

Season 1970/71: (Back) Wharton, Goldsworthy, Delaney (Capt.), Faulkner, Maskell, Maclean, Holt, Williams
(Middle) B.R.Lee (Man.), Nobbs, Rundle, Fuschillo, Searle, Gale, Bremer, Powell, Pritchard, Blunt, T.Thomas, J.Reardon(Asst.Man.)
(Front) Hutchinson, Anthony, Crump (Sec.), Seymour (President), Adams (Patron), Smethurst (Chairman),
R.N. Lee (Treasurer), Horseman, Baker (Front sitting) Sheppard (Attendant)

SEASON 1968-69
ISTHMIAN LEAGUE

No.	Date	Opposition	Res.	Att.	Goalscorers
1	17 Aug	BARKING	4-0		Samuels, Horseman(2), Merrick
2	20	Hitchin Town	2-3		O.G. Merrick
3	24	Leytonstone	2-1		Horseman, Merrick
4	27	HENDON	2-0		Merrick, Horseman
5	31	DULWICH HAMLET	1-0		Merrick
6	7 Sep	Maidstone United	1-3		Horseman
7	11	WOKING	4-0		Samuels(2), Horseman, Merrick
8	14	Sutton United	1-0		Busby
9	17	CORINTHIAN-CASUALS	8-0		Horseman(4,1pen), OG, Worley(2), Samuels
10	28	CLAPTON	1-0		O.G.
11	1 Oct	Wealdstone	0-2	1900	
12	5	Dulwich Hamlet	2-0		Temel, Busby
13	8	ST. ALBANS CITY	1-0	1250	Samuels
14	12	KINGSTONIAN	1-1		Samuels
15	15	Tooting & Mitcham United	2-2		Merrick(2)
16	19	Ilford	2-1		Worley, Thomas
17	22	St. Albans City	0-2		
18	2 Nov	BROMLEY	4-0		Horseman(2), Faulkner(2)
19	9	MAIDSTONE UNITED	2-3		Faulkner, Merrick
20	16	Kingstonian	0-3		
21	23	LEYTONSTONE	2-1		Horseman, Faulkner
22	7 Dec	WEALDSTONE	0-1		
23	21	HITCHIN TOWN	3-0		Samuels(2), Horseman
24	28	Clapton	0-0		
25	4 Jan	OXFORD CITY	3-0		Thomas, Horseman(2)
26	11	Woking	3-2		Samuels, Horseman(2)
27	15 Feb	ILFORD	1-0		Samuels
28	22	Bromley	1-0		Horseman
29	8 Mar	Corinthian-Casuals	2-0		Worley, Horseman
30	15	TOOTING & MITCHAM UTD	0-0		
31	17	Enfield	2-4		Samuels, O.G.
32	26	Oxford City	2-2		Faulkner, Horseman
33	29	Walthamstow Avenue	4-3		Faulkner(2), Busby, Horseman
34	4 Apr	ENFIELD	1-0	5000	Faulkner
35	12	Barking	0-0		
36	19	SUTTON UNITED	0-1		
37	3 May	WALTHAMSTOW AVENUE	4-1		Horseman(2), Samuels(2)
38	12	Hendon	2-1		Horseman, Busby

F.A. CUP

1QR	21 Sep	ST. ALBANS CITY	0-0	2651	
1QRr	26	St. Albans City	0-1	2300	

F.A. AMATEUR CUP

1R	14 Dec	Oxford City	2-3		Horseman, Rundle

BERKS & BUCKS SENIOR CUP

3R	1 Feb	Wokingham Town	0-1		

Final League Table

	P	W	D	L	F	A	Pts
Enfield	38	27	7	4	103	28	61
Hitchin Town	38	23	10	5	67	41	56
Sutton United	38	22	9	7	83	29	53
Wycombe Wanderers	38	23	6	9	70	37	52
Wealdstone	38	20	11	7	73	48	51
Hendon	38	22	5	11	69	47	49
St. Albans City	38	17	13	8	75	44	47
Barking	38	20	7	11	69	46	47
Oxford City	38	18	8	12	76	64	44
Tooting & Mitcham Utd.	38	18	10	12	68	55	42
Leytonstone	38	15	4	16	71	53	40
Kingstonian	38	15	8	15	62	56	38
Walthamstow Avenue	38	10	10	18	47	71	30
Maidstone United	38	10	8	20	47	75	28
Clapton	38	10	7	21	52	76	27
Woking	38	8	7	23	45	77	23
Bromley	38	8	7	23	52	95	23
Dulwich Hamlet	38	6	9	23	31	77	21
Ilford	38	6	8	24	33	77	20
Corinthian Casuals	38	2	4	32	23	120	8

SEASON 1969-70
ISTHMIAN LEAGUE

No.	Date	Opposition	Res.	Att.	Goalscorers
1	9 Aug	BROMLEY	5-0		Busby, Horseman(2), Hatt, Anthony
2	12	WEALDSTONE	2-2	1690	Delaney, Anthony
3	16	Sutton United	2-1		Horseman, Worley
4	19	Hitchin Town	2-1		Delaney(pen), Hatt
5	23	ILFORD	2-0		Rundle, Samuels
6	26	ENFIELD	1-2	2527	Horseman
7	30	Tooting & Mitcham United	0-0		
8	2 Sep	St. Albans City	0-3		
9	6	LEYTONSTONE	0-0	1342	
10	9	Dulwich Hamlet	4-0		Anthony, Horseman(3)
11	13	Hendon	1-0		Anthony
12	23	ST. ALBANS CITY	0-0	1676	
13	27	Bromley	1-0		Worley
14	30	DULWICH HAMLET	2-1		Horseman(2)
15	11 Oct	WALTHAMSTOW AVENUE	3-0		Searle, Rundle, Anthony
16	15	Corinthian-Casuals	3-0		Horseman(2), Searle
17	25	Enfield	2-2		Searle, Delaney
18	8 Nov	CLAPTON	4-1	1701	Searle, Busby, Anthony, Horseman(p)
19	15	Maidstone United	2-1	697	Anthony, Horseman
20	29	MAIDSTONE UNITED	4-0		Anthony(2), Horseman(pen), Searle
21	6 Dec	Woking	1-1	567	Delaney(pen)
22	26	Oxford City	3-0		Delaney(pen), Searle, Horseman
23	27	OXFORD CITY	6-1	2724	Hutchinson(2), Searle, Horsemn(2), Anthn
24	3 Jan	Clapton	2-0	450	Searle, Delaney(pen)
25	7 Feb	KINGSTONIAN	3-0		Hutchinson(2), Suddaby
26	16 Mar	HENDON	0-0		
27	21	Ilford	3-2		Horseman, Delaney, Suddaby
28	24	WOKING	3-0		Horseman, Searle, Anthony
29	28	Walthamstow Avenue	5-1		Delaney, Anthony, Horseman(3)
30	30	HITCHIN TOWN	2-0		Delaney, Searle
31	3 Apr	CORINTHIAN CASUALS	7-0		Hutchinsn, Horsemn(2), Searle(3), Faulknr
32	10	Barking	1-1		Horseman
33	14	Wealdstone	0-0		
34	18	SUTTON UNITED	2-2	2580	Hutchinson, Searle
35	25	Leytonstone	1-0		O.G.
36	2 May	TOOTING & MITCHAM U.	2-1	2043	Delaney(pen), Suddaby
37	6	BARKING	3-0		Delaney(pen), Horseman(2)
38	9	Kingstonian	1-1		Searle

F.A. CUP

1QR	20 Sep	DULWICH HAMLET	2-1		Worley, Faulkner
2QR	4 Oct	ERITH & BELVEDERE	2-0		Delaney(pen), Busby
3QR	18	HITCHIN TOWN	1-0		Delaney(pen)
4QR	1 Nov	BARNET	0-0	4200	
4QRr	4	Barnet	0-3	2956	

F.A. AMATEUR CUP

4QR	22 Nov	HERTFORD TOWN	5-1	2705	Blunt, Busby(2), Delaney(p), Searle
1R	13 Dec	Croydon Amateurs	1-0		Searle
2R	10 Jan	TOOTING &	0-0	3127	
2Rr	17	Tooting & Mitcham United	2-1	2100	Blunt, Anthony
3R	31	Wealdstone	1-0	4129	Horseman
4R	21 Feb	ST. ALBANS CITY	0-2	9520	

BERKS & BUCKS SENIOR CUP

2R	20 Dec	HAZELL'S (AYLESBURY)	10-0		Blunt, Horseman, Baker(2) *
3R	24 Jan	WOKINGHAM TOWN	2-1	2040	Delaney, Hutchinson
SF	14 Mar	Maidenhead United	0-1		

* Extra scorers - Lailey(2), Busby(3), Suddaby

Final League Table

	P	W	D	L	F	A	Pts
Enfield	38	27	8	3	91	26	62
Wycombe Wanderers	38	25	11	2	85	24	61
Sutton United	38	24	9	5	75	35	57
Barking	38	21	9	8	83	47	51
Hendon	38	19	12	7	77	44	50
St. Albans City	38	21	8	9	69	40	50
Hitchin Town	38	19	10	9	71	40	48
Tooting & Mitcham Utd.	38	19	5	14	88	62	43
Leytonstone	38	17	7	14	57	41	41
Wealdstone	38	15	10	13	53	48	40
Oxford City	38	15	7	16	81	78	37
Kingstonian	38	13	9	16	55	57	35
Ilford	38	8	15	15	42	73	31
Dulwich Hamlet	38	8	12	18	46	66	28
Woking	38	10	7	21	46	69	27
Walthamstow Avenue	38	11	5	22	52	81	27
Clapton	38	9	7	22	45	87	25
Maidstone United	38	7	8	23	48	84	22
Corinthian Casuals	38	3	9	26	30	99	15
Bromley	38	3	4	31	28	111	10

SEASON 1970-71
ISTHMIAN LEAGUE

No.	Date	Opposition	Res.	Att.	Goalscorers
1	15 Aug	WALTHAMSTOW AVENUE	3-2	1825	Delaney(2,1pen), Anthony
2	18	Wealdstone	6-1	2000	Searle,Pritch(2),Hutch,Anthony,Delney
3	22	Maidstone United	4-1	583	Searle, Bremer(2), Anthony
4	25	CORINTHIAN-CASUALS	3-0	2194	Searle(3)
5	29	SUTTON UNITED	4-0	2892	O.G., Pritchard, Delaney, Bremer
6	31	Hitchin Town	2-1		Bremer, Blunt
7	5 Sep	Clapton	1-0		Hutchinson
8	8	ENFIELD	1-0	4182	Hutchinson
9	12	Bromley	4-0		Horsemn,Htchinsn,Dlaney(p),Anthny
10	15	Tooting & Mitcham United	0-0		
11	26	LEYTONSTONE	3-1	2858	Horseman(2), Delaney
12	28	WEALDSTONE	2-1	2999	Delaney, Bremer
13	3 Oct	Walthamstow avenue	1-1		Searle
14	6	Kingstonian	1-2		O.G.
15	17	DULWICH HAMLET	1-0	2600	O.G.
16	27	ST. ALBANS CITY	3-2	3136	MacLean, Bremer(2)
17	31	BARKING	1-2	3000	Bremer
18	14 Nov	Leytonstone	2-2		Horseman, Delaney
19	28	KINGSTONIAN	4-0	1820	Searle, Blunt, Horseman, Bremer
20	1 Dec	St. Albans City	0-2		
21	12	MAIDSTONE UNITED	5-0	1963	Horseman(2), Searle(3)
22	19	Ilford	2-0		Bremer, Horseman
23	16 Jan	TOOTING & MITCHAM UTD	5-2	2215	Searle(3), Horseman, Bremer
24	27	OXFORD CITY	3-0		Hutchinson, Pritchard, Searle
25	9 Feb	Woking	2-0		Horseman, Searle
26	27	HITCHIN TOWN	4-1	2628	Hutchinson, Searle(2), Pritchard
27	1 Mar	Enfield	1-1		Hutchinson
28	6	Dulwich Hamlet	1-1		Delaney
29	16	HENDON	2-1	1618	Horseman(pen), Delaney
30	20	CLAPTON	5-1	2151	Delaney,Pritchard,Searle(2),Bremer
31	25	Corinthian-Casuals	4-0		Bremer, Horseman(2), Delaney
32	27	Barking	3-2		Horseman, Hutchinson(2)
33	29	WOKING	2-0	2056	Delaney, Searle
34	3 Apr	BROMLEY	2-0		Searle, Horseman
35	6	Hendon	3-1	1103	Horseman, Anthony, Hutchinson
36	17	Sutton United	1-0	3000	Pritchard
37	22	Oxford City	1-1		Searle
38	1 May	ILFORD	1-3	2528	Horseman

F.A. CUP

1QR	19 Sep	WOLVERTON TOWN & B.R.	8-1	2304	Baker, Pritchard, O.G., Searle, *
2QR	10 Oct	Banbury United	3-0	2787	Searle, O.G., Pritchard
3QR	24	Dunstable Town	4-0	2348	Htchinsn,Dlaney(p),Searle,Prtchrd
4QR	7 Nov	KETTERING TOWN	5-0	4518	Delaney(2,1p),Horseman(2),Searle
1R	21	SLOUGH TOWN	1-1	6662	Horseman
1Rr	25	Slough Town	0-1	6800	

Extra scorers - Hutchinson(3), Horseman

F.A. AMATEUR CUP

1R	9 Jan	WEALDSTONE	1-0	4345	Pritchard
2R	30	ENFIELD	2-1	6144	Delaney(2)
3R	13 Feb	OLDBURY UNITED	4-0	7066	Searle,Bremer,Pritchard,Horseman
4R	13 Mar	SKELMERSDALE UNITED	0-3	10203	

BERKS & BUCKS SENIOR CUP

3R	6 Feb	Didcot Town	5-2		Hutch'son,Pritchard,Horseman(3)
SF	20	WOKINGHAM TOWN	2-0	2770	Searle, Delaney(pen)
F*	28 Apr	Slough Town	0-0	3794	
Fr#	10 May	Slough Town	0-1	3400	

* Played at Reading # Played at Marlow

Final League Table

	P	W	D	L	F	A	Pts
Wycombe Wanderers	38	28	6	4	93	32	62
Sutton United	38	29	3	6	76	35	61
St. Albans City	38	23	10	5	87	26	56
Enfield	38	24	7	7	67	24	55
Ilford	38	21	7	10	74	51	49
Hendon	38	18	11	9	81	37	47
Barking	38	20	4	14	89	59	44
Leytonstone	38	17	10	11	68	50	44
Woking	38	18	6	14	57	50	42
Walthamstow Avenue	38	14	11	13	63	52	39
Oxford City	38	13	10	15	51	48	36
Hitchin Town	38	12	9	17	46	60	33
Wealdstone	38	12	8	18	45	64	32
Tooting & Mitcham Utd.	38	11	9	18	44	66	31
Kingstonian	38	11	8	19	53	71	30
Bromley	38	10	6	22	34	77	26
Dulwich Hamlet	38	7	10	21	30	66	24
Maidstone United	38	7	6	25	42	84	20
Clapton	38	5	7	26	33	101	17
Corinthian Casuals	38	2	8	28	23	103	12

SEASON 1971-72
ISTHMIAN LEAGUE

No.	Date	Opposition	Res.	Att.	Goalscorers
1	14 Aug	ILFORD	2-0	2700	Birdseye, Bremer
2	17	HENDON	1-0	2700	Pritchard
3	21	Leytonstone	0-0		
4	24	ST. ALBANS CITY	4-1	3500	Searle, Waughman, Pritchard, Horseman(p)
5	28	BROMLEY	3-0	2800	Birdseye, Searle(2)
6	30	Barking	1-2		Horseman
7	4 Sep	Dulwich Hamlet	4-0		Waughman, Searle, Horseman, Brmer
8	7	CLAPTON	8-0	2600	Delaney(2,1p), Searle, Waughmn(2), *
9	11	Enfield	4-0	1800	Delaney(3,2pens), Searle
10	14	HITCHIN TOWN	4-0		Delaney, Pritchard(2), Williams
11	20	Hayes	0-0		
12	25	Bishop's Stortford	1-0		Waughman
13	28	OXFORD CITY	6-2	3000	OG, Holifield, Dlaney, Searle(2), Waughmn
14	2 Oct	WALTON & HERSHAM	2-0	3200	Hutchinson, Holifield
15	9	Kingstonian	1-0		Searle
16	12	Hitchin Town	3-0	784	Pritchard, Searle, Delaney
17	16	WALTHAMSTOW AVENUE	2-0	2000	Horseman, Hutchinson
18	23	TOOTING & MITCHAM UTD	1-0		Delaney(pen)
19	26	Woking	4-0		Pritchard(4)
20	30	Sutton United	2-1		Delaney, Searle
21	6 Nov	BARKING	2-1	2800	Holifield, Horseman
22	13	Corinthian-Casuals	4-0		Searle, Birdseye, Delaney(2,1pen)
23	20	HAYES	0-1	2400	
24	24	St. Albans City	0-1		
25	27	Bromley	2-1		Horseman(pen), Pritchard
26	11 Dec	WOKING	1-0	2100	Searle
27	18	CORINTHIAN CASUALS	5-0	2100	Pritchard(2), Searle(2), Waughman
28	27	Oxford City	4-1		Horseman(3), Williams
29	1 Jan	DULWICH HAMLET	6-0	2400	Prtchrd(2), Searle, Htchinsn, Hrsemn
30	12 Feb	LEYTONSTONE	3-1	2700	Horseman(2), Delaney(pen)
31	19	Clapton	7-0		Hrsemn(3), Dlaney(p), Waughmn(2), Prchrd
32	26	Walthamstow Avenue	1-1		Searle
33	25 Mar	Tooting & Mitcham United	4-0		Mellows, Searle(2), Delaney(pen)
34	1 Apr	KINGSTONIAN	2-0		Searle, Hutchinson
35	8	Ilford	3-1		Searle(2), Horseman
36	21	Walton & Hersham	0-2	1800	
37	29	SUTTON UNITED	3-0	2200	Horseman(2,1pen), Searle
38	6 May	Hendon	1-0	1298	Williams
39	13	BISHOP'S STORTFORD	1-3	1350	Waughman
40	17	ENFIELD	0-1	1800	

* Extra scorers – Horseman(2), Birdseye

F.A. CUP

1QR	18 Sep	Maidenhead United	0-2		

F.A. AMATEUR CUP

1R	8 Jan	Aveley	2-2	1612	Horseman, Williams
1Rr	15	AVELEY	5-1	4907	Searle(2), Mellws, Horsemn, Prtchrd
2R	29	SPENNYMOOR UNITED	2-1	5625	Mellows, Delaney
3R	4 Mar	Walton & Hersham	2-1	5320	Mellows, Horseman
4R	11	HAYES	1-0	5273	Searle
SF*	18	Hendon	1-2	9210	Hutchinson

* Played at Brentford

BERKS & BUCKS SENIOR CUP

3R	22 Jan	MAIDENHEAD	3-1	2680	Waughman, O.G., Pritchard
SF	5 Feb	ABINGDON TOWN	3-1	2046	Holifield(2), Pritchard
F*	3 Apr	Slough Town	0-3		

* Played at Maidenhead

Final League Table

	P	W	D	L	F	A	Pts.
Wycombe Wanderers	40	31	3	6	102	20	65
Enfield	40	26	8	6	90	41	60
Walton & Hersham	40	24	8	8	69	25	58
Hendon	40	23	10	7	78	35	56
Bishops Stortford	40	24	5	11	61	37	53
Sutton United	40	21	10	9	77	43	52
St. Albans City	40	23	4	13	74	47	50
Ilford	40	17	11	12	62	52	45
Barking	40	20	4	16	65	61	44
Hitchin Town	40	17	10	13	68	66	44
Bromley	40	16	10	14	67	64	42
Hayes	40	14	12	14	50	48	40
Oxford City	40	13	9	18	67	74	35
Woking	40	11	10	19	52	58	32
Kingstonian	40	10	12	18	49	59	32
Walthamstow Avenue	40	12	8	20	58	70	32
Leytonstone	40	11	9	21	48	68	30
Tooting & Mitcham Utd.	40	6	9	25	38	93	21
Clapton	40	7	7	26	45	118	21
Dulwich Hamlet	40	4	12	24	35	81	20
Corinthian Casuals	40	3	4	33	21	116	10

Season 1971/72 (Back) Gamblin, Williams, Bullock, Rundle, Searle, Holifield, Powell, Horseman (Middle) Wharton, J.Reardon (Asst. Manager), T.Thomas, Wright, Birdseye, Mellows, Maskell, Delaney (Capt.), Hutchinson, Waughman, Pritchard, Avery, B.R. Lee (Manager), Cox, Holt (Front) Pearce, Williams, Crump (Sec.), Smethurst (Chairman), Seymour (President), R.N. Lee (Treasurer), Rackstraw, Goldsworthy (Front sitting) Sheppard (Trainer)

Season 1973/74: (Back) Perrin, Mead, Searle, Evans, Grant, Pritchard (Capt.), Birdseye, Mackenzie, Horseman (Middle) B.Lee(Man.), Avery,Holifield,Bullock,Price,Raine,Maskell,Rundle,Wood, T.Reardon,T.Thomas,Roberts, J.Reardon(Asst.Man.) (Front) Hart, Pearce, R.Lee (Treasurer), Seymour (President), Smethurst (Chairman), Crump (Sec.), Goldsworthy, Williams, Wharton(Front sitting) Sheppard (Team-Attendant).

Final League Tables 1972/73 - 1979/80 Isthmian League

1972/73

	P	W	D	L	F	A	Pts
Hendon	42	34	6	2	88	18	74
Walton & Hersham	42	25	11	6	60	25	61
Leatherhead	42	23	10	9	76	32	56
Wycombe Wanderers	42	25	6	11	66	32	56
Walthamstow Avenue	42	20	12	10	66	48	52
Tooting & Mitcham Utd.	42	20	11	11	73	39	51
Sutton United	42	21	9	12	69	48	51
Kingstonian	42	20	10	12	60	49	50
Enfield	42	20	8	14	90	54	48
Bishops Stortford	42	18	12	12	58	51	48
Hayes	42	19	8	15	69	42	46
Dulwich Hamlet	42	18	9	15	59	52	45
Ilford	42	18	9	15	61	59	45
Leytonstone	42	17	11	14	55	54	45
Woking	42	18	8	16	61	56	44
Hitchin Town	42	15	9	18	52	64	39
Barking	42	8	7	27	45	88	23
St. Albans City	42	5	12	25	34	76	22
Oxford City	42	6	7	29	30	101	19
Bromley	42	4	10	28	31	70	18
Clapton	42	3	11	28	31	100	17
Corinthian Casuals	42	3	8	31	30	106	14

1973/74

	P	W	D	L	F	A	Pts
Wycombe Wanderers	42	27	9	6	96	34	90
Hendon	42	25	13	4	63	20	88
Bishops Stortford	42	26	9	7	78	26	87
Dulwich Hamlet	42	22	11	9	71	38	77
Leatherhead	42	23	6	13	81	44	75
Walton & Hersham	42	20	12	10	68	50	72
Woking	42	22	6	14	63	55	72
Leytonstone	42	20	9	13	63	44	69
Ilford	42	20	8	14	60	44	68
Hayes	42	17	14	11	65	43	65
Oxford City	42	15	16	11	45	47	61
Sutton United	42	13	16	13	51	52	55
Hitchin Town	42	15	10	17	68	73	55
Barking	42	14	12	16	57	58	54
Kingstonian	42	12	15	15	47	46	51
Tooting & Mitcham Utd.	42	14	9	19	57	62	51
Enfield	42	13	11	18	50	57	50
Walthamstow Avenue	42	11	13	18	46	62	46
Bromley	42	7	9	26	37	81	30
Clapton	42	8	3	31	36	128	27
St. Albans City	42	4	7	31	30	92	19
Corinthian Casuals	42	3	4	35	31	107	13

1974/75 Division I

	P	W	D	L	F	A	Pts
Wycombe Wanderers	42	28	11	3	93	30	95
Enfield	42	29	8	5	78	26	95
Dagenham	42	28	5	9	95	44	89
Tooting & Mitcham Utd.	42	25	9	8	78	46	84
Dulwich Hamlet	42	24	10	8	75	38	82
Leatherhead	42	23	10	9	83	42	79
Ilford	42	23	10	9	98	51	79
Oxford City	42	17	9	16	63	56	60
Slough Town	42	17	6	19	68	52	57
Sutton United	42	17	6	19	68	63	57
Bishops Stortford	42	17	6	19	56	64	57
Hitchin Town	42	15	10	17	57	71	55
Hendon	42	15	7	20	59	74	52
Walthamstow Avenue	42	13	9	20	56	62	48
Woking	42	12	10	20	53	73	46
Hayes	42	10	14	18	52	66	44
Barking	42	12	8	22	57	81	44
Leytonstone	42	12	7	23	42	61	43
Kingstonian	42	13	4	25	48	73	43
Clapton	42	12	4	26	46	96	40
Walton & Hersham	42	9	4	29	37	108	31
Bromley	42	6	3	33	25	110	21

1975/76 Division 1

	P	W	D	L	F	A	Pts
Enfield	42	26	9	7	83	38	87
Wycombe Wanderers	42	24	10	8	71	41	82
Dagenham	42	25	6	11	89	55	81
Ilford	42	22	10	10	58	39	76
Dulwich Hamlet	42	22	5	15	67	41	71
Hendon	42	20	11	11	60	41	71
Tooting & Mitcham	42	19	11	12	73	49	68
Leatherhead	42	19	10	13	63	53	67
Staines Town	42	19	9	14	46	37	66
Slough Town	42	17	12	13	58	45	63
Sutton United	42	17	11	14	67	60	62
Bishops Stortford	42	15	12	15	51	47	57
Walthamstow Avenue	42	14	11	17	47	60	53
Woking	42	14	9	19	58	62	51
Barking	42	15	6	21	57	70	51
Hitchin Town	42	13	11	18	45	57	50
Hayes	42	10	19	13	44	48	9
Kingstonian	42	13	8	21	53	87	47
Southall & Ealing Boro'	42	11	9	22	56	69	42
Leytonstone	42	10	10	22	41	63	40
Oxford City	42	9	8	25	29	65	35
Clapton	42	3	3	36	19	112	12

1976/77 Division I

	P	W	D	L	F	A	Pts
Enfield	42	24	12	6	63	34	84
Wycombe Wanderers	42	25	8	9	71	34	83
Dagenham	42	23	10	9	80	39	79
Hendon	42	19	10	13	60	48	67
Tilbury	42	18	13	11	57	49	67
Tooting & Mitcham Utd.	42	18	10	14	85	72	64
Walthamstow Avenue	42	19	7	16	61	55	64
Slough Town	42	18	9	15	51	46	63
Hitchin Town	42	19	6	17	60	66	63
Leatherhead	42	18	7	17	61	47	61
Staines Town	42	16	13	13	52	48	61
Leytonstone	42	16	11	15	59	57	59
Barking	42	16	9	17	63	61	57
Southall & Ealing Boro'	42	15	8	19	52	64	53
Croydon	42	13	10	19	38	52	49
Sutton United	42	14	7	21	40	55	49
Kingstonian	42	13	7	22	45	60	46
Hayes	42	12	10	20	49	69	46
Woking	42	11	12	19	47	61	45
Bishops Stortford	42	11	11	20	51	71	44
Dulwich Hamlet	42	11	8	23	52	68	41
Ilford	42	10	8	24	32	73	38

1977/78 Premier Division

	P	W	D	L	F	A	Pts
Enfield	42	35	5	2	96	27	110
Dagenham	42	24	7	11	78	55	79
Wycombe Wanderers	42	22	9	11	66	41	75
Tooting & Mitcham	42	22	8	12	64	49	74
Hitchin Town	42	20	9	13	69	53	69
Sutton United	42	18	12	12	66	57	66
Leatherhead	42	18	11	13	62	48	65
Croydon	42	18	10	14	61	52	64
Walthamstow Avenue	42	17	12	13	64	61	63
Barking	42	17	7	18	76	66	58
Carshalton Athletic	42	15	11	16	61	63	56
Hayes	42	15	11	16	46	53	56
Hendon	42	16	7	19	57	55	55
Woking	42	14	11	17	62	62	53
Boreham Wood	42	15	8	19	48	65	53
Slough Town	42	14	8	20	52	69	50
Staines Town	42	12	13	17	46	60	49
Tilbury	42	11	12	19	57	68	45
Kingstonian	42	8	13	21	43	65	37
Leytonstone	42	7	15	20	44	71	36
Southall & Ealing Boro'	42	6	15	21	43	74	33
Bishops Stortford	42	7	8	27	36	83	29

1978/79 Premier Division

	P	W	D	L	F	A	Pts
Barking	42	28	9	5	92	50	93
Dagenham	42	25	6	11	83	63	81
Enfield	42	22	11	9	69	37	77
Dulwich Hamlet	42	21	13	8	69	39	76
Slough Town	42	20	12	10	61	44	72
Wycombe Wanderers	42	20	9	13	59	44	69
Woking	42	18	14	10	79	59	68
Croydon	42	19	9	14	61	51	66
Hendon	42	16	14	12	55	48	62
Leatherhead	42	17	9	16	57	45	60
Sutton United	42	15	15	12	69	51	60
Tooting & Mitcham Utd.	42	15	14	13	52	52	59
Walthamstow Avenue	42	15	6	21	61	69	51
Tilbury	42	13	11	18	60	76	50
Boreham Wood	42	13	10	19	50	67	49
Hitchin Town	42	12	11	19	59	71	47
Carshalton Athletic	42	10	16	16	49	69	46
Hayes	42	9	18	15	45	58	45
Oxford City	42	12	7	23	50	80	43
Staines Town	42	6	16	20	40	64	34
Leytonstone	42	8	7	27	36	75	31
Kingstonian	42	3	15	24	35	72	24

1979/80 Premier Division

	P	W	D	L	F	A	Pts
Enfield	42	25	9	8	74	32	84
Walthamstow Avenue	42	24	9	9	87	48	81
Dulwich Hamlet	42	21	16	5	66	37	79
Sutton United	42	20	13	9	67	40	73
Dagenham	42	20	13	9	82	56	73
Tooting & Mitcham Utd.	42	21	6	15	62	59	69
Barking	42	19	10	13	72	51	67
Harrow Borough	42	17	15	10	64	51	66
Woking	42	17	13	12	78	59	64
Wycombe Wanderers	42	17	13	12	72	53	64
Harlow Town	42	14	12	16	54	60	54
Hitchin Town	42	13	15	14	54	68	54
Hendon	42	12	13	17	50	57	49
Slough Town	42	13	10	19	54	71	49
Boreham Wood	42	13	10	19	50	69	49
Staines Town	42	14	6	22	46	67	48
Hayes	42	12	9	21	48	68	45
Leatherhead	42	11	11	20	51	60	44
Carshalton Athletic	42	12	7	23	48	78	43
Croydon	42	10	10	22	51	59	40
Oxford City	42	10	9	23	49	87	39
Tilbury	42	7	11	24	41	90	*30

* 2 points deducted for playing an ineligible player

SEASON 1972-73
ISTHMIAN LEAGUE

No.	Date	Opposition	Res.	Att.	Goalscorers
1	12 Aug	DULWICH HAMLET	3-0	1700	Delaney(pen), Pritchard, Williams
2	15	Woking	2-0		Delaney, Gane
3	19	Sutton United	2-0		Searle, Delaney
4	22	HAYES	1-0	2450	Delaney(pen)
5	26	LEYTONSTONE	1-0	1950	Holifield
6	29	Kingstonian	1-0		Holifield
7	2 Sep	Walthamstow Avenue	0-2		
8	5	HENDON	0-1	2100	
9	9	ENFIELD	2-2	2100	Holifield, Amos
10	12	St. Albans City	1-1		Searle
11	19	HITCHIN TOWN	4-0	1800	Delaney, Amos, Searle, Horseman
12	23	BISHOP'S STORTFORD	0-1	1700	
13	30	Ilford	1-2		Pritchard
14	2 Oct	Hayes	1-0		Hutchinson
15	9	Oxford City	8-0		Pritchard(2), Horseman(2), Holifield(2) *
16	14	BARKING	2-1	2150	Searle, Delaney(pen)
17	24	ST. ALBANS CITY	2-1	1084	Holifield, Amos
18	28	LEATHERHEAD	1-2	1506	Searle
19	31	Hendon	0-2	1250	
20	4 Nov	Dulwich Hamlet	2-0		Amos(2)
21	11	TOOTING & MITCHAM UTD	0-2	1177	
22	14	Hitchin Town	2-0	413	Jameson, Searle
23	18	Barking	3-1		Horseman(2), Pritchard
24	21	WOKING	1-2	809	Searle
25	16 Dec	Corinthian-Casuals	2-1		Amos, Horseman
26	26	OXFORD CITY	1-0		Hutchinson
27	30	Walton & Hersham	0-1		
28	6 Jan	SUTTON UNITED	3-1	1004	Horseman(2,1pen), Birdseye
29	13	ILFORD	0-0	982	
30	27	Leatherhead	0-1		
31	3 Feb	WALTON & HERSHAM	1-0	1385	Langfield
32	10	KINGSTONIAN	2-0	1086	Horseman, O.G.
33	3 Mar	CLAPTON	1-0	836	Gane
34	10	Leytonstone	1-1		Langfield
35	17	Enfield	0-2		
36	24	BROMLEY	2-1	720	Horseman(pen), Langfield
37	31	Bishop's Stortford	5-1		Prtchrd,Htchnsn,Hrsemn(2),Searle
38	7 Apr	Bromley	2-0		Searle(2)
39	10	CORINTHIAN-CASUALS	1-1		Searle
40	21	WALTHAMSTOW AVENUE	2-1		Hutchinson, Pritchard
41	28	Clapton	2-0		Delaney, Swain
42	1 May	Tooting & Mitcham United	1-1		Searle

* Extra scorers – Searle, Amos

F.A. CUP

1QR	16 Sep	Tooting & Mitcham United	3-1		Pritchard, Holifield, Hutchinson
2QR	7 Oct	Egham Town	6-2	2000	Horseman, Holifield(2), Searle(3)
3QR	21	Walton & Hersham	0-1		

F.A. AMATEUR CUP

1R	9 Dec	CHESHUNT	0-1	1809	

BERKS & BUCKS SENIOR CUP

3R	20 Jan	CHALFONT ST. PETER	9-0	724	Gamblin, Rundle, Horseman, #
SF	17 Feb	Bracknell Town	2-2		Hutchinson, Amos
SFr	24	BRACKNELL TOWN	1-0	1412	Pritchard
F*	23 Apr	Slough Town	1-0	3359	Searle

* Played at Chesham
# Extra scorers – Delaney, Pritchard(3), Williams, Amos

SEASON 1973-74
ROTHMANS ISTHMIAN LEAGUE DIV. 1.

No.	Date	Opposition	Res.	Att.	Goalscorers
1	18 Aug	Ilford	3-1		Holifield, Horseman(2,pen)
2	21	HAYES	4-3	1900	Gamblin, Holifield, Horseman(2,1pen)
3	25	BARKING	5-2		Searle(2), Perrin, Horseman(2)
4	28	LEATHERHEAD	2-0		Horseman, Searle
5	1 Sep	Bromley	2-0	1000	Brothers, Horseman
6	4	Hitchin Town	1-2	850	Holifield
7	8	TOOTING & MITCHAM UTD	2-2	1800	Bullock, Price
8	11	Walton & Hersham	1-4		Pritchard
9	18	OXFORD CITY	1-0	1200	Perrin
10	22	BISHOP'S STORTFORD	2-0	1850	Bullock(pen), Perrin
11	29	Sutton United	2-0		Holifield, Searle
12	2 Oct	WOKING	3-2		Searle, Perrin, Horseman(pen)
13	13	Kingstonian	0-0		
14	23	Hendon	1-2		Horseman
15	27	DULWICH HAMLET	1-1	2100	Searle
16	6 Nov	ST. ALBANS CITY	7-0	1500	Searle(2), Pritchard, Williams, *
17	10	ENFIELD	2-1	2250	Holifield, Horseman
18	13	St. Albans City	3-0		Searle, Horseman, Perrin
19	17	Walthamstow Avenue	4-0		Evans(4)
20	22 Dec	Tooting & Mitcham United	3-0		Horseman(2), Evans
21	26	Dulwich Hamlet	1-1		Horseman
22	29	CLAPTON	4-0	1400	Pritchard(2), Holifield, MacKenzie
23	13 Jan	CORINTHIAN-CASUALS	7-0	2200	Reardon, Horseman(pen), O.G., #
24	2 Feb	KINGSTONIAN	1-0	2100	Holifield
25	23	BROMLEY	7-0		Price, Perrin(2), Holifield(3), Mead
26	2 Mar	Corinthian-Casuals	4-0	300	Perrin(2), Horseman, O.G.
27	9	Clapton	3-2		Perrin(2), Horseman
28	16	Oxford City	0-1		
29	23	SUTTON UNITED	0-0	1900	
30	26	Woking	0-1		
31	30	Enfield	0-0		
32	1 Apr	Hayes	3-0		Horseman, Perrin, Pritchard
33	6	WALTHAMSTOW AVENUE	3-1		Horseman, O.G.
34	9	HITCHIN TOWN	2-1		Perrin, Holifield
35	13	Barking	0-0		
36	25	Leatherhead	1-1		Searle
37	27	Ilford	2-1	1600	Searle, Perrin
38	30	HENDON	2-0	3500	Horseman(2)
39	7 May	Bishop's Stortford	0-2	3800	
40	13	WALTON & HERSHAM	2-2	2300	Searle, Holifield
41	15	Leytonstone	2-1		Holifield, Perrin
42	18	LEYTONSTONE	3-0	2500	Holifield, Pritchard(2)

* Extra scorers – Perrin, Horseman(pen), Evans
# Extra scorers – Holifield(2), Pritchard, Evans

F.A. CUP

Round	Date	Opposition	Res.	Att.	Goalscorers
1QR	15 Sep	Tilbury	3-0	856	Holifield(2), Searle
2QR	6 Oct	WOKING	1-0	2133	Searle
3QR	20	Chatham Town	7-0	1102	Prrin(2), Prtchrd, Hrsemn(2), Searle(2)
4QR	3 Nov	Worthing	3-0	1249	Perrin, Pritchard, Holifield
1R	24	NEWPORT COUNTY	3-1	6888	Perrin(2), Evans
2R	15 Dec	PETERBOROUGH UNITED	1-3	10200	Pritchard

F.A. AMATEUR CUP

Round	Date	Opposition	Res.	Att.	Goalscorers
1R	5 Jan	HORNCHURCH	5-0	1900	Perrin(3), Evans, Horseman
2R	26	Evenwood Town	3-0	980	Pritchard(2), Perrin
3R	9 Feb	Blyth Spartans	1-2	1900	Perrin

BERKS & BUCKS SENIOR CUP

Round	Date	Opposition	Res.	Att.	Goalscorers
3R	20 Jan	Bracknell Town	4-1		Horseman(2), Price(2)
SF	16 Feb	Chesham United	3-1	1750	O.G., Holifield, Evans
F*	15 Apr	Slough Town	3-1	1920	Pritchard, Horseman(2,1pen)

* Played at Wokingham

SEASON 1974-75
ROTHMANS ISTHMIAN LEAGUE DIV. 1.

No.	Date	Opposition	Res.	Att.	Goalscorers
1	17 Aug	KINGSTONIAN	2-0	1400	Mead, Perrin
2	20	SLOUGH TOWN	1-0	2100	Perrin
3	24	Sutton United	2-2		Horseman, MacKenzie
4	27	Hendon	2-1		Kennedy, Horseman
5	31	TOOTING & MITCHAM UTD	2-1	1500	Holifield, Kennedy
6	7 Sep	Dagenham	0-1		
7	10	Hayes	2-1		Perrin, Evans
8	17	Leatherhead	1-2		Searle
9	21	WALTON & HERSHAM	1-0	1500	Horseman
10	24	Slough Town	1-1		Holifield
11	1 Oct	HENDON	5-0	1500	Knnedy(p),Prrin,Evns,Hlifield,Searle
12	8	HAYES	2-2	1750	Horseman, O.G.
13	12	Dulwich Hamlet	0-0	727	
14	15	LEATHERHEAD	1-0	1800	Mead
15	22	OXFORD CITY	2-1	1250	Searle, Kennedy
16	26	Barking	1-1		Holifield
17	9 Nov	CLAPTON	2-1	1480	Holifield, Perrin
18	16	ILFORD	3-3	2300	Perrin, Phillips, Horseman
19	7 Dec	WALTHAMSTOW AVENUE	1-0	1500	Evans
20	21	Kingstonian	2-3	500	Horseman, Perrin
21	28	SUTTON UNITED	3-2	2350	Bullock, Searle(2)
22	11 Jan	Oxford City	1-0	1500	Holifield
23	4 Feb	Woking	4-0		Alexander, Perrin(2), O.G.
24	11	Hitchin Town	1-0	540	Holifield
25	18	HITCHIN TOWN	2-0	1000	Perrin(2)
26	22	Clapton	2-1		Reardon, Kennedy
27	1 Mar	LEYTONSTONE	5-1	2000	Perrin(2),Kennedy,Hlifield,Horsemn
28	4	WOKING	3-0	1800	Kennedy, Phillips, Holifield
29	8	Ilford	2-0		Kennedy, Perrin
30	22	Leytonstone	2-0		Mead, Perrin
31	5 Apr	Bishop's Stortford	1-1		Horseman(pen)
32	8	Enfield	2-2		Horseman(pen), Reardon
33	12	Bromley	7-0		Searle(3),Prrin,Knnedy,Alxndr,Hrsemn
34	15	DULWICH HAMLET	1-1	1850	Evans
35	19	BARKING	5-1		Evans, Searle(3), Phillips
36	22	Walton & Hersham	4-0		Horseman(2), Evans, Holifield
37	24	Walthamstow avenue	2-0		Phillips, Holifield
38	29	BROMLEY	8-0	1900	Searle(3),Evans(3),Horseman(2,1p)
39	8 May	ENFIELD	0-0	4500	
40	10	Tooting & Mitcham United	1-1		Horseman
41	13	BISHOP'S STORTFORD	3-0	2350	Alexander(pen), Perrin
42	17	DAGENHAM	1-0	3800	Searle

F.A. CUP

Rd	Date	Opposition	Res.	Att.	Goalscorers
1QR	14 Sep	Marlow	1-0		Perrin
2QR	5 Oct	MILTON KEYNES CITY	2-0	1600	Searle(pen), Perrin
3QR	19	Chesham United	3-1	1800	Reardon, Mead, Searle
4QR	2 Nov	MARGATE	2-1	2891	Kennedy, Horseman
1R	23	CHELTENHAM TOWN	3-1	5001	Horseman(pen),Holifield,Birdseye
2R	14 Dec	AFC BOURNEMOUTH	0-0	7442	
2Rr	18	AFC Bournemouth	2-1	5407	Horseman, Perrin
3R	4 Jan	MIDDLESBROUGH	0-0	12000	
3Rr	7	Middlesbrough	0-1	30128	

F.A. TROPHY

Rd	Date	Opposition	Res.		
3QR	30 Nov	Ilford	0-3		

BERKS & BUCKS SENIOR CUP

Rd	Date	Opposition	Res.	Att.	Goalscorers
3R	8 Feb	Slough Town	3-0	2000	Perrin(2), Searle
SF*	15	Rivets Sports	7-1	1522	Mead,Alex'(2),Ken'dy(2),Perrin,Evans
F#	31 Mar	Thatcham Town +	4-0		Horseman(3), Searle

* Played at Aylesbury   # Played at Chesham

+ Wycombe not allowed by Berks & Bucks F.A. to compete in the London Senior Cup - as a protest they refused to collect the trophy, which was subsequently awarded to Thatcham.

SEASON 1975-76
ROTHMAN'S ISTHMIAN LEAGUE DIV 1

No.	Date	Opposition	Res.	Att.	Goalscorers
1	16 Aug	STAINES TOWN	2-1	1900	Horseman, Kennedy
2	19	SLOUGH TOWN	0-1	1900	
3	23	Kingstonian	1-0		Horseman
4	26	Hayes	1-0		Horseman(pen)
5	30	SUTTON UNITED	2-1	1950	Delaney, Horseman(pen)
6	2 Sep	OXFORD CITY	0-0	1550	
7	6	Tooting & Mitcham United	1-0		O.G.
8	9	Hendon	0-2		
9	13	BISHOP'S STORTFORD	1-1	1500	Horseman
10	20	Dagenham	0-1		
11	27	ENFIELD	2-1	1500	Mead, Evans
12	30	Slough Town	3-4	2000	Anthony, Evans, Horseman(pen)
13	4 Oct	Hitchin Town	0-2		
14	11	Bishops' Stortford	2-2		Horseman, Delaney
15	18	Walthamstow Avenue	5-2		Horseman, Holifield, Evans, Anthony(2)
16	21	HENDON	4-2	1800	O.G., Evans, Alexander, Holifield
17	25	ILFORD	1-1	1950	Horseman(pen)
18	29	Oxford City	1-1		Price
19	8 Nov	CLAPTON	5-0	1300	Anthny, Evns(2), Hrseman(p), McCrae
20	11	HAYES	2-1	1400	Kennedy, Holifield
21	15	Leytonstone	2-1		Horseman(2)
22	18	Southall & Ealing Borough	1-1		Evans
23	9 Dec	SOUTHALL & EALING BOR.	1-0	1000	Kennedy(pen)
24	27	TOOTING & MITCHAM UTD	3-2	2050	Evans(2), O.G.
25	3 Jan	Dulwich Hamlet	1-0		Anthony
26	17	Enfield	0-0	1450	
27	31	DULWICH HAMLET	0-1	1100	
28	7 Feb	KINGSTONIAN	4-0	1200	Horseman, Evans, Anthony(2)
29	28	WOKING	1-1	1500	Evans
30	6 Mar	Sutton United	1-3		Horseman(pen)
31	13	HITCHIN TOWN	1-0		Kennedy
32	20	Barking	2-1		Alexander, Horseman
33	27	Leatherhead	0-1		
34	30	Staines Town	1-0	1300	Evans
35	3 Apr	LEYTONSTONE	4-3	950	Anthony(2), Holifield, Kennedy
36	6	Woking	2-1		Mead, Kennedy
37	13	LEATHERHEAD	1-0	1000	Alexander(pen)
38	16	WALTHAMSTOW AVENUE	0-0	1300	
39	23	Clapton	0-0		
40	27	BARKING	4-0	800	MacKenzie, Evans, Mead, Reardon
41	6 May	DAGENHAM	6-2	900	Evans(3), Kennedy, Anthony(2)
42	8	Ilford	3-1		O.G., Holifield, Evans

F.A. CUP

4QR	1 Nov	Croydon	2-2	1450	Horseman, Evans
4QRr	5	CROYDON	5-2	2664	Anthony(2), Horseman(3,1pen)
1R	22	BEDFORD TOWN	0-0	4100	
1Rr	24	Bedford Town	2-2	4267	Delaney, Horseman
1R2r	1 Dec	BEDFORD TOWN	2-1	2710	Bullock, Evans
2R	13	Cardiff City	0-1	11607	

F.A. TROPHY

| 3QR | 29 Nov | Slough Town | 0-1 | 1700 | |

BERKS & BUCKS SENIOR CUP

1R	6 Dec	Buckingham Town	7-1	800	Knndy,Hlifield,Hrris,Dlaney(2),Evns,OG
2R	20	Chalfont St. Peter	2-0	600	Harris, Mead
2R	24 Jan	Rivets Sports	6-2		Hrsemn(2),Knnedy,Alxnder,Evns,Anthny
SF*	21 Feb	Chesham United	4-2	1600	OG,Mead,Horseman,MacKenzie

* Wycombe withdrew after discovering MacKenzie had played in a previous round for Hungerford.

ROTHMAN'S ISTHMIAN LEAGUE SUBSIDIARY CUP

1R	10 Mar	Oxford City	1-0		McCrae
2R	23	BOREHAM WOOD	3-2	550	McCrae, Horseman(2)
3R	8 Apr	Chesham United	2-1	900	Bullock, Alexander
SF	26	SLOUGH TOWN	1-2	950	Kennedy

ANGLO-ITALIAN TROPHY

| F/1 | 24 Sep | Monza A.C. | 0-1 | 4000 | |
| F/2 | 8 Oct | MONZA A.C. | 2-0 | 3351 | Delaney, Evans |

SEASON 1976-77
ROTHMAN'S ISTHMIAN LEAGUE DIV 1

No.	Date	Opposition	Res.	Att.	Goalscorers
1	21 Aug	TOOTING & MITCHAM UTD	4-2	1400	Pearson(3,2pens), A.Davies
2	24	HAYES	0-1	1450	
3	28	Dulwich Hamlet	1-0		Holifield
4	31	Hendon	0-3		
5	4 Sep	DAGENHAM	1-2	1300	Pearson(pen)
6	6	Southall & Ealing Borough	2-1		Evans, Horseman
7	11	Enfield	2-0		Kennedy, Pearson(pen)
8	14	STAINES TOWN	3-2	1300	Kennedy(2), Pearson
9	18	HITCHIN TOWN	0-1	1350	
10	21	Kingstonian	3-1		Kennedy(2), Priestley
11	25	BISHOP'S STORTFORD	2-2		Kennedy, Holifield
12	28	KINGSTONIAN	2-0	1150	Priestley, Pearson
13	2 Oct	WALTHAMSTOW AVENUE	4-0	1050	Kttleborough,Hrsemn,Hlifield,Pearsn
14	6	Hayes	1-0		Kettleborough
15	9	Ilford	1-1		Holifield
16	12	HENDON	1-0	1250	O.G.
17	16	Slough Town	2-3	1700	Kettleborough, Evans
18	23	Tilbury	2-0	491	Pearson, Phillips
19	26	Staines Town	1-1	900	Kettleborough
20	30	Leatherhead	0-0		
21	13 Nov	WOKING	1-0	1400	Evans
22	27	Sutton United	0-1		
23	4 Dec	SOUTHALL & EALING BOR.	2-0	1200	Pearson, Evans
24	28	CROYDON	3-0	1000	Pearson, Horseman, Mead
25	1 Jan	Dagenham	1-2		Pearson
26	8	ENFIELD	0-0	1600	
27	8 Feb	LEATHERHEAD	1-1	830	Kettleborough
28	12	Barking	2-0	360	Pearson(2)
29	19	TILBURY	0-0	1100	
30	26	Leytonstone	3-1	469	Pearson(2), Kettleborough
31	12 Mar	Woking	3-0		Kettleborough(2), Hill
32	19	Bishop's Stortford	1-1		Kettleborough
33	26	SUTTON UNITED	3-0	1300	O.G., Holifield(2)
34	29	ILFORD	4-0	1000	Pearson,Priestley,MacKenzie,Hill
35	2 Apr	Croydon	0-1		
36	9	Hitchin Town	2-1	763	Holifield, Phillips
37	16	LEYTONSTONE	1-0	1300	Pearson
38	21	SLOUGH TOWN	1-0	1350	Pearson
39	23	BARKING	3-0	1250	Kettleborough, Pearson, Phillips
40	26	Walthamstow Avenue	2-3		Holifield, Fraser
41	30	Tooting & Mitcham Utd	3-2		Kettleborough, Pearson, B.Davies
42	7 May	DULWICH HAMLET	3-1	1800	Pearson(3)

F.A. CUP

4QR	6 Nov	MERTHYR TYDFIL	3-1	2182	Holifield, Phillips, Pearson
1R	20	Waterlooville	2-1	3377	Priestley, Kennedy
2R	11 Dec	READING	1-2	7747	Pearson

F.A. TROPHY

1R	15 Jan	Barnet	1-0	1541	Kettleborough
2R	5 Feb	Runcorn	1-2	1880	Holifield

BERKS & BUCKS SENIOR CUP

4R	22 Jan	Chesham United	2-1		Kettleborough(2)
SF	5 Mar	Hungerford Town	1-2		Kettleborough

ROTHMAN'S ISTHMIAN LEAGUE CUP

2R	9 Nov	LEATHERHEAD	1-0	1250	Pearson
3R	15 Mar	KINGSTONIAN	3-0	600	Pearson(2,1pen), Evans
4R	18 Apr	Staines Town	1-3	700	Kettleborough

SEASON 1977-78
ISTHMIAN LEAGUE PREMIER DIVISION

Players (column headers): Maskell J., Birdseye P., Davies Bobby, Mead K., Phillips A., Priestley J., MacKenzie G., Kennedy H., Evans D., Holifield M., Horseman A., Spittle P., Vass S., Pratt S., Day R., Quraishi F., Harris D., Strong R., Bullis D.

No.	Date	Opposition	Res.	Att.	Goalscorers
1	20 Aug	Croydon	2-1		Evans, Phillips
2	23	Hayes	0-1		
3	27	LEATHERHEAD	1-1	1100	Priestley
4	30	HENDON	2-1	1000	Kennedy, Evans
5	3 Sep	Sutton United	0-1		
6	6	SOUTHALL & EALING BOR.	3-2	700	Evans(2), Horseman
7	10	TOOTING & MITCHAM UTD	0-2	1150	
8	13	Staines Town	3-1		Birdseye, Holifield, Pratt
9	17	Hendon	2-1	543	Horseman, Mead
10	20	KINGSTONIAN	3-0	1000	Day, Horseman, Evans
11	24	BOREHAM WOOD	3-0	1250	Evans, Holifield, Harris
12	27	Kingstonian	1-1		Horseman
13	1 Oct	Hitchin Town	3-1	600	Horseman(pen), Harris(2)
14	4	HAYES	0-2	1100	
15	8	BISHOP'S STORTFORD	3-0	950	Evans, Kennedy, Horseman
16	15	Enfield	0-3		
17	17	Southall & Ealing Borough	3-0		Evans, Horseman, MacKenzie
18	22	BARKING	1-0	1200	Kennedy
19	25	STAINES TOWN	4-0	1050	Holifield, Kennedy, Evans, Vass
20	29	Tilbury	3-2		MacKenzie, O.G., Holifield
21	5 Nov	LEYTONSTONE	1-0	1100	Phillips
22	12	Dagenham	2-1		MacKenzie, Evans
23	3 Dec	SLOUGH TOWN	1-3	1200	Holifield
24	17	Leatherhead	0-1		
25	31	Slough Town	3-0		Evans, Kennedy(pen), MacKenzie
26	7 Jan	Tooting & Mitcham United	2-1		Horseman, Harris
27	21 Feb	Woking	1-1		Kennedy(pen)
28	25	TILBURY	0-2		
29	11 Mar	Bishop's Stortford	1-0		Horseman
30	18	Carshalton Athletic	1-1		Evans
31	25	WOKING	0-0		
32	1 Apr	Boreham Wood	5-0		Hrsemn, Hlifield, Dvies, Hrris, Priestley
33	4	Leytonstone	0-2		
34	6	CARSHALTON ATHLETIC	3-2		MacKenzie, Harris, Horseman
35	8	Walthamstow Avenue	0-1		
36	11	DAGENHAM	3-0		Holifield, Harris, MacKenzie
37	15	ENFIELD	0-1		
38	17	HITCHIN TOWN	1-1		Evans
39	22	CROYDON	1-1		Evans
40	25	WALTHAMSTOW AVENUE	0-0		
41	5 May	SUTTON UNITED	1-1		Holifield
42	13	Barking	3-2		Harris, MacKenzie, Birdseye

Apps. 13 40 27 38 42 28 36 27 35 38 34 29 9 16 13 27 9 1
Subs. 2 1 7 3 4 1 3 1 4 1
Goals 2 1 1 2 2 7 6 14 8 11 1 1 1 8

F.A. CUP

| 1R | 26 Nov | Minehead | 0-2 | 1400 | |

F.A. TROPHY

| 1R | 14 Jan | Bridgend Town | 1-0 | 1000 | Holifield |
| 2R | 4 Feb | Goole Town | 1-2 | 1156 | Evans |

BERKS & BUCKS SENIOR CUP

1R	19 Nov	Maidenhead United	2-0	883	Mead, Kennedy
2R	10 Dec	HUNGERFORD TOWN	4-2	850	MacKnzie, Hrsemn, Priestley, Knnedy
3R	14 Feb	Slough Town	4-1	600	MacKenzie, Kennedy(2), Horseman
SF	4 Mar	Chesham United	3-1		Harris, Phillips, O.G.
F*	27	Chalfont St. Peter	2-0	1700	MacKenzie, Harris

* Played at Aylesbury

HITACHI LEAGUE CUP

1R	24 Jan	STAINES TOWN	3-1		O.G. Kennedy(pen), Phillips
2R	28 Feb	MAIDENHEAD UNITED	1-0		O.G.
3R	20 Apr	Leatherhead	0-1		

SEASON 1978-79
BERGER ISTHMIAN LEAGUE PREM DIV

Players (columns): Spittle P., Birdseye P., Davies Bobby, Mead K., Phillips A., Allanson D., Atkins S., Holifield M., Evans D., Kennedy H., Long S., Priestley J., Scott T., Harris D., Maskell J., Hardwick S., Fowles G., Reed L., Judd M., Way C., Pearce G.

No.	Date	Opposition	Res.	Att.	Goalscorers
1	19 Aug	Dagenham	0-1		
2	23	BOREHAM WOOD	1-0		Long
3	26	HENDON	5-0		Atkins(3), Phillips, Holifield
4	28	Walthamstow Avenue	0-2		
5	2 Sep	Enfield	4-1		Allanson, Evans, Harris, Scott
6	5	SLOUGH TOWN	0-1	900	
7	9	TOOTING & MITCHAM UTD	3-1	1150	Long(2), Evans
8	12	Hayes	1-0		Hardwick
9	16	DAGENHAM	1-1		Priestley
10	19	Staines Town	1-2		Harris
11	23	LEATHERHEAD	2-0		Holifield(2)
12	26	Boreham Wood	1-1		Evans
13	30	Barking	2-2	307	Atkins(2)
14	3 Oct	HAYES	3-2		Long(2), Phillips
15	7	HITCHIN TOWN	2-0		Long, Atkins
16	10	Slough Town	0-0		
17	14	WALTHAMSTOW AVENUE	1-2		Scott
18	21	CARSHALTON ATHLETIC	0-2	700	
19	28	Sutton United	1-1		O.G.
20	4 Nov	CROYDON	0-0	800	
21	11	Carshalton Athletic	3-2		Long, Phillips, Scott
22	21	STAINES TOWN	1-1	900	Davies
23	2 Dec	Kingstonian	2-0		Atkins, Birdseye
24	16	Hendon	0-1		
25	26	OXFORD CITY	2-0		Atkins, Scott
26	30	Hitchin Town	1-2		Evans
27	20 Jan	KINGSTONIAN	2-1		Long, Priestley
28	3 Mar	DULWICH HAMLET	1-0		Scott
29	10	WOKING	3-1	750	Atkins(2), O.G.
30	17	Leytonstone	2-1	200	Holifield, Scott
31	19	Croydon	0-3		
32	27	Oxford City	3-0		Scott, Long, Evans
33	31	Dulwich Hamlet	1-3		Scott
34	7 Apr	LEYTONSTONE	2-0	530	Atkins, Holifield
35	13	TILBURY	2-0	750	Kennedy, Scott
36	14	Leatherhead	2-1		Kennedy, Long
37	21	ENFIELD	0-0		
38	23	Tooting & Mitcham United	0-2		
39	24	Woking	1-1		Scott
40	30	BARKING	1-4		Atkins
41	1 May	Tilbury	1-0		O.G.
42	5	SUTTON UNITED	1-2		Atkins

Apps: 10, 37, 37, 30, 33, 19, 25, 42, 30, 34, 29, 14, 31, 7, 25, 32, 3, 16, 2, 6
Subs: 1, 1, 8, 5, 4, 2, 2, 2, 2
Goals: 1, 1, 3, 1, 13, 5, 5, 2, 10, 2, 10, 2, 1

F.A. CUP

1R	25 Nov	Maidstone United	0-1	1904	

F.A. TROPHY

1R	16 Jan	BARKING	1-0		Judd
2R	10 Feb	Blyth Spartans	1-1	2000	Scott
2Rr	24	BLYTH SPARTANS	3-0	2400	Hardwick, Atkins, Long
3R	6 Mar	Hayes	2-2		Kennedy(pen), Long
3Rr	12	HAYES	2-3	2050	Kennedy(pen), Scott

BERKS & BUCKS SENIOR CUP

2R	18 Nov	Chalfont St. Peter	2-1		Kennedy, Birdseye
3R	13 Feb	MAIDENHEAD UNITED	6-1	500	Knnedy(2,1p),Sctt,Judd,Evns,Lng
SF	27	SLOUGH TOWN	1-1	750	Holifield
SFr	24 Mar	Slough Town	1-0	1100	Scott
F*	16 Apr	Hungerford Town	2-2	1200	Atkins, Kennedy(pen)
Fr#	26	Hungerford Town	3-1		Evans, Atkins, Scott

* Played at Marlow   # Played at Slough

HITACHI LEAGUE CUP

| 3R | | LEATHERHEAD | 1-2 | | Kennedy |

SEASON 1979-80
BERGER ISTHMIAN LEAGUE PREM DIV

No.	Date	Opposition	Res.	Att.	Goalscorers	Maskell J.	Birdseye P.	Eaton R.	Barr I.	Fowles G.	Allanson D.	Murray J.	Holifield M.	McCarthy J.	Kennedy H.	Price A.	Miles P.	Mead K.	Long S.	Way C.	Priestley J.	Scott T.	Hardwick S.	Jacobs J.	Smith S.	Lester G.	Powles I.	Dell R.	Toll G.	Borg G.
1	18 Aug	BOREHAM WOOD	1-2		Allanson	1	2	3	4	5	6	7	8	9*	10	11	12													
2	25	Dagenham	1-1		Murray	1	2	3		5	6	7*	8	12	10	11	9	4												
3	27	Tilbury	2-0		Kennedy, Holifield	1	2	3		5	6	7*	8	12	10	11	9	4												
4	1 Sep	Dulwich Hamlet	1-2		Fowles		2	3		5	6	7	8			11*	9	4	12	1	10									
5	4	WALTHAMSTOW AVENUE	1-1	600	Kennedy(pen)			3*	12	5		9	6		10	11	8	4	7	1	2									
6	8	Hendon	2-2		Miles, Holifield		2	3		5	11	7*	6	10	9		8	4	12	1										
7	11	Hitchin Town	3-2	455	Price(3)			3		5	11		6	10	7	9	8	4		1	2									
8	15	TOOTING & MITCHAM UTD	0-0	805				3		5	11		6	10	7	9	8	4	12	1	2*									
9	18	ENFIELD	0-4	760				3		5	9*		6	10	2	12	8	4	7	1		11								
10	22	SLOUGH TOWN	1-0	792	Miles	1		3*		5			8	9	10		12	4	7			11	2	6						
11	29	Leatherhead	2-2		Kennedy, Scott	1	3			5			6	9	8	11*		4	12			10	2	7						
12	2 Oct	STAINES TOWN	4-0		Scott(2), Kennedy(2,1pen)		3			5			8	9*	10		12	2	7	1		11	4	6						
13	6	HARROW BOROUGH	5-0	924	Price(3), Long, Scott		2	3		5			7		10	12	8*		9	1		11	4	6						
14	9	Woking	0-0					3		5			8	12	10	9		4	7	1		11	2	6*						
15	13	Barking	1-2		McCarthy		3			5*			8	12	10	9		4	7	1		11	2	6						
16	16	SUTTON UNITED	2-2	824	Long, Price	1	2	3					8		10	9		4	7			11	5	6						
17	20	DULWICH HAMLET	2-1	1103	Scott, Kennedy	1	2	3					8		10	9		4	7			11	5	6						
18	23	Hayes	0-1				2	3					8	12	10	9		4	7*	1		11	5	6						
19	27	HARLOW TOWN	2-3	849	Kennedy(2pens)			3					8	12	10	9		4	7	1	2*	11	5	6						
20	6 Nov	Boreham Wood	0-0				2	3						12	10	9*		4	7	1		11	5	6	8					
21	10	DAGENHAM	0-0			1	2	3							10	9		4	7			11	5	6	8					
22	17	Walthamstow Avenue	1-2		Price	1	2	3		5				9	10	11	8	4	7*				6		12					
23	27	TILBURY	2-2	380	McCarthy, Miles		2	3		5				8*	10		12	4	9	1		11		7	6					
24	1 Dec	Croydon	1-0		Fowles		2	3		5					10	9		4				11	4	6	7	1				
25	8	HENDON	1-1	691	Smith		2	3		5					10	9	8*		12			11	4	6	7	1				
26	15	Enfield	0-2				2	3							10	9	8*	4	12			11	6	7	5	1				
27	18	HITCHIN TOWN	1-0		Price		2	3		5					10	9	8		11			12	4	6*	7	1				
28	26	Oxford City	5-0	800	Long, Smith, Kennedy, Miles, Jacobs		2	3		5					10	9*	8	4	11			12		6	7	1				
29	29	BARKING	1-2	820	Long		2	3							10	9	8	4	11			12	5	6	7*	1				
30	5 Jan	Slough Town	1-2		Kennedy(pen)		2	3							10	12	8	4	7*			11	5	6		1	9			
31	19	Harlow Town	1-2	350	Long	6	3			5				8		11	9	2	7			12	4		10*	1				
32	16 Feb	WOKING	1-1	609	Kennedy(pen)	7	3			5				8		9		2	11			10	4			1		6		
33	23	Sutton United	1-1		Scott	2				5				8		11		3	9			10	4			1		6		
34	1 Mar	HAYES	3-1	710	Miles(3)	2				5				8		11	9	3	7			10	4	12		1		6*		
35	4	Staines Town	1-4		Kennedy(pen)		3			5				8		11	9	2	7			10	4	6		1				
36	15	Carshalton Athletic	1-0		Fowles					5				8		11	9	3	7			4	2		1		6	10		
37	22	CROYDON	5-1		Hardwick, Toll, Long, Miles, Price					5				8		11	9	2	7			4	3		1		6	10		
38	29	Harrow Borough	2-1		Kennedy(pen), Toll					5				8		11	9*	2	7			4	12		1		6	10	3	
39	5 Apr	OXFORD CITY	5-3	1047	Scott(3), Kennedy, Toll					5				8		11		4	7			10	2		1		6	9	3	
40	19	LEATHERHEAD	3-1	802	Scott(2), Price		2									11		4	7			10	5	8		1		6	9	3
41	26	CARSHALTON ATHLETIC	4-1	585	Long(3), Toll		2			5						11*	12		7			10	4	8		1		6	9	3
42	3 May	Tooting & Mitcham United	2-1		Long Toll		2			5				6					7			10	4	8		1		11	9	3
					Apps.	9	27	33	1	32	8	6	19	10	39	33	25	35	31	14	5	26	30	27	10	19	1	10	7	5
					Subs.				1					7		3	5		6			4		2	1					
					Goals			3	1	1	2	2	14	11	8		10		11	1	1	2			5					

F.A. CUP

4QR	3 Nov	Barnet	2-0	1028	Long, Scott	1	2	3					7		10	9		4	8			11	5	6						
1R	24	CROYDON	0-3	1832			2	3		5				8	10	9		4	12	1		11*	6	7						

F.A. TROPHY

1R	21 Jan	BEDFORD TOWN	0-0	831		1	6			5					10	11	9	2	7			8	4	3						
1Rr	24	Bedford Town	1-0	401	Long	1	6			5					10	11*	9	2	7			8	4	3	12					
2R	2 Feb	Burton Albion	2-4	1387	Kennedy(pen), Miles	1	6	3						8		11	9	4	7			10	5	2						

BERKS & BUCKS SENIOR CUP

2R	13 Nov	Slough Town	1-3	550	Jacobs		2	3		5				8	12	10	9			7	1		11	4	6*					

HITACHI LEAGUE CUP

3R	30 Oct	Harlow Town	3-4		Scott(2), Jacobs		2	3						9*	10	7	12	4		1		11	5	6	8					

Season 1974/75: (Back) Evans, Searle, Mead, Maskell, Bullock, Perrin.
(Front) Horseman, Alexander, Kennedy, Phillips(Capt.), T.Reardon.

Season 1982/83 (Back) Davie (Asst.Manager), Dell, Perrin, Vircavs, Hill, Kennedy, Springell (Physio.)
(Middle) Keen (Manager), Borg, Wilson, P.West, Way, Lester, Thorne, Jacobs, Glynn, Pitwell
(Front) Schofield, Daglish, Hart, Cleere, Cox(Treas.), Lee(Chair.), Goldsowrthy(Sec.), Hobbs, Hutton, Holt

Final League Tables 1980/81 - 1987/88 Isthmian League (Unless shown otherwise)

1980/81 Premier Division

	P	W	D	L	F	A	Pts
Slough Town	42	23	13	6	73	34	82
Enfield	42	23	11	8	81	43	80
Wycombe Wanderers	42	22	9	11	76	49	75
Leytonstone/Ilford	42	19	12	11	78	57	69
Sutton United	42	19	12	11	82	65	69
Hendon	42	18	10	14	66	55	64
Dagenham	42	17	11	14	79	66	62
Heyes	42	18	8	16	45	50	62
Harrow Borough	42	16	11	15	57	52	59
Bromley	42	16	9	17	63	69	57
Staines Town	42	15	9	18	60	61	54
Tooting & Mitcham	42	15	8	19	49	53	53
Hitchin Town	42	14	10	18	64	62	52
Croydon	42	12	15	15	51	51	51
Dulwich Hamlet	42	13	12	17	62	67	51
Leatherhead	42	12	14	16	36	50	50
Carshalton Athletic	42	14	8	20	57	82	50
Barking	42	13	12	17	55	72	*49
Harlow Town	42	11	15	16	54	66	48
Walthamstow Avenue	42	13	7	22	51	82	46
Boreham Wood	42	10	13	19	46	69	43
Woking	42	11	7	24	40	70	+37

* 2 points deducted   + 3 points deducted

1981/82 Premier Division

	P	W	D	L	F	A	Pts
Leytonstone/Ilford	42	26	5	11	91	52	83
Sutton United	42	22	9	11	72	49	75
Wycombe Wanderers	42	21	10	11	63	48	73
Staines Town	42	21	9	12	59	46	72
Walthamstow Avenue	42	21	7	14	81	62	70
Harrow Borough	42	18	13	11	77	55	67
Tooting & Mitcham Utd.	42	19	10	13	58	47	67
Slough Town	42	17	13	12	64	54	64
Leatherhead	42	16	12	14	57	52	60
Hayes	42	16	10	16	58	52	58
Croydon	42	16	9	17	59	57	57
Barking	42	14	14	14	53	51	56
Hendon	42	13	13	16	56	65	52
Dulwich Hamlet	42	14	10	15	47	59	52
Bishops Stortford	42	15	5	22	50	70	50
Carshalton Athletic	42	14	8	20	58	86	50
Billericay Town	42	11	16	15	41	50	49
Hitchin Town	42	12	11	19	56	77	47
Bromley	42	13	7	22	63	79	46
Woking	42	11	13	18	57	75	46
Harlow Town	42	10	11	21	50	73	41
Boreham Wood	42	8	13	21	47	58	37

1982/83 Premier Division

	P	W	D	L	F	A	Pts
Wycombe Wanderers	42	26	7	9	79	47	85
Leytonstone/Ilford	42	24	9	9	71	39	81
Harrow Borough	42	24	7	11	91	58	79
Hayes	42	23	9	10	63	41	76
Sutton United	42	20	8	14	96	71	68
Dulwich Hamlet	42	18	14	10	59	52	68
Slough Town	42	18	13	11	73	36	67
Bognor Regis Town	42	19	8	15	53	48	65
Tooting & Mitcham Utd.	42	18	9	15	58	56	63
Billericay Town	42	17	10	15	54	51	61
Croydon	42	17	9	16	68	58	60
Hendon	42	18	6	18	68	61	60
Bishops Stortford	42	17	9	16	61	58	60
Barking	42	14	14	14	47	55	56
Bromley	42	14	12	16	51	50	54
Carshalton Athletic	42	15	9	18	58	60	54
Wokingham Town	42	13	9	20	37	51	48
Walthamstow Avenue	42	12	11	19	48	64	47
Staines Town	42	12	11	19	62	79	47
Hitchin Town	42	11	9	22	49	77	42
Woking	42	6	6	30	30	79	24
Leatherhead	42	4	5	33	36	121	17

1983/84 Premier Division

	P	W	D	L	F	A	Pts
Harrow Borough	42	25	13	4	73	42	88
Worthing	42	20	11	11	89	72	71
Slough Town	42	20	9	13	73	56	69
Sutton United	42	18	12	12	67	45	66
Hayes	42	17	13	12	56	41	64
Hitchin Town	42	16	15	11	58	57	63
Wycombe Wanderers	42	16	14	12	63	52	62
Wokingham Town	42	18	10	14	78	55	*61
Hendon	42	17	10	15	62	51	61
Dulwich Hamlet	42	16	11	15	61	64	59
Bishops Stortford	42	15	13	14	56	57	58
Harlow Town	42	15	11	16	64	70	56
Bognor Regis Town	42	14	13	15	62	69	55
Staines Town	42	15	9	18	63	72	54
Billericay Town	42	15	8	19	53	73	53
Barking	42	13	13	16	60	64	52
Croydon	42	14	10	18	52	58	52
Walthamstow Avenue	42	13	10	19	53	67	49
Leytonstone/Ilford	42	13	9	20	54	67	48
Carshalton Athletic	42	11	10	21	59	72	43
Tooting & Mitcham Utd.	42	10	13	19	50	63	43
Bromley	42	7	11	24	33	72	32

* 3 points deducted

1984/85 Premier Division

	P	W	D	L	F	A	Pts
Sutton United	42	23	15	4	115	55	84
Worthing	42	24	8	10	89	59	80
Wycombe Wanderers	42	24	6	12	68	46	78
Wokingham Town	42	20	13	9	74	52	73
Windsor & Eton	42	19	10	13	67	55	67
Bognor Regis Town	42	20	6	16	67	58	66
Dulwich Hamlet	42	16	17	9	82	57	65
Harrow Borough	42	18	8	16	70	56	62
Hayes	42	17	8	17	60	58	59
Tooting & Mitcham	42	16	11	15	64	66	59
Walthamstow Avenue	42	15	11	16	64	65	56
Croydon	42	15	12	15	62	63	**54
Epsom & Ewell	42	13	14	15	63	62	53
Slough Town	42	13	12	17	69	74	51
Carshalton Athletic	42	14	8	20	55	68	50
Bishops Stortford	42	12	12	18	48	67	48
Hendon	42	9	19	14	62	65	46
Billericay Town	42	11	14	17	53	74	*46
Barking	42	13	7	22	43	75	46
Hitchin Town	42	10	15	17	55	70	45
Leytonstone/Ilford	42	11	10	21	37	72	43
Harlow Town	42	5	12	25	45	95	27

* 1 point deducted   ** 2 points deducted.

1985/86 GM Vauxhall Conference

	P	W(H)	D(H)	L(H)	F(H)	A(H)	W(A)	D(A)	L(A)	F(A)	A(A)	Pts
Enfield	42	15	4	2	48	20	12	6	3	46	27	76
Frickley Athletic	42	16	4	1	46	21	9	6	6	32	29	69
Kidderminster Harr.	42	12	4	5	51	28	12	3	6	48	34	67
Altrincham	42	14	3	4	42	27	8	8	5	28	22	63
Weymouth	42	11	8	2	43	24	8	7	6	32	36	61
Runcorn	42	11	6	4	40	17	8	8	5	30	27	60
Stafford Rangers	42	10	7	4	30	22	9	6	6	31	32	60
Telford United	42	13	5	3	42	24	5	5	11	26	42	51
Kettering Town	42	11	6	4	37	24	4	9	8	18	29	49
Wealdstone	42	10	5	6	35	28	6	4	11	22	28	47
Cheltenham Town	42	13	4	4	47	27	3	7	11	22	42	46
Bath City	42	5	8	8	28	25	8	3	10	25	29	45
Boston United	42	11	5	5	41	26	5	2	14	25	50	44
Barnet	42	9	4	8	32	23	4	7	10	24	37	41
Scarborough	42	10	4	7	35	31	3	7	11	19	35	40
Northwich Victoria	42	5	6	10	24	25	5	6	10	18	29	37
Maidstone United	42	7	9	5	35	29	2	7	12	22	37	36
Nuneaton Boro'	42	8	3	10	27	27	5	2	14	31	46	36
Dagenham	42	6	7	8	23	29	4	5	12	25	37	36
Wycombe Wands.	42	7	6	8	30	35	3	7	11	25	49	36
Dartford	42	7	6	8	36	33	1	3	17	15	49	26
Barrow	42	5	6	10	26	34	2	2	17	15	52	24

Points: Home win = 2 pts. Away win = 3 pts. Draw = 1 pt.

1986/87 Premier Division

	P	W	D	L	F	A	Pts.
Wycombe Wanderers	42	32	5	5	103	32	101
Yeovil Town	42	28	8	6	71	27	92
Slough Town	42	23	8	11	70	44	77
Hendon	42	22	7	13	67	53	73
Bognor Regis Town	42	20	10	12	85	61	70
Harrow Borough	42	20	10	12	68	44	70
Croydon	42	18	10	14	51	48	64
Barking	42	16	14	12	76	56	62
Farnborough Town	42	17	11	14	66	72	62
Bishops Stortford	42	15	15	12	62	57	60
Bromley	42	16	11	15	63	72	59
Kingstonian	42	16	9	17	58	50	57
Windsor & Eton	42	13	15	14	47	52	54
St. Albans City	42	14	9	19	61	70	51
Carshalton Athletic	42	13	9	20	55	68	48
Hayes	42	12	12	18	45	68	48
Wokingham Town	42	14	6	22	47	61	48
Dulwich Hamlet	42	12	10	20	62	71	46
Tooting & Mitcham Utd.	42	12	9	21	41	53	45
Hitchin Town	42	13	5	24	56	69	44
Worthing	42	8	9	25	58	107	53
Walthamstow Avenue	42	4	6	32	36	113	18

1987/88 G.M. Vauxhall Conference

	P	W(H)	D(H)	L(H)	F(H)	A(H)	W(A)	D(A)	L(A)	F(A)	A(A)	Pts
Lincoln City	42	16	4	1	53	13	8	6	7	33	35	82
Barnet	42	15	4	2	57	23	8	7	6	36	22	80
Kettering Town	42	13	5	3	37	20	9	4	8	31	28	75
Runcorn	42	14	4	3	42	20	7	7	7	26	27	74
Telford United	42	11	5	5	33	23	9	5	7	32	27	70
Stafford Rangers	42	12	4	5	43	25	8	5	8	36	33	69
Kidderminster Harr.	42	11	8	2	42	28	7	7	7	33	38	69
Sutton United	42	9	8	4	41	25	7	10	4	36	29	66
Maidstone United	42	8	5	8	38	33	10	4	7	41	31	63
Weymouth	42	13	7	1	33	13	5	2	14	20	30	63
Macclesfield Town	42	10	5	6	36	27	8	4	9	28	35	63
Enfield	42	8	5	8	35	34	7	5	9	33	44	55
Cheltenham Town	42	14	1	6	36	32	5	9	7	28	35	53
Altrincham	42	11	5	5	41	21	3	5	13	18	38	52
Fisher Athletic	42	8	7	6	28	23	5	6	10	30	38	52
Boston United	42	9	5	7	33	25	5	2	14	27	50	49
Northwich Victoria	42	8	6	7	30	25	2	11	8	16	32	47
Wycombe Wand's	42	8	6	7	32	43	3	8	10	18	33	46
Welling United	42	8	4	9	33	32	3	5	13	17	40	42
Bath City	42	7	5	9	27	32	2	5	14	21	44	37
Wealdstone	42	3	11	7	20	33	2	6	13	19	43	32
Dagenham	42	4	3	14	20	46	1	3	17	17	58	21

SEASON 1980-81
BERGER ISTHMIAN LEAGUE PREM DIV

No.	Date	Opposition	Res.	Att.	Goalscorers
1	16 Aug	LEYTONSTONE/ILFORD	0-2	800	
2	18	Harrow Borough	1-1		Price
3	23	Dulwich Hamlet	2-2		Kennedy(pen), Davies
4	30	Sutton United	0-2		
5	2 Sep	BOREHAM WOOD	1-0	550	Glynn
6	6	CARSHALTON ATHLETIC	2-0	650	Long, Kennedy(pen)
7	9	Hitchin Town	0-0		
8	13	DAGENHAM	4-4	850	Kennedy(pen), Glynn(2), Price
9	20	Harlow Town	3-1		Kennedy, Long, Glynn
10	27	TOOTING & MITCHAM UTD	1-0		Kennedy
11	30	LEATHERHEAD	0-0	753	
12	4 Oct	Barking	0-2		
13	7	Staines Town	1-2		Long
14	11	WALTHAMSTOW AVENUE	5-0	730	Dell, Glynn(2), Long(2)
15	14	WOKING	4-0	770	Glynn, Jacobs, Long, Holifield
16	21	Hayes	1-2		G.Toll
17	25	ENFIELD	1-1	1400	Jacobs
18	28	HARROW BOROUGH	3-2	769	Long, Borg(pen), Miles
19	8 Nov	Dagenham	0-5		
20	11	HITCHIN TOWN	2-0	750	Price, Jacobs
21	15	BARKING	2-0	850	Borg(2pens)
22	25	HAYES	3-1	718	Long, Jacobs(2)
23	29	BROMLEY	5-0	737	O.G., Glynn, Price, Long, Holifield
24	6 Dec	Walthamstow Avenue	2-2		Price, Kennedy
25	9	STAINES TOWN	1-0	580	Glynn
26	13	SUTTON UNITED	3-1	1106	Glynn, Long, G.Toll
27	16	Woking	4-0		Glynn(2), Holifield, Long
28	27	SLOUGH TOWN	1-4	2010	Glynn
29	1 Jan	Slough Town	1-2	2112	Birdseye
30	3	Hendon	1-0		Kennedy(pen)
31	24	Leytonstone/Ilford	1-0		Scott
32	7 Feb	Carshalton Athletic	1-1		Kennedy
33	14	HARLOW TOWN	1-0	756	G.Toll
34	21	Tooting & Mitcham United	2-1		Glynn, West
35	28	DULWICH HAMLET	4-1	827	G.Toll, Kennedy, Glynn, Long
36	7 Mar	Enfield	0-2		
37	21	CROYDON	2-0	603	Scott(2)
38	4 Apr	HENDON	1-2	708	Long
39	11	Boreham Wood	4-0		Glynn, Long, O.G., Scott
40	18	Croydon	3-2		Scott(2), Holifield
41	25	Leatherhead	1-1		Holifield
42	2 May	Bromley	2-3		Scott, Glynn

F.A. CUP

4QR	1 Nov	Worcester City	1-1	2561	Glynn
4QRr	4	WORCESTER CITY	1-0	1993	Davies
1R	22	AFC BOURNEMOUTH	0-3	4768	

F.A. TROPHY

1R	10 Jan	Cheltenham Town	1-0	862	Glynn
2R	31	Sutton United	1-5	885	Kennedy(pen)

BERKS & BUCKS SENIOR CUP

1R	18 Oct	HUNGERFORD TOWN	3-2		Glynn(2), G.Toll
2R	18 Nov	AYLESBURY UNITED	2-2	850	Long(2)
2Rr	2 Dec	Aylesbury United	1-2	1003	Long

HITACHI LEAGUE CUP

1R	25 Aug	Hayes	1-2		Glynn

SEASON 1981-82
BERGER ISTHMIAN LEAGUE PREM DIV

Players (columns): Way C., Birdseye P., Toll S., Davies Bobby, Vircavs A., Dell R., Jacobs J., Kennedy H., Glynn T., Long S., West P., Wilson K., Lester G., Mead K., Harman A., Toll G., Longstaff A., Hunt A., Borg G., Rutledge B., Murphy M., Lee T., Smith M.

No.	Date	Opposition	Res.	Att.	Goalscorers
1	15 Aug	SUTTON UNITED	0-3	750	
2	18	STAINES TOWN	1-1	565	Glynn
3	22	Bromley	2-1		Long, West
4	29	CROYDON	3-1	650	West, Glynn, Long
5	5 Sep	Hitchin Town	2-4	325	Long, G.Toll
6	8	BOREHAM WOOD	1-0	606	Glynn
7	12	WALTHAMSTOW AVENUE	2-0	721	Kennedy, Glynn
8	15	Woking	1-2		Birdseye
9	19	Croydon	1-0		Kennedy
10	22	HENDON	3-1	790	Glynn, Kennedy, Wilson
11	26	Carshalton Athletic	3-0		Long, Glynn, Kennedy
12	3 Oct	TOOTING & MITCHAM UTD	1-1	855	Glynn
13	10	BARKING	0-0	803	
14	17	Harlow Town	1-1		Dell
15	24	CARSHALTON ATHLETIC	3-0	789	Glynn, Dell, Wilson
16	27	Slough Town	3-3	1072	Dell(2), Long
17	3 Nov	Boreham Wood	1-0		Glynn
18	7	BISHOP'S STORTFORD	2-1	925	Long, Glynn
19	10	WOKING	0-0	701	
20	14	DULWICH HAMLET	3-0	861	Long, Vircavs, Glynn
21	16	Harrow Borough	3-2		Hunt, Glynn, Jacobs
22	28	Leytonstone/Ilford	2-2		O.G. Glynn
23	2 Jan	Hayes	0-2		
24	2 Feb	HAYES	2-0	573	Wilson, Kennedy(pen)
25	13	Walthamstow Avenue	1-3		Dell
26	20	HARLOW TOWN	2-0	585	Glynn(2)
27	6 Mar	Billericay Town	0-2	537	
28	9	Hendon	1-1		Glynn
29	13	LEATHERHEAD	1-3	712	Kennedy
30	16	SLOUGH TOWN	3-2	711	Long, Glynn(2)
31	27	BROMLEY	0-0	650	
32	3 Apr	Barking	1-1		Jacobs
33	6	LEYTONSTONE/ILFORD	2-1	785	Glynn, Long
34	22	Sutton United	1-2		Kennedy(pen)
35	24	Dulwich Hamlet	0-2		
36	27	Staines Town	1-0		Wilson
37	29	HITCHIN TOWN	2-1	321	Glynn, Wilson
38	1 May	Leatherhead	2-1		Wilson, Kennedy
39	4	Tooting & Mitcham United	3-0		Kennedy, Longstaff(2)
40	6	HARROW BOROUGH	1-2	402	Glynn
41	8	BILLERICAY TOWN	2-0	527	Glynn, Long
42	11	Bishop's Stortford	0-2		

Apps: 10, 25, 42, 30, 29, 39, 39, 36, 40, 37, 28, 34, 32, 3, 3, 1, 6, 2, 21, 2, 3
Subs: 1, 3, 1, 2, 3, 6, 1, 6, 5, 1, 2, 1, 1, 1
Goals: 1, 1, 5, 2, 9, 22, 10, 2, 6, 1, 2, 1

F.A. CUP

4QR	31 Oct	Witney Town	1-0	975	Long
1R	21 Nov	Hendon	1-1	1353	Vircavs
1Rr	24	HENDON	2-0	2507	Kennedy, Glynn
2R	15 Dec	Barnet	0-2	2015	

F.A. TROPHY

1R	19 Jan	Walthamstow Avenue	1-1	280	S.Toll
1Rr	25	WALTHAMSTOW AVENUE	1-1	785	Long
1R2r	28	WALTHAMSTOW AVENUE	5-1	512	Vircavs,Glynn(2),Long,Kennedy(p)
2R	6 Feb	Hyde United	0-0	1127	
2Rr	9	HYDE UNITED	3-2	1263	Glynn, Long, Kennedy
3R	27	BISHOP AUCKLAND	4-1	2597	Glynn, Vircavs, Long(2)
4R	20 Mar	Kidderminster Harriers	1-0	2984	Glynn
SF1	10 Apr	Altrincham	1-1	2367	Wilson
SF2	17	ALTRINCHAM	0-3	4896	

BERKS & BUCKS SENIOR CUP

1R	7 Oct	Newbury Town	5-1	302	Glynn,Long,Hunt,Kennedy(p),Jacobs
2R	5 Dec	CHESHAM UNITED	3-1	561	Borg(pen), Davies, Wilson
3R	30 Jan	Burnham	4-2		Kennedy(3,2pens), Glynn
SF	23 Feb	MILTON KEYNES CITY	4-2	412	Vircavs,Glynn,Long,Kennedy(pen)
F*	12 Apr	Hungerford Town	0-1	875	

* Played at Wokingham

HITACHI LEAGUE CUP

1R	31 Aug	Rainham Town	1-0		Glynn
2R	13 Oct	Cheshunt	4-1		Long(2), Dell, Longstaff
3R	5 Jan	Slough Town	3-2	703	Kennedy(pen), Glynn, Long
4R	2 Mar	Carshalton Athletic	3-0		Vircavs, Kennedy(pen), Wilson
SF1	23	Kingstonian	0-2		
SF2	30	KINGSTONIAN	5-3		Birdseye, Glynn(3), Kennedy(pen)
SFr	20 Apr	Kingstonian	1-2		Birdseye

SEASON 1982-83
SERVOWARM ISTHMIAN LGE PREM DIV

Players: Lester G., Norman Steve, Hill M., Toll S., Vircavs A., Dell R., Jones C., Kennedy H., Glynn T., Long S., Wilson K., Borg G., Suddaby P., Thorne S., Davies A., Longstaff A., Jacobs J., Keen K., West P., Kiely M., Perrin S., Kotvics J., Way C., Hubbick B., Harman A.

No.	Date	Opposition	Res.	Att.	Goalscorers
1	21 Aug	Barking	2-3		Kennedy(pen), Glynn
2	24	BOGNOR REGIS TOWN	1-0	551	Wilson
3	28	CROYDON	2-1		Thorne, Long
4	4 Sep	Leytonstone/Ilford	3-2	219	Long(2), Dell
5	7	Tooting & Mitcham United	0-1		
6	11	HAYES	0-1	554	
7	14	Wokingham Town	1-1	435	Borg
8	18	LEATHERHEAD	5-0	502	Longstaff, Borg, Kennedy, Long(2)
9	21	Hendon	4-3		Long, Suddaby, Dell, Wilson
10	25	Staines Town	1-1	239	Long
11	2 Oct	Bishop's Stortford	1-3		Wilson
12	5	WOKING	1-0	464	Long
13	9	DULWICH HAMLET	2-2	705	Long, Wilson
14	12	Billericay Town	2-1	416	Borg(pen), O.G.
15	16	Bromley	3-0		Long(2), Glynn
16	19	HENDON	1-0	581	Dell
17	23	HITCHIN TOWN	2-0	751	Long, Kennedy
18	30	Croydon	0-2		
19	1 Nov	Bognor Regis Town	4-0		Jacobs, Long(2), Glynn
20	6	Sutton United	2-1		Glynn(2)
21	9	WOKINGHAM TOWN	1-1		Long
22	16	BILLERICAY TOWN	4-1	565	Vircavs,Wilson,Long(pen),Norman
23	27	WALTHAMSTOW AVENUE	2-0	570	Glynn, Borg
24	4 Dec	SLOUGH TOWN	1-1	1300	Dell
25	11	BROMLEY	1-0	670	Wilson
26	18	BISHOP'S STORTFORD	1-3	503	Dell
27	27	Harrow Borough	2-4	700	Perrin, Vircavs
28	1 Jan	HARROW BOROUGH	2-1	1039	Borg(2,1pen)
29	4	Walthamstow Avenue	1-1		Wilson
30	8	Hayes	1-4		Long
31	22	TOOTING & MITCHAM UTD	3-0	736	Kennedy, Borg(pen), Wilson
32	19 Feb	Dulwich Hamlet	1-2		Perrin
33	26	STAINES TOWN	4-3	613	Wilson, Jacobs, Hill, Dell
34	5 Mar	LEYTONSTONE/ILFORD	1-0	637	Perrin
35	8	CARSHALTON ATHLETIC	1-0	511	Borg(pen)
36	12	Hitchin Town	3-0		Hill, Thorne, Wilson
37	19	SUTTON UNITED	2-0	809	Thorne, Kennedy
38	26	Carshalton Athletic	1-0		Dell
39	5 Apr	Slough Town	3-2	1005	Perrin(2), Vircavs
40	9	Woking	2-0		Hill, Dell(pen)
41	16	Leatherhead	3-0		Perrin(2), Wilson
42	19	BARKING	2-2	801	Perrin(2)

F.A. CUP

| 1R | 20 Nov | Bristol Rovers | 0-1 | 6420 | |

F.A. TROPHY

1R	18 Jan	WEALDSTONE	2-1	1069	Hill, Wilson
2R	5 Feb	BOSTON UNITED	0-0	1522	
2Rr	14	Boston United	1-1	2017	Kotvics
2R2r*	17	Boston United	0-2	790	

* Played at Kettering

BERKS & BUCKS SENIOR CUP

| 2R | 13 Nov | Wallingford Town | 7-1 | | Vircavs,Dell,Long,Wilson(3),Glynn |
| 3R | 29 Jan | Bracknell Town | 1-2 | | Kennedy |

HITACHI LEAGUE CUP

1R	31 Aug	HARROW BOROUGH	2-1	527	Dell, Long
2R	28 Sep	Carshalton Athletic	4-3		Borg(pen), Suddaby, Dell, Long
3R	21 Dec	METROPOLITAN POLICE	3-2	303	Vircavs, Hil, Perrin
4R	22 Feb	Kingstonian	1-0		West
SF	22 Mar	Bromley	2-0		Perrin, Wilson
F1	12 Apr	SUTTON UNITED	0-1	842	
F2	30	Sutton United	1-1		Dell

SEASON 1983-84
SERVOWARM ISTHMIAN LGE PREM DIV

Players (columns): Lester G., How T., Hill M., Harman A., Vircavs A., Dell R., Jacobs J., Glynn T., Perrin S., Long S., West P., Wilson K., Borg G., Thorne S., Crook D., Riley A., Way C., Edwards K., Pacquette H., Mikurenda R., Kotvics J., Pearce G., Dell A., Tate C., Moore R.

No.	Date	Opposition	Res.	Att.	Goalscorers
1	20 Aug	BROMLEY	1-0	600	Glynn
2	23	Dulwich Hamlet	1-1		Glynn
3	27	Barking	0-0		
4	3 Sep	CARSHALTON ATHLETIC	2-0	550	Perrin(2)
5	6	SUTTON UNITED	2-2	750	Long, Borg(pen)
6	10	Bishop's Stortford	0-2		
7	13	Leytonstone/Ilford	2-1		Glynn, Borg
8	24	HITCHIN TOWN	0-2	450	
9	1 Oct	Harlow Town	5-3		How, Glynn(2), Long(2)
10	4	Hayes	0-2		
11	8	Hendon	1-2	350	Long
12	15	BISHOP'S STORTFORD	2-2		O.G., Long
13	22	HARROW BOROUGH	0-1	512	
14	5 Nov	Bognor Regis Town	2-1		Jacobs, Perrin
15	12	BARKING	3-2		Long(2), Wilson
16	15	Sutton United	1-2		Glynn
17	26	STAINES TOWN	0-2		
18	3 Dec	HENDON	1-2		Borg(pen)
19	10	TOOTING & MITCHAM UTD	2-2		Long, Perrin
20	26	Slough Town	0-3	855	
21	31	BILLERICAY TOWN	4-0		Vircavs,Wilson(pen),OG,Pacquette
22	7 Jan	Bromley	2-0		Glynn, Vircavs
23	21	Billericay Town	2-1	313	Dell, Pacquette
24	18 Feb	Worthing	2-2		Glynn(2)
25	21	Walthamstow Avenue	2-0		Perrin(2)
26	25	BOGNOR REGIS TOWN	2-2	507	Pacquette, Glynn
27	3 Mar	Staines Town	1-1		Glynn
28	10	Harrow Borough	1-1		How
29	12	Wokingham Town	2-2		Edwards, Jacobs(pen)
30	17	LEYTONSTONE/ILFORD	2-2	515	Pacquette(2)
31	24	Hitchin Town	0-0		
32	27	WALTHAMSTOW AVENUE	1-0	469	Vircavs
33	31	Carshalton Athletic	2-3		Glynn(2)
34	7 Apr	Tooting & Mitcham United	0-0		
35	10	HAYES	1-1	454	Glynn
36	12	HARLOW TOWN	1-2	349	How
37	14	WORTHING	5-1	455	Tate(2), Dell(pen), Glynn(2)
38	17	WOKINGHAM TOWN	1-0	482	Tate
39	21	Croydon	1-0		Glynn
40	23	SLOUGH TOWN	1-2	929	Pacquette
41	28	CROYDON	2-0		Mikurenda, Edwards
42	1 May	DULWICH HAMLET	3-0	450	Dell, Vircavs, Moore

Apps: 32, 40, 26, 30, 32, 31, 35, 39, 33, 15, 17, 19, 14, 4, 4, 10, 11, 20, 13, 6, 14, , 9, 4
Subs: , , 4, , , 1, , , , 1, , 2, 1, 1, 4, 1, 2, , 7, , 1, 2, 1, , 2
Goals: , 3, , , 4, 3, 2, 17, 6, 8, , 2, 3, , , , 2, 6, 1, , , , 3, 1

F.A. CUP

4QR	29 Oct	Eastwood Town	2-2	800	Glynn, Wilson
4QRr	1 Nov	EASTWOOD TOWN	2-1	1023	Long, Vircavs
1R	19	Chelmsford City	0-0	2277	
1Rr	22	CHELMSFORD CITY	1-2	1937	Glynn

F.A. TROPHY

1R	17 Jan	DORCHESTER TOWN	4-0	559	O.G., Wilson(2), Pacquette
2R	4 Feb	Bromsgrove Rovers	0-2	1195	

BERKS & BUCKS SENIOR CUP

PR	17 Sep	DIDCOT TOWN	2-0	382	Wilson, Borg
1R	8 Nov	CHESHAM UNITED	3-0	531	Vircavs, Glynn, Borg(pen)
2R	29	Bracknell Town	2-3		Borg, Glynn

HITACHI LEAGUE CUP

1R	29 Aug	LETCHWORTH GARDEN C.	6-0	359	Wilson(2), Glynn, West(2)
2R	27 Sep	Hayes	1-0		Thorne
3R	6 Dec	Grays Athletic	1-0		Perrin
4R	14 Feb	WOKINGHAM TOWN	1-0	516	Kotvics
SF	20 Mar	OXFORD CITY	1-0	554	Glynn
F1	5 May	SUTTON UNITED	1-1	597	Dell(pen)
F2	7	Sutton United	0-2	897	

Season 1983/84: (Back) Keen (Manager), Davies (Asst. Manager), Glynn, Perrin, Vircavs, Lester, Harman, Hill, How, Springell (Physio) (Front) P.West, Dell, Jacobs, Thorne, Wilson

Season 1984/85: (Back) Richardson, Springell(Phys.), How, Pearce, Burgess, Lester, Read, Collins, D Link, Gane (Asst. Mgr), Bence (Mgr.) (Front) Russell, Wanklyn, Dell, Vircavs, Tilley, Fairchild, M West, Wilson

SEASON 1984-85
SERVOWARM ISTHMIAN LGE PREM DIV

Players (columns): Lester G., Tilley K., Pearce G., How T., Burgess D., Dell R., Doherty M., Broome B., Link D., Tate C., Richardson John, Read S., Jacobs J., Pentland S., Harman A., Wanklyn W., Long S., Vircavs A., Mikurenda R., Russell D., Fairchild R., Collins K., Wilson K., West M., Riley A.

No.	Date	Opposition	Res.	Att.	Goalscorers
1	25 Aug	Wokingham Town	0-2		
2	28	EPSOM & EWELL	0-0	461	
3	1 Sep	BILLERICAY TOWN	1-2	464	Read
4	4	Hayes	0-1		
5	8	Bognor Regis Town	2-3		Read, Link(pen)
6	15	BARKING	3-0	459	Richardson, Read(2)
7	22	Harlow Town	1-0		Read
8	29	BISHOP'S STORTFORD	5-0	520	Jacobs, Read(3), Richardson
9	6 Oct	Dulwich Hamlet	2-0		Link(2)
10	13	WINDSOR & ETON	0-4	703	
11	20	Croydon	1-1		Long
12	3 Nov	Leytonstone/Ilford	0-2		
13	6	SLOUGH TOWN	3-1	766	Long(2,1pen), Fairchild
14	24	Sutton United	0-1		
15	1 Dec	HARLOW TOWN	5-1	496	Link(3), Read, Long
16	8	Harrow Borough	3-2		Read(2), Link
17	15	BOGNOR REGIS TOWN	0-2	464	
18	26	WOKINGHAM TOWN	1-1	533	Burgess
19	1 Jan	Windsor & Eton	0-1		
20	19	WALTHAMSTOW AVENUE	1-0	608	Read
21	26	Worthing	1-2	472	Russell
22	5 Feb	HAYES	1-0	463	Link
23	23	Bishop's Stortford	1-0		Link
24	26	Carshalton Athletic	3-3		Read, O.G.(2)
25	5 Mar	Slough Town	2-2		Link, Read
26	9	Epsom & Ewell	2-1	249	Wilson, Link
27	12	SUTTON UNITED	3-2	534	West, Read, Link
28	16	WORTHING	1-1	473	West
29	19	HITCHIN TOWN	2-0	424	Read(2)
30	23	Billericay Town	1-0		Link
31	30	Tooting & Mitcham United	2-1		Link(2)
32	2 Apr	CARSHALTON ATHLETIC	1-0	456	Read
33	6	LEYTONSTONE/ILFORD	1-0	477	Read
34	9	Hitchin Town	4-1	268	Burgess, Wilson, Read, Link(pen)
35	13	Barking	2-1		Burgess, Fairchild
36	16	Hendon	2-0		Link, Read
37	18	TOOTING & MITCHAM UTD	2-3	637	Read, How
38	23	Walthamstow Avenue	2-0		Link(2,1pen)
39	25	HENDON	1-3	474	Read
40	27	DULWICH HAMLET	2-1	567	Burgess, Pearce
41	30	HARROW BOROUGH	2-0	580	Wilson, Link
42	2 May	CROYDON	2-1	580	Link(2)

Apps: 42, 39, 37, 27, 42, 37, 6, 3, 38, 6, 8, 38, 2, 6, 7, 1, 10, 20, 7, 11, 17, 28, 21, 9
Subs: -, -, -, 1, -, -, 3, -, -, 1, 2, -, 1, 1, 2, -, -, 1, -, 1, -, -, 8, 2
Goals: -, -, 1, 1, 4, -, -, -, 22, 2, 23, 1, -, -, 4, -, 1, 2, -, 3, 2

F.A. CUP

4QR	27 Oct	BURTON ALBION	1-1	928	Vircavs
4QRr	31	Burton Albion	1-2	3442	Link

F.A. TROPHY

1R	12 Jan	DARTFORD	6-1	646	Read(2), Vircavs, Russell, Pearce, OG
2R	2 Feb	Wealdstone	1-2	852	Read

BERKS & BUCKS SENIOR CUP

1R	16 Oct	Burnham	3-5	500	Long, Link, O.G.

HITACHI LEAGUE CUP

1R	9 Oct	BRACKNELL TOWN	3-3	355	Tate(2,1pen), How
1Rr	23	Bracknell Town	4-0	265	Read(2), Link(2)
2R	13 Nov	Billericay Town	3-2	387	Long, Pentland(2)
3R	14 Mar	BISHOP'S STORTFORD	4-0	292	Burgess, West, Link, Fairchild
4R	28	HARROW BOROUGH	2-0	426	Read(2)
SF	4 Apr	Staines Town	2-0	389	Link(2)
F1	4 May	Farnborough Town	3-0	824	Read, West, Link
F2	6	FARNBOROUGH TOWN	2-1	1228	Read(2)

SEASON 1985-86
GOLA LEAGUE

Players (columns): Lester G., Collins K., Pearce G., Burgess D., Vircavs A., McMahon D., West M., Read S., Dell R., Link D., Stanley N., Fairchild R., Price S., Richardson John, Riley A., Snow M., Harman A., Boyle G., Blochel J., Hubbick B., Toll S., Price N., Bressington G., Connolly K., Bradley D., Longstaff A., Bunting T.

No.	Date	Opposition	Res.	Att.	Goalscorers
1	24 Aug	RUNCORN	0-1	1036	
2	26	Barnet	1-0	1081	Link(pen)
3	31	Altrincham	3-4	1006	Read, Link(2)
4	3 Sep	DARTFORD	3-2	886	Link(2pens), Pearce
5	7	Dagenham	1-1	584	Read
6	10	Dartford	0-1	437	
7	14	STAFFORD RANGERS	2-4	787	Read, Link
8	21	Barrow	1-1	517	West
9	28	ENFIELD	1-0	1068	Link
10	1 Oct	NUNEATON BOROUGH	2-0	786	O.G., West
11	5	Scarborough	2-1	805	West, Dell
12	9	Maidstone United	1-1	770	Link
13	12	WEYMOUTH	0-3	1001	
14	15	CHELTENHAM TOWN	3-3	825	Read, O.G., Link
15	19	Northwich Victoria	0-4	787	
16	2 Nov	BARROW	1-1	761	Link
17	9	Wealdstone	0-2	925	
18	23	Bath City	1-3	758	West
19	30	NORTHWICH VICTORIA	1-1	663	Link
20	14 Dec	BOSTON UNITED	4-1	741	Read, West(2,1pen), Stanley
21	28	Nuneaton Borough	0-3	649	
22	11 Jan	MAIDSTONE UNITED	2-2	794	West(pen), Blochel
23	25	Enfield	3-2	1112	Dell(2pens), West
24	1 Feb	SCARBOROUGH	2-1	680	Blochel, Stanley
25	5	Weymouth	1-1	630	Stanley
26	15	Boston United	1-1	1231	West
27	8 Mar	Frickley Athletic	2-2	537	West, Blochel
28	15	BARNET	2-0	832	Read, Stanley
29	22	TELFORD UNITED	1-2	754	West
30	25	BATH CITY	1-4	540	Read
31	29	Stafford Rangers	1-1	1035	O.G.
32	31	FRICKLEY ATHLETIC	1-3	831	Burgess
33	5 Apr	KIDDERMINSTER HARRIERS	2-5	621	West, Read
34	8	Runcorn	1-2	550	Dell
35	14	Kettering Town	1-4	662	West
36	19	WEALDSTONE	1-0	889	Read
37	22	Telford United	1-3	1066	Blochel
38	24	Kidderminster Harriers	2-8	704	Connolly, Collins
39	26	Cheltenham Town	2-4	894	Collins, Read
40	28	DAGENHAM	1-1	537	Read
41	30	ALTRINCHAM	0-1	544	
42	3 May	KETTERING TOWN	0-0	715	

Apps: 42, 36, 26, 37, 41, 18, 35, 38, 32, 19, 37, 7, 6, 2, 25, 2, 9, —, 21, 1, 7, 5, 8, 6, 1, —, —
Subs: —, 2, —, —, —, 2, 2, —, —, 1, —, 2, 8, —, 1, 3, 6, 3, 1, 1, —, —, 4, —, 1, —, —
Goals: —, 2, 1, 1, —, —, 13, 11, 4, 11, 4, —, —, —, —, —, —, —, 4, —, —, —, —, 1, —, —, —

F.A. CUP

Rnd	Date	Opposition	Res.	Att.	Goalscorers
4QR	26 Oct	BURTON ALBION	1-0	1157	Read
1R	16 Nov	COLCHESTER UNITED	2-0	3089	West, Read
2R	7 Dec	CHELMSFORD CITY	2-0	3816	Read, McMahon
3R	4 Jan	York City	0-2	5532	

F.A. TROPHY

Rnd	Date	Opposition	Res.	Att.	Goalscorers
1R	21 Dec	Barnet	1-0	882	West(pen)
2R	18 Jan	Crawley Town	2-0	1150	O.G., Blochel
3R	12 Feb	LEEK TOWN	2-2	417	Dell(pen), Read
3Rr	4 Mar	Leek Town	5-5	1081	Dell, Read(2), West, Stanley
3R2r*	10	Leek Town	1-1	696	Stanley
3R3r*	13	Leek Town	1-0	690	West
4R	17	Kettering Town	1-2	2312	Read

* Played at Worcester

BERKS & BUCKS SENIOR CUP

Rnd	Date	Opposition	Res.	Att.	Goalscorers
1R	12 Oct	Buckingham Town	2-1	400	Link(2,1pen)
2R	12 Nov	HUNGERFORD TOWN	9-0	179	Read(2),West,Dell,Brgess,McMahn#
3R	21 Jan	MAIDENHEAD UNITED	3-1	448	Read, Vircavs, Hubbick
SF	6 Mar	FLACKWELL HEATH	3-0	428	Dell(pen), Read, Harman
F*	12 Apr	Aylesbury United	2-2	1064	Read, Dell(pen)
Fr*	5 May	Aylesbury United	0-1	1306	

* Played at Slough   # Extra scorers: Link(2), Stanley.

BOB LORD TROPHY

Rnd	Date	Opposition	Res.	Att.	Goalscorers
1R/1	17 Sep	WEYMOUTH	1-3	682	Link(pen)
1R/2	25	Weymouth	2-4	740	Stanley, Vircavs

Season 1985/86 (Back) Stanley, Burgess, Lester, Read, Harman, S.Price, Springell (Physio)
(Front) Riley, M.West, Dell, Vircavs (Capt.), Collins, McMahon, D.Link.

Season 1986/87 (Back) Seacole, D.Link, Corbin, Durham, Bressington, Lester, M.West, Dawber, G.Link, N.Price
(Middle) Schofield (Committee), Cleere (Comm.), Jones (Physio), Day, Burgess, Barrett (Capt.), Ashford, Graham, Reardon (Asst. Manager), Holt (Comm.), Sutton (Comm.)
(Front) Hutton (Comm.), Richards (Director), Beeks (Director), Goldsworthy (Sec.), Adams (Patron), Lee (Chairman), Gane (Manager), Peart (Director), Roberts (Director), Cox (Director), Hart (Comm.)

SEASON 1986-87
VAUXHALL-OPEL LEAGUE PREM DIV

Players (column headers): Lester G., Riley A., Pearce G., Bressington G., Barrett K., Hackett P., Collins K., Durham K., Walton B., Ashford N., West M., Day K., Stanley N., Price N., Blue R., Bates J., Graham A., Seacole J., Connolly K., Burgess D., Silkman B., Moore S., Fisher B., Simpson R., Corbin K., Dawber M., Collier R., Link D., Link G., Hoddle C.

No.	Date	Opposition	Res.	Att.	Goalscorers
1	16 Aug	CROYDON	3-1	806	Walton, West(2)
2	19	Kingstonian	1-0	379	West
3	23	Walthamstow Avenue	2-1	312	West, Walton
4	26	WINDSOR & ETON	4-1	675	West(2), Ashford, Stanley
5	30	BOGNOR REGIS TOWN	2-1	857	Collins, O.G.
6	2 Sep	Hayes	2-0	633	Walton(2)
7	6	Bromley	4-0	448	West, Walton(2), Collins
8	9	ST. ALBANS CITY	3-0	1089	Ashford(2), West
9	20	FARNBOROUGH TOWN	1-2	1151	West
10	27	Yeovil Town	1-2	3169	Ashford
11	4 Oct	BISHOP'S STORTFORD	0-0	965	
12	7	Harrow Borough	1-2	647	West
13	11	Slough Town	3-0	1435	Ashford, Graham(2)
14	18	TOOTING & MITCHAM UTD	4-0	1243	Connolly, Graham, West(2)
15	1 Nov	WORTHING	4-2	853	Seacole(3), Ashford
16	4	HAYES	2-1	773	Graham, Seacole
17	8	Wokingham Town	1-0	640	Ashford
18	15	HENDON	5-0	1042	Barrett, Ashford, Walton, Graham(2)
19	22	Bishop's Stortford	4-1	450	Ashford(2), Seacole, Durham
20	29	Barking	4-3	305	Day, Walton, Graham, Durham
21	6 Dec	Hendon	3-2	489	Durham, Graham, West
22	9	WOKINGHAM TOWN	2-0	889	West(2)
23	13	DULWICH HAMLET	4-1	964	West, Graham(2), Riley
24	27	KINGSTONIAN	3-2	1084	Seacole, West(2)
25	3 Jan	Croydon	0-1	458	
26	6	HITCHIN TOWN	1-0	794	Ashford(pen)
27	10	WALTHAMSTOW AVENUE	7-1	1010	OG, Brrett, West(p), Durhm, Seacole(2), D.Link
28	24	BROMLEY	3-0	954	G.Link, Bressington, D.Link(pen)
29	31	St. Albans City	4-1	1173	Bressington, D.Link(2), Seacole
30	7 Feb	Farnborough Town	0-0	1120	
31	14	YEOVIL TOWN	0-1	2473	
32	24	Windsor & Eton	5-1	680	D.Link, Bressington(2), Dawber, Price
33	28	SLOUGH TOWN	1-1	2144	Seacole
34	7 Mar	Tooting & Mitcham United	0-0	380	
35	14	HARROW BOROUGH	0-0	1465	
36	21	Worthing	3-0	556	D.Link(2), Graham
37	28	Carshalton Athletic	2-0	600	West(pen), D.Link
38	4 Apr	BARKING	2-1	1161	Graham, D.Link
39	11	CARSHALTON ATHLETIC	4-0	1333	Durham, Graham, D.Link(p), Barrett
40	16	Bognor Regis Town	2-1	1030	Durham, O.G.
41	18	Hitchin Town	2-1	606	D.Link, Graham
42	2 May	Dulwich Hamlet	4-1	580	Ashford, Graham, West, Dawber

F.A. CUP

4QR	25 Oct	V.S. RUGBY	1-5	1362	Seacole

F.A. TROPHY

| 1R | 20 Dec | LEATHERHEAD | 0-0 | 834 | |
| 1Rr | 23 | Leatherhead | 0-1 | 385 | |

BERKS & BUCKS SENIOR CUP

2R	27 Jan	WINDSOR & ETON	11-1	577	Graham(4), Seacole(2), Burgess(2)*
3R	17 Feb	MARLOW	3-0	938	Riley, West(2pens)
SF	24 Mar	ABINGDON TOWN	5-0	691	D.Link(2), O.G., Graham, West
F**	25 Apr	Aylesbury United	3-2	1638	G.Link, D.Link, Ashford

* Extra scorers: Bressington, Moore(2). ** Played at Wolverton

A.C. DELCO (LEAGUE) CUP

1R	16 Sep	HORNCHURCH	3-2	582	Collins, West(2)
2R	18 Nov	WORTHING	2-1	827	Seacole, West
SR	16 Dec	YEOVIL TOWN	1-2	1087	Graham

G.M.A.C CUP

| 1R | 11 Nov | YEOVIL TOWN | 1-4 | 1255 | Graham |

SEASON 1987-88
GM VAUXHALL CONFERENCE

No.	Date	Opposition	Res.	Att.	Goalscorers
1	22 Aug	STAFFORD RANGERS	0-4	1217	
2	26	Maidstone United	1-0	1043	West(pen)
3	29	Kidderminster Harriers	2-0	1126	Durham(2)
4	5 Sep	Northwich Victoria	1-2	716	Gray
5	8	FISHER ATHLETIC	1-1	1169	West(pen)
6	15	BARNET	0-7	1606	
7	19	TELFORD UNITED	2-1	1069	Price, Westley
8	23	Cheltenham Town	2-2	1529	West(pen), Westley
9	29	BATH CITY	2-2	1386	Dodds, Westley
10	3 Oct	RUNCORN	2-2	1362	West, Dodds
11	10	ENFIELD	1-5	1459	Dodds
12	17	KETTERING TOWN	0-3	1387	
13	21	Welling United	0-1	732	
14	24	Stafford Rangers	0-3	1185	
15	31	Enfield	2-3	671	Carmichael, West
16	7 Nov	LINCOLN CITY	1-2	2105	West
17	14	Boston United	0-4	1321	
18	17	SUTTON UNITED	1-1	1217	Carmichael
19	21	Altrincham	2-4	1370	Graham, Lovell
20	24	DAGENHAM	2-1	1225	Day, Westley
21	28	Weymouth	0-0	1678	
22	5 Dec	BOSTON UNITED	1-2	1287	Boyland
23	12	Runcorn	2-1	582	Norman(pen), Boyland
24	16	Kettering Town	0-3	1462	
25	2 Jan	MAIDSTONE UNITED	1-5	1344	Graham
26	9	Wealdstone	0-0	1134	
27	16	CHELTENHAM TOWN	5-3	1361	Boyland, West(2), Norman(p), Barrett
28	6 Feb	WEALDSTONE	1-0	1773	West
29	13	Dagenham	1-2	595	Norman
30	20	Sutton United	2-2	983	West(2,1pen)
31	27	MACCLESFIELD TOWN	5-0	1492	Boyland(3), Barrett, Greenaway
32	29	Fisher Athletic	0-0	544	
33	8 Mar	KIDDERMINSTER HARRIERS	0-1	1583	
34	12	Northwich Victoria	1-1	1531	West(pen)
35	19	WELLING UNITED	3-1	1404	Mann(2), Boyland
36	26	Bath City	1-2	932	West
37	2 Apr	Macclesfield Town	1-1	1163	Boyland
38	4	WEYMOUTH	2-1	2066	West, Mann
39	9	Barnet	1-1	2956	Durham
40	16	Telford United	0-0	1610	
41	30	ALTRINCHAM	1-0	1607	Greenaway
42	2 May	Lincoln City	0-2	9432	

Extra players: T.Barry 28/7*, 29/7*, 33/9   M.Barnes 29/4   P.Collins 12/6,13/7,14/7   S.Cox 20/2,21/2,22/2#   I.Fergusson 20/6,21/6,22/6   L.Osborne 37/6,38/6,39/6#   J.Ray 34/4   M.Roderick 40/7,42/14

F.A. CUP

1QR	12 Sep	Aylesbury United	0-2	1530	

F.A. TROPHY

1R	19 Dec	CHELTENHAM TOWN	2-3	1557	Westley, Boyland

BERKS & BUCKS SENIOR CUP

| 2R | 23 Jan | Didcot Town | 4-0 | 442 | West, Boyland, Corbin, Norman(p) |
| 3R | 22 Feb | Windsor & Eton | 1-3 | 541 | Durham |

Extra player - T.Barry 3R/7

G.M.A.C. CUP

1R	27 Oct	BOGNOR REGIS TOWN	0-1	730	

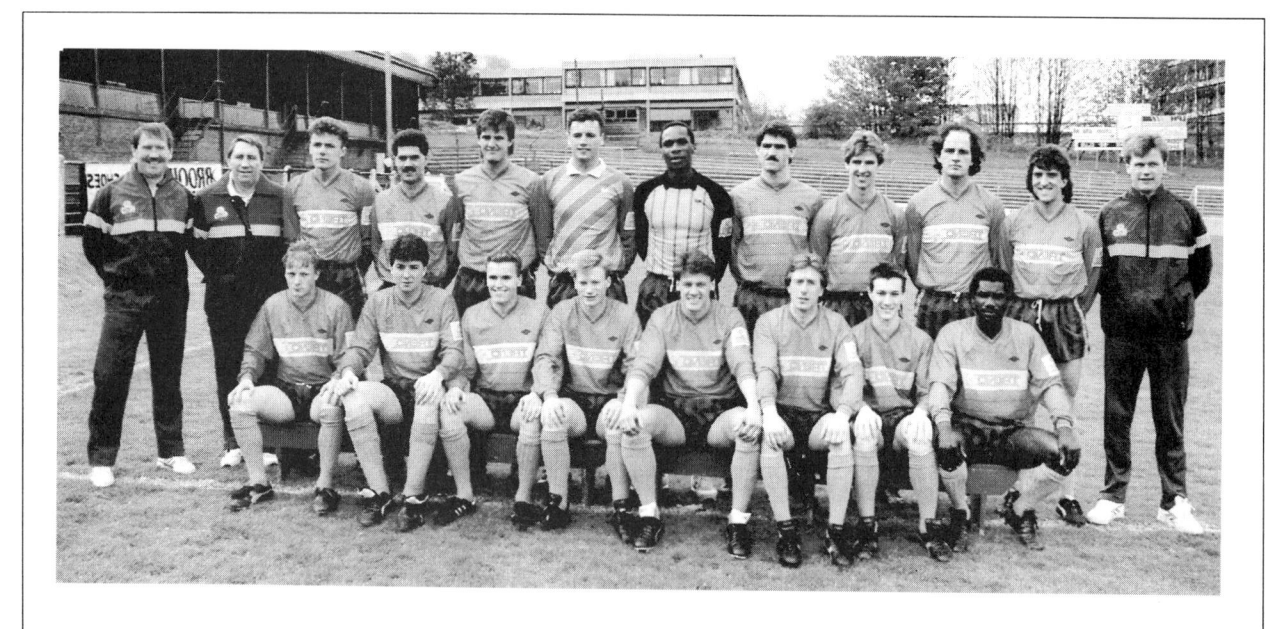

Season 1987/88: (Back) Jones (Phys.), Durham, Graham, Day, Barrett, Granville, Lester, Crossley, M West, Osborne, J Reardon (Asst. Mgr.), Kelman (Mgr.)
(Front) Corbin, Roderick, Greenaway, Boyland, Young, Norman, Taylor, Mann

Season 1988/89:
(Back) Hutchinson (Youth Man.), Jones (Physio), Ray, Taylor, Carroll, Vasey, Crompton, West, Greenaway, Osborne, Mulvaney, Lissaman, Dell (Caoch), Kelman (Manager)
(Front) Day, Regan, Young, Barrett, Norman, Durham, Boyland, Blackler, Abbley, Robinson.

Final League Tables 1988/89 - 1992/93 GM Vauxhall Conference

1988/89

	P	Home					Away					Pts
		W	D	L	F	A	W	D	L	F	A	
Maidstone United	40	12	5	3	48	22	13	4	3	44	24	84
Kettering Town	40	16	1	3	35	15	7	6	7	21	24	76
Boston United	40	12	3	5	36	28	10	5	5	25	23	74
Wycombe Wand's	40	9	7	4	34	25	11	4	5	34	27	71
Kidderminster Harr.	40	10	4	6	32	32	11	2	7	36	25	69
Runcorn	40	11	3	6	39	22	8	5	7	38	31	65
Macclesfield Town	40	9	5	6	31	26	8	5	7	32	31	61
Barnet	40	11	2	7	36	30	7	5	8	28	39	61
Yeovil Town	40	8	5	7	34	30	7	6	7	34	37	56
Northwich Victoria	40	8	5	7	31	30	6	6	8	33	35	53
Welling United	40	8	6	6	27	16	6	5	9	18	30	53
Sutton United	40	10	5	5	43	26	2	10	8	21	28	51
Entield	40	7	4	9	33	32	7	4	9	29	35	50
Altrincham	40	6	8	6	24	23	7	2	11	27	38	49
Cheltenham Town	40	7	7	6	32	29	5	5	10	23	29	48
Telford United	40	5	5	10	17	24	8	4	8	20	19	48
Chorley	40	6	4	10	26	32	7	2	11	31	39	45
Fisher Athletic	40	6	4	10	31	32	4	7	9	24	33	41
Stafford Rangers	40	7	4	9	27	32	4	3	13	22	42	40
Aylesbury United	40	7	4	9	27	30	2	5	13	16	41	36
Weymouth	40	6	7	7	27	30	1	3	16	10	40	31

1989/90

	P	Home					Away					Pts
		W	D	L	F	A	W	D	L	F	A	
Darlington	42	13	6	2	43	12	13	3	5	33	13	87
Barnet	42	15	4	2	46	14	11	3	7	35	27	85
Runcorn	42	16	3	2	52	20	3	10	8	27	42	70
Macclesfield Town	42	11	6	4	35	16	6	9	6	21	25	66
Kettering Town	42	13	5	3	35	15	5	7	9	31	38	66
Welling United	42	11	6	4	36	16	7	4	10	26	34	64
Yeovil Town	42	9	8	4	32	25	8	4	9	30	29	63
Sutton United	42	14	2	5	42	24	5	4	12	26	40	63
Merthyr Tydfil	42	9	9	3	41	30	7	5	9	26	33	62
Wycombe Wand's	42	11	6	4	42	24	6	4	11	22	32	61
Cheltenham Town	42	9	6	6	30	22	7	5	9	28	38	59
Telford United	42	8	7	6	31	29	7	6	8	25	34	58
Kidderminster Harr.	42	7	6	8	37	33	8	3	10	27	34	54
Barrow	42	11	8	2	33	25	1	8	12	18	42	52
Northwich Victoria	42	9	3	9	29	30	6	2	13	22	37	50
Altrincham	42	8	5	8	31	20	4	8	9	18	28	49
Stafford Rangers	42	9	6	6	25	23	3	6	12	25	39	48
Boston United	42	10	3	8	36	30	3	5	13	12	37	47
Fisher Athletic	42	9	1	11	34	34	4	6	11	21	44	46
Chorley	42	9	5	7	26	26	4	1	16	16	41	45
Farnborough Town	42	7	5	9	33	30	3	7	11	27	43	42
Enfield	42	9	3	9	36	34	1	3	17	16	55	36

1990/91

	P	Home					Away					Pts
		W	D	L	F	A	W	D	L	F	A	
Barnet	42	13	4	4	50	23	13	5	3	53	29	87
Colchester United	42	16	4	1	41	13	9	6	6	27	22	85
Altrincham	42	12	6	3	48	22	11	7	3	39	24	82
Kettering Town	42	12	6	3	38	19	11	5	5	29	26	80
Wycombe Wand's.	42	15	3	3	46	17	6	8	7	29	29	74
Telford United	42	11	3	7	30	21	9	4	8	32	31	67
Macclesfield Town	42	11	4	6	38	22	6	8	7	25	30	63
Runcorn	42	12	4	5	44	29	4	6	11	25	38	58
Merthyr Tydfil	42	9	5	7	37	24	7	4	10	25	37	57
Barrow	42	10	8	3	34	24	5	4	12	25	41	57
Welling United	42	7	10	4	33	27	6	5	10	22	30	54
Northwich Victoria	42	8	7	6	33	30	5	6	10	32	45	52
Kidderminster Harr.	42	8	5	8	33	30	6	5	10	23	37	52
Yeovil Town	42	9	5	7	38	29	4	6	11	20	29	50
Stafford Rangers	42	7	9	5	30	26	5	5	11	18	25	50
Cheltenham Town	42	8	6	7	29	25	4	6	11	25	47	48
Gateshead	42	10	3	8	32	38	4	3	14	20	54	48
Boston United	42	9	4	8	40	31	3	7	11	15	38	47
Slough Town	42	9	4	8	31	29	4	2	15	20	51	45
Bath City	42	9	4	8	39	27	1	8	12	16	34	42
Sutton United	42	6	6	9	29	33	4	3	14	33	49	39
Fisher Athletic	42	3	9	9	22	30	2	6	13	16	49	30

1991/92

	P	Home					Away					Pts
		W	D	L	F	A	W	D	L	F	A	
Colchester United	42	19	1	1	57	11	9	9	3	41	29	94
Wycombe Wands.	42	18	1	2	49	13	12	3	6	35	22	94
Kettering Town	42	12	6	3	44	23	8	7	6	28	27	73
Merthyr Tydfil	42	14	4	3	40	24	4	10	7	19	32	68
Farnborough Town	42	8	7	6	36	27	10	5	6	32	26	66
Telford United	42	10	4	7	32	31	9	3	9	30	35	64
Redbridge Forest	42	12	4	5	42	27	6	5	10	27	29	63
Boston United	42	10	4	7	40	35	8	5	8	31	31	63
Bath City	42	8	6	7	27	22	8	6	7	27	29	60
Witton Albion	42	11	6	4	41	26	5	4	12	22	34	58
Northwich Victoria	42	10	4	7	40	25	6	2	13	23	33	54
Welling United	42	8	6	7	40	38	6	6	9	29	41	54
Macclesfield Town	42	7	7	7	25	21	6	6	9	25	29	52
Gateshead	42	8	5	8	22	22	4	7	10	27	35	48
Yeovil Town	42	8	6	7	22	21	3	8	10	18	28	47
Runcorn	42	5	11	5	26	26	6	2	13	24	37	46
Stafford Rangers	42	7	8	6	25	24	3	8	10	16	35	46
Altrincham	42	5	8	8	33	39	6	4	11	28	43	45
Kidderminster Harr.	42	8	6	7	35	32	4	3	14	21	45	45
Slough Town	42	7	3	11	26	39	6	3	12	30	43	45
Cheltenham Town	42	8	5	8	28	35	2	8	11	28	47	43
Barrow	42	5	8	8	29	23	3	6	12	23	49	38

1992/93

	P	Home					Away					Pts.
		W	D	L	F	A	W	D	L	F	A	
Wycombe Wands.	42	13	5	3	46	16	11	6	4	38	21	83
Bromsgrove Rov.	42	9	7	5	35	22	9	7	5	32	27	68
Dagenham & Red.	42	10	5	6	48	29	9	6	6	27	18	*67
Yeovil Town	42	13	5	3	42	21	5	7	9	17	28	66
Slough Town	42	12	3	6	39	28	6	8	7	21	27	65
Stafford Rangers	42	7	6	8	22	24	11	4	6	33	23	64
Bath City	42	9	8	4	29	23	6	6	9	24	23	59
Woking	42	9	2	10	30	33	8	6	7	28	29	59
Kidderminster Harr.	42	9	5	7	26	30	5	11	5	34	30	58
Altrincham	42	7	7	7	21	25	8	6	7	28	27	58
Northwich Victoria	42	5	6	10	24	29	11	2	8	44	26	56
Stalybridge Celtic	42	7	10	4	25	26	6	7	8	23	29	56
Kettering Town	42	10	5	6	36	28	4	8	9	25	35	55
Gateshead	42	9	6	6	27	19	5	4	12	26	37	52
Telford United	42	9	5	7	31	24	5	5	11	24	36	52
Merthyr Tydfil	42	4	9	8	26	37	10	1	10	25	42	52
Witton Albion	42	5	9	7	30	34	6	8	7	32	31	50
Macclesfield Town	42	7	9	5	23	20	5	4	12	17	30	49
Runcorn	42	8	3	10	32	36	5	7	9	26	40	49
Welling United	42	8	6	7	34	37	4	6	11	23	35	48
Farnborough Town	42	8	5	8	34	36	4	6	11	34	51	47
Boston United	42	5	6	10	23	31	4	7	10	27	38	40

* 1 point deducted

1993/94 - 1995/96 Football League

1993/94 Division Three

	Pl.	Home					Away					F.	A.	Pts
		W	D	L	F	A	W	D	L	F	A			
1 Shrewsbury Town	42	10	8	3	28	17	12	5	4	35	22	63	39	79
2 Chester City	42	13	5	3	35	18	8	6	7	34	28	69	46	74
3 Crewe Alexandra	42	12	4	5	45	30	9	6	6	35	31	80	61	73
4 Wycombe Wanderers	42	11	6	4	34	21	8	7	6	33	32	67	53	70
5 Preston North End	42	13	5	3	46	23	5	8	8	33	37	79	60	67
6 Torquay United	42	8	10	3	30	24	9	6	6	34	32	64	56	67
7 Carlisle United	42	10	4	7	35	23	8	6	7	22	19	57	42	64
8 Chesterfield	42	8	8	5	32	22	8	6	7	23	26	55	48	62
9 Rochdale	42	10	5	6	38	22	6	7	8	25	29	63	51	60
10 Walsall	42	7	5	9	28	26	10	4	7	20	27	48	53	60
11 Scunthorpe United	42	9	7	5	40	26	6	7	8	24	30	64	56	59
12 Mansfield Town	42	9	3	9	28	30	6	7	8	25	32	53	62	55
13 Bury	42	9	6	6	33	22	5	5	11	22	34	55	56	53
14 Scarborough	42	8	4	9	29	28	7	4	10	26	33	55	61	53
15 Doncaster Rovers	42	8	6	7	24	26	6	4	11	20	31	44	57	52
16 Gillingham	42	8	8	5	27	23	4	7	10	17	28	44	51	51
17 Colchester United	42	8	4	9	31	33	5	6	10	25	38	56	71	49
18 Lincoln City	42	7	4	10	26	29	5	7	9	26	34	52	63	47
19 Wigan Athletic	42	6	7	8	33	33	5	5	11	18	37	51	70	45
20 Hereford United	42	6	4	11	34	33	6	2	13	26	46	60	79	42
21 Darlington	42	7	5	9	24	28	3	6	12	18	36	42	64	41
22 Northampton Town	42	6	7	8	25	23	3	4	14	19	43	44	66	38

1994/95 Division Two

	Pl.	Home					Away					F.	A.	Pts.
		W	D	L	F	A	W	D	L	F	A			
1 Birmingham City	46	15	6	2	53	18	10	8	5	31	19	84	37	89
2 Brentford	46	14	4	5	44	15	11	6	6	37	24	81	39	85
3 Crewe Alexandra	46	14	3	6	46	33	11	5	7	34	35	80	68	83
4 Bristol Rovers	46	15	7	1	48	20	7	9	7	22	20	70	40	82
5 Huddersfield Town	46	14	5	4	45	21	8	10	5	34	28	79	49	81
6 Wycombe Wanderers	46	13	7	3	36	19	8	8	7	24	27	60	46	78
7 Oxford United	46	13	6	4	30	18	8	6	9	36	34	66	52	75
8 Hull City	46	13	6	4	40	18	8	5	10	30	39	70	57	74
9 York City	46	13	4	6	37	21	8	5	10	30	30	67	51	72
10 Swansea City	46	10	8	5	23	13	9	6	8	34	32	57	45	71
11 Stockport County	46	12	3	8	40	29	7	5	11	23	31	63	60	65
12 Blackpool	46	11	4	8	40	36	7	6	10	24	34	64	70	64
13 Wrexham	46	10	7	6	38	27	6	8	9	27	37	65	64	63
14 Bradford City	46	8	6	9	29	32	8	6	9	28	32	57	64	60
15 Peterborough Utd.	46	7	11	5	26	29	7	7	9	28	40	54	69	60
16 Brighton & Hove A.	46	9	10	4	25	15	5	7	11	29	38	54	53	59
17 Rotherham United	46	12	6	5	36	26	2	8	13	21	35	57	61	56
18 Shrewsbury Town	46	9	9	5	34	27	4	5	14	20	35	54	62	53
19 Bournemouth	46	9	4	10	30	34	4	7	12	19	35	49	69	50
20 Cambridge United	46	8	9	6	33	28	3	6	14	19	41	52	69	48
21 Plymouth Argyle	46	7	6	10	22	36	5	4	14	23	47	45	83	46
22 Cardiff City	46	5	6	12	25	31	4	5	14	21	43	46	74	38
23 Chester City	46	5	6	12	23	42	1	5	17	14	42	37	84	29
24 Leyton Orient	46	6	6	11	21	29	0	2	21	9	46	30	75	26

1995/96 Division Two

	Pl.	Home					Away					F.	A.	Pts.
		W	D	L	F	A	W	D	L	F	A			
1 Swindon Town	46	12	10	1	37	16	13	7	3	34	18	71	34	92
2 Oxford United	46	17	4	2	52	14	7	7	9	24	25	76	39	83
3 Bl ackpool	46	14	5	4	41	20	9	8	6	26	20	67	40	82
4 Notts County	46	14	6	3	42	21	7	9	7	21	18	63	39	78
5 Crewe Alexandra	46	13	3	7	40	24	9	4	10	37	36	77	60	73
6 Bradford City	46	15	4	4	41	25	7	3	13	30	44	71	69	73
7 Chesterfield	46	14	6	3	39	21	6	6	11	17	30	56	51	72
8 Wrexham	46	12	6	5	51	27	6	10	7	25	28	76	55	70
9 Stockport County	46	8	9	6	30	20	11	4	8	31	27	61	47	70
10 Bristol Rovers	46	12	4	7	29	28	8	6	9	28	32	57	60	70
11 Walsall	46	12	7	4	38	20	7	5	11	22	25	60	45	69
12 Wycombe Wanderers	46	9	8	6	36	26	6	7	10	27	33	63	59	60
13 Bristol City	46	10	6	7	28	22	5	9	9	27	38	55	60	60
14 Bournemouth	46	12	5	6	33	25	4	5	14	18	45	51	70	58
15 Brentford	46	12	6	5	24	15	3	7	13	19	34	43	49	58
16 Rotherham United	46	11	7	5	31	20	3	7	13	23	42	54	62	56
17 Burnley	46	9	8	6	35	28	5	5	13	21	40	56	68	55
18 Shrewsbury Town	46	7	8	8	32	29	6	6	11	26	41	58	70	53
19 Peterborough Utd.	46	9	6	8	40	27	4	7	12	19	39	59	66	52
20 York City	46	8	6	9	28	29	5	7	11	30	44	58	73	52
21 Carlisle United	46	11	6	6	35	20	1	7	15	22	52	57	72	49
22 Swansea City	46	8	8	7	27	29	3	6	14	16	50	43	79	47
23 Brighton & Hove Albion	46	6	7	10	25	31	4	3	16	21	38	46	69	40
24 Hull City	46	4	8	11	26	37	1	8	14	10	41	36	78	31

SEASON 1988-89
GM VAUXHALL CONFERENCE

League

No.	Date	Opposition	Res.	Att.	Goalscorers
1	20 Aug	Yeovil Town	1-1	3106	West
2	23	MAIDSTONE UNITED	2-3	1674	West, Carroll
3	27	Chorley	2-3	870	Abbley, Durham
4	29	NORTHWICH VICTORIA	1-4	1541	O.G.
5	3 Sep	CHELTENHAM TOWN	1-0	1304	West(pen)
6	6	BARNET	2-3	1815	Durham, A.Kerr
7	10	Kettering Town	1-2	1520	Blackler
8	14	Welling United	1-0	848	Carroll
9	19	Fisher Athletic	3-3	805	Durham(2), Day
10	24	RUNCORN	3-3	1304	Norman, Robinson, Carroll
11	8 Oct	WELLING UNITED	1-1	1552	O.G.
12	11	Weymouth	3-0	801	West, J.Kerr, Blackler
13	22	TELFORD UNITED	1-0	1477	West
14	5 Nov	Boston United	1-0	1741	Norman(pen)
15	8	ENFIELD	3-2	1549	West, Osborne, J.Kerr
16	12	SUTTON UNITED	2-2	1884	West, Durham
17	19	Kidderminster Harriers	0-2	1505	
18	26	Altrincham	2-2	1229	J.Kerr, Durham
19	10 Dec	Barnet	0-1	2434	
20	17	CHORLEY	1-1	1577	Durham
21	24	Aylesbury United	2-0	2406	Durham, West
22	31	Maidstone United	3-1	1127	West(2,1pen), J.Kerr
23	2 Jan	AYLESBURY UNITED	1-0	3211	West
24	7	Runcorn	3-2	774	West, Durham, J.Kerr
25	21	FISHER ATHLETIC	3-0	1694	West, Carroll, Durham
26	31	Stafford Rangers	1-1	999	J.Kerr
27	11 Feb	STAFFORD RANGERS	6-1	2040	West(3), J.Kerr(3,1pen)
28	18	KIDDERMINSTER HARRIERS	1-0	4239	A.Kerr
29	4 Mar	YEOVIL TOWN	1-1	3103	West
30	18	BOSTON UNITED	2-1	2073	Evans(2)
31	25	Telford United	2-1	1515	J.Kerr, Evans
32	27	MACCLESFIELD TOWN	1-1	3873	J.Kerr
33	1 Apr	Cheltenham Town	1-0	1772	Durham
34	8	KETTERING TOWN	0-1	4890	
35	11	Enfield	4-3	843	West(3,1pen), Carroll
36	15	ALTRINCHAM	2-1	2115	Carroll, J.Kerr
37	22	Sutton United	0-3	1224	
38	29	Macclesfield Town	1-0	1006	O.G.
39	1 May	WEYMOUTH	0-0	2052	
40	6	Northwich Victoria	3-2	609	Creaser, West, Russell

F.A. CUP

Rd	Date	Opposition	Res.	Att.	Goalscorers
1QR	17 Sep	Haverhill Rovers	4-1	1012	Durham(2), Regan, Young
2QR	1 Oct	Finchley	3-0	400	Durham, West(2)
3QR	15	Staines Town	1-0	1100	West
4QR	29	KETTERING TOWN	1-2	2454	West

F.A. TROPHY

Rd	Date	Opposition	Res.	Att.	Goalscorers
3QR	3 Dec	CAMBRIDGE CITY	2-0	1272	West, Carroll
1R	15 Jan	Bath City	0-0	1174	
1Rr	18	BATH CITY	4-0	1177	J.Kerr(3), Robinson
2R	4 Feb	Wealdstone	1-0	1469	Blackler
3R	25	MERTHYR TYDFIL	2-0	3434	West, Creaser
4R	11 Mar	Hyde United	0-1	2341	

BERKS & BUCKS SENIOR CUP

Rd	Date	Opposition	Res.	Att.	Goalscorers
1R	29 Nov	CHESHAM UNITED	4-1	678	Blackler, A.Kerr, J.Kerr(2)
2R	11 Jan	WINSLOW UNITED	2-1	556	J.Kerr, West
3R	22 Feb	Marlow	0-5	1502	

Extra players – A.Markwell 2R/7, D.Meli 2R/12,3R/14, M.Wilson 2R/14,3R/12, M. Elworthy 3R\3, T.Hinton 3R/5, K.Sullivan 3R/6, A.Spur 3R/7, S.Dale 3R/10, D.Kipping 3R/11,

CLUBCALL CUP

Rd	Date	Opposition	Res.	Att.	Goalscorers
1R	4 Oct	Wokingham Town	2-1	695	Regan, Young
2R	24	Kidderminster Harriers	1-4	929	Young(pen)

SEASON 1989-90
GM VAUXHALL CONFERENCE

No.	Date	Opposition	Res.	Att.	Goalscorers
1	26 Aug	Northwich Victoria	0-3	740	
2	28	ALTRINCHAM	1-1	2078	Robinson
3	2 Sep	DARLINGTON	0-1	2620	
4	6	Welling United	0-0	910	
5	9	Stafford Rangers	0-1	1137	
6	19	Enfield	5-3	1001	Carroll,Stapleton(2),West(pen),Gipp
7	23	KIDDERMINSTER HARRIERS	3-3	1913	West(2), J.Kerr
8	26	FISHER ATHLETIC	6-1	1850	Stapleton, West(3),Gipp(2)
9	3 Oct	Kettering Town	0-1	2405	
10	7	RUNCORN	5-0	1885	Robinsn,Crssley,Durhm,West(p),Gipp
11	21	TELFORD UNITED	1-1	1838	Durham
12	4 Nov	Chorley	0-1	687	
13	7	YEOVIL TOWN	1-2	1659	West
14	11	BOSTON UNITED	1-0	1649	Guppy
15	18	BARROW	4-0	1673	Guppy, Durham, Evans, Carroll
16	25	Yeovil Town	2-4	2212	Carroll, Evans
17	28	MERTHYR TYDFIL	1-2	1655	Franklin
18	2 Dec	NORTHWICH VICTORIA	3-3	1548	Evans(2), Durham
19	9	Boston United	0-2	1397	
20	16	BARNET	1-0	2128	Lambert
21	26	Sutton United	2-1	1153	Durham, Guppy
22	30	CHELTENHAM TOWN	0-4	2166	
23	1 Jan	SUTTON UNITED	3-2	1745	Robinson, Carroll, Durham
24	6	Telford United	1-4	1345	West
25	20	Barrow	3-0	1178	Creaser, Carroll, West
26	27	MACCLESFIELD TOWN	1-1	2002	Stapleton
27	10 Feb	Merthyr Tydfil	1-1	1251	West
28	17	WELLING UNITED	1-0	1745	Carroll
29	20	KETTERING TOWN	2-2	1996	Lambert, Carroll
30	3 Mar	Macclesfield Town	0-1	1210	
31	10	ENFIELD	1-0	1740	West
32	17	Cheltenham Town	1-1	1411	West
33	24	CHORLEY	4-0	1706	Carroll, West(pen), Lambert(2)
34	27	Barnet	0-2	3707	
35	31	Kidderminster Harriers	2-0	1225	A.Kerr, Durham
36	14 Apr	Darlington	1-0	4297	Lambert
37	21	FARNBOROUGH TOWN	1-0	2268	Thorpe
38	23	Fisher Athletic	1-3	838	Stapleton
39	25	Farnborough Town	1-1	1925	Carroll
40	30	Runcorn	0-2	650	
41	3 May	STAFFORD RANGERS	2-1	1818	West, Carroll
42	5	Altrincham	2-1	541	Smith, Thorpe

F.A. CUP

1QR	16 Sep	Baldock Town	2-0	671	West, A.Kerr
2QR	30	BOREHAM WOOD	3-1	1460	A.Kerr, J.Kerr(2)
3QR	14 Oct	GRAVESEND & N/FLEET	1-1	1561	Durham
3QRr	17	Gravesend & Northfleet	1-1	840	Guppy
3QR2r	23	Gravesend & Northfleet	3-0	1205	J.Kerr, Carroll, Evans(pen)
4QR	28	Stafford Rangers	1-4	953	Evans

F.A. TROPHY

1R	13 Jan	METROPOLITAN POLICE	1-3	1128	West(pen)

BERKS & BUCKS SENIOR CUP

1R	9 Jan	Flackwell Heath	3-0	843	Robinson, Guppy, West(pen)
2R	15 Feb	WINDSOR & ETON	3-2	514	Guppy, West(2,1pen)
SF	7 Mar	Chesham United	2-0	1200	West
F*	16 Apr	Slough Town	2-1	1567	Carroll, Lambert

* Played at Hungerford

BOB LORD TROPHY

2R	23 Jan	MERTHYR TYDFIL	2-0	703	Crossley, West
3R	14 Mar	Boston United	2-0	1425	Lambert, West
SF1	4 Apr	Yeovil Town	1-2	1403	O.G.
SF2	10	YEOVIL TOWN	3-2*	1556	Carroll(2), Lambert

* lost on away goal rule

Season 1989/90: (Back) Sutton, Goldsworthy, Schofield, Melvin (Youth Team Man.), Crossley, Franklin, Evans, Carroll, Creaser, Blackler, Jones (Physio), Lavers (Groundsman), Robson (Comm. Man.), Hutton
(Middle) Simmonds, O'Neill (Manager), Guppy, Robinson, Granville, Smith, A.Kerr, Pearson, Lambert, Durham, M.West, Thorpe, Stapleton, Reardon (Asst. Manager)
(Front) Hart, Cleere, Peart (Fin. Dir.), Cox (Dir.), Hutchinson (Sec.), Adams (Patron), Beeks (Chairman), Seymour (President), Roberts (Co. Sec.), Lee (Dir.), Richards (Dir.), Parry (Dir.), Holt.

Season 1990/91:
(Back) Walford, Hanlan, Cash, Smith, Stapleton, Creaser, Crossley
(Middle) O'Neill (Manager), Jones (Physio), Robinson, Melvin (Res.Manager), Scott, Whitby, Kerry, Granville, Ryan, Nuttell, Hutchinson, Franklin (Coach), Reardon (Asst.Manager),
(Front) Guppy, Price, Moussaddik, Blackler, West, Carroll.

SEASON 1990-91
GM VAUXHALL CONFERENCE

Players (column headers): Granville J., Whitby S., Crossley M., Kerr A., Creaser G., Carroll D., Stapleton S., Smith G., West M., Robinson A., Guppy S., Durham K., Lambert M., Ryan K., Hutchinson S., Walford S., Evans N., Blackler M., Cook M., Moussaddik C., Nuttell M., Cash S., Scott K., Scope D., Hanlan M., Price J., Thorpe R., Sciaraffa M.

No.	Date	Opposition	Res.	Att.	Goalscorers
1	18 Aug	Runcorn	1-1	839	Carroll
2	25	Macclesfield Town	0-0	1370	
3	27	WELLING UNITED	4-1	3035	Smith, Carroll, Kerr, O.G.
4	1 Sep	ALTRINCHAM	3-0	2216	West(2), Kerr
5	8	NORTHWICH VICTORIA	3-0	2563	Kerr, Robinson, Ryan
6	18	Barnet	2-3	4579	West(2)
7	22	RUNCORN	1-1	2576	Hutchinson
8	6 Oct	Telford United	0-1	1087	
9	9	FISHER ATHLETIC	2-0	1978	Evans(2)
10	16	Slough Town	3-3	3394	West, Carroll, Evans
11	20	Gateshead	1-2	658	Hutchinson
12	3 Nov	KETTERING TOWN	5-1	4146	West(4), Carroll
13	10	YEOVIL TOWN	2-0	3485	Creaser, West(pen)
14	12	Fisher Athletic	3-2	651	Carroll(2), West
15	24	Colchester United	2-2	2970	Ryan(2)
16	27	BOSTON UNITED	3-0	2764	West, Creaser, Blackler
17	1 Dec	KIDDERMINSTER HARRIERS	2-3	3041	Evans(2)
18	15	SUTTON UNITED	4-1	2469	West(4)
19	22	Merthyr Tydfil	4-2	910	Evans, Carroll, Ryan, West(pen)
20	26	CHELTENHAM TOWN	0-2	3048	
21	29	Yeovil Town	2-2	2661	O.G., West(pen)
22	5 Jan	TELFORD UNITED	3-2	2608	Evans, Creaser, West
23	19	Kidderminster Harriers	2-1	1521	West, Nuttell
24	26	BARROW	2-1	2883	O.G., West
25	29	Bath City	2-1	832	Ryan, West
26	16 Feb	MACCLESFIELD TOWN	0-0	2816	
27	19	Stafford Rangers	1-2	856	Nuttell
28	26	BATH CITY	0-0	1991	
29	2 May	Altrincham	0-1	1698	
30	9	SLOUGH TOWN	2-1	3183	Scott, Ryan
31	12	Kettering Town	1-0	3020	Kerr
32	19	Cheltenham Town	0-1	1012	
33	23	Barrow	2-2	1432	Robinson, Scope
34	26	COLCHESTER UNITED	1-0	3367	Scott
35	28	Welling United	1-1	811	Guppy
36	30	Sutton United	0-1	1373	
37	18 Apr	GATESHEAD	4-0	1657	Creaser, Scott(2), Stapleton
38	20	Boston United	1-0	1188	West
39	23	MERTHYR TYDFIL	2-1	2106	Scott, Stapleton
40	227	Northwich Victoria	1-1	645	West
41	29	BARNET	1-3	4402	Nuttell
42	4 May	STAFFORD RANGERS	2-0	2460	Scott, Carroll

Apps: 33 24 32 34 40 28 34 19 36 19 26 — — 24 22 20 13 12 1 9 8 11 11 1 2 3
Subs: — 2 — — — 2 2 5 — 11 4 2 4 6 9 — — 2 1 — 5 1 1 2 — — —
Goals: — — — 4 4 8 2 1 24 2 1 — — 6 2 — 7 1 — — 3 — 6 1 — — —

F.A. CUP

1QR	15 Sep	MAIDENHEAD UNITED	3-0	1932	West(pen), Kerr, Creaser
2QR	29	Trowbridge Town	0-0	839	
2QRr	2 Oct	TROWBRIDGE TOWN	2-1	1870	Evans(2)
3QR	13	WOKINGHAM TOWN	4-1	2319	Kerr(2), West(2)
4QR	27	BASINGSTOKE TOWN	6-0	2203	Kerr, Evns(2), Htchinsn, Stpletn, West
1R	17 Nov	Boston United	1-1	2755	Evans
1Rr	21	BOSTON UNITED	4-0	4954	West(2), Ryan, Creaser
2R	12 Dec	PETERBOROUGH UNITED	1-1	5695	Blackler
2Rr	17	Peterborough United	0-2	5692	

F.A. TROPHY

1R	12 Jan	WEALDSTONE	1-0	2692	Guppy
2R	2 Feb	V.S. Rugby	1-0	1835	West
3R	28	CHELTENHAM TOWN	2-1	3143	Creaser, Kerr
4R	16 Mar	Northwich Victoria	3-2	1968	West, Scott(2)
SF1	6 Apr	ALTRINCHAM	2-1	5248	Carroll, Scott
SF2	13	Altrincham	2-0	3500	West, Scott(pen)
F*	11 May	Kidderminster Harriers	2-1	34842	Scott, West

* Played at Wembley

BERKS & BUCKS SENIOR CUP

1R	17 Jan	BRACKNELL TOWN	3-0	542	West(pen), Lambert, Guppy
2R	5 Feb	CHALFONT ST. PETER	7-0	638	Nuttell(2), West(3), Kerr, Ryan
SF	6 Mar	CHESHAM UNITED	3-1	1239	Nuttell(2), Ryan
F*	16 Apr	Marlow	2-3	1941	Robinson, Carroll

* Played at Slough

BOB LORD TROPHY

1R1	4 Sep	Bath City	1-0	445	Kerr
1R2	25	BATH CITY	0-0	1167	
2R	15 Jan	Kettering Town	0-1	1435	

SEASON 1991-92
GM VAUXHALL CONFERENCE

No.	Date	Opposition	Res.	Att.	Goalscorers
1	17 Aug	GATESHEAD	2-1	2603	West, Carroll
2	24	Witton Albion	2-1	1242	Guppy, Nuttell
3	26	YEOVIL TOWN	1-0	3360	Nuttell
4	31	ALTRINCHAM	4-2	3245	Nuttell(3), West
5	4 Sep	Welling United	3-1	1337	Guppy, West(2)
6	7	Stafford Rangers	2-0	1381	West(2,1pen)
7	17	Merthyr Tydfil	2-1	1088	Ryan, Nuttell
8	21	MACCLESFIELD TOWN	0-1	3821	
9	28	COLCHESTER UNITED	1-2	5184	Guppy
10	5 Oct	Runcorn	2-1	951	Scott, Guppy
11	12	TELFORD UNITED	6-1	4283	Gppy,Smth,West(2,1p),Kerr,Htchinsn
12	19	Boston United	2-2	1706	Stapleton(2)
13	26	Kidderminster Harriers	0-1	2037	
14	2 Nov	REDBRIDGE FOREST	1-0	2285	Cousins
15	9	MERTHYR TYDFIL	4-0	3339	Carroll, Smith, Kerr, Hutchinson
16	23	Barrow	1-0	1438	Scott
17	30	CHELTENHAM TOWN	2-2	3060	Scott, Hutchinson
18	7 Dec	Colchester United	0-3	5083	
19	21	RUNCORN	1-0	2688	Hutchinson
20	26	Slough Town	1-0	3703	Guppy
21	1 Jan	SLOUGH TOWN	3-0	5162	Crossley, West(pen), Guppy
22	4	Bath City	1-1	1386	Carroll
23	17	KIDDERMINSTER HARRIERS	2-0	3913	Creaser, O.G.
24	4 Feb	Cheltenham Town	1-2	1320	Stapleton
25	8	Telford United	0-1	1520	
26	15	Northwich Victoria	1-0	1043	Casey
27	29	BARROW	3-2	3699	Scott(2), Creaser
28	7 Mar	Yeovil Town	0-1	2901	
29	10	BOSTON UNITED	2-1	2580	Greene(2)
30	18	FARNBOROUGH TOWN	2-1	2275	Creaser, Scott
31	21	STAFFORD RANGERS	3-0	3202	Scott(2pens), Thompson
32	24	NORTHWICH VICTORIA	2-0	2750	Greene, Kerr
33	28	KETTERING TOWN	1-0	4069	O.G.
34	4 Apr	Farnborough Town	3-1	2236	Greene, Scott, Stapleton
35	11	Altrincham	4-0	1166	Greene(4)
36	14	Macclesfield Town	1-3	693	Scott
37	18	WELLING UNITED	4-0	3910	Scott(2), Greene, Kerr
38	20	BATH CITY	1-0	4263	Scott
39	22	Kettering Town	1-1	2918	Casey
40	25	Gateshead	3-2	912	Scott(2,1pen), Creaser
41	30	Redbridge Forest	5-0	2891	Scott(2,1pen), Casey(2), Carroll
42	2 May	WITTON ALBION	4-0	6035	Casey, Stapleton, Scott, Greene

F.A. CUP

| 1R | 16 Nov | Kettering Town | 1-1 | 3317 | Carroll |
| 1Rr | 27 | KETTERING TOWN | 0-2 | 5299 | |

F.A. TROPHY

1R	11 Jan	SALISBURY	2-0	2917	Carroll, Scott
2R	1 Feb	WOKING	1-0	5801	Casey
3R	23	Bath City	1-1	2899	Carroll
3Rr	25	BATH CITY	2-0	3542	Carroll, Casey
4R	14 Mar	WITTON ALBION	1-2	4636	West(pen)

BERKS & BUCKS SENIOR CUP

| 1R | 15 Jan | READING | 1-2 | 461 | O.G. |

Extra players — M.Poole 12   P.Kelloway 14

BOB LORD TROPHY

2R	15 Oct	Merthyr Tydfil	3-1	526	Crossley, Hutchinson, Gooden
3R	16 Dec	Colchester United	6-2	919	West(2),Scott, Htchinsn(2),Creasr
SF1	11 Feb	Yeovil Town	0-0	1816	
SF2	18	YEOVIL TOWN	2-0	1883	Creaser, Greene
F1	31 Mar	Runcorn	0-1	853	
F2	7 Apr	RUNCORN	2-0	2519	Guppy, O.G.

Extra players — M.Blackler SF1/6#   J.Muttock SF2/6#

Season 1991/92: (Back) Franklin (Coach), Melvin (Youth Mgr.), A Kerr, Ryan, Carroll, Nuttell, Scott, Hyde, Crossley, Hutchinson, Guppy, Covington, Blackler, Jones (Phys.), Reardon (Asst. Mgr.)
(Front) Walford, Gooden, Stapleton, M West, Creaser, O'Neill (Mgr.), Whitby, J Price, Smith, Cousins

Season 1992/93: (Back) Guppy, Stapleton, Scott, Crossley, Vircavs, Hayrettin.
(Middle) Jones (Physio), Melvin (Youth Coach), Carroll, Cousins, Kerr, Hyde, Ryan, Cooper, Horton, Reardon (Asst.Man.) (Front) Creaser, West, Langford, O'Neill (Manager), Franklin (Coach), Greene, Thompson, Casey, Hutchinson.

SEASON 1992-93
GM VAUXHALL CONFERENCE

Players (columns): Hyde P., Cousins J., Crossley M., Kerr A., Creaser G., Thompson S., Carroll D., Casey K., Stapleton S., Scott K., Guppy S., Ryan K., Hutchinson S., West M., Greene D., Covington G., Buckle P., Dewhurst R., Thompson L., Gooden T., Langford T., Sorrell T., Vircavs A., Hayrettin H., Aylott T., Cooper G., Moussaddik C., Barrowcliff P., Norman A., Waitman G.

No.	Date	Opposition	Res.	Att.	Goalscorers
1	22 Aug	Macclesfield Town	1-1	1397	Casey
2	25	WELLING UNITED	3-0	3530	S.Thompson, Scott, Casey
3	29	GATESHEAD	2-1	3290	Stapleton, West
4	31	Farnborough Town	2-0	2678	Scott, Stapleton
5	5 Sep	TELFORD UNITED	4-0	3414	Scott, Carroll, Kerr, Casey
6	9	Boston United	3-0	1460	S.Thompson(2), O.G.
7	12	Merthyr Tydfil	4-1	1408	Casey, S.Thompson, Scott(2)
8	15	YEOVIL TOWN	5-1	3769	Kerr, Scott(p), Casey, Stapleton, O.G.
9	19	BROMSGROVE ROVERS	4-0	4282	Carroll(2), Casey, O.G.
10	26	Kettering Town	4-0	3021	Casey, Stapleton, Carroll, Scott
11	29	Bath City	0-2	1283	
12	3 Oct	STALYBRIDGE CELTIC	4-0	4120	Casey, Scott, Guppy, Stapleton
13	10	Bromsgrove Rovers	0-1	3675	
14	17	BATH CITY	2-0	4085	Scott, Kerr
15	24	WITTON ALBION	2-1	4731	Kerr, Casey
16	31	Kidderminster Harriers	4-1	3064	S.Thompson, Scott(p), Guppy, Casey
17	7 Nov	STAFFORD RANGERS	2-2	4569	Scott, Hutchinson
18	21	Runcorn	1-2	850	Stapleton
19	28	Altrincham	2-0	1512	Scott, Stapleton
20	12 Dec	Witton Albion	2-2	1272	Scott, Greene
21	19	MERTHYR TYDFIL	4-0	3716	Carroll, Scott(2), Guppy
22	26	Woking	3-0	4911	Guppy(2), Scott
23	2 Jan	Welling United	2-2	2616	Carroll, Creaser
24	16	NORTHWICH VICTORIA	1-0	4060	Dewhurst
25	23	Stalybridge Celtic	2-2	1694	Scott, Kerr
26	6 Feb	KIDDERMINSTER HARRIERS	1-1	4353	Hutchinson
27	16	DAGENHAM & REDBRIDGE	1-0	5106	Carroll
28	27	Northwich Victoria	0-0	1860	
29	6 Mar	KETTERING TOWN	1-2	4430	Kerr
30	16	Yeovil Town	0-3	2667	
31	20	FARNBOROUGH TOWN	1-1	4141	Scott
32	23	SLOUGH TOWN	1-0	7230	Scott
33	25	Dagenham & Redbridge	2-1	2542	West(2,1pen)
34	30	BOSTON UNITED	3-3	4560	Ryan(2), West
35	6 Apr	WOKING	0-0	5000	
36	13	Slough Town	1-1	4500	Langford
37	15	RUNCORN	5-1	6220	Scott, Hutchinson(2), Langford, Guppy
38	17	ALTRINCHAM	0-2	6284	
39	18	Gateshead	1-0	815	S.Thompson
40	24	Telford United	3-2	1741	Langford(2), Hutchinson
41	29	Stafford Rangers	1-0	1631	Langford
42	1 May	MACCLESFIELD TOWN	0-1	5748	

Apps.: 40 39 35 37 20 30 34 20 33 36 38 14 21 5 9 1 1 2 7 3 11 10 5 3 5 2 1
Subs.: 2 5 9 5 8 15 1 1 1 1 1 1
Goals: 6 1 6 7 10 7 20 6 2 5 4 1 1 5

F.A. CUP

1R	14 Nov	MERTHYR TYDFIL	3-1	4322	Scott, Carroll, Stapleton
2R	6 Dec	WEST BROMWICH ALBION	2-2	6904	Creaser, S.Thompson
2Rr	15	West Bromwich Albion	0-1	17640	

F.A. TROPHY

1R	9 Jan	CHELTENHAM TOWN	3-1	3964	Carroll, Scott, Kerr
2R	30	Morecombe	1-1	2192	Scott
2Rr	2 Feb	MORECOMBE	2-0	4490	Kerr, Scott
3R	20	BROMSGROVE ROVERS	2-0	4907	Stapleton, Scott(pen)
4R	13 Mar	GATESHEAD	1-0	4795	Guppy
SF1	3 Apr	SUTTON UNITED	2-3	5600	Guppy, Carroll
SF2	10	Sutton United	4-0	5002	Crossley(2), Scott, Carroll
F*	9 May	Runcorn	4-1	32968	Cousins, Kerr, S.Thompson, Carroll

* Played at Wembley

BERKS & BUCKS SENIOR CUP

1R	19 Jan	Flackwell Heath	0-1	700	

Extra players — M.Sciaraffa 3, D.Owen 4, M.Keen 5*, A.Giamattei 7, N.Poffley 9, M.Poole 11#, G.Eaton 12, G.Wood 14

DRINKWISE CUP

2R	20 Oct	Welling United	3-2	452	Scott, West, Greene
3R	9 Feb	Yeovil Town	1-0	2330	Scott
SF1	23	DAGENHAM & R/BRIDGE	3-1	1901	Casey, Guppy, Ryan
SF2	9 Mar	Dagenham & Redbridge	0-0	1247	
F1	20 Apr	Northwich Victoria	0-0	1005	
F2	27	NORTHWICH VICTORIA	2-3	3784	Guppy, West

SEASON 1993-94
ENDSLEIGH INSURANCE LEAGUE DIV 3

No.	Date	Opposition	Res.	Att.	Goalscorers
1	14 Aug	Carlisle United	2-2	7752	O.G., Guppy
2	21	CHESTER CITY	1-0	6507	Scott
3	28	Wigan Athletic	1-1	2388	Guppy
4	31	Hereford United	4-3	2847	Scott(2,1pen), Kerr(2)
5	4 Sep	GILLINGHAM	1-1	6226	Scott(pen)
6	11	Bury	2-1	2559	Kerr, Langford
7	18	COLCHESTER UNITED	2-5	6025	Scott(pen), Langford
8	25	DONCASTER ROVERS	1-0	4905	Langford
9	2 Oct	Chesterfield	3-2	2956	Scott(2), Evans
10	9	Northampton Town	1-1	5197	Guppy
11	16	LINCOLN CITY	2-3	5623	Carroll, Thompson
12	23	Darlington	0-0	2057	
13	30	SHREWSBURY TOWN	1-1	5064	Scott
14	2 Nov	SCARBOROUGH	4-0	3975	Carroll, Crossley, Scott(2)
15	6	Scunthorpe United	0-0	3604	
16	20	CREWE ALEXANDRA	3-1	6137	Evans, Hemmings(2)
17	27	Preston North End	3-2	9265	Langford(2), Hayrettin
18	11 Dec	Chester City	1-3	3195	Hemmings
19	18	CARLISLE UNITED	2-0	5044	Evans, Ryan
20	27	Torquay United	1-1	4991	Evans
21	1 Jan	Walsall	2-4	6473	Hemmings(2)
22	3	HEREFORD UNITED	3-2	5528	Guppy, Carroll, Evans
23	15	Lincoln City	3-1	3735	Langford(2), Evans
24	22	NORTHAMPTON TOWN	1-0	6737	Guppy
25	25	MANSFIELD TOWN	1-0	4424	Cooper
26	29	Shrewsbury Town	0-1	5967	
27	12 Feb	Mansfield Town	0-3	3009	
28	19	WIGAN ATHLETIC	0-1	4846	
29	26	Gillingham	1-0	4292	Langford
30	5 Mar	BURY	2-1	4737	Garner, Carroll
31	12	Colchester United	2-0	3932	Stapleton, Titterton
32	19	Doncaster Rovers	3-0	2358	Brown, Guppy(2)
33	26	CHESTERFIELD	0-1	5752	
34	29	DARLINGTON	2-0	4491	Hemmings, Guppy
35	2 Apr	TORQUAY UNITED	1-1	5808	Crossley
36	4	Rochdale	2-2	2575	Carroll, Garner
37	9	WALSALL	3-0	5512	Garner, Carroll, Hemmings
38	16	Scarborough	1-3	2090	Cusack
39	19	ROCHDALE	1-1	5226	Garner
40	23	SCUNTHORPE UNITED	2-2	5755	Cousins, Creaser
41	30	Crewe Alexandra	1-2	6182	O.G.
42	7 May	PRESTON NORTH END	1-1	7442	Creaser

F.A. CUP

1R	14 Nov	Bristol Rovers	2-1	6421	Langford, Carroll
2R	4 Dec	CAMBRIDGE UNITED	1-0	6313	Hemmings
3R	8 Jan	NORWICH CITY	0-2	7802	

COCA-COLA CUP

1R1	17 Aug	Leyton Orient	2-0	4151	Thompson, Langford
1R2	24	LEYTON ORIENT	1-0	4906	Scott
2R1	22 Sep	Coventry City	0-3	9615	
2R2	5 Oct	COVENTRY CITY	4-2	5933	Ryan, Scott, Evans, Cousins

ENDSLEIGH INSURANCE LEAGUE PLAY-OFFS

SF1	15 May	Carlisle United	2-0	10862	Thompson, Garner
SF2	18	CARLISLE UNITED	2-1	6265	Carroll, Garner
F*	28	Preston North End	4-2	40109	Thompson, Garner, Carroll(2)

*Played at Wembley

AUTOGLASS TROPHY

1RG	28 Sep	BARNET	1-0	2323	Scott
1RG	9 Nov	Brentford	3-2	3165	Scott, Creaser(2)
2R	14 Dec	CARDIFF CITY	3-2	2703	Langford, Evans, Guppy
SAQF	11 Jan	Colchester United	1-0	2751	Guppy
SASF	8 Feb	Fulham	2-2p	8733	Langford(2)
SAF/1	1 Mar	Swansea City	1-3	6335	Garner
SAF/2	22	SWANSEA CITY	1-0	6710	Hemmings

p – won on penalties Extra players – A.Norman IRG (Barnet)/14

Season 1993/94
(Back) Crossley, Creaser, Hyde, Moussaddik, Evans, Turnbull, Carroll
(Middle) Melvin (Youth Team), Cunningham, Stapleton, Ryan, Hemmings, Norman, Reid, Titterton, Garner, Horton, Jones (Physio). (Front) Guppy, Thompson, Langford, Brown, Franklin (Coach), O.Neill (Manager), Hayrettin, Kerr, Hutchinson, Cousins.

Season 1994/95
(Back) Guppy, Stapleton, Creaser, Evans, Carroll, Garner, Horton. (Middle) Jones (Physio), Smith, Stevens, Crossley, Ryan, Hyde, Moussaddik, Turnbull, Titterton, Cousins, Walford (Youth Coach) (Front) Thompson, Hutchinson, Hemmings, O'Neill (Manager), Franklin (Coach), Brown, Langford, Reid.

SEASON 1994-95
ENDSLEIGH INSURANCE LEAGUE DIV 2

No.	Date	Opposition	Res.	Att.	Goalscorers
1	13 Aug	CAMBRIDGE UNITED	3-0	5782	Garner, Hemmings, Cousins(pen)
2	20	Huddersfield Town	1-0	13334	Garner
3	27	BRISTOL ROVERS	0-0	5895	
4	30	Birmingham City	1-0	14305	Regis
5	3 Sep	Bradford City	1-2	8010	Cousins(pen)
6	10	BRENTFORD	4-3	6847	Evans, Garner(2), Regis
7	13	HULL CITY	1-2	4676	Evans
8	17	Crewe Alexandra	2-1	4466	Regis, Carroll
9	24	Stockport County	1-4	4607	Turnbull
10	1 Oct	SWANSEA CITY	1-0	4388	Carroll
11	8	LEYTON ORIENT	2-1	5668	Regis, Thompson
12	15	Plymouth Argyle	2-2	6864	Regis(2)
13	22	Peterborough United	3-1	5924	Regis, Garner, Thompson
14	29	YORK CITY	0-0	7140	
15	1 Nov	SHREWSBURY TOWN	1-0	4626	Regis
16	5	Wrexham	1-4	3747	Ryan
17	19	CARDIFF CITY	3-1	5391	Ryan(2), Hemmings
18	26	Blackpool	1-0	4846	Kerr
19	10 Dec	HUDDERSFIELD TOWN	2-1	6790	Evans, Garner
20	16	Cambridge United	2-2	3713	Patterson, Evans
21	26	BRIGHTON & HOVE ALBION	0-0	7085	
22	27	Oxford United	2-0	9540	Ryan, Garner
23	31	A.F.C. BOURNEMOUTH	1-1	5990	Carroll
24	14 Jan	Rotherham United	0-2	3537	
25	31	Chester City	2-0	1524	Desouza(2)
26	4 Feb	BLACKPOOL	1-1	6380	Desouza
27	11	Shrewsbury Town	2-2	3945	Stapleton, Desouza(pen)
28	18	ROTHERHAM UNITED	2-0	5153	Desouza, Stapleton
29	21	Cardiff City	0-2	3024	
30	25	Swansea City	1-1	3699	Desouza
31	4 Mar	STOCKPORT COUNTY	1-1	5265	Evans
32	11	Bristol Rovers	0-1	5118	
33	14	York City	0-0	2800	
34	18	BIRMINGHAM CITY	0-3	7289	
35	21	Brentford	0-0	9530	
36	25	CREWE ALEXANDRA	0-0	6288	
37	28	PETERBOROUGH UNITED	3-1	4590	Garner(2), Brown
38	1 Apr	Hull City	0-0	5054	
39	4	BRADFORD CITY	3-1	4522	Soloman, Hemmings, Carroll
40	8	A.F.C. Bournemouth	0-2	5816	
41	11	WREXHAM	3-0	5115	McGavin, O.G., Bell
42	15	OXFORD UNITED	1-0	7683	Carroll
43	19	Brighton & Hove Albion	1-1	8095	Carroll
44	22	CHESTER CITY	3-1	5284	Hemmings(2), McGavin
45	29	PLYMOUTH ARGYLE	1-2	6850	Bell
46	6 May	Leyton Orient	1-0	4698	Regis

Extra player – A.Clark 46/10*

F.A. CUP

1R	12 Nov	CHELMSFORD CITY	4-0	5654	Stapleton(2), Bell, Ryan
2R	3 Dec	Hitchin Town	5-0	2765	Garner(3), Ryan, Bell
3R	7 Jan	WEST HAM UNITED	0-2	9007	

COCA-COLA CUP

1R1	17 Aug	Brighton & Hove Albion	1-2	6884	Regis
1R2	23	BRIGHTON & HOVE ALB	1-3	5281	Turnbull

AUTO WINDSCREENS SHIELD

2R	29 Nov	Shrewsbury Town	0-2	1785	

SEASON 1995-96
ENDSLEIGH INSURANCE LEAGUE DIV 2

No.	Date	Opposition	Res.	Att.	Goalscorers
1	12 Aug	CREWE ALEXANDRA	1-1	5281	McGavin(pen)
2	19	Notts County	0-2	5552	
3	26	A.F.C. BOURNEMOUTH	1-2	4749	Desouza
4	29	Brighton & Hove Albion	2-1	5360	Desouza(2)
5	2 Sep	Bradford City	4-0	9748	Desouza(3), Castledine
6	9	PETERBOROUGH UNITED	1-1	5637	Garner
7	12	CHESTERFIELD	1-0	3617	Castledine
8	16	Stockport County	1-1	5588	Castledine
9	23	WREXHAM	1-1	4649	Desouza
10	30	Bristol City	0-0	5564	
11	7 Oct	Burnley	1-1	8029	Williams
12	14	WALSALL	1-0	4724	Carroll
13	21	Oxford United	4-1	7731	Farrell, Howard, Desouza, McGavin(p)
14	28	HULL CITY	2-2	5021	Evans, Bell
15	31	YORK CITY	2-1	4038	Desouza(pen), Garner
16	4 Nov	Swansea City	2-1	2809	Carroll, Garner
17	18	BRISTOL ROVERS	1-1	4886	Farrell
18	26	Carlisle United	2-4	4459	Carroll(2, 1pen)
19	9 Dec	Wrexham	0-1	3468	
20	16	BRISTOL CITY	1-1	4020	Blissett
21	23	SHREWSBURY TOWN	2-0	4131	Blissett, Howard
22	26	Swindon Town	0-0	12976	
23	13 Jan	NOTTS COUNTY	1-1	4908	Williams
24	20	Crewe Alexandra	0-2	4150	
25	23	Blackpool	1-1	4040	Desouza
26	30	Brentford	0-1	4668	
27	3 Feb	A.F.C. Bournemouth	3-2	4447	O.G., Patterson, Williams
28	10	BLACKPOOL	0-1	5285	
29	17	Chesterfield	1-3	4571	Desouza
30	24	STOCKPORT COUNTY	4-1	4246	Williams(3), Carroll
31	27	Peterborough United	0-3	3670	
32	2 Mar	SWINDON TOWN	1-0	6457	Desouza
33	6	BRIGHTON & HOVE ALBION	0-2	3466	
34	9	Shrewsbury Town	1-1	2866	Ryan
35	16	BRENTFORD	2-1	4912	Carroll, Evans
36	23	Rotherham United	0-0	2775	
37	28	BRADFORD CITY	5-2	3021	Desouza(3), Ryan, Evans
38	30	BURNLEY	4-1	4921	Ryan(2), Desouza, Farrell
39	2 Apr	Walsall	1-0	3252	Carroll(pen)
40	6	Hull City	2-4	3065	Carroll(pen), Desouza
41	8	OXFORD UNITED	0-3	6727	
42	13	York City	1-2	3113	Skiverton
43	16	ROTHERHAM UNITED	1-1	2836	Desouza
44	20	SWANSEA CITY	0-1	3672	
45	27	CARLISLE UNITED	4-0	3964	Crossley, Williams, Farrell(2)
46	4 May	Bristol Rovers	1-2	6621	Carroll

F.A. CUP

1R	13 Nov	GILLINGHAM	1-1	5064	Patterson
1Rr	21	Gillingham	0-1		

COCA-COLA CUP

1R1	15 Aug	LEYTON ORIENT	3-0	3310	Desouza(2), Crossley
1R2	22	Leyton Orient	0-2	2478	
2R1	19 Sep	MANCHESTER CITY	0-0	7443	
2R2	4 Oct	Manchester City	0-4	11474	

AUTO WINDSCREENS SHIELD

1RG	10 Oct	FULHAM	1-1	2756	Howard
1RG	7 Nov	Walsall	0-5	2592	

Season 1995/96:
(Back) Soloman, Stevens, Howard, Hyde, Evans, Moussaddik, Crossley, Stapleton, Patterson.
(Middle) Jones(Physio), Melvin(Youth Officer), Desouza, Hemmings, Ryan, Cousins, Carroll, Thompson, Kemp, Smillie (Youth Man.). (Front) Brown, Bell, Hardyman, Smith (Manager), Clark, Garner, McGavin.

Season 1996/97:
(Back) McCarthy, Carroll, Cousins, Kemp (Asst.Man.), Hall, McGavin, Ryan.
(Middle) Melvin (Youth Dev.Off.) Jones (Physio), Markman, Clark, Cheesewright, Parkin, Crossley, Patterson, Smillie (Youth Man.), M.Smith (Community Off.),
(Front) Skiverton, Lawrence, Bell, Brown, A.Smith (Manager), Evans, Desouza, Farrell, Williams..

ADVANCED SUBSCRIBERS

Roger Vere-Verco Office Furniture Ltd.
Mr. R. Hance, Amersham
Brian Shirley, Holmer Green
Peter Howland, High Wycombe
Alan Cockram, High Wycombe
Alan Russell, High Wycombe
Sarah J. Beeks
Ian Mitchell, Flackwell Heath
Peter Stears, High Wycombe
Peter Hunt, High Wycombe
Chris Trower, Gerrards Cross
Gordon Anning
David Austin, Beaconsfield, Bucks.
J.E.G. McKiernon, Bledlow Ridge
William Folds, Farnham Common
Shaun Cross, High Wycombe
Kelvin Thorn, Beaconsfield, Bucks
Vincent Faulkner, Naphill, Bucks
Peter Grey, Beaconsfield, Bucks
Neil Rabone, Worthing, West Sussex
John Finch, High Wycombe
Ron Monk, High Wycombe
Bill Lowe, High Wycombe
Mark & Simon Nelson, G.Missenden
Brian Rumsey, High Wycombe
Robert Filer, High Wycombe
Nigel Penn, High Wycombe
Patrick Botell, Great Kingshill
George Maloney, High Wycombe
Keith Clayton, High Wycombe
John Parslow, High Wycombe
Clifford Sharp, High Wycombe
Kevin A. Saunders, High Wycombe
Graham Worley, High Wycombe
David Goulding, High Wycombe
Dennis Ford, High Wycombe
Mr. M. Tapping, Totteridge
Frank Bartley, Ickenham, Middlesex
Neil Townsend
Anthony Hill, Tring, Herts.
Chris Jefferies
Gerald Eggleton, Bledlow
Stuart Stanley, Booker
David Loveday, High Wycombe
John A. Burnard, High Wycombe
Tracy Wyatt, High Wycombe
Graham Townsend, Edgware
Trevor Cox, Widmer End
Stephen Daglish, Burnham
Sandie Searle, Milton Keynes
Frederick G. Cox, Kennington
Mr. Wright, High Wycombe
Roger Clarke, Speen, Bucks.

Mr. Sewell, Chalfont St.Peter
Mark Hamilton, Lucerne, Switzerland
Steve Redfern, Basingstoke
Sharon and Gary Trimby
Glenn and Sarah, Cheltenham
John W. Maskell, High Wycombe
Gary Dean, Hazlemere
Robert Priestley, High Wycombe
The Skedge Family, Winslow
Dylan Van Looy, Antwerp
G.J. Oliver, Manchester
Darren Peart, High Wycombe
Jason Newton, High Wycombe
Mark Allan, Widmer End
Stuart A. Redding, Deeds Grove
Dave & Gerry Gardner, Chinnor
Richard Frame, Abingdon
Leslie Munday, Stokenchurch
Michael Pym, Brisbane, Australia
Ian Monk, Loughborough, Leicestershire
Tony Phillips, Hazlemere
Elaine Humphrey
Graham Lacey, High Wycombe
Cliff Buckle, Altrincham
Mick Bowden, High Wycombe
John Scurrell, Tylers Green
John Howland, New Zealand
George Kent, High Wycombe
Michael Collins, High Wycombe
Roger & Gill Hazell, HighWycombe
Kevin Bye, Watchet, Somerset
John Hobley, Holmer Green
Jim & Janet Ryan, The Chequers
Andrew Tillman, Swanage, Dorset
John E. Keep, Thatcham, Kent
Timothy William Newman Bower
Jim Gallagher, Holmer Green
Jennie Garlick, Slough, Berks.
Ken Townsend, Bourne End
Paul Davies, Green Hill, H.Wycombe
David Townsend, Worcester
Chris Neal, Hove, Sussex
Mike Perkins
Peter Nunn
Mark Berry, High Wycombe
Paul Berry, High Wycombe
Tony Hudson, High Wycombe
Wayne Newton, Maidenhead
Chris Mohin, Syston, Leicester
Ben Gilby, New Malden
Stuart Latham, Swindon, Wilts.
Chris Hardy, Seer Green
Charles Scully, Thurston, Suffolk

Dennis J.D. Jones, High Wycombe
C.J. Hayfield, Beaconsfield
David Mason, Wendover
Andrew Nicholls, High Wycombe
R.J. Spring, Maidenhead
David J. Avery, Aylesbury
Rob Collins, Hughenden Valley
David Goff, Stokenchurch
K. Saunders, High Wycombe
Stephen Walmsley, Gerrards Cross
Pat Quinn, Billericay, Essex
Mr. R.R. Fawkes, High Wycombe
Mr. G. Crisp, Great Kingshill
Calvin Marks, Egham, Surrey
Anthony Ball, Birmingham
Mr.M.I.Anderson, Ramsey, Isle of Man
Ian Crossley, Basingstoke, Hampshire
Ernie Anderson, Chinnor, Oxon
Andrew Walters, Ashford, Middlesex
Bob Horner, Maidenhead
John Clegg, Princes Risborough
Martin Cooper, Amersham
John Glenister, Ashford, Kent
Jack Sparke, Chalfont St. Giles
Vince Lynch, West Wycombe
Colin Macklen, Ashford, Middlesex
Jim Kielty, Ashford, Middlesex
Miss.C. Barnett, High Wycombe
Andrew Hearn, Aylesbury
David Rutland, Hazlemere
Jane Alison Oliver, Aylesbury
Geoff Sutton, Stokenchurch
Adam Cecil, Hazlemere
Mick Burt, Cippenham
Paul Skeates, Biggleswade
Ian Newman, Bedale, N.Yorks.
Barry Lewis, Bexhill, Sussex
A.C. Carter, Swindon
Mark West, WWFC 1984-93
John Luckett, London E.7.
The Blagboroughs, Walters Ash
Paul Hudson, Princes Risborough
J.A. Piercy
Chris Turner, Dawlish, Devon
Mrs. B. Cooper, High Wycombe
Matthew Hutton, Holmer Green
Jack Adams, Patron WWFC
The McColm Family, Downley
The Reddington Family, Booker
Tony Poth, High Wycombe
Vernon Lewis, Reading, Berks.
Matthew Coles, High Wycombe
Jeff Woodbridge, Happy Christmas

David Woodbridge, Happy Christmas
John Twigg, Hemel Hempstead
Eric S. Woodhall
Mr. A.J. Chester, Poole, Dorset
Hayward Family, High Wycombe
Michael T. Hughes, Hazlemere
Phil Rowe, Reading
Pat Hawkes, Flackwell Heath
Diet Townend, Little Chalfont
Chris Jones, Widmer End
Philip Starkey, Milton Keynes
Graham Starkey, High Wycombe
Malcolm Price, London
Algis & Kestutis Kuliukas, Penn
Buzz
James Mott, Haddenham, Bucks.
Reginald Hall, Beaconsfield
Philip Capron, Marlow Bottom
Andrea Webster-Brown, Bracknell
John Day, High Wycombe
Richard Bolton, High Wycombe
Peter C. Glenister
David R. Glenister
Robert Evans, High Wycombe
Michael Barker, Sands, H.Wycombe
Happy Christmas, Trevor Austin
David Peatey, Newbury, Berks.
John (Wigga) Pierce
Bill Kukstas, Reading
Tony Keen, Piddington
Simon Armitage, High Wycombe
Bob Graham, High Wycombe
Brian North, High Wycombe
Carl Ashby, London W10
Mr. G.P. Dormer, High Wycombe
Stephen Coton, Cookham, Berks.
Robert Sanderson, Hughenden Valley
Ian Peart, Edinburgh
Ben Peart, Swindon
K. Pink, Salisbury
Robin Plumridge, Ashdon, Essex
Ian Jolliffe, Cowling, Yorkshire
Ian Blacklidge, High Wycombe
Cameron Scott, Kilmarnock, Scotland
Nick Tolerton, Christchurch, N. Zealand
Leslie Pearce, Skewen, West Glam.
Tim Hardy, London SW19
R.K. Chown, Hazlemere, Bucks.
Stephen Heather, High Wycombe
Alec Mercer, Hemel Hempstead
David Bassett, High Wycombe
Christopher Perrin, Lane End
Nigel Belsham, Hazlemere
Neil Hurford, High Wycombe
Peter Loftus, Holmer Green
Martin (Buchanan) Ball
Norman Anthony, High Wycombe
Peter John Emery, Eastbourne
Mike Rolfe, High Wycombe

Roy Hazell, High Wycombe
K.N. Proctor, Bicester
Richie Johnson, Amersham, Bucks
Jason Anthony, Cubbage, Basingstoke
Stuart Aiden, Cubbage, Basingstoke
Mr. J. Paul, Buckinghamshire
David Williams, Beaconsfield
Barry White, Hackney, London
Nigel King, Caversham, Reading
Leonard Roy Buckle, Twyford
Roy Buckle, Sands
John Hanson, Princes Risborough
Philip Barker
Jack Harris, Wooburn Green
Alan Barks of Penn
Robin & Timothy Harris, Spalding
Stephen Rabone, Cardiff
Peter Reaer (Ex-Holmer Green)
Andrew Martin, Skibbereen, Eire
Rod Lavers, Chinnor, Oxfordshire
Carole Linda Little, Naphill, H.W.
Neil Smith, Long Eaton
Mark Overall, Seer Green
Mark Austin B.A.
Jim Abram, Abingdon, Oxon.
Adrian Dodds, Alvechurch
Alan Hodder, Widmer End
Peter Sommers, High Wycombe
Andrew Bernard, Cirencester
Wallington Family, Wokingham, Berks
Emily & Isobelle Atkinson
Christine Bye, Wooburn Green
David Chandler, High Wycombe
Steve Kemsley, Aylesbury
Viv Pike, Widmer End
Geoff Harrison, Dewsbury, Yorkshire
Jonathon Vasbenter, Stokenchurch
Alison, Anna, Mark Rimmer
Brian Reynolds, Lane End
Ron Barrington, Flackwell Heath
Martin Bailey, Widmer End
Terry Holt, Princes Risborough
Reg Holt, High Wycombe
Barry Witham, High Wycombe
Helen Goddard, High Wycombe
Mark & Lisa Murphy, Shoreham
Martyn Fox, Princes Risborough
Olly Britnell, High Wycombe
Nick Parkinson, Stokenchurch
Roger Long
Lloyd Long, Diss, Norfolk
Patricia Long, Little Chalfont
Diane Bishop, Barnhurst, Kent
Paul.Lewis@Molins.Com
Harry Deaney, Holmer Green
C.R.Grace, St.Austell
Robin Prickett, High Wycombe
Gerry Croxford, High Wycombe
Andrew Eastwood, High Wycombe

Raymond Shaw
R.V. Calmels, Sports Programmes
Peter Cogle, Aberdeen
David Keats, Thornton Heath
Martin Cripps
David Downs and Marion
Derek Hyde
Graham Spackman
Michael John Griffin
John R. Orton
Robert M. Smith
John Motson
R. Bickel
John Rawnsley
Jonny Stokkeland, Norway
Gordon Macey (Q.P.R. Historian)
Steve Emms, Evesham
W.D. Phillips
Geoff Allman
J. Ringrose
Richard Wells
Mark Tyler, Rayleigh, Essex
Chris. Marsh, Chesterfield
Paul Johnson, Birmingham City
Geoffrey Wright
Alan Davies
Philip H. Whitehead
Peter and Christopher Thorn
Martin Simons-Lambrechts, Belgium
Fred Lee - Plymouth Argyle
Dave Parine
Richard Stocken
Bob Lilliman
Christer Svensson, Sweden
Keith Coburn
Chris Harte
Jonathan Hall
Michael Campbell
Peter Kirby, Maidstone
Mr. R. Smith, Abingdon
John & James Davies
Gareth A. Evans
Ingemar Strömberg, Sweden
David and Martin Fleckney
Robin John Walsh
Peter Baxter
Richard W. Lane, Newark
Alexander David Newcombe, Muskham
David Jowett
Mr. S. Metcalfe
Malcolm Smith
L.A. Zammit
Trond Isaksen, Norway
John Treleven
Philip Buchanan Ball
Jeffrey and Irene Peart
Debbie Peart
Andy Worboys
Arran & Nicholas Matthews

A SELECTION OF TITLES
From
'YORE PUBLICATIONS'
12 The Furrows, Harefield,
Middx. UB9 6AT

(Free lists issued 3 times per year. For your first list please send a S.A.E.)
Current titles include:

NOTTS COUNTY - The Official History (1862 - 1995) (Tony Brown) The Author, a prominent member of the Association of Football Statisticians, has put together the detailed history of his local club - the oldest team in the Football League. Statistics commence, including line-ups, from 1864 (all 18 players for the first game!), and other sections provide the full well illustrated written history (with a concentration on the early days), named team groups (every season from 1898/99), a Who's Who, plus a most interesting 'A-Z' of the Club: 272 large page hardback, price £16-95 plus £3-80 P/P.

THE LADS IN BLUE (The complete history of Carlisle United) (Paul Harrison). This detailed written history from the first days, with many illustrations, also includes full statistics and a Players Who's Who - from the team's entry into the Football League in 1928. Other Chapters deal with The Managers, the Great Games, the complete record of matches against every other League Club, etc. 256 large pages (hardback), price £16-45 plus £3-80 P/P.

BREATHE ON 'EM SALOP - THE OFFICIAL HISTORY OF SHREWSBURY TOWN (Mike Jones).
Written by long time supporter and local radio broadcaster, and aided by the club's official statistician, this 256 large page hardback book tells the full story - including statistics from 1886. It is very well illustrated, and includes a 'one-liner' Who's Who section, and a feature on all the managers. Price £14-95 plus £3-80 P/P.

Other Club histories include :
Kilmarnock, Bristol City, Southend United., Maidstone United, Doncaster Rovers & Colchester United

FORGOTTEN CAPS (England Football Internationals of two World Wars) (Bryan Horsnell and Douglas Lamming)
A much acclaimed book written by the two leading authorities on the subject. A complete Who's Who record of every England player (including non playing reserves) - over 100. Includes biographies and photographs of **every** player; plus much more, a truly complete record! 112 large pages, price £8-95 plus 85p P/P.

REJECTED F.C. VOLUMES 2 and 3 (Reprints) (Dave Twydell) The Histories of all the ex-Football League Clubs (Volume 1 - reprint - now sold out). Clubs consist: Accrington/Acc. Stanley, Barrow, Darwen, Merthyr Town, Thames Assoc. plus Leeds City (Volume 2), and Durham City, Gainsborough Trin., Middlesbrough Ironopolis, New Brighton/New Brighton Tower, Northwich Vics., Southport plus Wigan Borough (Volume 3).
Each 256 pages (hardback), and priced £12-95 (per copy), plus £1-55 P/P for each volume.

Also: REJECTED F.C. OF SCOTLAND: Vol. 1 covers Edinburgh and The South (Edinburgh City, Leith Ath., St.Bernards, Armadale, Broxburn United, Bathgate, Peebles Rovers, Mid-Annandale, Nithsdale Wanderers and Solway Star - 288 pages). Volume 2 covers Glasgow and District (Abercorn, Arthurlie, Beith, Cambuslang, Clydebank, Cowlairs, Johnstone, Linthouse, Northern, Third Lanark, and Thistle - 240 pages). Each priced £12-95 plus £1-35 P/P (each)

FOOTBALL LEAGUE - GROUNDS FOR A CHANGE (By Dave Twydell). Published 1991. A 424 page, A5 sized, Hardback book. A comprehensive study of all the Grounds on which the current English Football League clubs previously played. Includes 250 illustrations, with plenty of 'reading' material. Price £13-95 Plus £1-75 Postage.

THE CODE WAR (Graham Williams) A fascinating look on the history of football (in the broadest sense) - from the earliest days up to the First World War. The book delves into the splits within Rugby Union, Rugby League, as well as Football (Soccer). 192 page hardback, price £10-95 plus £1-25 postage.

SIMPLY THE BEST (David Ross) 'The Greatest hour-and-a-half of every Football League and Scottish League Club - 132 well written stories of each club's greatest match. Well illustrated large pages, price £9-75 plus £1-15 P/P.

Non-League football is also covered, including the 'Gone But Not Forgotten' series (histories of defunct non-League clubs and grounds). Plus unusual items, e.g. 'The Little Red Book of Chinese Football', etc.